Truth for Today
Commentary

Eddie Cloer, D.Min.
General Editor

Timothy Paul Westbrook, M.A.
Assistant Editor

Don Shackelford, Th.D.
Associate Old Testament Editor

Duane Warden, Ph.D.
Associate New Testament Editor

Truth for Today
Commentary

An Exegesis & Application of the Holy Scriptures

Ezekiel

Denny Petrillo, Ph.D.

Resource □
Publications
2205 S. Benton
Searcy, AR 72143

Truth for Today Commentary
Ezekiel
Copyright © 2004 by Resource Publications
2205 S. Benton, Searcy, AR 72143

All rights reserved. No portion of the text of this book may be reproduced in any form without the written permission of the publisher.

ISBN:0-9760327-0-8

Scripture taken from the NEW AMERICAN STANDARD BIBLE®, © Copyright 1960, 1962, 1963, 1968, 1971, 1972, 1973, 1975, 1977, 1995 by The Lockman Foundation. Used by permission. (www.Lockman.org)

CONTENTS

Editor's Preface	ix
Abbreviations	xi
Application Authors	xiii
Hebrew Transliteration	xv
Introduction	1
The Expanded Outline	13

Part I: The Prophecy of Judgment on Judah and the Pronouncement of Sin (1—24) 21

Chapter 1:	The First Vision: The Glory of the Lord	23
Chapter 2:	Ezekiel's Call from the Lord	42
Chapter 3:	Ezekiel's Call from the Lord (Continued)	50
Chapter 4:	The Prophecies of Punishment Dramatized	70
Chapter 5:	The Prophecies of Punishment Dramatized (Continued)	83
Chapter 6:	The Prophecy of Israel's Doom And the Promise for a Remnant	96
Chapter 7:	The Prophecy of Israel's Doom And the Promise for a Remnant (Continued)	106
Chapter 8:	Idolatry in the Temple	119
Chapter 9:	The Lord's Punishment: The Six Executioners	134
Chapter 10:	The Withdrawal of the Glory Of the Lord from the Temple	145
Chapter 11:	The Promise for a Remnant And the Withdrawal Of His Glory from the City	153
Chapter 12:	Symbolizing the Siege	166

Chapter 13: Condemnations of False Prophets And Prophetesses	182
Chapter 14: Consequences Will Come	198
Chapter 15: Jerusalem: A Fruitless and Faithless People	211
Chapter 16: Jerusalem: An Unfaithful Wife	216
Chapter 17: National Disobedience	240
Chapter 18: Individual Responsibility	253
Chapter 19: Lamentation for the Leaders	275
Chapter 20: The Wayward People	283
Chapter 21: The Sword of God's Judgment	307
Chapter 22: The Oracle Against Jerusalem	326
Chapter 23: An Allegory of Two Sisters: Oholah and Oholibah	338
Chapter 24: The End of Jerusalem	359

Part II: The Prophecies Against Foreign Nations (25—32) — 373

Chapter 25: Prophecies Against Ammon, Moab, Edom, and Philistia	375
Chapter 26: The Fall of Tyre	389
Chapter 27: A Lamentation for Tyre	401
Chapter 28: Judgment of Tyre's Leaders and Sidon	413
Chapter 29: The Prophecy Against Egypt	432
Chapter 30: The Invasion of Egypt	447
Chapter 31: Pharoah Is Judged: The Allegory of the Cedar	456
Chapter 32: A Lamentation for Pharaoh and Egypt	464

Part III: The Prophecy of Israel's Restoration— The Return of the Glory of the Lord (33—48) — 477

An Overview of Ezekiel 33—39: Six Messages from God	479
Chapter 33: The Watchman and News Of the Fall of Jerusalem	481
Chapter 34: The Return of Israel To Their Own Land: The Good Shepherd	495

Chapter 35: The Return of Israel To Their Own Land: Edom To Be Destroyed	510
Chapter 36: The Return of Israel To Their Own Land: Restoration	522
Chapter 37: The Return of Israel To Their Own Land: A New Life	542
Chapter 38: Oracles 1–4 Against Gog and Magog	558
Chapter 39: Oracles 5–7 Against Gog and Magog	571
An Overview of Ezekiel 40—48: The New Temple and God's Kingdom	587
Chapter 40: The New Temple: Its Outer and Inner Courts	597
Chapter 41: The Temple Itself	611
Chapter 42: The Priests' Chambers And the Temple Measurements	618
Chapter 43: God's Glory Returns to the Temple; The Altar of Burnt Offerings	624
Chapter 44: The New Worship: Servants in the Temple	638
Chapter 45: The "Holy Portion" Allotted And Temple Regulations	651
Chapter 46: Additional Regulations	661
Chapter 47: The New Land (Part 1)	668
Chapter 48: The New Land (Part 2)	676
Appendix 1: Additional Studies	685
Appendix 2: Charts and Maps	703
Selected Bibliography	707
Have You Heard . . . About Truth for Today?	713

FIGURES, TABLES, AND MAPS

Possible Location of the "Idol of Jealousy" at the Temple	125
Tyre: The Island Fortress (c. 330 B.C.)	396
Seven Dates Given During Oracles Against the Nations (25—32)	433
The Fall of Egypt and Other Events	472
The Temple Complex in Ezekiel's Vision in 40:1—47:2	586
The Outer East Gate	600
The Land Allotment Showing the "Holy Portion," The City Possession, and the Surrounding Area	653
The Land Allotment in Ezekiel's Vision	678

FOR FURTHER STUDY

Old Testament Cruelty and the Goodness of God (9:6)	141
The Glory and Dwelling of the Lord	151
Was "the King of Tyre" an Allusion to Satan? (28:11–19)	427
"Sheol," the Realm of the Dead	473
"My Servant David"	506
The Two Sticks and Mormon Doctrine	555
An Analysis of Four Views For Interpreting Ezekiel 40—48	589

Editor's Preface

This printing marks the eighth volume in a series of commentaries on the Holy Scriptures that will eventually cover every book in God's divine revelation to us. This is an ambitious undertaking, to be sure, but one that we believe should be done. May the Lord in His gracious providence allow us to complete the effort that is planned. More important, may the work be as faithful and true to His will as we can possibly make it.

No one can spend his or her time upon this earth more nobly than in an earnest study of the Scriptures. A handy assistant in such a pursuit is a reliable commentary. Any study of the Scriptures, however, should be predicated upon the realization that the Word of God and the Word of God alone is our guide from earth to heaven. A commentary must never be allowed to take the place of God's precious Word; it must be viewed as a printed teacher that seeks to guide the reader to a better understanding of the Word that God has given.

The author of a commentary does not intend for his comments on the sacred Word to be regarded as infallible; he knows that he is subject to mistakes, as is the case with all other humans. Consequently, we must admit at the start that perfection is beyond our reach. This commentary is not perfect, and no commentary ever will be. In writing a commentary, the author only wishes to share with others the fruits of his lifelong study of the Scriptures, with the hope that this sharing will aid, encourage, and enrich the reader in his or her pursuit of the knowledge of God as revealed in the sacred Scriptures.

Dennis Petrillo and I have been friends for several years and brothers in Christ for much longer. He has proven himself to be one of God's great servants. He has taught God's Word in the classroom for many years and now serves as the President of the Bear Valley School of Biblical Studies in Denver, Colorado. His students and those who have heard him preach have found him to be a faithful presenter of the Holy Scriptures. We believe this commentary will bring anyone who reads it to a better understanding of the great Book of Ezekiel.

So far as we know, the churches of Christ have never completed a multi-authored commentary series on the entire Bible. Surely, the time for producing such a set has come. We can leave to the generations that will follow us no finer legacy than presentations on every book of the Scriptures that have resulted from our faithful scholarship and responsible handling of these Scriptures. We hope this commentary series will serve this grand purpose.

A project of this magnitude will require many faithful laborers, much time, and a great, enduring persistence. Let us join together, as brothers and sisters bought by Christ's blood, and work together until the task is completed.

May all of us, through a diligent study of God's Word, walk in God's will for us and for the world.

Eddie Cloer
General Editor

Abbreviations

OLD TESTAMENT

Genesis	Gen.	Ecclesiastes	Eccles.
Exodus	Ex.	Song of Solomon	Song
Leviticus	Lev.	Isaiah	Is.
Numbers	Num.	Jeremiah	Jer.
Deuteronomy	Deut.	Lamentations	Lam.
Joshua	Josh.	Ezekiel	Ezek.
Judges	Judg.	Daniel	Dan.
Ruth	Ruth	Hosea	Hos.
1 Samuel	1 Sam.	Joel	Joel
2 Samuel	2 Sam.	Amos	Amos
1 Kings	1 Kings	Obadiah	Obad.
2 Kings	2 Kings	Jonah	Jon.
1 Chronicles	1 Chron.	Micah	Mic.
2 Chronicles	2 Chron.	Nahum	Nahum
Ezra	Ezra	Habakkuk	Hab.
Nehemiah	Neh.	Zephaniah	Zeph.
Esther	Esther	Haggai	Hag.
Job	Job	Zechariah	Zech.
Psalms	Ps.	Malachi	Mal.
Proverbs	Prov.		

NEW TESTAMENT

Matthew	Mt.	1 Timothy	1 Tim.
Mark	Mk.	2 Timothy	2 Tim.
Luke	Lk.	Titus	Tit.
John	Jn.	Philemon	Philem.
Acts	Acts	Hebrews	Heb.
Romans	Rom.	James	Jas.
1 Corinthians	1 Cor.	1 Peter	1 Pet.
2 Corinthians	2 Cor.	2 Peter	2 Pet.
Galatians	Gal.	1 John	1 Jn.
Ephesians	Eph.	2 John	2 Jn.
Philippians	Phil.	3 John	3 Jn.
Colossians	Col.	Jude	Jude
1 Thessalonians	1 Thess.	Revelation	Rev.
2 Thessalonians	2 Thess.		

AB	Amplified Bible
ASV	American Standard Version
KJV	King James Version
NASB	New American Standard Bible
NIV	New International Version
NKJV	New King James Version
NRSV	New Revised Standard Version
RV	English Revised Version

Application Authors

D.P.   Denny Petrillo

E.C.   Eddie Cloer

T.P.W.   Timothy Paul Westbrook

J.L.K.   John L. Kachelman, Jr.

A.J.   Ancil Jenkins

O.D.O.   Owen D. Olbricht

Hebrew Transliteration

Studying the Word of God in the original languages brings out more fully the richness of the biblical texts. This series attempts to incorporate a healthy number of Greek and Hebrew words that help clarify the passages under investigation. Although translating and transliterating are difficult tasks with any language, Hebrew poses a particular challenge. First, it is an old language, and spelling and pronunciation have evolved over time. Second, there are multiple methods for transliterating Hebrew words into English. Therefore, the editorial committee has discussed how we will transliterate Hebrew, and we have adapted our own method for the series. It is assumed that not all of our readers will have a working knowledge of Hebrew. Our system attempts to present a transliteration that will simplify pronunciation and assist in word studies. In order to accomplish this, we have applied the following rules throughout the commentary.

Rule 1. No difference is indicated by the hard/soft pronunciation of "Begad Kapath" letters: תתפפככ דדגגבב. The meaning of a word is not affected by whether or not these letters are hard or soft.

Rule 2. When the *Daghesh Forte* indicates a doubling of consonants, the letter is doubled in the transliteration.

Rule 3. The Tetragrammaton (יְהוָה) is transliterated *YHWH* and written "Yahweh" in the text. Since the original vowel pointings are unknown for this word, they have been left out when it appears in the commentary, thus forming יהוה.

Rule 4. The transliteration distinguishes between ה when used as a consonant and ה when used as a vowel letter to lengthen the vowel *Qamets*.

Rule 5. The vocalized *sheva* is indicated by ^{e}.

Rule 6. Since the word "torah" (law) is a commonly known word, the ת that begins this word is transliterated as *t* rather than *th*.

Examples of transliterated words:

לְדָוִד, *lᵉdawid*; חַטָּאִים, *chatta'im*; תּוֹרָה, *torah*; אַשְׁרֵי, *'ashrey*; and אִישׁ, *'ish*

Consonants

There are twenty-three consonants in the Hebrew text. They are listed below by name, Hebrew symbol, and transliteration.

Name	Hebrew	Transliteration
Aleph	א	'
Beth	ב	b
Gimel	ג	g
Daleth	ד	d
He	ה	h
Vav	ו	w
Zayin	ז	z
Heth	ח	ch
Teth	ט	t
Yodh	י	y
Kaph	כ ך	k
Lamedh	ל	l
Mem	מ ם	m
Nun	נ ן	n
Samekh	ס	s
Ayin	ע	ʻ
Pe	פ ף	p
Tsadhe	צ ץ	ts
Qoph	ק	q
Resh	ר	r
Sin	שׂ	ś
Shin	שׁ	sh
Tav	ת	th

Vowels

The vowels in Hebrew are used more for determining the form of a word rather than the root meaning. We have tried to differentiate between these vowels to help guide their pronunciation and grammatical function. They are listed here by name, Hebrew symbol, and transliteration.

Name	Hebrew	Transliteration
Qamets	ָ	a (long)
Patach	ַ	a (short)
Tsere	ֵ	e (long)
Segol	ֶ	e (short)
Hireq Yodh	יִ	i (long)
Hireq	ִ	i (short)
Qamets Yodh	יָ	ay
Segol Yodh	יֶ	ey
Tsere Yodh	יֵ	ey
Holem	וֹ	o (long)
Qamets-Hatuph	ָ	o (short)
Shureq	וּ	u (long)
Qibbuts	ֻ	u (short)
Hatep-Patach	ֲ	a
Hatep-Segol	ֱ	e
Hatep-Qamets	ֳ	o

Suggested Hebrew Grammar Books

For further study of the Hebrew language, we recommend the following books:

Kelly, Page H. *Biblical Hebrew: An Introduction Grammar*. Grand Rapids, Mich.: Wm. B. Eerdmans Publishing Co., 1992.

Pratico, Gary D. and Miles Van Pelt. *Basics of Biblical Hebrew Grammar*. Grand Rapids, Mich.: Zondervan, 2001. This book includes an interactive CD-ROM.

Seow, Choon Leong. *A Grammar for Biblical Hebrew*. Nashville: Abingdon Press, 1987.

Weingreen, J. *A Practical Grammar for Classical Hebrew*, 2d ed. New York: Oxford University Press, 1959.

INTRODUCTION

The Book of Ezekiel has been lauded by scholars and Bible students for centuries. Its text captivates; its message enthralls. As we read these chapters, we are drawn into fellowship with Ezekiel—the man, the prophet, the priest, the husband. Our hearts are filled with sorrow as the sinfulness of God's people is detailed; we rejoice as God announces forgiveness and restoration. We struggle alongside Ezekiel as he is burdened with the message of God's wrath. We smile with Ezekiel as he witnesses God's promises of a glorious resurrection for a dead nation.

The diligent reader of Ezekiel's message will be changed forever. The power of God's inspired Word is vividly seen in this rich book. No human being could have created such a masterpiece of literature. Evidences of inspiration permeate the book, from its historical accuracies and the preciseness of its prophecies to the beauty of its poems and prose.

In the midst of these great attributes, we are reminded of the connection between Ezekiel and Jesus. Ezekiel was the Old Testament "son of man." This phrase, which occurs a remarkable ninety-three times in the book, provides a fascinating background for the study of Jesus, who frequently referred to Himself as the "Son of Man" (thirty-one times in Matthew alone, twenty-six times in Luke).

Ezekiel was the ultimate servant of mankind. Like Jesus, he gave himself totally to God's will and purpose in trying to provide a bridge between God and man. While Jesus drew this designation from the famous passage in Daniel 7:13, 14, the connection with Ezekiel is unmistakable.

THE AUTHOR

Ezekiel: The Name

The meaning of the name Ezekiel (יְחֶזְקֵאל, *y'chezqe'l*) is "God strengthens" (24:21; 30:18; 33:28). This is based on the Hebrew word חָזַק (*chazak*), meaning "strength, power, or might." As with all the prophets, Ezekiel had a significant name. Weak and broken by the Babylonian Captivity, where was the nation of Judah to find strength? Indeed, as Ezekiel's name beautifully illustrated, her strength would come from God (34:16), as is true in the new covenant as well (Eph. 6:10). If Israel had relied upon the strength of the Lord while in the Promised Land, she would still be there. Instead, her leaders had encouraged and strengthened the people to sin against the covenant, and thereby they had led them to the Captivity and the eventual destruction of Jerusalem by enemy nations (see 13:22; 33:28; 34:8). These nations had success against Israel because God *strengthened* the nations (30:24). In order for Israel to return to her former glory, she would have to return to God and again rely upon *His* strength.

Ezekiel: The Man

Ezekiel was a priest (1:3). As a true priest of God, he was naturally concerned about the open and blatant disobedience to God's law. The fact that he was a priest compounded his sadness when he saw the abominations taking place in Jerusalem (ch. 8).

When God called Ezekiel to be a prophet, he was thirty years old and was in exile in Babylonia. At the age of twenty-five, he had been deported from Jerusalem in 598(7) B.C.,[1] among ten thousand captives (2 Kings 24:14).

He was contemporary with Daniel, who had been taken in the first exile in 606(5) B.C., and Jeremiah, who remained with

---

[1] Scholars are divided on how to date many of these events. When a year is in question, it will be presented in this form with the later year in parentheses or brackets. (See also "A Timeline of Ezekiel" in Appendix 2.)

the poorest of the people in Judea. He was influenced by the preaching of Jeremiah, and he knew of Daniel (14:14, 20).

Ezekiel was God's spokesman for twenty-two years, serving until age fifty-two (1:1–3; 40:1; 29:17). He was one of the most imposing prophets of God and ranked among the most noted of God's Old Testament spokesmen.

He was a married man (24:15–18). This prophet was convicted that God's hand was upon him. He was deep and thoughtful—one who meditated; everything he did had a meaning. In his condemnation of sin, he was harsh and blunt—in both word and action. A strict moralist, zealous for righteousness, he boldly proclaimed God's word. He was uncompromising (and unpopular), yet sensitive to the suffering of his people in captivity.

THE MESSAGE AND DATE

The message delivered by Ezekiel was one of doom. He explained the reason for Judah's captivity (1—24). At the same time, his message was one of hope. He prophesied that Judah's restoration was assured (25—48).

The prophecies of Ezekiel were presented between 593(2) and 571(0) B.C. (1:2; 29:17). The book has thirteen dates included, seven of which are dated during oracles against the nations (25—32). The remaining ones are in chronological order. John B. Taylor suggested the following precise dates for the oracles, in relation to the Julian calendar:[2]

1:2	July 31, 593 B.C.
8:1	September 17, 592 B.C.
20:1	August 9, 591 B.C.

---

[2]John B. Taylor, *Ezekiel: An Introduction and Commentary*, Tyndale Old Testament Commentaries (Downers Grove, Ill.: Inter-Varsity Press, 1969), 36. Dating these references is an inexact science. Not only are we uncertain as to the type of calendar Ezekiel was using (from fall to fall or spring to spring), but we are also unsure as to days and months when no clear reference is given. In 1:1 a reference is made to a date, but it is another way of calculating the date in 1:2.

24:1	January 15, 588 B.C.
26:1	February 12, 586 B.C.
29:1	January 7, 587 B.C.
29:17	April 26, 571 B.C.
30:20	April 29, 587 B.C.
31:1	June 21, 587 B.C.
32:1	March 3, 585 B.C.
32:17	March 17, 585 B.C.
33:21	January 19, 586 B.C.
40:1	April 28, 573 B.C.

Ezekiel used several methods to convey God's message: symbolic (apocalyptic) visions, imagery (visual aids), allegories, parables, acted symbols, riddles/proverbs, and prophecy. These methods will be discussed as we come to examples in the text. Some overlapping of categories will occur.

THE PURPOSE AND THE THEMES

Students of God's Word often approach the books of the Bible by identifying themes suggested by key words and/or phrases. Quality exegetical work recognizes the inspired author's continued emphasis upon key ideas. Ezekiel is typical in this regard. This forty-eight-chapter book is full of recurring words and phrases:

- "Blood" (דָּם, *dam*—occurs 55 times)
- "Bring," "brought" (בּוֹא, *bo'*—56 times)
- "Sword" (חֶרֶב, *chereb*—83 times)
- "Idols" (גִּלּוּל, *gillul*—39 times)
- "Abominations" (תּוֹעֵבָה, *tho'ebah*—43 times)
- "Middle," "midst" (תָּוֶךְ, *thawek*—118 times)
- "Slain" (חָלָל, *chalal*—32 times)
- "Righteous[ness]" (צֶדֶק, *tsedeq*—29 times)
- "Prophesy"/"prophet" (נָבָא, *naba'*—54 times)
- "The word of the Lord came to me" (46 times); "the word of the Lord" (60 times)
- "Will [shall] know that I am the Lord" (63 times)

INTRODUCTION

- "Live" (61 times); variations of "'As I live,' says the Lord GOD" (16 times)
- "Son of man" (93 times)[3]

Awareness of the use of these words and phrases will help us to understand the book's purpose and themes. (See the italicized words below.)

The Purpose

Ezekiel's task was to impress upon (that is, *prophesy* to) the exiles *the word of the Lord,* explaining that their enslavement was due to their own sinfulness. They had committed *abominations* by their continued worship of *idols*. Therefore, God was *bringing* upon them a *sword* that would shed their *blood*—the penalty for their sinfulness. God said that these events occurred so that they would *"know that I am the Lord."*

Ezekiel was to destroy the people's false hopes of an early return (see Jer. 28:1–17). However, he had a message of hope for their return and restoration. If they would *return* to the Lord in *righteousness*, He would *bring* them back home.

The Themes

The main theme of the book is "the person who sins will die" but "to turn [repent] is to live" (18:20–23; 33:7–16). Ezekiel set forth individual (personal) responsibility, a theme not emphasized by other prophets. The Israelites, while in captivity, had determined that their captivity was not due to their own sin, but to the sins of their fathers. Ezekiel reminded them of their own rebellion against the law of God.

The message of Ezekiel emphasized the promise of God's faithfulness in carrying out His eternal purpose: This sinful nation had to die, but the penitent remnant would be saved.

---

[3]Textual counts can be achieved in several different ways. While counts may vary, the repetition of key words and phrases indicates their importance in God's message given through Ezekiel. The counts in this series are based on searches in the updated edition of the New American Standard Bible and the Hebrew Masoretic Text (MT), using *Accordance,* 5.6.1 [CD-ROM] (Altamonte Springs, Fla.: OakTree Software, 2002).

Five themes are predominant:

(1) *The holiness of God.* In the midst of an evil nation, God's eternal attribute of righteousness was manifested.

(2) *The sinfulness of Israel.* The word "sin" occurs twenty times in the book. Three chapters chronicle Israel's sinfulness. The evil progression of Jerusalem is detailed in chapter 1, the four abominations of Israel are enumerated in chapter 8, and the evil sisters Oholah and Oholibah are discussed in chapter 23.

(3) *God will not allow sinfulness to continue: He will punish sin.* Ezekiel often portrayed Israel's sin as having accumulated, until finally the "cup" was full. She would now receive the extent of God's wrath, which He would "spend" (see 5:13 [twice]; 6:12; 7:8; 13:15) or "pour out" (see 7:8; 9:8; 14:19; 20:8, 13, 21; 30:15; 39:29).

(4) *Individual responsibility.* While this theme is repeated often in the text, the prophet especially focused on it in chapter 18: "The person who sins will die."

(5) *God will restore.* The forgiving nature of God is beautifully illustrated. God's *righteousness* required punishment, but His *compassion* allowed forgiveness and restoration. This truth is most powerfully illustrated in the vision of the valley of dry bones (ch. 37).

Another key idea is God's Spirit, or "glory," leaving and returning. He left the temple in chapters 8 through 11 and returned in chapter 43. He left when there was judgment, then returned after restoration.

THE TEXT

Perhaps no other book has endured as much criticism as has Ezekiel. Within the last fifty years, many authors have offered a wide range of criticisms regarding its unity,[4] its authenticity, and

---

[4]S. R. Driver's assessment still stands true: "No critical question arises in connexion with the authorship of the book, the whole from beginning to end bearing unmistakably the stamp of a single mind" (S. R. Driver, *An Introduction to the Literature of the Old Testament* [New York: C. Scribner, 1891; reprint, New York: Meridian Books, 1956], 279).

its accuracy, as well as the credibility of the prophet himself.[5] Nevertheless, these critics have themselves endured numerous criticisms, with other authors finding significant faults with their evaluation of Ezekiel. While the Book of Ezekiel still stands, these critics have passed away. No critical theory has emerged that undermines the traditional view that Ezekiel was written by a Jewish prophet around 570 B.C., living with the Jewish captives in Babylonia.[6]

The Hebrew text of Ezekiel is admittedly difficult. The book is filled with words whose meanings are still uncertain to modern Hebrew scholars. This explains why some English translations contain alternative readings in their marginal notes. The problem, generally speaking, is not confusion about *what* Hebrew word appeared in the original. The Dead Sea Scrolls, for example, provided significant testimony to the Hebrew text of Ezekiel. Cave 4 alone yielded fragments from three manuscripts of Ezekiel, affirming the accuracy of the Masoretic Text (the standard Hebrew Old Testament text abbreviated as "MT"). It is the *meaning* of these rarely occurring words that is difficult to determine. As a result, modern translators have leaned heavily upon the Septuagint (a Greek translation of the Hebrew, c. 150 B.C., abbreviated as "LXX").

THE HISTORICAL BACKGROUND

In a remarkably swift turn of events, the Babylonians disposed of the powerful Assyrians in 612 B.C. This shift of power had a profound impact upon Judah, and Ezekiel would have been a witness to many changes that were taking place. During his lifetime five kings reigned, with Josiah being the most noteworthy:

---

[5]Perhaps the most radical is in Charles Cutler Torrey, *Pseudo-Ezekiel and the Original Prophecy* (New York: KATV Publishing House, 1970).

[6]A good overview of positions is found in William H. Brownlee, "Ezekiel," in *The International Standard Bible Encyclopedia*, rev., ed. Geoffrey W. Bromiley (Grand Rapids, Mich.: Wm. B. Eerdmans Publishing Co., 1982), 2:250–63. He also asserted that some of Ezekiel's prophecies may have been given in Gilgal as well as Egypt.

Josiah (640–609 B.C.)
Jehoahaz (also called Shallum—609 B.C.)
Jehoiakim (609–598[7] B.C.)
Jehoiachin (also called Coniah and Jeconiah—598[7] B.C.)
Zedekiah (598[7]–587[6] B.C.)

As the Books of 2 Kings and Jeremiah bear witness, these kings attempted to provide a measure of stability to Judah during these troubled times. Sadly, most of them sought to acquire this stability by foreign alliances (with Egypt proving to be the most popular—and equally unreliable). Making foreign alliances, however, proved catastrophic in several areas:

1. It was in direct rebellion against the will of God.
2. It weakened the economy, since the people paid tribute to the other nations.
3. It introduced the pagan beliefs and practices of these heathen nations.
4. It encouraged rebellion against the governing nation and "jumping" to another nation for protection. This created distrust of Judah and led to its eventual destruction at the hands of Nebuchadnezzar and his Chaldean armies.

History records that Nebuchadnezzar attempted to work with the kings of Judah. He allowed them to serve as leaders of their subjugated state, but their continued rebellion against the Babylonians led to three deportations:

1. 606(5) B.C. The wealthiest and most powerful were transported to Babylonian exile. Daniel was among this first group.
2. 598(7) B.C. The eighteen-year-old king Jehoiachin surrendered and was exiled along with another group of powerful individuals of Judah (2 Kings 24:12–14).
3. 587(6) B.C. King Zedekiah made an alliance with the Egyptian Pharaoh. This action prompted Nebuchadnezzar to dispatch his armies to destroy the remaining

fortified cities of Judah—Jerusalem, Lachish, and Azekah. The Babylonian army arrived at Jerusalem in January 589(8) B.C. (Ezek. 24:1, 2). It took eighteen months, but the Babylonians eventually breached the walls of Jerusalem in July of 587(6) B.C. and destroyed the city in the next several weeks (see 33:21). A majority of the remaining inhabitants of Judah were transported to Babylon. However, the prophet Jeremiah, the appointed governor Gedaliah, and a few of the poorest of the people were allowed to stay in Judah.

During these events, God had three prophets ministering at the same time. Daniel was working in the palace of the kings of Babylonia, and Ezekiel was with the Judean captives in Babylonia. Jeremiah was prophesying to the people who remained in destroyed Jerusalem and the surrounding regions.[7] (See the map of "Babylon in the Time of Ezekiel" in Appendix 2.)

BIBLICAL AND APOCALYPTIC SYMBOLISM[8]

Ezekiel is classified as "apocalyptic" literature. The term "apocalyptic" is from the Greek word ἀποκάλυψις (*apokalupsis*), which means "a revelation" (see 1 Cor. 14:6). Other biblical books that use apocalyptic language include Isaiah, Jeremiah, Daniel, Joel, Amos, Zechariah, and Revelation. In recording his vision, John often used Old Testament apocalyptic symbols.

Apocalyptic books are noted for their figures, symbols, and imagery. They have a particularly artistic arrangement and finish, and they feature "double vision."

---

[7]Evidently, Jeremiah and Ezekiel were quite familiar with each other's prophecies and work. A comparison of their messages is given in Taylor, 34–35.

[8]Most of this information is from D. S. Russell, *The Method and Message of Jewish Apocalyptic* (Philadelphia: Westminster Press, 1964) and Edward P. Myers, "Interpreting Figurative Language," in *Biblical Interpretation: Principles and Practices*, ed. F. Furman Kearley, Edward P. Myers, and Timothy D. Hadley (Grand Rapids, Mich.: Baker Book House, 1986), 91–92.

Books of this nature emphasize the divine intervention of God in the affairs of mankind and nations. Written during times of trial, these books of comfort assured God's people that His faithful followers would be delivered—and that judgment would be poured out upon their enemies. The double vision is seen in that inspired writers were allowed to see beyond their own times, to the coming day of the Lord, when every wrong would be recompensed. Imbedded within these strange images was a promise that righteousness, glory, joy, and peace would return to the faithful ones of God.

In interpreting apocalyptic symbolism, we should not get lost in the symbols themselves but must discern the great truths which they embody. The apocalypses should be compared with each other. This study method cannot be overemphasized because the symbols almost always have the same meaning. Competent interpretation can be made based upon symbols explained or interpreted in other places.

Here are three fundamental rules for interpreting symbolic language:

1. The names of symbols are to be understood literally.
2. When symbols are interpreted by inspired writers, the given interpretation is to be accepted (see, for example, Dan. 2:31, 36; Rev. 1:12, 13, 20).
3. A resemblance is to be found between the symbol and the thing signified. When Ezekiel saw a resurrection of dry bones, it represented Israel's restoration from exile (Ezek. 37). Daniel saw a male goat which symbolized the Grecian conqueror Alexander the Great (Dan. 8:5, 21). Zechariah saw two olive trees that stood for God's anointed ones, Joshua and Zerubbabel (Zech. 4:2–4; see vv. 11–14).

The chief question to be answered is "What are the probable points of resemblance between the symbol (or sign) and the thing which it is intended to represent?" In some symbols, resemblances are many and detailed, while in others they are few and incidental (see Ezek. 1—3; Is. 6:1–8).

INTRODUCTION

Strict regard should be given to the historical standpoint of the writer, the scope and context of the writing, and the meaning of similar symbols elsewhere in the Scriptures. The application of symbols is consistent and uniform, not shifting from the symbolic to the literal without indication in the original text. Ignorance of this rule leads to confusion. Without adhering to such a rule, there can be no certainty as to the interpretation; the deducted meanings would be countless and contradictory!

Each symbol should be considered in its broader and more common aspects, as it would naturally present itself to the view of those acquainted with the ways of God. A figure should not be connected with small incidents or peculiar uses known only to a few.

The meaning of a symbol has to be determined by an accurate knowledge of its nature. The importance of each separate symbol must be sought from its name. In general, a symbol has just one signification. (One exception occurs in Revelation 17:9, 10, which has two meanings.)

THE OUTLINE

I. THE PROPHECY OF JUDGMENT ON JUDAH AND THE PRONOUNCEMENT OF SIN (1—24)
  A. The Prophet's Call and the First Vision (1—3)
    1. The First Vision: The Glory of the Lord (1)
    2. His Call from the Lord (2; 3)
  B. The Prophecy of Judgment Through Signs and Oracles (4—7)
    1. The Prophecies of Punishment Dramatized (4; 5)
    2. The Prophecy of Israel's Doom and the Promise for a Remnant (6; 7)
  C. The Prophetic Utterance of Jerusalem's Sin and Judgment (the Second Vision)—The Withdrawal of the Glory of the Lord (8—11)
    1. Idolatry in the Temple (8)
    2. The Lord's Punishment by Six Executioners (9)
    3. The Withdrawal of the Glory of the Lord from the Temple (10)

  4. The Promise for a Remnant and the Withdrawal of His Glory from the City (11)
 D. The Prophetic Utterances Against Jerusalem Continued (12—24)
  1. Reproofs and Warnings and the Message of Personal Judgment (12—19)
  2. Renewed Proofs and Predictions of Doom of Judah and Jerusalem (20—24)

II. THE PROPHECIES AGAINST FOREIGN NATIONS (25—32)
 A. The Prophecies Against Four Surrounding Nations: Ammon, Moab, Edom, and Philistia (25)
 B. The Prophecies Against Tyre (and Sidon) (26—28)
 C. The Prophecies Against Egypt (29—32)

III. THE PROPHECY OF ISRAEL'S RESTORATION—THE RETURN OF THE GLORY OF THE LORD (33—48)
 A. The Fall of Jerusalem and the Promised Restoration of Israel (33—37)
  1. The Watchman and News of the Fall of Jerusalem (33)
  2. The Return of Israel to Their Own Land (34—37)
 B. Gog of Magog Defeated and God's People Delivered (38; 39)
 C. The Temple and People in God's Kingdom (40—48)
  1. The New Temple (40—43)
  2. The New Worship (44—46)
  3. The New Land (47; 48)

THE EXPANDED OUTLINE

I. THE PROPHECY OF JUDGMENT ON JUDAH AND THE PRONOUNCEMENT OF SIN (1—24)
   A. The Prophet's Call and the First Vision (1—3)
      1. The First Vision: The Glory of the Lord (1)
         a. The Time of the Vision (1:1–3)
         b. The Vision (1:4–28)
            (1) The Four Living Creatures (1:4–14)
            (2) The Wheels (1:15–21)
            (3) The Expanse (1:22–25)
            (4) The Throne (1:26–28)
      2. His Call from the Lord (2; 3)
         a. The Commission Received (2:1—3:11)
            (1) "Go to the House of Israel" (2:1–7)
            (2) "Eat the Scroll" (2:8—3:3)
            (3) "Speak My Message" (3:4–11)
         b. Instructions About His Ministry (3:12–27)
            (1) "Go to Babylon" (3:12–15)
            (2) "Be a Watchman" (3:16–21)
            (3) "Be Confined" (3:22–27)
   B. The Prophecy of Judgment Through Signs and Oracles (4—7)
      1. The Prophecies of Punishment Dramatized (4; 5)
         a. First Symbolic Act: The Siege Against a Model of Jerusalem (4:1–3)
         b. Second Symbolic Act: Lying on His Side (4:4–8)
         c. Third Symbolic Act: Eating the Unclean Bread (4:9–17)

            d. Fourth Symbolic Act: Dividing His Cut Hair into Thirds (5:1–4)
            e. An Explanation of the Acts (5:5–17)
         2. The Prophecy of Israel's Doom and the Promise for a Remnant (6; 7)
            a. Destruction and Hope (6)
               (1) The Destruction of High Places (6:1–7)
               (2) A Remnant to Be Preserved (6:8–10)
               (3) The Desolate Land (6:11–14)
            b. Three Oracles of Disaster (7:1–13)
               (1) First Oracle (7:1–4)
               (2) Second Oracle (7:5–9)
               (3) Third Oracle (7:10–13)
            c. The Resulting Desolation (7:14–27)
   C. The Prophetic Utterance of Jerusalem's Sin and Judgment (the Second Vision)—The Withdrawal of the Glory of the Lord (8—11)
      1. Idolatry in the Temple (8)
         a. Ezekiel Taken to the Scene of the Vision (8:1–4)
         b. Four Abominable Acts (8:5–18)
            (1) The Idol of Jealousy (8:5, 6)
            (2) The "Hidden" Idolatry of the Elders of Judah (8:7–13)
            (3) The Women Weeping for the God Tammuz (8:14, 15)
            (4) The Sun Worshipers (8:16–18)
      2. The Lord's Punishment by Six Executioners (9)
         a. The Innocent Marked (9:1–4)
         b. The Guilty Slaughtered (9:5–11)
      3. The Withdrawal of the Glory of the Lord from the Temple (10)
         a. Instructions to the Man Clothed in Linen and Activity of the Cherubim (10:1, 2, 5–17)
         b. From the Holy of Holies to the Threshold of the Temple (10:3, 4)
         c. From the Threshold to the East Gate (10:18–22)
      4. The Promise for a Remnant and the Withdrawal of His Glory from the City (11)
         a. The Leaders to Be Slain (11:1–12)
         b. The Promise for a Remnant (11:13–21)

c. From the East Gate out of Jerusalem; the Vision Ends (11:22–25)
D. The Prophetic Utterances Against Jerusalem Continued (12—24)
   1. Reproofs and Warnings and the Message of Personal Judgment (12—19)
      a. The Sign of Baggage for Those in Jerusalem (12:1–16)
      b. The Sign of Terror (12:17–20)
      c. A Warning Concerning God's Messages (12:21–28)
      d. The Message Against the False Prophets and Prophetesses (13)
         (1) Against the False Prophets (13:1–16)
         (2) Against the False Prophetesses (13:17–23)
      e. The Message Against the Elders (14:1–11)
      f. God's Judgment Illustrated (14:12–23)
      g. The Parable of the Vine (15)
      h. The Parable of the Unfaithful Wife (16)
         (1) Jerusalem Adopted (16:1–7)
         (2) God's Love Demonstrated (16:8–14)
         (3) Her Rejection of God (16:15–34)
         (4) God's Punishment (16:35–59)
         (5) God's Promise of Restoration (16:60–63)
      i. The Parable of the Two Eagles (17)
         (1) The Telling of the Parable (or Riddle) (17:1–10)
         (2) The Interpretation of the Parable (or Riddle) (17:11–21)
         (3) The Message of Hope (17:22–24)
      j. The Message of Personal Judgment (18)
         (1) The Declaration (18:1–4)
         (2) The Five Examples (18:5–29)
            (a) The Righteous Father (18:5–9)
            (b) The Unrighteous Son (18:10–13)
            (c) The Righteous Grandson (18:14–20)
            (d) The Unrighteous Man (18:21–23)
            (e) The Righteous Man (18:24–29)
         (3) The Command to Repent (18:30–32)
      k. Lament for the Kings of Judah (19)
         (1) Jehoahaz (19:1–4)
         (2) Jehoiachin (19:5–9)

(3) Zedekiah (19:10-14)
2. Renewed Proofs and Predictions of Doom of Judah and Jerusalem (20—24)
   a. The Elders' Inquiry of Ezekiel for a Message from the Lord and the Basis for the Reply (20:1-4)
   b. Making Known the Abominations of the People Through an Historical Survey (20:5-32)
      (1) Apostasies in Egypt (20:5-9)
      (2) Apostasies in the Wilderness (20:10-26)
      (3) Apostasies in the Promised Land (20:27-32)
   c. The Result of Their Apostasies—Israel to Be Purged (20:33-44)
   d. The Prophecies of the Sword (20:45—21:32)
      (1) The Sword of the Lord Unsheathed (20:45—21:7)
      (2) The Song of the Sword (21:8-17)
      (3) The Sword of Nebuchadnezzar En Route to Jerusalem (21:18-27)
      (4) The Sword of Chaldean Conquest (21:28-32)
   e. The Sins of Jerusalem (22)
      (1) An Indictment of the City (22:1-16)
      (2) The Refiner's Furnace (22:17-22)
      (3) The Evil of the Whole Population (22:23-31)
   f. The Parable of Judgment on Jerusalem: The Two Sisters (23)
      (1) Introduction to the Two Sisters (23:1-4)
      (2) Oholah's Harlotries (23:5-10)
      (3) Oholibah's Harlotries (23:11-21)
      (4) The Fate of Oholibah (23:22-35)
      (5) God's Judgment (23:36-49)
   g. The Parable of Judgment on Jerusalem: The Boiling Pot (24:1-14)
      (1) The Siege Begun; The Date (24:1, 2)
      (2) The Siege Illustrated (24:3-14)
   h. Ezekiel Himself a Sign upon the Death of His Wife (24:15-27)
      (1) Her Death and Ezekiel's Reactions (24:15-18)
      (2) The Meaning of the Sign (24:19-21)
      (3) The Application and Ezekiel's Message (24:22-27; see 33:21, 22; 34—39)

EXPANDED OUTLINE

II. THE PROPHECIES AGAINST FOREIGN NATIONS (25—32)
   A. The Prophecies Against Four Surrounding Nations (25)
      1. Ammon (25:1–7)
      2. Moab (25:8–11)
      3. Edom (25:12–14)
      4. Philistia (25:15–17)
   B. The Prophecies Against Tyre (and Sidon) (26—28)
      1. The Predicted Destruction of Tyre (26)
         a. The Overall Description of the Destruction of Tyre (26:1–6)
         b. The Specific Military Campaign of Nebuchadnezzar (26:7–11)
         c. The Future Destruction of Tyre (26:12–21)
      2. A Lamentation for Tyre (27)
         a. The Description of Tyre as a Ship (27:1–9)
         b. The Directory of Tyre's Trade Partners (27:10–25)
         c. The Shipwreck of Tyre (27:26–36)
      3. Judgment of Tyre's Leaders and of Sidon (28)
         a. Judgment Against the Prince of Tyre (28:1–10)
         b. A Funeral Song for the King of Tyre (28:11–19)
            (1) What God Had Given to Tyre (28:11–15)
            (2) God's Judgment That Would Fall upon Tyre (28:16–19)
         c. God's Judgment Against Sidon (28:20–24)
         d. The Restoration of Israel (28:25, 26)
   C. The Prophecies Against Egypt (29—32)
      1. The Sins of Egypt (29:1–16)
      2. Egypt Becomes Compensation for Babylon (29:17–21)
      3. Nebuchadnezzar's Invasion of Egypt (30:1–19)
      4. The Defeat of Pharaoh (30:20–26)
      5. Pharaoh Is Judged: The Allegory of the Cedar (31)
      6. A Lament for Pharaoh (32:1–16)
      7. Final Lamentation for Egypt and Her Allies (32:17–32)

III. THE PROPHECY OF ISRAEL'S RESTORATION—THE RETURN OF THE GLORY OF THE LORD (33—48)
   A. The Fall of Jerusalem and the Promised Restoration of Israel (33—37)
      1. The Watchman and News of the Fall of Jerusalem (33)

      a. The Watchman's Duties Restated (33:1–20)
         (1) The Watchman's Duties (33:1–9)
         (2) The Importance of Individual Responsibility (33:10–20)
      b. Ezekiel's Reputation Established by the Report of the Fall of Jerusalem (33:21–33)
    2. The Return of Israel to Their Own Land (34—37)
      a. The True Shepherd, the False Shepherds, and the Flock of God (34)
         (1) The Evil Shepherds (34:1–10)
         (2) The Concerned Shepherd (34:11–16)
         (3) The Good Shepherd (34:17–24)
         (4) A Covenant of Peace (34:25–31)
      b. Removal of a Threat to Peace: Edom (35)
      c. The Restoration of Israel (36)
         (1) Judgment on Her Enemies (36:1–7)
         (2) God Promises to Bless the Land (36:8–15)
         (3) Protecting God's Name: An Historical Review (36:16–23)
         (4) God Promises to Cleanse Israel (36:24–32)
         (5) God Rebuilds the Nation and Repopulates the Land (36:33–38)
      d. A New Life for the People (37)
         (1) The Vision of the Valley of Dry Bones (37:1–14)
         (2) The Two Sticks: Reuniting the Two Kingdoms Under One Head (37:15–28)
B. Gog of Magog Defeated and God's People Delivered (38; 39)
    1. Oracle 1: The Description of Gog and His Forces (38:1–9)
    2. Oracle 2: Gog's Evil Plan (38:10–13)
    3. Oracle 3: Gog's Army Mobilized (38:14–16)
    4. Oracle 4: The Destruction of Gog (38:17–23)
    5. Oracle 5: The Defeat and Burial of Gog (39:1–16)
    6. Oracle 6: God's Great Bird Feast (39:17–24)
    7. Oracle 7: The Restoration of Israel (39:25–29)
C. The New Temple and God's Kingdom (40—48)
    1. The New Temple (40—43)
      a. The Outer Court (40:1–27)
         (1) The Man with the Measuring Rod (40:1–4)

EXPANDED OUTLINE

        (2) The Wall and the East Gate (40:5–16)
        (3) The Outer Court Itself (40:17–19)
        (4) The North and South Gates (40:20–27)
    b. The Inner Court (40:28–47)
        (1) The Three Gates (40:28–37)
        (2) The Equipment for Sacrifices (40:38–43)
        (3) The Priests' Chambers (40:44–47)
    c. The Temple Porch (or Vestibule) (40:48, 49)
    d. The Temple Itself (41)
        (1) The Holy Place and the Most Holy Place (41:1–4)
        (2) The Side Chambers (41:5–12)
        (3) The Measurements, Furnishings and Decorations (41:13–26)
    e. The Priests' Chamber-Buildings in the Outer Court (42:1–14)
    f. The Measurements of the Temple Area (42:15–20)
    g. The Return of the Glory of God to the Temple (43:1–12)
        (1) The Glory of the Lord Coming to the Temple (43:1–5)
        (2) The Lord Speaking Within His Temple (43:6–12)
    h. The Altar of Burnt Offerings (43:13–27)
        (1) The Description and Measurements of the Altar (43:13–17)
        (2) The Statutes Concerning the Altar (43:18–27)
2. The New Worship (44—46)
    a. The Duties and Inheritance for the Priests (44:1—45:8)
        (1) The Closed East Gate (44:1–3)
        (2) The Qualifications for Service in the Temple (44:4–27)
            (a) Foreigners Excluded (44:4–9)
            (b) Levites Given Only Menial Tasks (44:10–14)
            (c) Zadokites Selected to Serve as Priests (44:15–27)
        (3) The Inheritance of Land for the Priests (44:28–31)
        (4) The Land Allotted as a "Holy Portion" (45:1–8)

b. Regulations Regarding the Temple and Community (45:9—46:24)
   (1) A Plea to Deal Justly and Righteously (45:9–12)
   (2) Sacrifices and Sacred Days (45:13—46:15)
       (a) The People's Obligations to the Prince (45:13–17)
       (b) Sin Offering Regulations (45:18–20)
       (c) The Passover (45:21–24)
       (d) The Feast of Tabernacles (45:25)
       (e) Sacrifices for the Sabbath and New Moon (46:1–8)
       (f) Crowd Control in the Temple (46:9, 10)
       (g) Further Regulations (46:11–15)
   (3) Giving Land as Gifts (46:16–18)
   (4) Cooking Sacrificial Meals (46:19–24)
3. The New Land (47; 48)
   a. The River of the Water of Life from the Temple (47:1–12)
   b. The Division of the Land (47:13—48:29)
      (1) The Boundaries (47:13–21)
      (2) An Inheritance for the Alien (47:22, 23)
      (3) The Tribal Allotments (48:1–29)
          (a) The Seven Northern Tribes (48:1–7)
          (b) The Central Tribe, "the Holy Portion," the City Possession, and the Surrounding Area (48:8–22)
          (c) The Five Southern Tribes (48:23–29)
   c. The City: The Size, Gates, and Name (48:30–35)
      (1) The Size and the Gates (48:30–35a)
      (2) The Name: "The Lord Is There" (48:35b)

Part I

The Prophecy of Judgment on Judah and The Pronouncement of Sin (1—24)

1. The Prophet's Call and the First Vision (1—3)
2. The Prophecy of Judgment Through Signs and Oracles (4—7)
3. The Prophetic Utterance of Jerusalem's Sin and Judgment (the Second Vision)—The Withdrawal of the Glory of the Lord (8—11)
4. The Prophetic Utterances Against Jerusalem Continued (12—24)

Chapter 1

The First Vision: The Glory of the Lord

THE TIME OF THE VISION (1:1–3)

¹Now it came about in the thirtieth year, on the fifth day of the fourth month, while I was by the river Chebar among the exiles, the heavens were opened and I saw visions of God. ²(On the fifth of the month in the fifth year of King Jehoiachin's exile, ³the word of the LORD came expressly to Ezekiel the priest, son of Buzi, in the land of the Chaldeans by the river Chebar; and there the hand of the LORD came upon him.)

Verses 1, 2. Ezekiel's account of his prophecies begins with a narrative about his **visions of God**. These "visions" occurred in **the thirtieth year**. There is much discussion as to the meaning of this date.[1] Some scholars think that it is an attempt to date the prophecy more specifically than "in the fifth year of King Jehoiachin's exile" (v. 2). Others suggest that this is an attempt to identify the date as the "thirtieth year" from the time when Hilkiah the high priest found the book of Torah in the temple (2 Kings 22:8–13). In other words, Bible historians have counted backward from the fifth year of Jehoiachin's exile (mentioned in v. 2), arriving at the eighteenth year of Josiah's reign, when he found "the book of the law."

However, the more logical explanation is to link this date to

---

[1] Anthony D. York offered several explanations as to the meaning of the "thirtieth year" in "Ezekiel 1: Inaugural and Restoration Visions?" *Vetus Testamentum* 27 (January 1977): 82–98.

the age of Ezekiel. (See "A Timeline of Ezekiel" in Appendix 2.) Ezekiel was a priest (v. 3), and a Levite entered his priestly ministry at the age of thirty (Num. 4:3, 23, 30, 39, 43; see 1 Chron. 23:3). Therefore, Ezekiel apparently received this vision and his commission in the very year he began his priestly service. Thus God involved Ezekiel in a ministry immediately upon his becoming a priest, and we are allowed to witness the work of Ezekiel from his first commission.

The statement **I saw visions** is the first direct claim of inspiration for the book (v. 1; see Is. 1:1). As is explained in 1 Samuel 9:9, one who saw visions was a prophet. The fact that **the heavens were opened** indicates that God was allowing Ezekiel to see things both in and from the heavenly realm. No indication is given as to whether or not this event took place in a dreamlike state. Notice that Ezekiel also saw "visions of God." These incredible visions of God are described—in symbolic details—beginning in verse 4.

The vision came to Ezekiel by **the river Chebar**, a minor river or a canal in Babylonia. The location of the Chebar, if it can be identified with the Babylonian *naru kabari*, was between Babylon and Nippur.

The fifth [day of the fourth] **month in the fifth year of King Jehoiachin's exile** would be July 593(2) B.C. Jehoiachin was deported to Babylonia in 598(7) B.C. Therefore, Ezekiel received his commission in 593(2) B.C. It is significant that the year of King Jehoiachin's exile is the focal point of all dating within the book.

Although Zedekiah was king in Jerusalem at this time, Ezekiel chose to date the prophecy from the reign of Jehoiachin, because Jehoiachin was still considered king. Zedekiah was not really the king; he was made king by Nebuchadnezzar in 598(7) B.C., after the second deportation, in which both the legitimate king and Ezekiel were among ten thousand captives taken to Babylonia (see 2 Kings 24:10–17).

Verse 3. The phrase **Ezekiel the priest** presents some grammatical ambiguity; the phrase "the priest" could either be referring to the father or to the son. It does seem, though, that Ezekiel himself was a priest. This makes two sections especially significant: (1) chapter 4, where Ezekiel is asked to eat unclean food and (2) chapter 8, where Ezekiel is taken, in a vision, to see the abominations associated with the temple in Jerusalem. Ezekiel is called by his name only one other time within this book (24:24). He is described as a "sign" in 12:6, 11; 24:24, 27. "By his action what Yahweh is about to bring upon his people is already present. The prophet belongs inseparably to the 'message.'"[2]

Ezekiel was a priest and the **son of Buzi**. Nothing is known about Buzi—though, as Ezekiel's father, he also would have been a priest. The fact that Ezekiel was a priest is significant to the whole of his book and his ministry. The text is filled with allusions to the law of Moses, including priestly responsibilities, the temple, and personal purity. Ezekiel was able to convict the people of violating God's covenant and ignoring His laws and statutes.

The word of the Lord should be linked with the vision mentioned in verse 1. Those visions were, in fact, the word of the Lord. Ezekiel was not about to embark upon a discussion of his personal view of the ills of Israel. His ministry, like that of every true prophet of God, was to deliver the divine message. The phrase "the word of the Lord" occurs sixty times in the text of Ezekiel, clearly indicating the origin of his message (see 6:3; 25:3; 36:4).

Verse 3 says that **the hand of the Lord** came upon Ezekiel (see 3:14, 22; 8:1; 33:22; 37:1; 40:1). This phrase conveys more than just the idea that the prophet received a message from God; it implies the power of God and the submissiveness of Ezekiel. The word "hand" is often equivalent to power. (Compare Gen. 39:8 and Ex. 3:8 in the KJV and the NASB.)

Verses 1 through 3 provide evidence of Ezekiel's divine call:

1. "The heavens were opened," affording Ezekiel a special revelation given only to the true prophets of God. (Compare Ezekiel's vision to the one given to John in Rev. 4.)

---

[2]Walther Zimmerli, *Ezekiel 1: A Commentary on the Book of the Prophet Ezekiel, Chapters 1—24*, trans. Ronald E. Clements, Hermeneia (Philadelphia: Fortress Press, 1979), 54.

2. "I saw visions of God." Ezekiel was allowed to see God in a special way.

3. "The word of the LORD" came expressly to Ezekiel. We see a clear indication of inspiration; Ezekiel was given—directly—a message from God.

4. "The hand of the LORD came upon him." God was going to give Ezekiel the strength to bear and proclaim the message. According to Ralph H. Alexander, "'The hand of the Lord was upon him' connotes the idea of God's strength on behalf of the person involved (3:14; cf. Isa 25:10; 41:10, 20), a concept . . . in the name 'Ezekiel' (*yehezqel*), which means 'God strengthens.'"[3]

THE VISION (1:4–28)

Ezekiel described his vision in figurative ("apocalyptic") language. Many people have decided to read the book, only to be discouraged after encountering the first chapter. While some find the apocalyptic images fascinating as well as challenging, others would prefer to receive their information without so much effort. Simply stated, the goal of this vision was to give a demonstration of God and His magnificent glory (vv. 1, 28). Why did God not just state truths about His glory in decisive terms? Why did He use the figurative method of establishing such concepts?

First, we must remind ourselves of the perfect nature of God and His omniscience. God knows the best and the most perfect way to communicate important truths. Since God is spirit (Jn. 4:23, 24), human terms cannot fully convey His glory. Therefore, the use of apocalyptic visions such as this one enables us to see His awesomeness and His magnificent glory in terms that we are more likely to appreciate.

Second, a difficult task lay ahead of Ezekiel. He was being sent to a stubborn and obstinate people (3:7). This vision would help him to recall the greatness of the God he was serving. By

---

[3]Ralph H. Alexander, "Ezekiel," in *The Expositor's Bible Commentary*, ed. Frank E. Gaebelein (Grand Rapids, Mich.: Zondervan Publishing House, 1986), 6:755.

remembering this vision, Ezekiel would be continually strengthened and motivated to face the obstacles of preaching to such a people.

Third, we must remember that many people during Old Testament times believed that the gods of conquering nations were the stronger gods. This is the reason they deserted their gods to serve the gods of a conquering army. This point is illustrated throughout the Old Testament. What is remarkable is how the Israelites were so inclined to idolatry that they did what the other nations did not do: adopt the gods of the defeated nations! (See 2 Kings 16:3; 17:8.)

Ezekiel, as a result of the vision, would have sufficient evidence that the Babylonian gods—or any other gods for that matter—were powerless, unlike the one true God. He would be motivated to proclaim the excellencies of the Lord and encourage the people to renew their covenant with Him. If they would do this, they would find a God who was willing to forgive and reestablish them in their land.

What should we keep in mind when we are interpreting this type of literature? Ezekiel was painting a picture, and all the parts help to form a whole. These parts do not necessarily have meanings in and of themselves. Many times, phrases with the word "like" or "as" are used. This construction, called a "simile," tells us that Ezekiel's description is, at best, a likeness—an approximation—of what he was actually seeing. "Likeness" (דְּמוּת, $d^e muth$) occurs sixteen times in Ezekiel, and "like" is the preposition k^e (כְּ), found eighteen times in chapter 1 (166 times in Ezek.). In addition, notice the use of "like" with "appearance" (כְּמַרְאֶה, $k^e mar'eh$).

In preparation for studying this incredible vision, we should note the four predominant aspects of the vision. Each one should be considered in regard to how it contributes to the picture of the glory, majesty, and power of God.

1. The four living creatures (vv. 4–14)
2. The wheels (vv. 15–21)
3. The expanse (vv. 22–25)
4. The throne (vv. 26–28)

The Four Living Creatures (1:4–14)

1:4–6

⁴As I looked, behold, **a storm wind was coming from the north, a great cloud with fire flashing forth continually and a bright light around it, and in its midst something like glowing metal in the midst of the fire.** ⁵**Within it there were figures resembling four living beings. And this was their appearance: they had human form.** ⁶**Each of them had four faces and four wings.**

Verse 4. As the stage was set for this vision, Ezekiel noted four features that seemed to indicate that severe weather was approaching. (1) He said that **a storm wind was coming from the north** which is frequently the direction from which God's judgments are said to come (see Jer. 1:14; 4:6; 6:1, 22; 10:22; 13:20). (2) He saw **a great cloud with fire flashing forth continually**—suggesting a powerful electrical storm with continual lightning flashes. (3) He saw **a bright light** round about it, apparently shining brightly behind and around the storm clouds. (4) He saw **something like glowing metal**—lights in this storm that were atypical of any storm Ezekiel had ever seen. It had flashing lights with the vividness of hot metal when it was brought out of a fire.

Verse 5. Within this storm, Ezekiel saw four figures resembling **living beings** (see Rev. 4). Though the beings looked like men (having **human form**), each one "had four faces and four wings" (vv. 6, 9, 11; 10:5, 12, 14; 10:21, 22; see Rev. 4:8, where the living beings had six wings). Perhaps the reference to "human form" is because the creatures stood upright, with their legs straight (v. 7).

The use of "four" is thought by some to suggest completeness (see Is. 11:12). Notice the four faces and wings here, the four scenes of false worship in chapter 8, and the four plagues in chapter 14. In this context, "four" suggests God's omnipresence: With His servants facing every direction at once, nothing can escape His notice. The face of a man was predominant, facing to the front on each being (v. 10), while the lion's face was on the right, the bull's (or cherub's; see 10:14, 22) face on the left, and the eagle's face on the back. The "four wings" would provide an extra degree of mobility. These beings were cherubim (10:18–22).

Verse 6. This verse refers to **each of them**. In the description, the gender of the verb and pronoun references to the creatures change. Out of forty-five references, twelve are the grammatically proper feminine plural; the others are masculine plural.[4] The significance of this, as with other unusual grammatical features of the chapter, is unknown.[5] Those who draw attention to these anomalies must remember that such inconsistency is common in apocalyptic literature.

1:7–14

[7]Their legs were straight and their feet were like a calf's hoof, and they gleamed like burnished bronze. [8]Under their wings on their four sides were human hands. As for the faces and wings of the four of them, [9]their wings touched one another; their faces did not turn when they moved, each went straight forward. [10]As for the form of their faces, each had the face of a man; all four had the face of a lion on the right and the face of a bull on the left, and all four had the face of an eagle. [11]Such were their faces. Their wings were spread out above; each had two touching another being, and two covering their bodies. [12]And each went straight forward; wherever the spirit was about to go, they would go, without turning as they went. [13]In the midst of the living beings there was something that looked like burning coals of fire, like torches darting back and forth among the living beings. The fire was bright, and lightning was flashing from the fire. [14]And the living beings ran to and fro like bolts of lightning.

---

[4]Moshe Greenberg, *Ezekiel 1—20: A New Translation with Introduction and Commentary*, The Anchor Bible, vol. 22 (Garden City, N.Y.: Doubleday & Co., 1983), 44.

[5]See Daniel C. Fredericks, "Diglossia, Revelation, and Ezekiel's Inaugural Rite," *Journal of the Evangelical Theological Society* 41 (June 1998): 197.

Verse 7. While the **straight** legs mentioned depict the creature standing upright like a man, the **feet** are like those of a **calf**, providing a high degree of stability and durability, as well as mobility. These feet also drew Ezekiel's attention because they were glowing brightly like **burnished bronze**.

Verse 8. Ezekiel observed **human hands** under the wings (see 10:8, 21). Perhaps this feature would provide the ability to do the many versatile works that human hands can do. The description reminds us that one of the primary functions of these beings is to serve God in ministering to mankind.

Verse 9. Two of the four **wings** were in the act of flying, so stretched out that the extremity of each touched a wing of the next living creature, which also had its wings outstretched (vv. 9, 11, 23). This was when they were in motion, although the text never says that the wings were *moving*. Movement of the wings might be assumed from the noise they made (v. 24). While Ezekiel described these beings as cherubim, the four wings mentioned here remind us of the description of the seraphim mentioned in Isaiah 6:2 (see Ezek. 1:6, 9, 11; 10:5, 12, 14, 21, 22; Rev. 4:8). The Jewish Targum on this passage explained the meaning of these wings and their respective positions: "Holy ministers are in the sky before Him, each with six wings. With two they are covering their faces, lest they see the Lord. With two they are covering their bodies, lest they be seen; and with two they are ministering."[6] Ezekiel explained that two of the wings cover "their bodies" (v. 11). He also noted that when they stood still, they "dropped their wings" (vv. 24, 25).

Before describing the appearance of their faces, Ezekiel observed that their faces **did not turn when they moved, each went straight forward**. This point is repeated in verse 12 (also in 10:22). The four together formed a square and never altered their respective positions. The significance of this is seen in that the creatures never needed to be delayed by the act of turning. With astonishing quickness ("like bolts of lightning"; v. 14), they were able to respond to the bidding of God.

---

[6]A Targum is a somewhat paraphrased translation of a portion of the Old Testament in Aramaic. Tg. Ezek. 1:9 [Targum of Ezekiel].

Verse 10. Their "four faces"—those of a man, a bull, an eagle, and a lion—represent the major areas of created life.

Man is God's ultimate creation commissioned to subdue the earth; the lion is the king of wild beasts; the ox (or bull) is the strongest of domesticated animals; and the eagle rules the air. The chariot was borne aloft above the totality of creation, a symbol of the fact that nature is under the domination of the Lord.[7]

A Midrash to Exodus 15:1 supports the idea presented above:

> ... four kinds of proud beings were created in the world: the proudest of all—man; of birds—the eagle; of domestic animals—the ox; of wild animals—the lion; and all of them are stationed beneath the chariot of the Holy One...."[8]

Only the greatest of animals are worthy to be the bearers to God Almighty.

The general meaning of the faces could be as follows:

- **Man**—rational and moral nature, suggesting wisdom and intelligence.
- **Lion**—majesty and strength, suggesting power, rule, and authority.
- **Bull** ("ox"; KJV)—patient and productive service, representing labor, strength, and energy.
- **Eagle**—winged velocity and swiftness, indicating vision and flight.

Ezekiel wrote, "... so I knew that they were cherubim" (10:20;

---

[7]Carl G. Howie, *The Book of Ezekiel, The Book of Daniel*, The Layman's Bible Commentary, vol. 13 (Richmond, Va.: John Knox Press, 1961), 22.

[8]*Exodus Rabba* 23:13. A Midrash is a commentary on the Scriptures. The word transliterated "Midrash" occurs twice in the Old Testament (2 Chron. 13:22; 24:27).

see 10:21, 22). What are cherubim? These creatures always appear in a most intimate relation to the glory of God. They are seen as engaging in worship and service to God. In Ezekiel's vision, they were bearing up and transporting the throne of God (see 10:1–4).

Cherubim are spiritual creatures (Ps. 18:10; Heb. 9:5). Some think they are angels of the highest order, but that idea is not provable by Scripture; they are never called angels.

In ancient Israel, the cherubim were God's attendants and messengers. Representations of cherubim were found in the tabernacle (Ex. 36:35). Having these did not violate Exodus 20:4 because they were not worshiped. When Solomon built the temple, he had two gold cherubim, fifteen feet high, standing separately from the ark but still located in the most holy place (2 Chron. 3:10). Passages for further study include Genesis 3:24; Exodus 25:18–22; 26:31; 1 Samuel 4:4; 2 Samuel 22:11; 1 Kings 6:26–35.

Verses 11, 12. Ezekiel noted concerning the wings that **each had two touching another being** (v. 11). This is reminiscent of the cherubim on the ark of the covenant, whose wings touched above the ark (Ex. 25:18–22).

The spirit provided the leadership for the four living beings. Wherever the spirit would go, these beings would follow (see v. 20). Since this is a section about God's glory, it is logical that this spirit would be the Holy Spirit, or the Spirit of God. While it is possible that "the spirit" within them is a reference to their own spirit, it seems that the creatures were following the lead of the spirit (v. 12)—suggesting that they were following something independent of themselves. However "spirit" is understood, it would be contrary to the vision for these creatures to be operating apart from the will of God.

Verses 13, 14. Ezekiel saw something that looked like **torches** or **burning coals of fire**, as if coming from the bodies of the living beings themselves (v. 13). In apocalyptic literature, fire frequently symbolizes God's judgment (see Ps. 18:8; 50:3). This image seems to demonstrate that His judgment is quick and decisive, covering all the earth. Not only was **lightning** flashing from the coals of fire, but the living beings themselves **ran**

to and fro like bolts of lightning (v. 14). Their movements were quick and awe-inspiring. A vision of power was found among these creatures.

The Wheels (1:15–21)

¹⁵Now as I looked at the living beings, behold, there was one wheel on the earth beside the living beings, for each of the four of them. ¹⁶The appearance of the wheels and their workmanship was like sparkling beryl, and all four of them had the same form, their appearance and workmanship being as if one wheel were within another. ¹⁷Whenever they moved, they moved in any of their four directions without turning as they moved. ¹⁸As for their rims they were lofty and awesome, and the rims of all four of them were full of eyes round about. ¹⁹Whenever the living beings moved, the wheels moved with them. And whenever the living beings rose from the earth, the wheels rose also. ²⁰Wherever the spirit was about to go, they would go in that direction. And the wheels rose close beside them; for the spirit of the living beings was in the wheels. ²¹Whenever those went, these went; and whenever those stood still, these stood still. And whenever those rose from the earth, the wheels rose close beside them; for the spirit of the living beings was in the wheels.

Verses 15–17. The wheels are the *second part* of the vision. Translating the description is challenging. The Hebrew term תַּרְשִׁישׁ (*tharshish*) has been suggested to mean **sparkling beryl** (v. 16), chrysolite, yellow jasper, or topaz.[9] It is important to remember that the wheels are a symbol for something and are not meant to be interpreted literally. The wheels probably represent the idea of the activity of God or His *movement*. The Jews in Babylonia perhaps did not believe that God could come to them there. The idea existed in the ancient world, and in many Jewish people's minds, that God was confined to one geographical

---

[9]John B. Taylor, *Ezekiel: An Introduction and Commentary*, Tyndale Old Testament Commentaries (Downers Grove, Ill.: Inter-Varsity Press, 1969), 56–57.

area (1 Kings 20:23, 28). They may have believed that He was limited to the area surrounding Jerusalem and therefore could not be with them in Babylonia. These wheels show otherwise. The omnipresence of God is being described in apocalyptic terms.

Within another could mean that the second wheel was concentric to the first wheel, like an archery target, or that it was perpendicular to the first wheel. This construction would allow the wheels to be rolling constantly, never needing to turn (v. 17).

Verses 18, 19. While discussing the wheels of this divine chariot, Ezekiel described the rims as **lofty and awesome** (v. 18). This expression indicates not only that the rims were very high or tall, but also that they had a frightening appearance.[10] It has been well documented that kings in ancient cultures surrounded themselves with various objects signifying power. This vision far surpasses anything an earthly king could create or anything one could imagine for a pagan god. The **eyes** emphasize the all-seeing nature of God. Even though the children of Israel were in Babylonia, a faraway country, God could still see what they were doing—both good and bad. This introduces the concept of individual responsibility, which is covered more completely in chapter 18 (see 8:12; 9:9; Ps. 94:7). The wheels and eyes, combined, demonstrate both the omnipresence and the omniscience of God. Certainly, the "glory of God" is being fully realized in this spectacular vision. Moving in complete harmony, **the living beings** did not move independently of the wheels (v. 19).

Verses 20, 21. These wheels were not inanimate objects; they had spirits inside them (v. 20). The fact that Ezekiel repeated this point is noteworthy. How were the wheels and the living beings able to move in perfect harmony? Ezekiel explained: **For the spirit of the living beings was in the wheels** (v. 21b; emphasis added). The same spirit that led the living beings also dwelt within the wheels. Such a characteristic is apparently not

---

[10]Nahum M. Waldman, "A Note on Ezekiel 1:18," *Journal of Biblical Literature* 103 (December 1984): 614–18. Waldman offered this translation: "As for their rims—these having majesty and fearfulness—their rims were filled with eyes all around, all four of them" (617).

something Ezekiel could witness, but he knew this truth through revelation.

The Expanse (1:22–25)

²²Now over the heads of the living beings there was something like an expanse, like the awesome gleam of crystal, spread out over their heads. ²³Under the expanse their wings were stretched out straight, one toward the other; each one also had two wings covering its body on the one side and on the other. ²⁴I also heard the sound of their wings like the sound of abundant waters as they went, like the voice of the Almighty, a sound of tumult like the sound of an army camp; whenever they stood still, they dropped their wings. ²⁵And there came a voice from above the expanse that was over their heads; whenever they stood still, they dropped their wings.

Verse 22. The **expanse** is the *third part* of the vision. This word is the Hebrew word רָקִיעַ (*rakia'*), the same word used in Genesis 1:6–8 for the hard plane dividing the upper from the lower waters. The word "firmament" is used in the KJV, although this is not a good translation. The expanse seems to represent the widespread influence of God. Ezekiel did not dwell upon the expanse. He merely described that which provided the inspiring backdrop to the whole scene. Nevertheless, it appears that the expanse provided a firm, level surface upon which the throne of God was resting (see Rev. 4:6).

Verses 23, 24. It is obvious that the **wings** of the living beings continued to impress Ezekiel (v. 23). In this section he repeated their location, but this time elaborated on the tremendous sound (v. 24) being made by these wings. He offered three analogies: The noise was **like the sound of abundant waters**, which provide a tremendous roar—almost a deafening sound to one standing near a waterfall. It was **like the voice of the Almighty**—a voice that completely terrified those gathered around Mount Sinai in Exodus 20, but sometimes a term referring to thunder. The **sound of tumult** [was] **like the sound of an army camp**—which would involve a variety of sounds, from the clanking of gear and weapons to the grunts, groans, and cries of the soldiers. Not only was Ezekiel impressed with what he was *seeing*, but he was also awestruck with what he was *hearing*. He was able to witness God's glory in different ways.

Verse 25. In spite of all the noise generated by the wings of the four living creatures, Ezekiel was able to hear **a voice from above the expanse**—from the location of the throne of God. Ezekiel mentioned no words that were uttered, at least not yet, but the Lord spoke to him (see ch. 2).

The Throne (1:26–28)

²⁶**Now above the expanse that was over their heads there was something resembling a throne, like lapis lazuli in appearance; and on that which resembled a throne, high up, was a figure with the appearance of a man.** ²⁷**Then I noticed from the appearance of His loins and upward something like glowing metal that looked like fire all around within it, and from the appearance of His loins and downward I saw something like fire; and there was a radiance around Him.** ²⁸**As the appearance of the rainbow in the clouds on a rainy day, so was the appearance of the surrounding radiance. Such was the appearance of the likeness of the glory of the** Lord. **And when I saw it, I fell on my face and heard a voice speaking.**

Verse 26. The **throne** is the *fourth part* of the vision. What Ezekiel saw was not an actual throne but something **resembling a throne**. It was **like lapis lazuli**, a sapphire-like stone that was very valuable in the ancient world. Ezekiel did not dwell on the throne itself, because He who is on the throne is far more important. Nevertheless, a throne is always an image of power and authority. The word "throne" is a key word in the revelation. Here, Ezekiel was relating the universal power of the "King of kings." God's throne rises above the feeble attempts of authority and rule of man; it is far more glorious than the imagined thrones of pagan gods.

Ezekiel described God in symbolic terms, saying that He had **the appearance of a man.** He took great pains to avoid making

God creature-like, because God is indescribable and cannot be compared to anything or anyone.

Verse 27. The awe-inspiring portrayal of God in this verse emphasizes three primary features: His *fearsomeness*, His *radiance*, and His *majesty*. God is depicted as being surrounded from His waist up by something glowing like electrum (**glowing metal**). From His waist down, Ezekiel said that He was encompassed by what **looked like fire**. The entire figure, then, was encompassed with splendor (נֹגַהּ, *nogah*).[11] "Fire" is that which can destroy (in judgment) or can illuminate. Ezekiel would announce the fiery judgments of God.

Verse 28. The description in this verse includes the image of a **rainbow**. For Jews, the rainbow was a symbol of God's mercy and God's covenant (see Gen. 9:13). A rainbow comes after a storm. In this case, the storm of God's judgment was coming—but there was hope. There would be a rainbow after the storm, providing hope for the future. "Just as the colors of the rainbow are not real but merely the effect of sunlight, so the likeness of the glory of the Lord as visualized by the prophet was only the reflection of the Divine light."[12]

The Hebrew word translated "glory" (כָּבוֹד, *kabod*) is a technical term describing God (Ex. 16:7; 24:16; 40:34; Lev. 9:6, 23; Num. 14:10; 16:19; 1 Kings 8:11; 2 Chron. 7:1). His "glory" was generally associated with either the tabernacle or the temple. It was not seen elsewhere. By having Ezekiel see His glory far from the temple, God helped the Israelites to understand that He is not limited to one place—specifically, the temple at Jerusalem. Before, they would have felt cut off from God Almighty, but now He made them realize that they could still have a relationship with Him. The divine glory was not identified with storm clouds, angelic beings, or flashes of lightning. It was something peculiar to God Himself. While He exhibited certain human appearances or characteristics (1:28; 3:12, 23; 8:4; 9:3; 10:4, 18; 11:22, 23), God obviously is something far different than human beings.

---

[11] Ibid., 618.

[12] S. Fisch, *Ezekiel: Hebrew Text and English Translation with an Introduction and Commentary*, Soncino Books of the Bible (London: Soncino Press, 1950), 8.

In each vision Ezekiel was careful to distinguish between God's glory and its attendant circumstances.[13]

This is the first occurrence of the phrase **the glory of the LORD**, one of the key phrases in the book (1:28; 3:12, 23; 10:4, 18; 11:23; 43:4, 5; 44:4). Ezekiel seems to have structured his book around this phrase; the word "glory" occurs twenty-three times. In chapter 1 the glory is described, in 10:18 the glory departs, and in 43:5 the glory returns.

When Ezekiel saw the glory of the Lord, he said, **I fell on my face**. Why did he do this? Death resulted if one looked upon the face of God (Ex. 33:20). When Ezekiel realized who he was seeing, he dropped to the ground and covered his face so that he might live. Ezekiel is one of many who were overwhelmed by witnessing the glory of the Lord: Jacob (Gen. 32:30), Jeremiah (Jer. 1:6), Isaiah (Is. 6:5), Daniel (Dan. 10:8, 9), and John (Rev. 1:17) all responded with similar reactions.

APPLICATION

God's Great Attributes

This apocalyptic vision presents God's greatness and majesty.

Three truths are taught about the nature and the attributes of God: (1) He can bring judgment. He has the power—*omnipotence*—to do this, as represented by the four living creatures. (2) He can bring about righteous judgment. He has the knowledge—*omniscience*—to do this, as represented by the wheels and the eyes (see Eccles. 12:13, 14). (3) He will bring about universal judgment. Because of His ability to be everywhere—*omnipresence*—His power is not limited to Judea, and no man can escape justice (see Rev. 20:11–14).

The rainbow reminds us of God's mercy. God made the rainbow as a sign of His covenant with Noah. Though we are sinful, God has shown us mercy. His new covenant offers hope for salvation through Jesus' blood (see 1 Jn. 1:7; Eph. 1:7).

D.P.

---

[13]Everett F. Harrison, "A Neglected Apologetic," *Bibliotheca Sacra* 95 (October-December 1938): 478.

Preaching in a Difficult Time (1:1–3)

Every preacher should observe the kind of prophet Ezekiel was: He was a unique prophet for an extreme time in history.

He had a divine ministry. Ezekiel had a word from God. Through him, God was going to reveal His message to the people in captivity.

He had a relevant ministry. Ezekiel was placed among the people. He would not be sending them a letter, but he would give out God's message from the midst of them, as one of them.

He had a compassionate ministry. Ezekiel stood with God's message at a stressful time. From the viewpoint of Judah, these were the worst of times. They had been driven from their land and had received the sentence of living in a foreign land. This tragedy resulted from their sin, but God's mercy was still extended to them.

Ezekiel's Vision of God (1:4–22)

What does this vision tell us about God? Ezekiel saw God in a representative way, as he had never seen Him before.

First, we are reminded that God had not forgotten His people. We will give up on ourselves before God does.

Second, God is glorious and beyond our ability to picture. These symbols leave our minds spinning with wonder and amazement.

Third, God is almighty and omnipresent. The vision suggests God's greatness and His eternal nature.

We should fall on our knees in reverence and respect for God. In the presence of the true and living God, Ezekiel's heart quaked with the solemn reverence that is due Him.

E.C.

"Ezekiel Saw the Wheel" (1:15–21)

The wheels of Ezekiel 1 have received much attention and spark the imagination to ponder what they looked like and what purposes they served. Did they look like ancient chariot wheels? Could they have looked more like a space station or transporter? Questions like these are sometimes asked when reading apocalyptic literature.

One must approach prophetic studies responsibly. While an

eager literalist can misinterpret the symbolism found in Ezekiel, another reader may have an aversion to difficult passages in the Scriptures. This person may erroneously conclude that the Book of Ezekiel is not worth the effort to read. What we must recognize is that apocalyptic literature, although both sensational and difficult, has its own unique beauty.

Try to imagine the exiled Jews' situation. They were displaced. Not only were they suffering the pains of a foreign military's occupation and the destruction of their way of life, but they also were learning how to live in a new culture and speak a new language. The gods of Babylonia seemed to be the victors of this terrible battle; and the Jews' own conception of Yahweh, who allowed these things to happen, was being challenged.

As a people defeated, displaced, and distressed, they needed theological answers for their plight. How appropriate were the wheels of God's transport! At a time when they needed Him the most, the message Ezekiel delivered from his vision reassured them of God's universal presence. Indeed, even though the nation of Israel had rebelled against their Lord, He continued to move among them—no matter where they were—and to provide another opportunity for their deliverance.

The Voice of the Lord (1:24, 25)

In verses 24 and 25 we see two references to a voice. One sound was "like the voice of the Almighty," and another was the "voice" from the throne of the Lord. This theophany must have been an amazing and fearful experience. In several places in Scripture, God's powerful voice is compared to earth-shaking thunder.

In Exodus 20, when God announced the Ten Commandments, we read that "the people perceived the thunder and the lightning flashes and . . . when they saw it, they trembled and stood at a distance" (v. 18).

When God interrogated Job from the whirlwind, He asked, "Do you have an arm like God, and can you thunder with a voice like His?" (Job 40:9).

Psalm 29 is perhaps one of the most elaborate depictions of

God's voice as thunder in the Bible.[14] In this psalm God is represented as a thunderstorm moving across Palestine, and "the voice of the LORD" serves as a metaphor for thunder. As we read "the voice of the LORD is powerful" and "the voice of the LORD shakes the wilderness," we are to imagine His presence and might as awesome as this severe weather wreaking havoc in the wilderness.

The Almighty knows how to capture our attention. When His Word is brought before us, the question we must ask ourselves is whether or not we are ready and willing to obey.

T.P.W.

---

[14]For a good discussion of Psalm 29 see Eddie Cloer, *Psalms 1—50*, Truth for Today Commentary Series (Searcy, Ark.: Resource Publications, 2004), 383–95.

Chapter 2
Ezekiel's Call from the Lord

THE COMMISSION RECEIVED (2:1—3:11)

"Go to the House of Israel" (2:1–7)

2:1

¹Then He said to me, "Son of man, stand on your feet that I may speak with you!"

Verse 1. Based upon the incredible vision of chapter 1, Ezekiel was to be given his commission. God was not expecting His prophet to go preach without a full vision of His greatness and glory. Ezekiel's task was to convey to an exiled, discouraged people the wonderful attributes of their God. The Lord continued to appear to Ezekiel in this same fashion, to encourage him and remind him that he was a servant of the almighty God (3:12, 23, 24; 8:2–4; 9:3; 10:1–20; 11:22, 23; 43:2–4).

The phrase **son of man** occurs first here and is found ninety-three times in Ezekiel. It means "man of service," or "servant."

> In this summons the prophet was not being addressed in the uniqueness of his particular personal being, as would be expressed by his proper name, nor according to his office, but as an individual within the created order, the servant, who is summoned by his master. . . .[1]

---

[1] Walther Zimmerli, *Ezekiel 1: A Commentary on the Book of the Prophet Ezekiel, Chapters 1—24,* trans. Ronald E. Clements, Hermeneia (Philadelphia: Fortress Press, 1979), 131.

The expression most related to Christ is found in Daniel 7:13, where the Son of Man is given the kingdom by the Ancient of Days. This is an obvious prophetic passage, referring to Christ. The phrase is one that Christ used often to refer to Himself. Why did Jesus call Himself the "Son of Man"? These words stress His humanity, underscore His intention to be a servant (like Ezekiel), and identify Him as a representative for all mankind on the cross.[2]

The command to "stand on your feet" is reminiscent of Romans 14:4. God will help us to do everything He wants us to do (see Phil. 2:12, 13; Heb. 13:20, 21). Ezekiel was commanded to stand, and in verse 2 the Spirit gave him the strength to stand.

2:2–4

[2] As He spoke to me the Spirit entered me and set me on my feet; and I heard Him speaking to me. [3] Then He said to me, "Son of man, I am sending you to the sons of Israel, to a rebellious people who have rebelled against Me; they and their fathers have transgressed against Me to this very day. [4] I am sending you to them who are stubborn and obstinate children, and you shall say to them, 'Thus says the Lord GOD.'"

Verse 2. When God **spoke**, He gave Ezekiel the ability to understand His communication. God was going to equip him to understand the message he was about to deliver. The same was true with the apostles of Christ (see Mt. 10:19, 20; Jn. 15:26, 27; 16:13). **The Spirit** had to help Ezekiel stand because he was so weak. The vision described in chapter 1 was of such magnitude that it took all of Ezekiel's strength. Since God was "sending" Ezekiel to the people, he needed to be standing (see 3:24).

Verse 3. God's **rebellious people** are described further in verses 4 through 8. He had to punish them because of their disobedience to Him. The ten northern tribes were defeated and

---

[2] A good source for further study is F. F. Bruce, "The Background to the Son of Man Sayings," in *Christ the Lord: Studies in Christology Presented to Donald Guthrie*, ed. Harold H. Rowden (Downers Grove, Ill.: Inter-Varsity Press, 1982), 50–70.

assimilated into the Assyrian culture in 722(1) B.C., and the southern tribes were carried into Babylon in 587(6) B.C. Unfortunately, this condition of rebellion described the Israelites for centuries. They had continually rebelled against God's law, against God's prophets, and against God Himself. Ezekiel, like the prophets before him (see Is. 6), was being told exactly what kind of people he would try to warn. To be a successful man of God, it is necessary to see people *the way God sees them*. The tendency is to view the people in light of more wicked people or nations, as did Habakkuk (see Hab. 1:2–4, 12, 13). Ezekiel had to realize that the transgressions of the people remained **to this very day**. Even in captivity, the people would not repent and turn to the Lord. They were still rebellious.

Verse 4. How did God see these people? They were **stubborn**. "Brazen" would be a better translation, because these individuals refused to admit guilt; they were shameless (Is. 50:7; see Jer. 5:3). The people were also **obstinate**. They had hearts of stone (Ezek. 36:26). In such a condition, the person has an unyielding will and refuses to humble himself, even when he is found guilty. Ezekiel was not left to offer his own perspective on the ills of the people. His message was to be clear: **"Thus says the Lord GOD."** Throughout the Old and New Testaments, God held men accountable for the messages delivered by His prophets. Those who refused to listen to them were refusing God Himself (see 1 Cor. 14:37, 38; 1 Thess. 2:13).

2:5–7

⁵"As for them, whether they listen or not—for they are a rebellious house—they will know that a prophet has been among them. ⁶And you, son of man, neither fear them nor fear their words, though thistles and thorns are with you and you sit on scorpions; neither fear their words nor be dismayed at their presence, for they are a rebellious house. ⁷But you shall speak My words to them whether they listen or not, for they are rebellious."

Verse 5. God's purpose in sending Ezekiel was to let the people know that **a prophet** of God had been **among them**. Obviously, God wanted them to "repent and live" (see 18:23, 32). However, if they failed to heed the pleadings of this prophet of God, at least they would not be able to say that God had given them no *opportunity* to repent. They could never deny that God had tried to restore them. Ezekiel was supposed to present his messages, **whether they listen**[ed] **or not**. To God, successful evangelism is the *faithful* proclamation of His Word, regardless of the people's response (see 3:7). Ezekiel was not to hold back because of opposition. *When* he presented this message, *then* the people would know that a prophet had been among them.

Rebellious house (vv. 5–8; 3:9, 26, 27; 12:2, 3, 9, 25; 17:12; 24:3) is the counterpart to the expression "house of Israel." By renaming His people, God expressed as fully as possible the depth of their sin. It was appropriate that God renamed them. When He renamed Jacob in Genesis 33:24–28, He changed his name to "Israel," or "he who strives with God." Ezekiel was being sent to a nation that was striving against God.

Why did God send Ezekiel to the people? They already knew that they were being punished. Jeremiah, who had been preaching since 627 B.C., had sent a letter to the captives (see Jer. 29). For almost thirty years, He had told the people that the city would be destroyed and that they would be taken captive. God sent Ezekiel because of His great love for the people (2 Chron. 36:15; 1 Tim. 2:4; 2 Pet. 3:9).

Verses 6, 7. When God told Ezekiel, **"Neither fear"** (v. 6), He was talking about personal safety. Ezekiel had good reason to "fear" for his safety; yet God told him not to think about that, but only to preach. Whenever one preaches the message of God, opposition will come. Whenever the truth is preached, opposition will arise (Gal. 4:16). As others have observed, the preacher should either comfort the afflicted or afflict the comfortable. Ezekiel had a difficult job ahead of him. God was not softening the truth, but He offered His prophet strength and encouragement (v. 6; see 3:8–11, 22, 23). The temptation to fear opposition would be great, because the people would rise up as **thorns** pricking him and **scorpions** stinging him.

God specified, **"But you shall speak My words . . ."** (v. 7). This instruction took the pressure off Ezekiel; the "words" which he was to speak were not his, but God's. If the people rejected the prophet, they were rejecting God.

Twice, God said that Ezekiel should not fear "their words" (v. 6). Rather, he (and they) were to fear the word of God. Ezekiel would be far worse off if he chose to yield to the people rather than to the God whose glory he had witnessed. All Ezekiel had to do was "speak" (v. 7). If he chose not to speak because he knew the people would not listen, then he would be in rebellion with them. If he spoke, God would be pleased. This is all God wants from us today—to be faithful to Him. If our gift is showing mercy or helping others, we need to use that gift, regardless of what other people may do or think. Servants serve because that is *who they are*, not because of the worthiness of those served.

"Eat the Scroll"
(2:8—3:3)

2:8–10
⁸**"Now you, son of man, listen to what I am speaking to you; do not be rebellious like that rebellious house. Open your mouth and eat what I am giving you." ⁹Then I looked, and behold, a hand was extended to me; and lo, a scroll was in it. ¹⁰When He spread it out before me, it was written on the front and back, and written on it were lamentations, mourning and woe.**

Verse 8. God told Ezekiel, "**. . . listen to what I am speaking to you.**" God was not giving this commission to others; the responsibility was Ezekiel's. If he did not listen, then he himself would be **rebellious**. The prophet's rebellion would have been seen in a refusal to preach the message God was giving him to preach. Ralph H. Alexander explained,

> The Lord's charge to Ezekiel emphasized the absolute necessity of hearing, understanding, and assimilating God's message prior to going forth as a spokesman for the Lord. Ezekiel was to listen to God (2:8a) and not rebel

against him as did the people of Israel, who failed to listen to his word.[3]

This is the seventh occurrence of the word "rebellious" in this chapter.

Next, God told Ezekiel to **eat** what would be given to him (v. 8c). What Ezekiel was to eat was at first left vague to stress the unconditional submission of the prophet. If he did not surrender to God completely, he would be considered rebellious, like the house of Israel. To "eat" the book signifies being thoroughly possessed with its contents (compare 3:10; Jer. 15:16).

Verses 9, 10. The prophet was given a **scroll** (v. 9), literally, a "scroll of a book" (see Ps. 40:7). This was the ancient kind, with the text written on animal skins that were sewn and rolled together. The writing was usually on one side; but in this case, **it was written on the front and back** (v. 10a), that is, on both sides. The writing seemed to be running over, expressing the abundance of calamities in store for the rebellious people. Also, this would allow no further words to be added to the scroll. Its overwhelming fullness signified the completeness of God's message. Nothing was to be added by the prophet (or anyone else).

The subject matter of this scroll was **lamentations, mourning and woe** (v. 10b). It was filled with "lamentations" (songs like funeral dirges, full of sadness and tears), "mourning" (bemoaning a sad situation or tragedy), and "woe" (words of warning that, despite present difficulties, a situation can get worse).

APPLICATION

Obedience to God's Word

All God wants us to do is be faithful to Him. God tells us in His Word how to be faithful.

The majority of people may be rebellious to the Word of God (and probably will be; see Mt. 7:13, 14). It is each person's

---

[3]Ralph H. Alexander, "Ezekiel," in *The Expositor's Bible Commentary*, ed. Frank E. Gaebelein (Grand Rapids, Mich.: Zondervan Publishing House, 1986), 6:763.

responsibility to be faithful—regardless of what others may do.

God's preachers will always face the temptation to yield to the feelings of the hearers (see 2 Tim. 4:3, 4). The preacher must speak the truth, whether or not it is popular or accepted (Acts 20:27; 2 Tim. 2:15; Jas. 3:1).

The revelation of God is complete (Jude 3; see Rev. 22:18, 19). He has given us all that is needed for life and godliness (2 Pet. 1:3). There is no room for people to add to or take away from what God has given.

D.P.

Obeying God's Commission

The commission of God is a theme that pervades the whole Bible. His commission always involves three parties: the Sender, the messenger, and the target. Each of these can be seen in this chapter.

God was the Sender (vv. 3, 4). God had a message for the people. He was hurt by their transgressions and sought an opportunity to relay His words to them.

Ezekiel was the messenger (vv. 3–7). God chose Ezekiel. He had no need to fear, for the Sender would be with him. God did not promise an easy mission, but implied in this commission was His presence and guidance throughout the endeavor.

The people of Israel were the target (vv. 3–7). God acknowledged at the beginning that Ezekiel's target was a rebellious nation. Built into this situation was frustration and disappointment. Perhaps Ezekiel even wondered to himself, "What's the point?" The point was, however, that God had called him to preach His Word. Paul wrote to Timothy to "preach the word . . . in season and out of season" (2 Tim. 4:2a). One Hungarian translation says, ". . . whether it is appropriate or not."

Not all of us are sent to easy targets, but we are all called. In both receptive and resistant fields, we must take seriously the burden of the gospel that God puts on our hearts. We should trust in His sovereign plan to prepare the soil before us in His own good time.

EZEKIEL 2

Counting the Cost of God's Commission

Ezekiel's ministry involved difficult visual demonstrations of the severity of God's message. When he modeled the siege of Jerusalem, he suffered discomfort and perhaps public humiliation (ch. 4).

God forewarned Ezekiel that this mission would be hard when He mentioned "thistles," "thorns," and "scorpions" (v. 6). He did not explicitly tell Ezekiel what he would suffer, but the point was clear, "Ezekiel, this job won't be easy."

Jesus warned His disciples that they should count the cost of their commitment to Him. He asked, "What king, when he sets out to meet another king in battle, will not first sit down and consider whether he is strong enough with ten thousand men to encounter the one coming against him with twenty thousand?" (Lk. 14:31; see vv. 28–33).

When God sends His people on a mission, they must be ready for a battle. Accepting God's commission must not be about glamor or pride, but rather humility and a willingness to serve. As we ponder over and seek out our ways to serve the Lord, may we, too, consider the depth of our commitment to Him. The road ahead may not be easy, but since God is with us, we shall not fear! (Ezek. 2:6; Mt. 10:28; Rom. 8:31).

T.P.W.

CHAPTER 3
EZEKIEL'S CALL FROM THE LORD (CONTINUED)

"Eat the Scroll" (Continued)
(2:8—3:3)

3:1–3
¹Then He said to me, "Son of man, eat what you find; eat this scroll, and go, speak to the house of Israel." ²So I opened my mouth, and He fed me this scroll. ³He said to me, "Son of man, feed your stomach and fill your body with this scroll which I am giving you." Then I ate it, and it was sweet as honey in my mouth.

Verse 1. No chapter break should have been made between 2:10 and 3:1, for the same thought is being continued. After being offered the scroll, Ezekiel was told, "... **eat what you find.**" Whether or not he found something appetizing was unimportant. His job was simple: to eat what he found—as it was—and *then* go and **speak** the message. One should not embark upon the task of preaching God's Word without having first digested the message. Much damage has been done to the truth by unqualified, unlearned men (see 2 Pet. 3:15, 16).

Verses 2, 3. God's Word is **sweet** (v. 3; Ps. 19:10; 119:103). This implies that the Word of God is always good—even when it is a message of "lamentations, mourning and woe" (2:10). Ralph H. Alexander explained that "this was not a joyous note to begin on. But even when the ministry would seem difficult and distasteful, the Lord would cause his word to be as sweet as honey (3:3; cf. Pss 19:10; 119:103; Prov 16:24; 24:13–14; Jer

15:16)."¹ As John was told in Revelation 10:9, Ezekiel was told here to eat the scroll.

> Before, there was a direct commission, now there is a symbolic action. . . . John has the same vision [Rev. 10:8–10], but there that is expressed, which is here left to be inferred, [namely,] that *as soon as he had eaten it his belly was bitter.* The sweetness in the mouth denoted that it was good to be a messenger of the Lord . . . , but the bitterness which accompanied it, denoted that the commission brought with it much sorrow.²

This illustrates how God's prophets were responsible for making the message a part of themselves—taking it deep inside them. In Jeremiah 20:9 the message was a burning fire in the prophet's bones. No faithful preacher can separate himself from the Word. It is a part of his life, a part of his thinking.

"Speak My Message" (3:4–11)

3:4–7
⁴Then He said to me, "Son of man, go to the house of Israel and speak with My words to them. ⁵For you are not being sent to a people of unintelligible speech or difficult language, but to the house of Israel, ⁶nor to many peoples of unintelligible speech or difficult language, whose words you cannot understand. But I have sent you to them who should listen to you; ⁷yet the house of Israel will not be willing to listen to you, since they are not willing to listen to Me. Surely the whole house of Israel is stubborn and obstinate."

Verse 4. The house of Israel refers to all the Israelites—both the northern ten tribes and the southern two tribes. Ezekiel's

---

¹Ralph H. Alexander, "Ezekiel," in *The Expositor's Bible Commentary*, ed. Frank E. Gaebelein (Grand Rapids, Mich.: Zondervan Publishing House, 1986), 6:763.

²Albert Barnes, *The Bible Commentary: Proverbs to Ezekiel*, Barnes' Notes, ed. F. C. Cook, abr. and ed. J. M. Fuller (Grand Rapids, Mich.: Baker Book House, 1983), 312.

mission was to all the "sons of Israel" (see 2:3). Second Chronicles 30 specifies that a number of Israelites from the northern kingdom had moved down to Judah. The dispensationalist idea of the "ten lost tribes" is not biblically supportable. In this chapter we find that people from Asher, Manasseh, Zebulun, Ephraim, and Issachar were living in the southern kingdom. This also explains how Anna in Luke 2:36 was able to know that she was of the tribe of Asher (see Acts 26:7).

Verse 4 provides the basic definition of preaching: **go**—the preacher is one who is sent (Rom. 10:14, 15); **speak**—preaching requires the man of God to make audible the message; and speak **My words**—it is not true preaching unless it is God's Word that is preached (see 2 Tim. 4:2).

Verses 5, 6. When Ezekiel began his ministry, he did not encounter some of the difficulties so frequently associated with mission work. God noted that he was not dealing with people of **unintelligible speech** (vv. 5, 6a)—literally, "deepness of lip." This phrase is found only here and in Isaiah 33:19, where it refers to foreign peoples who speak a language that cannot be understood. The next phrase—**difficult language**—was used by Moses (Ex. 4:10), who considered himself inadequate as God's spokesman; perhaps he was not fluent or eloquent as a speaker. Ezekiel was being sent to his own people. He spoke a language familiar to them. This made the commission easier for Ezekiel, but it also added to the responsibility of **the house of Israel** (v. 6b). They were without excuse; they could not claim that they would have obeyed the message if they had understood it. Therefore, God said that they **should listen** to Ezekiel. Far too often, preachers assume that just because they are preaching the Word people will listen. They "should" listen, but not all do. Those who refuse to listen will be held accountable.

Verse 6b has an alternative translation in the NKJV and in a footnote in some printings of the NASB: "Surely, had I sent you to them, they would have listened to you." God said that if Ezekiel had preached to the nations around him, they would have listened to the message, even though it came from a "foreign God" (Yahweh). In contrast, Israel, who should have listened to him, would not. The NIV translates the statement this way: "Surely if I had sent you to them, they would have listened to you."

Verse 7. God revealed to Ezekiel the hard reality: The people would **not be willing to listen**. Throughout the Bible, and especially in the Gospel of John, it is evident that people have to be predisposed to listen. Paul would say that a "love of the truth" is required to be saved (2 Thess. 2:10). God does not force-feed truth to anyone. As Ezekiel willingly "opened [his] mouth" (3:2) to be fed God's word, so people today ought to be willing to learn the truth. Every student of the Bible should ask, "Am I open to the truth? Am I willing to challenge my previously held beliefs when they come in conflict with the inspired Word of God?"

We must not find ourselves in the same situation as those in Romans 10:2: "For I testify about them that they have a zeal for God, but not in accordance with knowledge," or Hosea 4:6a: "My people are destroyed for lack of knowledge." Jesus taught that only in *knowing* the truth can one be free (Jn. 8:32). Why did Israel refuse to listen? They were **stubborn and obstinate** (see Is. 48:4; Jer. 3:3). These unfortunate attributes explained to Ezekiel the reason his message would be rejected. The rejection would not be of the prophet personally. The people, God said, **"[were] not willing to listen to Me."** God had, through the ages, spoken to them through other prophets—yet with the same results (see Mt. 5:12; Jn. 15:18–20).

3:8–11
⁸"Behold, I have made your face as hard as their faces and your forehead as hard as their foreheads. ⁹Like emery harder than flint I have made your forehead. Do not be afraid of them or be dismayed before them, though they are a rebellious house." ¹⁰Moreover, He said to me, "Son of man, take into your heart all My words which I will speak to you and listen closely. ¹¹Go to the exiles, to the sons of your people, and speak to them and tell them, whether they listen or not, 'Thus says the Lord GOD.'"

Verses 8, 9. How would God equip His prophet to deal with such a stubborn people? He planned to make Ezekiel's **face as hard as their faces** (v. 8; see Jer. 1:18).

The word "hard" (חָזָק, *chazaq*) is repeated in verse 9. This is a play on Ezekiel's name, which means "God makes strong or hard." Indeed, God would strengthen Ezekiel for the difficult task ahead. He was to become the ultimate "hardheaded preacher." Perhaps we could use a few more of these today, as opposed to the "ear-ticklers" whose preaching is often popular (2 Tim. 4:3, 4).

Ezekiel's forehead would be **like emery harder than flint** (v. 9). The word translated "emery" ("adamant"; KJV) is apparently used here metaphorically to represent something extremely hard, like a diamond used to cut flint (see Jer. 17:1). As Ezekiel's firmness became like that of a diamond, he should be able to cut through the hard hearts of the people.

It seems sad that God had to make the prophet this way, but the people were so **rebellious** that extreme measures were required to try to reach them. This philosophy is in sharp contrast to the religious world of today, in which the operative word is "tolerance." There is only *one* way and *one* truth. Such narrowness is unpopular, but being swept away "by every wind of doctrine" is contrary to the plan of God (Eph. 4:14).

Verse 10. God wanted Ezekiel to take His message into his **heart** (see Job 22:22). God's prophet needed to develop a love for His word. Truth becomes a part of the one who teaches it, defining who he is, his character, and his life's aim. God wanted **all** of His words to be taken in by Ezekiel. The preacher cannot pick and choose which of God's laws to preach and obey. True devotion to God requires attention to all of His commands (see Mt. 23:23). When Jeremiah wanted to quit preaching (Jer. 20:9), his *heart* would not let him because God's word was in his heart.

Verse 11. While there may be no fine distinction between "speaking" and "telling," God's point was clear when He told Ezekiel, **". . . speak to them and tell them."** God wanted Ezekiel to communicate His word decisively and constantly. Although Ezekiel would encounter rejection, he was to preach, **whether they listen or not**. This phrase has now been used three times, in 2:5, 7 and 3:11. The power of the prophet's message would be found in his opening line: "Thus says the Lord GOD."

Ezekiel must, therefore, go and proclaim God's message—faithfully, skillfully, and courageously. Moshe Greenburg wrote,

> . . . this is a revelation of God's concern for his people, even when, as here, the content of his message is wrath and doom. In his wrath over their evildoing he does not abandon them but sends them repeated warnings of the misfortune that must overtake them; this constant theme of Jeremiah (7:25; 25:4; 26:5; 35:15; 44:4) is elaborated in II Chron 36:15—"YHWH [Yahweh] God of their fathers sent word to them by his messengers, sending every day anew, because he had compassion for his people and his house." Even when there is little hope of averting the misfortune, a prophet is still sent, so that afterward the people will realize that a prophet had been among them, that is, God had given them warning in due time; it was no lack of consideration on his part but their own heedlessness that caused their downfall.[3]

INSTRUCTIONS ABOUT HIS MINISTRY (3:12–27)

"Go to Babylon" (3:12–15)

[12]Then the Spirit lifted me up, and I heard a great rumbling sound behind me, "Blessed be the glory of the LORD in His place." [13]And I heard the sound of the wings of the living beings touching one another and the sound of the wheels beside them, even a great rumbling sound. [14]So the Spirit lifted me up and took me away; and I went embittered in the rage of my spirit, and the hand of the LORD was strong on me. [15]Then I came to the exiles who lived beside the river Chebar at Tel-abib, and I sat there seven days where they were living, causing consternation among them.

---

[3]Moshe Greenberg, *Ezekiel 1—20: A New Translation with Introduction and Commentary*, The Anchor Bible, vol. 22 (Garden City, N.Y.: Doubleday & Co., 1983), 75.

Verses 12, 13. Ezekiel had received his commission. Now **the Spirit** (v. 12) that filled and strengthened Ezekiel transported him to the place of his ministry. It was time to get to work. Meanwhile, Ezekiel was given another glimpse of the wonderful vision of chapter 1—with **the living beings** and the tremendous sound of power. It is no wonder that the sound behind him cried, **"Blessed be the glory of the Lord in His place."** The place where the Lord revealed Himself in the vision—with the expanse, the throne and all the glorious details—provides a powerful reminder of the "glory" of God.

Verse 14. Ezekiel went **embittered in the rage of** [his] **spirit**. This could either refer to his righteous anger at the people's sinfulness or to his anger at being given such a hopeless job. Jeremiah sometimes experienced such feelings (see Jer. 20:7–10). The former seems to be the better choice: Ezekiel, as a result of the heavenly vision, now shared the righteous anger of God. He embarked upon his ministry with a heart full of "rage" that this people—*his* people—could be so stubborn and rebellious against their one true God. Fellow Israelites would mock and persecute him; even friends and relatives would reject him and his message. Nevertheless, **the hand of the Lord** provided the strength Ezekiel needed to go forth.

Verse 15. After he came to the place where the exiles were living, Ezekiel **sat there seven days**. It could be that God allowed Ezekiel this period of time to grow accustomed to his role as a prophet. More likely, God wanted him to get an accurate measure of the people's spiritual and emotional condition. Every minister needs to understand the people before he can relate to them and preach a message that touches them "where they live."

The Spirit placed Ezekiel in **Tel-abib**, which was the location of the Jewish settlement along the banks of **the river Chebar** in Babylon. "Tel-abib" means "the mound of the deluge" in Chaldean, "the mound of corn ears" in Hebrew, and "sand heap" or "stone heap" in Assyrian.

Ezekiel sat in this place, **causing consternation among** his countrymen. "Causing consternation" is not an accurate translation. The Hebrew word (מַשְׁמִים, from the root שָׁמֵם, *shamem*) is a

Hiphil participle and means to "be desolated, appalled, . . . shewing horror."[4] The NRSV seems to have the best translation: "And I sat there among them, stunned, for seven days." This, then, describes Ezekiel's condition among the exiles. He was "overwhelmed, overcome with a mixture of horror and wonderment at what he had seen and heard."[5]

"Be a Watchman" (3:16–21)

¹⁶At the end of seven days the word of the LORD came to me, saying, ¹⁷"Son of man, I have appointed you a watchman to the house of Israel; whenever you hear a word from My mouth, warn them from Me. ¹⁸When I say to the wicked, 'You will surely die,' and you do not warn him or speak out to warn the wicked from his wicked way that he may live, that wicked man shall die in his iniquity, but his blood I will require at your hand. ¹⁹Yet if you have warned the wicked and he does not turn from his wickedness or from his wicked way, he shall die in his iniquity; but you have delivered yourself. ²⁰Again, when a righteous man turns away from his righteousness and commits iniquity, and I place an obstacle before him, he will die; since you have not warned him, he shall die in his sin, and his righteous deeds which he has done shall not be remembered; but his blood I will require at your hand. ²¹However, if you have warned the righteous man that the righteous should not sin and he does not sin, he shall surely live because he took warning; and you have delivered yourself."

Verses 16, 17. The phrase **the word of the LORD** occurs sixty times in this book. Earlier, God had commissioned Ezekiel to preach only His word (3:4). Now Ezekiel received that word. However, the initial message is not so much a message to be preached as a caution regarding the responsibility of the prophet. God viewed him as **a watchman**. The image is often applied to

---

[4]Francis Brown, S. R. Driver, and Charles A. Briggs, *A Hebrew and English Lexicon of the Old Testament* (Oxford: Clarendon Press, 1972), 1030–31.
[5]John B. Taylor, *Ezekiel: An Introduction and Commentary,* Tyndale Old Testament Commentaries (Downers Grove, Ill.: Inter-Varsity Press, 1969), 67.

God's prophets (see Is. 52:8; 56:10; 62:6; Jer. 6:17; Hos. 9:8; Mic. 7:4). Watchmen, stationed in strategic locations on the city walls, looked out for impending danger. They were the city's security system. When these lookouts saw danger, they were to warn the people immediately so that they might prepare themselves for the danger. The application to the prophet is powerful. He was charged with being alert to God's word and then making the people aware of the danger of disobedience. He was to **warn them** regarding the consequences of sin and the inevitable judgment of God if they continued to neglect His will. The truth to learn here is that God is the true watchman. His prophets merely function as servants of the true watchman.

Verse 18. "**When I say. . . .**" The people needed to listen to Ezekiel because God was talking and not Ezekiel. He was not speaking his own ideas or of his own volition, as did the false prophets around him. When the Almighty said that the wicked would die, He charged His prophet to **warn him**, to **speak out to warn the wicked**. These two phrases indicate that the prophet was expected to raise his voice—that is, to preach the message—with greater urgency as time passed. The warning given was "**You will surely die.**" While false watchmen (prophets) often declared a message of peace (Jer. 6:14; 8:11), the true prophet was to explain the sad reality. There was no escaping death. The self-deceived hearer would **die in his iniquity**, even if the watchman did not warn him.

God expected His watchman to warn of coming dangers. If he failed in that task, God would hold him responsible for the destruction that would follow. In such a case, the watchman would be guilty of failing to obey a command of God—and disobedience results in death.[6] In this context, "die" refers only to physical death. Alexander wrote,

> "Life" and "death" in this context are to be understood as physical, not eternal, life and death. The concept of life and death in the Mosaic covenant is primarily

---

[6]See Gen. 9:5, 6; Judg. 9:24; 2 Sam. 4:5–12; Acts 18:6; 20:26; Ps. 37:35, 36; 55:23; Prov. 10:27; 1 Jn. 5:16.

physical. The Mosaic covenant was given to guide those who had already entered into a relationship with God by faith (Lev 18:5; Deut 4:37–40; ch. 6; 7:6–11; 10:15–17; 30:15–20). The Hebrews could live righteously and freely by keeping these commands (Lev 18:5; Deut 16:20; cf. John 14:15). But if they disobeyed, physical death, resulting in a shortened life, was the normal result.[7]

Preaching the Word of God is no light matter. It is a paramount responsibility, and the watchman must be faithful to the charge given to him.[8]

Ezekiel was to warn the whole "house of Israel" (v. 17; 33:7). In using the singular for "house," God was not saying that Ezekiel had to warn every individual. He was clarifying the principle found in the object lesson of the watchman in 33:2–6.

Verse 19. The prophet's task was to *warn, speak up to warn, so as to keep alive* the doomed. Failing to do so, he would forfeit his own life.[9] If the **wicked** one was warned but did not respond to the warning, he would **die in his iniquity**. A man who remained in wickedness—whether warned or not—would die because of his wickedness. However, to the faithful prophet who had warned the guilty, God said, **"You have delivered yourself."**

God had already told Ezekiel that the people were stubborn and rebellious and that they would not listen to him. The passage shows how God assured Ezekiel that he would not be held accountable for their failure to heed the message. The preacher is not responsible for whether the message is rejected or accepted. He is responsible only for the proclamation of that message. This parallels what the Lord said in Jeremiah 6:17:

"And I set watchmen over you, saying,

---

[7]Alexander, 766.

[8]Greenberg translated the verse this way: "When I say to a wicked man, 'You shall die,' and you do not warn him—you do not speak up to warn the wicked man against his wicked course so as to keep him alive, he, [the] wicked man, shall die because of his iniquity, but I will hold you responsible for his death" (Greenberg, 82).

[9]Ibid., 87.

'Listen to the sound of the trumpet!'
But they said, 'We will not listen.'"

Verse 20. The watchman's responsibilities are now expanded. He also is expected to warn the **righteous man [who] turns away from his righteousness**. God does not want any to perish (18:23, 32; 2 Pet. 3:9; 1 Tim. 2:4); but if some turn from Him, then He will allow them to do so (2 Thess. 2:9–12; 1 Kings 22:22; Rom. 1:24, 26, 28). He will even provide **an obstacle**:

> Though this is conventional rendering of [the Hebrew word] *miksol*, its meaning here is closer to "calamity"—not an occasion for sin but a cause of downfall and ruin. Cf. Jer 6:21: "I shall put before this people stumbling blocks over which they shall stumble (=calamities by which they shall be destroyed)—fathers and children alike; neighbor and friend shall perish."[10]

An often repeated biblical truth is that when one is not seeking to do right, but wants to do and believe what is wrong, then God will help him along his path to destruction. Taylor said,

> It does not here indicate that God deliberately sets out to trip up the righteous and bring him crashing to the ground, but that He leaves opportunities for sin in the paths of men, so that if their heart is bent on sin they may do so and thus earn their condemnation. There is no sense in which stumbling is inevitable: it always involves moral choice, and there was also the watchman's word of warning to point out where and what the stumbling-blocks were.[11]

The doctrine of the impossibility of apostasy is not biblical in regard to either the Old Testament or the New Testament. God allows people to operate with free moral choice. Even those who were once counted as "righteous" by God can decide to

---

[10]Ibid., 85.
[11]Taylor, 71–72.

leave that righteous condition by committing **iniquity**.[12]

Verse 21. The best possible outcome is described: **"The righteous man** [will] **live because he took warning."** This is why preachers preach. They always hope that the gospel will fall upon good soil, so that some people will respond and live faithfully.

Throughout this section, the idea of *individual responsibility* has been emphasized. As noted in the introduction, this is a key idea in the book. While people sometimes blame others for their fate (see ch. 18), it is clear that each one, individually, will give an account for his or her decisions.

Note the four potential situations involving the watchmen:

1. The watchmen fail to do their duty (v. 18).
2. The watchmen give the warning, but with no positive response (v. 19).
3. The watchmen fail to warn those who have fallen away (v. 20).
4. The watchmen warn the righteous who have fallen away, and they heed the warning (v. 21).

There are four corresponding outcomes for the watchmen and the hearers:

1. The watchmen are lost, and the wicked are lost.
2. The watchmen are saved, and the wicked are lost.
3. The watchmen are lost, and the righteous turned wicked are lost.
4. The watchmen are saved, and the righteous hearers are saved.

"Be Confined" (3:22–27)

3:22–24

[22]The hand of the LORD **was on me there, and He said to me, "Get up, go out to the plain, and there I will speak to you."**

---

[12]See Heb. 3:12–15; Gal. 6:1; Jas. 5:19, 20; 2 Pet. 1:9, 10; Rev. 2:5, 16, 21; 3:3, 19.

²³So I got up and went out to the plain; and behold, the glory of the LORD was standing there, like the glory which I saw by the river Chebar, and I fell on my face. ²⁴The Spirit then entered me and made me stand on my feet, and He spoke with me and said to me, "Go, shut yourself up in your house."

Verse 22. After seeing the wicked condition of the people and the need for a faithful witness, Ezekiel was called away to "think about it." Again, he saw "the glory of the LORD." Albert Barnes summarized this experience by writing,

> A fresh revelation of the glory of the Lord, to impress upon Ezekiel another characteristic of his mission. Now he is to learn that there is *a time to be silent* as well as *a time to speak*, and that both are appointed by God. This represents forcibly the authoritative character and Divine origin of the utterances of the Hebrew prophets.[13]

Verse 23. This verse does not tell about the same vision as in chapter 1, but relates one similar to it. It appears to be nothing more than a "mini-vision." Nevertheless, Ezekiel responded in a similar way: He **fell on** [his] **face.** Seeing the glory of the Lord for a second time did not lessen the awesomeness of the event. The vision still weakened and humbled the reverent prophet.

Verse 24. After the vision, it appears that God sent Ezekiel to his own house to begin the first of the lessons that He wanted to teach the prophet. Ezekiel was told, **"Go, shut yourself up in your house."** The Spirit entered him and so commanded him. The shutting up was symbolic of the binding that Ezekiel would endure.

3:25–27

²⁵"As for you, son of man, they will put ropes on you and bind you with them so that you cannot go out among them. ²⁶Moreover, I will make your tongue stick to the roof of your mouth so that you will be mute and cannot be a man who

---

[13]Barnes, 314.

rebukes them, for they are a rebellious house. ²⁷But when I speak to you, I will open your mouth and you will say to them, 'Thus says the Lord God.' He who hears, let him hear; and he who refuses, let him refuse; for they are a rebellious house."

Verse 25. The statement **they will . . . bind you** could be interpreted either literally or figuratively. There is no record of any physical restraint of Ezekiel, and a figurative application would mean that Ezekiel was unable to impart his message. Jesus would perform no powerful miracles in His own country because of the people's unbelief (Mk. 6:5, 6). In effect, they bound Jesus' hands. This could be what happened to Ezekiel. Others see in this binding a perfect illustration of the stubbornness and rebelliousness of the people. They were so adamantly opposed to the message that they would resort to extreme measures—even tying up the messenger. Being tied up, Ezekiel could not **go out among them**. As a result, those who were seeking a message from God would have to come to Ezekiel (see 8:1; 14:1, 2; 20:1).

Verse 26. The prophet was also told that he would be **mute**. The purpose of this silence was to prevent Ezekiel from being **a man who rebukes them**.

> It is far more satisfying and realistic to understand this as a ritual dumbness, or a divinely commanded refusal to make public utterances except under the direct impulse of God's word. From that moment onwards, Ezekiel was to be known as nothing but the mouthpiece of Yahweh. When he spoke, it was because God had something to say; when he was silent, it was because God was silent.[14]

The people would silence Ezekiel by closing their minds to the message (because they were a rebellious house). God, in turn, would silence the prophet, not allowing him to talk for a time. However, God said that Ezekiel's silence would not last forever

---

[14]Taylor, 74.

(24:27; 33:22). He was to be released from it after news of the destruction of Jerusalem reached Babylon (see 29:21).

Alexander thought that Ezekiel's "muteness" lasted approximately seven and one-half years, until the fall of Jerusalem (see dates in 1:1–3; 33:21, 22). Nevertheless, he said, the prophet delivered several oral messages in the intervening period (see 11:25; 14:1; 20:1). This concept of muteness, therefore, was not one of total speechlessness throughout the seven and one-half years. Rather, Ezekiel was restrained from speaking publicly among the people, in contrast to the normal vocal ministry of the prophets. The prophets usually moved among their people, speaking God's message as they observed the contemporary situation. Ezekiel remained in his home, except when he was dramatizing God's messages (see 4:1—5:17).[15]

When Jerusalem was destroyed, it proved that Ezekiel had been preaching the truth. The vindication that he felt might have been the reason God opened his mouth. With the people's hopes of a quick return to Jerusalem destroyed, and their punishment for sin realized, Ezekiel was given a different commission—to preach a message of hope and restoration.

Verse 27. Again, Ezekiel's message was to be **thus says the Lord**. God emphasized that Ezekiel would be speaking God's words and not his own; he would have the opportunity to utter the words only when God was ready to **open [his] mouth**. When he did speak, some would **hear** and some would **refuse** to hear, because they were **a rebellious house**. However, their refusal to hear did not mean that Ezekiel should stop preaching—even though they were an audience that had shut him out.

APPLICATION

Our Responsibility to God

God wants us to be faithful to Him and use the gifts that He has given to us. In the parable of the talents (which is talking about money), the criterion for being faithful was not how much money one had to begin with or how much he made, but that he

---

[15]Alexander, 767.

did something with it (Mt. 25:14–29; see Prov. 24:30–34).

The concept of a watchman applies to all of us. With increased knowledge comes increased responsibility (Mt. 13:10–12; Jas. 3:1). We have an obligation to alert our families to the dangers of sin (see Gal. 6:1).

No matter how difficult it is to be faithful, God will prepare us adequately to accomplish our task (v. 8). We will not, cannot, be successful unless we are filled with His Word.

If no problems had existed between God and mankind, there would have been no need for prophets. Today, a preacher is to try to resolve problems in the God/man relationship. It is unrealistic to expect the church not to have struggles. A preacher should approach his work with the view that there will be some difficulties. The task of ministering includes helping to mend broken relationships, strengthen the faith of those who are weak, and reunite people with God (see 2 Tim. 2:24–26).

The preacher must be as determined to preach the truth as the people are determined to reject it.

All people have the responsibility to be open to the truth and willing to learn it.

Will God Condemn Those Who Never Heard? (3:17–21)

Ezekiel 3:17–21 needs to be considered carefully. A question might be asked: "How can God condemn a person who did not receive the warning?" The question assumes that the person never received *any* warning, which is not stated in this passage. God was dealing here with the possibility of *Ezekiel* failing in his charge (v. 18). It is not a biblical truth that people at the Judgment will say, "If you had only given me the gospel, I would be saved. Since you didn't, I am lost." It implies that the person *would have* obeyed, if given the opportunity. Such, however, is not necessarily the case. God wants *all* to be saved (1 Tim. 2:4). We know that He is patient with people, giving them time to get their lives in order (2 Pet. 3:9). In light of these passages, it may well be that no one on the Day of Judgment will ask God, "If I had had another year to live, would I have repented?" and receive the answer "Yes, you would have repented, but Jesus came before you had that opportunity."

Jesus has promised that truth-seekers will be truth-finders (Mt. 7:7, 8). There will be no people on the Day of Judgment who were genuine truth-seekers but never received the opportunity to hear and obey the truth. Again, the argument about the person in the "deepest part of Africa"—far removed from the rest of humanity—is offered. How can God hold him responsible for the gospel?

Note carefully 2 Thessalonians 1:7–9:

> . . . the Lord Jesus will be revealed from heaven with His mighty angels in flaming fire, dealing out retribution to those who do not know God and to those who do not obey the gospel of our Lord Jesus. These will pay the penalty of eternal destruction, away from the presence of the Lord and from the glory of His power.

God will deal out punishment (a) to those who know not God and (b) to those who do not obey the gospel of Christ. All people, this side of the cross, will be judged by the gospel. If it were possible for one to be saved without hearing and obeying the gospel, then why did Christ urgently command His followers to "go into all the world and preach the gospel to all creation" (Mk. 16:15)? Those who are not taught will *not* be saved in their ignorance (Acts 17:30, 31).

Consider this scenario: A person living in a remote part of the earth comes to understand God's "invisible attributes, His eternal power and divine nature" through the wonders of creation (Rom. 1:20). He desires to know more about this God who made the world. God, in His providence, will provide a messenger to provide the truth to this truth-seeker.

Ezekiel was expected to be a faithful watchman. If he was not faithful, he would pay the penalty for disobeying God's call. While nothing further is said, it is logical to assume that God would have raised up another watchman, a faithful watchman. It must be that God works within the confines of His will to give every honest heart an opportunity to obey His gospel.

D.P.

The "Hardheaded" Prophet (3:8)

As God prepared Ezekiel to preach among the exiles, He warned him that the people would not listen. He told the prophet, "Behold, I have made your face as hard as their faces and your forehead as hard as their foreheads" (3:8). This text helps us to understand how a "hardheaded" believer can be accepted, and even complimented, by God. The prophet's character challenges Christians today to be commended by God as "hardheaded" believers. Ezekiel had to be "hardheaded" so that he would accept nothing but the whole, unpolluted truth of God.

Compassion and Sympathy. Ezekiel said, in effect, "I sat where they sat" (see 3:15). The prophet's message was one of judgment and retribution; his face was to be set against the hardhearted people. Before delivering his message, however, he "sat" with them for seven days. During this period he gained understanding of the lives of those in the audience. This helped him as he presented God's truth.

Some think "hardheaded" people are void of compassion. When a Christian refuses to compromise, he is viewed as being unloving. Ezekiel shows that this is not necessarily true. When one possesses compassion or sympathy for another, he will refuse to allow the object of compassion to do wrong and face injury.

Devotion to God's Will. We should be "hardheaded" in our loyalty to God. He is to be feared more than men.

One of the most admirable qualities of this "hardheaded" prophet was his dedication to God. An illustration of this dedication is seen when Ezekiel's wife died (24:16–18). In the fourth year of his ministry, his wife suddenly died; but Ezekiel's dedication caused him to do exactly as God commanded. A deep conviction that the Scriptures teach truth and that one must therefore follow the Scriptures will make us "hardheaded" like Ezekiel.

In the tumult of upsetting situations, the "hardheaded" prophet was able to endure because he was devoted to God's will. When life falls apart and seemingly impossible situations arise, such devotion enables us to persevere.

Obedience to God's Will. A commendable statement was made

by Ezekiel in 24:18c: "I did as I was commanded." Ezekiel was determined to obey the Lord God, regardless of what happened.

What an admirable goal for us to emulate! How determined are we to obey God? Do we allow the situations of life to dictate the degree of our compliance to the divine will? A "hardheaded" believer will make obedience to God's Word the top priority in his life.

Respect for the Almighty. The vision of chapter 1 portrayed the glory of the Lord God. This vision made an indelible mark on Ezekiel. He would always remember the assuring truths this vision taught him about God: His divine majesty and glory, His sovereign rule, His activity in history. Ezekiel's understanding of the Almighty was what encouraged him to be "hardheaded" in religious matters. Such a God as the One presented by this vision must be revered and obeyed. Only a fool would dare to refuse such a God!

Confidence in the Future. Ezekiel 33—48 contains assurances for the future. God would provide a great city, a great temple, and a great river of life to those who followed His word. Only those who maintain purity in their religious practices can partake of God's eternal blessings!

Conclusion. Those who understand the wonderful blessings of eternity will share the "hardheaded" nature of Ezekiel. They will not pollute God's eternal promises by compromising the truth. They will confront and refute those who try to serve God without full devotion.

God's Love (2; 3)

The prophecy of Ezekiel proclaims the great love of Yahweh. Throughout the prophecy, God urged people to return to Him. In the opening chapters is found a wonderful illustration of God's tender concern for erring man. Chapters 2 and 3 present three truths about God's great love.

His Love Solicits (2:1). God called Ezekiel to go and teach the truth. God desires for all people to hear, understand, obey, and faithfully live according to His directions. This loving God still solicits a willing response to the message of forgiveness and life (3:6b, 19, 21). He still solicits responses to His offer of salvation.

His Love Sends (2:3; 3:16, 17). Ezekiel was to "go"; the prophet was "sent" (3:4, 5). Why? In order for God's gracious offer of "life" to be accepted, the message had to be heard. An obligation was placed upon Ezekiel to go and speak of God's love even if those hearing would not respond (3:4–7). God still sends us today to proclaim His truth to all who are in sin.

His Love Saves (3:21). Those who heard, believed, and obeyed would be saved. Many in our world are eager to hear and obey God's commands. God still saves those who obey.

This Old Testament passage wonderfully illustrates the "better hope" of salvation that is offered in the New Testament (see Heb. 7:19). God's great love provides for all a plan of salvation (Mk. 16:15, 16). His love solicits those who are eager to hear, believe, confess, repent, and be immersed for the forgiveness of sins (Rom. 10:17; Acts 3:19; 2:38).

God has granted each of us the right and the responsibility to choose how we will respond. Ezekiel 3:27 says, "'... He who hears, let him hear; and he who refuses, let him refuse. ...'" How have you responded to God's great love?

J.L.K.

A Watchman's Duty (3:17–21)

The watchman's duty is to the wicked (3:17–19). The wicked one can turn from his sin and be saved. God is willing to forgive and save such a person. Christians are commissioned to watch and warn those in sin.

The watchman's duty is to the righteous (3:20, 21). It *is* possible for a righteous person to turn from his righteousness and commit sin that would involve death. Sadly, none of his righteous deeds will be remembered in the Day of Judgment. He will be judged as a wicked person, not as a righteous one. Christians are to watch for the welfare of one another and warn those brethren who are in sin.[16]

The watchman's duty is to himself (3:18–21). If he warns, he lives; if he does not warn, his blood will be required.

---

[16]*Teacher's Annual Lesson Commentary*, Gospel Advocate Series (Nashville: Gospel Advocate Co., 1957), 128–30.

CHAPTER 4
THE PROPHECIES OF PUNISHMENT DRAMATIZED

In chapters 4 and 5 we see Ezekiel performing *four symbolic acts*. Carl G. Howie said,

> The reader should remember the Hebrew prophets proclaimed the word of God through action as well as through word. For example, Isaiah walked naked through the streets to dramatize the fact that Egypt and Ethiopia would be captured by Assyrian power (Isa. 20:1–2). Jeremiah broke a pottery jar as a symbol of God's intent with respect to Judah (Jer. 19), and when Hananiah broke the yoke of wood, a yoke of iron indicated the Captivity which would become unbreakable (Jer. 27:1—28:16).[1]

Ahijah, Zedekiah, Elisha, and Agabus also conveyed messages with symbolic actions (1 Kings 11:30; 22:11; 2 Kings 13:17; Acts 21:10, 11). Ezekiel's strange actions were done in a public place, perhaps just outside his house. No doubt word would have spread quickly that the prophet was acting strangely—thereby drawing considerable crowds to witness the "show."

FIRST SYMBOLIC ACT: THE SIEGE AGAINST A MODEL OF JERUSALEM (4:1–3)

¹"Now you son of man, get yourself a brick, place it before

---

[1] Carl G. Howie, *The Book of Ezekiel, The Book of Daniel*, The Layman's Bible Commentary, vol. 13 (Richmond, Va.: John Knox Press, 1961), 25.

you and inscribe a city on it, Jerusalem. ²Then lay siege against it, build a siege wall, raise up a ramp, pitch camps and place battering rams against it all around. ³Then get yourself an iron plate and set it up as an iron wall between you and the city, and set your face toward it so that it is under siege, and besiege it. This is a sign to the house of Israel."

Verse 1. *The first symbolic act is that of Ezekiel's laying siege against a model of Jerusalem.* He took **a brick** and was told to **inscribe** Jerusalem on it. Sun-dried or kiln-burned bricks were used for centuries for building walls throughout the plain of Mesopotamia. The bricks of Nineveh and Babylon were sometimes stamped with the image or insignia of the king who was then in power. Symbols or scenes were stamped into some bricks, and others were covered with an enamel-type coating. Castles and forts are depicted on bricks and bas-reliefs that have been discovered at Nimrod. Ezekiel was merely duplicating this ancient practice, except that he was drawing a map of Jerusalem on the brick.[2]

Verse 2. Ancient military strategy of the day is described. When attacking, or **lay**[ing] **siege** to a city, an army would first **build a siege wall**, which was a wheeled tower used by archers. Often, several of these towers would be built, encompassing the city (see 2 Kings 25:1). Next, they would **raise up a ramp** ("mound"; KJV, ASV). This was a heap of dirt raised to the level of the city wall. The ramp allowed the attackers to be even with the defenders on the walls. The mounds would be used for observation as well as attacks. Then the attackers would **pitch camps**, arranging for a strategic location of the army around the city in mini-encampments. Finally, they would **place battering rams**, heavy beams designed to swing like a pendulum and pound against the wall or gates. These were often hung by chains near the bottom of the tower. Something iron or bronze placed on the end of the beam would smash against the wall. The

---

[2]See T. C. Mitchell, *The Bible in the British Museum: Interpreting the Evidence* (London: British Museum Press, 1988), 52; and D. J. Wiseman, *Illustrations from Biblical Archaeology*, 3d ed. (London: The Tyndale Press, 1966), 12.

Romans placed a bronze ram's head on the end of this type of beam. This phraseology occurs only in Ezekiel (v. 2; 21:22).

Verse 3. The **iron plate** probably represents God and His anger toward the holy city. This "plate" or "pan" (NIV, KJV, ASV), shaped like a griddle, was a typical household utensil used in baking. It was also the kind of pan used by the priests for certain offerings (Lev. 2:5; 6:21; 7:9). Ezekiel was told to place this iron plate **between** [himself] **and the city**. Thus the plate represented a wall of hostility that the Lord was directing against Jerusalem. God's purpose in having Ezekiel lay siege to a representation of Jerusalem was to give **a sign to the house of Israel**. Verse 7 indicates that Ezekiel continued to lay siege to the city, and verse 8 mentions "days" (plural) of the siege. Indeed, Ezekiel was giving a "sign" of events that would come to pass. The people mistakenly thought they would return to Jerusalem in a short time. That would not be the case.

SECOND SYMBOLIC ACT: LYING ON HIS SIDE (4:4–8)

⁴"As for you, lie down on your left side and lay the iniquity of the house of Israel on it; you shall bear their iniquity for the number of days that you lie on it. ⁵For I have assigned you a number of days corresponding to the years of their iniquity, three hundred and ninety days; thus you shall bear the iniquity of the house of Israel. ⁶When you have completed these, you shall lie down a second time, but on your right side and bear the iniquity of the house of Judah; I have assigned it to you for forty days, a day for each year. ⁷Then you shall set your face toward the siege of Jerusalem with your arm bared and prophesy against it. ⁸Now behold, I will put ropes on you so that you cannot turn from one side to the other until you have completed the days of your siege."

Verse 4. Here is described the *second symbolic act* of this chapter. *Ezekiel was to lie on his left side for "three hundred and ninety days" (v. 5) and on his right side for "forty days" (v. 6)*. In the first symbolic act, Ezekiel inflicted the punishment upon Jerusalem.

Second, he would have to endure the affliction. Since the city was under attack in the first symbolic act, the natural second event would be the capture and the exile of its inhabitants. In the second symbolic act, *Ezekiel was to represent the punishment which God would dispense to Israel for their wickedness.* In other words, Ezekiel was going to **bear their iniquity**. Did he literally lie on his side for this period of time (a total of 430 days—well over one year)? Doing so would have been possible only through the power provided by the Spirit within Ezekiel (see 3:24). Such an illustration would have no impact if it did not actually take place. If it did literally happen, it would have been one of the most powerful illustrations given by any of the Old Testament prophets. Second, Ezekiel's actions would have made a lasting impression upon the people. Third, these actions would have been a firm proof that Ezekiel was a genuine prophet of God. No man could perform such a feat without divine assistance.

Verse 5. The **days** represented **years**—more specifically, the years **of their iniquity**. This number, regardless of its exact meaning, represented a set period of punishment. God would not punish *too much* or *too little* for the corresponding offenses.

The figure "390" presents some difficulty for scholars in regard to the text and its interpretation. The LXX has 190 days in verse 5 and 150 inserted into verse 4. The rationale for this (while not preferred or accepted by most major translations) seems to be as follows: Israel fell to the Assyrians in 722(1) B.C., almost 150 years before Ezekiel's vision. By adding the number "forty" (v. 6), the number 190 is attained. Thus the LXX has the prophet lying on his left side for 150 days and his right side for 40 days. Aligning the number "190" chronologically is somewhat difficult. Perhaps the best suggestion is this: Around 734 B.C. the Assyrian king Tiglath-pileser III deported a number of people from the northern kingdom (2 Kings 15:29). Jerusalem was destroyed in 587(6) B.C., 148 years later (rounded to 150 years). The forty days that Ezekiel lay on his right side (representing forty years) would roughly represent the time from the destruction of Jerusalem (587[6] B.C.) to the time the Babylonian Captivity ended (537[6] B.C.).

Knowing when the counting started or ended would be helpful in understanding the 390 days, but neither is revealed. It is helpful to remember that:

1. In both cases the period of time represents the period of suffering for sins previously committed.
2. Restoration would not take place until these periods of atonement for past sins had been endured. Only then could it be said, "Speak tenderly to Jerusalem, and cry to her that her warfare is ended, that her iniquity is pardoned, that she has received from the LORD's hand double for all her sins" (Is. 40:2; RSV).
3. While many scholars say that a *total* of 390 days was given (because Israel and Judah were released at the same time), that total does not seem to be supported by the text. Rather, it appears that God wanted the iniquity of Israel to be represented separately from that of Judah. (Verse 6 says, "When you have completed these, you shall lie down a *second time*. . . .")[3]

The word "iniquity" (עָוֹן, *'awon*) is found forty-four times in this book, and the phrase **bear the iniquity** appears twice. It can refer to the atoning act, as in Leviticus 16:21, 22 (see Ex. 28:38; Lev. 10:17), or to punishment (consequences of iniquity), as in Numbers 14:33, 34. In context, the second definition is better: Ezekiel was symbolically bearing the punishment for Israel's sins. It also seems that we should understand *'awon* as "[past] iniquity" in verse 5 and "punishment" in verse 6. This first set of days (390) was specifically in reference to **the house of Israel**—that is, the northern ten tribes that had been carried into captivity by Assyria. Those tribes had been gone for a long time, but they had not been forgotten by God.

Verse 6. Here we see that God intended for Ezekiel to complete the first set of days—390 days—assigned for Israel. Then,

---

[3]John B. Taylor disagreed: "Restoration *will* come eventually (*cf.* 37:16ff.) and it will be simultaneous for Judah and Israel. These considerations lead to the conclusion that the two periods are to be taken as ending concurrently" (John B. Taylor, *Ezekiel: An Introduction and Commentary*, Tyndale Old Testament Commentaries [Downers Grove, Ill.: Inter-Varsity Press, 1969], 79).

when he had **completed** them, God assigned him a new set of days—forty—for **Judah**, the southern kingdom composed of the two tribes, Judah and Benjamin. The "forty years" given to Judah are a reminder of the forty years the Israelites had spent in the wilderness during the days of Moses. Those forty years were for the purpose of discipline and punishment for their rebellion—a definite parallel to the text of Ezekiel and the reason for the punishment of Judah.

Verse 7. As Ezekiel prophesied against his model siege, he was to leave his **arm bared**. "In this gesture, the prophet's representation of God as the enemy reaches maximum clarity."[4] (See Is. 52:10.) Verse 7 shows that, during the period he was lying on his side, Ezekiel maintained his earlier siege that he had set up against Jerusalem. Returning to that earlier illustration, Ezekiel began to "preach" to it. The message, for those who gathered to watch, would be plain and powerful.

As noted in the introduction, one of the key words in the Book of Ezekiel is **prophesy** (נָבָא, *naba'*). Forms of the verb occur thirty-eight times.[5] The significance of the verb (occurring for the first time here) and the noun help to define the ministry of Ezekiel. The *nabi'* in Old Testament times was a voice for God. He served as a spokesman for God, an intercessor, communicating the divine will to the people. One of the tragedies found in ancient Israel was the corruption of this sacred calling (see Jer. 14:14).

Verse 8. The phrase **put ropes** is a metaphor either for divinely imposed restraint or for restraint that Ezekiel felt was being imposed by outside forces (see 3:25). Remember that Ezekiel was to do other things during this time period (see vv. 7, 9, 11). Therefore, he could not have been tied up completely.

Taylor suggested that Ezekiel did various tasks in parts. Once

---

[4]Moshe Greenberg, *Ezekiel 1—20: A New Translation with Introduction and Commentary*, The Anchor Bible, vol. 22 (Garden City, N.Y.: Doubleday & Co., 1983), 106.

[5]See 4:7; 6:2; 11:4 (twice), 13; 12:27; 13:2 (three times), 16, 17 (twice); 20:46; 21:2, 9, 14, 28; 25:2; 28:21; 29:2; 30:2; 34:2 (twice); 35:2; 36:1, 3, 6; 37:4, 7 (twice), 9 (twice), 10, 12; 38:2, 14, 17; 39:1. Also see "prophet" (נָבִיא)—2:5; 7:26; 13:2, 3, 4, 9, 16; 14:4, 7, 9 (twice), 10; 22:25, 28; 33:33; 38:17.

he had finished one task (spending part of the day lying toward the model of the besieged city), he would then bare his arm in another symbolic act. After these duties were performed, "when no spectators were around, he could revert to a more normal manner of conduct within his house."[6] There is, however, no indication that Ezekiel was ever allowed to return home during this 430-day period. He may possibly have done his tasks at different times. It seems inconceivable that he could have done all that was asked of him while bound, lying on his side, for 430 days.

Nevertheless, God told him to remain tied so that he could not **turn from one side to the other**. Captivity is unpleasant, but Ezekiel's immobility was to last **until you have completed the days of your siege**.

Nothing given in the chronology of the Book of Ezekiel would forbid taking these days to be literal. For example, considering the dates in 1:2 and 8:1, we may suppose that Ezekiel had anywhere from 413 days (according to the lunar calendar) to 442 days (if it was a leap year). Henry L. Ellison wrote,

> Between 1:2 and 8:1 are exactly a year and two months. The Jewish year is a lunar year of 354 days, the months being alternatively 30 and 29 days in length. So we are dealing with a period of 413 days. If it was a leap year, which today comes round about twice in five years, and which is formed by the insertion of an extra 29-day month, we can extend the period to 442 days.[7]

Ezekiel had ample time to perform these actions.

Therefore, to what do these numbers refer? No significant date is found by counting back 390 years. The same is true when the forty years are applied to Judah. One solution that has merit is to understand the 430 years *in a figurative sense*. If we set the chronological notion aside, we can, with some justice, say that

---

[6]Taylor, 81.

[7]Henry L. Ellison, *Ezekiel: The Man and His Message* (Grand Rapids, Mich.: Wm. B. Eerdmans Publishing Co., 1956), 33.

the whole thing is symbolic of another national captivity. Hosea, who preached for thirty-eight years starting in 750 A.D., spoke of the captivity of the northern kingdom under Assyrian domination as a "return to Egypt" (8:13). He repeated the threat in 9:3 and then explained that he was warning Assyria rather than Egypt. Why did the prophet say that Israel would return to Egypt when he really meant Assyria? Was it because "Egypt" had become synonymous with captivity? To threaten the people with "Egypt" was to speak to them of bondage! How long was Israel enslaved in Egypt? For 430 years (Ex. 12:40; Gal. 3:17). This is the only number that has a *clear link* to the numbers given in Ezekiel (390 + 40 = 430). The 430 years represented the total time spent in captivity in Egypt, so it here symbolizes the total amount of time Israel and Judah would spend in captivity. Jim McGuiggan rightly stated, "Each of us has a number or a name which brings thoughts to our mind when and every time we think of it. 430 years spoke to the Jew of the terrible time when all twelve tribes endured the house of bondage."[8] This interpretation seems most logical and does not require wild interpretations that stretch the text.

Ezekiel brought up this point to emphasize the fact that Judah (along with Israel) would go into captivity (Ezek. 11:14, 15). This means that all of Judah would go into captivity—including those who were left in the city. There remained yet one more deportation (in 587[6] B.C., when the city was destroyed). Those in captivity were hoping for an early return to Jerusalem, but that would not happen. They would have to spend their time (given as forty years) in captivity.

THIRD SYMBOLIC ACT: EATING THE UNCLEAN BREAD (4:9–17)

4:9–13

⁹"But as for you, take wheat, barley, beans, lentils, millet and spelt, put them in one vessel and make them into bread

---

[8]Jim McGuiggan, *The Book of Ezekiel*, Looking Into The Bible Series (Lubbock, Tex.: Montex Publishing Co., 1979), 53.

for yourself; you shall eat it according to the number of the days that you lie on your side, three hundred and ninety days. ¹⁰Your food which you eat shall be twenty shekels a day by weight; you shall eat it from time to time. ¹¹The water you drink shall be the sixth part of a hin by measure; you shall drink it from time to time. ¹²You shall eat it as a barley cake, having baked it in their sight over human dung." ¹³Then the LORD said, "Thus will the sons of Israel eat their bread unclean among the nations where I will banish them."

Verse 9. This verse introduces the *third symbolic action* Ezekiel performed before the captives of Tel-abib (see 3:15). This all took place during the 390 days while Ezekiel was lying on his side to symbolize the captivity of Israel. This symbol also represented the siege which was to come against Jerusalem (see 4:16). *Ezekiel was portraying the difficulty experienced during a siege—famine.* **Take wheat, barley, beans, lentils, millet and spelt, put them in one vessel and make them into bread for yourself.** Why was the bread composed of so many different items? To indicate the scarcity of food. It was crude and unappealing. "The Babylonian Talmud (*Erubin* 81a) relates an experiment made in the third century C.E. [Common Era] proving that Ezekiel's bread would not be touched even by a dog."⁹ However, a study of Leviticus 19:19, Deuteronomy 22:9, and the *Mishna* reveals no ritual defilement involved in the mixing of grains for bread.

Verse 10. Ezekiel was to eat his food **by weight**. Rationed food is another indication of a siege (see Lev. 26:26). He was to have **twenty shekels a day** of food. From archaeological findings, we know that a shekel could be 12.2, 11.5, or 9.82 grams. If we use the 11.5 grams, approximately equal to four-tenths of an ounce, for a shekel, then this would be about eight ounces. Eight ounces of bread a day is not far from starvation rations—and this was all Ezekiel had to eat for a year! He ate this bread **from time to time**. A similar phrase is found in 1 Chronicles 9:25, in reference to a recurring action which was to take place at the same time each day. G. A. Cooke translated the phrase "'at stated

---

⁹Greenberg, 106.

times,' but this is not sufficiently clear without his explanatory note, 'i.e. at a certain time on one day and at the corresponding time on the next.'"[10]

Verse 11. The prophet's water was measured as **the sixth part of a hin**. This measurement can equal from one to two pints (sixteen to thirty-two ounces). This was an extremely small amount of water, considering the extremely hot climate. Any siege brings a terrible time for humanity! During the actual siege against Jerusalem, Jeremiah received only one loaf of bread a day until it was all gone (Jer. 37:21). In addition, the water was almost gone (Jer. 38:6).

Verses 12, 13. The application of this symbolic act is partially explained in verse 13: Ezekiel's meals represented the pitiful rations the Israelites would have to eat **among the nations where [God] will banish them**. As if the quality of food and the portions were not pathetic enough, the Israelites would also prepare the food in an **unclean** condition. Though eating combined grains was acceptable, using human dung in a cooking fire (v. 12) was defiling. Eating unclean food was forbidden by the Mosaic covenant.

4:14–17
[14]But I said, "Ah, Lord God! Behold, I have never been defiled; for from my youth until now I have never eaten what died of itself or was torn by beasts, nor has any unclean meat ever entered my mouth." [15]Then He said to me, "See, I will give you cow's dung in place of human dung over which you will prepare your bread." [16]Moreover, He said to me, "Son of man, behold, I am going to break the staff of bread in Jerusalem, and they will eat bread by weight and with anxiety, and drink water by measure and in horror, [17]because bread and water will be scarce; and they will be appalled with one another and waste away in their iniquity."

Verse 14. When God commanded Ezekiel to cook his food

---

[10]Taylor, 83. His reference is to G. A. Cooke, *A Critical and Exegetical Commentary on the Book of Ezekiel*, International Critical Commentary (Edinburgh: T. & T. Clark, 1936), 55.

over human dung, the prophet spoke out for the first time, in a spontaneous outburst. God had commanded him to defile his food![11] Ezekiel detailed how he had grown up in the sanctuary and had never eaten what **died of itself** (Deut. 14:21), what was **torn by beasts** (Ex. 22:31; Lev. 17:15), or any **unclean meat** (Deut. 14:3–21). He had taken great pains to keep pure, and he did not desire to do something defiling now.

Verse 15. God relented, allowing Ezekiel to cook his food over **cow's dung**. This would not make the food unclean. In Eastern countries, where fuel is scarce, dried cow dung is laid up for the winter and used as fuel. Bread was (and is) baked under hot ashes without an oven.[12] In response to Ezekiel's concern, God allowed dried animal dung to replace human dung as a means of fuel.

Verses 16, 17. What was the point of all of this? God wanted the people to realize that they would become unclean. Ezekiel was performing the actions God commanded him "in their sight" (v. 12); the captives saw what he was doing.

> The point Jehovah is making is abundantly clear. *It is not* that the Jews would bake their food this way (literally in captivity) for in fact, the Jew was rather well off after the initial shocks of exile were over and they settled into a fairly prosperous life (see Isaiah. 55:1ff). No. [T]he uncleanness didn't derive from the way in which the food was literally baked, it would result from their being removed from the temple and the sacrificial system.[13]

---

[11]See Ex. 22:31; Lev. 7:18; 17:11; 19:7; 22:8; Deut. 12:16; 14:21.

[12]"God was not changing his law when he commanded Ezekiel to do all this. God temporarily caused Ezekiel to disregard the principle of eating unclean food to dramatize in an extreme way how abhorrent the Captivity would be. God used an acted parable to convey this truth in a way that would surely be understood. However, this was only symbolic; the eating of unclean food as a normal practice was not being condoned. God sovereignly protected Ezekiel against any ill effects of eating defiled food" (Ralph H. Alexander, "Ezekiel," in *The Expositor's Bible Commentary*, ed. Frank E. Gaebelein [Grand Rapids, Mich.: Zondervan Publishing House, 1986], 6:770).

[13]McGuiggan, 56.

Amos had threatened the priest Amaziah, "You . . . will die upon unclean soil" (Amos 7:17). A similar prediction is given in Hosea 9:3: "Ephraim will return to Egypt, and in Assyria they will eat unclean food." Jews had so many particulars to follow in order to remain pure that it would be difficult, in a foreign land, to keep from being defiled. This would be especially true when dealing with the diet. However, we know from Daniel 1 that it was possible for some captives to avoid gross uncleanness, even in the royal court. Ezekiel 11:16 also points to the possibility of a pure life, although at a reduced level. Perhaps, then, God's concession to Ezekiel in verse 15 provided hope that the truly righteous could find a way to remain pure, even amidst the most difficult circumstances.

God declared that He would **break the staff of bread in Jerusalem** (v. 16; see Lev. 26:26; Ps. 105:16). Bread sustained people. Even now, it is a staple of almost every meal (see Gen. 18:5; Judg. 19:5, 8). The people's abundant bread would be "broken"; in its place would be rationed food and water. Food would be so scarce that the Israelites would face rapid weight loss, being reduced to nothing more than "skin and bones." They would **be appalled with one another and waste away** (v. 17). The reason for this tragedy was **their iniquity**.

APPLICATION

Punishment and Restoration

God will not tolerate sin indefinitely. A time comes when He dispenses punishment. Ezekiel was not providing chronological statistics. He was proclaiming judgment and hope.

The time given before punishment should be viewed as compassion from God. He gives an opportunity to repent (2 Pet. 3:9).

After punishment God offers restoration. This demonstrates that our God is rich in mercy and forgiveness (see Eph. 2:1–10). Nevertheless, God's people must "bear their iniquity." God's righteousness will not allow Him to let sin go unpunished.

People are the ones who have failed. God has always maintained His faithfulness. "If we are faithless, He remains faithful, for He cannot deny Himself" (2 Tim. 2:13).

Even in the most difficult circumstances, God will provide a way for the faithful to remain true to His Word. He will live up to the promise of 1 Corinthians 10:13.

D.P.

Simulating the Siege of Jerusalem (4:1–8)

Ezekiel was made to act out the siege of Jerusalem (vv. 1–8). What possible meaning could this symbolic action have for us?

First, we see that God is a righteous God. He will not overlook sin. Ezekiel was to bear the iniquity of Israel by pretending to lay siege to Jerusalem.

Second, we see that God is a truthful God. He wanted Israel to know the reason for the chastisement. He was going to great extremes so that Israel, Judah, and all people (through His record of it) would know what had happened and why.

Third, we see that sin is serious business. No wonder God had to send Jesus to die for sins. Being the righteous God that He is, God cannot deal with sin by the wave of His hand.

Bread Fit for No One (4:9–15)

Such a command as in 4:9–15 was difficult for Ezekiel to fulfill; however, a nation's waywardness called for drastic measures. What can we learn from this special command?

Sin must be paid for in personal sacrifice. With these extreme measures, God was asking Ezekiel to illustrate with his life the results of sin. The people in and around Jerusalem would suffer far more.

Sin affects the innocent. Ezekiel illustrated the punishment that had come to Israel and Judah. As God's faithful prophet, he endured humiliation and discomfort because of their sins.

The remedy for sin is costly. There is no easy route to dealing with sin. The true remedy of sin cost Jesus Christ His life; it was even expensive to Ezekiel.

What if we were given the command that Ezekiel was given? Would we have obeyed it? All of us say, "I hope so, but I am sure glad I did not get the command!" Ezekiel obeyed, and we learn much from what he did. Behold the wisdom of God!

E.C.

Chapter 5

The Prophecies Of Punishment Dramatized (Continued)

FOURTH SYMBOLIC ACT: DIVIDING HIS CUT HAIR INTO THIRDS (5:1–4)

¹"As for you, son of man, take a sharp sword; take and use it as a barber's razor on your head and beard. Then take scales for weighing and divide the hair. ²One third you shall burn in the fire at the center of the city, when the days of the siege are completed. Then you shall take one third and strike it with the sword all around the city, and one third you shall scatter to the wind; and I will unsheathe a sword behind them. ³Take also a few in number from them and bind them in the edges of your robes. ⁴Take again some of them and throw them into the fire and burn them in the fire; from it a fire will spread to all the house of Israel."

Verse 1. This is the *fourth symbolic act* of Ezekiel. Imagine the scene Ezekiel was creating. The prophet was likely the topic of everyone's conversation. He cut off the hair of his **head** as well as his **beard**. The people might have thought that this indicated mourning (see Is. 15:2; Jer. 48:37) or disgrace (2 Sam. 10:4, 5). According to Ralph H. Alexander,

> If an Israelite priest shaved his head, he was defiled and no longer holy to the Lord (Lev 21:5). Ezekiel defiled and humiliated himself as a symbol of the humiliation of the people of Judah who were defiled and no longer holy to

the Lord. Nothing was left to do but to mourn their death as a nation.[1]

Then, however, he was to divide the hair into three equal parts; he was told, "... **take scales for weighing and divide the hair."**

Verses 2, 3. The first part of his hair, he was to **burn**. This act represented those who would perish within the city during the siege of Jerusalem. The second part of his hair, he was to hack at with a **sword**, symbolizing those who would be killed around the city during the same period. The third part, he was to throw to **the wind**, signifying those who, after the siege, would be dispersed in foreign lands. Concerning the third group, God said that He would **unsheathe a sword behind them**: Those scattered might not escape death by an enemy sword. **When the days of the siege are completed** probably means when Ezekiel ended his 390 (or 430) days of lying on his side.

Having completed these signs, the prophet gathered some of the scattered hair, binding a few strands on his garment and burning the rest. John B. Taylor commented,

> The symbolism is obvious: a third of the inhabitants of Jerusalem would be destroyed within the city, a third would be killed by the sword in fighting around the city [see 2 Kings 25:4–7], and a third would be scattered among the nations and would continue to be harried by hostile forces. From among these survivors would emerge the handful of those who would be preserved.[2]

Verse 4. God said that **a fire** [would] **spread to all the house of Israel**. This could refer to "further devastation flaming forth from Jerusalem, possibly a reference to the debased remnant who were left in the vicinity of the destroyed city and who had to be

---

[1] Ralph H. Alexander, "Ezekiel," in *The Expositor's Bible Commentary*, ed. Frank E. Gaebelein (Grand Rapids, Mich.: Zondervan Publishing House, 1986), 6:771.

[2] John B. Taylor, *Ezekiel: An Introduction and Commentary*, Tyndale Old Testament Commentaries (Downers Grove, Ill.: Inter-Varsity Press, 1969), 84.

purged out after the return from exile (see Ezr. 4:1–4)."³ Another possibility is that the fire refers to purification and not judgment. This seems to be the thrust of Zechariah 13:8, 9. Whereas Ezekiel was instructed to bind a few hairs in the edge of his robe (seemingly safe from destruction), he was next told to take **some of them** and **burn them**. Thus the message was that those who initially escaped would still face death.

This concludes the *four symbolic acts* done by Ezekiel. Each act dealt with an aspect of the punishment which was about to befall God's people:

1. The siege (4:1–3). Jerusalem would be attacked.
2. The length of the punishment (4:4–8). Both Israel and Judah would have to endure, for a time, punishment for their iniquity.
3. The conditions during the siege and subsequent exile (4:9–17): famine, starvation, and uncleanness.
4. The fate of the inhabitants of Jerusalem (5:1–4). Divided into thirds, all of God's people would suffer, except for a small remnant.

AN EXPLANATION OF THE ACTS (5:5–17)

God gave the interpretation for His symbolic action. Because of the sin of the city, it would be destroyed.

5:5, 6
⁵**"Thus says the Lord God, 'This is Jerusalem; I have set her at the center of the nations, with lands around her. ⁶But she has rebelled against My ordinances more wickedly than the nations and against My statutes more than the lands which surround her; for they have rejected My ordinances and have not walked in My statutes.'"**

Verse 5. Jerusalem was **the center** for the Jews—not only

---

³Ibid., 85.

physically, but also spiritually. Albert Barnes provided the following insight into the importance of Jerusalem:

> It was not unusual for nations to regard the sanctuary, which they most revered, as the centre of the earth. In the case of the Holy Land this was both natural and appropriate. Egypt to the South, Syria to the North, Assyria to East and the Isles of the Gentiles in the Great Sea to the West, were to the Jew proofs of the central position of his land in the midst of the nations [see Jer. 3:19]. The habitation assigned to the chosen people was suitable at the first for separating them from the nations; then for the seat of the vast dominion and commerce of Solomon; then, when they learnt from their neighbours idol-worship, their central position was the source of their punishment. Midway between the mighty empires of Egypt and Assyria the Holy Land became a battlefield for the two powers, and suffered alternately from each as for the time the one or the other became predominant.[4]

Ezekiel 38:12 is the passage that gave the Jews, especially the rabbis, the idea that Jerusalem was the exact center of the earth. Jerusalem should have been an example among the nations, but she committed sins worse than all the pagan nations around her. She should have known better and done better. She could have demonstrated to the whole world the glory of God.

Verse 6. This verse speaks of God's **ordinances** (מִשְׁפָּטִים, *mishpatim*). This word refers to general religious obedience, including proper relationships between individuals. **Statutes** (חֻקּוֹת, *chuqqoth*) deal with man's responsibilities to God. According to Anthony Tomasino,

> Many of the prescriptions in the Pentateuch are called

---

[4]Albert Barnes, *The Bible Commentary: Proverbs to Ezekiel*, Barnes' Notes ed. F. C. Cook, abr. and ed. J. M. Fuller (Grand Rapids, Mich.: Baker Book House, 1983), 317.

"a lasting ordinance" [חֻקַּת עוֹלָם, *chuqqath 'olam*], which were to be carried out regularly: the observance of the Passover and other feasts (Exod 12:14, 17, 24; Lev 23:14, 21, 41), the lighting of lamps in the temple (Exod 27:21; 28:43), the blowing of the trumpets for assembly (Num 10:8), and the various regulations regarding the preparations and presentations of sacrifices (Exod 29:9, 28; 30:21; Lev 3:17; 6:18 [11]; 7:34, 36; 10:9, 15; 16:29, 31, 34; Num 15:15; 18:8, 11, 19, 23; Ezek 46:14).[5]

This double expression (ordinances and statutes) is found in 11:20; 18:9, 17; 20:11, 13, 16, 19, 21, 24; 37:24. (The masculine plural חֻקִּים [*chuqqahim*] is used in 11:12; 20:18, 25; 36:27.) "Jerusalem's sin is not something vague, but an affront to the clear, revealed law of God. This is shown in a particular way in ch. 22."[6] What was especially troubling was the fact that Israel had not only disobeyed but had *exceeded* the wickedness of **the lands which surround her.**

5:7–10
[7]"Therefore, thus says the Lord GOD, 'Because you have more turmoil than the nations which surround you and have not walked in My statutes, nor observed My ordinances, nor observed the ordinances of the nations which surround you,' [8]therefore, thus says the Lord GOD, 'Behold, I, even I, am against you, and I will execute judgments among you in the sight of the nations. [9]And because of all your abominations, I will do among you what I have not done, and the like of which I will never do again. [10]Therefore, fathers will eat their sons among you, and sons will eat their fathers; for I will execute judgments on you and scatter all your remnant to every wind.'"

---

[5]Anthony Tomasino, "עוֹלָם," in *New International Dictionary of Old Testament Theology & Exegesis,* ed. Willem A. VanGemeren (Grand Rapids, Mich.: Zondervan Publishing House, 1997), 3:349.

[6]Walther Zimmerli, *Ezekiel 1: A Commentary on the Book of the Prophet Ezekiel, Chapters 1—24,* trans. Ronald E. Clements, Hermeneia (Philadelphia: Fortress Press, 1979), 175.

Verse 7. Ezekiel 11:12 says that God's people had "acted according to the ordinances of the nations around [them]," which seems to contradict verse 7. Regarding this, S. Fisch said,

> To reconcile the apparent contradiction between these words and the statement in xi. 12 the Talmud (Sanh. 39b) interprets the passage to mean: "In your conduct you have not followed the example of the righteous Gentiles, but you have copied the evils of the corrupt peoples." The phrase may, however, be explained in this sense: You have not fallen to the level of heathens but sunk even deeper in wickedness. Cf. the indictment in xvi. 47 [2 Kings 21:11; Jer. 2:11].[7]

A simple truth is being stated: The Israelites were characterized by lawlessness. They did not obey God's laws or man's laws—neither their own nor those of neighboring nations. They refused to obey anybody's law.

Verse 8. Because of their unparalleled sin, God said, **"I, even I, am against you."** This is the phrase הִנְנִי עָלַיִךְ (*hinni 'alayik*), and it occurs, with variations, twenty-two times in the Old Testament.[8] God would make a public example of His people **in the sight of the nations**, vindicating His holy name.

Verse 9. The statement **I will do among you what I have not done, and the like of which I will never do again** might be understood as a proverbial remark, thereby not contradicting Jesus' words in Matthew 24:21. Otherwise, it could be viewed as a unique judgment of God, in which He would withdraw

---

[7]S. Fisch, *Ezekiel: Hebrew Text and English Translation with an Introduction and Commentary*, Soncino Books of the Bible (London: Soncino Press, 1950), 26.

[8]This basic construction appears in Jeremiah 21:13; 23:30–32; 50:31; 51:25; Ezekiel 5:8; 13:8, 20; 21:3; 26:3; 28:22; 29:3, 10; 30:22; 34:10; 35:3; 36:9; 38:3; 39:1; Nahum 2:13; 3:5. "Accordingly the saying only occurs in prophecy at about the turn of the seventh/sixth centuries B.C., and, apart from Ezek 36:9, it always has a threatening meaning. It is also regularly (with the exception of 29:10) connected with the messenger formula or an oracle-formula. Thus in its present connection it contains a wholly threatening divine announcement" (Ibid.).

from the temple and execute judgments without any degree of pity. When viewed this way, this passage indicates an act of God without parallel in history—and such was certainly the case.

Verse 10. The prediction that **sons** [would] **eat their fathers** goes beyond what was mentioned in Leviticus 26:29 and Deuteronomy 28:53. God's unprecedented punishment would be heightened by unheard-of cannibalism. Although cannibalism was known in desperate siege conditions (2 Kings 6:28, 29), God said that, when this punishment came, family members would consume each other.

5:11, 12

¹¹"'So as I live,' declares the Lord GOD, 'surely, because you have defiled My sanctuary with all your detestable idols and with all your abominations, therefore I will also withdraw, and My eye will have no pity and I will not spare. ¹²One third of you will die by plague or be consumed by famine among you, one third will fall by the sword around you, and one third I will scatter to every wind, and I will unsheathe a sword behind them.'"

Verse 11. Two variations of the oath formula found in this verse occur sixteen times in Ezekiel. **"As I live," declares the Lord GOD** appears fourteen times (5:11; 14:16, 18, 20; 16:48; 17:16; 18:3; 20:3, 31, 33; 33:11; 34:8; 35:6, 11). Twice, the structure of the formula is reversed: "Thus says the Lord GOD, 'As I live . . .'" (17:19; 33:27). Evidently, this phrase was used to increase the seriousness of the oath, since it was being made by God Himself (speaking through the mouth of the prophet). It is noteworthy that the contemporary prophets Ezekiel and Jeremiah used this phraseology far more than any other prophets. The reason for this is clear. Both prophets lived in a time when false prophets were numerous. These deceivers frequently made the claim that they were speaking for God, when, in fact, He had not spoken to them at all (see Jer. 14:14; Ezek. 22:28).

The double appellation "Lord GOD" occurs 218 times in Ezekiel, in talking about Israel's sinfulness. Moshe Greenberg said,

... it is the prophet's duty to take them to task in the name of their Lord, against whom they have rebelled. The very pairing of YHWH with "Lord" aims to force upon them awareness of their true state—subjection to a Lord whom they refuse to acknowledge.[9]

God told His people, "... **you have defiled My sanctuary.**" The details are given in chapters 8 and 11 (see 2 Kings 21:7). They had committed many sins against God; but the ultimate sin was that they had defiled His sanctuary, insulting the very character and holiness of God. Therefore, He would **have no pity**. This phrase in Ezekiel (7:4; 8:18; 9:10; see 7:9; 9:5) demonstrates a bitter truth. Whereas God wanted to exercise His basic characteristics of love and mercy, repeated rejection of Him, His law, and His sanctuary provoked the strongest of retributions. The time came when there was no more room for mercy. The full force of God's anger and wrath would be spent.

Verse 12. The use of **one third** justifies the interpretation presented earlier in verse 2. The biblical narratives of the actual siege and destruction may be read in 2 Kings 25:1–21, 2 Chronicles 36:17–21, and Jeremiah 39:1–18. The first third is explained more fully here. These people would not be consumed by literal fire, but by pestilence and famine. Perhaps fire destroyed their crops and lands, causing the pestilence and famine. By breaking down judgment into thirds, God was demonstrating the full measure, the completeness, of His punishment. The phrase **I will unsheathe a sword behind them** is a reminder of King Zedekiah's ill-advised attempt to escape. As a result of this vain attempt, many more died by the sword as they were captured (2 Kings 25:1–21).

5:13–17

¹³"'Thus My anger will be spent and I will satisfy My wrath on them, and I will be appeased; then they will know that I,

---

[9]Moshe Greenberg, *Ezekiel 1—20: A New Translation with Introduction and Commentary*, The Anchor Bible, vol. 22 (Garden City, N.Y.: Doubleday & Co., 1983), 65.

the LORD, have spoken in My zeal when I have spent My wrath upon them. ¹⁴Moreover, I will make you a desolation and a reproach among the nations which surround you, in the sight of all who pass by. ¹⁵So it will be a reproach, a reviling, a warning and an object of horror to the nations who surround you when I execute judgments against you in anger, wrath and raging rebukes. I, the LORD, have spoken. ¹⁶When I send against them the deadly arrows of famine which were for the destruction of those whom I will send to destroy you, then I will also intensify the famine upon you and break the staff of bread. ¹⁷Moreover, I will send on you famine and wild beasts, and they will bereave you of children; plague and bloodshed also will pass through you, and I will bring the sword on you. I, the LORD, have spoken.'"

This final section expands what the judgment would entail, and exactly why it would happen—to warn the nations around Jerusalem (v. 15). Israel had broken God's covenant; therefore, He was no longer bound to bless them as promised in the covenant (see Gen. 12:1–3; 22:18). They were not the shining light to the world that He wanted them to be. Instead, they were the worst possible example (v. 15).

Verse 13. The expression **then they will know** occurs for the first time in this verse, meaning that only when judgment had passed would the people recognize that God's hand had been behind the destruction. In order for them to "know" that the Lord had brought this judgment, God would perform a series of actions. He said,

(1) **"My anger will be spent."** His anger had been building up, accumulating with the continued disobedience of Israel. Now it was time for God to "spend" the wrath that He had accumulated (see 6:12; 7:8).

(2) **"I will satisfy My wrath."** He is a righteous God. It is not part of His character to allow sin to go unpunished. There must be "satisfaction," or justice, meted out.

(3) **"I will be appeased"** ("comforted"; KJV, ASV; "eased and comforted"; AB; "satisfy myself"; NRSV; "avenged"; NIV). When God brings His punishments, His need for justice is satisfied.

He will not be pacified until full vengeance is dispensed. "... and the phrase *I will be comforted* ... similarly implies the relief that comes after the unburdening of powerful emotions, such as grief or anger."[10]

The reference to **My zeal**, or "My jealousy" is the Hebrew word קִנְאָתִי (*qin'athi*), which is common in Ezekiel (8:3, 5; 16:38, 42; 23:35; 36:6; 38:19).[11] God is zealous for righteousness and justice.

Verse 14. God announced that instead of glorifying Israel, which was His desire, He would **make you a desolation and a reproach among the nations which surround you, in the sight of all who pass by**. "Desolation" meant that the cities would be without inhabitants, and "reproach" would come because God's people were an example of failure, despite abundant blessings and opportunities.

Verse 15. God said the surrounding nations would view the demise of Israel in several ways:

1. **A reproach**—The nation would be looked at with disgust, as something worthy of criticism.
2. **A reviling** ("taunt"; KJV, NIV)—Judah would become an object of jokes and proverbs.
3. **A warning** ("instruction"; KJV)—His chosen nation would serve as a powerful example regarding the consequences of sin. It would warn and instruct others that God cannot overlook sin.
4. **An object of horror** ("astonishment"; KJV)—Others would be appalled at how completely devastated a people can become.

---

[10]Taylor, 87.

[11]"By *qin'a* is meant the resentful rage of one whose prerogatives have been usurped by, or given to, another. Among humans, it seizes the husband who suspects his wife of adultery (Num 5:14ff.) or knows her to have been faithless (Prov 6:34). Since YHWH's relation to Israel is figured as a marriage ..., *qin'a* is appropriate for his rage at Israel's breach of faith with him" (Greenberg, 115).

God's judgments would be dispensed in . . .

1. **Anger** (אַף, *'ap*),[12] a word that occurs eighteen times in Ezekiel. This word conveys a strong emotional reaction. God was not simply displeased; He was *angry* because of Israel's disobedience.
2. **Wrath** (חֵמָה, *chemah*),[13] which occurs thirty-three times in the book.
3. **Raging rebukes** (תֹּכְחוֹת חֵמָה, *thok‛choth chemah*). This phrase contains two occurrences of the nominative form חמה. It means a "stinging rebuke" or, literally, a "rebuke of wrath."

Defeated nations were always an object of shame and derision. This is the exact opposite of what God wanted for His people. Judah should have been receiving the blessings promised in Deuteronomy 28:1–14.

Verses 16, 17. God promised to send the **deadly arrows of famine** upon the Israelites (v. 16). Famine and pestilence are represented as poisoned arrows ("evil"; KJV), inflicting death wherever they landed. The ancients represented them in the same way. God had prepared these harmful arrows for others; they were **for the destruction** of enemy nations. Now God would

---

[12]"The nom. [אַף], conveying an intense emotional state, usually refers to divine anger, although it can also refer to human anger. To be angry is not simply being upset or indignant at someone or something. It is the type of anger in which the face may turn red and the passions are aroused. This type of anger in humans may indicate an irrational, out-of-control anger (cf. Num 22:27; 1 Sam 20:30). However, the Lord's anger is rational and controlled" (Gale B. Struthers, "אָנַף," in *New International Dictionary of Old Testament Theology & Exegesis*, ed. Willem A. VanGemeren [Grand Rapids, Mich.: Zondervan Publishing House, 1997], 1:463).

[13]"An examination of the prophecies of Jeremiah and Ezekiel illustrates that the nom. [חֵמָה] conveys a stronger emotion than [אַף] when [אַף] is without modifiers. These men prophesied in the time surrounding the fall of Judah and the subsequent exile. It was at this point that the patience of the Lord had reached its end" (Gale B. Struthers, "חֵמָה," in *New International Dictionary of Old Testament Theology & Exegesis*, ed. Willem A. VanGemeren [Grand Rapids, Mich.: Zondervan Publishing House, 1997], 2:170–71).

give those arrows to the very nations they were intended to defeat, using them to destroy His own people.

The punishments promised in verse 17 fall into these areas:

1. **Famine**—which would "break the staff of bread," a phrase representing the blessings of abundant food.
2. **Wild beasts**[14]—a danger in ancient times, and certainly a concern for parents who wanted to protect their children.
3. **Plague**—under which the land would be ravished, unable to produce crops or fruits, often accompanied with sickness and disease.
4. **Bloodshed**—continual conflict with enemies, who would take advantage of her weakness (from the first three punishments) and come bearing arms (חֶרֶב, *chereb*, "sword," one of the key words in the Book of Ezekiel, occurring eighty-three times).

APPLICATION

Disobedience and Discipline

God does discipline people, especially His children. He said that His punishment would be severe—so severe in fact, that the inhabitants of Jerusalem would resort to cannibalism in order to survive (vv. 9, 10).

There is always a reason for the punishment God brings. In 5:5–8, we see the reason for Jerusalem's punishment: She did not allow her light to shine before the nations, but instead "rebelled . . . more wickedly than the nations" surrounding her, rejecting God's ordinances.

The temporal punishments from God do not last forever

---

[14]"Wild beasts always multiply in depopulated countries. . . . Nebuchadnezzar and his Chaldeans may be called here *evil beasts*. He is often compared to a *lion* [Jer. 4:7; Dan. 7:4] on account of the ravages made by him and his Chaldean armies" (Adam Clarke, *The Holy Bible with a Commentary and Critical Notes*, vol. 4, *Isaiah to Malachi* [New York: Abingdon-Cokesbury Press, n.d.], 437).

(v. 13). He does not punish His children from spite or vindictiveness as a human might, but only to get His people to repent (see Rev. 2:21; 16:9, 11).

The people of God can fall into such rebellion and lawlessness that they become even more wicked than the wicked people around them.

God expects *all* of His laws, ordinances, and statutes (v. 6) to be obeyed.

D.P.

A Hair-Raising Experience (5:1–12)

Ezekiel was told to cut his hair and his beard and then use the hair in a series of object lessons. What could we possibly learn from this incident in Ezekiel's life? Does it have any meaning for us? In fact, this event is quite revealing.

We see here what happens when God withdraws His hand of grace. God said, "I will have no pity, and I will not spare" (v. 11). Life has been exceedingly good to us because God's hand has been upon us. Just think what would happen if God should withdraw His hand!

We see what it is like to be fully punished by the sin we have committed. We will be punished *for* our sins in eternity; but in this life we are mostly punished *by* our sins. God allowed His people to receive the full results of their sins. Look at the crumbled heap of human wreckage along the roadway of life. People who give themselves to sin eventually have their lives torn apart by it.

We see that the results of sin are tragic. The results of sin are not splinters in the hand, but whole lives consumed by slavery and deprivation. Sin is not a toy; it is the major issue in life.

God wanted His people to learn important lessons about life from Ezekiel. He asked His prophet to go to a great extreme to convey the messages because they were so valuable. Will we learn the lessons?

E.C.

CHAPTER 6

THE PROPHECY OF ISRAEL'S DOOM AND THE PROMISE FOR A REMNANT

Thematically, chapter 6 continues what is introduced in chapters 4 and 5: Because of the people's idolatry, the land of Israel would be devastated and its inhabitants would be killed or dispersed. God's message to His people through Ezekiel was "I . . . am going to bring a sword on you" (v. 3; see 5:17); "Thus will I spend My wrath on them" (v. 12; see 5:13); ". . . the house of Israel . . . will fall by sword, famine and plague!" (v. 11; see 5:17). The indirect contact of prophet and audience continues. At the start, the address is to the countryside; later (v. 4b), to the inhabitants of the land. God had Ezekiel talking to just about everything except the exiles. This preaching device was powerful and effective.

DESTRUCTION AND HOPE (6)

The Destruction of High Places (6:1–7)

6:1–4

¹And the word of the LORD came to me saying, ²"Son of man, set your face toward the mountains of Israel, and prophesy against them ³and say, 'Mountains of Israel, listen to the word of the Lord GOD! Thus says the Lord GOD to the mountains, the hills, the ravines and the valleys: "Behold, I Myself am going to bring a sword on you, and I will destroy your high places. ⁴So your altars will become desolate and your incense altars will be smashed; and I will make your slain fall in front of your idols."'"

EZEKIEL 6

Verses 1–3. The word of the LORD occurs sixty times in the book and is often used to introduce a new section. **Set your face** occurs repeatedly (13:17; 21:2; 25:2; 28:21; 29:2; 35:2; 38:2). The phrase **mountains of Israel** is often mentioned also (19:9; 33:28; 34:13, 14; 35:12; 36:1, 4, 8; 37:22; 38:8; 39:2, 4, 17). It refers to the whole land of Israel and is not meant to be interpreted literally. Notice how well balanced the book is: In 6:2 the mountains are rebuked, while in 36:6–15 they are consoled.

God had commanded that all the **high places** be destroyed (Deut. 12:2). Throughout the Old Testament, God condemned these high places. Judah practiced idolatry "on every high hill" (Jer. 3:6). That is why Ezekiel was preaching to the mountains: They were filled with idolatrous places of worship.

Verse 4. This verse contains the first occurrence in the book of the word translated **idols** (גִּלּוּלִים, *gillulim*). This word only occurs forty-eight times in the Old Testament, and thirty-nine of these are within this book (see Lev. 26:30; Deut. 29:17; 1 Kings 15:12; 21:26; 2 Kings 17:12; 21:11, 21; 23:24; Jer. 50:2 for examples outside Ezekiel). These were the gods which the people thought would protect them; instead, the people would die in front of them. Walther Zimmerli wrote,

> In the book of Ezekiel we find in the foreground the idea of abominable uncleanness . . . , which was brought into Israel by the representatives of a non-Yahwistic cultic holiness and which rendered the Israelites who used them unclean (20:7; 23:7). . . .
>
> The judgment which Yahweh brings upon the land by the sword has, by a deep inner logic of righteousness, the consequences that the cult places of the mountains of Israel, which are outwardly places of venerable sanctity, although in Yahweh's eyes they are places of abominations, are to be publicly desecrated by the dead of Israel lying there.[1]

---

[1]Walther Zimmerli, *Ezekiel 1: A Commentary on the Book of the Prophet Ezekiel, Chapters 1—24*, trans. Ronald E. Clements, Hermeneia (Philadelphia: Fortress Press, 1979), 187.

Of all the kings of Judah, only Hezekiah (c. 690 B.C.) and Josiah (c. 625 B.C.) removed these condemned high places. Sadly, their efforts had little impact upon the idolatrous tendencies of the people, who kept returning to these practices.

6:5–7

⁵"'"I will also lay the dead bodies of the sons of Israel in front of their idols; and I will scatter your bones around your altars. ⁶In all your dwellings, cities will become waste and the high places will be desolate, that your altars may become waste and desolate, your idols may be broken and brought to an end, your incense altars may be cut down, and your works may be blotted out. ⁷The slain will fall among you, and you will know that I am the LORD."'"

Verse 5. God said, **"I will scatter your bones."** The lack of a proper burial was considered a terrible punishment in the ancient world (see Ps. 53:5; 141:7). This was a fitting demonstration of the futility of idol worship. The most devoted worshipers would be killed; then the **altars** would be defiled by the bones of their own worshipers (see 2 Kings 23:15–20). Josiah was most noted for attempting to defile high places in this way. The worshipers considered the altars unusable after Josiah burned bones on the pagan altars. The people believed that human bones defiled such a place.

Verse 6. Cities could mean small settlements and also large populations of people. They would become **waste and desolate**. **Works** could refer to the construction of idols (see Hos. 14:3; Jer. 10:3, 9) or perhaps altars (see Is. 17:8). These were carefully made, occasionally being overlaid with gold or silver. "Works" could also refer to the religious practices associated with these high places of worship. God specifically targeted the following areas to be punished because of idolatrous practices:

1. "Cities" would become waste.
2. "High places" would be desolate.
3. "Altars" would become waste and desolate.
4. "Idols" would be broken and brought to an end.

5. "Incense altars" would be cut down.
6. "Works" would be blotted out.

Ideas like these in verses 5 through 7, when remembered, contributed to the people's abandoning their idolatrous ways after the Exile.

Verse 7. The phrase **you will know that I am the L**ORD occurs sixty-three times in the book. Moshe Greenberg wrote,

> The name YHWH is properly synonymous with power (to punish and to rescue), sovereignty, holiness, and authorship and control of events. Presently it is not recognized as such either in Israel, who are apostate or faithless, or among the nations, who are idolatrous. But when disaster strikes them or they experience a miraculous deliverance, the God who announced the event through the prophet will be acknowledged as possessing the attributes properly attached to his name [see Jer. 16:21; Is. 52:6].[2]

Although God gave Ezekiel a message of destruction, He also offered hope.

A Remnant to Be Preserved (6:8–10)

⁸"'"However, I will leave a remnant, for you will have those who escaped the sword among the nations when you are scattered among the countries. ⁹Then those of you who escape will remember Me among the nations to which they will be carried captive, how I have been hurt by their adulterous hearts which turned away from Me, and by their eyes which played the harlot after their idols; and they will loathe themselves in their own sight for the evils which they have committed, for all their abominations. ¹⁰Then they will know that I am the

---

[2]Moshe Greenberg, *Ezekiel 1—20: A New Translation with Introduction and Commentary*, The Anchor Bible, vol. 22 (Garden City, N.Y.: Doubleday & Co., 1983), 133.

LORD; I have not said in vain that I would inflict this disaster on them.'"''

Verse 8. The mention of **a remnant** indicated that some of the people would survive (see 12:16; 14:22). After this terrible ordeal, they would recognize that God had been right all along and that they had been properly punished for their sins. Then they would turn to the Lord and worship only Him (see Is. 17:7; Lev. 26:40, 41). Those who survived in exile would confess their guilt; their uncircumcised hearts would be humbled. A didactic role was envisaged for the remnant: to teach, by the tale of their wicked conduct, the justice of God's punishment. The statements in 14:22, 23 show marked progress. From the ruin of Jerusalem, a remnant would be taken for the sake of the exiles: "'. . . you will see their conduct and actions; then you will be comforted for the calamity which I have brought against Jerusalem. . . . you will know that I have not done in vain whatever I did to it,' declares the Lord GOD." Greenberg said, "The purpose of preserving them is to vindicate God's evil decree: the manifest depravity of the survivors will convince the exiles that the fall of Jerusalem was deserved, and that will be their consolation."³ Here, for the first time, the exiles were explicitly brought into the picture of why God preserved a remnant. They needed to see their depraved state firsthand.

Verses 9, 10. The **escape** of the remnant is mentioned. These people would survive not because of their righteousness, but in order to testify to the truthfulness of God's judgment (v. 11). God named three events that would occur among the remnant:

1. "[They] **will remember Me**" (v. 9), even though they had been carried away and were living in foreign lands as captives.
2. **"They will loathe themselves"** (v. 9). When they looked at themselves, they would feel disgust **for the evils which they** [had] **committed, for all their abominations**.

---

³Ibid., 141.

"Abominations" (תּוֹעֵבָה, *tho'ebah*) is one of the key words in Ezekiel, occurring forty-three times.

3. **"They will know that I am the Lord"** (v. 10). They would come to realize that the Lord is God, and that He was true to His word when He promised that He would **inflict this disaster on them.**

God said, **"I have been hurt."** He is hurt every time we sin. Specifically, He had been hurt by their **hearts**, which had committed adultery when they forsook God and went after other "lovers," the pagan gods and their **eyes**, which had lusted after the idols, desiring their high places and wanting to worship them. Zimmerli wrote,

> ... man's responsibility is described not only by his inner being (לב), but also by an organ which opens the inner life of man to the external world and gives access from the physical world to the inner life (עין). It was in this totality of heart and eye that Israel had sinned. This shows a genuine awareness that it is the eyes in particular which turn in faithlessness to idols, flattered by a sense of their beauty. It is through the gate of the eye that temptation comes to man (Gen. 3:6; Mt. 5:28f; 6:22f), so that the heart, which should not only be regarded as the center of feeling but as the center of man's thought and will, breaks faith with Yahweh [cf. Num. 15:39].[4]

The destruction of Jerusalem and the death of so many people would not be **in vain** because then the people would understand what God meant when He said, **"I am the Lord"** (vv. 7, 10, 13, 14). This gives one of the reasons for God's judgment. Everything God does has a purpose; for every cause there is an intended effect. All that God did, He did to chasten, purge, and cleanse His people. When He disciplines, He is attempting to bring people to repentance.

---

[4]Zimmerli, 189.

The Desolate Land (6:11–14)

¹¹"Thus says the Lord God, 'Clap your hand, stamp your foot and say, "Alas, because of all the evil abominations of the house of Israel, which will fall by sword, famine and plague! ¹²He who is far off will die by the plague, and he who is near will fall by the sword, and he who remains and is besieged will die by the famine. Thus will I spend My wrath on them. ¹³Then you will know that I am the Lord, when their slain are among their idols around their altars, on every high hill, on all the tops of the mountains, under every green tree and under every leafy oak—the places where they offered soothing aroma to all their idols. ¹⁴So throughout all their habitations I will stretch out My hand against them and make the land more desolate and waste than the wilderness toward Diblah; thus they will know that I am the Lord.""'"

Verse 11. The clapping of hands and the stamping of feet seem to indicate either triumph at the vindication of God (see 21:14, 17) or actions of grieving and mourning. These were the actions of the Ammonites of Ezekiel's time (see 25:5, 6). Here, perhaps Ezekiel was told, **"Clap your hand, stamp your foot,"** because justice was finally being done. Such a reaction would not take place because of joy at the destruction, but because God's action vindicated him and the message of God that he preached.

> ... the prophet was not expressing by his action a gloating gesture of an onlooker, but was giving expression to the action of Yahweh himself in which he triumphantly settled accounts with his enemies, and "vented his fury" on them (21:22; cf. 5:13).[5]

Verse 12. God's wrath is inescapable. No matter where these people might go, be it **near** or **far**, or even **remain**[ing] in the land, they would face God's judgment because God would find them.

---

[5]Ibid., 184.

The anger of God is not like the anger of people. When God gets angry, He does not stay angry. Rather, the anger of God is more of a releasing of anger because of the continual stubbornness of His people. He said, **"Thus will I spend My wrath on them."** Once He has spent His anger, then He has no more of it left (at that point in time).

Verse 13. Then you will know that I am the Lord. It was important that God's people learn three vital lessons:

1. The Lord alone is God.
2. The Lord alone is Judge.
3. The Lord alone is Savior.

In the fulfillment of the prophesied events, these three vital lessons would be learned. People of every generation need to know these same three truths. What happened in the Book of Ezekiel is merely a demonstration of what everyone will learn in the final judgment (see Phil. 2:9–11; Rev. 20:11–14).

When judgment came upon Judah, there would be the **slain** in every key idolatrous location: around their altars, on every high hill, on the tops of the mountains, under every green tree, and under every leafy oak. This verse reveals the widespread practice of their idolatry. Indeed, one would never have to go far in Judah to find a place to worship a pagan god!

Verse 14. Since their idolatry was so prevalent, God's judgment would have to be thorough: Desolation would go **throughout all their habitations**. God would **stretch out [His] hand against them**—which is what He told Ezekiel to do symbolically in 4:7. By way of illustration, God said that He would **make the land more desolate and waste** than some of the most useless land in the area, namely **Diblah**. Some translations have "Riblah," which is in the far northern region of the Orontes River in the district of Hamath, on the northeastern coast of the Mediterranean Sea.

APPLICATION

Giving Our All to God

There is no middle ground in the worship of God. The people of Judah were trying to worship Him in the temple and serve their false gods in the "high places." This is wrong! God demands all or nothing from us. What sort of "idols" have we put on an equal level with God (if not higher)? Where are our priorities?

Ezekiel 6:9 tells us something about our relationship with God. Our sinful actions hurt God. If we say that we love God, then we should not want to hurt Him. If we do not want to hurt Him, then we should not make idols in any area of our lives. God is not emotionally detached from us. He is involved in our lives.

God disciplines us for our good (see Eph. 6:1–4; Heb. 12:5–13; 2 Thess. 3:6, 7). He wants to use the discipline to bring us back to Him through repentance and obedience.

D.P.

"Then You Will Know That I Am the Lord"

We see a glimpse of how angry God can become when His people sin against Him. God will not tolerate idolatry of any kind. His response to serving other gods is simple, sincere, and severe.

The simplicity of His message. The first of the Ten Commandments forbade the Israelites from serving other gods. The second commandment ruled out idols or graven images (Ex. 20:3, 4). It should have been clear that they were not to join the polytheistic culture around them in the Promised Land in pagan worship.

The sincerity of God's covenant. Joshua's warning to the victorious conquerors of Canaan was not to be taken lightly. He said, "If you forsake the Lord and serve foreign gods, then He will turn and do you harm and consume you . . . " (Josh. 24:20). God is just, which means that when His followers break the covenant, they will be punished.

The severity of God's judgment. A quick glance through the chapter shows how severe God's wrath can be. He said, "I will scatter your bones"; "Your . . . cities will become waste . . . and desolate" (vv. 5, 6). People will die by the "plague," "sword," and "famine" (v. 12).

When God gives us instructions through His Word, we must take them seriously. Whether these instructions involve codes of morality, the order of worship, or becoming a Christian, we must take care to obey all that He commands. May we praise Him and know that He is the Lord without having to suffer the wrath described in this chapter!

God, Judge, and Savior

Every generation needs to learn that the Lord is God, Judge, and Savior.

The Lord is God. There are no other gods before Him. He created the heavens and the earth. No work, dream, or material blessing is more important than our Creator.

The Lord is Judge. God advocates His right to judge. He does not judge because He is angry or unfair. It is His righteous nature that compels Him to judge. In addition, He conveys strong emotions when He said, "I have been hurt by their adulterous hearts which turned away from Me" (v. 9).

When there is a crime, there must be a penalty. When one sins, that person deserves to receive the due punishment—punishment for breaking the law and for hurting God.

The Lord is Savior. When God punishes people for their trespasses, He always holds out a "remnant" (v. 8). This is a sign of His mercy. He could easily destroy everyone and start again, but His compassion compels Him to extend His grace. As people under the new covenant, we are truly blessed. We are guilty of sin, but Christ has paid our debt on the cross. Therefore, when we believe in Him, repent of our sins, confess His name, and are baptized, God cancels our debt and removes our punishment. How wonderful it is to have God, the Judge, also to be our Savior!

T.P.W.

CHAPTER 7
THE PROPHECY OF ISRAEL'S DOOM AND THE PROMISE FOR A REMNANT (CONTINUED)

A message of destruction extends into chapter 7 to convince the disobedient people of God that He was about to bring an end to their disobedience. John B. Taylor said,

> Verses 2–13 consist of three short oracles, all in similar vein, linked together by the common phrase "the end has come", "your doom has come", "the time has come". The fact that the message needed so much reiteration can only be understood against the background of popular belief in the inviolability of Jerusalem. Its destruction was inconceivable to the Israelite mind. As long as God was God, God's Temple and God's city would stand.[1]

THREE ORACLES OF DISASTER (7:1–13)

First Oracle (7:1–4)

¹Moreover, the word of the LORD came to me saying, ²"And you, son of man, thus says the Lord GOD to the land of Israel, 'An end! The end is coming on the four corners of the land. ³Now the end is upon you, and I will send My anger against you; I will judge you according to your ways and bring all your abominations upon you. ⁴For My eye will have no pity

---

[1] John B. Taylor, *Ezekiel: An Introduction and Commentary*, Tyndale Old Testament Commentaries (Downers Grove, Ill.: Inter-Varsity Press, 1969), 92.

on you, nor will I spare you, but I will bring your ways upon you, and your abominations will be among you; then you will know that I am the LORD!'"

Verse 1. This verse begins the three oracles of disaster and the description of the desolation.

Verse 2. The phrase translated **the land of Israel** is יִשְׂרָאֵל אַדְמַת (*ʾaḏmath yiśraʾel*). *ʾAdmath* means "soil of" and "evokes the earth of the cultivated homeland lived on by Israel; it is particularly poignant in the mouth of an exile."[2] The Hebrew phrase occurs seventeen times in Ezekiel,[3] but nowhere else in the Bible. Isaiah 19:17 contains the closest expression, "land of Judah." Walther Zimmerli explained the significance of this verse,

> "Israel" is addressed as "the land of Israel," although in Ezekiel's day the people were only living in the Judean remnant of the land. The address "land of Israel" shows that this Israel was an entity which possessed its secret in its divine election (Ezek 20:5), but which could be described not only as a phenomenon preserved by a purely spiritual bond, but also as a land. Thus conversely this land also defined Israel because it was the physical pledge of the people's election by God.[4]

The end is coming was a standard announcement of doom (see Gen. 6:13; Lam. 4:18; Amos 8:2). The fact that it was coming **on the four corners of the land** is proof of the thoroughness of God's judgment.

Verse 3. God said, **"I will judge you."** The Hebrew word

---

[2]Moshe Greenberg, *Ezekiel 1—20: A New Translation with Introduction and Commentary*, The Anchor Bible, vol. 22 (Garden City, N.Y.: Doubleday & Co., 1983), 145.

[3]The Hebrew phrase appears in Ezekiel 7:2; 11:17; 12:19, 22; 13:9; 18:2; 20:38, 42; 21:7, 8; 25:3, 6; 33:24; 36:6; 37:12; 38:18, 19.

[4]Walther Zimmerli, *Ezekiel 1: A Commentary on the Book of the Prophet Ezekiel, Chapters 1—24*, trans. Ronald E. Clements, Hermeneia (Philadelphia: Fortress Press, 1979), 204.

שָׁפַט (shapat) has the sense of "punish" here. The word occurs thirty-five times in the text of Ezekiel. It demonstrates that God had evaluated the evidence and the people of Israel had been found guilty. The parallel phrase (נָתַתִּי עָלַיִךְ, naththi ʽalayik), translated **bring** ("repay"; NKJV, NIV; "send"; KJV) does not mean "charge you with," as it is usually rendered, but "impose on you [the penalty for]."[5] Notice the obvious repetition of the word "you"—which occurs no less than twelve times, either as "you" or "yours," in verses 3 and 4. The point is clear. What Israel had done was resulting in painful consequences. She was reaping what she had sown.

Verse 4. "My eye will have no pity, nor will I spare you," God said. While He is presented as a God of love, mercy, and compassion in the Old Testament, He is also a just God. When His continual extensions of mercy (seen, for example, in the gift of time) are ignored, God will act. In this case, His act of vengeance would be thorough. He would have "no pity." This is the second time we have encountered this phrase in the book (see 5:11). "Spare" is translated from the Hebrew word חָמַל (chamal), meaning "to look upon with compassion or regret." Mike Butterworth wrote,

> In the prophecies of Ezekiel, "my eye will not/your eyes shall not spare" occurs with the root [חָמַל]; ("pity"; the nom. [חֶמְלָה, chumlah], compassion, occurs in 16:5; otherwise it is the vb.). In most cases the intention is similar to that expressed in Deuteronomy: judgment must be carried out, unhindered by pity. (Ezek 16:5 is a historical reference: no one but the Lord showed any pity for Israel on the day she was born.) In 24:14 the gram-

---

[5]"This is seen in Jonah 1:14, where the desperate sailors, about to throw Jonah into the sea, pray to God, 'Do not lay upon us [the penalty for shedding] the blood of an innocent man.' What they fear is not a divine indictment but a divine punishment. Similarly, in Ezek 23:49, '[Your executioners] shall lay upon you [the penalty of] your depravity, and you shall bear the guilt (= suffer the punishment . . .) of your idolatry.' Again, since the subjects are not judges (or plaintiffs) but executioners, their acts are not a mere proffering of charges, but a carrying out of a penal verdict" (Greenberg, 147).

matical construction is different but the emphasis is the same: "I the Lord have spoken. The time has come for me to act. I will not hold back; I will not have pity, nor will I relent [לֹא אֶנָּחֵם, *lo' 'ennachem*]."[6]

"Pity" is the translation of חוּס (*chus*), which also occurs in 5:11; 7:9; 8:18; 9:5, 10; 16:5; 24:14. Unlike Jeremiah, Ezekiel did not talk about Judah's repentance (see Jer. 18:7–11; 25:4–7; 26:3–6; 35:15) or the people's failure to repent (see Jer. 5:1–6, 21, 23, 25; 6:19, 27–30; 7:23–29; 9:5–9; 13:22; 15:6–9; 19:15). Why should God have "pity"? In view of the years of opportunities He had given Judah to repent and the fact that His prophets had come to them "again and again" (as is so often repeated in Jeremiah), they were beyond being given further opportunities. God did not feel sorry for them now. They were getting their just reward. Such are the wages of sin (see Rom. 6:23).

Thomas M. Raitt observed,

> He begins with the assumption that there is no hope for Judah, and thus he preaches denied mercy, rejection, and annihilation from the outset. His public ministry begins in chapter 4 with punishment already inevitable, beyond a chastising or purgative level.[7]

Second Oracle (7:5–9)

⁵"Thus says the Lord God, 'A disaster, unique disaster, behold it is coming! ⁶An end is coming; the end has come! It has awakened against you; behold, it has come! ⁷Your doom has come to you, O inhabitant of the land. The time has come, the day is near—tumult rather than joyful shouting on the mountains. ⁸Now I will shortly pour out My wrath on you and spend My anger against you; judge you according to your ways

---

[6]Mike Butterworth, "חָמַל," in *New International Dictionary of Old Testament Theology & Exegesis*, ed. Willem A. VanGemeren (Grand Rapids, Mich.: Zondervan Publishing House, 1997), 2:174–75.

[7]Thomas M. Raitt, *A Theology of Exile: Judgment/Deliverance in Jeremiah and Ezekiel* (Philadelphia: Fortress Press, 1977), 47.

and bring on you all your abominations. ⁹My eye will show no pity nor will I spare. I will repay you according to your ways, while your abominations are in your midst; then you will know that I, the LORD, do the smiting.'"

Verse 5. The picture of unprecedented destruction is painted here. The idea was that evil (**disaster**) would follow after evil, with one instantly succeeding another. This would culminate in the destruction of the temple. Thus this verse says the same thing as 5:9: Because of Judah's terrible wickedness, God would do equally terrible things—destroy the city, destroy the people, and destroy the temple. The short, broken phrasing in this proclamation adds force to the message. Only **the Lord GOD** has the power or authority to make and carry out such a pronouncement. Only He would know for certain to say, **"Behold it is coming!"**

Verses 6, 7. The terminology used here emphasizes the *certainty* of God's coming judgment. It was something that had **awakened** and was **coming**—there was no avoiding it now. The hostile troops were on their way. Israel could hear them approaching; no attempt was made to bring about a surprise attack. The **joyful shouting on the mountains** might refer to the festivals that took place there, the shouts of joy from the farmers who harvested there, or perhaps the joy of the pagan worship services conducted there. Those sounds were soon to be replaced by noise from the country that was about to defeat Israel.

Verses 8, 9. The pronounced acts of God make these verses humbling and frightening. Notice what God announced that He would do: "I will . . ."

1. ". . . pour out My wrath."
2. ". . . spend My anger."
3. ". . . judge you according to your ways."
4. ". . . bring on you all your abominations."
5. ". . . will show no pity."
6. ". . . [not] **spare.**"
7. ". . . repay you according to your ways."

In conclusion, God declared, **"Then you will know that I, the LORD, do the smiting"** (יהוה מָכָּה, *YHWH makah*; "the smiting LORD"). The word translated "smite" is a common word meaning to "hit, punch, wound." It emphasizes here the physical nature of God's judgment. Israel would *feel* the consequences of God's wrath. Taylor said,

> To hearers and readers who were used to names of God like "Jehovah-jireh" and "Jehovah-nissi" (Gn. 22:14; Ex. 17:15), it must have come home with tremendous force to have Him described as "Jehovah-makkeh". The Lord who had provided and protected was about to strike.[8]

Third Oracle (7:10–13)

10"'Behold, the day! Behold, it is coming! Your doom has gone forth; the rod has budded, arrogance has blossomed. 11Violence has grown into a rod of wickedness. None of them shall remain, none of their people, none of their wealth, nor anything eminent among them. 12The time has come, the day has arrived. Let not the buyer rejoice nor the seller mourn; for wrath is against all their multitude. 13Indeed, the seller will not regain what he sold as long as they both live; for the vision regarding all their multitude will not be averted, nor will any of them maintain his life by his iniquity.'"

Verse 10. God's punishment would come soon. A budding **rod** is a sure sign that a blossom will quickly follow. The certainty of the day of doom is compared to a budding rod. The blossom could be referring to Nebuchadnezzar (see Is. 10:5; Jer. 51:20).

Verse 11. The "rod" of judgment in verse 10 is now the **rod of wickedness**. Everything important to the people of Judah—jobs, houses, wealth—would be lost. Theirs was the classic and often repeated problem of misplaced priorities. Jesus dealt with this same problem when He asked, "For what will it profit a

---

[8]Taylor, 93.

man if he gains the whole world and forfeits his soul?" (Mt. 16:26a).

Verse 12. Let not the buyer rejoice. . . . According to Moshe Greenberg,

> It is customary that a buyer rejoices in his purchase and a seller is sorry that out of need he had to part with his property; compare the talmudic adage, "People say, If you've bought, you've gained, if you've sold, you've lost" [BT *Baba Mesi'a*, p. 51a].[9]

The buying and selling of land was not wrong or sinful (see Jer. 32:6–12), but the attitude was in question. Normal sounds of everyday life, like hearing others **rejoice** or **mourn**, would be gone. There was to be no normalcy. About to enter their otherwise peaceful lives was something quite *abnormal*: **wrath**.

Verse 13. Whatever work one did in order to better his life would be lost, and it was never to be regained. Social dealings would become meaningless. Purchases would be wasted efforts. Land acquisitions would be of no value. What God was bringing upon them could **not be averted**. God had no intention of backing down. His warnings through the years had fallen on deaf ears. People had continued in their **iniquity**, supposing that their choice to live this way had somehow provided a better life. The same kind of self-deception occurs today. A man may choose a life of sin—stealing, lying, or adultery—because he supposes that it provides some measure of the "good life." Indeed, as Moses discovered, such a life is built only on the "passing pleasures of sin" (Heb. 11:25, 26). When God's judgment came, no one would be able to buy, bribe, or beg his way to safety.

THE RESULTING DESOLATION (7:14–27)

7:14–18
¹⁴"'They have blown the trumpet and made everything

---

[9]Greenberg, 149.

ready, but no one is going to the battle, for My wrath is against all their multitude. ¹⁵The sword is outside and the plague and the famine are within. He who is in the field will die by the sword; famine and the plague will also consume those in the city. ¹⁶Even when their survivors escape, they will be on the mountains like doves of the valleys, all of them mourning, each over his own iniquity. ¹⁷All hands will hang limp and all knees will become like water. ¹⁸They will gird themselves with sackcloth and shuddering will overwhelm them; and shame will be on all faces and baldness on all their heads.'"

Verse 14. They have blown the trumpet . . . but no one is going to the battle. This shows the futility of armed resistance. With God against them, who could stand?

Verse 15. There was no good news anywhere. If a person should venture inside the city, he would find **plague** and **famine**. If he should venture outside the city into the field, he would encounter **the sword**. There was no place to hide. God's judgment cannot be avoided or postponed.

Verse 16. A comparison is given: **. . . they will be on the mountains like doves of the valleys, all of them mourning. . . .** The people would be like mourning doves (הַגֻּאָיוֹת, *hagge'aywoth*), chased from their dovecotes and separated from their mates.

Verse 17. Another comparison is given: **All knees will become like water.** This indicates their extreme fear.

Verse 18. The people would be shamed and humiliated by their sins that brought this **overwhelm**[ing] destruction. They would put on **sackcloth** in mourning, demonstrate their **shame** by their facial expressions, and shave their **heads**, totally humiliated (see Gen. 37:34; 1 Kings 20:31; Is. 15:2, 3; Jer. 16:6; 48:37).

7:19, 20

¹⁹"'They will fling their silver into the streets and their gold will become an abhorrent thing; their silver and their gold will not be able to deliver them in the day of the wrath of the LORD. They cannot satisfy their appetite nor can they fill their stomachs, for their iniquity has become an occasion of stumbling. ²⁰They transformed the beauty of His ornaments into

pride, and they made the images of their abominations and their detestable things with it; therefore I will make it an abhorrent thing to them.'"

Verse 19. The **abhorrent thing** is the Hebrew word נִדָּה (*niddah*). This word refers to menstrual impurity (Lev. 15:19; 18:19; see Ezek. 22:10). S. Fisch said, "On the day of reckoning, the desperate inhabitants will cast away their wealth as something of extreme impurity (see 36:17), because they will neither be able to buy food nor ransom their lives with it."[10]

For once, money would be viewed in a proper light. It is basically worthless in relation to the really important matters in life. At this time of destruction, it would no longer have "power." It would be unable to do anything: Money could not buy one's freedom; it could not even buy food. Whereas men sometimes can be bought by the lure of money, God is not so deceived. Verse 19 declares that **their silver and their gold will not be able to deliver them in the day of the wrath of the Lord**. Money cannot avert God's wrath. There would be no way to **satisfy their appetite** for the basic needs of life. Why? **Their iniquity** [had] **become an occasion of stumbling** (מִכְשׁוֹל עֲוֺנָם, *mikshol ᵃwonam*, "a stumbling block of their iniquity").[11]

Verse 20. These people who were supposed to have been God's special people had **made . . . images of their abominations and their detestable things**.

7:21, 22

21"'I will give it into the hands of the foreigners as plunder and to the wicked of the earth as spoil, and they will profane

---

[10]S. Fisch, *Ezekiel: Hebrew Text and English Translation with an Introduction and Commentary*, Soncino Books of the Bible (London: Soncino Press, 1950), 38.

[11]"This expression is peculiar to Ezekiel; it recurs in 14:3, 4, 7 applied to idols; in 18:30 to unrepented transgression; in 44:12 to Levites who served at the illegal shrines. . . . In accord with Ezekiel's use of 'stumbling-block,' the phrase means 'cause of downfall (consisting) of iniquity'; or 'the iniquitous cause of their downfall.' . . . How their gold and silver became an iniquitous cause of their downfall is told in the next verse" (Greenberg, 152–53).

it. ²²I will also turn My face from them, and they will profane My secret place; then robbers will enter and profane it."'

Verses 21, 22. Riches that had been a source of pride—everything treasured—would become unclean. Such things had brought about their fall. God announced that He would **turn** [His] **face** from them. He only does this when sin is involved (Is. 59:1, 2). According to Taylor, "The emotive words used are a healthy reminder to the reader that when God acts in judgment He Himself suffers pain and grief as well as those whom His holiness has condemned."¹²

My secret place is the temple. God would allow even the temple to be profaned—something the Jewish people never thought would happen (see Jer. 7). The Babylonians would not only destroy the city; but they would also enter the temple, deface it, plunder it, and burn it to the ground. This took place in 587(6) B.C., about seven years after this prophecy was made.

7:23–27
²³"'Make the chain, for the land is full of bloody crimes and the city is full of violence. ²⁴Therefore, I will bring the worst of the nations, and they will possess their houses. I will also make the pride of the strong ones cease, and their holy places will be profaned. ²⁵When anguish comes, they will seek peace, but there will be none. ²⁶Disaster will come upon disaster and rumor will be added to rumor; then they will seek a vision from a prophet, but the law will be lost from the priest and counsel from the elders. ²⁷The king will mourn, the prince will be clothed with horror, and the hands of the people of the land will tremble. According to their conduct I will deal with them, and by their judgments I will judge them. And they will know that I am the LORD.'"

Verse 23. They were told to **make the chain**—the chain that would bind the captives together as they were led to Babylon.
Verse 24. The worst of the nations was the ruthless Baby-

---
¹²Taylor, 94–95.

lon (see 28:7; 30:11). The Babylonians were feared warriors, known for their brutality and cruelty (Hab. 1:6, 7). The prophet Habakkuk was amazed that God would send a wicked nation to destroy His people. God explained to the prophet that the Chaldeans' day of judgment was also coming—but, for a time, God intended to use them as His rod of judgment against the Israelites. **The pride of the strong ones** refers to the magnificence of their greatest and haughtiest princes, who gloried in their wealth and high position. **Their holy places** refers to the various parts of the temple.

Verse 25. Naturally, one who is afflicted is going to **seek peace**—an end to the torment. However, no such relief would come to Judah (see Jer. 6:14). As noted several times already, the full amount of God's wrath would be poured out. There would be no peace until His wrath was "spent."

Verses 26, 27. The situation would go from bad to worse. When the people thought their plight could not get any worse, another **disaster** would come. They would **seek a vision** from a prophet, but there would be no such word from the Lord. When God no longer spoke to the people, especially through His prophets, it was a signal of His displeasure with them (1 Sam. 14:37, 38; Lam. 2:9). Ralph H. Alexander wrote the following:

> None could offer help. They had no answers at all! The leadership had failed in its responsibility to lead the people in God's ways. It was too late! The anguish of judgment had come! If the people had sought peace earlier, it would have been available; but now there was no peace. Kings and princes would be horrified and mourn (v. 27). God had judged Israel by her own judgments—by the Mosaic covenant they should have known and followed. The only redeeming factor was that they would learn that the Lord truly was God and that his covenants were to be obeyed![13]

---

[13]Ralph H. Alexander, "Ezekiel," in *The Expositor's Bible Commentary*, ed. Frank E. Gaebelein (Grand Rapids, Mich.: Zondervan Publishing House, 1986), 6:780.

Those most relied upon for guidance would be silent:

1. **The prophet** would have nothing to say because he had received nothing from God.
2. **The priest** would be silenced, having to admit his utter ignorance of the Law—the very tool he was commanded to use to instruct the people.
3. **The elders**—who were given the charge to oversee the people, to judge them righteously, to encourage them to be faithful to the covenant in their secular and religious activities—would be unable to give counsel.

APPLICATION

God's Judgment

God postpones judgment as long as He possibly can—but eventually, if they do not change, punishment must come upon the guilty (see Rev. 2:21). God wants us to repent and be saved, and He gives us the time. If we ignore Him, then we will be lost.

The wages of sin is death (Rom. 6:23). The Israelites had filled up their measure of sin. It was time for them to be paid according to their sinful choices.

In Ezekiel 7:25–27, God said that the people would realize that His judgment had come upon them. They would long to turn to God, to hear a word of comfort from God's prophets or priests—but there would be none, because it was too late. We also need to repent while there is opportunity (see Acts 17:30, 31; Heb. 3:13).

People are often self-deceived, thinking that sin brings some measure of joy and the best that life has to offer. Like the Israelites, they fail to consider the *whole* picture. A judgment day is coming, when everyone must give an account (Eccles. 12:13, 14; 2 Cor. 5:10; Rev. 20:11–14).

D.P.

The Tragedy of Idol Worship

What is the tragedy of worshiping idols? Is it a harmless pastime or a serious matter?

We are worshiping a lie. Idol worship is based on absolute error. One who bows down and pays homage to wood or stone as if it were God has traded the truth for falsehood.

God can no longer bless us. When someone is worshiping idols, he will no longer receive God's blessings. After he passes the time God has given for repentance, God turns the worshiper over to the results that idol worship brings.

Idol worship eventually brings God's judgment. The fall of the northern and southern kingdoms came as His judgment upon idol worship. Their captivities were times of discipline for the two kingdoms. When the remnant went to Jerusalem and rebuilt the city and the temple, idol worship did not occur again. The people had learned their lesson.

God is a jealous God—jealous concerning the truth. He is God, and there is no other God.

The Wrath of God (7:12, 13)

Two great questions are "What is the wrath of God?" and "When does He bestow it?"

One lives under the wrath of God when he is separated from God. He stands in a state of condemnation. He is apart from God's grace and lives under His legal wrath.

God has bestowed His wrath upon sinful people at different times in history. When He destroyed the world with the flood, sinful people saw His horrible wrath. History reflects His judgment.

God's wrath will descend upon the sinner at the final judgment in the form of eternal punishment. The one who is separated from God experiences God's legal wrath now. The Old Testament pictures His wrath being poured out upon sin at different times. The final judgment pictures His eternal wrath for all eternity.

When someone becomes a Christian, he is forgiven and removed from the wrath of God. The redeemed person can sing with Paul, "Therefore there is now no condemnation for those who are in Christ Jesus" (Rom. 8:1).

E.C.

CHAPTER 8

IDOLATRY IN THE TEMPLE

Chapters 8 through 11 form a unit, telling about Ezekiel's second vision. Around fourteen months had passed since the opening vision of the book. In this second vision, Ezekiel witnessed the idolatrous practices at the temple in Jerusalem (ch. 8) and learned what God planned to do about these abominations. He saw the destruction of the people (ch. 9) and the departure of God's glory from the temple, but was given hope concerning the remnant to be saved (chs. 10; 11).

God had declared, ". . . the end has come" in 7:6, but now the reasons for this condemnation are given in chapters 8 through 11. Ezekiel was allowed to see the extent to which religious corruption had overcome Israel's leaders. He observed that the people of Jerusalem were immoral, and he was told that those who did not have the mark of God on them were doomed. In these four chapters, then, we will see different aspects of why "the end" had come.

EZEKIEL TAKEN TO THE SCENE OF THE VISION (8:1–4)

¹It came about in the sixth year, on the fifth day of the sixth month, as I was sitting in my house with the elders of Judah sitting before me, that the hand of the Lord GOD fell on me there. ²Then I looked, and behold, a likeness as the appearance of a man; from His loins and downward there was the appearance of fire, and from His loins and upward the ap-

pearance of brightness, like the appearance of glowing metal. ³He stretched out the form of a hand and caught me by a lock of my head; and the Spirit lifted me up between earth and heaven and brought me in the visions of God to Jerusalem, to the entrance of the north gate of the inner court, where the seat of the idol of jealousy, which provokes to jealousy, was located. ⁴And behold, the glory of the God of Israel was there, like the appearance which I saw in the plain.

Verse 1. These events occurred in **the sixth month**. If this was during a leap year, then Ezekiel had finished his symbolic action of chapter 4 twelve days before this vision came to him. If it was not a leap year, then Ezekiel was still lying on his right side, bearing the punishment for the iniquity of Judah, when the elders came to him.[1] It seems logical that Ezekiel would be in the middle of Judah's judgment when this vision came to him. By comparing the date given here with the first dated vision (ch. 1), this account would be fourteen months later—around September of 592 B.C.

Ezekiel sat with **the elders of Judah**. The people realized that Ezekiel was a prophet (see 2:5), and they wanted to hear a word from the Lord. Several times throughout the book, the elders came to consult with Ezekiel (14:1; 20:1; see 33:31). Ralph H. Alexander wrote,

> These elders were not contemporary elders in Judah who had come from Judah to Babylonia to seek counsel from Ezekiel. This would be most unlikely in light of the distance and time involved. Moreover, the depraved character of the Judean elders revealed in this vision would not have led them to take such an arduous journey to Babylonia for genuine spiritual reasons. The elders sitting before Ezekiel were the leaders of the Judean exiles in Babylonia who had already been deported from Judah

---

[1]The Jews used a lunar calendar, which they aligned with the solar year by adding a 29-day "intercalary" month between Adar and Nisan (perhaps twice in five years).

in the captivities of Daniel (605 B.C.) and Jehoiachin (597 B.C.).[2]

Ezekiel was a man of God, the type of person who would not answer unless **the hand of the Lord God** moved him to speak (according to the directive of God given in 3:26, 27).

Verse 2. A figure in Ezekiel's vision had **a likeness as the appearance of a man.** Ezekiel had seen "a figure with the appearance of a man" in 1:26. While most versions say "man" here, the NKJV and the KJV have "fire" instead. If this is correct, then the verse must still be talking about God (see 1:27). S. Fisch wrote, "Modern commentators follow the LXX and read *ish* (man) for *esh* (fire) in conformity with 1:26; but there the noun is *adam* and no explanation is offered why Ezekiel did not use it here. This verse is obviously based on 1:27 which supports the M.T."[3]

Verse 3. The figure in the vision **stretched out the form of a hand.** The context lets us know that this is talking about God. As in chapter 1, Ezekiel avoided using anthropomorphic language to describe God. This second vision does not end until 11:24. While Ezekiel referred to **visions of God,** the events in the vision depicted the reality of the situation in Jerusalem.[4] Since the section was given to justify God's condemnation of the people, it has to reflect accurately the corruption found in Jerusalem.

Ezekiel was taken **to Jerusalem**[5]—and, more specifically, **to the entrance of the north gate of the inner court.** The northern gate was one of three which provided access from the outer court of the temple to the inner court. This was the location of **the seat**

---

[2]Ralph H. Alexander, "Ezekiel," in *The Expositor's Bible Commentary*, ed. Frank E. Gaebelein (Grand Rapids, Mich.: Zondervan Publishing House, 1986), 6:781.

[3]S. Fisch, *Ezekiel: Hebrew Text and English Translation with an Introduction and Commentary*, Soncino Books of the Bible (London: Soncino Press, 1950), 41.

[4]Many scholars believe that Ezekiel was literally transported to Jerusalem. Several reasons to justify that conclusion are offered in William H. Brownlee, *Ezekiel 1—19*, Word Biblical Commentary (Waco, Tex.: Word Books, 1986), 129–30.

[5]Babylon is approximately five hundred miles from Jerusalem.

of the idol of jealousy, which provokes to jealousy. The rendering of the noun קִנְאָה (*qin'ah*) in relation to God as "jealousy" has caused confusion among biblical scholars. The noun, when it relates to divine disfavor, has nothing in common with human jealousy. It is derived from the verb *qanah*, meaning "to acquire as one's own property," and denotes in the first instance the vindication of one's rights. The phrase "the idol of jealousy, which provokes to jealousy" means "the image of outrage against authority, which provokes Him to vindicate His exclusive rights."

The term *qin'ah*, describing God as being zealous, or jealous, for His violated rights, is used in Ezekiel and in other parts of the Old Testament only in respect to the sins of idolatry and immorality. The word occurs in Exodus 20:5; 34:14; Deuteronomy 4:24; 5:9; 6:15; Joshua 24:19; and Nahum 1:2. In Ezekiel, it is used in 5:13; 8:3; 16:38, 42; 23:25; 31:9; 35:11; 36:5, 6; 38:19; and 39:25. An explanation for its meaning is in *The Soncino Chumash* (an English translation and commentary of the Pentateuch) on Numbers 25:11. Fisch concluded,

> Attributing *kin'ah* [*qin'ah*] to God is simply an expression of certain retribution for these offenses which undermine the existence of human society. Ezekiel, in particular, laid stress on this doctrine in repeatedly employing the term *kin'ah* with reference to these sins.[6]

Exactly what was this "idol of jealousy"? The reference could be to the graven image of Asherah, which Manasseh put in the house of the Lord (2 Kings 21:7). He eventually removed it (2 Chron. 33:7, 15), but then it was returned. Josiah disposed of the idol (2 Kings 23:6). John B. Taylor suggested the possibility that one of Josiah's successors may have made another one and set it up by the northern gate.[7] Others speculate that Zedekiah reestablished this altar. Another possibility is that the reference is to what Ahaz had done years earlier (2 Kings 16). Ahaz had

---

[6]Fisch, xv.

[7]John B. Taylor, *Ezekiel: An Introduction and Commentary*, Tyndale Old Testament Commentaries (Downers Grove, Ill.: Inter-Varsity Press, 1969), 98.

moved the brazen altar from the front of the Lord's house to the north of the altar which he himself had erected. The locality of the idol before God's own altar enhances the heinousness of the sin. Whatever this idol was, it provoked God. It was an insult to Him, to His character, and to His holiness. The idol mocked His law regarding worship and the sanctity of the temple. God had declared in the Mosaic covenant that He alone was God (Ex. 20:1–3) and that all idolatry was forbidden (Deut. 4:16; 32:16, 21; see 1 Kings 14:22, 23; Ps. 78:58).

Verse 4. The glory of the God of Israel was part of this vision. It is remarkable, in view of the corruption in Jerusalem, that "the glory of the God of Israel" was still there. According to Taylor,

> It was as if he wanted to throw into sharp relief the difference between the God who belonged there and the deviations which were practised there, so making the crimes all the more heinous. Perhaps he was also trying to say that God would stay with His people until the very last moment of their rejection of Him.[8]

However, in a short time, God's glory would depart (ch. 11).

FOUR ABOMINABLE ACTS (8:5–18)

In 8:5–18, God showed Ezekiel four abominable acts being committed by His people:

1. The idol of jealousy (vv. 5, 6).
2. The "hidden" idolatry of the elders of Judah (vv. 7–13).
3. The women weeping for the god Tammuz (vv. 14, 15).
4. The sun worshipers (vv. 16–18).

Each of the abominations is described with repetitive phrases, which are used for emphasis and dramatic effect:

---

[8]Ibid., 97–98.

1. "Then He said" (vv. 5, 12) and "Then He brought . . ." (vv. 7, 14, 16). He brought Ezekiel to the very locations where these sins were being perpetuated.
2. "Do you see . . . ?" (vv. 6, 12, 15, 17). God wanted to make sure that Ezekiel observed the totality of the situation, noticing every aspect of the evil that had been done by His people.
3. "You will see still greater abominations" (vv. 6, 13, 15). As if that sin were not bad enough, God prepared Ezekiel for something even worse. The fourth abomination serves as the climax of this section.

The Idol of Jealousy (8:5, 6)

⁵Then He said to me, "Son of man, raise your eyes now toward the north." So I raised my eyes toward the north, and behold, to the north of the altar gate was this idol of jealousy at the entrance. ⁶And He said to me, "Son of man, do you see what they are doing, the great abominations which the house of Israel are committing here, so that I would be far from My sanctuary? But yet you will see still greater abominations."

Verse 5. Ezekiel began describing the first abomination. When God told him, "**. . . raise your eyes now toward the north,**" He was asking the prophet to recognize the significance of what he was seeing. It had been more than five years since Ezekiel had seen the city that he loved and the center of the city, the temple. Whatever concept Ezekiel may have had of the daily events at the temple—perhaps of faithful priests serving according to the law of God—that notion was about to be shattered. The degree of wickedness in Jerusalem and, more astonishingly, at the temple, would have stunned even the most pessimistic prophet. The text describes the **idol of jealousy at the entrance** of the north gate. The north gate is called **the altar gate** because animals were slaughtered there (Lev. 1:11). It is not exactly clear where this idol of jealousy was set up. Was it actually inside the temple proper or just outside the north gate? Was it actually something that was carved into the north wall? The following illustration shows the probable location of this idol. There, it would have been easily seen by those entering by the north gate, and perhaps by those coming in the east gate. The true altar of burnt offerings may have been removed, leaving only this pagan idol.

Verse 6. God was asking the prophet to see why He should

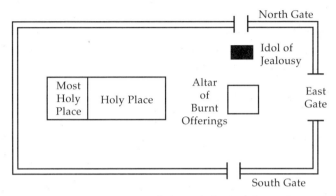

Possible Location of the "Idol of Jealousy" At the Temple

be **far from** [His] **sanctuary**. Some versions translate this "removing themselves from my sanctuary." The NIV translates the phrase as "things that will drive me far from my sanctuary." God's people were actually doing things that would *force Him out* of His "sanctuary."

The "Hidden" Idolatry of the Elders of Judah (8:7–13)

8:7–10
⁷Then He brought me to the entrance of the court, and when I looked, behold, a hole in the wall. ⁸He said to me, "Son of man, now dig through the wall." So I dug through the wall, and behold, an entrance. ⁹And He said to me, "Go in and see the wicked abominations that they are committing here." ¹⁰So I entered and looked, and behold, every form of creeping things and beasts and detestable things, with all the idols of the house of Israel, were carved on the wall all around.

Verse 7. Here begins the second abomination God showed to Ezekiel. The "entrance of the court" is presumably still referring to the north entrance that was mentioned earlier. In this area was a large chamber (see 40:44–46) where the priests and Levites would reside. Ezekiel found **a hole in the wall**. Apparently, the hole was not big enough for him to climb through, but still this lack of maintenance and upkeep reflects the people's disregard for the temple area.

Verse 8. God told Ezekiel to **dig through the wall**. He wanted Ezekiel to enter the area where the elders were engaging in their abominable practices. "Digging" represents a search for truth.

Verses 9, 10. When Ezekiel dug through the wall, he discovered a door leading to another area. He was instructed to go beyond that entrance, where he would **see the wicked abominations that** [the seventy elders were] **committing** (v. 9). Carved on the wall were images of **every form of creeping things and beasts and detestable things** (v. 10). God's law (see Deut. 4:16–18) had clearly delineated these three categories as unclean:

1. "Creeping things"—images of reptiles.
2. "Beasts"—representations of animals declared unclean (such as the pig).
3. "Detestable things"—a reference to the heathen gods.

It is inconceivable that such unclean animals—which they were not even to eat—could now be engraved upon their walls. The people had made all the walls of this holy place into murals to worship along with their idols. Apparently, each elder had a room where he did this (v. 12).

8:11–13
¹¹**Standing in front of them were seventy elders of the house of Israel, with Jaazaniah the son of Shaphan standing among them, each man with his censer in his hand and the fragrance of the cloud of incense rising.** ¹²**Then He said to me, "Son of man, do you see what the elders of the house of Israel are committing in the dark, each man in the room of his carved images? For they say, 'The Lord does not see us; the Lord has**

forsaken the land.'" ¹³And He said to me, "Yet you will see still greater abominations which they are committing."

Verse 11. The **seventy elders** were most likely the leaders of the nation, who based their traditional position on Moses' appointment of the seventy elders to assist him in governing God's people (Ex. 24:1, 9; Num. 11:16–25). What Ezekiel was seeing were heads of the tribes or families—men who should have been examples of godliness, not promoters of idolatry. This large number demonstrates how widespread idolatry was in Israel. The corruption was not just on a "wall," but also in their hearts.

Jaazaniah the son of Shaphan was probably the leader of the seventy idolaters. He can be identified as the son of the scribe who read the book of the Law to Josiah. His brother—or half brother, Ahikam—was involved in the work of Jeremiah (Jer. 26:24). Sadly, Jaazaniah decided to go a much different direction from his family; he was "the black sheep of a worthy family."⁹ His name means "Yahweh hears," but he was offering worship to gods who could not hear, because they did not exist. Further, the offering **of incense** was the religious duty of the priests, not the elders. As a priest, Ezekiel must have been disgusted at this blatant usurpation of the priestly duties. These men were not even attempting to be priests *of God*; they were worshiping the unclean, detestable animals which the Egyptians, the Canaanites, and the Babylonians worshiped.

Verse 12. The elders did not engage in these practices publicly. They were committing these acts **in the dark**, that is, in secret. The idolatries were taking place in secret, apparently with **each man** in his own room. In Ezekiel's time, various buildings stood on the space around the inner court. There would be space for such activities in the outer court, but probably not in the inner court. Ezekiel initially was outside the wall of the outer court; then he dug through, into a room which was inside the wall of the outer court but against the gate. Of course, no room is so dark or so secluded that it is beyond the sight of the Lord. Whereas these men might have said, **"The LORD does not see"**

---

⁹Taylor, 99.

(see 9:9), such is far from the truth! The Lord is immanently qualified to judge, because He sees everything (see Job 7:18, 19; 22:13, 14; Ps. 10:11; 94:7; Is. 29:15). The statement of the elders, **"The LORD has forsaken the land,"** may provide some insight into their thinking. They no longer believed that the Lord was with them; they thought that He had, in fact, deserted them.

> The motive of the two constitutive elements of the vision is provided by the repeated, twofold assertion of the culprits, "YHWH does not see us; YHWH has left the land" (8:12; 9:9). By way of confuting the first part, God takes the prophet on a tour of the temple area, showing him the various abominations practiced there, and checking on the prophet's observation by asking him at each site, "Do you see, man?" The prophet knows that God has seen all, including the clandestine rites of the elders who believe him blind to them.[10]

Verse 13. Even **greater abominations** were to be seen.

The Women Weeping For the God Tammuz (8:14, 15)

> **¹⁴Then He brought me to the entrance of the gate of the LORD's house which was toward the north; and behold, women were sitting there weeping for Tammuz. ¹⁵He said to me, "Do you see this, son of man? Yet you will see still greater abominations than these."**

Verse 14. God showed Ezekiel a third abomination. Like his contemporary Jeremiah, Ezekiel witnessed abominations being committed by the women of the land (see Jer. 7:18; 44:15–30). God took Ezekiel to the entry way of the north gate, not far from where the first two abominations were seen. He found women

---

[10]Moshe Greenberg, *Ezekiel 1—20: A New Translation with Introduction and Commentary*, The Anchor Bible, vol. 22 (Garden City, N.Y.: Doubleday & Co., 1983), 200.

sitting there weeping for Tammuz.[11] Tammuz was a male deity whose origin was in Babylonia. Worship to him can be traced back as far as 3,000 B.C., making it one of the oldest known forms of ancient worship. Tammuz later became associated with Adonis and Aphrodite. He was viewed as the husband, son, or brother of Ishtar, the Babylonian goddess of fertility. Worshiped as the god of rain and vegetation, he was similar to the Canaanite gods Hadad and Baal.

According to pagan belief, Tammuz would die in the early fall—when the scorching heat came, the plants withered, and the rivers were dry. His worshipers would weep for his resurrection, joining his wife, Ishtar, who was said to be in mourning. Proof of his resurrection was claimed in the springtime, when the land once again received rains and the plants began to grow.[12] The belief regarding Tammuz is similar to that of the Sumerian god Dumuzi or the Babylonian god Duzo. Probably, these names refer to the same god, who was named according to geographical location and the people who worshiped him.[13]

The Jewish women, then, were worshiping a *Babylonian* God. This is consistent with the ancient practice of adopting the gods of the conquering nation. Since the Babylonians were able to defeat the Israelites and take them into captivity, their gods were assumed to be stronger than Israel's God. Also, conditions in Israel may already have been as God had promised, including drought and famine. The "staff of bread" had been broken (see 5:16). To whom did the women turn in order to bring back the crops? Not to the Lord, the One who could truly help them, but to some non-god of the Babylonians!

---

[11]"The date of this vision was in the months of August/September, when Tammuz 'died.' This month later became known in the Hebrew calendar as the month of Tammuz. At the time of this vision the land of Palestine would have been parched from the summer sun; and the women would have been lamenting Tammuz's death" (Alexander, 784).

[12]Some scholars question the validity of the resurrection theme in Tammuz worship (see Edwin Yamauchi, "Tammuz and the Bible," *Journal of Biblical Literature* 84, no. 3 [1965]: 283–90).

[13]T. Jacobsen, *The Treasures of Darkness* (New Haven: Yale University Press 1976), 25–73.

Verse 15. God next took Ezekiel to the fourth abomination being committed by the Israelites in Jerusalem. Again, God declared that this **abomination** was **greater** than the ones before.

The Sun Worshipers (8:16–18)

> ¹⁶**Then He brought me into the inner court of the Lord's house. And behold, at the entrance to the temple of the Lord, between the porch and the altar, were about twenty-five men with their backs to the temple of the Lord and their faces toward the east; and they were prostrating themselves eastward toward the sun.** ¹⁷**He said to me, "Do you see this, son of man? Is it too light a thing for the house of Judah to commit the abominations which they have committed here, that they have filled the land with violence and provoked Me repeatedly? For behold, they are putting the twig to their nose.** ¹⁸**Therefore, I indeed will deal in wrath. My eye will have no pity nor will I spare; and though they cry in My ears with a loud voice, yet I will not listen to them."**

Verse 16. This time, God took Ezekiel to the area (**the inner court**, the court of the priests) between the altar of burnt offerings and **the porch** which was **at the entrance to the temple**. **Twenty-five men** were there. They were probably priests, because the priests were to offer prayers between the porch and the altar (Joel 2:17). The number "twenty-five" may have some significance. David organized the priesthood into twenty-four divisions (1 Chron. 24:3–18). Counting the high priest, that would make twenty-five. Therefore, the twenty-five men could be representative of the whole priesthood.

In 9:6 these men are called "elders," perhaps meaning that they were among the older members of the priesthood. They should have been praying to the Lord. Instead, they had **their backs to the temple of the Lord**—in effect, turning their backs on God. The entrance to the temple was on the east side, and the most holy place was positioned on the west. These idolaters turned deliberately toward the east, demonstrating their denial of God and their belief in the sun-god.

The Rabbis detected in the phrase "with their backs toward the temple" as a wanton affront of the divine presence whose abode was in the west.[14] The *Mishna* records a time when this passage was recalled in the celebration of the drawing of water during the Festival of Tabernacles:

> When the celebrants reached the gate which leads out to the east, they turned their faces from east to west (thus facing the Temple) and said, "Our fathers who were in this place stood with their backs toward the Temple of the Lord and their faces towards the east, and they worshipped the sun towards the east; but as for us, our eyes are turned to the Lord."[15]

The "elders" **were prostrating themselves eastward toward the sun.** Scholars say that the word translated "prostrating" is an unusual Hebrew word, intentionally corrupted to express the wickedness of such a practice.[16] The worship of the heavenly bodies was one of the earliest forms of idolatry (Job 31:26, 27) and was expressly forbidden in the Law (Deut. 17:3). Josiah destroyed "the horses which the kings of Judah had given to the sun" and "the chariots of the sun" (2 Kings 23:11).

Verses 17, 18. After showing Ezekiel the evils being done in Jerusalem, God asked, **"Is it too light a thing for the house of Judah to commit the abominations which they have committed here. . . ?"** People today must not think, "How we worship isn't important to God as long as we worship." Seeing for himself how abhorrent these practices were to God, the young priest would understand God's reasons for sending destruction. **Putting the twig to their nose** was an act of pagan worship. The ritual is of uncertain origin and purpose, but it certainly angered God. Some scholars believe that this was a practice done out of

---

[14]*Yoma* 77a.

[15]*Sukkah* 5.4.

[16]"The unusual Hebrew form *mishtachawithem* is traditionally explained as a compound of two verbs, *mashchithim* (they destroy) and *mishtachawim* (they worship), signifying the dual nature of their offense: the degradation of the temple and the worshiping of the sun-god . . ." (Fisch, 45).

respect for the sun-god, to "filter" one's breath[17] so as not to defile the solar rays. The Israelites had **repeatedly** done that which was forbidden by God's law. Their open disregard for the will of God **provoked** God, leaving Him no option but to punish. Although He would have preferred to extend compassion and mercy, God had to **deal in wrath** (v. 18). As is so often discussed in the Bible, actions bring forth consequences. The Israelites were going to reap what they had sown.

Four times God asked Ezekiel if he had seen specific abominations. God was proving to him how wicked Jerusalem was, and how deserving of destruction. Finally, He said, **"My eye will have no pity nor will I spare."**

APPLICATION

Daily Living Before Our God

We cannot overestimate the significance of the father in the home. An ungodly father deprives his children of a great blessing. However, if the mother is serving God and teaching the children, then the children may be able to overcome a bad influence from the father.

In the second abomination, God pointed out that He sees everything we do—even what we do in secret. It is possible to fool a community, the church, and even our families in regard to our spirituality; but we cannot fool God. Someday "God will bring every act to judgment, everything which is hidden, whether it is good or evil" (Eccles. 12:14).

Religious error not only angers God, but it is also disgusting to Him. It is an abomination (vv. 6, 13, 15, 17).

God is not pleased with just any kind of worship. He is only pleased with worship that is done specifically according to His divine instructions. We may think a change to be a "light thing," but God does not view it that way (v. 17; see Mt. 15:8, 9; Jn. 4:34, 35).

D.P.

---

[17]H. W. F. Saggs, "Notes and Studies: The Branch to the Nose," *Journal of Theological Studies* 11 (October 1960): 318–29.

What Does the Lord See? (8:12)

We know that the Lord is "all-seeing" and "all-knowing," but sometimes we fail to live according to what we know.

The "elders" of Israel were accused of secretly worshiping false gods. They believed that what they did in the dark would not be seen by God; however, Ezekiel's warning proved otherwise. No one is able to sin without God's knowing it.

Jesus also discussed "secret" worship. In the Sermon on the Mount, He said, "But . . . when you pray, go into your inner room, close your door and pray to your Father who is in secret, and your Father who sees what is done in secret will reward you" (Mt. 6:6). Just as some may think that God does not see their sins, others may wonder if He sees their own good deeds.

What does God see when He looks at His children? Everything! He sees our shortcomings and our successes. He knows of sins that we commit in secret, but we must also trust that He sees our righteousness performed behind closed doors.

Christianity vs. Culture (8:13, 14)

One of the greatest challenges that Christians face is how to be faithful to God's Word and yet be heard by the people around them. How are we to be "in the world but not of the world"?

The Jewish women in verses 13 and 14 who turned toward Tammuz (the Babylonian god) were following the accepted customs of worshiping the gods of their nation's conqueror. Their practice pleased society, but not God.

Shadrach, Meshach, and Abed-nego, three men under severe pressure to yield to Babylonian customs and laws, jeopardized their lives in order to please God, and not society.

It is natural to desire acceptance by the mainstream, but this can make a person vulnerable to unhealthy change. When our integrity and morality are challenged by society, we ought to strive to please God rather than culture.

T.P.W.

CHAPTER 9

THE LORD'S PUNISHMENT: THE SIX EXECUTIONERS

In 8:18 God pronounced Judah's coming punishment. Now, in Ezekiel's vision, this punishment was executed. God first directed His attention to individuals who were disobedient to Him. This is consistent with the overall theme of Ezekiel, which emphasizes individual responsibility.

THE INNOCENT MARKED (9:1–4)

9:1, 2
¹Then He cried out in my hearing with a loud voice saying, "Draw near, O executioners of the city, each with his destroying weapon in his hand." ²Behold, six men came from the direction of the upper gate which faces north, each with his shattering weapon in his hand; and among them was a certain man clothed in linen with a writing case at his loins. And they went in and stood beside the bronze altar.

Verse 1. In Ezekiel's **hearing**, God cried out for action. He summoned His **executioners of the city** to come and do their work. Each executioner had his "battle ax" ready for judgment. The identity of these executioners is not stated, although the seven executing angels of Revelation 8:1–6 may provide a parallel. Most likely, these men represent the Babylonian soldiers who would soon be entering the city.
Verse 2. Six men came, and with them **a certain man clothed in linen**. This brings the number involved in the punishment to seven—a significant number in the Bible, representing perfec-

tion. Thus the idea is conveyed that this is the perfect and complete judgment of God. The man was wearing "linen," a reminder of the clothing of other divine messengers (see Dan. 10:5; 12:6, 7; Rev. 15:6), as well as that worn by priests (Ex. 28:6, 8, 42; Lev. 16:4; 1 Sam. 2:18; 22:18). The linen here seems to represent the purity and holiness of God. In addition, the man had **a writing case**, an "inkhorn" that was frequently carried by scribes. This included a writing stylus, a bottle of ink, and a container of water to mix with the ink.

The inkhorn was usually a flat case about nine inches long, by an inch and a quarter wide, and half an inch thick. It would contain several reed pens (since the tips would wear out or break) and a penknife. The scribe would mix his ink according to the anticipated amount he would need, because the ink would dry out relatively quickly. Archaeologists have discovered a number of these inkhorns in Israel.[1]

The man with the inkhorn had the responsibility of marking those who grieved over Jerusalem's sin and perhaps writing in the Book of Life the names of those who were marked. "The [Book of Life] metaphor is from the custom of registering the names of the Israelites in public rolls [see Ex. 32:33; Ps. 69:28; Is. 4:3; Phil. 4:3; Rev. 3:5]."[2] It is noteworthy that judgment was to begin at the **altar**, because it was there that the people had defiled God's sanctuary and set up the altar of jealousy.

9:3, 4

³Then the glory of the God of Israel went up from the cherub on which it had been, to the threshold of the temple. And He called to the man clothed in linen at whose loins was the writing case. ⁴The LORD said to him, "Go through the midst of the city, even through the midst of Jerusalem, and put a mark on the foreheads of the men who sigh and groan over all the abominations which are being committed in its midst."

---

[1] Albert Barnes, *The Bible Commentary: Proverbs to Ezekiel*, Barnes' Notes, ed. F. C. Cook, abr. and ed. J. M. Fuller (Grand Rapids, Mich.: Baker Book House, 1983), 325.

[2] Ibid.

Verse 3. This verse indicates that God was preparing to leave His temple (see ch. 11). He made a preliminary move here. Ralph H. Alexander said,

> With judgment imminent, God's glory could not be present over the ark of the covenant in the Most Holy Place or in the presence of the divine Judge. Therefore, the Lord vividly demonstrated his readiness to judge by withdrawing his glory from his people. God's glory moved from the Most Holy Place to the entry of the temple to assign the tasks of judgment.[3]

The glory of the God of Israel went up from the cherub. Barnes explained this imagery as follows:

> The singular is put collectively for the *Cherubim*, which were upon the mercy-seat of the Ark in the Holy of Holies, the proper seat of the glory of the Lord in the midst of Israel. God is represented as *arising* from between the Cherubim to scatter His enemies [Num. 10:35].[4]

The first of the seven summoned was **the man clothed in linen**. He had to do his job before the six executioners could do theirs.

Verse 4. The man in linen was instructed to **put a mark on** the righteous few found in the city. The word for "mark" is the Hebrew letter ת (*Tav*), which had the shape of an "x" or a "t" during this time period. The significance of this has been interpreted in various ways.

(1) Some Jews noted that the letter was the last of the Hebrew alphabet. Therefore, since it closed the alphabet, it represents the complete sorrow for sin felt by the righteous. In other words, those bearing the mark fully felt the anguish and disappointment for the wickedness of their people.

---

[3] Ralph H. Alexander, "Ezekiel," in *The Expositor's Bible Commentary*, ed. Frank E. Gaebelein (Grand Rapids, Mich.: Zondervan Publishing House, 1986), 6:786.
[4] Barnes, 325.

(2) Some rabbis noted that the *Tav* was the first letter of the Torah, and those who had this mark had been faithful to the law.

(3) Christian commentators have sometimes seen an analogy between the mark and the cross of Christ. Those who have taken advantage of the cross will not suffer God's execution.

The idea of a "mark" being put on the foreheads of men is a biblical idea. Note the similarity with Revelation 7:2, 3, where righteous people were to be marked (as in this text), and Revelation 13:16, where evil people were marked.

Those to be marked in this case were the people said to **sigh and groan over all the abominations**. Jesus taught that those who "mourn" are blessed (Mt. 5:4; see Is. 61:2; Jn. 16:20; Rev. 7:17). Here, the righteous are described as men who "sighed"—perhaps as a result of discouragement and sad resolve over the sin that permeated the city. They also "groaned"—an indication of the inner agitation and sorrow over the open rebellion they saw from their own people. Regarding this display of compassion, John B. Taylor said,

> It is worth noting that the procedure for inflicting God's punishment was selective, in keeping with the principle of 18:4, "the soul that sins shall die". The basis for exemption from the slaughter was the individual's deep concern . . . over the city's apostasy. This was what Amos had looked for among the luxury-loving revellers of Jerusalem and Samaria whom he castigated with his tongue. Their most guilty sin was that they "did not grieve over the ruin of Joseph" (Am. 6:6). In both cases the criterion that was needed was not strictly a religious quality, like faith, or an outward act, like sacrifice, but an affair of the heart—a passionate concern for God and for His people.[5]

---

[5] John B. Taylor, *Ezekiel: An Introduction and Commentary*, Tyndale Old Testament Commentaries (Downers Grove, Ill.: Inter-Varsity Press, 1969), 102–3.

THE GUILTY SLAUGHTERED (9:5–11)

9:5, 6
⁵But to the others He said in my hearing, "Go through the city after him and strike; do not let your eye have pity and do not spare. ⁶Utterly slay old men, young men, maidens, little children, and women, but do not touch any man on whom is the mark; and you shall start from My sanctuary." So they started with the elders who were before the temple.

Verse 5. The executioners were instructed to follow the scribe who marked the righteous. The order to **go through the city** indicates the thoroughness required for the job they had before them. God also instructed them concerning the *attitude* they were to have as they embarked upon this awful task: **"Do not let your eye have pity and do not spare."** Human compassion is sometimes misplaced. It may be offered to one who makes a good impression (called a "hypocrite" or "a wolf in sheep's clothing" in the New Testament) but is inwardly "full of dead men's bones and all uncleanness" (Mt. 23:27). God's judgment is always right. The punishment itself and the degree of the punishment are exactly what is required.

Verse 6. These executioners were told, **"Utterly slay. . . ."** regarding unrighteous who were **old men, young men, maidens, . . . and women**. This was not a punitive judgment, by which one would merely be disciplined. This was a judgment of death. **Little children** were also to be slain. This is a perfect example of innocents suffering because of the sinful choices of others. The children obviously were not guilty of the "abominations" described in Ezekiel. Nevertheless, the judgment of God was to cover all; sadly, the children would suffer as well.

Then the executioners were told, **"Start from My sanctuary."** The first to be punished were those who had brought idolatry nearest to the holy place. The twenty-five men who had stood with their backs to the temple (8:16) were the first to be slain. The righteous, in this vision, were not to die; yet, in 21:3, 4, God mentioned that the righteous would also "be cut off." When the judgment came upon Jerusalem, both wicked and righteous people died—but God spared a few, those who had the mark. These would serve as the remnant.

9:7, 8

⁷And He said to them, "Defile the temple and fill the courts with the slain. Go out!" Thus they went out and struck down the people in the city. ⁸As they were striking the people and I alone was left, I fell on my face and cried out saying, "Alas, Lord GOD! Are You destroying the whole remnant of Israel by pouring out Your wrath on Jerusalem?"

Verse 7. God next instructed, **"Defile the temple."** In view of the texts in the law of Moses regarding the temple, with all of the provisions to maintain its purity and holiness, this command is extraordinary. It powerfully demonstrates how unworthy the temple had become to house the glory of the Lord.[6] The executioners proceeded to do God's bidding, and they **struck down the people in the city**.

Verse 8. When Ezekiel said, **"I alone was left,"** he could have meant that he was the only righteous individual in the city, the only righteous individual within the temple, or the only one in the city who "sighed and groaned" over the wickedness of the city. Regardless of the specific meaning, this statement is astonishing. As Jesus taught in Matthew 7:13, 14, the number of those who walk on the path to eternal life are "few."

The compassion of the prophet is seen in his words, **"Alas, Lord GOD!"** Moshe Greenberg wrote,

> As he beholds the sentence of death being executed in this vision, the prophet twice cries out on behalf of the condemned people (9:8; 11:13). These are the only

---

[6]"Contrast [this situation with] II Kings 11:15: Athaliah is deliberately dragged out of the temple before being executed; here, since these men had already defiled the house with their idolatry, it is no matter if they are killed there.... God's shocking command expresses the total unfitness of the temple for his presence..." (Moshe Greenberg, *Ezekiel 1—20: A New Translation with Introduction and Commentary*, The Anchor Bible, vol. 22 [Garden City, N.Y.: Doubleday & Co., 1983], 177–78).

instances of Ezekiel's attempt to intercede for his people, and they may have to do with his (visionary) presence amidst the slain. The otherwise striking omission of intercession from the book is perhaps connected with its unconditional message of doom; compare how God repeatedly thwarts Jeremiah's attempts at intercession (Jer 7:16; 14:7—15:4 . . .).[7]

He could have had the attitude "They're getting what they deserve" (which, as has been established, is certainly true). Nevertheless, Ezekiel was concerned that even the **remnant** might be eliminated, making the nation of Israel a footnote in history, alongside other nations which no longer exist.

9:9, 10

⁹Then He said to me, "The iniquity of the house of Israel and Judah is very, very great, and the land is filled with blood and the city is full of perversion; for they say, 'The LORD has forsaken the land, and the LORD does not see!' ¹⁰But as for Me, My eye will have no pity nor will I spare, but I will bring their conduct upon their heads."

Verse 9. God responded to Ezekiel's appeal with a further explanation for the judgment. He reminded Ezekiel of these truths:

1. **The iniquity of the house of Israel and Judah is very, very great.**
2. **The land is filled with blood.**
3. **The city is full of perversion.**

Those sins were bad enough, but God added that the people had failed to understand Him. Jesus would later say that "eternal life" is dependent upon knowing God and knowing Him (Jn. 17:3). Paul would write that God will deal out retribution to those who "do not know God" (2 Thess. 1:7–9). In this case, the

---

[7]Ibid., 203.

people failed to appreciate God's omnipresence (**the LORD has forsaken the land**) and His omniscience (**the LORD does not see**). In chapter 11 the first declaration came true: God left. "God had in fact not left the land when the people believed he had, but now their behavior brought it about...."[8]

Verse 10. Ezekiel pleaded for mercy, but there would be none. He may have been given a hard forehead (3:8), but he had a soft heart. God had declared earlier (8:18) that there would be **no pity** and He would not **spare**. The people's wicked choices, **their conduct**, had brought this judgment upon them. As Paul taught, the "wages" of sin is death (Rom. 6:23). The people of Judah had "earned" this punishment.

9:11
¹¹**Then behold, the man clothed in linen at whose loins was the writing case reported, saying, "I have done just as You have commanded me."**

Verse 11. Some of the people were still righteous. Apparently, the man clothed in linen had *someone* to mark.

This chapter reflects Ezekiel's continuing education, the continued sinfulness of the people, and the absolute necessity of God's judgment.

FOR FURTHER STUDY: OLD TESTAMENT CRUELTY AND THE GOODNESS OF GOD (9:6)

"How can God allow the innocent to suffer?" is an honest question, but not one that is easily answered. It usually arises when one reads a passage such as Deuteronomy 20:16, 17, where God commanded His people, "... you shall not leave alive anything that breathes. But you shall utterly destroy them...." The question may also be asked in connection with Deuteronomy 7:1–3 or Joshua 6:21. A dilemma arises when one sees such commands and their fulfillment. Knowing that God is good and that

---

[8]Ibid., 200.

everything He does is right (see Ps. 100:5; 119:68; Is. 6:3), the Bible-believer may sincerely ask, "How could a loving God command such a slaughter?" Here are several truths to consider when studying this subject.

(1) *God has the right, as God, to deal with mankind as His infinite wisdom dictates.* God's ways and thoughts are superior to ours. He does not look at situations the way man does.

(2) *God had given these people hundreds of years to repent, but they failed to take advantage of their opportunities.* God told Abraham that he could not have the land of Canaan because "the iniquity of the Amorite is not yet complete" (Gen. 15:16). Their wickedness did not yet warrant destruction.

(3) *God's righteousness and justice are meaningless if wickedness is not punished.* These attributes are the foundation of God's throne (Ps. 89:14; 97:2). The Israelites had always been a stubborn people (see Deut. 9:4–6). God's goodness is seen in the hundreds of years He gave them to repent, and justice is seen in that their continual rejection of His grace finally resulted in punishment. How could God demand righteousness if there were no consequences for unrighteousness? (See Ex. 34:6, 7.)

(4) *The destruction of the wicked helps to preserve the morality of the masses.* The punishment of wicked nations served as a vital lesson to the Israelites (Deut. 8:20; 20:17, 18) and as examples for us (1 Cor. 10:5, 6, 11, 12). God is set against sin. He will pay the wages "earned" by the sinner (Rom. 6:23).

(5) *The death of children is one of the consequences of humanity's free moral choice.* When one sins, it often adversely affects others. Many died because of Achan's sin (Josh. 7:5, 20, 24, 25). An entire generation spent forty years in the wilderness because of their fathers' sins (Num. 14:33; see Ex. 34:7; Num. 14:18). The consequences these others faced had *nothing* to do with their own eternal salvation. They were to be judged on the basis of their own lives (see 2 Cor. 5:10; Rev. 20:12, 13).

(6) *The destruction of the children was a blessing instead of a curse.* When we view this destruction of the innocent from a *temporal* viewpoint, it seems tragic. However, when viewed from an *eternal* standpoint, the children were much better off dying. Having no sin to their charge, they would spend eternity with

God (Mt. 18:1–4; Ezek. 18:20). If they had grown up, they would most likely have become wicked like their parents (consider Jeroboam's son; 1 Kings 14:12, 13).

Even with these considerations, we still may not know all of God's reasons for certain acts. We must learn to trust in Jesus' words: Our heavenly Father is perfect (Mt. 5:48). We ought also to learn the biblical truths taught in Romans 12:19; Hebrews 10:30, 31 (see Deut. 32:35; Rom. 11:22; 2 Pet. 3:9, 15).

APPLICATION

Righteousness and Judgment

The time comes when judgment must begin. God will not tolerate sin forever.

God knows those who are His; they obey Him and abstain from wickedness (2 Tim. 2:19).

The truly righteous are those who sigh and groan over the evil in the world around them. Let those who have sinned the most be the first victims of justice. Those who know the Lord's will but do not obey it shall be beaten with many stripes (see Lk. 12:48). The unfaithful members of Christ's church will be the first visited and most punished. However, those who belong to the synagogue of Satan should not exult in this, for if judgment is to "begin with the household of God . . . what will be the outcome for those who do not obey the gospel of God?" (1 Pet. 4:17). Only the truly penitent will be safe. God's command here was to "put a mark on . . . the men who sigh and groan" (Ezek. 9:4); and his command to the destroyers was "Come not near any man upon whom is the mark" (v. 6).[9]

It is upsetting to God when people do not know Him and, as a result, make false statements about Him (v. 9).

God will render to each one according to his deeds (v. 10; Rom. 2:6; 2 Cor. 5:10; Jn. 5:28, 29).

D.P.

---

[9]Barnes, 325.

Spiritual Assurance (9:4–6)

God's disciples enjoy wonderful spiritual assurance. Knowing that they possess the joys of heaven gives them great peace. In His vision to Ezekiel (vv. 4–6), God announced for His angels to punish those who had committed evil. In contrast to those who were to suffer destruction, the faithful would enjoy protection.

Recognized by God. The angels were sent into the city, but they were told that the faithful would be easily recognized. Those who are obedient to God's commands are always set apart (Jn. 3:19, 20). God recognizes their devotion.

Owned by God. Each person belongs either to God or Satan and will bear the "mark" of ownership. The faithful follower has been identified as God's possession (2 Tim. 2:19).

Directed by God. The "forehead" symbolizes one's thoughts, desires, and decisions. The one who has given his "forehead" to God has been transformed by God's truth (Eph. 4:17–24).

Comforted by God. Living in the world, surrounded by abominations, the Christian "sighs and groans" over great burdens and sorrows. However, spiritual assurance offers comfort (Rom. 8:31–39).

Protected by God. Those who are faithfully following God are in an invincible position (Jn. 10:27–29).

God's assurance is available to all, but it is not given without requirements. God urges us, "Make certain about His calling and choosing you" (2 Pet. 1:10).

J.L.K.

Chapter 10

The Withdrawal of the Glory Of The Lord from the Temple

God was in control of all the vengeance described in chapter 9. Now chapter 10 demonstrates the glory of God and His right to act in judgment (see Rom. 12:19–21).

Chapter 10 curiously repeats much of the imagery that is in chapter 1. (Review the discussion of the cherubim and the wheels given in the lesson on chapter 1, since that material will not be repeated here.) Why would God inspire Ezekiel to repeat information given earlier (1:4–25)? Several reasons may be offered:

1. This is a separate vision, so God has given it its own place.
2. These verses provide further information on the "man clothed in linen" who was introduced in 9:2.
3. More information is given on the living creatures of chapter 1. Now they are more fully identified as cherubim.
4. The repetition reestablishes and expands the discussion concerning the *glory* of God.
5. These descriptions emphasize that the Lord was justified in declaring and dispensing this punishment against Judah. His glory is the primary basis of His judgment.
6. The passage takes the student one step closer to understanding the reason for God's departure from the sanctuary.

INSTRUCTIONS TO THE MAN CLOTHED IN LINEN AND ACTIVITY OF THE CHERUBIM (10:1, 2)

10:1, 2
¹Then I looked, and behold, in the expanse that was over the heads of the cherubim something like a sapphire stone, in appearance resembling a throne, appeared above them. ²And He spoke to the man clothed in linen and said, "Enter between the whirling wheels under the cherubim and fill your hands with coals of fire from between the cherubim and scatter them over the city." And he entered in my sight.

Verses 1, 2. God instructed **the man clothed in linen** to take **coals of fire** from the center of the cherubim throne-chariot and to pour out the coals in judgment on the city to purify it. Coals of fire were often symbolic of cleansing in the Old Testament (see Is. 6). These coals, having been taken from this location, could offer legitimate cleansing. Only God has the power to wipe away sins (see Mt. 9:1–8).

FROM THE HOLY OF HOLIES TO THE THRESHOLD OF THE TEMPLE (10:3, 4)

³Now the cherubim were standing on the right side of the temple when the man entered, and the cloud filled the inner court. ⁴Then the glory of the LORD went up from the cherub to the threshold of the temple, and the temple was filled with the cloud and the court was filled with the brightness of the glory of the LORD.

Verse 3. The cherubim are portrayed in verse 3 as standing ready in the temple. Before God would leave His sanctuary, they had work to do.

Verse 4. The throne-chariot of God "landed" in the inner courtyard, on the right side. The work of the executioners in chapter 9 had cleansed the area, for this was where they had begun their work. In verse 4 is the first mention, in this vision, of **the glory of the LORD** (כְּבוֹד־יהוה, *kᵉbod YHWH*). The word "glory" (כָּבוֹד, *kabod*; Gk.: δόξα, *doxa*)¹ is a key Bible word and makes an essential study for one who is trying to understand the nature and the character of God. Fundamentally, it deals with the presence of God. However, His presence is not all that is significant—it is *who* is present. When the word כָּבוֹד is applied to the Lord, its basic meaning includes honor, splendor, magnificence, power, superiority, and holiness. Israel seems not to have appreciated all that she was about to give up in losing the Lord. Why would anyone exchange "the glory of the incorruptible God for an image in the form of corruptible man and of birds and four-footed animals and crawling creatures" (Rom. 1:23)? That is exactly what the Israelites had done.

When the glory of the Lord went up from the cherub, it went to the threshold of the temple. Two events took place as a result of this: The temple was filled with the cloud, and the court was filled with the brightness of His glory.

ADDITIONAL INSTRUCTIONS TO THE MAN CLOTHED IN LINEN AND ACTIVITY OF THE CHERUBIM (10:5–17)

10:5–7
⁵**Moreover, the sound of the wings of the cherubim was heard as far as the outer court, like the voice of God Almighty when He speaks.**

⁶**It came about when He commanded the man clothed in linen, saying, "Take fire from between the whirling wheels, from between the cherubim," he entered and stood beside a**

---

¹"[כָּבוֹד is] a technical term for God's manifest presence. The normal use of the expression [כְּבֹד יהוה], the glory of the Lord (including use with suffixes; occasionally [אֱלֹהִים], God, is the genitive), is as a technical term for the Lord's manifest presence with his people" (C. John Collins, "כָּבוֹד," in *New International Dictionary of Old Testament Theology & Exegesis*, ed. Willem A. VanGemeren, [Grand Rapids, Mich.: Zondervan Publishing House, 1997], 2:581).

wheel. ⁷Then the cherub stretched out his hand from between the cherubim to the fire which was between the cherubim, took some and put it into the hands of the one clothed in linen, who took it and went out.

Verses 5–7. We are brought back to **the man clothed in linen**, the one with the writing case (ch. 9), who marked those who were faithful to God. He had been instructed in 10:2 to "fill [his] hands with coals of fire," and he obeyed that command. He received some help from the cherub, who took some of the coals and put them into his hands (v. 7). He had been told to take the coals and "scatter them over the city." We might expect a description of the city bursting into flames. Rather, Ezekiel returned to discussing the cherubim.

10:8–17

⁸The cherubim appeared to have the form of a man's hand under their wings.

⁹Then I looked, and behold, four wheels beside the cherubim, one wheel beside each cherub; and the appearance of the wheels was like the gleam of a Tarshish stone. ¹⁰As for their appearance, all four of them had the same likeness, as if one wheel were within another wheel. ¹¹When they moved, they went in any of their four directions without turning as they went; but they followed in the direction which they faced, without turning as they went. ¹²Their whole body, their backs, their hands, their wings and the wheels were full of eyes all around, the wheels belonging to all four of them. ¹³The wheels were called in my hearing, the whirling wheels. ¹⁴And each one had four faces. The first face was the face of a cherub, the second face was the face of a man, the third the face of a lion, and the fourth the face of an eagle.

¹⁵Then the cherubim rose up. They are the living beings that I saw by the river Chebar. ¹⁶Now when the cherubim moved, the wheels would go beside them; also when the cherubim lifted up their wings to rise from the ground, the wheels would not turn from beside them. ¹⁷When the cherubim stood still, the wheels would stand still; and when they rose

up, the wheels would rise with them, for the spirit of the living beings was in them.

Verses 8, 9. Four wheels [were] beside the cherubim. This is similar to the account given in chapter 1. Some scholars think that this section is too repetitious and has been added by someone else. However, having this repetition may indicate the opposite. No editor would add such to the text, knowing that the material was already present. Rather than serving as evidence of an editor, the description supports the idea of a single hand.[2]

Verses 10–13. With Ezekiel listening, a voice called upon the wheels (v. 13). Obedient to the call, the cherubim were lifted up and the wheels rolled on. God was leaving.

Verse 14. Why does this verse change the description from a bull's face (in 1:10) to that of a cherub? Perhaps Ezekiel had a better, closer look and now recognized the face as that of a cherub. Maybe a cherub had the look of a bull or an ox. Other explanations have been offered, but the text gives no answer.

Verses 15–17. Why did Ezekiel not call the "living beings" of chapter 1 "cherubim"? John B. Taylor said,

> . . . it may be that Ezekiel is saying that only when he saw the cherubim in the Temple did he realize that these were the very creatures which he had seen in his vision by the river Chebar. This is a reasonable explanation, because Ezekiel had not yet qualified as a priest before he went into exile and so he would never in person have seen the cherub-figures carved on the inside walls of the Temple (1 Ki. 6:29) and on the double doors (1 Ki. 6:35) and on the Temple furnishings (1 Ki. 7:29, 36), where only priests could see them clearly. But there is no need to press the point too much, for he could hardly have been brought up in a priestly family without this kind of

---

[2] "The point is one of emphasis. Ezekiel is being told of the terror that is to come (and is thus emboldened to speak) and we are being told that the judgment is just and is being carried out, not irrationally, but with forethought." (Jim McGuiggan, *The Book of Ezekiel*, Looking Into The Bible Series [Lubbock, Tex.: Montex Publishing Co., 1979], 105).

knowledge. It is just that for reasons of literary artifice he deliberately withholds the identification until this stage, and in so doing he cleverly fills in the moment of suspense which follows the angel's departure from the presence of the Lord to carry out his destructive task.[3]

We must also bear in mind that Ezekiel is the only person who claims to have seen the heavenly cherubs. "The only cherubs previously seen by humans were the statues in the inner sanctum, which were only approximations."[4]

FROM THE THRESHOLD TO THE EAST GATE (10:18–22)

10:18–22
[18]Then the glory of the LORD departed from the threshold of the temple and stood over the cherubim. [19]When the cherubim departed, they lifted their wings and rose up from the earth in my sight with the wheels beside them; and they stood still at the entrance of the east gate of the LORD's house, and the glory of the God of Israel hovered over them.
[20]These are the living beings that I saw beneath the God of Israel by the river Chebar; so I knew that they were cherubim. [21]Each one had four faces and each one four wings, and beneath their wings was the form of human hands. [22]As for the likeness of their faces, they were the same faces whose appearance I had seen by the river Chebar. Each one went straight ahead.

Verses 18, 19. We see more significance in this repeated section, for God was departing from the temple. It is almost as if He was reluctant to leave, yet the people did nothing to keep this glory with them. The glory of God would completely abandon the city in 11:23. The people were wrong in assuming that

---

[3]John B. Taylor, *Ezekiel: An Introduction and Commentary*, Tyndale Old Testament Commentaries (Downers Grove, Ill.: Inter-Varsity Press, 1969), 104.
[4]Moshe Greenberg, *Ezekiel 1—20: A New Translation with Introduction and Commentary*, The Anchor Bible, vol. 22 (Garden City, N.Y.: Doubleday & Co., 1983), 183.

God would continue to make His abode among an adulterous people. God had established that He would depart and not dwell with them forever if they persisted in lawlessness (Deut. 31:17; Hos. 9:12). In an ironic way, there is a repetition of the events of 1 Samuel 4. There, because of sin and rebellion, the people lost the ark of the covenant to the Philistines. The high priest, Eli, died upon hearing that news, and his pregnant daughter-in-law responded to the loss by naming her newborn "Ichabod" (1 Sam. 4:21), which means "no glory." In Ezekiel's time, there was to be "no glory" in Jerusalem. Another "Ichabod" had been "born."

Six centuries later, another generation was to reject the "glory of God" in the person of Jesus Christ. Jesus said to them, "Behold, your house is left to you desolate!" (Mt. 23:38).

Verses 20–22. Ezekiel concluded his description by confirming that these were the same living beings that he had seen earlier. As mentioned in chapter 1, each one went straight ahead—intent upon the object of the collective aim, not deviating from the way or losing sight of the end.

FOR FURTHER STUDY: THE GLORY AND DWELLING OF THE LORD[5]

As the new covenant was initiated through Jesus, a new dawning of the God's glory was revealed. John 1:14 refers to the apostles as having witnessed Jesus' "glory" (Gk.: δόξα, *doxa*) and calls Jesus "full of grace and truth" (Gk.: πλήρης χάριτος καὶ ἀληθείας, *plērēs charitos kai alētheias*). This appears to be a deliberate reference to Exodus 33:18—34:6, where the Lord's glory passed before Moses. Thus John 1:14 should be understood in light of the expression כְּבוֹד־יהוה (*kᵉbod YHWH*, "the glory of the LORD"). The verb he used, σκηνόω (*skēnoō*, "live" or "dwell") evokes the Hebrew שָׁכַן (*shakan*, "abide" or "dwell"), which is used with כָּבוֹד in Exodus 24:16 and 40:35, where it depicts "the glory of the Lord" resting or settling. Therefore, the statement "The Word became flesh, and dwelt among us" should be seen as another way of stating the doctrine of John 1:1—

---

[5]Much of this material, as well as a full discussion of "glory" can be found in the excellent word study of "כָּבוֹד" by C. John Collins (Collins, 581).

namely, that Jesus was the manifest presence of Yahweh. According to John, Jesus was God, and in Him the glory of God was seen. John used the word "glory" forty times in his Gospel Account, usually expanding the thought expressed in 1:14.

APPLICATION

God's Glory Among Us

God dwells with those who are His children (Jn. 14:23; Rev. 3:20; 21:3; Eph. 3:17; 2 Cor. 6:16).

He will not dwell with those who are unfaithful to Him. Our bodies are the temple of God today. Therefore, we are to "glorify God" in our bodies, according to 1 Corinthians 6:19, 20.

He has powerful and awesome heavenly creatures that answer to His will. Even though the cherubim are described figuratively, they confirm God's greatness and the magnificence of the heavenly host.

D.P.

God's Presence (10:18)

When Christians gather for worship, God is with us (Mt. 18:20). However, we must not delude ourselves into thinking that our gathering guarantees His presence. He is not necessarily found in large or rich congregations. Past blessings are not evidence of present favor. His presence departed from the temple because of the people's wickedness.

During Christ's earthly ministry, He often sought out the poor, weak, and downtrodden. If He were here physically today, where would He be?

We must not presume on the presence of the Lord. We must not be like Samson, who thought that God would be with him regardless of the way he lived (Judg. 14—16).

The Lord's presence brings hope through a new heart and a new spirit. God pleaded with the Israelites to leave their ways and let Him soften their hard hearts (Ezek. 18:31; 36:26). He calls on us to do the same. The one who begins living for Christ will surely declare, "I'm glad I do not have my old heart any more!"

A.J.

CHAPTER 11

THE PROMISE FOR A REMNANT AND THE WITHDRAWAL OF HIS GLORY FROM THE CITY

From its beginning in chapter 8, Ezekiel's vision has been filled with images of Jerusalem's destruction and God's departure. Finally, in chapter 11, the scenes of abomination come to a close, and a reference is made to a remnant, hinting that some hope will remain for God's people.

THE LEADERS TO BE SLAIN (11:1–12)

11:1
¹**Moreover, the Spirit lifted me up and brought me to the east gate of the LORD's house which faced eastward. And behold, there were twenty-five men at the entrance of the gate, and among them I saw Jaazaniah son of Azzur and Pelatiah son of Benaiah, leaders of the people.**

Verse 1. Ezekiel remained in the vision while sitting in his house. The elders who had come to inquire of him were still present.

The Spirit is said to have lifted up Ezekiel, taking him **to the east gate of the LORD's house**. This was the main gate of the temple. While the twenty-five sun-worshipers in chapter 8 were priests, these **twenty-five men** were representatives of the leaders of Judah. The numbers are the same, but the groups are different. There may be a special symbolism in the number (as there appeared to be with the group in 8:16). The meaning of this number is unknown, but it probably represents the totality of the political leaders of Israel.[1] These men were led by **Jaazaniah son of Azzur**, and **Pelatiah son of Benaiah**. This Jaazaniah should not be identified as the son of Shaphan in 8:11. Although the names are the same, the fathers are different. These men were **leaders of the people**. As is frequently demonstrated in the Scriptures, poor leadership results in disaster for the people. Such was the case here. These men were wicked, and they led the people far from God.

11:2, 3
²He said to me, "Son of man, these are the men who devise iniquity and give evil advice in this city, ³who say, 'Is not the time near to build houses? This city is the pot and we are the flesh.'"

Verse 2. These leaders were said to **devise iniquity**. They openly opposed the direction given by God's prophets. Jeremiah, for example, had frequently encouraged the people to surrender to the Babylonians. Men like these opposed Jeremiah (Jer. 27:12–16) and Ezekiel (ch. 17) and encouraged continued resistance against Babylon. This resistance was a rejection of the will of God.

Verse 3. They offered evil advice: **"Is not the time near to build houses?"** The Hebrew here can be translated differently, giving a number of possible interpretations:

1. "Judgment is not near, so let us build houses." This was a message of peace and security (see 28:26), when in fact there was trouble on the horizon (as was being continually pronounced by God's prophets). The KJV translation favors this interpretation, saying, "It is not near; let us build houses."
2. "Jeremiah is right; let us prepare to relocate in captivity." This view, which was proposed by Carl F. Keil

---

[1]It was not unusual for each tribe to have two representatives, giving a total of twenty-four. By adding the king, we arrive at the number "twenty-five."

(based on Jer. 29:5), sarcastically mocked Jeremiah's prophecies. It meant, "There is no immediate danger, so ignore Jeremiah."[2]

3. "Is not the time near to build houses?" This is the reading of the NASB, as well as the RSV margin note. The NIV translates, "Will it not soon be time to build houses?" This makes the phrase an interrogative (following the LXX) and also demonstrates a smug arrogance. The thought was "We are safe; there is nothing to worry about. Carry on your normal activities."

4. "The time is not near to build houses" (RSV, ASV). This statement would have been understood as a call to arms: "Don't spend time building houses. It is time to sharpen our swords and prepare for battle against the Babylonians!"

The fourth interpretation seems most logical. First, it is easy to see how this would be classified as "devising iniquity" and giving **evil advice**, as the leaders were accused of doing in verse 2. Second, it fits most logically with the next clause: **This city is the pot and we are the flesh.** This declaration would be understood to mean that, as long as they were in the city, they were as safe as flesh is from the fire when it is in the pot. (See 24:3–10 for another illustration using a pot or a caldron.) Also, this fits with the arrogance of the Israelites. They assumed that, because they had the temple in Jerusalem, they were invincible. S. Fisch said,

> In assuring themselves of the adequate protection which the walls of Jerusalem would afford them in the event of an attack by the army of Babylon, the planners of the rebellion used a simile familiar at the time. The pot protects the flesh within it from the fire, and the meat is only removed after it has been sufficiently cooked. Similarly, the walls of the city would give protection to

---

[2]Adapted from Carl F. Keil, *Biblical Commentary on the Prophecies of Ezekiel*, trans. James Martin, Biblical Commentary on the Old Testament (Grand Rapids, Mich.: Wm. B. Eerdmans Publishing Co., 1950), 1:144–45.

its inhabitants, and only a natural death, not the sword of the enemy, would end their lives.³

John B. Taylor added,

> Such an attitude would readily be seen by Ezekiel to be sheer folly and deserving of the sternest condemnation. It not only ignored the explicit warnings of Jeremiah that resistance to Babylon would bring greater disaster than submission (cf. Je. 21:8–10), but it also reeked of the sublime self-confidence which was to be Jerusalem's undoing.⁴

11:4, 5
⁴"Therefore, prophesy against them, son of man, prophesy!"
⁵Then the Spirit of the Lord fell upon me, and He said to me, "Say, 'Thus says the Lord, "So you think, house of Israel, for I know your thoughts."'"

Verse 4. The command **"Prophesy!"** was given. Twice, Ezekiel was called upon to do this, underscoring the importance of what he was about to say. "Prophesy" is one of the key words in the book, occurring thirty-one times.

Verse 5. **"I know your thoughts,"** God said. Throughout his book, Ezekiel emphasized that God knows everything, even our thoughts and what we do in secret. God was aware of the evil intentions of Jaazaniah and Pelatiah. God knew that their counsel was self-serving.

11:6–8
⁶"'"You have multiplied your slain in this city, filling its streets with them." ⁷Therefore, thus says the Lord God, "Your slain whom you have laid in the midst of the city are the flesh and

---

³S. Fisch, *Ezekiel: Hebrew Text and English Translation with an Introduction and Commentary*, Soncino Books of the Bible (London: Soncino Press, 1950), 57.
⁴John B. Taylor, *Ezekiel: An Introduction and Commentary*, Tyndale Old Testament Commentaries (Downers Grove, Ill.: Inter-Varsity Press, 1969), 109.

this city is the pot; but I will bring you out of it. ⁸You have feared a sword; so I will bring a sword upon you," the Lord GOD declares.'"

Verse 6. A reference is made to **your slain**. Rather than being safe in the city, the people would find the opposite to be true. The streets would be filled with the dead.

Verse 7. God used their own parable, giving it a new interpretation. The flesh in the pot would be **your slain**, representing innocent and/or righteous people who had been killed by evil leaders like Jaazaniah and Pelatiah. **The pot** still represented the city, but it would not provide a safe haven for these wicked men. God said, **"I will bring you out of it"**—that is, out of the city—where the people would come face to face with the Babylonian soldiers.[5]

Verse 8. He also said that the people had **feared a sword**. Any normal, thinking person would be terrified at the thought of facing the cruel Babylonians. Their reputation was one of total brutality and no compassion (see Hab. 1:5–10). That is why Judah endeavored to secure protection from Egypt (see 17:15), but the alliance proved worthless. God would make their fears a reality. They would face the sword.

11:9–12
⁹"'"And I will bring you out of the midst of the city and deliver you into the hands of strangers and execute judgments against you. ¹⁰You will fall by the sword. I will judge you to the border of Israel; so you shall know that I am the LORD. ¹¹This city will not be a pot for you, nor will you be flesh in the midst of it, but I will judge you to the border of Israel. ¹²Thus you will know that I am the LORD; for you have not walked in My statutes nor have you executed My ordinances, but have acted according to the ordinances of the nations around you."'"

---

[5]"The figure of the pot and flesh is given a new meaning. The corpses of innocent people slain in the streets of Jerusalem will be the flesh which will remain in the pot, but they who engineered the rebellion and shed blood will be dragged out of the city to suffer the punishment they deserve" (Fisch, 58).

Verse 9. **"I will bring [יָצָא, *yatsa'*]"** is another recurring term in Ezekiel. It was frequently used by Ezekiel and the other prophets[6] to describe how God delivers His people in a way similar to how He delivered them out of Egyptian bondage. Ezekiel also used it this way in 20:34–38, giving it a positive sense. They would be a "soothing aroma" ("fragrant incense"; NIV) on the day when God brought them out (20:41). He would "bring them out from the peoples and gather them from the countries and bring them to their own land" (34:13). However, the word is not used in a positive sense here. God would bring (as in v. 7) these evil counselors out of the safe confines of Jerusalem and deliver them to their tormentors. God would take three actions: **"I will bring you out . . . deliver you . . . and execute judgments against you."**

Verse 10. They would die in the way they feared most: **by the sword**. Whereas these men believed that they would die naturally, that belief was far from the truth. In powerful prophetic language, God told them exactly how they would meet death. They would be judged **to the border of Israel**. Zedekiah and the princes with him were judged and killed at Riblah, on the borders of Israel, according to 2 Kings 25:1–7. They died, as prophesied, by the sword of the Babylonians.

Verse 11. Next, God said, **"This city will not be a pot for you. . . ."** The leaders were referring to Jerusalem as a pot and to the people as flesh. The pot meant security and protection. God told them that the danger they would face was not to be in the city, but on the borders of the nation. With the coming of this judgment (and with the prophecy accurately fulfilled), they would know "that I am the LORD" (v. 12). God, upon the fulfillment of His word, would be vindicated.

Verse 12. The people had **acted according to the ordinances of the nations**. Israel had made choices that put them in league with the wicked nations around them. Nothing was unique or peculiar about them (see 1 Pet. 2:9), although they were supposed to behave as God's people. Actually, when this is viewed

---

[6]See, for example, Is. 42:3; 43:14–17; 49:9, 17; 51:4, 5; 54:16. (Translations of the word vary.)

in light of the final phrase in 5:7, it shows that they were not faithful to foreign laws either. They were a lawless people! Their corruption exceeded that of even the most vile nations (16:47).

God repeated the significant phrase **Thus you will know that I am the LORD**. They learned this when Jerusalem fell to Nebuchadnezzar and the Babylonian army in 587(6) B.C. (see 2 Kings 25:18–21). God had said that if they were true to His covenant they would live (Lev. 18:5; Deut. 28:1–14). The choice they made, however, brought death.

THE PROMISE FOR A REMNANT (11:13–21)

11:13
¹³**Now it came about as I prophesied, that Pelatiah son of Benaiah died. Then I fell on my face and cried out with a loud voice and said, "Alas, Lord GOD! Will You bring the remnant of Israel to a complete end?"**

Verse 13. Pelatiah son of Benaiah died. Ezekiel was in Babylonia, and Pelatiah was in Jerusalem. Through the medium of this vision, God allowed Ezekiel to see a current event (**as I prophesied**). As word came to the exiles that Pelatiah had, in fact, died, the report confirmed the legitimacy of Ezekiel's words (as did the fulfillment of other prophecies; for example, those in 24:2, 16, 27).

Next, Ezekiel said, **I fell on my face and cried out**. He was not glad that an evil man had died (see 9:8). The name "Pelatiah," meaning "God has delivered," suggested hope for the remnant. Now Ezekiel was concerned that God would destroy the entire **remnant of Israel**. Taylor said, "The incident so frightened Ezekiel . . . that he again pleaded with God for his people (*cf.* 9:8). It is this intercession which leads into the second of his messages in this chapter, relating to a hopeful future for the despised exiles."[7] While Judah's judgment was deserved, annihilation was something that the compassionate prophet feared.

---

[7]Taylor, 110.

11:14-16

¹⁴**Then the word of the LORD came to me, saying,** ¹⁵**"Son of man, your brothers, your relatives, your fellow exiles and the whole house of Israel, all of them, are those to whom the inhabitants of Jerusalem have said, 'Go far from the LORD; this land has been given us as a possession.'** ¹⁶**Therefore say, 'Thus says the Lord GOD, "Though I had removed them far away among the nations and though I had scattered them among the countries, yet I was a sanctuary for them a little while in the countries where they had gone."'"**

Verses 14, 15. For a prophecy of hope and restoration to be given this early in Ezekiel's ministry seems strange. However, this is related to Ezekiel's cry for God to spare the remnant (v. 13). God continually gave hints that a period of restoration would come (see 5:3; 6:8, 9; 12:16; 16:60). The concept of the remnant is more fully developed later, beginning in chapter 33.

God wanted Ezekiel to appreciate the extent of the rebellion, which included [his] **brothers** (the only reference that Ezekiel had brothers), [his] **relatives**, [his] **fellow exiles and the whole house of Israel, all of them**. Moshe Greenberg explained,

> The threefold repetition of kinship expressions at the beginning of the statement, followed by the elaboration "all . . . Israel entire," underlines the extent of the diaspora, as if answering the prophet's concern (vs. 13) over Israel's extinction: the destruction of Jerusalem and Judah can hardly be complete when the diaspora is taken into consideration. . . . "All the house of Israel entire" (recurs only in restoration prophecies 20:40; 36:10), as opposed to those in the homeland, must include all Israelites in exile, the northern deportees as well as the exiles of Judah.[8]

In a remarkable display of arrogance, the poor who remained

---

[8]Moshe Greenberg, *Ezekiel 1—20: A New Translation with Introduction and Commentary*, The Anchor Bible, vol. 22 (Garden City, N.Y.: Doubleday & Co., 1983), 189.

in Jerusalem declared, **"This land has been given us."** They assumed that the Lord had removed the exiles because of their wickedness and had left them in Judah because of their righteousness. Jeremiah had encountered this arrogance, and he described those remaining as "bad figs" and the exiles as "good figs." The exiles would be returned to the land after renewing their relationship with the Lord (see Jer. 24).

Verse 16. God responded to the arrogance of those remaining in the land, saying, **"I was a sanctuary for them a little while."** He corrected their false impression of the exiles by confirming that these exiles were under divine protection (God's "sanctuary")[9] and that they would only be in captivity "a little while." Ezekiel had never indicated a short period of exile, and Jeremiah had prophesied that the Captivity would last seventy years (Jer. 25:11). God's mention of **countries** suggests that the promise was for all of God's people, not solely for Judah.

11:17–21

[17]**"Therefore say, 'Thus says the Lord G**OD**, "I will gather you from the peoples and assemble you out of the countries among which you have been scattered, and I will give you the land of Israel."'** [18]**When they come there, they will remove all its detestable things and all its abominations from it.** [19]**And I will give them one heart, and put a new spirit within them. And I will take the heart of stone out of their flesh and give them a heart of flesh."**

[20]**"That they may walk in My statutes and keep My ordinances and do them. Then they will be My people, and I shall be their God.** [21]**But as for those whose hearts go after their detestable things and abominations, I will bring their conduct down on their heads," declares the Lord G**OD.

---

[9]"To the humiliating allegation of the inhabitants of Jerusalem that the exiles, being far removed from the Temple, forfeited the Fatherhood and protection of God, comes the Divine retort that they still preserve their relationship to Him by means of their Houses of Worship and Houses of Learning, each of them serving the purpose of a miniature Temple in which the spirit of God was present (Meg. 29a). The Synagogue is even now called *a little sanctuary* in allusion to this verse" (Fisch, 60).

Verse 17. A message of hope is seen in this verse. There would be a time when God would **gather** His people, just as He had **scattered** them. This reiterated a key theological point to the Israelites: God was the One who had brought about their captivity—it was no one else. Judah's defeat was not because of the superiority of the Babylonian gods. Neither was their defeat brought about by bad fortune. God had scattered, and God would gather. Equally, He said that He would give them **the land of Israel**. This prophecy came true in 536 B.C., when the Persian king Cyrus issued a decree allowing the Jews to return to Palestine (see Ezra 1:1–4).

Verse 18. When the Israelites finally returned to the Promised Land, they would be through with idolatry. Passages like this provided them the incentive to rid themselves of idolatrous practices. They remembered what idolatry had cost them, and they did not want to pay that price again.

Verse 19. God said, **"I will give them one heart."** As is clarified in verse 20, God will not force a new heart or a new spirit into a person who is stubborn and rebellious. He transforms the heart only when that heart is soft and pliable, willing to conform to His will. God can and will do something with such a heart.[10]

Anyone who sees God bringing about a new Israel without Israel's consent is reading too much into this passage. God has always operated on the principle of free will and the human right to choose. Jim McGuiggan wrote,

> Note the divine initiative of verse 19—it is *God* who gives the new heart, and the new spirit within them. Here the stress is on the divine initiative but in 18:31 the stress is on the human cooperation with God. The story here of God making the first move in the direction of a reconciliation between himself and his creatures is taught all through the Bible. 2 Corinthians 5:17ff and Romans 5:6ff

---

[10]"In Jer 32:39 'one heart' is complemented and explained by 'one way'—singleness of mind and constancy of conduct. The contrasting expression is $b^e leb\ waleb$ (Ps 12:3) 'with two hearts,' i.e., insincerely . . ." (Greenberg, 190).

give us that story in explicit terms. But surely 1 John 4:19 is as clear as any passage in the Bible on the matter.[11]

Once a person has (through his own rebellion and lawlessness) created a **heart of stone** within himself, God must perform the spiritual surgery required to remove the wickedness from that heart. He performs such an "operation" only upon the penitent soul. The transplanted heart is **a heart of flesh**—that is, one capable of loving and staying loyal to God.
Verses 20, 21. God declared, **"I shall be their God"** (v. 20).

As always, the covenant-promise of blessing and union with God as His peculiar people (20) is set alongside the solemn consequences that will come upon the heads of those *whose heart goes after* all the corrupt practices from which they are to keep themselves free (*cf.* 18). . . . Moses set before the people "a blessing and a curse" (Dt. 11:26); Christ spoke of two ways, one leading to life and the other to destruction (Mt. 7:13f). The infinite gain of heaven is always matched in Scripture by the irreparable loss of hell.[12]

After the completion of their discipline in the land of exile, God would initiate four significant blessings. He would gather the people (v. 17); and He would bring them back to the land (v. 17). He would cleanse the land by removing the detestable things, the abominations, and those who persisted in idolatry (vv. 18, 21). Finally, He would once again be "their God" as He had been when they were faithful to the Law (vv. 19, 20).

In order for this arrangement to work, He said that the people must **walk in My statutes, keep My ordinances**, and **do them**. We must note the conditionality of this promise. Only in connection with faithfulness to His covenant would God re-adopt them. Notice that He said, "Then . . . I shall be their God."

---

[11]Jim McGuiggan, *The Book of Ezekiel*, Looking Into The Bible Series (Lubbock, Tex.: Montex Publishing Co., 1979), 114–15.
[12]Taylor, 112.

FROM THE EAST GATE OUT OF JERUSALEM; THE VISION ENDS (11:22–25)

²²**Then the cherubim lifted up their wings with the wheels beside them, and the glory of the God of Israel hovered over them. ²³The glory of the LORD went up from the midst of the city and stood over the mountain which is east of the city. ²⁴And the Spirit lifted me up and brought me in a vision by the Spirit of God to the exiles in Chaldea. So the vision that I had seen left me. ²⁵Then I told the exiles all the things that the LORD had shown me.**

Verses 22, 23. The promise of blessings given in the previous section did not mean that God had decided not to depart from Jerusalem. He still had to leave, but He left with a message of hope and reconciliation. Nevertheless, there could be no reconciliation until He returned (43:1–4). With **the glory of the LORD** having departed, nothing good could be expected to happen in that place. As Paul mentioned in 2 Thessalonians 1:7–9, when one is away from "the presence of the Lord," nothing good will result.

Verses 24, 25. The Spirit returned Ezekiel to **Chaldea** (v. 24a). There was nothing further to show him in Jerusalem. He had seen enough. He knew exactly why God was departing from this wicked city. At this point, **the vision ... left** Ezekiel (v. 24b), concluding the vision that began in chapter 8. No longer in a visionary state, Ezekiel related to the exiles all that he had seen (v. 25). How interesting it must have been to sit at Ezekiel's feet that day! One can only imagine the passion, sadness, and vividness with which Ezekiel told this incredible story. For one who has a heart like Ezekiel's, this account brings great sadness.

In a sense, the false prophets were right in believing that their enemies could never take Jerusalem because that was the location of the temple, the dwelling place of God. However, they were wrong in assuming that God would continue to make His abode in the midst of a lawless and rebellious people. A temple without God is just a building of mortar and bricks. Once He left, there was nothing special about the site.

APPLICATION

God's Withdrawal

God expects His people to be different from the world (v. 12).

Temporal "blessings" are not an indication of God's approval (v. 15).

God never withdraws from His people by His own will, sin forces Him to do so. In fact, James said, "Draw near to God and He will draw near to you" (Jas. 4:8a). God's leaving, however, signals trouble (2 Thess. 1:7–9).

God's departure does not mean that all have lost His presence or that He will never return.

The Glory of the Lord
And the Indwelling of the Holy Spirit

God's glory and His presence left the temple in chapter 11 and would not return until 43:1–5. One of the reasons we study the Old Testament is to try to understand some of the concepts found in the New Testament. One such concept is the indwelling of the Holy Spirit (Acts 2:38; 5:32; Rom. 8:9–11; 1 Cor. 6:19; 1 Thess. 4:8; Gal. 4:6; Acts 13:52; 11:24; 6:3). The temple in which God dwelt during Old Testament times was a physical structure. The New Testament, however, emphasizes the spiritual over the physical. The body of the Christian is God's temple, and He dwells in it (1 Cor. 6:19). Many people misunderstand this teaching and present arguments to disprove this statement of Paul. One argument is that if God dwells in us, then when we sin He must leave. By looking at Ezekiel 8—11, we see that God stayed in His temple until the last moment—when the people had completely apostatized. Before that, even though the people had been sinning for several centuries, God did not leave His temple. The same is true with us. God will not leave His temple, our bodies, until the last possible moment—when the time comes that we will not repent. Even then, if we were to repent, God would return, just as He did in the Book of Ezekiel.

D.P.

CHAPTER 12
SYMBOLIZING THE SIEGE

Ezekiel was called upon to demonstrate to the exiles in Babylon the certain doom of Jerusalem. The reason for this vivid demonstration was the people's stubborn refusal to believe that their captivity would be long, not short. They were still deceived into believing that as long as the temple stood, their nation would stand. Ezekiel was to enact, in order, the following:

1. The people being carried off into exile (12:3–7).
2. The king of Judah attempting to escape, only to be captured and brought to Jerusalem to die (12:10–13).
3. The hardships to be experienced by the people remaining in Jerusalem (12:17–20).

THE SIGN OF BAGGAGE FOR THOSE IN JERUSALEM (12:1–16)

12:1, 2
¹**Then the word of the Lord came to me, saying, ²"Son of man, you live in the midst of the rebellious house, who have eyes to see but do not see, ears to hear but do not hear; for they are a rebellious house."**

Verses 1, 2. Ezekiel lived in the middle of a **rebellious house**. This phrase is used five times in this chapter alone (vv. 2 [twice], 3, 9, 25). God had described the people this way in chapters 2 and 3 as well (2:3, 5, 6, 7, 8; 3:9). Their self-centered attitude caused rebellion—which, in turn, caused blindness. The refrain **who have eyes to see but do not see** is familiar in the prophets (see Is. 6:9; Jer. 5:21). It indicates the stubbornness of the people. Isaiah had preached more than 180 years earlier, and the people were still guilty of the same sins. For fourteen months Ezekiel had been telling the people that the city would be destroyed, but they refused to listen to him. God had given them the physical equipment (eyes and ears) to understand His message, but they did not use that equipment. Therefore, they were held accountable and this judgment was given.

12:3–6
³"Therefore, son of man, prepare for yourself baggage for exile and go into exile by day in their sight; even go into exile from your place to another place in their sight. Perhaps they will understand though they are a rebellious house. ⁴Bring your baggage out by day in their sight, as baggage for exile. Then you will go out at evening in their sight, as those going into exile. ⁵Dig a hole through the wall in their sight and go out through it. ⁶Load the baggage on your shoulder in their sight and carry it out in the dark. You shall cover your face so that you cannot see the land, for I have set you as a sign to the house of Israel."

Verse 3. This verse describes a visual aid being given to the people. Seeing the message should have helped them to understand exactly what was going to happen. The phrase **in their sight** (literally, "to their eyes") is used seven times in verses 3 through 7, emphasizing that the prophet was to force himself on their attention. ("Understand" in the next clause is literally "see.") Even so, being so rebellious, they could refuse to take notice. Ezekiel was told to **prepare . . . baggage for exile**. The people to whom this illustration was given were in Tel-abib. They had already experienced the trauma of being taken into exile. Now they were going to see a demonstration of what would happen to those in Jerusalem. The statement **perhaps they will understand** indicates that there is always hope that people will listen to the message of God, even though they have not heeded previous messages. The idea that people will not listen should never be used as an excuse not to give the message. Whether or not people listen to His message is not as important to God as the fact that we proclaim the message. God wants *us* to be faithful and do our jobs, regardless of what results.

Verse 4. Ezekiel was instructed to **bring [his] baggage out by day in their sight**. This baggage was **baggage for exile**. A person being carried into exile was allowed to take a small bag of personal belongings—and that was all. The captives' whole world was being left behind. The accumulation of possessions, the houses they had built, the businesses they had established—everything had to be abandoned. We can only imagine the utter depression they would feel, walking away from their homes and their homeland, saying goodbye to the lives they knew. Ezekiel was then to **go out at evening**, signifying that many of the exiles would begin their long journey to Babylon at nightfall.

Verse 5. Next, he was to **dig a hole through the wall**. This particular action has been interpreted in several ways, but it seems logical to see Ezekiel as presenting two exile possibilities: those who were easily taken captive and led off to exile during the day and those who had packed with plans to make a nighttime escape.[1] They did not realize that, at the time that they were packing their bags, they were actually packing for "exile" and not "escape." Also, Ezekiel was told, "You shall cover your face." This act would reflect the following:

1. The ignorance of those attempting a night escape. They were too blind to see that there was no escape.
2. The humiliation and embarrassment felt by the exiles as they were unceremoniously led into exile. Their dignity and self-respect were gone. The Babylonian soldiers were insensitive to their despair about leaving their land.

---

[1]"The Hebrew noun is not the usual *choshech*, but *alatah*—which, apart from verse 12, occurs again only in Genesis 15:17. It signifies the darkness which follows a sunset" (S. Fisch, *Ezekiel: Hebrew Text and English Translation with an Introduction and Commentary*, Soncino Books of the Bible [London: Soncino Press, 1950], 64).

3. A sign of mourning and grief felt by the exiles.
4. A preview of the literal blindness to be experienced by Zedekiah (v. 12).

Verse 6. God was making Ezekiel **a sign to the house of Israel**. A "sign" is that which conveys a message. It represents or points to something else. Ezekiel's sign conveyed the fact that the coming exile was real. When these events became a reality, the standing of the prophet would be more certain. He was a genuine prophet, and his accurate prophecies would confirm him. What Ezekiel prophesied here did, in fact, take place (2 Kings 25:4; Jer. 39:4). At the time of this prophecy, though, it did not seem possible. King Zedekiah was doing well, and the Jews in Jerusalem anticipated that he would have a long tenure, since he was just a puppet king of the Babylonians (see Ezek. 17:1–16).

12:7

⁷I did so, as I had been commanded. By day I brought out my baggage like the baggage of an exile. Then in the evening I dug through the wall with my hands; I went out in the dark and carried the baggage on my shoulder in their sight.

Verse 7. Ezekiel recorded, **I did so, as I had been commanded.** Once again, he showed himself to be very different from his people. He obeyed, though they were rebellious. He saw even though they did not, and he heard when they refused to do so. **Wall** is from the Hebrew word קִיר (*qir*) and usually refers to the walls of a "house or chamber,"² as opposed to the walls of a "city"³ (which is חוֹמָה, *chomah*). Ezekiel, then, was illustrating the vain attempts of people to flee their homes (obviously out of desperation and panic, unable to depart by normal means). The house where Ezekiel lived would most likely have been a typical Babylonian house, made of sun-dried bricks (see

---

²Francis Brown, S. R. Driver, and Charles A. Briggs, *A Hebrew and English Lexicon of the Old Testament* (Oxford: Clarendon Press, 1972), 885.
³Ibid., 327.

8:1, 7; Jer. 29:5; 1 Sam. 18:11; Amos 5:19). These bricks could be removed by hand, but not without much effort. Again, this would represent the actions of people in a difficult and desperate situation.

12:8–11

⁸**In the morning the word of the LORD came to me, saying,** ⁹**"Son of man, has not the house of Israel, the rebellious house, said to you, 'What are you doing?'** ¹⁰**Say to them, 'Thus says the Lord GOD, "This burden concerns the prince in Jerusalem as well as all the house of Israel who are in it."'** ¹¹**Say, 'I am a sign to you. As I have done, so it will be done to them; they will go into exile, into captivity.'"**

Verses 8, 9. The next morning God again spoke to Ezekiel. It had been a busy night for Ezekiel, and now it was time to elaborate on the meaning of his demonstration. Ezekiel had drawn the desired attention; his fellow exiles had inquired about his actions. They wanted to know, **"What are you doing?"** They apparently recognized Ezekiel's actions as a "sign" (v. 6), but what did the sign mean? Why would a man purposely damage his own home?

Verse 10. God answered, **"This burden concerns the prince."** In Hebrew, this phrase is הַנָּשִׂיא הַמַּשָּׂא הַזֶּה (*hannaśi' hammaśśa' hazzeh*). It is obviously a play on words, perhaps used to draw more careful attention to what the prophet was about to explain (see Jer. 23:33). The "burden" reminds us of the "baggage" Ezekiel was told to carry in verse 6. A "burden" (מַשָּׂא, *maśśa'*) was a load that was carried, something that had to be lifted. In this case, Ezekiel's message was a burden that the "prince" and the people (**the house of Israel**) would have to carry, as Ezekiel had carried his exile bag. The king and his people would have to bear this burden equally, for all of them were being charged with sin.

Verse 11. God told Ezekiel to say, **"I am a sign to you."** He wanted Ezekiel to explain what his symbolic actions meant. Actually, they were more than symbolic: They were prophetic. Ezekiel announced that **they** (the inhabitants of Jerusalem) would **go into exile, into captivity**. It was assured. The exiles' belief that the people in the city were safe was ill-founded.

12:12, 13

[12]"The prince who is among them will load his baggage on his shoulder in the dark and go out. They will dig a hole through the wall to bring it out. He will cover his face so that he can not see the land with his eyes. [13]I will also spread My net over him, and he will be caught in My snare. And I will bring him to Babylon in the land of the Chaldeans; yet he will not see it, though he will die there."

Verse 12. Unable to save the city, the humiliated king would try to escape under the cover of darkness. Like his people, he would have to pack his **baggage**. He would also experience the humiliation of having to leave under such conditions, closing his eyes because he could not bear to **see the land with his eyes**. His poor leadership had brought this event to reality. Jeremiah had warned him, but he had failed to listen.

Verse 13. God said, **"I will also spread My net over him."** King Zedekiah was unable to escape God's judgment. While the Babylonians would actually capture him, it was because of the **snare** God laid and the "net" God had cast. According to S. Fisch,

> The king's intended flight from the doomed city will be frustrated by God. Rashi and Kimchi [Rashi was Rabbi Solomon ben Isaac (1040–1105), a Jewish commentator, and David Kimchi (1160–1235) was also a Jewish commentator] quote a legend that there was a subterranean passage from Zedekiah's palace to the plains of Jericho through which he attempted to escape. To thwart his plan, God caused a gazelle to run along the top of that passage pursued by Babylonian soldiers. When they reached the exit of the passage, they saw Zedekiah coming from it and so captured him.[4]

---

[4]Fisch, 66.

God said, ***"I will bring him to Babylon"*** (emphasis added). This was clearly a judgment of God. When the Babylonian soldiers finally captured Zedekiah, they slew his sons before his eyes, then immediately blinded him. (Thus the last event he saw was the slaughter of his sons. See Jer. 39:6, 7; 52:4–11 and 2 Kings 25:1–7.) Zedekiah was never to return to Jerusalem; he was to **die** in Babylon.

12:14–16

¹⁴"I will scatter to every wind all who are around him, his helpers and all his troops; and I will draw out a sword after them. ¹⁵So they will know that I am the LORD when I scatter them among the nations and spread them among the countries. ¹⁶But I will spare a few of them from the sword, the famine and the pestilence that they may tell all their abominations among the nations where they go, and may know that I am the LORD."

Verse 14. I will scatter to every wind. As Ezekiel had scattered his hair to the wind (5:2), God would scatter His people. The cohort of Zedekiah was divided into three groups: **all who are around him**—a group of commoners involved in service to the king; **his helpers**—those closest advisors, his cabinet; and **his troops**—at this point not a very substantial army. Each of these would face **a sword** and be forced to flee from his pursuers.

Verse 15. The reason for this tragic scene is given: **So they will know that I am the LORD.** Everything that God had done and would do to these people had the direct purpose of forcing them to recognize Him as Lord. It is sad that the people did not see God during their days of prosperity. Now, in the midst of tragedy, God would make certain that they recognized His hand. Fisch said,

> When the prophecies of doom are fulfilled, the remnant of Israel which is scattered among the nations will realize that God is not only the Creator, but also the Ruler of the universe, and that punishment of the wicked is an essential feature of His sovereignty over mankind.

This they will transmit to their conquerors, so that these will also learn the true nature of God.[5]

Verse 16. Still, God said, **"But I will spare a few of them."** God again announced that He would preserve a few. These few were not spared because of righteousness, but to serve as witnesses to the events of judgment. They would announce **among the nations** the acts of the one true God, so that they—the exiles as well as the inhabitants of the nations—would come to know one great, fundamental truth: the truth of God's statement **"I am the Lord."** John B. Taylor said,

> Only as they confess their people's sins among the nations will it be seen that Israel's God is both holy and powerful: without such admissions He would simply be regarded as incapable of protecting His own people against the enemy. Ezekiel here shows his passion for Yahweh's vindication in circumstances which, without his message, would have brought nothing but disgrace in heathen eyes upon His name.[6]

THE SIGN OF TERROR (12:17–20)

12:17, 18
[17]**Moreover, the word of the Lord came to me saying,** [18]**"Son of man, eat your bread with trembling and drink your water with quivering and anxiety."**

Verses 17, 18. Ezekiel's next assignment was **Son of man, eat your bread . . .** (v. 18). In 4:10 his eating of the meal was to symbolize the scarcity of the food, but here it was to indicate the terror that would seize the people when Babylon laid siege to the city. God let them know that this judgment would come about because of "the violence" of the people. When it was all

---

[5]Ibid.
[6]John B. Taylor, *Ezekiel: An Introduction and Commentary*, Tyndale Old Testament Commentaries (Downers Grove, Ill.: Inter-Varsity Press, 1969), 116.

done, they would "know that I am the LORD" (vv. 16, 20). Notice the range of emotions experienced by people under siege, knowing that their days were numbered:

1. **Trembling** (רַעַשׁ, *ra'ash*)—a word typically associated with an earthquake or, in poetry, the rumbling and tumult caused by a mighty army (see 27:28; Is. 9:4; Jer. 47:3; Job 39:24).
2. **Quivering** (רְגַז, *ragaz*)—"be agitated, quiver, quake, be excited, perturbed."[7] This word indicates the inner turmoil and nervousness caused by the siege.
3. **Anxiety** (דְּאָג, *da'ag*)—"be anxious, concerned . . . fear, dread."[8] There would be no peace for the people under siege. Verse 19 says that they would "eat their bread with anxiety." Their concern would be whether or not they would have any more bread for tomorrow.
4. **"Horror"** (שִׁמָּמוֹן, *shimmamon*)—a word added in verse 19, meaning "appalment, horror."[9] They could hardly believe that they had been reduced to such meager supplies. They had only the bare necessities.

12:19, 20

[19]"Then say to the people of the land, 'Thus says the Lord GOD concerning the inhabitants of Jerusalem in the land of Israel, "They will eat their bread with anxiety and drink their water with horror, because their land will be stripped of its fullness on account of the violence of all who live in it. [20]The inhabited cities will be laid waste and the land will be a desolation. So you will know that I am the LORD."'"

Verses 19, 20. God's message concerned **the inhabitants of Jerusalem in the land of Israel** (v. 19). This phrase is used here to refer to the poorest people of the land. The lifestyle of this

---

[7]Brown, Driver, and Briggs, 919.
[8]Ibid., 178.
[9]Ibid., 1031.

class was in contrast to the kings and the wealthy inhabitants. (See Ezek. 7:27.) According to Walther Zimmerli,

> . . . before the exile it was the designation of the land-owning full citizens of Judah with military responsibility. Only after the exile did the title drop to becoming a deprecatory designation by the pious of the poorer part of the nation, who were despised for their unfaithfulness to the law.[10]

The emotions experienced by those under siege came, in part, **because their land [would] be stripped of its fullness**. It would be horrifying to see their once beautiful, productive land lose its productivity as well as its beauty. Because they had sown violence, they were to reap violence.

A WARNING CONCERNING GOD'S MESSAGES (12:21–28)

12:21, 22
²¹**Then the word of the LORD came to me, saying,** ²²**"Son of man, what is this proverb you people have concerning the land of Israel, saying, 'The days are long and every vision fails'?"**

Verse 21. In Ezekiel, the phrase **the word of the LORD** signals the beginning of a new series of messages. Beginning here and going through 14:11, a series of oracles is given. These deal specifically with prophecy. Taylor said,

> This must have been an acute problem for all the prophets of Old Testament times and especially for men like Jeremiah and Ezekiel, whose message did not naturally commend itself to their hearers. The struggle between Jeremiah and Hananiah (Je. 28) illustrates the issue

---

[10]Walther Zimmerli, *Ezekiel 1: A Commentary on the Book of the Prophet Ezekiel, Chapters 1—24*, trans. Ronald E. Clements, Hermeneia (Philadelphia: Fortress Press, 1979), 209.

clearly. Here were two men speaking contradictory words, ostensibly from the Lord. The bystanders were helpless to know which was true. The simple rule of thumb given in Deuteronomy 18:22, the fulfillment of the word spoken, was too far distant to be an immediate guide, and the test of orthodoxy given in Deuteronomy 13:1ff was not relevant to the issue. In the event the verbal contest escalated until Jeremiah pronounced a death-prophecy, which did take effect and was his vindication. But this could hardly happen every time.[11]

Verse 22. The days are long and every vision fails. This is the first of two sayings that Ezekiel specifically addressed. The second is in verse 27. This apparently common saying reflected the people's skepticism about the prophecies they had heard. Far too frequently, such prophecies had failed. The people had listened to prophets, but they had not seen their words come true. One problem was that they looked for immediate fulfillment (see Zech. 1:12). When the event prophesied did not happen immediately, they believed the prophecy to have failed. The end result of this was a false sense of security. They said, in effect, "Why should we be upset by these prophecies of doom? We are still here, and our situation looks good—so relax!" This is an Old Testament parallel of 2 Peter 3:4.[12]

12:23–25

²³"Therefore say to them, 'Thus says the Lord GOD, "I will make this proverb cease so that they will no longer use it as a proverb in Israel." But tell them, "The days draw near as well as the fulfillment of every vision. ²⁴For there will no longer be any false vision or flattering divination within the house of Israel.

---

[11]Taylor, 117–18.

[12]"From God's retort (vs. 25b) that fulfillment will surely come 'in your time ([literally,] days),' it may be inferred that the 'time' alluded to here is to be measured in lifetimes. Generations have lived under the shadow of unfulfilled prophecies; this circumstance has given rise to the disbelief epitomized in the proverb" (Moshe Greenberg, *Ezekiel 1—20: A New Translation with Introduction and Commentary*, The Anchor Bible, vol. 22 [Garden City, N.Y.: Doubleday & Co., 1983], 227).

²⁵For I the LORD will speak, and whatever word I speak will be performed. It will no longer be delayed, for in your days, O rebellious house, I will speak the word and perform it," declares the Lord GOD.'"

Verse 23. Two popular sayings are refuted in verses 23 through 28. God was offended by the statement "The days are long and every vision fails." The proverb negatively reflected upon the truthfulness of His words and undermined the credibility of His prophets. Therefore, He intended to eliminate the saying. How? By bringing forth **the fulfillment of** [these] **vision**[s]. **"The days draw near,"** He said. Before long, the people would see these prophecies come true (see 7:7). It would not take years, but "days." God further qualified this by saying, "It will no longer be delayed" (v. 25).

Verse 24. The people would say, in effect, "Ezekiel is just another blabbering prophet. Why should we listen to him?" Generally speaking, the words of the prophets were classified in two very uncomplimentary categories, given in verse 24:

(1) **False vision** means something that either was no vision at all (that is, it was made up by a lying prophet), or was not a vision that originated with God.

(2) **Flattering divination** refers to attempts by prophets to make their prophecies believable. Various devices would be employed in order to give the impression of legitimacy. (Examples include Hananiah's breaking the yoke off of Jeremiah in Jeremiah 28:10 and the iron horns worn by Zedekiah, the son of Chenaanah, in 1 Kings 22:11.)

Jerusalem had been inundated with false prophets. God's true prophets had a difficult task in trying to combat the deluge of false prophecies and false teachings issued daily.

Verse 25. In powerful and emphatic terminology, God said, **"I the LORD will speak."** Such a speaker ought not to be taken lightly! Certainly, whatever He spoke would be completely and totally fulfilled. From Him there would be no inaccuracies and no half-truths. This time, God assured them that there would also be no delay. In the past, God had deferred judgment in order to provide the people an opportunity to repent. Such deferment would not happen this time. A show of love and compassion by God had been construed as ineffectiveness in the eyes of the people. Again, we see parallels between this passage and 2 Peter 3 (note vv. 3–15).

12:26–28

²⁶Furthermore, the word of the LORD came to me, saying, ²⁷"Son of man, behold, the house of Israel is saying, 'The vision that he sees is for many years from now, and he prophesies of times far off.' ²⁸Therefore say to them, 'Thus says the Lord GOD, "None of My words will be delayed any longer. Whatever word I speak will be performed,"'" declares the Lord GOD.

Verses 26, 27. God then directed His words to Ezekiel, clarifying what He was about to do. While addressing this, He mentioned a second saying that He would refute: **"The vision that he sees is for many years from now . . . he prophesies of times far off"** (v. 27). Part of the false security experienced by the people was their belief that, even if the prophecy did come true, it would not directly affect them because they would be dead long before it happened.

Verse 28. Ezekiel acknowledged that the fulfillment of other prophecies had been delayed, but he asserted that there would be no delay in his. These people were to see firsthand the fulfillment of Ezekiel's words.

APPLICATION

Seeking the Truth

God has given us the tools we need to understand His truths (eyes to see and study the Word, as well as ears to listen to it). We are without excuse when we choose not to study the Bible or when we fail to listen while the truth is being preached. Jesus said that if we have ears, we should hear (Mt. 13:9–17).

The truthfulness of God's prophecies is not dependent upon time. Man should learn that God operates on His own timetable (2 Pet. 3:3–13).

In our sophisticated, technological world, do we "know the

Lord"? Do our leaders know Him? By their failure, the leaders in Ezekiel's day brought doom upon themselves and their people. We should pray for our leaders that the same may not happen today (1 Tim. 2:1, 2).

Many false teachers and false teachings exist in the world today—as in Ezekiel's day. It is imperative that we "test the spirits to see whether they are from God" (1 Jn. 4:1). False teachers can appear to be "sheep," lovable, believable, spiritual, and holy—but they are wolves (Mt. 7:15–20).

Time is to be viewed as a gift of God, providing us an opportunity to repent.

D.P.

The Worst Thing Anyone Can Do (12:1–6)

Ezekiel was told that he was living among a people who had "eyes to see" but they were not seeing and who had "ears to hear" but they were not hearing (v. 2). God used this figurative language to say that they had rebelled against His Word. Instead of opening their hearts to His messages, they had lifted clinched fists to them. Instead of humbling themselves before His commands, they hardened themselves against them.

This severe evaluation of the people was not a mere guess or a simple possibility. God was the One who had conducted the examination, and upon His flawless evidence, He had given the diagnosis. The Doctor who tended to them was all-wise, all-knowing, and unerring. He had given them an accurate picture of their hearts, a picture that revealed that their condition was the most horrendous condition of all. They had heart trouble of the worst kind—they were a rebellious people!

With their rebellion, they had closed themselves off from God's will. The house of Israel had disobediently rejected God's will, the highest plan for their lives. It has been said, "None is so blind as the person who refuses to see." Deliberate blindness is the most terrible kind. Can you imagine someone who has perfect 20/20 vision choosing not to see? He has decided to live with closed eyes. Surrounded by a host of wonderful things to view, he has opted to live in darkness. No one would do such a thing physically, but Israel did it spiritually.

With their rebellion, they had closed themselves off from God's fellowship. The refusal of the house of Israel to obey God's commandments placed them in the middle of a life without God. Jonah soon realized that when one flees from God's will, he flees from God (Jon. 1:4, 5). We go through the Word to get to the Author of the Word. The Israelites missed out on the highest type of communion through their disobedience.

With their rebellion, they had closed themselves off from God's provisions. God has promised to guide, protect, and provide only for those who are within His will. Ezekiel was told that his enactment of a deportation would illustrate the actual experience that would come to the house of Israel. Even their king, the prince, would be taken in humiliation to Babylon; but he would not see Babylon, for he would be blinded in the land of Israel. When we do not humble ourselves before God's Word, He allows us to suffer humiliation so that we might learn to obey it.

How does God get through to a rebellious house? He issues a clarion call for repentance. God continued to plead with the house of Israel. They would not heed what He had put before their eyes and in their ears, so God told Ezekiel that maybe they would listen to Him if He showed His message to them with a vivid visual, Ezekiel himself simulating a deportation. Later, God allowed them to go into captivity as a harsh discipline so that they might recognize their sin and return to Him.

The people had put their eyes and ears to the worst possible use. With eyes to see God's will and ears to hear it, they said no to God. The worst thing anyone can do is to rebel against God. Such a spirit closes the door to God's will, fellowship, and provisions. The noblest thing anyone can do is to let his heart melt before the sunlight of God's truth, so that he might enter into God's spiritual life.

Is God's Word True? (12:17–28)

Ezekiel was God's prophet who ministered to those who were already in Babylon. The heart of his prophesying was to reveal to the people why Jerusalem would fall. It has been said that Jeremiah was a priest who became a prophet, while Ezekiel was a prophet who had to become a priest.

Before the fall of Jerusalem, spirituality was at an all-time low. The people of the land had forsaken God and were chasing after idols under every spreading tree. Another indication of their disobedience to God was the way they looked upon His Word, the words of His prophets. How did they see God's messages?

They saw His messages as unbelievable. They saw much of His Word as being unbelievable. They had made a proverb that said, "The days are long and every vision fails." They meant by their proverb that they were not seeing the reality of the fulfillment of the visions from God. They regarded the true visions from God as empty dreams that failed.

They saw them as irrelevant. They saw the prophetic portions of His Word as being irrelevant to their day. They would picture these prophecies as being for some day in the distant future that was far removed from their time. These revelations, they said, could contribute nothing meaningful to their current situation.

They saw them as uninteresting. They saw false teachings as being far more interesting and encouraging to them. The false prophets would say, "You people are doing well before God. There is nothing but peace and prosperity ahead of you." They did not want repentance preached to them. "Tell us to rejoice, not repent," they would say. They would only listen to sermons that made them feel good about themselves and their relationships with God.

When these three views of God's Word are combined, they dovetail into the single view that God's Word is untrue. Any individual or nation that takes such an attitude toward the Scriptures is swiftly headed for ruin.

God rebuked their view of His Word by saying to them, "I will show you what a prophecy is. You will hear it, and you will see its immediate fulfillment. No longer will you have your proverbs, and no longer will you take delight in preaching that flatters sinful people. Through what happens to you and your nation, you will come to know that a prophet has been among you."

E.C.

CHAPTER 13

CONDEMNATIONS OF FALSE PROPHETS AND PROPHETESSES

While God held His people responsible for listening to false prophets, He nevertheless was sympathetic to them. He knew how they had been overwhelmed by false teachers, becoming victims to these ravenous wolves.

The words in chapter 13 targeted these wolves—the false prophets and prophetesses. Their messages of peace and safety had led the nation of Judah down a path of self-indulgence and unfounded security. Now they were truly going to receive a word from the Lord, but it was not a message they would like.

THE MESSAGE AGAINST THE FALSE PROPHETS AND PROPHETESSES (13)

Against the False Prophets (13:1–16)

13:1–3

¹Then the word of the Lord came to me saying, ²"Son of man, prophesy against the prophets of Israel who prophesy, and say to those who prophesy from their own inspiration, 'Listen to the word of the Lord! ³Thus says the Lord God, "Woe to the foolish prophets who are following their own spirit and have seen nothing."'"

Verse 1. Then the word of the Lord came to me. While it has been noted that this phrase marks a new message, it takes on special significance in this chapter. Ezekiel, a true prophet of God, was receiving a true message from God. The false prophets, who continually created messages and then claimed that they were of divine origin, had none of the credibility of a prophet like Ezekiel.

Verse 2. God told Ezekiel to **prophesy against the prophets of Israel who prophesy**. There were few true prophets of the Lord at this time. However, there were scores of false prophets. These were generally men who prophesied for hire and were virtually "yes men" to the king. They spoke **from their own inspiration**; they were not genuinely inspired by God. Through their own creative means, they conjured messages and then cloaked them in lies, making them seem to be from the Lord. An element of self-deception may have affected many of these prophets. Perhaps they so desired a message from God that they construed any unusual events in their lives to be divine oracles. This is what happened with the prophets of Baal, whom Elijah confronted on Mount Carmel (1 Kings 18).

Verse 3. "Woe to the foolish prophets," God said.[1] The word here translated "foolish" (נָבָל, *nabal*) means more than stupidity or a lack of education. This describes a person who is devoid of a moral foundation. He could easily say, "There is no God" (Ps. 14:1), blaspheme (Ps. 74:18), or be involved in immorality (2 Sam. 13:13). Being devoid of ethics, he would willingly create and promote all sorts of messages and claim that they came from God. Why would anyone do such a thing? Perhaps for attention, fame, or fortune. Prophets in Old Testament times might receive an audience with the king or be given a position of authority. Much money could be made; prophets faced the temptation to "sell" favorable prophecies (see 1 Kings 22:6–13). This should remind us or convince us that history is full of corrupt people who used religion as their platform. The world is no different today. Listeners, beware! For further study on the problem of false teachers, consult Jeremiah 14; 23; 29; and Deuteronomy 13; 18. In addition, Peter wrote,

> But false prophets also arose among the people, just

---

[1] See Num. 16:28 as opposed to 1 Kings 12:33. Read Jer. 5:30, 31; 14:14; 23:16; 2 Pet. 1:21.

as there will also be false teachers among you, who will secretly introduce destructive heresies, even denying the Master who bought them, bringing swift destruction upon themselves. Many will follow their sensuality, and because of them the way of the truth will be maligned; and in their greed they will exploit you with false words; their judgment from long ago is not idle, and their destruction is not asleep (2 Pet. 2:1–3).

God revealed the truth behind these prophets: They had **seen nothing**. There can be no degree of sympathy for them. We must not say, "They just misunderstood the message; their hearts were in the right place" or "Their love for God and their desire to serve Him led them to claim to have a message from Him." Since they had seen nothing, their claim to have seen something could be nothing less than a lie.

13:4–7
⁴"'"O Israel, your prophets have been like foxes among ruins. ⁵You have not gone up into the breaches, nor did you build the wall around the house of Israel to stand in the battle on the day of the Lord. ⁶They see falsehood and lying divination who are saying, 'The Lord declares,' when the Lord has not sent them; yet they hope for the fulfillment of their word. ⁷Did you not see a false vision and speak a lying divination when you said, 'The Lord declares,' but it is not I who have spoken?"'"

Verse 4. The prophets are compared to **foxes among ruins**. These false prophets had no real concern for the people. The statement may be applied as follows: (1) Foxes run when confronted. Likewise, false prophets make their presence felt through the damage they do and then run when confronted. (2) Foxes enter vineyards in order to destroy. False prophets preach messages that destroy those who listen and believe them. (3) Foxes are drawn to areas in disarray and ruin, entering homes and fields through breaches (v. 5). False prophets are drawn to those people who are discouraged, downtrodden, and in desperate need of a good word. They offer these people the type of message they so badly want to hear. The false prophets among the exiles were ancient "ear ticklers" (see 2 Tim. 4:3, 4).

Verse 5. Farmers built fences around their fields to protect them from intruders. Foxes were not invited to enter into these fields; their presence was made possible through deception. In the same way, false prophets had entered into the general population through ignoble means. They were not invited there by God to serve His people. God said, **"You have not gone up into the breaches, nor did you build the wall around the house of Israel to stand in the battle on the day of the LORD."** God needed prophets and prophetesses who would help to make society better. He wanted servants who would address what was wrong with the nation. The walls were broken down or in need of repair, thus threatening the security of Israel on the day of battle. Walther Zimmerli wrote,

> Where, however, the enemy in war had already made breaches in the walls of a city . . . , then it was the duty of those who were concerned for their city to go into these breaches . . . and to climb up on the threatened places in the face of hostile fire. . . . Even this duty of defending the breaches and closing the threatened gaps the prophets have neglected towards their people.
>
> . . . True prophecy had to know that in a time of danger it had to choose, like Moses, to fulfill the responsibilities of its task in complete disregard of its own concerns. Instead of this the prophets of Israel had handed on uncritically their delusory visions . . . and spoken of them, perhaps personally quite sincere in their belief in their deceitful message. . . .[2]

This would prepare them for "the day of the LORD." That day, in context, was when Jerusalem fell in 587(6) B.C. God's true prophets were preparing the people for that day. False prophets, how-

---

[2]Walther Zimmerli, *Ezekiel 1: A Commentary on the Book of the Prophet Ezekiel, Chapters 1—24*, trans. Ronald E. Clements, Hermeneia (Philadelphia: Fortress Press, 1979), 292–93.

ever, were trying to undo the work of the true prophets by preaching messages of peace and security.

Verse 6. Whereas true prophets saw revelations from God, false prophets . . .

. . . saw **falsehood** (literally, "vanity"). They had not seen anything.

. . . saw **lying divination.** Their messages were made up or were entirely lies.

. . . said, **"The LORD declares,"** yet God never gave them a message to deliver.

. . . **hope[d] for the fulfillment of their word.** They did not know what would happen in the future. They could only invent a prophecy and then hope for it to come true.

Verse 7. In highly confrontational language, God asked these false prophets to be truthful. They knew that God had not spoken to them, but they persisted in giving their messages. Their dishonesty and evil intent is made clear.

13:8–13

⁸Therefore, thus says the Lord GOD, "Because you have spoken falsehood and seen a lie, therefore behold, I am against you," declares the Lord GOD. ⁹"So My hand will be against the prophets who see false visions and utter lying divinations. They will have no place in the council of My people, nor will they be written down in the register of the house of Israel, nor will they enter the land of Israel, that you may know that I am the Lord GOD. ¹⁰It is definitely because they have misled My people by saying, 'Peace!' when there is no peace. And when anyone builds a wall, behold, they plaster it over with whitewash; ¹¹so tell those who plaster it over with whitewash, that it will fall. A flooding rain will come, and you, O hailstones, will fall; and a violent wind will break out. ¹²Behold, when the wall has fallen, will you not be asked, 'Where is the plaster with which you plastered it?'" ¹³Therefore, thus says the Lord GOD, "I will make a violent wind break out in My wrath. There will also be in My anger a flooding rain and hailstones to consume it in wrath."

God gave four reasons why He was against these false prophets:

1. They had "spoken falsehood," meaning that they had given the people things that had no spiritual value (v. 8).
2. They had "seen a lie," demonstrating that their "visions" were full of untruth and error (v. 8).
3. They had "misled" the people, promising peace, when God's true prophets were predicting calamity as a result of their sinfulness (v. 10).
4. They had "plastered" the truth, covering up the true problems of the nation and creating a spiritual wall that looked sound and strong. However, at the first blow this wall would crumble.

Verse 8. God made the frightening declaration **"I am against you."** These men should have been standing to fight against the enemies of Israel; instead, they had made themselves enemies of God. Friendship with the world makes one an enemy of God (Jas. 4:4).

Verse 9. Next, He announced, **"My hand will be against the prophets."** His opposition to the false prophets would bring three results. He said,

1. **"They will have no place in the council of My people."** The temptation to be a prophet was fame and fortune. These prophets would lose their place of honor and respect.
2. **"Nor will they be written down in the register of the house of Israel."** They would no longer be considered citizens of God's chosen nation.
3. **"Nor will they enter the land of Israel."** The people were to be returned to the land of Israel after seventy years in captivity (Jer. 25:11). However, these prophets would die in captivity. Jeremiah had delivered a similar message regarding the false prophet Shemaiah (Jer. 29:32).

Verse 10. God spoke **definitely** against these prophets because they had **misled** the people with a false message of **peace** and security, as a wall is plastered **with whitewash**. God used an illustration of **when anyone builds a wall**. The word "wall" (חַיִץ, *chayits*, "a thin or party-wall"[3]) refers to bricks or stones laid upon each other but not cemented together. According to the illustration, the false prophets observed the wall that someone else had built, and rather than pointing out that the wall needed to be secured, they covered the obvious weaknesses of the wall with **plaster**.[4] The people had developed their own "theology" regarding the state of the nation and their spiritual health. This was their "wall." The prophets needed to advise and warn the people that their nation was not in good spiritual health, that they were no longer a strong nation.

Verses 11–13. The dangers that would inevitably come were **a flooding rain**, **hailstones**, or **a violent wind** that would test the strength of the wall. These elements represent the forces of God's wrath (v. 13).

As is always the case when people build a wall against God's will, God said that He would bring resistance that would leave the wall **fallen**. Every attempt to establish something against God's Word must be brought down. However, the lesson here is not really about the building of the wall, but about the actions of the false prophets. When the wall came down, people would confront the prophets who had convinced them that the wall was solid. The imagery is similar to the idea of one who builds a house. The builder assures the buyer that the house is solidly built. If it falls when a storm comes, the buyer seeks the builder who offered such assurance. Likewise, people would return to

---

[3]Francis Brown, S. R. Driver, and Charles A. Briggs, *A Hebrew and English Lexicon of the Old Testament* (Oxford: Clarendon Press, 1972), 300.

[4]"As said expressly in 22:28, 'they' who daubed the wall were the prophets: the people built the dry wall—a figure of their unfounded optimism, while the prophets daubed it with worthless stuff [the whitewash]—their self-inspired predictions of well-being. Such a structure will offer no shelter from the storm (God's wrath)" (Moshe Greenberg, *Ezekiel 1—20: A New Translation with Introduction and Commentary*, The Anchor Bible, vol. 22 [Garden City, N.Y.: Doubleday & Co., 1983], 238).

the false prophets and ask, "What happened to your prophecies? You promised us that the land was safe!" Jesus later said, "Every plant which My heavenly Father did not plant shall be uprooted" (Mt. 15:13).

13:14–16
¹⁴"So I will tear down the wall which you plastered over with whitewash and bring it down to the ground, so that its foundation is laid bare; and when it falls, you will be consumed in its midst. And you will know that I am the LORD. ¹⁵Thus I will spend My wrath on the wall and on those who have plastered it over with whitewash; and I will say to you, 'The wall is gone and its plasterers are gone, ¹⁶along with the prophets of Israel who prophesy to Jerusalem, and who see visions of peace for her when there is no peace,' declares the Lord GOD."

Verse 14. God specified, **"I will tear down the wall"** (v. 14a). Using terminology similar to Isaiah 30:13, God said that His "wrath" would come against the feeble wall. God's anger is sure to come against the false teachings (the "walls") of men. False teachers today continue to support and promote teachings that are not biblical. They manage through smoothness of speech or deception to make the unlearned believe their message. Meanwhile, the anger of God is kindled against those who "suppress the truth in unrighteousness" (Rom. 1:18).

The wall of false teaching would be brought **down to the ground** (v. 14b). When God's wrath came to bring it down, the foundation upon which the wall was built would be exposed. All teaching must be built upon fundamental truth. God planned to expose everything that the false prophets had done. In the New Testament a parallel is seen: "For no man can lay a foundation other than the one which is laid, which is Jesus Christ" (1 Cor. 3:11). Men have built many churches that are not built upon the foundation of Jesus Christ. If the gospel He preached is not adhered to, then it has no claim to Christ.

When the wall supported by these false teachers came down, it would not simply mean that another wall needed to be built.

In this case, God said, **"And when it falls, you will be consumed in its midst"** (v. 14c). The switch from a masculine word meaning "wall" to a feminine form translated "it" demonstrates that the prophet was now speaking about Jerusalem. The city would come down; and the false prophets, who had directly contributed to her demise, were to go down with her. The destruction of Jerusalem would be so thorough that her foundations would be exposed—**laid bare**. John B. Taylor wrote,

> At this stage the figure of the wall, which began by representing popular optimism, comes to be identified with the city of Jerusalem, on whose impregnability their empty hopes had centred. The strongest condemnation, however, goes not to the people but to those who led them into error. "Woe to the man by whom the temptation comes!" (Mt. 18:7).[5]

Verses 15, 16. God said that He would **spend** His wrath (v. 15; see the notes on 5:13). This terminology represents God as being patient, but to a point. Finally, after His cup of wrath becomes full, He "spends" it. Indeed, it would be a terrifying thing to be a part of that day (see Heb. 10:31). In addition to the destruction of the city itself, God said, **"[The] plasterers are gone."** Those false prophets who did not die within the city would be carried into captivity. As noted in verse 9, they would never again enter the land, but would die as captives. The primary guilt of the prophets lay in their claims to see **visions of peace for her when there is no peace** (v. 16). Feelings of peace and security have always given people attitudes of indifference.

Against the False Prophetesses (13:17–23)

13:17–19
¹⁷**"Now you, son of man, set your face against the daughters of your people who are prophesying from their own inspira-**

---

[5]John B. Taylor, *Ezekiel: An Introduction and Commentary*, Tyndale Old Testament Commentaries (Downers Grove, Ill.: Inter-Varsity Press, 1969), 123.

tion. Prophesy against them ¹⁸and say, 'Thus says the Lord GOD, "Woe to the women who sew magic bands on all wrists and make veils for the heads of persons of every stature to hunt down lives! Will you hunt down the lives of My people, but preserve the lives of others for yourselves? ¹⁹For handfuls of barley and fragments of bread, you have profaned Me to My people to put to death some who should not die and to keep others alive who should not live, by your lying to My people who listen to lies."'"

Verse 17. Like the false prophets, false prophetesses were **prophesying from their own inspiration**. God had not spoken to these women; their messages were not of divine origin. The people's acceptance of error opened the door for several abuses, and these women walked through that door. They were not prophetesses, as one might think of a role for a prophetess (similar to that of a prophet). Instead, the women were soothsayers, witches, or sorceresses. They were involved in divination. Although the practice of witchcraft was common then, it was condemned in the law of Moses (Lev. 19:26).

Verse 18. These women would sew **magic bands** ("pillows"; KJV) upon their wrists. These bracelets were thought to transmit the power of the sorceress to the prophetess. Also, they would **make veils for the heads**. Whether they made these veils for themselves (NIV) or for their victims (NASB; KJV; ASV; RSV) is unclear. If the veils were for themselves, the idea is that of wearing the dress of a sorceress and casting spells on people. If they were placing the veils on their victims, it would be for the purpose of identifying a subject and then proceeding with incantations (perhaps so that the victim would be partially blinded to what the sorceress was doing). The goal, however, is clear: These prophetesses intended to **hunt down lives**. The word here translated "lives" is the Hebrew word נֶפֶשׁ (*nepesh*). This has led some to believe that these women were somehow controlling disembodied spirits. There is no way the Hebrew word will allow this idea. It refers to the total person—his entire composition. While the ultimate goal was perhaps the person's death (see v. 19), that was not the immediate goal. These women wanted to control their subjects, making them slaves and involving them in their idolatrous practices.⁶

Verse 19. God said, **"For handfuls of barley . . . you have profaned Me."** Some have supposed that this refers to the price of their services (which would have been rather cheap), but such is unlikely. Recent archeological findings have revealed that Hittite and Syrian rituals used barley bread as part of the pagan sacrificial ritual—perhaps being used to determine whether the subject would live or die.⁷ The verse says that the women **put to death some who should not die**. It is not known exactly how these women were "killing" the people, or if, in fact, they literally killed anybody. Their entire work centered on **lies**. William H. Brownlee said,

> In order to make a living, the sorceresses require a brisk business, demand for which could arise from their claim to powers of life and death over other people through mantic gifts in some way connected with the bands and veils. Will they for hire kill off the enemies of aggrieved parties? Their vaunted powers are in any case "lies" which deceive the people.⁸

If they did bring about death, it was sometimes the death of people "who should not die," referring to people who were generally well-meaning people but were deceived by the women's "powers." Those **who should not live** means those who led lives of wickedness, illustrated by their willingness to be involved

---

⁶"Hunt" is the Hebrew word *tsoded* (צוֹדֵד) which is "an intensive of *sud*, 'hunt down' (not kill), probably with reference to many objects. . . . A like phrase recurs in Prov 6:26, 'a married woman can trap [*tasud*] an honorable person (*nepes*)' with her wiles; it is a figure for the enticement of gullibles. Theories based on the notion of the magical catching of disembodied souls . . . disregard the absence of evidence that *nepes* ever has such a sense in Hebrew" (Greenberg, 239–40).

⁷Ralph H. Alexander, "Ezekiel," in *The Expositor's Bible Commentary*, ed. Frank E. Gaebelein (Grand Rapids, Mich.: Zondervan Publishing House, 1986), 6:803.

⁸William H. Brownlee, *Ezekiel 1—19*, Word Biblical Commentary, vol. 28 (Waco, Tex.: Word Books, 1986), 196.

with these women. God's law declared that witches should die, and those who sought their services deserved the same fate. Nothing in this text indicates that these women had mystical powers to give life or cause death. The Bible makes it plain that the ultimate power of life and death belongs to God.

13:20–23

²⁰Therefore, thus says the Lord GOD, "Behold, I am against your magic bands by which you hunt lives there as birds and I will tear them from your arms; and I will let them go, even those lives whom you hunt as birds. ²¹I will also tear off your veils and deliver My people from your hands, and they will no longer be in your hands to be hunted; and you will know that I am the LORD. ²²Because you disheartened the righteous with falsehood when I did not cause him grief, but have encouraged the wicked not to turn from his wicked way and preserve his life, ²³therefore, you women will no longer see false visions or practice divination, and I will deliver My people out of your hand. Thus you will know that I am the LORD."

Verse 20. As God announced to the prophets in verse 8, so He repeated the warning: **"I am against [you]."** God detailed that He was against everything these women were doing, especially their **magic bands**—part of their arsenal that they used to **hunt lives . . . as birds**.

Verse 21. God's judgment on the prophetesses is stated. He would remove the items of their trade. Presumably, this would happen when the women were taken into Babylonian captivity. The prophetesses, who supposed that they had power, would **know that I am the LORD**.

Verse 22. Besides the earlier charges of taking the lives of those who should not die, God presented two other charges:

1. **"You disheartened the righteous."** They did this with falsehood, saying and doing things that would cause grief. These women undermined faith, causing individuals to abandon their trust in the Lord.

2. **"[You] have encouraged the wicked not to turn from his wicked way."** These women kept people walking with them on the path of rebellion against God's laws. They promoted immorality, when they could have used their influence to **preserve ... life**. Death would result—both for them and for those they influenced.

Verse 23. The announcement of God's judgment is given: **Therefore**, these women would no longer see false visions and no longer practice divination. God would take away their "tricks of the trade," and they would be helpless. Meanwhile, God planned to **deliver** His people from these ensnaring women. The powerful admonition **Thus you will know that I am the LORD** provided a lesson for these prophetesses, as it does for all others: When these events come to pass, remember that they came from God.

APPLICATION

Truth vs. False Hope

There is a difference between the true prophet of God and the false prophet. The false prophets were spreading a message that the people wanted to hear. They were more numerous than the true prophets, and they were giving the people hope (but a false hope). They were "foolish" and followed "their own spirit," "prophesying from their own inspiration." Their behavior among the people of God was like "foxes among the ruins." They would prophesy and "yet hope for the fulfillment of their word."

Contrast their characteristics with those of Ezekiel, who always spoke with a "thus says the Lord." He was not foolish but obedient. He was a watchman helping the nation of Israel, and he knew that what he said would come true.

Today, when we are examining a person and his teaching, we need to see if that teaching agrees with the Bible, and if the teacher's characteristics are those of a man like Ezekiel or of the false prophets. Jim McGuiggan said, "Self-made religion is vain (Matthew 15:9). Self-made religion is in conflict with God (Matthew 15:3, 6). Self-made religion will be rooted up (Matthew 7:24–27; 15:13)."[9]

Many religions have been built, but only the church that has Christ as its foundation will stand (1 Cor. 3:11; Eph. 2:20).

God condemns all witchcraft and sorcery: voodoo, séances, horoscopes, astrology, fortunetelling, and every other such practice. The child of God will not be involved in any of these.

D.P.

Preaching That Always Fails (13:1–7)

It can almost be said, "As goes the preaching, so goes the spirituality of a people." The house of Israel was in an awful shape, for the prophets within her, for the most part, had taught her to believe, think with, and practice error.

Even though we know that God will not allow us to blame what we have chosen to do on someone else, we frequently permit others to tell us what to do. In fact, the individual usually does what the many do. It is hard to go against the flow, and it is especially difficult to stand up against the will of the majority when it is misled or wrong. Smooth-talking, listener-friendly preachers or prophets easily persuaded Judah.

What kind of preaching brought on Judah's demise?

Uninspired preaching. Much of the preaching heard by Israel was preaching that was self-inspired or of human origin. They needed divinely inspired preaching, but they were listening to messages that had been invented by the prophets themselves. Ezekiel was told, "Son of man, prophesy against the prophets of Israel who prophesy . . . from their own inspiration. . . . Woe to the foolish prophets who are following their own spirit and have seen nothing" (vv. 2, 3). These prophets had no divine message because God had been silent to them.

Inadequate preaching. These false prophets had failed the people because they had not prepared them for the dark, hard days ahead. God said of them, ". . . nor did you [the false prophets] build the wall around the house of Israel to stand in the

---

[9]Jim McGuiggan, *The Book of Ezekiel,* Looking Into The Bible Series (Lubbock, Tex.: Montex Publishing Co., 1979), 135.

battle on the day of the LORD" (v. 5). It was a crucial time in Israel's history. The people needed to harden into a wall of spiritual conviction that would keep them strong as they approached the even rougher days that lay ahead of them. The preaching they had received put in them a time bomb that would go off when they needed God the most.

Cowardly preaching. God said, "O Israel, your prophets have been like foxes among ruins" (v. 4). In other words, He compared the false prophets to the field and wilderness foxes that would sneak in under the cover of darkness, gather up what they wanted, and then disappear into the night. The false prophets would get out of the people what they wanted from them; then, when the time of calamity came and the people needed them to show them the way, they were long gone. Their preaching served the prophet, not the people.

Uncommissioned preaching. These false prophets were missing divine credentials. The Holy Spirit was not in charge of what they were saying. God did not choose them, and He had not commissioned them. The Lord said of them, "They see falsehood and lying divination who are saying, 'The LORD declares,' when the LORD has not sent them; yet they hope for the fulfillment of their word" (v. 6). Their preaching was a human exercise which only had human wisdom and energy of the flesh.

Judah had failed because her prophets had failed. How differently the story might have read had they been faithful to God and to the nation! Tragedy came because they had not been God's men, giving God's message in God's way. They were self-seekers, devising their own pleasing platitudes for selfish and sinful reasons. They did not feed the flock; they fleeced it. They were prophets who preached for personal profit. They should have scorned the values of their world, lived by rigid discipline, and given God's divine message so that the people would know that God and God's men had been among them and would be with them in the crises that were in front of them.

Preaching That Has No Future (13:8–23)

The false prophets might have received some benefits here from their preaching. They preached for profit and remuneration, and they received some. They traded God and the truth for "handfuls of barley and fragments of bread." However, one day they had to give an account for the preaching that they had done, and what a day of accounting that was!

They faced the wrath of God. Instead of receiving God's congratulation, they received His condemnation. When the day of reckoning came, they found that they had been living under God's wrath and that His wrath was to be poured out upon them even more fully. False preaching misrepresents God and His truth, and it leads people into ruin. Why should it not receive the sternest sentence?

They faced the exposure of truth. They would also discover that the truth of God would expose what they had done in their preaching and what their preaching really was. What they said could not stand the test of the facts; the sunlight of God's righteousness revealed its shame, dishonor, and emptiness. They whitewashed the wall instead of repairing the wall. They painted the car instead of putting a new motor in it. They said "peace," when they should have prepared the people for war. God said of them, "Thus I will spend My wrath on the wall and on those who have plastered it over with whitewash" (v. 15a).

They faced the reality of a misspent life. On the day of the Lord, they were confronted with the tragedy of a wasted life. How devastating it would be to realize that you have thrown away the precious gift of life! They had lived in vain; their lives could be summarized with a zero. The greatest of all tragedies is that of giving time, talent, and treasures to the propagation of falsehood. The most useless thing anyone can do is to dedicate his life to error. False preaching cannot save, does not honor God, and is destined for humiliation.

Judgment comes for all, especially to teachers and preachers. James warned that a greater responsibility and judgment falls upon those who lead others (Jas. 3:1–4). No one can do anything greater than preach the truth; and the supreme tragedy of life is to preach what is not true for personal gain. At the end, the righteous preacher will hear the Lord's "Well done!" while the wicked prophet will hear "Depart from Me!"

E.C.

CHAPTER 14
CONSEQUENCES WILL COME

False prophets could not exist if they had no audiences. Sadly, Judah had given them their attention and their support. Ezekiel addressed the consequences of such actions. The elders and others who had sought these false prophets would have to take partial responsibility for the plight of the nation.

THE MESSAGE AGAINST THE ELDERS (14:1–11)

14:1–3
¹Then some elders of Israel came to me and sat down before me. ²And the word of the LORD came to me, saying, ³"Son of man, these men have set up their idols in their hearts and have put right before their faces the stumbling block of their iniquity. Should I be consulted by them at all?"

Verse 1. Some elders of Israel went to Ezekiel. As noted in 3:25–27, God had confined him to his house. Anyone who wanted to hear from the prophet had to go to his house. Here, as in 8:1, the elders went to Ezekiel. Perhaps they wanted to learn about the situation in Jerusalem. They received a scorching sermon instead!

Verses 2, 3. God told Ezekiel, **"These men have set up their idols in their hearts"**—an idiom which meant that they had set their minds upon idols. These elders were not guilty of literally worshiping idols. However, they had adopted beliefs and practices associated with idolatry. They may have placed value on divination and incantations. Perhaps they had adopted the idolatrous ways of the Babylonians. Regardless of the details, their hearts were corrupt. They failed to see that the problem with Jerusalem was **right before their faces**! These idolatrous beliefs had become a **stumbling block** leading them to sin. Therefore, they had made themselves unfit for divine truth (see 2 Thess. 2:10). Why, since their hearts were inclined toward wickedness, should God **be consulted by them at all?** They came to Ezekiel to inquire of the Lord and to receive counsel. God was asking, "Should I give it to them?" The answer to this question is clearly "Of course not!"

14:4, 5

⁴"Therefore speak to them and tell them, 'Thus says the Lord God, "Any man of the house of Israel who sets up his idols in his heart, puts right before his face the stumbling block of his iniquity, and then comes to the prophet, I the Lord will be brought to give him an answer in the matter in view of the multitude of his idols, ⁵in order to lay hold of the hearts of the house of Israel who are estranged from Me through all their idols."'"

Verse 4. The word **therefore** begins this verse, showing that a verdict was about to be issued. God would give them a message, but it would not be what they wanted. He told Ezekiel to **speak to them**. These elders, who were guilty of this heart-idolatry, were arrogant to come and seek a word from the prophet. By doing so, they gave the impression that they were genuine truth-seekers, sincere worshipers of Yahweh. Each of these leaders had set up **his idols in his heart**. They were not guilty of open, public idolatry; their idolatry was a heart problem. Nevertheless, they were there to inquire of the Lord. In today's world, there are people who "hesitate between two opinions" (see 1 Kings 18:21). They have one foot in the world and one foot in the church. When these people appear to be genuinely spiritual and interested in the things of God, they anger God. His words in verse 4 were not directed solely to the elders, but to **any man of the house of Israel** who would commit the same abomination. This sort of hypocrisy provokes God so that He personally is **brought to give him an answer**.

Verse 5. God desired to reclaim the hearts that had been lost to idolatry. As long as the people allowed the corruption of idolatry to dwell in their hearts—as long as they were devoted to idolatry—there would be no room for the truth of God.

14:6–8

⁶"Therefore say to the house of Israel, 'Thus says the Lord God, "Repent and turn away from your idols and turn your faces away from all your abominations. ⁷For anyone of the house of Israel or of the immigrants who stay in Israel who separates himself from Me, sets up his idols in his heart, puts right before his face the stumbling block of his iniquity, and then comes to the prophet to inquire of Me for himself, I the Lord will be brought to answer him in My own person. ⁸I will set My face against that man and make him a sign and a proverb, and I will cut him off from among My people. So you will know that I am the Lord."'"

Verse 6. Another **therefore** indicates that words of judgment were about to be issued. God called upon these idol-worshipers to do the following:

Repent. This was a call to go in a different direction. Their present course had led the nation to ruin and had jeopardized their own souls. The word here is not the typical Hebrew word for "repentance," נָחַם (*nacham*), meaning "to be sorry, moved to pity, suffer grief"¹; rather, it is the word שׁוּב (*shub*), which means to "turn back, return."² This was a call to come back, to return to God.

Turn away from your idols. Again using the word *shub*, Ezekiel specified that God wanted His people to desert their heart-idols.

Turn your faces away from all your abominations. They

---

¹Francis Brown, S. R. Driver, and Charles A. Briggs, *A Hebrew and English Lexicon of the Old Testament* (Oxford: Clarendon Press, 1972), 637.
²Ibid., 996–1000.

must make a conscious choice never again to give their attention to these idolatries and the abominations that were associated with them. If they were going to turn to the Lord, they needed to turn to Him with their whole hearts. Halfhearted religion angers God and is profitless to the worshiper.

Verse 7. The immigrants ("strangers that sojourn in Israel," RSV, ASV, see the KJV; or "aliens who reside in Israel," NRSV, see the NIV) were not Israelites, but they lived among the people of Israel. God expected these people to abstain from idolatry (Lev. 17:10; 20:2). God was emphasizing that the idolater puts his problem **right before his face** (see v. 4), and yet he cannot see what is causing him to stumble into a life of **iniquity**. These people, who in self-deception and arrogance presumed to inquire of God, were going to hear from God personally.

Verse 8. Three acts of God are listed with regard to the heart-idol-worshiper. He said, "I will . . ."

1. "**. . . make him a sign**"—an example and a warning (Deut. 28:46).[3]
2. "**. . . [make him] a proverb**"—a byword.
3. "**. . . cut him off from among My people**"—deserted and isolated, no longer a member of God's covenant family, with all of its blessings and privileges (see Gen. 17:14).

God's statement of these three punishments leads into a familiar refrain. He declared, **"So you will know that I am the Lord."** The repetition of this phrase reminds us that these people were woefully ignorant of God, His law, and His ways. This book contains many lessons that God would have to teach the people about Himself.

---

[3] "A warning, a lesson, as in Num 17:25 the sprouted staff of Aaron is to be preserved as 'a sign to rebels' of the election of the priestly line. The doom of the inquirer will serve as a warning for all who would force themselves on God" (Moshe Greenberg, *Ezekiel 1—20: A New Translation with Introduction and Commentary*, The Anchor Bible, vol. 22 [Garden City, N.Y.: Doubleday & Co., 1983], 250).

14:9–11

⁹"'"But if the prophet is prevailed upon to speak a word, it is I, the LORD, who have prevailed upon that prophet, and I will stretch out My hand against him and destroy him from among My people Israel. ¹⁰They will bear the punishment of their iniquity; as the iniquity of the inquirer is, so the iniquity of the prophet will be, ¹¹in order that the house of Israel may no longer stray from Me and no longer defile themselves with all their transgressions. Thus they will be My people, and I shall be their God,'" declares the Lord GOD."

Verse 9. I, the LORD, . . . have prevailed upon that prophet. This unique phrase has generated considerable discussion. It appears that God was giving additional evidence that a man was a false prophet. In the Law, God identified a false prophet either as one who predicted accurately but encouraged departure from the law of God (Deut. 13:1–5) or as one who predicted events that did not come true (Deut. 18:20).

Here, we see that a false prophet could be identified if he presumed to answer an inquirer who worshiped idols in his heart. In a way similar to what happened in 1 Kings 22:18–23, God "prevailed" upon that prophet to give an answer that was not from God. Thus a biblical truth is repeated: When a person is not genuinely seeking truth, God will allow him to believe a lie and will even contribute to the false evidences he uses to support his lie (see 2 Thess. 2:10). John B. Taylor explained,

> This does not mean that the prophet who acts wrongly is not a free agent and bears no responsibility. He is deceived because he has lost his spiritual perception. He fails to detect the insincerity of his inquirer and he works up some answer, as the false prophets of chapter 13 did, without a true divine inspiration.[4]

According to Moshe Greenberg, "prevailed" is a rather poor translation. He had this to say about the Hebrew word:

---

[4]John B. Taylor, *Ezekiel: An Introduction and Commentary*, Tyndale Old Testament Commentaries (Downers Grove, Ill.: Inter-Varsity Press, 1969), 127.

putta [פָּתָה, *pathah*]—to fall into error—see Jer 20:10, which Moffatt excellently renders, "perhaps he will make a slip"; the implied agency—temptation, sin—is here startlingly identified in the next clause as God.[5]

Other translations include "befooled,"[6] "enticed,"[7] "misled,"[8] and "deceived."[9] When such men decided to speak falsely, God allowed them to do so. These prophets were to be punished in the same way the inquirers would be punished: God would **stretch out** [His] **hand** and **destroy** them.

Verse 10. These individuals had free will—**the prophet** and **the inquirer** alike. Thus they would have to **bear the punishment of their iniquity**. Each one would bear the responsibility for his own rebellious decisions.

Verse 11. God was doing what He must **in order that the house of Israel may no longer stray** from Him. The word translated "stray" conveys the idea of a gradual departure. The Israelites had gradually adopted the idols of the foreign peoples in the Promised Land. God wanted them to stop **defil**[ing] **themselves** with their many sins. God is a holy God, and those who come before Him must be holy (1 Pet. 1:13–16). The desired result of God's actions is stated plainly: **"They will be My people, and I shall be their God."** This important phrase—repeated often in the Old Testament—describes the fundamental principle of the covenant. God could be their God and they could be His people only if they were faithful to His words (see Ex. 19:5, 6; Lev. 26:12; Jer. 7:23; 31:33; Ezek. 11:20).

---

[5]Greenberg, 250. His reference is to James Moffatt, *The Bible: A New Translation* (New York: Harper & Brothers, 1954), 848.

[6]Walther Zimmerli, *Ezekiel 1: A Commentary on the Book of the Prophet Ezekiel, Chapters 1—24*, trans. Ronald E. Clements, Hermeneia (Philadelphia: Fortress Press, 1979), 302.

[7]S. Fisch, *Ezekiel: Hebrew Text and English Translation with an Introduction and Commentary*, Soncino Books of the Bible (London: Soncino Press, 1950), 77.

[8]Greenberg, 247.

[9]Walther Eichrodt, *Ezekiel: A Commentary*, trans. Cosslett Quin, The Old Testament Library (Philadelphia: Westminster Press, 1970), 179.

TRUTH FOR TODAY COMMENTARY

GOD'S JUDGMENT ILLUSTRATED (14:12–23)

14:12–14

¹²Then the word of the LORD came to me saying, ¹³"Son of man, if a country sins against Me by committing unfaithfulness, and I stretch out My hand against it, destroy its supply of bread, send famine against it and cut off from it both man and beast, ¹⁴even though these three men, Noah, Daniel and Job were in its midst, by their own righteousness they could only deliver themselves," declares the Lord GOD.

Verses 12, 13. In 14:12–23, God clarified who would and would not be delivered and why. "Famine" was the *first of four illustrations* of God's punishment (v. 13). An entire country could be guilty of sinning against God by **committing unfaithfulness**. This unfaithfulness primarily took the form of idolatry—because the people were not faithful to the covenant promise they had made when they became God's children. Therefore, God would **stretch out [His] hand against** [the nation]. What does this phrase mean? First, God would **destroy its supply of bread**. When God stretches out His hand, He can cause the earth no longer to be productive. As our Creator, God knows our fundamental needs. Bread is one of those fundamentals. However, God does not guarantee even one's basic survival needs when His law is broken. Second, He would **send famine against it**. The ultimate of unproductive land is described. A famine can occur from a variety of causes—from the lack of rainfall, disease on the crops, or as a result of insects. Next, He would **cut off from** [the country] **both man and beast** ("kill its men and their animals"; NIV). The area would be so unproductive that no man or beast would survive there.

God specified the cause for such conditions: **"If a country sins against Me."** The Hebrew word here, חָטָא (*chata'*, "to miss or go wrong"), is strong. This country was dealing treacherously, acting wickedly against God and His word. (For another occurrence of this term, see Josh. 7:11.) Because of Israel's sin, she was deserving of God's full wrath.

Verse 14. Noah, Daniel and Job are mentioned. The righteousness or blamelessness of these men was legendary. (Consider this: If they were not real people, the point here would be futile.) The naming of Daniel is especially worthy of note, since he was a contemporary of Ezekiel. Daniel was in the palace in Babylon, and Ezekiel was with the common people. Thus all the people would be able to hear God's word. This reference verifies that Daniel was recognized in his own time and by his own people as a prophet of God. When Daniel spoke or wrote, the people would instantly accept his work as canonical and of equal merit with earlier writings. There is no truth to modern theories that Old Testament books, such as the writings of Daniel and Ezekiel, were composed over long periods of time and were not officially accepted until a century or two before Christ.

These three men are specifically mentioned to show that a righteous few will not prevent the destruction of the many. Noah, Daniel, and Job would **only deliver themselves** by their **own righteousness**. Their righteousness would not avail for others. The righteousness of Noah (Gen. 6:9; Heb. 11:7), Daniel (Dan. 6:4, 5, 22), and Job (Job 1:1, 8; 2:3) delivered each of them, respectively, out of danger; but they succeeded only in delivering themselves. Righteous men did not always change God's judgments against nations (see 22:30; Ps. 106:23).

The truth, then, is clear. When the majority of a nation is evil, God's judgment will come.

14:15, 16

¹⁵"If I were to cause wild beasts to pass through the land and they depopulated it, and it became desolate so that no one would pass through it because of the beasts, ¹⁶though these three men were in its midst, as I live," declares the Lord GOD, "they could not deliver either their sons or their daughters. They alone would be delivered, but the country would be desolate."

Verse 15. God gave a *second illustration*. He described the horrible effect that **wild beasts** would have upon **the land**. When uncontrolled, those beasts would leave the land **depopulated** (literally, "bereaved of its children"). Although the land might otherwise be desirable and productive, **no one would pass through it because of the beasts**. The Old Testament frequently mentions the problems and fears caused by wild beasts (see, for example, 2 Kings 17:24–26; Jer. 12:5; Ezek. 5:17).

Verse 16. Again there is a reference to the **three men** named in verse 14, saying, **"They alone would be delivered."** Perhaps the people of Ezekiel's day had "run too far" with the discussion between God and Abraham regarding Sodom. From Genesis 18:22–33, it might be presumed that a few righteous men, like Abraham or Lot (see 2 Pet. 2:7), could save a city from destruction. This hope is a vain one. Ezekiel clarified that if Noah, Daniel, and Job were in the midst of Israel, they could deliver only themselves. Even **their sons or their daughters** would not be delivered by their fathers' righteousness.

14:17, 18

¹⁷**"Or if I should bring a sword on that country and say, 'Let the sword pass through the country and cut off man and beast from it,' ¹⁸even though these three men were in its midst, as I live," declares the Lord God, "they could not deliver either their sons or their daughters, but they alone would be delivered."**

Verse 17. The *third illustration* is **the sword**. This act was one of man—not of nature, as in the first two illustrations. In ancient times the fear of foreign invasion robbed the people of peace. It was not unusual for enemy armies to destroy everything in their path—people, beasts, crops, and towns.

Verse 18. Again, **these three men** would be unable to save their own children. It is clear through these illustrations that God is in control of every situation. If He were not, how could He declare that Noah, Daniel, and Job would be spared? In the Old Testament God used enemy armies to punish His people (see Hab. 1). They brought "the sword" upon the people because of their sin. God promised blessings for faithfulness; but when the people were unfaithful, nothing was left for them except curses.

14:19, 20
[19]"Or if I should send a plague against that country and pour out My wrath in blood on it to cut off man and beast from it, [20]even though Noah, Daniel and Job were in its midst, as I live," declares the Lord GOD, "they could not deliver either their son or their daughter. They would deliver only themselves by their righteousness."

Verse 19. God moved to His *fourth illustration*: **a plague** ("pestilence"; KJV). The plague would bring about premature death (**in blood**), having the power to eliminate all life through disease.
Verse 20. For the last time, the three faithful men are mentioned. In the midst of the plague, these men **could not deliver either their son or their daughter**. The benefits God gives to the righteous are not transferable.

14:21–23
[21]For thus says the Lord GOD, "How much more when I send My four severe judgments against Jerusalem: sword, famine, wild beasts and plague to cut off man and beast from it! [22]Yet, behold, survivors will be left in it who will be brought out, both sons and daughters. Behold, they are going to come forth to you and you will see their conduct and actions; then you will be comforted for the calamity which I have brought against Jerusalem for everything which I have brought upon it. [23]Then they will comfort you when you see their conduct and actions, for you will know that I have not done in vain whatever I did to it," declares the Lord GOD.

Verse 21. God reviewed the dangers to His disobedient people: **sword, famine, wild beasts and plague.** Here we have Ezekiel's and Jeremiah's "triad of doom" (see Jer. 16:4), plus one—wild beasts. There is no way to escape God's judgment! God called these **My four severe judgments against Jerusalem**. Many tools are in the hand of God, available for His use in dispensing judgment and punishment upon the unfaithful. All of these could have been avoided by obedience.

Verses 22, 23. In spite of these horrors, God said, **"Yet, behold, survivors will be left"**! (v. 22). He added, **"You will see their conduct and actions"** (v. 23). These survivors were not righteous individuals but evil people preserved by God for the purpose of setting an example and teaching important spiritual lessons. Their "conduct and actions" (words that always have a bad sense) would be proof of the justice of God's punishment. In a strange way, their (the "survivors") evil actions (which provided a reason for divine judgment) would **comfort** the exiles (those already in Babylonia). How? They would assure the exiles that God's actions were justified. (**I have not done in vain whatever I did to it.**) The thought of an angry God punishing without cause would be unsettling and disturbing, but knowing the reasons why God does what He does provides a measure of "comfort," or consolation. This word in Hebrew (נָחַם, *nacham*) has the idea of calming, soothing, or bringing relaxation. These current exiles were not being comforted in God's punishment, but were finding comfort in seeing His justice meted out. A measure of peace is obtained when one sees the reasons why God does what He does (and agrees with it). According to Taylor, "It is with this very purpose in view that the unrighteous survivors of Jerusalem's overthrow were to be allowed to escape. Only then would the embittered exiles see the justice of it all."[10]

APPLICATION

Each Must Choose

When people separate themselves from God's truth, they get the kind of preaching and teaching they desire or choose (2 Tim. 4:2–4).

Those who refuse to submit to God's will are submitting to the will of sin or Satan, becoming "instruments of unrighteousness" (Rom. 6:13).

The righteousness of another person, even a family member, will not affect God's judgment upon us.

---

[10]Taylor, 130–31.

The anger of God is kindled against "fence straddlers." He would prefer that one be either hot or cold (Rev. 3:15, 16).

When God does something, He has a good reason (v. 23). While we may not understand God's reason for doing something, we must learn to trust His infinite wisdom.

D.P.

According to the Idols in One's Heart (14:1–14)

God answers people according to the idols in their hearts. What is in the heart produces one's words and deeds. How does God answer a person according to the idols in his heart?

Illustration 1: Balaam (Num. 21—25). Balak, the king of Moab, offered to reward Balaam if he would curse Israel. Balaam apparently wanted that reward more than he wanted to do God's will. God intervened, using teaching, warning, and providential obstruction. He even rebuked Balaam through his donkey! However, driven by the idol of his heart, Balaam would not listen. God would not allow the prophet to curse Israel, but eventually He turned him over to the god he had worshiped all along. Love for the false god in his heart brought Balaam's destruction.

Illustration 2: Judas. Judas was privileged to be among the apostles and live with Jesus; he ate with Jesus, prayed with Him, and listened as He preached. He was with Jesus daily. One might think that, in an environment like this, he could not be tempted to sin. However, there was a secret idol in Judas' heart—a love of money. Even in the glow of our Lord's spotless life, Judas would not turn loose of his idol. Eventually, God turned him over to the idol of his heart, and that cherished idol destroyed him.

Illustration 3: The acceptance of error. Second Thessalonians 2:1–10 is one of the most moving passages in the New Testament. It tells of a great apostasy that was to come (and now has come) upon the world. It is personified in the phrase "man of sin." This man of sin was to take his seat in the temple and insist that he be worshiped as God. How can we be sure not to be deceived by him? Paul said that the only means of escape from his grasp is to love the truth (v. 10). Anyone who does not love the truth is open to strong delusions and will believe a lie. If a person wants error, eventually God will give him over to it; God will allow him to be so overtaken by falsehood that he embraces it as truth.

Yes, God will answer people according to the idols of their hearts. Therefore, we should ask ourselves, "What do I have in my heart? Am I following the Lord sincerely, or do I have an idol hidden within me?" God will try to rid us of our idols. However, if we do not listen to Him, He will turn us over to them.

E.C.

A Tale of Two Prophets

In the Scriptures we have two major prophets in Babylonia who answered God's call:

Daniel prophesied before the kings of Babylonia and Persia, while reassuring the Jews that God is always in control.

Ezekiel preached repentance to captives, encouraging them to take responsibility for their sins. He dramatized the imminent destruction of Jerusalem.

Although they had different messages and modes of delivery, they both filled important roles. We, too, serve God in a variety of ways. Some people walk with kings, while others walk with paupers; but both groups can be invaluable assets to the kingdom of God. When God calls us to serve Him, will we be ready to respond with humility and obedience, no matter what the price?

T.P.W.

Chapter 15

Jerusalem: A Fruitless and Faithless People

The figure of a vine is a familiar one (Gen. 49:22; Jer. 2:21; Is. 5:1–7; Hos. 10:1; Jn. 15:1–5). Ezekiel used this parable to explain why the nation would fall. God had done everything necessary to make Jerusalem beautiful and productive. Instead, she turned to wickedness, making herself ugly and worthless.

THE PARABLE OF THE VINE (15)

15:1–3
¹**Then the word of the LORD came to me, saying,** ²**"Son of man, how is the wood of the vine better than any wood of a branch which is among the trees of the forest?** ³**Can wood be taken from it to make anything, or can men take a peg from it on which to hang any vessel?"**

Verses 1, 2. In the new oracle which marks this chapter, God asked Ezekiel a question from nature: **"How is the wood of the vine better than any wood . . . ?"** The answer reveals that value is found only in productivity.

Verse 3. The wood of the vine was worthless. It could not be used for woodworking because it was too soft, crooked, and weak. It could not even be used to make **a peg** from which to hang anything (see Is. 22:23, 25).

15:4, 5
⁴**"If it has been put into the fire for fuel, and the fire has consumed both of its ends and its middle part has been charred,**

is it then useful for anything? ⁵Behold, while it is intact, it is not made into anything. How much less, when the fire has consumed it and it is charred, can it still be made into anything!"

Verse 4. The vine wood was already worthless; yet, to further illustrate its worthlessness, God asked about its usefulness after being **consumed [on] both of its ends**. Even wood that is ideal for woodworking would not be used if it had been burned on both ends.

Verse 5. Even while the wood was **intact**, it was worthless. There was little possibility that it could be made into anything at first; now that it was **charred**, it certainly could not be used. S. Fisch said,

> The meaning of the parable is: Israel, numerically smaller than other peoples, is compared to a vine (Isa. v. 1ff) which has thinner branches than other trees. By failing to produce the spiritual fruits for which he is destined, Israel becomes comparable to the wild vine and is therefore only fit for the fire of Divine punishment. This process of judgment has already begun. Its *ends* are already consumed in the destruction of the Northern Kingdom and the Judean captivity in 597 B.C.E. [Before Common Era]. What remains, Jerusalem, is like the singed wood from which nothing can be made.
>
> ... When the whole branch is valueless, how can a fragment of it be of use! So, if the whole nation, consisting of the twelve tribes, failed in its purpose, what hope is there of the remnant in Jerusalem?[1]

15:6–8

⁶"**Therefore, thus says the Lord GOD, 'As the wood of the vine among the trees of the forest, which I have given to the fire**

---

[1] S. Fisch, *Ezekiel: Hebrew Text and English Translation with an Introduction and Commentary*, Soncino Books of the Bible (London: Soncino Press, 1950), 82.

for fuel, so have I given up the inhabitants of Jerusalem; ⁷and I set My face against them. Though they have come out of the fire, yet the fire will consume them. Then you will know that I am the LORD, when I set My face against them. ⁸Thus I will make the land desolate, because they have acted unfaithfully,'" declares the Lord GOD.

Verse 6. God provided the application to this parable. When a man throws wood into the fire, he has given up on that wood being of any use for construction, building, or fruit-bearing. Equally, God had given up on **the inhabitants of Jerusalem**. These people were intended to be a blessing to the people around them, bearing fruit for God by living lives in accordance to His law. This would have been highly productive for the name and glory of God. Instead, God's reputation was damaged by the worthlessness of the people of Jerusalem. Moshe Greenberg said,

> The figure of the vine aptly expressed several aspects of Israel's relation to its God. As the vinedresser lovingly cultivated his vineyard, expecting a good reward, so God cultivated and tended Israel, expecting its faithful obedience (Isa 5:1–7); as the vinedresser transplanted shoots into good soil, so God transplanted Israel from Egypt to Canaan (Ps 80:9). Israel was God's "beloved planting" (Isa 5:7). While this figure was used in eulogistic self-description in Israel's prayers ("Turn . . . and attend to this vine!" Ps 80:15), prophets turned it to polemical purpose: both Isaiah (5:1ff.) and Jeremiah (2:21) spoke of the disappointment of the divine vinedresser, whose labors yielded only bad grapes.[2]

Though God said, **"So have I given up,"** He did not want to give up on them. A vinedresser has hopes for the vine which he tends.

---

[2]Moshe Greenberg, *Ezekiel 1—20: A New Translation with Introduction and Commentary*, The Anchor Bible, vol. 22 (Garden City, N.Y.: Doubleday & Co., 1983), 268.

The language here seems to indicate that Jerusalem had already been thrown into the fire. When God decrees something, it is as good as done. When it became apparent that God's people would not be productive, the fire was the only logical alternative. John 15:6 says, "If anyone does not abide in Me, he is thrown away as a branch and dries up; and they gather them and cast them into the fire, and they are burned."

Verse 7. God **set** [His] **face against** the people of Judah. Before, His face had been turned *toward* them, as He cared for them, watched over them, and loved them. Their continued disobedience had brought about this rejection. The people had **come out of the fire**—perhaps referring to the two previous attacks by the Babylonians and the subsequent deportations in 606(5) B.C. and in 598(7) B.C. However, they would go into the fire one more time, and this time it would **consume them**. This occurred during the final attack and capture of Jerusalem in 587(6) B.C.

Verse 8. They have acted unfaithfully (see 14:13). In their wicked idolatry, the people had been unfaithful to their only true God.

APPLICATION

Being Fruitful

God wants us to be fruitful and faithful. (We cannot be one without the other.) Our lives should show the world who God is and the greatness of His name. If we are not being fruitful, either as individuals or in a corporate sense—that is, in the church—then God will bring upon us what He brought upon the Israelite nation: punishment.

We have all been given the necessary attributes to be fruitful. If we do not bear fruit for God, it is our own fault.

A faithless nation is a worthless nation.

D.P.

The Tragedy of Uselessness

God had cultivated Israel. He desired for Israel to be a productive vine, bringing forth fruit to God's glory. However, Israel had failed. She had become like charred wood, partially burned in a fire—useless. This parable of Israel's non-productivity brings before us the tragedy of uselessness. What happens when a nation or an individual degenerates into worthlessness?

God's purposes for that nation or individual are not fulfilled. When His plan is thwarted, His plan to save the individual or bless that nation is corrupted. The supreme calamity is for God's design for His people to be destroyed.

The individual or the nation descends in value. A person or nation who deviates from God's divine will falls in worth and productivity. By rejecting God's plan, we curse ourselves.

The judgment of God becomes necessary. The gardener must prune his vineyard to remove the dead branches; nature demands it. Even so, judgment must come to those who live outside of God's purpose. Eventually, God says, "I have set My face against them" (v. 7).

Worthless wood is a disappointment, but a worthless human being or nation is a tragedy. The soul, the spiritual being, is a terrible thing to waste!

E.C.

Chapter 16

Jerusalem:
An Unfaithful Wife

The story of Jerusalem in chapter 16 is fascinating—one filled with adventure and intrigue. Unfortunately, the story has few happy moments. The city was given every opportunity for happiness, but the people made terrible choices that turned the beautiful city of God into a worn-out, undesirable harlot. We cannot help but see the parallels of this story to the famous love story of Hosea. His relationship with his wife echoed that of the Lord and His people. A covenant was made, and the future looked bright. However, in the same way Hosea's wife turned to other lovers, the people gave their attention to the idols of foreign nations, which was an affront to their loving God. Hosea never stopped loving Gomer, and God never stopped loving Israel.

During this historical journey, a question frequently comes to mind: "What is the purpose of this passage?" God wanted the prophet to educate Jerusalem regarding her "abominations." Was she self-deceived? Probably. Did she consider herself safe within her city walls? Certainly. Through this powerful story, Ezekiel was to reveal to Jerusalem how wicked she was. Why was Jerusalem chosen for this extended illustration? Because she was the heart and soul of Israel. She was the chief city. As she went, so went the nation of Israel. (Notice how the exiles mourned for Jerusalem; Ps. 137:1–6.)

Upon close examination, we can see the lessons for us in this historical survey of Jerusalem: (1) The people were nothing before God adopted them; (2) His love for Jerusalem—that is, all of His people—was seen from the outset; (3) Israel's venture into adultery was not because of an absence of God's love, but because of her failure to control idolatrous desires; (4) her punishment was both needed and deserved; and (5) restoration was still available, for God was willing to forgive if she was willing to repent.

THE PARABLE OF THE UNFAITHFUL WIFE (16)

Jerusalem Adopted (16:1–7)

16:1–5

¹Then the word of the LORD came to me, saying, ²"Son of man, make known to Jerusalem her abominations ³and say, 'Thus says the Lord GOD to Jerusalem, "Your origin and your birth are from the land of the Canaanite, your father was an Amorite and your mother a Hittite. ⁴As for your birth, on the day you were born your navel cord was not cut, nor were you washed with water for cleansing; you were not rubbed with salt or even wrapped in cloths. ⁵No eye looked with pity on you to do any of these things for you, to have compassion on you. Rather you were thrown out into the open field, for you were abhorred on the day you were born."'"

Verses 1–3. Ezekiel received the command to **make known to Jerusalem . . .** (vv. 1, 2). Jerusalem, symbolic of the entire nation of Israel, was a worthless city when she began. Her origin and birth were **from the land of the Canaanite** (v. 3). This is true in at least two senses. First, she was a city in Canaanite territory. Second, her character was like that of her parents. The word "Canaan" became synonymous with idolatry and immorality. Canaan was known as "the land of the Amorites" (Ex. 23:23; Num. 21:31; Josh. 24:8; Judg. 10:8) and "the land of the Hittites" (Josh. 1:4; Judg. 1:26). The object here, though, is not to look for literal parentage, but to observe that God's people assimilated foreign influences to make her the kind of city she was. As far as idolatry was concerned, she was multicultural.

Benjamin Mazar combined the meager data on pre-Davidic Israelite contact with Jerusalem (including traditional data that Ezekiel may have known) as follows: In Joshua's time, Adonizedek, king of Jerusalem, headed an alliance of Amorite kingdoms in the south of the country (Josh. 10:1, 3, 4). After Joshua's death (in the second half of the thirteenth century B.C.), the city was razed and the Amorite element wiped out (Judg. 1:8–36). The Jebusites, apparently belonging to the Hittites and their satellites, migrated from the north during the first half of the twelfth century B.C., after the destruction of the Hittite empire. This is the background of Ezekiel 16:3.[1]

Verses 4, 5. From the perspective of the nations, Jerusalem was not a desired child. Notice the lack of care and attention given to her at her birth:

1. **Your navel cord was not cut** (v. 4).
2. **Nor were you washed with water** (v. 4). A newborn needs to be cleansed of blood and fluids.
3. **You were not rubbed with salt** (v. 4). Rubbing a newborn with salt was practiced for antiseptic reasons.[2]
4. **No eye looked with pity on you** (v. 5). She obviously was a struggling city, but no one cared enough to help. She was like a child no one wanted.
5. No one was willing **to have compassion on you** (v. 5). Seeing a child like this should evoke some feelings of

---

[1] See Benjamin Mazar, *The Mountain of the Lord: Excavating in Jerusalem* (Garden City, N.Y.: Doubleday & Co., 1975); and Arieh Shachar, *Jerusalem Through the Ages* (Jerusalem: Israel Exploration Society, 1968).

[2] "It was an ancient custom to rub a child at birth with salt to harden and strengthen its body. In connection with childbirth Dr. E. W. G. Masterman describes present-day custom in Palestine: As soon as the navel is cut, the midwife rubs the child all over with salt, water and oil, and tightly swathes it in clothes for seven days; at the end of that time she removes the dirty clothes, washes the child and anoints it, and then wraps it up again for seven days—and so until the fortieth day" (S. Fisch, *Ezekiel: Hebrew Text and English Translation with an Introduction and Commentary*, Soncino Books of the Bible [London: Soncino Press, 1950], 84). The student will note that this quotation is now over fifty years old. With modern medical advances, it is unlikely that women today continue this procedure.

sympathy, but Jerusalem received none.
6. **You were thrown out into the open field** (v. 5). Jerusalem was left alone, like an abandoned child.
7. **You were abhorred on the day you were born** (v. 5). Jerusalem was viewed as worthless. Not even her "parents" (foreign nations) cared for her. No people or nation claimed Jerusalem as "theirs."

16:6, 7

⁶""""When I passed by you and saw you squirming in your blood, I said to you while you were in your blood, 'Live!' Yes, I said to you while you were in your blood, 'Live!' ⁷I made you numerous like plants of the field. Then you grew up, became tall and reached the age for fine ornaments; your breasts were formed and your hair had grown. Yet you were naked and bare."""**

Verse 6. Like a sensitive traveler, the Lord passed by and saw Jerusalem **squirming in . . . blood**. She was sick, bleeding, and dying. The Almighty saw this struggling city and said, **"Live!"** The repetition emphasizes the basic truth: She would not have lived if God had not provided life. We read,

> The Lord saw Jerusalem in her ignoble condition and sent David, the newly anointed king over Israel (2 Sam 5:6–10), to rescue her from the Jebusites and her maltreatment. God determined Jerusalem's destiny when he found her and stressed that she would live![3]

Verse 7. The growth of the nation is described figuratively under the imagery of a girl developing to maturity. As the image continues, Israel is described as reaching **the age for fine ornaments**. This phrase literally means "ornament of ornaments" and is defined as the physical attributes of a beautifully

---

[3]Ralph H. Alexander, "Ezekiel," in *The Expositor's Bible Commentary*, ed. Frank E. Gaebelein (Grand Rapids, Mich.: Zondervan Publishing House, 1986), 6:811.

formed woman. She was obviously very beautiful, but she was still naked (defenseless).

God's Love Demonstrated (16:8–14)

16:8–12

⁸""""Then I passed by you and saw you, and behold, you were at the time for love; so I spread My skirt over you and covered your nakedness. I also swore to you and entered into a covenant with you so that you became Mine," declares the Lord GOD. ⁹"Then I bathed you with water, washed off your blood from you and anointed you with oil. ¹⁰I also clothed you with embroidered cloth and put sandals of porpoise skin on your feet; and I wrapped you with fine linen and covered you with silk. ¹¹I adorned you with ornaments, put bracelets on your hands and a necklace around your neck. ¹²I also put a ring in your nostril, earrings in your ears and a beautiful crown on your head."""

Verse 8. As if departing for a time and then returning, God once again **passed by** and took notice of the city. This time, she was **at the time for love**—a phrase meaning that she was ready for a mature relationship (see 23:17). The statement **I spread my skirt over you** alludes to a symbolic act in which the prospective husband would put the lower part of his robe over his bride, making a claim for her to be his wife. The spreading of the skirt had a second purpose: to cover her **nakedness.** While she had become beautiful and developed, she was still naked and dirty (defenseless).

God desired to make her His own, so He **swore** allegiance to her and **entered into a covenant** with her. John B. Taylor wrote,

> The reference in verse 8 to entering *into a covenant with you*, while being a legitimate expression for the marriage contract (*cf.* Pr. 2:17; Mal. 2:14), hints at the historical reality of which this story is but the allegory. It seems therefore quite permissible to historicize the description of this courtship and to see the covenant of

marriage as a reference to the Sinai covenant, the time at which Israel in the purpose of God had come of age as a nation.[4]

This covenant, like any marriage contract, was to be faithful and to provide the care and protection that a husband should provide for his wife. God did not actually enter into a covenant with the city but with the people of Israel; yet the story is based heavily upon the history of the city itself. In trying to equate historical events with this illustration, it seems best to envision the young, unattended girl as Israel in Egyptian bondage. Then, immediately preceding the ten plagues, God adopted Israel to be His people. The adoption occurred in Exodus 6:6, although verse 5 says that He "remembered [His] covenant." This would be the covenant that God had made with Abraham, Isaac, and Jacob. In a sense, when God first said, "Live!" He entered into the covenant. However, He did not directly act on that covenant until the deliverance of Israel from Egypt (see Gen. 15:8–18).

Verses 9–12. Once God had entered into this covenant, He immediately demonstrated His love and devotion. Thirteen actions are mentioned as examples of God's love. He said,

1. **"I bathed you with water"** (v. 9). She was finally given the bath a newborn baby would have normally received.
2. **"[I] washed off your blood"** (v. 9). This is not just cleaning off the blood left on the child from birth; the phrasing "your" blood implies blood from wounds received while left in the open.
3. **"[I] anointed you with oil"** (v. 9). She received the medical attention needed.
4. **"I also clothed you with embroidered cloth"** (v. 10). Multicolored cloth is often associated with a queen or a person of great wealth (Ps. 45:13, 14; Judg. 5:30).

---

[4]John B. Taylor, *Ezekiel: An Introduction and Commentary*, Tyndale Old Testament Commentaries (Downers Grove, Ill.: Inter-Varsity Press, 1969), 135–36.

5. **"[I] put sandals . . . on your feet"** (v. 10). These sandals were made of **porpoise skin**. The KJV has "badgers' skin," but this translation is incorrect. This was the same material used in the covering of the tabernacle (Num. 4:6–25; Ex. 26:14). Whether the skin was that of a seal-like animal, a goat, or a sheep is uncertain.
6. **"I wrapped you with fine linen"** (v. 10). The Hebrew word translated "linen" is שֵׁשׁ (*shesh*). This fabric, or possibly cotton, was probably used as headgear.
7. **"[I] covered you with silk"** (v. 10). The actual translation for this Hebrew word is unknown. If "silk" is correct, it is the first reference to such in ancient literature.[5]
8. **"I adorned you with ornaments"** (v. 11). (See 23:40; Is. 61:10.)
9. **"[I] put bracelets on your hands"** (v. 11). Bracelets, necklaces, and earrings were frequently overlaid with gold or silver, several strands thick.
10. **"[I put] a necklace around your neck"** (v. 11).
11. **"I also put a ring in your nostril"** (v. 12). A gold or silver ring would have been clipped to the nose.
12. **"[I put] earrings in your ears"** (v. 12).
13. **"[I put] a beautiful crown on your head"** (v. 12). This final piece of bridal jewelry complemented the bracelets and rings.

16:13, 14

[13]**"'Thus you were adorned with gold and silver, and your dress was of fine linen, silk and embroidered cloth. You ate fine flour, honey and oil; so you were exceedingly beautiful and advanced to royalty. [14]Then your fame went forth among the nations on account of your beauty, for it was perfect because of My splendor which I bestowed on you," declares the Lord God.'"**

---

[5]G. A. Cooke, *A Critical and Exegetical Commentary on the Book of Ezekiel*, International Critical Commentary (Edinburgh: T. & T. Clark, 1936), 164.

Verse 13. Having thus adorned His bride, God provided food and clothing reminiscent of prosperous times (see Deut. 32:13, 14; Hos. 2:8). He said, **"You ate fine flour, honey and oil...."** He gave Jerusalem everything needed for her to be a growing, thriving city.

Verse 14. As a result of the Lord's abundant blessings, Jerusalem achieved international fame. She was the **perfect** city. Nevertheless, it was clear that all she possessed—her wealth, beauty, and reputation—was solely because of the blessings bestowed upon her by God. As with the grace of the New Testament, these blessings were undeserved and unmerited.[6]

Her Rejection of God (16:15–34)

16:15–22

¹⁵"'"But you trusted in your beauty and played the harlot because of your fame, and you poured out your harlotries on every passer-by who might be willing. ¹⁶You took some of your clothes, made for yourself high places of various colors and played the harlot on them, which should never come about nor happen. ¹⁷You also took your beautiful jewels made of My gold and of My silver, which I had given you, and made for yourself male images that you might play the harlot with them. ¹⁸Then you took your embroidered cloth and covered them, and offered My oil and My incense before them. ¹⁹Also My bread which I gave you, fine flour, oil and honey with which I fed you, you would offer before them for a soothing aroma; so it happened," declares the Lord God. ²⁰"Moreover, you took your sons and daughters whom you had borne to Me and sacrificed them to idols to be devoured. Were your harlotries

---

[6]"The same truth is expressed by Old Testament writers in Deuteronomy 7:7f.; 9:4ff.; 32:10; Jeremiah 2:2; Hosea 9:10. It is also carried over into New Testament thought, as it represents perfectly the love and initiative of God in finding, saving and entering into covenant with people who would otherwise be doomed to die. Then, having made them His, He pours upon them every gift and blessing that earth or heaven affords (*cf.* Rom. 8:32; Eph. 2:3–8)" (Taylor, 137).

so small a matter? ²¹You slaughtered My children and offered them up to idols by causing them to pass through the fire. ²²Besides all your abominations and harlotries you did not remember the days of your youth, when you were naked and bare and squirming in your blood."'"

Verse 15. We are now inundated with forms of the word **harlot** (twenty-one times in vv. 15–41). Having no regard for the covenant promise with God, Jerusalem used her **beauty** and **fame** to attract **every passer-by** (foreign nation).

Verses 16–21. The gifts God had given to her were being used to contribute to her idolatrous ways. What an affront to God! He had given priceless gifts to the people of Jerusalem— as undeserving as they were—and they used them in this offensive way. Notice what the city did with God's gifts:

(1) **Took . . . clothes** (v. 16) to adorn the idolatrous high places and commit spiritual adultery (see 2 Kings 23:7). God said such acts **should never come about nor happen**. Having received God's instructions and warnings, we—like they—are without excuse for our sins (Acts 17:30, 31; Eph. 5:17; 1 Tim. 2:4).

(2) **Took . . . jewels** (v. 17) to make **male images** and worship these images. Since Jerusalem was portrayed as a "woman," her idolatry involved "male" gods.

(3) **Took . . . embroidered cloth** (v. 18) to decorate the idols. God had given such cloth to her as part of the "wedding ceremony" (vv. 9, 10). Now she was acting as if she were marrying another.

(4) **Offered . . . oil** (v. 18) to the idols. This is probably referring to perfume (see Ps. 23:5; Lk. 7:38, 46). Again, the contrast is between the sinful actions of Jerusalem and what God had done for her in verse 9.

(5) "**Offered**" **. . . incense** (v. 18). Some have taken this to mean the fragrance given by the perfume; others, to mean the burning of incense as an act of worship.

(6) Took **bread**—along with **fine flour, oil and honey** (v. 19). She took the choice foods provided by the Lord and offered them to her idols **for a soothing aroma**.

(7) Took . . . sons and daughters . . . and sacrificed them to idols to be devoured (v. 20a). This was the ultimate of her idolatrous ways. Becoming involved in human sacrifice, she slaughtered children who were born of the union of love between the Lord and Israel. Child sacrifice is well attested in the Old Testament (2 Kings 23:10; 2 Chron. 28:3; 33:6; Jer. 7:31; 19:5; Ezek. 20:31; 23:37) and clearly condemned in the law of God (Lev. 18:21; 20:2–5; Deut. 18:10). Perhaps these idolatrous worshipers considered the offering of their children as the ultimate act to demonstrate love and devotion. However, God considered justice, kindness, and a humble walk the greatest acts (Mic. 6:6–8).

After reviewing these activities, God asked, **"Were your harlotries so small a matter?"** (v. 20b). She failed to understand the significance and consequences of what she was doing. She willingly had her children "sacrificed," "devoured," and **slaughtered**. The process of child sacrifice varied, but **causing them to pass through the fire** (v. 21) could indicate either offering children alive on a burning altar or offering them ritualistically, then giving the bodies as burnt sacrifices. The ancients believed that the spirit, as it left the body, passed through the fire and was perfected as it passed through.

Verse 22. He next said, **"You did not remember the days of your youth."** Revealing an attitude of ingratitude, she had forgotten her terrible beginning, her near-death experiences, and her nakedness. Failure to "count your many blessings" leads to destruction.

16:23–29

[23]**"'Then it came about after all your wickedness ('Woe, woe to you!' declares the Lord GOD), [24]that you built yourself a shrine and made yourself a high place in every square. [25]You built yourself a high place at the top of every street and made your beauty abominable, and you spread your legs to every passer-by to multiply your harlotry. [26]You also played the harlot with the Egyptians, your lustful neighbors, and multiplied your harlotry to make Me angry. [27]Behold now, I have stretched out My hand against you and diminished your rations. And I**

delivered you up to the desire of those who hate you, the daughters of the Philistines, who are ashamed of your lewd conduct. ²⁸Moreover, you played the harlot with the Assyrians because you were not satisfied; you played the harlot with them and still were not satisfied. ²⁹You also multiplied your harlotry with the land of merchants, Chaldea, yet even with this you were not satisfied."'"

Verse 23. God declared, **"Woe, woe to you!"** He was issuing a warning: Jerusalem's involvement in idolatry must end, or else she would suffer severe consequences.

Verses 24, 25. The **shrine** most likely refers to rooftop shrines used for sacred prostitution or fertility rites—acts included in the idolatrous practices of the nations. Using graphic language, Ezekiel said that Jerusalem **spread** [her] **legs**—not just to a select group of lovers, but **to every passer-by**. Israel was completely absorbed in idolatrous practices. High places for idol worship were found throughout the land; they were **in every square** (v. 24) and under "every green tree" (6:13).

Verses 26-29. As an illustration of the extent of Jerusalem's idolatry, several nations are named—and she had "spread [her] legs" to entice all of them: **Egyptians** (v. 26), **Philistines** (v. 27), **Assyrians** (v. 28), and **Babylonians** (v. 29). Her involvement with these nations centered on two primary areas: religious and political. Jerusalem had adapted their gods and their beliefs. Further, she had made political alliances with them. These alliances were often condemned, and they never provided the security the nation had sought (Is. 20:5, 6; 30:1-5; 31:1; Hos. 7:11; 12:1). In chapter 17 Ezekiel specifically targeted a contemporary alliance between King Zedekiah and Egypt. This alliance proved fatal for the nation, bringing about her destruction in 587(6) B.C. By that time, Egypt could have done nothing to save Israel—even if she had wanted to. These alliances were an affront to God, who considered them a demonstration of Israel's lack of faith and confidence in Him.

Because of Israel's sins and their lack of faith, God said, **"I have stretched out My hand against you"** (v. 27). Using familiar terminology of judgment (see 25:7), God said He would punish them. (1) He said, "[I have] **diminished your rations.**" God began withholding the fruit of the earth, perhaps through the annexation of Israelite territory by enemy armies. (2) He declared, **"I delivered you up to . . . the Philistines."** The **hate** which the Philistines felt toward Israel is well documented in the books of the Old Testament. This wicked nation, however, was **ashamed** of what she saw in Israel. Her **lewd conduct** (beyond sensual desire—base, degraded, unnatural) even embarrassed the Philistines! Foreign nations saw her fickle, inconsistent conduct, jumping from one god to another. These pagan nations were more loyal to their gods than Israel was to the one true God.

The alliance with Egypt proved unfulfilling; therefore Israel deserted that nation and went to **the Assyrians** (v. 28; see 2 Kings 16:7, 8; Hos. 5:13; 8:9). When the Assyrians weakened, she sought out **Chaldea** (v. 29; see 2 Kings 20:12, 13), which is called **the land of merchants.** Chaldea was a highly productive land, with plenty of opportunity for business growth.

16:30–34

³⁰**"How languishing is your heart," declares the Lord God, "while you do all these things, the actions of a bold-faced harlot. ³¹When you built your shrine at the beginning of every street and made your high place in every square, in disdaining money, you were not like a harlot. ³²You adulteress wife, who takes strangers instead of her husband! ³³Men give gifts to all harlots, but you give your gifts to all your lovers to bribe them to come to you from every direction for your harlotries. ³⁴Thus you are different from those women in your harlotries, in that no one plays the harlot as you do, because you give money and no money is given you; thus you are different."**

Verses 30, 31. "How languishing is your heart," God lamented. His people were degenerate, morally weak, and hardhearted. The word translated "heart" is feminine here (the only place it is found in the feminine) in order to be linked with the adulterous woman, Jerusalem. Indeed, Israel's problem was a heart problem. While most harlots exercised some measure of privacy and discretion, Israel knew no such boundaries. She was **a bold-faced harlot**. She was so callous, insensitive, and depraved that she flaunted her harlotry without limits or restraints. She did not act this way for money. In fact, she **disdain**[ed] **money**. She was motivated by lust.

Verse 32. Herein is the real sadness. Israel was an adulterous **wife**. She had no interest in **her husband**—God, the One to whom she was still married and to whom she was supposed to be committed (see 23:5).

Verses 33, 34. Harlotry is normally a profitable business, as **men give gifts** (v. 33) to purchase the harlot's services. Jerusalem had "to bribe" other nations to enter into an alliance with her. She had to purchase their affections. Thus God said, **". . . no one plays the harlot as you do"** (v. 34). She knew no moral boundaries.

**God's Punishment
(16:35–59)**

16:35–37
*35***Therefore, O harlot, hear the word of the LORD.** *36***Thus says the Lord GOD, "Because your lewdness was poured out and your nakedness uncovered through your harlotries with your lovers and with all your detestable idols, and because of the blood of your sons which you gave to idols,** *37***therefore, behold, I will gather all your lovers with whom you took pleasure, even all those whom you loved and all those whom you hated. So I will gather them against you from every direction and expose your nakedness to them that they may see all your nakedness."**

Verse 35. Beginning with the dreaded **therefore**, God now issued His verdict and subsequent punishment. The fact that He used the vocative **O harlot** indicates that, at this point, she deserved to be called no other name; this one was the most accurate and descriptive. The next section is introduced by the phrase **hear the word of the LORD**. Walther Zimmerli pointed out that this phrase is used "in direct address," acting as "a summons to pay attention" (see 6:3; 13:2; 18:15; 21:3; 25:3; 34:7, 9; 36:1, 4; 37:4).[7]

Verse 36. God's judgment was not based on insufficient evidence. As if in a courtroom, the charges against Israel are given. He said,

1. **"Because your lewdness was poured out."** Israel was given to unbridled passion, without shame or discretion.
2. **"[Because] . . . your nakedness [was] uncovered through your harlotries with your lovers."** As a husband or a wife wants the assurance of a faithful mate, so God desired Israel's complete devotion. He did not want His people even to mention the names of other gods (see Ex. 23:13; Deut. 12:30; Josh. 23:7; Hos. 2:17; 13:4; Ps. 16:4).
3. **". . . and with all your detestable idols."** The thought of Israel bowing down to these "non-gods" was nauseating to the Lord.
4. **". . . because of the blood of your sons which you gave to idols."** The giving of these children to an idol was a grievous charge. Rather than follow the admonition of the *Shemah* (Deut. 6:4ff.), they gave their children to other gods by taking these innocent lives.

Verse 37. The verdict is given: Guilty! God would punish Israel using the nations to whom she had given her affection. Jerusalem had even taken **pleasure** with nations whom she **hated**. Those nations, as well, would participate in her deserved punishment. When God gathered them **from every direction**, they would surround her and **expose** [her] **nakedness**. Moshe Greenberg wrote,

> The public degradation of a harlot by exhibiting her naked is mentioned in Hos 2:12; Nahum 3:5; Jer 13:22, 26.

---

[7]Walther Zimmerli, *Ezekiel 1: A Commentary on the Book of the Prophet Ezekiel, Chapters 1—24*, trans. Ronald E. Clements, Hermeneia (Philadelphia: Fortress Press, 1979), 346.

A modified form appears in *Mishnah Sotah* 1.5, inflicted on a suspected adulteress before her trial (as here); the rationale expressed there—"She exposed herself for sin, God therefore exposes her"—fits our case, for this humiliation corresponds to the indictment of vs. 36a. Such uncovering of nakedness or turning back clothing is distinct from the stripping of the adulteress, which occurs after her conviction (vs. 39).[8]

16:38–41

38"Thus I will judge you like women who commit adultery or shed blood are judged; and I will bring on you the blood of wrath and jealousy. 39I will also give you into the hands of your lovers, and they will tear down your shrines, demolish your high places, strip you of your clothing, take away your jewels, and will leave you naked and bare. 40They will incite a crowd against you and they will stone you and cut you to pieces with their swords. 41They will burn your houses with fire and execute judgments on you in the sight of many women. Then I will stop you from playing the harlot, and you will also no longer pay your lovers."

Verse 38. In an ironic twist, the very nations with whom she had played the harlot would serve as her **judge**[s]. If she had been familiar with the law of God, she would have known that those **who commit adultery** or **shed blood** deserve death! Because of His mercy, God would not bring about the death of the nation; but His **wrath** and **jealousy** demanded justice.

Verses 39–41. When God gave her into the hands of her **lovers**, He said they would . . .

1. **". . . tear down your shrines"** (v. 39). Her places of cultic prostitution within the city would be destroyed.
2. **". . . demolish your high places"** (v. 39). The places of idol worship on every high hill would be destroyed.

---

[8]Moshe Greenberg, *Ezekiel 1—20: A New Translation with Introduction and Commentary*, The Anchor Bible, vol. 22 (Garden City, N.Y.: Doubleday & Co., 1983), 286.

3. "... strip you of your clothing, take away your jewels, and will leave you naked and bare" (v. 39). The ornaments, signs of a loving husband, would be removed. She would return to the pitiful state in which God had found her—naked and alone.
4. "... incite a crowd against you" (v. 40). A crowd of people, upon hearing of the abominations committed by her, would be filled with outrage. The word translated "crowd" is קָהָל (*qahal*)—an assembly ("company"; 27:27, 34), often an army (17:17; 38:4). Here it no doubt refers to Nebuchadnezzar's armies.
5. "... stone you" (v. 40). The crowd would take the only thing she had remaining—her life (see Lev. 20:10; Deut. 22:23, 24).
6. "... cut you to pieces" (v. 40). Out of total disdain for what she was, the crowd would dismember her corpse.
7. "... burn your houses with fire" (v. 41). The city— once so beautiful, desirable, prosperous, and secure— would be reduced to ashes (see 23:47; 2 Kings 25:8, 9).
8. "... execute judgments on you in the sight of many women" (v. 41). Other nations (see 5:8)—Judah's allies and rivals—would witness her punishment.

16:42, 43

⁴²"So I will calm My fury against you and My jealousy will depart from you, and I will be pacified and angry no more. ⁴³Because you have not remembered the days of your youth but have enraged Me by all these things, behold, I in turn will bring your conduct down on your own head," declares the Lord God, "so that you will not commit this lewdness on top of all your other abominations."

Verses 42, 43. Then God said, "**I will calm My fury against you.**" In terminology similar to the "spending of God's wrath," Ezekiel showed that His "fury" is calmed when justice is meted out. God could be **pacified** only by the shedding of Jerusalem's blood. Punishment had to come upon her **because** [she had]

not remembered the days of [her] youth. Her primary sin was forgetting what God had done for her.

16:44–46
⁴⁴"Behold, everyone who quotes proverbs will quote this proverb concerning you, saying, 'Like mother, like daughter.' ⁴⁵You are the daughter of your mother, who loathed her husband and children. You are also the sister of your sisters, who loathed their husbands and children. Your mother was a Hittite and your father an Amorite. ⁴⁶Now your older sister is Samaria, who lives north of you with her daughters; and your younger sister, who lives south of you, is Sodom with her daughters."

Beginning here, Ezekiel changed his allegory, although the link to the previous one is clear. Earlier, he had mentioned how Jerusalem was born of mixed parentage. Now, dealing specifically with Judah, he spoke of the same parents as in verse 3, this time including two "sisters"—Samaria (the older sister) and Sodom (the younger sister).

Verse 44. A number of **proverbs** are given in this book regarding sins that anger God (see 12:24–28; 18:2). Here we see an example: **Like mother, like daughter.** God acknowledged that the proverb is true—and that it could be rightly spoken of Judah.

Verses 45, 46. Judah's Hittite mother produced children **who loathed their husbands and children.** Both **Samaria**, to the north, and **Sodom**, to the south, were guilty of this sin. Exactly what they did is unknown. Perhaps they, like Judah, rejected their own gods for the gods of others. They may also have offered their children in sacrificial rites, as did Judah. Canaan was fertile ground for religious syncretism—accepting and incorporating all kinds of heathen, idolatrous practices and beliefs.

16:47, 48
⁴⁷"Yet you have not merely walked in their ways or done according to their abominations; but, as if that were too little, you acted more corruptly in all your conduct than they. ⁴⁸As I live," declares the Lord GOD**, "Sodom, your sister and her**

daughters have not done as you and your daughters have done."

Verses 47, 48. Judah not only imitated the heathen nations' false religions, but even exceeded them in acting **corruptly**. Samaria and Sodom were destroyed for their wickedness, and God said that Judah's wickedness was so great as to make these other nations look good by comparison. (Verse 52 says, ". . . you have made your sisters appear righteous"; RSV) God said to Jerusalem, **"Sodom, your sister and her daughters** [other cities of Judah] **have not done as you and your daughters have done."**

16:49–52
[49]"Behold, this was the guilt of your sister Sodom: she and her daughters had arrogance, abundant food and careless ease, but she did not help the poor and needy. [50]Thus they were haughty and committed abominations before Me. Therefore I removed them when I saw it. [51]Furthermore, Samaria did not commit half of your sins, for you have multiplied your abominations more than they. Thus you have made your sisters appear righteous by all your abominations which you have committed. [52]Also bear your disgrace in that you have made judgment favorable for your sisters. Because of your sins in which you acted more abominably than they, they are more in the right than you. Yes, be also ashamed and bear your disgrace, in that you made your sisters appear righteous."

Verses 49, 50. What sins did Judah imitate and then exceed? God enumerated the sins of Sodom, adding to our previous lists of why she was destroyed with fire from God:

- **Arrogance.** With her abundant blessings, Sodom became full of pride for what she had built and what she had accomplished.
- **Abundant food.** She had what others wished they had, with plentiful crops and flocks.
- **Careless ease.** She was idle, doing nothing to make the world a better place.

- **Not help[ing] the poor and needy.** The Scriptures attest to the prosperity of the cities of the plain. (They were "like the garden of the LORD"; Gen. 13:10.) God held prosperous nations accountable for their lack of compassion toward those in need (see Amos 1).
- **Haught[iness].** In her prosperity, Sodom felt superior to other cities and nations.
- **Committ[ing] abominations.** This was the home of sodomy (see Gen. 19:5; Lev. 18:22; 20:13).

Verse 51. In comparing Jerusalem to others, God said, **"Samaria did not commit half of your sins"** (see Jer. 3:11). Samaria was extremely wicked, yet her wickedness was far from that committed by Judah. God had given Judah blessings and guidance not available to other nations (see Deut. 5:1–21). Unfortunately, Judah committed the same transgressions the other nations did—sins against humanity—and then added violations against God's law given through Moses.

Verse 52. God said, in effect, "You ought to be ashamed of yourself!" Her despicable conduct had made **judgment favorable for** [her] **sisters**. The sisters were destroyed, but their devastating punishment was less than Judah deserved! According to Ralph H. Alexander,

> This passage stands as both an exhortation and a warning against such wickedness and life styles today. As evil as Sodom was, she did not begin to do evil like Jerusalem. (Jeremiah described how the prophets of Jerusalem committed adultery, lied, and encouraged evildoers so that none turned from their wickedness, just like Sodom [Jer 23:14; cf. 2 Kings 15:37; 16:6; 24:2; 2 Chron 28:18–19; Isa 3:9; Ezek 22:15].) If God removed Sodom in judgment, as he did, certainly Jerusalem would receive greater punishment (vv. 48, 50; Lam 4:6; cf. Matt 11:23–24).[9]

---

[9]Alexander, 817.

16:53–55

⁵³"Nevertheless, I will restore their captivity, the captivity of Sodom and her daughters, the captivity of Samaria and her daughters, and along with them your own captivity, ⁵⁴in order that you may bear your humiliation and feel ashamed for all that you have done when you become a consolation to them. ⁵⁵Your sisters, Sodom with her daughters and Samaria with her daughters, will return to their former state, and you with your daughters will also return to your former state."

Verses 53–55. Next, God promised equal treatment to Judah and her sisters. This was to Judah's shame. God said, "... **bear your humiliation and feel ashamed**" (v. 54). Jerusalem had used Sodom as an illustration of evil and corruption. Now Edom and Philistia would use Jerusalem as the example of depravity (v. 57)! Judah was **a consolation to them**: They could reason that, if God restored her, He must assuredly restore those who had sinned less.

The idea of "restoration" mentioned in verse 53 is explained in verse 55. God, who allowed those peoples to be carried into captivity (along with Judah) would allow them to return to their own lands. This suggests that God had intended for those nations to vanish from the earth—however, because of Judah, they would be allowed to return. Jeremiah also prophesied the restoration of Israel's neighbors (Jer. 12:14–17; 48:47; 49:6, 39). They went into captivity together, and they would come out together.

16:56–59

⁵⁶"As the name of your sister Sodom was not heard from your lips in your day of pride, ⁵⁷before your wickedness was uncovered, so now you have become the reproach of the daughters of Edom and of all who are around her, of the daughters of the Philistines—those surrounding you who despise you. ⁵⁸You have borne the penalty of your lewdness and abominations," the LORD declares. ⁵⁹For thus says the Lord GOD, "I will also do with you as you have done, you who have despised the oath by breaking the covenant."

Verses 56, 57. Jerusalem, filled with **pride**, felt superior to Sodom, her **sister** (v. 56). The wickedness and punishment of Sodom was a popular theme for the prophets (Amos 4:11; Is. 1:9, 10; 3:9; 13:19; Jer. 49:18; 50:40). Judah had looked upon Sodom's sin and assumed an attitude of superior righteousness. However, God pointed out that this was **before your wickedness was uncovered** (v. 57). The other nations—**Edom** to the south and **the Philistines** to the west—were amazed to learn the extent of Judah's wickedness. These nations were led to **despise** the people God had intended for them to honor.

Verse 58. Judah's sinfulness was the reason this punishment was being brought upon them. They must not be deceived into thinking that this judgment was for *any other* reason.

Verse 59. This decree from God was made in regard to His covenant with Israel (see Deut. 29:12, 14). They had despised it, so He would despise them. No covenant is one-sided; Israel broke faith, so God's promise of favor ceased.

God's Promise of Restoration (16:60–63)

⁶⁰"**Nevertheless, I will remember My covenant with you in the days of your youth, and I will establish an everlasting covenant with you. ⁶¹Then you will remember your ways and be ashamed when you receive your sisters, both your older and your younger; and I will give them to you as daughters, but not because of your covenant. ⁶²Thus I will establish My covenant with you, and you shall know that I am the Lord, ⁶³so that you may remember and be ashamed and never open your mouth anymore because of your humiliation, when I have forgiven you for all that you have done," the Lord God declares.**

The destruction of Jerusalem was unavoidable, but all was not lost. In this final section, Ezekiel looked beyond the destruction of the city and the exile of its people. God planned to forge a new relationship, based upon His compassion and forgiveness! Fisch wrote,

The Hebrew prophets never left their people in despair. The most vehement denunciation and the direst threats are followed by words of hope. Judah has been unmindful of, and faithless to, the covenant with God and must suffer the consequences; but He will remember and renew it for ever. Whatever may be in store for the nation in the near future, He will not completely repudiate them.[10]

Jeremiah, preaching during the same time, announced the coming of a new covenant (Jer. 31:31–34). The covenant in Ezekiel 16 was one God would "remember"; it was not newly conceived, but had been made in "the days of [Judah's] youth." Therefore, the promise *here* ought not to be equated with that in Jeremiah 31, which is referring to the covenant of Christ in the New Testament (see Heb. 8:8–13). Ezekiel 34 also speaks of that new covenant, but the promise made in 16:60 was fulfilled when the Captivity ended. At that time the people reestablished themselves in the Promised Land under the leadership of Ezra and Nehemiah.

Verse 60. I will remember My covenant. In Hebrew, the pronoun "I," though implied in the verb, appears after the verb, providing a double emphasis (as occurs again in v. 62). God said, in effect, "Whereas *you* have been disobedient, *I* will be faithful to My covenant. I will establish an everlasting covenant with you." This is not the usual phrase indicating a new covenant; rather, it refers to one that already existed but needed to be reestablished—the covenant God had made with Israel at Mount Sinai.

Verses 61, 62. "Then you will remember your ways and be ashamed," God said (see 20:43; 36:31). He had frequently warned Israel of the dangers of forgetting His covenant (Deut. 8:2–20; 16:12). In contrast, God always remembered this covenant (see Gen. 9:15–17; Ex. 2:24; 6:5; Lev. 26:42–45). Even though Jerusalem was more wicked than Samaria and Sodom, God would exalt her to a position superior to them. These cities are no longer

---

[10]Fisch, 98.

mentioned as **sisters**, but now as **daughters**. As "daughters," they would be subsections of the greater nation of Israel and under the jurisdiction of Jerusalem. God was not obligated by the law of Moses to make them daughters. This clearly demonstrated His mercy.[11]

"**But not because of your covenant,**" God emphasized. Israel was learning about the Lord's willingness to forgive (v. 61). Israel did not have the right to reestablish the broken covenant, but God was willing to mend the relationship. Fortunately for her, God showed mercy. The rejected Lord said, **"I will establish My covenant with you"** (v. 62). What a tremendous example of the nature of God!

Verse 63. He said, **"When I have forgiven you. . . ."** With God, forgiveness includes "remembering no more" (see Heb. 8:12; 10:17). Such would not be the case with Israel. God wanted them to remember so that they might **be ashamed**—shame is always a great motivator to improve one's morality. He also wanted them to remember so that they would **never open** [their] **mouth**[s] **anymore**. Judah had no basis to brag about her righteousness. She had nothing to say, for everyone now knew the truth: She was the epitome of wickedness! Taylor said,

> When God forgives our sins, He also forgets them (Is. 43:25). But the sinner can never completely forget: Paul remembered that he had persecuted the Church (I Cor. 15:9; I Tim. 1:13). . . . The value of such memory is that it keeps a man back from pride. Not even the justified sinner should forget that he has a past of which he is right to be ashamed.[12]

APPLICATION

God's Loving Admonitions

God's love for an unlovable Jerusalem parallels our state before Him because of our sin (Rom. 5:1–11).

---

[11] M. H. Woudstra, "The Everlasting Covenant in Ezekiel 16:59–63," *Calvin Theological Journal* 6 (April 1971): 22–48.
[12] Taylor, 142.

He had provided Jerusalem with all that she needed to be beautiful. He has also given us what we need (2 Pet. 1:3).

God warned Jerusalem of the evils of idolatry, yet she failed to listen and did that which "should never come about nor happen" (Ezek. 16:16). Likewise, He has told us how to live holy and godly lives. We are without excuse if we fail to heed His instructions (Acts 17:30, 31; Eph. 5:17; 1 Tim. 2:4).

There is a danger of forgetting God's blessings (Ezek. 16:22). Let us not forget God's gift through Christ (Jn. 3:16; Eph. 1:3).

The wise man said, "Watch over your heart with all diligence, for from it flow the springs of life" (Prov. 4:23). The Scriptures have much to say about the heart: It can be . . .

- Languishing (Ezek. 16:30; "weak"; KJV)
- Adulterous (Ezek. 6:9)
- Transplanted (Ezek. 18:31; 36:26)
- Broken (Acts 21:13; see Rom. 9:2)
- Burning (Lk. 24:32)
- Perfect (Ps. 101:2; KJV)
- Pure (Ps. 24:4; Mt. 5:8; 1 Tim. 1:5; 2 Tim. 2:22)
- Circumcised (Deut. 10:16; see Acts 7:51)
- Upright (2 Chron. 29:34; KJV)
- Loving (see Deut. 6:5)
- Right (2 Kings 10:15)
- Wicked (1 Sam. 17:28; Deut. 15:9; KJV)

Attributes such as wrath, anger, and jealousy are applied to God. As we learn about His character, we learn that these emotions are part of the divine makeup. However, we must understand that they are attributes of the perfect God. Therefore, there is room for "jealousy" in the proper context (Ezek. 16:38, 42).

God will never leave the sinner who is humbled because of his sins and demonstrates a penitent attitude. By His grace and power, God—through the blood of Jesus—will reconcile him to Himself (Rom. 5:1–11) and will continually wash away his sins (1 Jn. 1:7). This promise is contingent upon the person's obedience to the gospel.

D.P.

Chapter 17
National Disobedience

The story of Jerusalem in chapter 16 portrays the city's sordid past. Such historical reflection might have made the exiles wonder why they were reaping the fruits of their fathers' sins. In the next two chapters Ezekiel addressed such a mentality. In chapter 17, through the visual of a parable or riddle about two eagles, Ezekiel demonstrated how the current generation had failed to heed God's warnings against foreign alliances (which showed a lack of trust in God). In chapter 18 Ezekiel turned the discussion from national disobedience to individual disobedience.

In studying chapter 17, notice the emphasis on dualism: (1) two methods of storytelling, parable and riddle; (2) two eagles; (3) two plants; and (4) two actions of God: punishment and consolation.

THE PARABLE OF THE TWO EAGLES (17)

The Telling of the Parable (or Riddle) (17:1–10)

17:1–6
¹Now the word of the LORD came to me saying, ²"Son of man, propound a riddle and speak a parable to the house of Israel, ³saying, 'Thus says the Lord GOD, "A great eagle with great wings, long pinions and a full plumage of many colors came to Lebanon and took away the top of the cedar. ⁴He plucked off the topmost of its young twigs and brought it to a

land of merchants; he set it in a city of traders. ⁵He also took some of the seed of the land and planted it in fertile soil. He placed it beside abundant waters; he set it like a willow. ⁶Then it sprouted and became a low, spreading vine with its branches turned before him, but its roots remained under it. So it became a vine and yielded shoots and sent out branches."'"

Verses 1, 2. The prophet received the Lord's instruction to **propound a riddle and speak a parable.** A "riddle" (חִידָה, *chidah*) is obscure and requires an explanation. The word meaning "parable" (מָשָׁל, *mashal*) is also translated as "allegory" (see the NIV) or "proverb" (as in 18:2, 3). A "parable" lays ideas side by side in order to make a comparison and is therefore more easily understood. This type of writing is found in Proverbs in its use of parallelism. While the Hebrew words *mashal* and *chidah* sometimes occur together (Ps. 49:4; 78:2; Prov. 1:6), they are not synonymous. Therefore, two interpretations are to be seen in this chapter: the obvious parallels (the *mashal*) and a deeper, more obscure meaning (the *chidah*). In this case, the "riddle" would be the spiritual application to be made from the story.

In order to understand the riddle better, we should consider some pertinent historical information in 2 Kings 24:6–20 and 2 Chronicles 36:8–16, as well as Jeremiah 37; 52:1–7. These passages show that the kings of Judah were weak, both morally and politically. While God provided them ample guidance through the Law and through His prophets, the kings continued to violate His commands. They persisted in idolatrous practices and ignored the prophets, making foreign alliances which God condemned. These foreign alliances stand at the center of this chapter.

Verse 3. The first eagle mentioned was **a great eagle with great wings.** Nebuchadnezzar, the mighty king of Babylon, was comparable to the eagle, the king of birds. Another point of comparison was the tendency of this king, like the eagle, to swoop down on his prey. The plunderer of a nation is often described as an eagle-like creature (see Deut. 28:49; Is. 46:11; Jer. 48:40; Dan. 7:4; Hos. 8:1). The eagle in this parable flew to **Lebanon** or the land of Canaan (see Josh. 1:4; 2 Kings 14:9) **and took**

away the top of the cedar, which is Israel or the land of Israel.

Verse 4. The topmost of its young twigs is an allusion to the young king Jehoiachin (Jeconiah) and his princes, who were taken to Babylon by Nebuchadnezzar in 598(7) B.C. (see 2 Kings 24:10–15). Jehoiachin was the nineteenth king of Judah. Babylon was called "a land of merchants"; the city was famous for its strategic location for commerce, using both the Tigris and the Euphrates rivers. It was also connected with the Persian Gulf, thereby allowing commerce with India (see 16:29).

Verse 5. The seed of the land may be referring to Zedekiah (or Mattaniah; see 2 Kings 24:17; Jer. 37:1), the twentieth and final king of Judah. The eagle **planted** [this seed] **in fertile soil**. Thus the plant was located in the most promising site: a fertile field with **abundant waters** (see Deut. 8:7; 11:11; Jer. 51:13). Nebuchadnezzar gave Zedekiah every opportunity to prosper, as a tree planted in fertile soil near abundant waters can prosper. He set him upon the throne in Judah and provided the economical and military backing required for him to prosper. Nebuchadnezzar gave Zedekiah privileges and status as the newly installed king of Judah. He set him up **like a willow**.[1]

Verse 6. What should have been a beautiful willow tree became, instead, **a low, spreading vine**, but the vine prospered under the sustenance provided by Babylon. It is clear from verse 14 that Nebuchadnezzar intended to keep Judah in subjection by taking away the mighty of the land. Nevertheless, he provided support for the kingdom to prosper as a vassal state.

17:7, 8

⁷"'"But there was another great eagle with great wings and much plumage; and behold, this vine bent its roots toward him and sent out its branches toward him from the beds where it was planted, that he might water it. ⁸It was planted in good

---

[1]"It became (the figure changes) a spreading vine instead of a willow tree. It was planted as a 'willow tree' and not as an oak. The oak or the cedar would speak too clearly of strength and independence. A 'willow' tree (with its bending and stooping stature) expresses just what Nebuchadnezzar intended (v. 14)" (Jim McGuiggan, *The Book of Ezekiel*, Looking Into The Bible Series [Lubbock, Tex.: Montex Publishing Co., 1979], 178).

soil beside abundant waters, that it might yield branches and bear fruit and become a splendid vine."'"

Verse 7. **Another great eagle** is introduced. While this eagle is also called "great," it is otherwise described in less glorious terms than the first one. The second eagle is Pharaoh Hophra, the king of Egypt to whom Zedekiah appealed for help (**bent its roots toward him**), thereby violating his covenant with Babylon. Pharaoh himself later fell to Nebuchadnezzar (see Jer. 37:7; 44:30).

Verse 8. The vine **was planted in good soil**. Zedekiah, whose throne was safe and protected by Babylon, could have succeeded in strengthening his kingdom and securing the throne for his children. He had no need to look to Egypt for support. Like so many before him, he foolishly sought security in foreign alliances. Some see "planted" as meaning "transplanted"— although there is no indication historically that Hophra intended to relocate Zedekiah. Regardless, Pharaoh Hophra and Zedekiah formed an alliance that both considered profitable ("in good soil"). The stated purpose of this alliance was that it **might yield branches and bear fruit**. Why Zedekiah believed that he could be more fruitful under Hophra is a mystery. Historical records indicate that Babylon provided him with everything he needed. The only fundamental requirement was to be subservient to Babylon. The same would have been expected by Egypt, so no discernible advantage was to be gained.

17:9, 10

⁹"Say, 'Thus says the Lord God, "Will it thrive? Will he not pull up its roots and cut off its fruit, so that it withers—so that all its sprouting leaves wither? And neither by great strength nor by many people can it be raised from its roots again. ¹⁰Behold, though it is planted, will it thrive? Will it not completely wither as soon as the east wind strikes it—wither on the beds where it grew?"'"

Verse 9. The question is **Will he not pull up its roots . . . ?** The subject of the verb is the first eagle, Nebuchadnezzar. While

Nebuchadnezzar exhibited a degree of compassion toward the people of Judah by making this arrangement with Zedekiah, he would not tolerate anarchy. He would take action to eliminate any possible hope of growth, prosperity, and fruitfulness. Nebuchadnezzar's army removed Zedekiah from the throne and destroyed all of his rightful heirs. This vine would be raised **neither by great strength nor by many people**. Neither Zedekiah and his people nor Pharaoh and his army had the strength to save Judah from Nebuchadnezzar's anger. In fact, Nebuchadnezzar did not himself need to send a large army to dispatch Zedekiah and his kingdom.

Verse 10. When Hophra's help was needed the most, he did not come to Zedekiah's aid. Therefore, all of the opportunities given to Zedekiah (having been **planted**) were lost. He would **completely wither** under the pressure of the Chaldean forces.

The Interpretation of the Parable (or Riddle) (17:11–21)

17:11–15
¹¹**Moreover, the word of the Lord came to me, saying,** ¹²**"Say now to the rebellious house, 'Do you not know what these things mean?' Say, 'Behold, the king of Babylon came to Jerusalem, took its king and princes and brought them to him in Babylon.** ¹³**He took one of the royal family and made a covenant with him, putting him under oath. He also took away the mighty of the land,** ¹⁴**that the kingdom might be in subjection, not exalting itself, but keeping his covenant that it might continue.** ¹⁵**But he rebelled against him by sending his envoys to Egypt that they might give him horses and many troops. Will he succeed? Will he who does such things escape? Can he indeed break the covenant and escape?'"**

Verses 11–13. Verse 12 is reminiscent of chapter 2; God labeled Judah as a **rebellious house. The king** whom Nebuchadnezzar took to Babylon was Jehoiachin (the "top of the cedar"; v. 3; see Jer. 22:15, 23). Zedekiah, Jehoiachin's uncle, is the **one of the royal family** with whom he made a covenant (v. 13). Nebuchadnezzar was **putting him under oath**, an oath made in the name of God to secure Zedekiah's loyalty to Babylonian leadership (see 2 Chron. 36:13). **The mighty** or the influential leaders of Judah were also taken to Babylon as hostages to guarantee the observance of the terms of the treaty (see 2 Kings 24:15).

Verse 14. Nebuchadnezzar thought that Zedekiah would be happy for this opportunity and be faithful to the oath. However, the king recognized by the people was Jehoiachin, even though he was in exile in Babylon. Perhaps Zedekiah was trying to win the people's support when he "rebelled" against Nebuchadnezzar (in spite of the prosperity enjoyed because of Babylon's support). Nebuchadnezzar's policies were intended to allow the people relative happiness and yet keep the nation (1) **in subjection**, (2) **not exalting itself**, and (3) **keeping his covenant** (v. 14). In return for their doing these three things, Nebuchadnezzar would allow Judah to **continue**.

Verse 15. Zedekiah **rebelled** against the king of Babylon **by sending his envoys to Egypt that they might give him horses and many troops**. God asked, "Can he indeed break the covenant and escape?" Why was God so concerned about the breaking of a political promise made to Babylon? As is seen in verses 18 and 19, since the oath was made in His name, God considered Zedekiah's covenant with Nebuchadnezzar to be "My oath" and "My covenant." God declared, "He shall not escape" (17:18).

17:16–18

[16]"'As I live,' declares the Lord GOD, 'Surely in the country of the king who put him on the throne, whose oath he despised and whose covenant he broke, in Babylon he shall die. [17]Pharaoh with his mighty army and great company will not help him in the war, when they cast up ramps and build siege walls to cut off many lives. [18]Now he despised the oath by breaking the covenant, and behold, he pledged his allegiance, yet did all these things; he shall not escape.'"

Verse 16. God predicted that Zedekiah, who broke that **covenant**, would die in Babylon. Zedekiah had sworn an oath to Nebuchadnezzar, using the name of the Lord. By such a careless use of God's name, Zedekiah showed little regard for the name of the Lord or for the principles of His law (such as honesty and integrity). By this disregard he showed himself unworthy to be a leader of God's people.

Verse 17. Pharaoh [would] not help him in the war. Egypt had never been faithful to alliances—why should that change now? (See Is. 36:6; Ezek. 29:6, 7.) Both Isaiah (Is. 30:1, 2) and Jeremiah (Jer. 37:7) rigorously opposed this act of trust in Egypt.

Verse 18. The anger of God in the threefold repetition of Zedekiah's sins is shown here: (1) **He despised the oath;** (2) he broke **the covenant;** and (3) **he pledged his allegiance.** When Nebuchadnezzar was seeking verbal commitment from Zedekiah, he got it. Zedekiah promised the Babylonian king that he would fulfill all the stipulations of the covenant he signed.

17:19–21

¹⁹**Therefore, thus says the Lord GOD, "As I live, surely My oath which he despised and My covenant which he broke, I will inflict on his head. ²⁰I will spread My net over him, and he will be caught in My snare. Then I will bring him to Babylon and enter into judgment with him there regarding the unfaithful act which he has committed against Me. ²¹All the choice men in all his troops will fall by the sword, and the survivors will be scattered to every wind; and you will know that I, the LORD, have spoken."**

Verse 19. God said, **"My oath . . . he despised and My covenant . . . he broke."** God considered this contract to be *His* contract. The situation is similar to the covenant made with the Gibeonites in Joshua 9:3–15. The use of God's name in any earthly promise made that promise binding (2 Chron. 36:13). It seems that Nebuchadnezzar made Zedekiah swear this allegiance to him and this covenant by the Lord, knowing (suspecting) that such an action would secure his loyalty. Such was not the case; therefore, God was displeased.

Verses 20, 21. Since Egypt was of no help to Judah, the inevitable happened: The people were carried off into Babylonian exile. This was a **judgment** of God because of Zedekiah's **unfaithful act.** He went to Babylon, and all the remaining members of his kingdom—with his **choice men**—faced death by the Babylonian **sword**. Those who escaped that sword would be **scattered to every wind**. God had a goal, even in the midst of this judgment: **And you will know that I, the Lord, have spoken.** God wanted Zedekiah to know Him because of these events. Jeremiah had tried in vain to teach him this, so perhaps this action of God would teach him.

The Message of Hope (17:22–24)

²²Thus says the Lord God, "I will also take a sprig from the lofty top of the cedar and set it out; I will pluck from the topmost of its young twigs a tender one and I will plant it on a high and lofty mountain. ²³On the high mountain of Israel I will plant it, that it may bring forth boughs and bear fruit and become a stately cedar. And birds of every kind will nest under it; they will nest in the shade of its branches. ²⁴All the trees of the field will know that I am the Lord; I bring down the high tree, exalt the low tree, dry up the green tree and make the dry tree flourish. I am the Lord; I have spoken, and I will perform it."

Verses 22–24. Thus says the Lord God. Notice the repetition of the personal pronoun "I," as God declared in this third section what He would do. He said,

1. "I will also take a sprig from the lofty top of the cedar."
2. "[I will] set it out."
3. "I will pluck from the topmost of its young twigs a tender one."
4. "I will plant it on a high and lofty mountain."
5. "**On the high mountain of Israel I will plant it.**"
6. "**I bring down the high tree.**"
7. "[I will] **exalt the low tree.**"
8. "[I will] **dry up the green tree.**"
9. "[I will] **make the dry tree flourish.**"
10. "**I am the Lord;** ... **I will perform it.**"

God promised to take from the twigs "a tender one" and "plant it" in an exalted place in Israel. This tender twig would then grow to the extent that **birds** would nest under the shade of its healthy branches.

By the repetition of the personal pronoun in verses 22 through 24, God made clear that, while Nebuchadnezzar had carried the people to Babylon, the Lord Himself would restore them and return them to the holy land. This would not be the work of any human instrument, as Nebuchadnezzar had been His instrument earlier. When He did this, the people would "flourish" and prosper. Prosperity was promised not only for what God planted in the land, but also for **all the trees of the field**. These, presumably, represent other nations that were also to be blessed by the Lord—again, for the purpose of teaching them about Himself. Meanwhile, those nations who were strong and prosperous (portrayed as "the high tree" and "the green tree") would be brought down.

What is the meaning of this passage, and to whom does it apply? As identified in verse 1, this chapter is a parable and a riddle. Herein lies the difficulty in identifying one interpretation. There are two predominant views:

(1) The chapter may be a messianic prophecy—with Christ Himself being the young twig. Ralph H. Alexander interpreted this symbolism as follows:

> This cutting of the cedar was not from the first cutting made by Nebuchadnezzar in vv. 4, 12, for Jeremiah 22:28–30 declared that the physical line of Jehoiachin (Coniah) would not continue to sit on the Davidic throne. Rather, the line would continue through other descendants of David. This new cutting was, however, from the "cedar," the messianic line. It was the "tender one," a concept that had messianic implications (Isa 11:1; Jer 23:5–6; 33:14–16; Zech 3:8; 6:12–13). This was the Messiah whom God would establish as King over Israel in the messianic kingdom. The high and lofty mountain may have reference to Mount Zion and the temple complex (cf. 20:40; Ps 2:6; Mic 4:1), but this is only conjecture. This messianic

kingdom would be great and fruitful as a stately cedar tree (v. 23). All the birds would nest in its branches—perhaps a figure of the nations of the world (cf. Dan 4:17, 32, 34–37; Matt 13:31–32). All the trees (or nations according to the immediate context) would submit to the Messiah and his rule (v. 24). God had spoken, he would do it![2]

This view has the advantage of providing a vivid portrayal of the success the messianic kingdom (the church) would have as a worldwide kingdom. However, there are no references to this passage in the New Testament, which makes this interpretation, at best, a guess.

(2) The twig may be a reference to a leader at the time of the Jews' return to the Promised Land after the Exile—that is, Zerubbabel, Ezra, or Nehemiah. These men were established in the Promised Land, and their work flourished because of the Lord's blessings. This interpretation has the advantage of referring to the next historical event that literally took place in Israel. This was the meaning accepted by the rabbis.

In memorable language, God spoke of Judah's history of missed opportunities. While specific interpretations may vary, the basic truth is unmistakable: God's people would have to suffer the consequences of their disobedience. At the same time, they were given hope for a glorious future because of God's faithfulness to His promises.

APPLICATION

Trust and Trustworthiness (17:16)

Trust in God is a fundamental element in our relationship with Him. Judah did not trust God; therefore, the leaders sought foreign alliances for protection. We must believe in God and His Word, not leaning on our own understanding.

---

[2]Ralph H. Alexander, "Ezekiel," in *The Expositor's Bible Commentary*, ed. Frank E. Gaebelein (Grand Rapids, Mich.: Zondervan Publishing House, 1986), 6:822.

Whether in business dealings or in religious life, God expects us to be true to our promises and to be people of our word.

D.P.

Undeniable Facts

Judah had forgotten critical truths. If we ignore these facts, we, too, will face God's justice.

Man's confidence is judged by God's purpose (vv. 1–10). Man often places great confidence in his strength, wisdom, and abilities, forgetting God. However, God will judge such arrogance!

Man's strength is conquered by God's power (vv. 11–21). Man may view military might and empires as invincible. However, the greatest nation is easily conquered by God!

Man's rebellion is corrected by God's purpose (vv. 22–24). God has designed a plan to redeem mankind. His scheme of redemption will lead many to "know" the Lord. The wonderful truth is that no one has gone so far away from God that he cannot choose to return.

Amazing Grace! (17:22–24)

The prophet's words speak of the wonderful blessings that are offered by the almighty God. These blessings are available to all (see Tit. 2:11). These blessings are the result not of any personal virtues of those receiving them but are the free gifts of God's grace. This amazing grace is extended to people today (Eph. 2:8–9). Those who acknowledge God's grace will find wonderful blessings. Notice the following aspects of this grace.

God's grace is sovereign—"*I will take*" (v. 22a). The almighty God is the sole controller of this amazing grace. God decides the basis for one receiving the blessings of this grace.

God's grace is specific—"*I will set it*" (v. 22b). God does not say that His grace can be obtained in a general way. God's grace is specific. His grace is bestowed according to how the Almighty determines. People may wish that His grace be available in a number of different ways, but God says He has "set it" in the way He chooses.

God's grace is significant—"*I will plant it on a high mountain*" (v. 22c). God's grace was planned to have a worldwide impact.

So significant is the amazing grace of God that it is set on the highest peak so it will have the widest influence!

God's grace is solemn—"*I am the* LORD" (v. 24). The amazing grace of God cannot be lightly regarded. Those who fail to honor the offered grace offer God a great insult.

God's amazing grace is available to all people. We should rejoice in the fact that God has offered us His grace and do everything God commands so we will enjoy the blessings of God's amazing grace. In order to receive this grace one must understand God's will by hearing and studying His Word (Acts 8:30-1). When one understands God's Word, then action will be taken to "repent" of wrong living choices and turn to God's directions (Acts 3:19). This repentance leads one to "confess" that Jesus is the Christ, the Son of God (Rom. 10:9–10) and then to be immersed for the forgiveness of sins (Acts 22:16). By doing this, one finds salvation through faith by grace (Tit. 3:4–5).

J.L.K.

God's Alternate Plan (17:1–6)

Too often, people get God's second best because of their failures and rebellion. This is illustrated in 17:1–6.

God had an ideal plan for His people. He desired to lead them to victory in every battle and purpose. He had the highest and best plan for Israel.

Sin often destroys God's first choice for His people. Salvation is full and free, but God's greatest blessings are reserved for His faithful ones. God pleaded through His prophets for Israel to repent of their idolatry. They were deaf to His words of salvation, and God's patience ran out.

God's second choice is sometimes expensive. The Lord made Nebuchadnezzar His instrument of chastisement and permitted His people to be taken into captivity. This was a trying time for Israel.

We might view God as having three plans for our lives. The first is an ideal plan: He wants us to be faithful to Him and receive His highest blessings. If we spurn the Lord's will and give ourselves to sin, that plan for us cannot be fulfilled. Instead, God takes us into a secondary will, allowing us to give Him what we have left. If we begin to live for Him, we will receive wonderful blessings; but we cannot receive His highest and best. By throwing away our opportunity for the best, we have settled for second best. God's final will for us is His eternal will. What will happen to us in eternity depends upon our final decision regarding Him.

The Futility of Disobeying God

We see in this chapter the pain caused by disobedience to God. In what ways does rebellion hurt?

Disobedience hurts God. God's heart is broken when His people disobey Him. He knows the tragedy that lies before them. How a father hurts for his child who rebels and heads for ruin!

It hurts the rebellious one. Perhaps, as the fruits of disobedience begin to come, he sees how harmful disobedience has been to him.

It hurts others around him. Innocent children and others may be affected by a person's disobedience.

How God Works

Presented here are some of the ways in which God works.

God works through His people. He wanted to work through His nation, Israel, to show every nation divine love and providence.

God works through powerful rulers. When His people were badly in need of discipline, God turned to pagan rulers like Nebuchadnezzar.

God works through trying circumstances. He allowed suffering to come upon Israel to teach them the error of idolatry.

God works through grace. He tempers judgment with mercy. He extends His lovingkindness to remind us that we are saved by grace.

E.C.

Chapter 18
Individual Responsibility

Every generation has had to deal with the temptation to blame someone else. It is easy to engage in finger-pointing and transferring of guilt. Ezekiel had to deal with the "poor me" mentality of the exiles. They laid the blame for their national condition upon the evil kings and the leaders before them—mainly King Manasseh, whose sins provided the focal point of their argument (2 Kings 21:10–12; 24:3). He was considered the single reason for their exile. This gave the exiles an excuse for their plight, as well as reason to consider themselves free from personal guilt. They did not recognize or believe in personal responsibility and individual sin.

The attitude of the exiles reflected poorly upon the nature and justice of God. In their view, God was making a terrible mistake by punishing them for the sins of their fathers. You can practically hear their cries of "Life isn't fair!" and "We don't deserve this!" Righteous in their own eyes, they blamed their fathers for their plight. They even made a proverb to illustrate their philosophy: "The fathers have eaten sour grapes, and the children's teeth are set on edge" (v. 2; Jer. 31:29). Ezekiel boldly attacked this proverb. He intended to kill this saying, once and for all, by doing the following:

(1) Demonstrating that every individual will be held personally responsible for his own decisions in life—whether good or bad. The judgment given to an individual will not be impacted by the sins of others *or* the righteous deeds of others (even the closest of relatives). The one who does good will find blessings from God; the one who does evil will find punishment.

(2) Showing that the concept of "predestination" is false. Man's sin is not something he has inherited apart from his own actions. He is not evil or good because of inherited traits. Each person is completely free to make his or her own life choices. Anyone can choose to repent and turn to God or decide to abandon faith and practice unrighteousness.

(3) Proving that God's ultimate desire is the salvation of every soul. God calls each person, individually, to "repent and live." Therefore, rather than viewing God as unfair and unjust, Ezekiel showed God to be a loving and merciful Father who longs for His children to return to Him. If they choose not to return to Him, they will find a just God who will dispense judgment. If they choose to turn to Him, they will find forgiveness. The same truth applies today. One who turns to God by obeying the gospel of Christ will find love and forgiveness. It is a choice each person must make (Acts 2:37–41; Rom. 6:3–11; Gal. 3:26–28).

Ezekiel supported his primary thesis in verse 20, "The person who sins will die," by giving these examples:

- *The righteous father* will live because of his righteousness (vv. 5–9).
- *The unrighteous son* will die because of his unrighteousness (vv. 10–13).
- *The righteous grandson* will live because of his righteousness (vv. 14–20).
- *The unrighteous man* who decides to pursue righteousness will live because of his righteousness (vv. 21–23).
- *The righteous man* who decides to pursue wickedness will die because of his unrighteousness (vv. 24–29).

THE MESSAGE OF PERSONAL JUDGMENT (18)

The Declaration (18:1–4)

¹Then the word of the Lord came to me, saying, ²"What do you mean by using this proverb concerning the land of Israel, saying,

'The fathers eat the sour grapes,
But the children's teeth are set on edge'?

³As I live," declares the Lord GOD, "you are surely not going to use this proverb in Israel anymore. ⁴Behold, all souls are Mine; the soul of the father as well as the soul of the son is Mine. The soul who sins will die."

Verses 1, 2. Both Jeremiah and Ezekiel had to deal with the proverb **The fathers eat the sour grapes, but the children's teeth are set on edge.** In Jeremiah 31:29 the Hebrew verb (אָכַל, 'akal) is in the perfect mood ("have eaten"), but here in the imperfect: "the fathers eat." The proverb means "Should one generation pay for the sins of earlier generations?" The people held this false philosophy for basically four reasons:

(1) Exodus 20:5: ". . . I, the LORD your God, am a jealous God, visiting the iniquity of the fathers on the children, on the third and the fourth generations of those who hate Me." Sinful choices affect generations to come, but God never said that those future generations were not free to make their own moral choices. Ralph H. Alexander said,

> This principle of the Decalogue teaches that children would be affected by their father's sin. Parents model for their children. The sinful behavior of parents is readily followed by their children. Regrettably, therefore, children frequently found themselves practicing the same sinful acts as their father. Likewise, they must accept the same just punishment for such actions. However, each child is still individually responsible. He can abort the "sin-punishment-inheritance" progression at any time. But he must repent and do what is right.[1]

The Old Testament always taught individual accountability (see

---

[1] Ralph H. Alexander, "Ezekiel," in *The Expositor's Bible Commentary*, ed. Frank E. Gaebelein (Grand Rapids, Mich.: Zondervan Publishing House, 1986), 6:823.

Gen. 2:17; 4:7; Deut. 24:16; 2 Kings 14:6; Ezek. 3:16–21; 14:12–20; 33:1–20). Note what God said to Moses in this passage:

> On the next day Moses said to the people, "You yourselves have committed a great sin; and now I am going up to the LORD, perhaps I can make atonement for your sin." Then Moses returned to the LORD, and said, "Alas, this people has committed a great sin, and they have made a god of gold for themselves. But now, if You will, forgive their sin—and if not, please blot me out from Your book which You have written!" The LORD said to Moses, *"Whoever has sinned against Me, I will blot him out of My book. But go now, lead the people where I told you. Behold, My angel shall go before you; nevertheless in the day when I punish, I will punish them for their sin."* Then the LORD smote the people, because of what they did with the calf which Aaron had made (Ex. 32:30–35; emphasis added).

(2) The people assumed that they were now paying the price for Manasseh's sins. This belief was based on the words from the Lord in 2 Kings 21:11, 12, even though almost fifty years had passed since they were uttered.

(3) The people could point to Ezekiel's and Jeremiah's preaching. Both prophets identified the suffering of Judah as the natural result of continually rebelling against God's law, committing idolatry, and breaking the Mosaic covenant. Ezekiel spoke of God's wrath as being accumulated until His cup was full; He would now "spend" that wrath on them.

(4) Suffering, the death of many by the sword, and then exile fell upon the entire nation, which included the righteous as well as the unrighteous who deserved punishment. The people thought that, since God made the righteous suffer, the cause for the suffering was the sins of those before them.

Verse 3. God told the people, **"You are surely not going to use this proverb ... anymore."** The Law and the Prophets should have convinced them that this proverb was not true (see Jer. 31:29, 30; Deut. 24:16), but they heard only what they wanted to hear. Their proverb was false; it fostered a mistaken belief that one was not individually responsible for the things that happened to him.

At the same time, elements of truth are seen in the proverb:

- A person does not live in a vacuum.
- Things done yesterday will affect today, and decisions/actions today will affect tomorrow.
- Each generation must deal with decisions made by previous generations (national alliances and trade contracts, individual business dealings, and personal promises; see Ex. 34:7; Num. 14:18; Rom. 5:12–21).

Although the consequences for sin may affect future generations (Lam. 5:7), each person will be judged for his own deeds (Jer. 31:30).

Verse 4. "All souls are Mine," the Lord declared. God has created (and as a result owns) all people. He does not view them collectively, but individually. He will not allow the moral choices of one to dictate the moral choices of another; each person must choose for himself. Moshe Greenberg wrote,

> This sentence appears to take the form of a syllogism, but the meaning of the premises and their relation to the conclusion are not perfectly clear. The argument seems to say: Since I, as the dispenser of life, own everybody; since, therefore, I have an equal stake in fathers and sons (or: therefore fathers and sons are alike to me); hence sinners appear to me not as fathers or sons but simply as sinful individuals, and as such each takes the consequences only for his own conduct. This denies that any person is morally an extension of another; God does not "get at" a sinner through his son, nor does He impose punishment on the son as a "limb" of the father. The sinner, like everybody, is a discrete moral entity in God's sight; he is not a father or a son.[2]

---

[2]Moshe Greenberg, *Ezekiel 1—20: A New Translation with Introduction and Commentary*, The Anchor Bible, vol. 22 (Garden City, N.Y.: Doubleday & Co., 1983), 286.

The word "souls" is not referring to disembodied spirits. The Hebrew word translated "soul" (נֶפֶשׁ, *nepesh*) represented the totality of the person or the life-force within him. The word here is best understood as "lives" and should be so translated. Every person belongs to God, and every person will be individually accountable to Him (vv. 5–9).

The Five Examples (18:5–29)

In verses 5 through 18, Ezekiel used examples to cover every conceivable scenario. By going through three generations, he demonstrated his primary thesis: "The person who sins shall die" (v. 20). It is noteworthy that these three generations perfectly describe three kings of the seventh century: Hezekiah, his son Manasseh, and Manasseh's grandson Josiah.

The Righteous Father (18:5–9)

⁵"But if a man is righteous and practices justice and righteousness, ⁶and does not eat at the mountain shrines or lift up his eyes to the idols of the house of Israel, or defile his neighbor's wife or approach a woman during her menstrual period—⁷if a man does not oppress anyone, but restores to the debtor his pledge, does not commit robbery, but gives his bread to the hungry and covers the naked with clothing, ⁸if he does not lend money on interest or take increase, if he keeps his hand from iniquity and executes true justice between man and man, ⁹if he walks in My statutes and My ordinances so as to deal faithfully—he is righteous and will surely live," declares the Lord God.

Verses 5–9. The character of the righteous father was defined first, according to his deeds:

(1) He practices **justice** (v. 5). Demonstrating a spirit of impartiality was essential in God's law (Lev. 19:15, 16, 35, 36; Deut. 25:13–16).

(2) He practices **righteousness** (v. 5). Righteousness is something that can be practiced; indeed, it is required of man by God.

For Judah, this involved obeying all of God's laws, statutes, and ordinances—neglecting nothing that He asked them to do, and doing nothing that He asked them to avoid. When a person did sin, he dealt with it according to the sacrificial laws of the Old Testament.

(3) He **restores to the debtor his pledge** (v. 7). This phrase refers to being a fair and merciful creditor (see Ex. 22:26). The righteous man today may find himself the borrower rather than the one who loans (indicating that being righteous does not mean he is without financial needs). He is true to his word. Whatever he borrows, he repays. If he borrows goods, he returns them in good condition. To do otherwise would fulfill neither the law of love nor the pledge of the righteous man.

(4) He **gives . . . bread to the hungry** (v. 7). If others are "hungry," a godly person is moved with compassion to help them. He is not righteous in word only, saying, "Be warmed and be filled" (see Jas. 2:14–17). When he sees a need, he will do something about it.

(5) He **covers the naked with clothing** (v. 7). The man interested in fulfilling every part of God's law takes special interest in the plight of others, making sure they have the necessities of life—such as adequate clothing (Deut. 15:11; 24:19–22).

(6) He **executes true justice** (v. 8). His fair treatment is genuinely fair; he does not pretend that he has been fair when, in fact, he has not been.

(7) He **walks in My statutes** (v. 9). He believes that God's law is true and right, and therefore commits his life to obedience. The word translated "statutes" (חֻקּוֹת, *chuqqoth*) refers to decrees or enactments by a king "for which no reason is given."[3]

(8) He "walks in" . . . **My ordinances** (v. 9). The word used here (מִשְׁפָּטִים, *mishpatim*) is generally connected with God's covenant law. He has chosen to walk in the path prescribed by God, following His direction in marriage, business dealings, and treatment of friends and neighbors. This word also involved instructions concerning the Jewish feasts and festivals. In all matters,

---

[3]Norman H. Snaith, *Leviticus and Numbers,* The Century Bible (Greenwood, S.C.: Attic Press, 1967), 132.

the righteous person does what God has commanded and avoids what He has forbidden.

Second, the character of righteousness was defined in terms of deeds avoided by the righteous man:

(1) He does not **eat at the mountain shrines** (v. 6). The high places so frequently mentioned in the Old Testament were often located on mountaintops. Worship at these shrines involved bowing down to idols, along with sacred rites that included a sacrificial meal.

(2) He does not **lift up his eyes to ... idols** (v. 6). He did not engage in the worship and entreaties ("lifting up the eyes for help") of pagan idols. This was condemned in Deuteronomy 12:2–4.

(3) He does not **defile his neighbor's wife** (v. 6). Respecting the sanctity of God's moral law, he did not have or desire to have sexual relations with the wife of another man (Ex. 20:14; Lev. 20:10; Deut. 22:22). He practiced the command to "love your neighbor as yourself" (Lev. 19:8).

(4) He does not **approach a woman during her menstrual period** (v. 6). Having sexual relations with a woman during her menstrual period was forbidden in the law of Moses (Lev. 15:24; 18:19; 20:18).

(5) He does not **oppress anyone** (v. 7). Oppression can occur in many forms, including physical mistreatment, extortion, intimidation, or threats. The wealthy often took advantage of those without wealth, such as the widows, orphans, and strangers (see Ex. 22:26, 27; Deut. 24:6; Amos 2:8).

(6) He does not **commit robbery** (v. 7). Stealing was forbidden in the Ten Commandments (Ex. 20:15; Lev. 19:13). Theft could occur in a number of different ways, from the overt taking of another man's goods or property to the misrepresentation of the value of something.

(7) He does not **lend money on interest or take increase** (v. 8; see Ex. 22:25; Lev. 25:35–37; Deut. 23:19, 20; Ps. 15:5). Both ideas indicate ways of receiving interest on loans. The first refers to loaning money as long as the borrower promises to pay back the principal with interest. The second seems to refer to accepting additional payments offered voluntarily by the

debtor (once the debt had been repaid). God's law established a fundamental principle related to the covenant people: love. It was considered an abuse of that love when one took advantage of his brother (who obviously was in need, since he was borrowing) by charging him interest—thereby increasing his poverty.

(8) He does not commit **iniquity** (v. 8). He did not associate with those who engaged in sinful activities, nor did he wander from the standard of God's law.

Verse 9 provides the summary of the first man. When he lives according to the divine standard, God—to whom all belong—declares him **righteous**. Being righteous, he shall **live** (see Lev. 18:1–5); and, being faithful to God's Word, he will enjoy all the blessings promised to the righteous man (see Deut. 11; 26:16–19; 30:15–20).

The Unrighteous Son (18:10–13)

> [10]**"Then he may have a violent son who sheds blood and who does any of these things to a brother** [11]**(though he himself did not do any of these things), that is, he even eats at the mountain shrines, and defiles his neighbor's wife,** [12]**oppresses the poor and needy, commits robbery, does not restore a pledge, but lifts up his eyes to the idols and commits abomination,** [13]**he lends money on interest and takes increase; will he live? He will not live! He has committed all these abominations, he will surely be put to death; his blood will be on his own head."**

Verses 10–13. Despite the good environment in which the son in verse 10 was reared, he exercised his own free will and went in a much different direction than did his father. This shows that even righteous parents can have unrighteous children. Jim McGuiggan wrote,

> This very passage makes it clear that a man may be righteous before God (and surely God wouldn't call him righteous and just and true if he made no attempt to bring up his child in the way of the Lord!) and have a child

who is an abomination. "Train up a child in the way that he should go and when he is old he will not depart from it." That's not intended to be an iron clad rule for it would work both ways and those trained in sin and debauchery would never be converted. No one would argue that the scripture cited would be the general rule; but no one with sense would deny the clear teaching of this section of Ezekiel.

We can't forever cast suspicion on the godly parents of wicked kids and inwardly hold them responsible. A child can have the greatest father possible and still become a rebel. I *know* that's right for *Adam* had the best possible Father and he went wrong.... ENVIRONMENT, GOOD OR BAD, IS NOT OMNIPOTENT![4]

Note how, in every way, the son described here is the opposite of the father: (1) The father fulfilled the letter and spirit of the Law as set forth in Exodus 20:3–6, while the son openly defied the Law. (2) The father was faithful to his marriage vows, as commanded in Exodus 20:14, while the son was not. (3) The father respected God's moral code for purity (Lev. 15:19–30), but the son did not respect those laws. (4) The father shunned sinful acts and practiced righteous acts (Ex. 22:25–27; Lev. 25:17, 35–37; Deut. 15:7–11), while the son was swift to do evil.

Therefore, verse 13b asks, **"Will [the son] live?"** Should such a wicked man escape punishment because of the righteousness of his father? The question assumes a no answer. That answer is obvious. Righteousness is not transferable.

The Righteous Grandson (18:14–20)

18:14–18
¹⁴"Now behold, he has a son who has observed all his father's sins which he committed, and observing does not do likewise. ¹⁵He does not eat at the mountain shrines or lift up

---

[4]Jim McGuiggan, *The Book of Ezekiel*, Looking Into The Bible Series (Lubbock, Tex.: Montex Publishing Co., 1979), 189.

his eyes to the idols of the house of Israel, or defile his neighbor's wife, ¹⁶or oppress anyone, or retain a pledge, or commit robbery, but he gives his bread to the hungry and covers the naked with clothing, ¹⁷he keeps his hand from the poor, does not take interest or increase, but executes My ordinances, and walks in My statutes; he will not die for his father's iniquity, he will surely live. ¹⁸As for his father, because he practiced extortion, robbed his brother and did what was not good among his people, behold, he will die for his iniquity."

Verses 14–16. Ezekiel said that this son **observed all his father's sins**, making the decision to act differently. He was not tied to the character of his father. He was not compelled, separate from his own free will, to make the same decisions his father had made; nor was he compelled to follow his righteous grandfather. Neither the righteousness of the one nor the wickedness of the other determined his character. He made a choice to develop the characteristics of righteousness listed earlier.

Verses 17, 18. The verdict for this man of the third generation was **he will surely live** (v. 17). The Hebrew word order here is emphatic. Could the wickedness of the father be imputed to the son? No! This refutes the doctrine of original sin, which says that babies inherit sin and need to be baptized.

18:19, 20

¹⁹"Yet you say, 'Why should the son not bear the punishment for the father's iniquity?' When the son has practiced justice and righteousness and has observed all My statutes and done them, he shall surely live. ²⁰**The person who sins will die. The son will not bear the punishment for the father's iniquity, nor will the father bear the punishment for the son's iniquity; the righteousness of the righteous will be upon himself, and the wickedness of the wicked will be upon himself."**

Verse 19. Yet you say begins this verse, and the first objection is given: **Why should the son not bear the punishment for the father's iniquity?** The belief that the innocent son is punished for the sin of his father was stated and refuted by the prophet. The people, believing that a son is tied to the father, assumed that he should also share the father's "punishment."

Verse 20. The fundamental principle of how God deals with man is stated here. The son, Ezekiel argued, is not affected by the evil deeds of his father. This eliminates the false doctrine of inherited sin. Only **the person who sins will die.** There is no need, nor is there any biblical teaching, for infants to be baptized for the forgiveness of sin. A child has no sin and therefore has no need for the forgiveness that baptism provides (Acts 2:38; 22:16; 1 Pet. 3:21; Mk. 16:15, 16; Mt. 28:18–20). This is why every biblical example of conversion involves adults who were capable of believing, repenting, and making a conscious choice to be baptized. An infant, who has no sin, is incapable of believing or repenting. Babies cannot make the mental choice to declare Jesus as Lord and to be immersed in the waters of baptism.

Further, the doctrine of unconditional election is proven false by these verses. If God predetermined one's eternal destiny, then the discussion in these verses would be a waste of time. Ezekiel showed that the person who sins will die, while the righteous person will live. If such choices were scripted for them by God, without their being able to decide on either course, then this entire chapter would be unnecessary. Note that **the righteousness** of the one is **upon himself, and the wickedness** of the other is **upon himself.** This phraseology means that an individual brings judgment upon himself by the choices he makes in life.

God desires for everyone to be saved (18:23, 32). If He desires salvation for all, then, according to Calvinistic logic, all should be saved. However, God created mankind as free moral agents. Each person, on the Day of Judgment, will be judged solely upon his or her life choices (Eccles. 12:13, 14; Rom. 2:6; 2 Cor. 5:10; Rev. 20:11–15).

The Unrighteous Man (18:21–23)

21"But if the wicked man turns from all his sins which he has committed and observes all My statutes and practices

justice and righteousness, he shall surely live; he shall not die. ²²All his transgressions which he has committed will not be remembered against him; because of his righteousness which he has practiced, he will live. ²³Do I have any pleasure in the death of the wicked," declares the Lord God, "rather than that he should turn from his ways and live?"

The doctrine of personal accountability is supported by biblical teaching on repentance. No individual is punished for his own sin after he has repented. Why, then, should he be penalized for the sins of another?

Verse 21. The penitent **turns from all his sins . . . and practices justice**. Genuine repentance involves two parts: to stop doing what is wrong and to start doing what is right. The man described here turned from his sinful activities and observed what God's law requires. S. Fisch said,

> The two stages of genuine repentance are defined: turning away from a sin committed and loyal obedience to the will of God. The essential elements of penitence, as taught in the Torah and by the Rabbis, are regret for past sins and a determination to avoid them in the future: remorse and amendment.[5]

As a result of his making this change in his life, God declared, **"He shall surely live; he shall not die."** This man's course was not preordained; he decided, after living a life of sinful rebellion, to change. It was totally his choice.

Verse 22. As the judge of the universe, God declared that **all** of the **transgressions** committed before repentance **will not be remembered**. God's law stated that even *one* violation of law brought death (see Mt. 5:19; Rom. 3:23; Gal. 5:3; Jas. 2:10). Therefore, the transgressor deserves to die. However, in a show of grace and mercy in the Old Testament, God decreed that He would forget those past sins. He can wash the sinner clean,

---

[5]S. Fisch, *Ezekiel: Hebrew Text and English Translation with an Introduction and Commentary*, Soncino Books of the Bible (London: Soncino Press, 1950), 112.

making him white as snow (see Is. 1:18–20). Does God dispense His mercy to an individual without reason? Of course not. His mercy is given **because of** [the man's] **righteousness which he has practiced**. In the New Testament, God gives His grace to the person who is trying to die to sin and live according to the gospel (Rom. 6:1–14). If one is not practicing what God has commanded, he has no grace, but is of the devil (1 Jn. 3:9).

Verse 23. God takes no pleasure in the death of the wicked, but desires **rather . . . that he should turn from his ways and live**. The repentance of the wicked causes no change in the will of God, since His will has always been that man should "live." The change in the fate of the individual is brought about by his own change of heart, which is subject to his will. God desires for everyone to be saved (1 Tim. 2:4; 2 Pet. 3:9). The exiles needed to be reminded of the characteristics of God: He is gracious and forgiving, and He wants to have a positive relationship with man. There is no perverted **pleasure** in God's nature when He dispenses the punishment of death. As God, He has to be true to His attribute of justice. He cannot, will not, overlook sin.

The Righteous Man (18:24–29)

²⁴"But when a righteous man turns away from his righteousness, commits iniquity and does according to all the abominations that a wicked man does, will he live? All his righteous deeds which he has done will not be remembered for his treachery which he has committed and his sin which he has committed; for them he will die. ²⁵Yet you say, 'The way of the Lord is not right.' Hear now, O house of Israel! Is My way not right? Is it not your ways that are not right? ²⁶When a righteous man turns away from his righteousness, commits iniquity and dies because of it, for his iniquity which he has committed he will die. ²⁷Again, when a wicked man turns away from his wickedness which he has committed and practices justice and righteousness, he will save his life. ²⁸Because he considered and turned away from all his transgressions which he had committed, he shall surely live; he shall not die. ²⁹But the house of Israel says, 'The way of the Lord is not right.' Are

My ways not right, O house of Israel? Is it not your ways that are not right?"

Verse 24. The discussion of choice continues in verses 24 through 29. The righteous man described was not locked into that lifestyle. His early wisdom, reflected in his decisions to live righteously, was foolishly forsaken. For reasons not stated, he turned away from his righteousness and entered a life of sin. God asked, **"Will he live?"** The answer should be obvious: Of course not. Perhaps the next statement is a surprise to some. God declared that the years of faithfulness **will not be remembered** (see 2 Pet. 2:20–22). These will be forgotten **for his treachery . . . and his sin**. The word "treachery" (מַעַל, *maʻal*) means to dishonor, ignore, or neglect a previous pledge. It is the breach of a relationship of trust with God or with man. This refutes the false doctrine of "once saved always saved." Obviously, this man was saved at one point—because God declared him to be **a righteous man**. If he had never been truly righteous, would God have declared him to be so? As stated in verses 9, 17, and 21, the righteous man "shall surely live."

Verse 25. This verse presents the second objection: **Yet you say, "The way of the Lord is not right"**[6]—that is, "His manner of ruling the universe is inconsistent." The argument seemed to claim, first, that it was unjust for God to allow a man who was once righteous to leave that lifestyle. This accusation implies a weakness in the way God rules mankind. If He wants people to be saved, why let a saved man lose that salvation by going into a life of sin? Why did God not stop him? Again, such an argument does not take into consideration God's determination to allow people to choose. Second, the argument claimed that God lacks fairness—since He will forget righteous deeds if one turns to wickedness. According to the exiles' thinking, God should have offered some reward for the years of righteousness. Equally, the man who committed abominable deeds before repenting

---

[6]"The wonder of these passages is that God bothers to justify himself at all. Here is the ungodly man calling God into question. Here's the sinful creature accusing the Creator of acting immorally" (McGuiggan, 193).

should have received at least some sort of punishment for those deeds. Fisch said,

> It seems that the doctrine taught by the prophet gave rise to the criticism: if man is free to change his way of life from wickedness to righteousness and *vice versa*, this implies a change in the attitude of God towards man and so points to a defect in His nature. To this reasoning the prophet replies that it is not God Who makes the change but man himself. God always bestows His blessing upon man, but it is for him to be worthy of receiving it. As rain cannot fertilize the soil unless it has been cultivated, so man can only benefit from God's benevolence when he has retained his moral capacity for its reception (Malbim). Biblical phrases which apparently ascribe inconstancy to God, such as *it repented the* Lord *that He had made man* (Gen. vi. 6), are only an anthropomorphic form of expression.[7]

God replied, **"Is it not your ways that are not right?"** Who was really to blame here: God, who set up His universe with free moral agency, or the man, who failed to exercise sound judgment and decided to follow a life of sin? God firmly declared that His way is "right." It is right because . . .

1. Each person determines his or her own eternal destiny.
2. People are allowed to serve God because they truly love Him and want to do His will. God would not be glorified by having servants who were made to serve Him.
3. A person can escape the penalty of past decisions. God allows people to repent and live.
4. One may come from a wicked environment (even having a wicked father) and yet become righteous.

Verse 26. God repeated what was stated in verse 24. Some-

---

[7]Fisch, 113.

times **a righteous man turns away from his righteousness.** Again, the principle is proven. Each is free to choose his own course. Here He stated that, because of a man's unrighteous deeds, **he will die.** This could mean that God would bring him to justice (for example, at the hands of the Babylonian soldiers and their swords) or that the elders of the land would sentence him to death (perhaps by stoning) for violating one of the laws given by Moses. Such a death is no accident—it is **for his iniquity.**

Verse 27. The word **again,** indicates that God was restating the positive side of His rule of free will. Here, **a wicked man** decided that he no longer wanted to live such a life. The wonderful element of God's plan is that a person can make such a determination, choosing to go in a different direction. In the course of this change, he practiced **justice and righteousness.** "Justice" deals with the fair treatment of others, whether neighbors, friends, relatives, or business associates; "righteousness" has to do with attention to the law of God in all matters. As Fisch stated, "Things 'lawful' are things which may be judged by the law courts; things 'right' are acts of righteousness, deeds of religious courage and of mercy of which God alone is judge."[8]

Verse 28. What was the reason for this man's change of heart? **He considered** the direction his life was going, certainly realizing the consequences of such a life. Satan's great ploy is to get people so busy that they do not take time to consider their eternal direction. People can also become deceived regarding consequences, believing that they will not pay an eternal price for living in sin. This is why we need to "encourage one another, day after day . . . so that none of you will be hardened by the deceitfulness of sin" (Heb. 3:13).

Verse 29. The house of Israel offered the third objection: **The way of the Lord is not right.** This repeats the objection given in verse 25. Unable to devise a new objection to the way the Lord rules His universe, the objector could only repeat himself. What logical argument could be offered at this point? The truth had been stated by God: **"Is it not your ways that are not right?"**

---

[8]Ibid., 114.

Certainly, the objector wanted to justify himself. He was comfortable in his philosophy regarding the fathers eating sour grapes and the children's teeth being affected as a result. He was comfortable in his finger-pointing and blame-shifting. Like many today, he viewed his wrongs as being everybody else's fault.

The Command to Repent (18:30–32)

³⁰"**Therefore I will judge you, O house of Israel, each according to his conduct,**" **declares the Lord God.** "**Repent and turn away from all your transgressions, so that iniquity may not become a stumbling block to you.** ³¹**Cast away from you all your transgressions which you have committed and make yourselves a new heart and a new spirit! For why will you die, O house of Israel?** ³²**For I have no pleasure in the death of anyone who dies,**" **declares the Lord God.** "**Therefore, repent and live.**"

Verse 30. If any of the previous teachings were unclear, verse 30 should resolve all doubt. Here God said definitively, **"I will judge you . . . each according to his conduct."** Judgment will be based on nothing else. Each will stand or fall based upon his own "conduct." Could God have stated the principle of free moral agency any more plainly? Again, there is no way the doctrine of unconditional election or total depravity can stand in light of this text. God offers His divine invitation: **"Repent and turn."** Each person should heed God's tender plea. He is willing to forgive, but only on the condition that the person does, in fact, turn. Good intentions are not enough. Those who say, "Tomorrow I will get right with God" may never be given that tomorrow. The one who does not repent will be brought down by his **iniquity**.

Verse 31. **"Make yourselves a new heart and a new spirit,"** the Lord urged. How is this done? In part, it is achieved by obeying the first instruction in the verse. He said, **"Cast away from you all your transgressions."** By so doing, a person demonstrates a change of heart—a new devotion. Now he is committed to God and His Word; before he was committed to obeying Satan. Unlike the language of 36:26, which has God providing the new heart, here God was challenging each to make for himself a "new heart" and "spirit." The "heart" represents his mode of thinking and his loyalties; the "spirit" represents his attitude and disposition. This certainly goes along with the theme of the chapter—individual choice and responsibility. God will not manipulate a person's heart, forcing it to be devoted to Him. John B. Taylor wrote,

> The language is that of human exhortation. It would be unfair to Ezekiel to suggest that he regarded these as being anything other than gifts of God. He himself says so in 36:26, "A new heart I will give you, and a new spirit I will put within you." Individual effort and activity are needed, however, at the human level in order to effect repentance and enable the spiritual reformation to take place. Fatalism results in inactivity and is deadly to the soul. To live by the proverb of verse 2 is to capitulate and die. *Why will you die, O house of Israel?*[9]

Verse 32. God's point given in verse 23 is restated. He wants to save people! This desire is revealed in the New Testament: That is why He sent His only begotten Son (Jn. 3:16). The problem is not God's unwillingness to save, but man's unwillingness to be saved. There is no victory when an evil man dies, except for the evil kingdom of Satan. There is no satisfaction in God's mind when a wicked person comes to the grave—only sadness. People today should see in this section the great love of God and His tender appeal to **repent and live**. Indeed, we still have such an opportunity—as long as we have life.

---

[9]John B. Taylor, *Ezekiel: An Introduction and Commentary*, Tyndale Old Testament Commentaries (Downers Grove, Ill.: Inter-Varsity Press, 1969), 151–52.

APPLICATION

Life Choices and Accountability

God's people must resist the temptation to blame others for their lives. Unrighteousness is not the fault of one's parents, spouse, or environment. Every person will face God and be judged solely for his or her own sin (Jas. 1:13–15; 2 Cor. 5:10; Jn. 5:28, 29).

Someone can "rise above" his or her environment and be truly righteous. Even having wicked parents does not prevent one from being righteous. The modern philosophy of moral determinism, which claims that a person is unable to make his or her own life choices, is false. We may have courtrooms that continually excuse lawbreaking citizens because of "insanity," but such is not found within the law of God. In addition, this philosophy, which claims that there is no such thing as "human freedom," has produced a world full of pessimism and helplessness. If one is not free to make choices, why try?

Genuine righteousness is found in paying attention to all of God's laws—even the "little ones." God's people do not overlook or minimize any of His commands, but try to be obedient to all (Mt. 23:23).

God's nature is such that He desires for all people to be saved and will give them every opportunity to obey Him (Ezek. 18: 23, 32; 1 Tim. 2:4; 2 Pet. 3:9).

Christians must operate with a deep conviction that each one will be held personally responsible and accountable to God for life choices. Each can be a good husband, wife, father, mother, child, grandparent, or worker. No script is written for our lives. We are not doomed to follow some predetermined plan.

The characteristics that describe a righteous person are intimately tied to his attitude and actions toward his fellow man, as well as his response to God's law (see Mt. 25:35–40).

The doctrine of inherited sin is false. Each person's choices will determine his or her own eternal destiny. There is no need to baptize infants who have not made such choices. An infant is without sin and is therefore a child of God (see Mt. 18:1–4).

The doctrine of "once saved, always saved" is false. It is

possible for a righteous person to turn from his righteousness and become wicked (Ezek. 18:24). One can certainly fall away from Christ (see Gal. 5:1–4).

D.P.

Four Truths About Individual Responsibility

Ezekiel 18 presents four important truths about individual responsibility: (1) No person is under the total dominion of others. (2) No person is a total slave to his own past. (3) Everyone chooses his own future. (4) Each one is responsible for his own conduct.

Personal Responsibility (18:5–32)

What Ezekiel said about personal responsibility is *true regarding relationships*. If a father is righteous, he shall live (vv. 5–9). If his son is wicked, that son shall die (vv. 10–13). If his son's son is righteous, that grandson shall live (vv. 14–18).

Personal responsibility is *true regarding repentance* (vv. 21–23). If a wicked man decides to be righteous, he shall live (vv. 21, 22). God takes no pleasure in the death of the wicked (v. 23).

Personal responsibility is *true regarding rebellion* (vv. 24–29). If a righteous man turns to wickedness, he shall die (v. 24). Someone might say, "This response is not right. Think of all the good he did." However, a person has the responsibility to live right at all times (vv. 25–29). In this fashion, God declared that He would judge the house of Israel (vv. 30–32).

E.C.

God's Purpose

God has designed a purpose for our lives, and we must fulfill that purpose by obeying Him. Ezekiel spoke of false prophets in Jerusalem who failed to fulfill God's purpose. They were called to tell the truth, but they softened the message and told lies. The priests were called to be holy and to discern between the clean and the unclean, but they also failed. The rulers were called to serve the people, yet they oppressed them for profit. How can we avoid failing to fulfill His purpose for us?

We must remember Him. The Lord warned the Israelites not

to forget Him. However, as they became comfortable with their prosperity in Canaan, that is what happened. We should be aware that the same sort of danger exists today (see 1 Tim. 6:9, 10). God will bring judgment on nations that disregard His laws.

We must take sin seriously. We must recognize sin for what it is and not be afraid to confront it in order to sweep it from our midst. God's holy nature will not allow sin to go unpunished (Hab. 1:13), but sin can be transferred (Is. 53:4, 5). Jeremiah's lesson about the potter shows that God's decisions to punish or reward are contingent, not fixed (Jer. 18:8–10). The same truth is emphasized in Ezekiel 18, where God urged His people to "repent and live" (v. 32).

A.J.

CHAPTER 19
LAMENTATION FOR THE LEADERS

The kings of Judah were given every opportunity to succeed. Not only did God give Judah a land that would provide prosperity, but He also supplied ample prophetic guidance to go along with His divine law. As if that were not enough, Judah had the benefit of history. Having seen what happened to her sister Israel, she could have learned not to make the same mistakes and suffer the same fate. However, because of passages like 2 Samuel 7 and Psalm 89, and because of promises made to David, the people did not believe that Judah would be destroyed the way Israel was. As seen in the "temple sermon" of Jeremiah 7, they believed that as long as they possessed the temple they were safe. We saw in Ezekiel 8 how corrupt the temple was. Both the king and his subjects were putting their faith in a vain and foolish hope. They were engaged in worthless idolatrous worship. Somehow they failed to see that they had put themselves on a course of destruction. A holy God cannot tolerate such blatant disregard for Himself, His holy place, and His holy law. What was intended to be a strong and righteous nation had become a pitiful example, lacking genuine devotion and allegiance to the one true God.

In this extended lamentation, Ezekiel compared the kings of Judah to lion whelps. These, by extension, represented the nation of Judah as a whole. This lamentation is a קִינָה (*qinah*), a mournful song or dirge. In the Hebrew it has rhythm, but this rhythm is nearly impossible to transfer to English. Since the chief concern is to make sense of the text, the meter has been lost in translation.

LAMENT FOR THE KINGS OF JUDAH (19)

Jehoahaz (19:1–4)

¹"As for you, take up a lamentation for the princes of Israel ²and say,

'What was your mother?
A lioness among lions!
She lay down among young lions,
She reared her cubs.
³When she brought up one of her cubs,
He became a lion,
And he learned to tear his prey;
He devoured men.
⁴Then nations heard about him;
He was captured in their pit,
And they brought him with hooks
To the land of Egypt.'"

Verses 1, 2. "Take up a lamentation for the *princes* of Israel," Ezekiel wrote (emphasis added). He refused to use the word "king" in reference to the kings of Israel. Ezekiel favored the word נָשִׂיא (*naśi'*, "prince") instead of מֶלֶךְ (*melek*, "king"). (See 7:27; 12:12.) In verse 2 he asked, **"What was your mother?"** and answered, **"A lioness among lions!"** The Davidic kingdom of Judah was symbolized by a lion (see Gen. 49:9; Mic. 5:8; 1 Kings 10:19, 20). The "mother," then, is not to be seen as a particular individual, but as the nation herself, who produced these kings.

Verses 3, 4. The first king represented is Jehoahaz (also called Shallum). He reigned for only three months in 609 B.C. before Pharaoh Neco deposed him and brought him to Egyptian exile, where he died (2 Kings 23:30–34). This was predicted by Jeremiah (Jer. 22:10–12). Jehoahaz was twenty-three years old when he became king, but he did not exercise good judgment so as to have a lasting reign (see 2 Chron. 36:1–4).

Jehoiachin (19:5–9)

> ⁵"'When she saw, as she waited,
> That her hope was lost,
> She took another of her cubs
> And made him a young lion.
> ⁶And he walked about among the lions;
> He became a young lion,
> He learned to tear his prey;
> He devoured men.
> ⁷He destroyed their fortified towers
> And laid waste their cities;
> And the land and its fullness were appalled
> Because of the sound of his roaring.
> ⁸Then nations set against him
> On every side from their provinces,
> And they spread their net over him;
> He was captured in their pit.
> ⁹They put him in a cage with hooks
> And brought him to the king of Babylon;
> They brought him in hunting nets
> So that his voice would be heard no more
> On the mountains of Israel.'"

Verses 5, 6. She took another of her cubs. Jewish commentators consider this second whelp to be Jehoiakim,[1] but the facts given here fit Jehoiachin better: (1) He fits the analogy of Jeremiah's two laments (Jer. 22:10–19). (2) He died in a foreign land as an exile (Jer. 22:24–30).

Verses 7–9. Jehoiachin came to the throne at the young age of eighteen. His short three-month reign is summarized in the

---

[1]Jehoiakim had a disastrous eleven-year reign. Having been placed on the throne by Pharaoh Neco in 609 B.C., he was eventually defeated by Nebuchadnezzar in 605 in the Battle of Carchemish. At that point Jehoiakim became a vassal for Babylon. Three years later he rebelled and was carried off to Babylon. Nebuchadnezzar reinstated him but then eventually had him assassinated because of a second rebellion (2 Kings 24:1–5; Jer. 22:19; compare Josephus *Antiquities* 10.6.3).

statement that he did evil in the sight of the Lord (2 Kings 24:8, 9). The city of Jerusalem came under siege during his reign; he, his mother, his servants, and his officials were taken into Babylonian captivity in the second deportation (598[7] B.C.). Ten thousand people went into this captivity along with Jehoiachin, leaving only the poorest people in the land (2 Kings 24:11–17). **The sound of his roaring** and **the land** being **appalled** fits Jehoiachin well. While his people suffered, he was involved in foolish building projects—all the while neglecting spiritual growth (Jer. 22:13–19). Ezekiel said that this whelp would be brought **to the king of Babylon**, something else that better fits Jehoiachin, since Jehoiakim was killed and buried outside the city wall of Jerusalem.

Zedekiah (19:10–14)

19:10, 11

> ¹⁰"'Your mother was like a vine in your vineyard,
> Planted by the waters;
> It was fruitful and full of branches
> Because of abundant waters.
> ¹¹And it had strong branches fit for scepters of rulers,
> And its height was raised above the clouds
> So that it was seen in its height with the mass of its branches.'"

Verse 10. The statement **Your mother was like a vine in your vineyard** changes the figure from whelps to vines. According to Moshe Greenberg,

> Some have taken this oracle to be a continuation of the eagle-cedar-vine allegory of ch. 17; the two are indeed similar. But our dirge differs from the political allegory of ch. 17 in its distinguishing between generations (parent-offspring) and its moral grounds for punishment (cruelty, pride), instead of the political ground of ch. 17. Both features reflect something of the themes of the intervening ch. 18. In the light of 18:10, "a violent [*prys*]

son," it is also interesting that Isaiah 35:9 parallels "lion" with "a violent [*prys*] beast"; could the unusual adjective in ch. 18 have triggered the lion figure of ch. 19?[2]

Ezekiel continued to represent the "mother" as the nation of Israel. This figure of the "vineyard" is common in Ezekiel (15:1–6; 17:1–10; see Is. 5:1–7; 27:2–6; Ps. 80:8–16; Mt. 21:33–41; Jn. 15:1–8). As indicated in this text, the vine was given every opportunity to succeed and be fruitful. It had been carefully **planted by the waters**, which gave it what it needed to be **fruitful and full of branches**.

Verse 11. The **strong branches**, strong because of the blessings provided by the Lord, were **fit for scepters of rulers**. That is, they were able to produce a succession of kings, each with the potential for great success. The greatness of the nation was such that **its height was raised above the clouds**. It was visible by many, even those in distant lands. This description best fits the reigns of David and Solomon. During their tenure the nation of Israel reached its greatest global impact.

19:12–14

¹²"'**But it was plucked up in fury;**
It was cast down to the ground;
And the east wind dried up its fruit.
Its strong branch was torn off
So that it withered;
The fire consumed it.
¹³**And now it is planted in the wilderness,**
In a dry and thirsty land.
¹⁴**And fire has gone out from its branch;**
It has consumed its shoots and fruit,
So that there is not in it a strong branch,
A scepter to rule.'"

This is a lamentation, and has become a lamentation.

---

[2]Moshe Greenberg, *Ezekiel 1—20: A New Translation with Introduction and Commentary*, The Anchor Bible, vol. 22 (Garden City, N.Y.: Doubleday & Co., 1983), 359.

Verses 12, 13. Because of disobedience and rebellion, the vine was pulled up by its roots, bringing certain death to this once strong and healthy vine. As is frequently described in the Scriptures, such a dried-out vine is good for nothing except to be thrown into **the fire**. The **strong branch** that was torn off certainly is a reference to Zedekiah, the twentieth and final king of Judah. **The east wind** refers to the Babylonians (see 17:6–15), who took the vine and transplanted it in **a dry and thirsty land**—the land of captivity.

Verse 14. Fire has gone out from its branch. This destructive "fire" that came out of one of the primary branches of the vine describes the demise of Zedekiah. Certainly, not all of the ills of Judah were Zedekiah's fault; nevertheless, he was accountable for refusing to hear God's prophets (especially Jeremiah). He failed in his responsibility to turn the people back to the Lord.

Ezekiel gave the exiles ample reason not to trust that Zedekiah would somehow deliver them. This **lamentation** depicted no **strong branch**, no **scepter to rule**. Judah had no king, for Zedekiah had been deported in 587(6) B.C. God's judgment was complete.

APPLICATION

God's Plan for Success

Of him to whom much is given will much be required. The kings of Israel were provided everything essential for success, yet they failed. Therefore, they were judged accordingly. The same will be true for people today (see Lk. 12:48; Mt. 13:11, 12).

People should learn not to follow others around them rather than God. The kings of Judah were unworthy of the people's trust and allegiance. Only God should be followed.

D.P.

The Path to Failure (19:1–9)

The history lesson in Ezekiel 19 cautions Christians not to forsake God's sovereignty. If we want to avoid disaster, then we must not live as the kings and citizens of Judah lived:

Arrogance in living—Judah "learned to tear his prey" (v. 3).

The people had neither respect nor sensitivity for their fellow man. They "consumed" others because of their self-centered desires.

Abuse toward others—The people "devoured men" (vv. 3, 6). They lived selfishly. Everything was done to satisfy self. Never was consideration given to the welfare of others.

Arrest by justice—Judah was "captured" (vv. 4, 8). The people thought they were "above" the limits of justice, but God's justice is always meted! No person, no position of sovereignty, can escape the justice of God.

Anguish in the future—"Hope was lost" (v. 5). Judah met God's justice and found anguish. The people's self-centered living also brought anguish to others. They thought nothing about the future, only their immediate desires.

Antagonism from others—Nations were "against him" (v. 8a). They thought they were "untouchable" and treated others callously. Eventually, their disregard for others brought a tragic harvest of woe as justice was served.

When we treat others with arrogant disregard and contempt, we will find failure in our lives. Selfishness makes enemies. If we live under the control of selfish dictates, we will bring anguish into our lives and the lives of those close to us. As we contemplate this "path to failure," we should listen well and avoid the tragedy that struck Judah!

J.L.K.

The Traits of Poor Leadership

The nation of Judah was likened to a lioness, and the young lion whelps mentioned in these verses represented kings of Judah. These kings were inept at leading the nation. They illustrate characteristics of leadership that all leaders should try to avoid:

First, we see the sin of being a copy instead of being a statesman. Jehoahaz reigned for only three months. He was deposed by the King of Egypt. He did evil, following in the footsteps of his fathers; and God withheld His hand of blessing (2 Kings 23:32).

Second, we see extravagance and rebellion. Not only did Jehoiachin do evil in the sight of the Lord, but he also foolishly engaged in an expensive building project at a time when his people needed his full attention.

Third, we see a failure to listen to God's Word and turn the people back to Him. Zedekiah was God's representative on earth. He was God's man for the people. Zedekiah refused to listen to the prophets; instead, he turned to human strength for deliverance.

What are the primary responsibilities of leadership? To stand with God, to put the needs of the people first, to listen carefully to God's Word (whether or not anyone else does), and to be to the people that God intended.

E.C.

Chapter 20
The Wayward People

Chapter 18 focused on individuals and their responsibility for their own lives, but in chapter 20 the emphasis is on the continuance of sin. Ezekiel was not saying that Jerusalem would be punished because of the sins of her forefathers, but that she had continued in the same sins for which Israel was punished. Since her behavior had not changed, she should not expect to be treated any differently than Israel was in the past. This is an illustration of the proverb "Like mother like daughter."

The background for the chapter is seen in verses 1 through 4. The elders of the people returned to Ezekiel to inquire of the Lord. From the answer given them, their appeal seems to have been for a reversal of God's announced judgment on Judah. Ezekiel told them that God's decision was final and would not be revoked. Then he gave the reason through an historical survey: Judah had continually rebelled against the Lord, engaging in abominable acts such as idolatry and disobedience. Now, these elders and their contemporaries were guilty of the same sins. Verse 32 indicates that these elders had even considered adopting the heathen practices of the Babylonians and other nations! It is unlikely that they would have reported this intention to Ezekiel (unless it was some kind of threat). This being the case, why should God revoke His judgment of doom on Jerusalem? She deserved this judgment. Still, Ezekiel ended with a message of hope. The entire population of Israel would not perish; God would preserve a remnant.

THE ELDERS' INQUIRY OF EZEKIEL FOR A MESSAGE FROM THE LORD AND THE BASIS FOR THE REPLY (20:1-4)

¹Now in the seventh year, in the fifth month, on the tenth of the month, certain of the elders of Israel came to inquire of the Lord, and sat before me. ²And the word of the Lord came to me saying, ³"Son of man, speak to the elders of Israel and say to them, 'Thus says the Lord God, "Do you come to inquire of Me? As I live," declares the Lord God, "I will not be inquired of by you."' ⁴Will you judge them, will you judge them, son of man? Make them know the abominations of their fathers."

Verse 1. The seventh year would have been 591 B.C. A little under a year had passed since the last noted date (8:1). A duration of about three years would elapse, and then the siege of Jerusalem would begin.

Verses 2, 3. The word of the Lord came to [Ezekiel]. God's message for the elders was, **"I will not be inquired of by you."** Whereas in Ezekiel 36:37 God allowed Himself to be inquired of, here He did not. The situation demanded a different response from the Lord. For men who persist in their sinfulness to seek a word from God is an affront to Him.

Verse 4. Next, God asked Ezekiel, **"Will you judge them, son of man?"** In other words, God asked if Ezekiel would act as a champion, or advocate, on their behalf. This was not the time for Ezekiel to assume such a role. His job was to **make them know** the reason for their dangerous plight, which would become evident to them as they surveyed the nation's past. John B. Taylor said,

> The reason given for the refusal to answer the elders' enquiry is cryptically given as *the abominations of the fathers* (4). To interpret this as an accusation against the elders on the grounds of their forefathers' sins would involve a denial of much that Ezekiel has been arguing in relation to individual responsibility. The point is that

for some unexplained reason the enquiry is an impertinent one and needs only a rehearsal of Israel's past sins to show that history has answered the question for them. This explains the impatience of the repeated *Will you judge them* (4), a phrase which has the force of an imperative: "set out the case against them".[1]

Ezekiel was called upon to make these leaders know **the abominations of their fathers**. There was to be no parable, no allegory, and no lamentation. Here, Ezekiel presented the clear, straightforward truth: Israel had persisted in unfaithfulness—even to this day—and therefore must be punished. God had to be true to Himself.

MAKING KNOWN THE ABOMINATIONS OF THE PEOPLE THROUGH AN HISTORICAL SURVEY (20:5–32)

Apostasies in Egypt (20:5–9)

⁵"And say to them, 'Thus says the Lord GOD, "On the day when I chose Israel and swore to the descendants of the house of Jacob and made Myself known to them in the land of Egypt, when I swore to them, saying, I am the LORD your God, ⁶on that day I swore to them, to bring them out from the land of Egypt into a land that I had selected for them, flowing with milk and honey, which is the glory of all lands. ⁷I said to them, 'Cast away, each of you, the detestable things of his eyes, and do not defile yourselves with the idols of Egypt; I am the LORD your God.' ⁸But they rebelled against Me and were not willing to listen to Me; they did not cast away the detestable things of their eyes, nor did they forsake the idols of Egypt.

⁹""Then I resolved to pour out My wrath on them, to accomplish My anger against them in the midst of the land of

---

[1] John B. Taylor, *Ezekiel: An Introduction and Commentary*, Tyndale Old Testament Commentaries (Downers Grove, Ill.: Inter-Varsity Press, 1969), 156–57.

Egypt. ⁹But I acted for the sake of My name, that it should not be profaned in the sight of the nations among whom they lived, in whose sight I made Myself known to them by bringing them out of the land of Egypt."'"

Verses 5, 6. The only place where Ezekiel said that God **chose Israel** was in verses 5 and 6 (see Jer. 33:24). This was a glorious day in the history of Israel. At the point of God's choosing, she was a lowly nation, enslaved and humiliated under the strong arm of the Egyptians. On that day God **swore** to the people that He would be their God. His swearing is mentioned three times here, then again in verses 15, 23, 28, and 42. God gave His chosen people these promises: (1) He would make Himself known to them, (2) deliver them, and (3) bring them to a land flowing with milk and honey.

This divine election and this divine revelation did not interfere with their free moral choice. The Lord God was giving them the blessings He had promised to their fathers. The fact that he "chose" them emphasizes the unique relationship between God and Israel. "Chose" (בָּחַר, *bachar*) is a key word in Deuteronomy. The election of Israel was a two-way process, involving God's blessings to the nation while requiring faithful obedience from the people.

God spoke of the **land that [He] had selected for them**. The word "selected" (תּוּר, *thur*, literally, "sought out") portrays God's advance scouting for campsites during Israel's trek through the wilderness. The same word is used regarding the twelve spies who spied out the land for the Israelites (Num. 13:1, 2, 16). This phrasing depicts God as surveying the earth to find the choicest land for Israel.

Verse 7. The Israelites were told to **cast away ... detestable things**. They followed some of the religious practices of their Egyptian neighbors (see Josh. 24:14). The golden calf they made in the wilderness was an outgrowth of what they had learned in Egypt (Ex. 32:4). God had laid the groundwork for faithfulness to Him. This newly adopted nation was not confused on the will of her God.

Verses 8, 9. God had taught them everything they needed to know, yet here He said, **". . . they rebelled against Me and were not willing to listen to Me"** (v. 8a). In open defiance to God's will, the people continued worshiping idols. Also, they were unwilling to listen to God. His warnings were ignored. The people continued in two discernible sins: (1) **They did not cast away the detestable things of their eyes,** and (2) they did not **forsake the idols of Egypt.**

Since the Israelites had persisted in idolatry, God knew that they had to be punished. This text tells us something that the narration in Exodus does not tell us—that God determined to **pour out** [His] **wrath** (v. 8b) upon those who continued in idolatry, even while he was in the process of bringing forth their deliverance. While we marvel at the great power God demonstrated in the ten plagues, some foolish Israelites who witnessed these miracles maintained their idolatrous ways! What were they thinking? What did their non-gods do for them, especially in view of the visible manifestation of God through the plagues? God did not tolerate their foolishness; He punished them, but in such a way as to avoid bringing reproach upon His **name** (v. 9). Were the Israelites not liberated from Egypt, the nations would not attribute it to divine retribution but to His lack of power (see Num. 14:16; Deut. 9:28).

> God's reluctance to punish His people *for the honour of (his) name,* or "for (his) name's sake", is the recurrent theme of this chapter. For the Israelite, a man's name represented what the person was in himself. So by God's *name* was meant all that he represented in terms of faithfulness and power. To prevent the misconception of God being limited to a given earthly locality, the stream of thought represented by Deuteronomy personified the name of God as the form of his presence in the Jerusalem temple. God dwells in heaven (Deut. 26:15), but he causes his name to dwell at his chosen sanctuary (12:5 and 11). Once God had revealed his name to Israel, respect for him among the nations was linked with the fate of his chosen people. The appropriate punishment for their idolatry—leaving them in Egypt—would have shown

him in the eyes of the nations to be fickle and powerless. But his name would thus have been profaned.[2]

He did not want that name to be **profaned in the sight of the nations**. If God had publicly smitten the idolatrous Israelites, their destruction would have cast a pall on the reputation of God. At that time, He was in the process of establishing that reputation. The rabbis believed that God had killed the idolaters during the plague of darkness. This allowed the Israelites to bury them without the Egyptians—or other nations—realizing what had happened.[3] Others, referring to the following verses, believe that God delayed the punishment upon the idolaters until they were in the wilderness. However, the first view seems to have more merit, since the last part of verse 8 has God vowing to **accomplish [His] anger against them in the midst of the land of Egypt**. Again, God declared that this was all done **for the sake of [His] name**. According to Taylor,

> The *name* of Yahweh expresses His nature, His total personality as He has revealed Himself. It is parallel to His "glory", *i.e.* His glorious majesty, and it can refer to His reputation in the eyes of men. If men think right thoughts about Him and recognize His attributes for what they are and so worship Him, they may be said to "sanctify" Him; and conversely, to misunderstand His nature and to regard Him less highly than He ought to be regarded is to *profane* His name. It is the duty of the new Israel, as it was of the old Israel, to see that God's name is not profaned through inadequate witness to His nature and His truth. The believer's sins and shortcomings inevitably result in such profanation. But God can and does frequently take special measures to counteract this and to ensure that faithful witness to Him and His power is not completely extinguished.[4]

---

[2]Keith W. Carley, *The Book of the Prophet Ezekiel*, The Cambridge Bible Commentary (Cambridge: Cambridge University Press, 1974), 129.
[3]*Midrash Rabba*; Ex. 4:3; see 10:22, 23.
[4]Taylor, 157–58.

In verse 9 He said, **"I made Myself known to them by bringing them out of the land of Egypt."** God had revealed Himself to Israel through the plagues and had conveyed to them His intention to liberate them. All this was likewise demonstrated to the Egyptians. Therefore, if the Israelites failed to follow God's procedure for their release, they would be profaning His name.

Apostasies in the Wilderness (20:10–26)

20:10–12
¹⁰"'"So I took them out of the land of Egypt and brought them into the wilderness. ¹¹I gave them My statutes and informed them of My ordinances, by which, if a man observes them, he will live. ¹²Also I gave them My sabbaths to be a sign between Me and them, that they might know that I am the LORD who sanctifies them."'"

Verses 10–12. In spite of their disobedience to His word while in Egypt, God **brought them into the wilderness** (v. 10). Even at this early stage of their relationship, God was showing His mercy, compassion, and longsuffering toward His people. He gave them His **statutes** and **ordinances** (v. 11), along with His **sabbaths** (v. 12). "Statutes" are generally considered to be laws which God gave without explanation as to why He made them law. "Ordinances" followed the principles given in the covenant (which would include circumcision and various requirements found in the Decalogue). "Sabbaths," in the plural, includes festivals given in the Pentateuch (see Lev. 23:24, 39). The Sabbaths were **a sign**, the identifying mark that separated Israel from the other nations. They signified that the Israelites were God's covenant people. As they observed the Sabbath laws, they honored the God who gave them. In response, God would identify Israel as His holy people (see Ex. 31:13).

All these laws were given at Sinai. (See Neh. 9:13, 14; Lev. 26:46; regarding the Sabbath, see Ex. 31:12–17.) The purpose of the given laws is clearly stated: **. . . if a man observes them, he will live** (v. 11). Literally, this means "which man will observe and live through them." (See Lev. 18:5 for the only occurrence of the phrase outside this prophecy.) The combination of the concepts of *observing* and *living* occurs in Ezekiel 18:9, and the phrase "statutes which ensure life" is found in 33:15. God's laws are intended to bring life; obedience to them benefits people (see Deut. 6:24, 25). Deuteronomy 30:15-19 states forcefully that to follow the commandments is to choose life and blessing; not to follow them is to choose death and the curse. God's promises indicated His desire to bless Israel, yet within His laws came a warning: Disobey, and face God's anger.

God had, therefore, made Himself known by three decisive acts: the deliverance from Egypt (v. 10), the giving of the Law (v. 11), and the giving of the Sabbaths (v. 12).

20:13, 14

¹³""But the house of Israel rebelled against Me in the wilderness. They did not walk in My statutes and they rejected My ordinances, by which, if a man observes them, he will live; and My sabbaths they greatly profaned. Then I resolved to pour out My wrath on them in the wilderness, to annihilate them. ¹⁴But I acted for the sake of My name, that it should not be profaned in the sight of the nations, before whose sight I had brought them out."""

Verse 13. After all He had done for Israel, God said, **"They did not walk in My statutes."** The giving of the Law was a vivid illustration of God's love and grace. He was doing what was best for His people, yet they "rebelled." Their disobedient attitude showed even here. Taylor said,

> It is worth noting that, despite New Testament strictures on the spiritual value of the law as an instrument of salvation (*e.g.* Jn. 1:17; Acts 13:39; Rom. 3:20; Gal. 3:19ff.), it is quite clearly regarded as a gracious gift of God through Moses to His people and it was ordained so that by the observance of it *man shall live, i.e.* "prosper", both materially and spiritually (*cf.* Dt. 4:40; Jos. 1:7f.). In face of Israel's rejection of His grace, the Lord *thought* to destroy them utterly (13) and *swore* not to allow them

into Canaan (15), but even these decisions were changed in the face of His overriding concern for His name. There is nothing inconsistent in the Deity changing His mind, or "repenting", under such circumstances.[5]

The texts of Exodus and Numbers record numerous sins of the people while they were in the wilderness: the worshiping of the golden calf (Ex. 32), ignoring God's instructions regarding the collection of manna (Ex. 16:20), the trying of God in Rephidim (Ex. 17:1–7), plus grumbling and murmuring many times (Num. 11:1; 21:5). In addition, the people violated God's Sabbath laws. This repeated disobedience so angered God that He determined to **annihilate them**. Had it not been for the intercession of Moses, Israel would have been destroyed. Moses' appeal was based upon the reputation of God's name.

Verse 14. God's decision to allow them to live was likewise based upon the protection of His **name**. After their continued rebellion, however, God determined that those who left Egypt would not enter into the Promised Land, except for a few faithful. In spite of this, **the nations** were impressed with the God of the Israelites, as noted by the comments of Rahab in Joshua 2:11: "For the LORD your God, He is God in heaven above and on earth beneath."

20:15–17
15""'Also I swore to them in the wilderness that I would not bring them into the land which I had given them, flowing with milk and honey, which is the glory of all lands, ¹⁶because they rejected My ordinances, and as for My statutes, they did not walk in them; they even profaned My sabbaths, for their heart continually went after their idols. ¹⁷Yet My eye spared them rather than destroying them, and I did not cause their annihilation in the wilderness."'"

Verse 15. God had warned that there would be consequences

---

[5]Ibid., 158.

if the people did not obey His laws and statutes. They disobeyed; therefore, God **swore to them** that they would not be allowed to enter into the Promised Land. His description of this land illustrated how much these people would be missing because of their rebellion. It was a land that was **flowing with milk and honey**. The potential for production was beyond description. Such a land would make it easy to grow crops and produce thriving herds. It was a land that was **the glory of all lands**. Nothing else could compare with its beauty.

Verses 16, 17. God gave His laws with great care and detail. The people, however, rejected His teachings. They had a heart problem: They loved **their idols** and **continually** sought to participate in their idolatrous rites. While God overlooked the people's unwillingness to obey His commands regarding marriage because of their "hardness of heart," (see Mt. 19:7, 8; Deut. 24:1–4), He was never willing to accept their idolatrous ways for the same reason. He said, **"Yet My eye spared them rather than destroying them"** (v. 17). This can only be seen as an act of compassion and longsuffering (see 39:25). At this point in Israel's history, they were not getting what they deserved.

20:18–20

¹⁸"'"I said to their children in the wilderness, 'Do not walk in the statutes of your fathers or keep their ordinances or defile yourselves with their idols. ¹⁹I am the Lord your God; walk in My statutes and keep My ordinances and observe them. ²⁰Sanctify My sabbaths; and they shall be a sign between Me and you, that you may know that I am the Lord your God.'"'"

Verse 18. God moved on to the next generation. They would be given the same opportunities as their fathers, hopefully with a different result. Therefore, they received **the statutes** and **ordinances** that were given before, in addition to the warning not to **defile [themselves] with their idols**.

Verse 19. The basis of God's commands is His very being. He referred to Himself as **the Lord your God**. Distinct from the gods their parents had worshiped, He has always been the true and living God. He identified Himself to the Israelites as "your"

God—so why would they want to worship the gods of other nations?

Verse 20. In addition, God repeated His laws regarding His **sabbaths**. These laws were said to be **a sign between Me and you**. (See the discussion on v. 12.) The earlier generation missed an opportunity to be marked as the special people of God—which would have been powerfully demonstrated in their victorious march through the Promised Land. Instead, they suffered the humiliation of dying in the wilderness. Now their children were given the opportunity to seize this promise and be marked as God's chosen nation—but only if they obeyed His laws and His sabbaths.

20:21, 22

²¹""*"But the children rebelled against Me; they did not walk in My statutes, nor were they careful to observe My ordinances, by which, if a man observes them, he will live; they profaned My sabbaths. So I resolved to pour out My wrath on them, to accomplish My anger against them in the wilderness. ²²But I withdrew My hand and acted for the sake of My name, that it should not be profaned in the sight of the nations in whose sight I had brought them out."""*

Verse 21. But the children rebelled against Me. The threat of punishment and exile did not deter their desire to serve idols. As their fathers had done, they rejected the three categories of instruction God had given them: His **statutes, ordinances,** and **sabbaths**. Since they were determined to disobey, God was equally **resolved** to punish. He declared that He will **pour out** [His] **wrath on them** and **accomplish** [His] **anger against them in the wilderness**.

Verse 22. As before, God **withdrew** [His] **hand**—and for the same reason: **for the sake of** [His] **name**. At this early stage in Israel's history, the reputation of God's name, especially **in the sight of the nations**, was of utmost importance.

20:23–26

²³""*"Also I swore to them in the wilderness that I would scatter

them among the nations and disperse them among the lands, ²⁴because they had not observed My ordinances, but had rejected My statutes and had profaned My sabbaths, and their eyes were on the idols of their fathers. ²⁵I also gave them statutes that were not good and ordinances by which they could not live; ²⁶and I pronounced them unclean because of their gifts, in that they caused all their firstborn to pass through the fire so that I might make them desolate, in order that they might know that I am the Lord."'"

Verses 23, 24. God had told them—in advance (while they were still **in the wilderness**) that He would **scatter them among the nations**. God did this because the people continued to hold a false belief that they somehow deserved the Promised Land, and that God would never forsake them—regardless of how unfaithful they became. They believed that, once they were located in the land, it would be forever theirs. Especially, once the temple was built as the "dwelling of God," the people felt assured that their land inheritance was guaranteed (see Jer. 7:1–11). The threat to "scatter them among the nations" must have been especially painful words to the elders as they sat listening to Ezekiel. They were already in exile. God had announced this punishment centuries before, and they were now living this nightmare.

Verse 25. I also gave them statutes that were not good. This passage has mystified scholars and theologians, because it seems to contradict other passages about the nature of God. How could God, or why would God, give them statutes that were "not good"? Passages like this offer an interesting glimpse into the nature of God. As Paul taught, one must have a love for the truth so as to be saved. If a person no longer maintains a "truth-seeker" mentality, God will send a deluding influence and allow him to believe a lie (2 Thess. 2:8–12). God desires for all men to be saved and come to a knowledge of the truth (1 Tim. 2:4); but if one persists in the path of sin and rebellion, God will give up on him (Rom. 1:24, 26, 28). Israel had lost her love for the truth of God. She was frequently guilty of ignoring God's laws and following after the idolatrous laws of the other nations. Consequently, Israel was to be given the same fate imposed on the Canaanites—expulsion from the land.

Because Israel consistently rejected God's good, life-giving laws, God's designed punishment was to replace them with laws that were "not good." By observing such laws, one would gain death rather than life (see 18:18). These laws are exemplified by child sacrifice (20:26), a murderous pagan practice and an abomination worthy of severest condemnation. By this "anti-gift," God confirmed the people in their choice of laws countering God's. Their choice led them, inevitably, to adopt the deadly laws of the pagans, including the pagan mode of worship by the custom of burning children.[6]

The shocking idea that God misleads those who anger Him—allowing them to participate in sin for which He then destroys them—has appeared before. In 3:20 God set a stumbling block before the sinner, and in 14:9 God prevailed upon a prophet to speak a word which He did not send. This practice is essentially the same as God's hardening Pharaoh's heart so that his ruin might be a lasting object lesson (Ex. 9:16; 10:2; Rom. 9:17). Consider also the charge to Isaiah to "render the hearts of this people insensitive, their ears dull, and their eyes dim, otherwise they might see with their eyes, hear with their ears, understand with their hearts, and return and be healed" (Is. 6: 10). Another example is the complaint in Isaiah 63:17: "Why, LORD, do you make us stray from your ways, and harden our hearts not to fear you?" (see 1 Kings 18:36b). The explanation is given in Psalm 81:11, 12: "But my people did not listen to My voice; so I gave them over to the stubbornness of their heart, to walk in their own devices."[7]

---

[6]"The penalty of sin is further delusion and worse sin, the end of which is death. God had ordained that the firstborn, 'all that openeth the womb,' should be 'sanctified' to Him (Exodus 13:2). So far as the children were concerned, this was a law which preserved them alive since nowhere does He command child-sacrifice. They rejected this law, and God allowed them to turn an act of 'sanctification' into an act of 'pollution' when they burnt their children to Molech" (S. Fisch, *Ezekiel: Hebrew Text and English Translation with an Introduction and Commentary*, Soncino Books of the Bible [London: Soncino Press, 1950], 126).

[7]See George C. Heider, "A Further Turn on Ezekiel's Baroque Twist in Ezek 20:25, 26," *Journal of Biblical Literature* 107 (December 1988): 721–24.

Verse 26. I pronounced them unclean because of their gifts. Greenberg translated this as "defiling them by their gifts."[8] "Gifts" here refers to religious sacrifices (see Ex. 28:38; Lev. 23:38). The specific offerings in this context were the child sacrifices of their firstborn to their pagan deities (Lev. 18:21; Deut. 18:10; 2 Kings 21:6; 2 Chron. 28:3; see Ex. 13:12). Taylor explained,

> The latter presents an acute problem of interpretation. It seems to refer to the unlawful practice of "passing children through the fire to Molech", a form of child-sacrifice so strongly and frequently condemned in the Old Testament that it may well have happened far more than the occasional times it is mentioned (*e.g.* 2 Ki. 21:6; 2 Ch. 28:3; *cf.* 2 Ki. 17:17; 23:10, 13; Je. 7:31; 32:35). But this could never be described as an ordinance of God. It may be that the ordinance referred to is that of the offering of the first-born with its insistence that everything that opens the womb belongs to the Lord. This is modified by the law of redemption whereby a substitute or a ransom-price can be provided for first-born children (Ex. 22:29; Nu. 18:15ff.). But the occasional continuance of child-sacrifice was probably due to a misinterpretation of this law, and so Ezekiel could imply that God had ultimately made it so. The alternative is to understand these verses in the manner of Romans 1:24, which is saying that the consequence of spiritual perversity is that God "gives men up" to grosser sins.[9]

Apostasies in the Promised Land (20:27–32)

20:27–29

[27]"Therefore, son of man, speak to the house of Israel and say to them, 'Thus says the Lord GOD, "Yet in this your fathers

---

[8]Moshe Greenberg, *Ezekiel 1—20: A New Translation with Introduction and Commentary*, The Anchor Bible, vol. 22 (Garden City, N.Y.: Doubleday & Co., 1983), 361.

[9]Taylor, 158–59.

have blasphemed Me by acting treacherously against Me. ²⁸When I had brought them into the land which I swore to give to them, then they saw every high hill and every leafy tree, and they offered there their sacrifices and there they presented the provocation of their offering. There also they made their soothing aroma and there they poured out their drink offerings. ²⁹Then I said to them, 'What is the high place to which you go?' So its name is called Bamah to this day.""'

Verse 27. Only by God's mercy did the people enter the Promised Land. They deserved to die in the wilderness. Incredibly, God brought them into their own land with a fascinating display of His power. Surely, this should have permanently convinced the Israelites of the greatness of their God. Instead, they used this beautiful land that God had given them as a shrine of idolatrous blasphemy. This blatant disregard for God and His laws was not overlooked. The verb **blasphemed** signifies, in a wider sense, that they committed a most serious sin. The phrase "the same blasphemes the LORD" (Num. 15:30) is interpreted in the *Talmud* as "idolatry."[10]

Verse 28. When God **brought them into the land**, what did they do? Did they immediately engage in worship and praise to the Lord who had blessed them so? No, their eyes saw the hills of the land and the beautiful trees as perfect places to honor false gods in these ways: (1) **They offered . . . their sacrifices;** (2) **they made their soothing aroma;** and (3) **they poured out their drink offerings.**

Each of these phrases presents a nauseating portrayal of idolatry. These places should have been viewed as testimony to the majesty of God and His awesome power to create (Ps. 19:1–6; Rom. 1:18–23). God's chosen people used His marvelous creation as the starting point for building their idolatrous shrines.

Verse 29. "What is the high place to which you go?" God asked them. In other words, He inquired, "Who permitted you the use of a 'high place'?" God had never allowed the use of high places for His worship. In studying through 1 and 2 Kings,

---

[10]Kerithoth 7b.

one finds that many of the kings of Judah and Israel were guilty of continuing this practice (and failing to learn from others; 2 Kings 17:11). Hezekiah and Josiah finally removed the high places (2 Kings 18:4; 23:13). The name of the high place mentioned was **Bamah**.[11]

20:30-32

30"Therefore, say to the house of Israel, 'Thus says the Lord God, "Will you defile yourselves after the manner of your fathers and play the harlot after their detestable things? 31When you offer your gifts, when you cause your sons to pass through the fire, you are defiling yourselves with all your idols to this day. And shall I be inquired of by you, O house of Israel? As I live," declares the Lord God, "I will not be inquired of by you. 32What comes into your mind will not come about, when you say: 'We will be like the nations, like the tribes of the lands, serving wood and stone.'"'"

Verse 30. Now turning to the elders, Ezekiel asked them a pertinent question: **"Will you defile yourselves after the manner of your fathers . . . ?"** These elders evidently desired to build a "high place" in Babylon.

Verses 31, 32. In reply to the inquiry of the elders of Israel, Ezekiel reviewed the nation's past. He applied the teaching to the future. **When you offer your gifts . . . you are defiling yourselves** (v. 31). By engaging in such worship, they had created a barrier between themselves and the Lord. Proverbs 28:9 says, "He who turns away his ear from listening to the law, even his prayer is an abomination." It is impossible to approach a holy God on the day of worship when one has engaged in rebellion

---

[11]"The meaning of the term *bamah* ('high place') is uncertain. . . . It is used in this context as a proper noun, designating a place. Perhaps the place that became known as the 'high place' was at the site of Gibeon. This city had played a significant religious role in Israel's early history in Canaan (cf. 1 Sam 9; 1 Kings 3:4; 11:7; 1 Chron 16:39; 21:29; 2 Chron 1:3, 13). However, there is insufficient data to confirm this interpretation" (Ralph H. Alexander, "Ezekiel," in *The Expositor's Bible Commentary*, ed. Frank E. Gaebelein [Grand Rapids, Mich.: Zondervan Publishing House, 1986], 6:837).

to Him throughout the week. These men, if they were honest with themselves, must have known that they were guilty. God said that they were doing these defiling acts **to this day**. This was not ancient history: God was recounting events that could have appeared in Israel's current newspaper.

THE RESULT OF THEIR APOSTASIES—ISRAEL TO BE PURGED (20:33–44)

20:33–35
³³"'"As I live," declares the Lord GOD, "surely with a mighty hand and with an outstretched arm and with wrath poured out, I shall be king over you. ³⁴I will bring you out from the peoples and gather you from the lands where you are scattered, with a mighty hand and with an outstretched arm and with wrath poured out; ³⁵and I will bring you into the wilderness of the peoples, and there I will enter into judgment with you face to face."'"

Verse 33. God would bring about another exodus. As He had brought about Israel's deliverance from Egypt with His **mighty hand** and His **outstretched arm**, so God would establish Himself as their **king** when He repeated His acts of greatness. God said that He would do this **with wrath poured out** (v. 34; see 7:8; 9:8; 14:19; 20:8, 13, 21; 21:36; 22:22, 31; 30:15; 36:18). This is interpreted to mean:

1. He would pour out wrath against the nations that held His people hostage (as He did to the Egyptians).
2. He would pour out His wrath against any nation that stood in the way of God's people as they again entered into the "wilderness."
3. He would pour out His wrath against the exiles who, even in exile, had persisted in their idolatrous ways. They would be left behind while the others were brought again to the land.

Verses 34, 35. God would **enter into judgment** with Israel, but not before bringing them out of their various lands of captivity. His judgment would be **face to face**—certainly not an inviting thought. "It is a terrifying thing to fall into the hands of the living God" (Heb. 10:31)!

20:36–39

³⁶"'"As I entered into judgment with your fathers in the wilderness of the land of Egypt, so I will enter into judgment with you," declares the Lord God. ³⁷"I will make you pass under the rod, and I will bring you into the bond of the covenant; ³⁸and I will purge from you the rebels and those who transgress against Me; I will bring them out of the land where they sojourn, but they will not enter the land of Israel. Thus you will know that I am the Lord.

³⁹"'"As for you, O house of Israel," thus says the Lord God, "Go, serve everyone his idols; but later you will surely listen to Me, and My holy name you will profane no longer with your gifts and with your idols."'"

Verses 36, 37. As discussed in verse 8, God would punish those who had brought shame to His name through their idolatrous ways. As stated in that verse, this judgment would take place **in the wilderness of the land of Egypt** (v. 36). There is some discussion as to the meaning of the phrase **I will make you pass under the rod** (v. 37). In Old Testament times, a sheep was made to pass under the shepherd's rod as evidence that the sheep belonged to that shepherd (see Lev. 27:32). Since the full phrase "pass under the rod" is used, this is the probable meaning. However, "the rod" also represents punishment and discipline (Ps. 89:32; Lam. 3:1). Certainly, there would be discipline. God would not allow this wayward child to go unpunished. S. Fisch said,

> In separating the tithe of herd or flock, it was the practice to make the animals pass one by one under the rod and the tenth was separated and declared holy (cf. Lev. 27:32). Similarly, the Judeans, before their deliverance from exile,

will be scrutinized by their Shepherd; the wicked will perish and the righteous be saved.[12]

The discipline must come first, then the reinstituting of **the bond of the covenant**. The exact time frame referred to here is unknown. Possibly, this is a reference to the challenges the exiles had while they were making their way back to Israel after their release from captivity.

Verse 38. As noted in the New Testament, a little leaven affects a whole lump of dough. Therefore, as Paul also advised, God planned to "clean out the old leaven" (1 Cor. 5:7). God would bring the people out of captivity—perhaps giving them the impression that all was well—but they would **not enter the land of Israel**. These **rebels** and **transgress**[ors] would not see good days. Why would God go through this process of bringing them out of captivity only to have them die in the wilderness? God Himself answered this question: **"Thus you will know that I am the Lord."**

Verse 39. Eventually, God said, **"Go, serve everyone his idols."** This interesting phrase could be understood in one of two ways: (1) It may have been an invitation to the present generation, who loved to engage in idolatrous practices, to continue in this "love affair." It would be better, for the sake of God's reputation, for them to forsake the God of Israel completely. This way no one could confuse their practices with the genuine religion given by the Lord. The time would come when God would bring them into judgment, and they would no longer have the opportunity to profane His name. (2) The statement could have been made as a point of irony—inviting them to go ahead and serve their idols (see Jer. 44:25; Amos 4:4). After they got their "fill" of idolatry, they might be more inclined to **listen to** the Lord and **no longer** be tempted to do things which **profane**[d] His **holy name**.

---

[12]Fisch, 129.

20:40–44

⁴⁰"'"For on My holy mountain, on the high mountain of Israel," declares the Lord God, **"there the whole house of Israel, all of them, will serve Me in the land; there I will accept them and there I will seek your contributions and the choicest of your gifts, with all your holy things. ⁴¹As a soothing aroma I will accept you when I bring you out from the peoples and gather you from the lands where you are scattered; and I will prove Myself holy among you in the sight of the nations. ⁴²And you will know that I am the Lord, when I bring you into the land of Israel, into the land which I swore to give to your forefathers. ⁴³There you will remember your ways and all your deeds with which you have defiled yourselves; and you will loathe yourselves in your own sight for all the evil things that you have done. ⁴⁴Then you will know that I am the Lord when I have dealt with you for My name's sake, not according to your evil ways or according to your corrupt deeds, O house of Israel,"** declares the Lord God.'"

Verse 40. My holy mountain refers to Zion, where the temple stood (see Is. 27:13; 56:7; 65:11; 66:20; Joel 2:1; 4:17; Zeph. 3:11; Zech. 8:3; Dan. 9:20). God would reinstitute proper worship in Jerusalem, on the site of the temple mount.

Verse 41. The worship offered on the holy mount would be accepted by God, for it would be **a soothing aroma**. God must first accept the person, and then He will accept his worship (see v. 40; Gen. 4:4). God vowed, **"I will prove Myself holy"** upon delivering His people from bondage. He planned to demonstrate in the sight of the nations that He is the one true God and that these were His people. The word "holy" here can be understood as "unique," since no other god could do what the Lord would do for Israel. In addition, it means that He was right in His previous judgments which had been questioned (see 18:25, 29).

Verse 42. After the long exile, they would realize a wonderful truth: **You will know that I am the Lord.** God's word, His promises, came true. The restoration of Israel was to impress the nations so that they would also seek Him (Is. 66:18; Zech. 14:16–19).

Verse 43. In God's plan, it is vital for people to **remember**. He did not want His people to forget their **ways** or their **deeds**—the actions, words, and practices by which they had **defiled** themselves. However, this remembrance would cause them to **loathe** themselves. It would be disgusting to them to think of all the abominable practices they used to do. How could they have been so foolish? How could they have resorted to such evil? These would be hard lessons to learn—but important ones.

Verse 44. They were to realize that God had remained faithful to them **for [His] name's sake, not according to [their] evil ways or ... corrupt deeds**. They would also remember that their restitution was based solely upon God's "name" and had nothing to do with their deeds. Their "evil ways" and "corrupt deeds" deserved punishment, but they would escape that punishment because of God's desire to protect His reputation. They were to learn from this, and in the future do all they could to preserve and enhance the name of the Lord.

THE PROPHECIES OF THE SWORD
(20:45—21:32)

The Sword of the Lord Unsheathed (20:45—21:7)

20:45-49

⁴⁵Now the word of the LORD came to me, saying, ⁴⁶"Son of man, set your face toward Teman, and speak out against the south and prophesy against the forest land of the Negev, ⁴⁷and say to the forest of the Negev, 'Hear the word of the LORD: thus says the Lord GOD, "Behold, I am about to kindle a fire in you, and it will consume every green tree in you, as well as every dry tree; the blazing flame will not be quenched and the whole surface from south to north will be burned by it. ⁴⁸All flesh will see that I, the LORD, have kindled it; it shall not be quenched."'" ⁴⁹Then I said, "Ah Lord GOD! They are saying of me, 'Is he not just speaking parables?'"

This paragraph begins chapter 21 in the MT, the LXX, and the Vulgate. It seems to fit better in that context than here.

Either way, it provides a link between chapter 20 and the discussion in chapter 21.

Verses 45, 46. Ezekiel was commanded to **speak out against the south** (v. 46). The Hebrew has three different words here (תֵּימָנָה, *theymanah*; דָּרוֹם, *darom*; and נֶגֶב, *negeb*). Of these, the first two are general poetic words to describe the southerly direction,[13] whereas the third refers to a named geographical area, called in modern Israel **the Negev**, which lay to the south of the Judean hills. Taylor wrote,

> Today this is a waterless desert, except where agricultural settlements have irrigated it into a state of cultivation, but we know that in Old Testament times there was greater afforestation throughout Palestine, and so a reference to *the forest of the Negeb* (RSV) does not have to be regarded as completely figurative. Ezekiel may have reinforced his words by facing southwards as he uttered his oracle, predicting that the Lord will cause a forest fire to sweep through the land from south to north. All will see it and no-one will be able to avoid its heat (47; *all faces . . . shall be scorched by it*). Men will realize that it has been sent by the Lord as an act of judgment.[14]

Verse 47. "I am about to kindle a fire in you," God warned. The "fire" of judgment is a frequent biblical theme, especially in Ezekiel (5:4; 10:2, 6; 15:4–7; 16:41; 19:12, 14; 21:37; 23:25, 47; 24:10, 12; see 22:21, 31; 38:19). The judgment would be thorough, covering all of the foliage, even the "whole surface from south to north."

Verse 48. God brought the fire of judgment upon Judah. The Babylonian soldiers, having captured Jerusalem in 587(6) B.C., burned it to the ground (Neh. 2:3). This judgment was not actu-

---

[13]The NASB has capitalized "Teman." Teman was one of the primary cities of Edom and had been targeted to be a recipient of God's wrath (Ezek. 25:13). It is possible that Ezekiel was using Teman to represent this southern region. However, it is preferable to adopt the NASB footnote "the South."

[14]Taylor, 160–61.

ally from the hand of the Babylonians. Rather, it was what the Lord had promised to **kindle**, and it could not be **quenched** until there was nothing left to consume. God's judgment would indeed be thorough.

Verse 49. The people asked concerning Ezekiel, **"Is he not just speaking parables?"** The "parable" of the fire did not make sense to them. Two meanings are possible: (1) Ezekiel was saying things that did not seem to make sense. Who could understand him? (2) His earlier prophecies had not come true, so the people were asking, "Why should we consider this one factual?"

If we link this text with that of chapter 21, then the first view would be correct. In 21:1–5, God stated that He would punish Judah and Jerusalem. This was also the meaning of the "parable" of the fire.

APPLICATION

God's Relationship with His People

History should teach God's people. God expects future generations to learn from, and not repeat, the failings of earlier generations.

Each generation is given new opportunities. Developing righteousness is their own responsibility, regardless of what earlier generations might have done.

God's patience should lead to repentance (see Rom. 2:4; 2 Pet. 3:9–15).

God maintains the reputation of His name. He wants His name to be glorified by His people. If they persist in disobedience, He will find other ways to glorify His name.

When a person's heart is not inclined toward the truth, God will allow him to believe a lie (see Ezek. 20:25).

God cannot be approached in worship by those who have, throughout the week, neglected His Word and led sinful lives (Prov. 28:9; 1 Pet. 3:8–12). God wants those who come before Him to have "holy hands" (1 Tim. 2:8).

D.P.

Patience and Punishment (20:9–26)

Punishment was due to those who rebelled against God. However, the chastisement was delayed because of God's patience. Ezekiel's message about how Judah scorned God's patience cautions us against sinning in the same manner.

God's patience is founded upon God's character, His "name" (vv. 9, 14). His patience is unquestioned because it is founded upon the holy "name." He will be patient because He is God.

God's patience is governed by His knowledge, given in His "statutes" (v. 11). He has always governed mankind with clearly revealed laws. Repeatedly, those laws have been broken; but, just as often, divine patience has "waited" for man to learn and obey God's statutes (2 Chron. 36:15; Acts 17:30, 31).

God's patience is tried by those who have "rebelled" (v. 13). Mankind has often refused to obey God's revealed will (Gen. 6:5–7; 2 Chron. 36:16–21). God's righteous nature must eventually respond to rebellion.

God's patience is terminated by God's justice when His people are "pronounced . . . unclean" (vv. 21–26). His patience has a limit. Ezekiel announced that God's patience had been exhausted by those who had not "observed [His] ordinances," had "rejected [His] statutes," and had "profaned" the holy practices (v. 24).

God is still exemplifying patience as He waits for souls to obey His commands and be saved (2 Pet. 3:9). Let us not show scorn and contempt toward God's patience, but let us obey His commands in humility!

J.L.K.

Chapter 21

The Sword of God's Judgment

Having been accused of speaking in "parables" in the preceding five verses (20:45–49), Ezekiel was given a plain message to deliver: Jerusalem was to be devastated, now by the sword. This sharpened and ready sword was in Nebuchadnezzar's hand; he was God's instrument to execute judgment without pity. After noting that Nebuchadnezzar was ready to act, Ezekiel depicted him as practicing divination in order to decide whether he should first attack Jerusalem or Ammon. Jerusalem was chosen, but the destruction of the Ammonites would soon follow.

Not since chapters 4 through 7 and chapter 9 has the theme of judgment been presented with such force and thoroughness as it is in the uninterrupted proclamation of doom. At least four oracles about the sword are intertwined in chapter 21: vv. 1–7, 8–17, 18–27, and 28–32.

The Sword of the Lord Unsheathed (Continued) (20:45—21:7)

21:1–5
¹And the word of the Lord came to me saying, ²"Son of man, set your face toward Jerusalem, and speak against the sanctuaries and prophesy against the land of Israel; ³and say to the land of Israel, 'Thus says the Lord, "Behold, I am against you; and I will draw My sword out of its sheath and cut off from you the righteous and the wicked. ⁴Because I will cut off from you the righteous and the wicked, therefore My sword

will go forth from its sheath against all flesh from south to north. ⁵Thus all flesh will know that I, the LORD, have drawn My sword out of its sheath. It will not return to its sheath again."'"

Verses 1, 2. Ezekiel was to **set [his] face toward Jerusalem** (v. 2). Those listening to Ezekiel at the time would have had no trouble understanding this message. In 20:46 he had been instructed to "set [his] face toward Teman," "speak out against the south," and "prophesy against the forest land of the Negev." God repeated the same three verbs as He gave Ezekiel new instructions: (1) "Set your face toward Jerusalem." The city would fall under the terrible judgment of the Lord, enduring His wrath. (2) **"Speak against the sanctuaries."** The pagan holy places would receive direct condemnation by God. (3) **"Prophesy against the land of Israel."** As is vividly illustrated in 20:15, God had brought His people to the "glory of all lands." Sadly, they used the land to establish idolatrous high places and its produce to finance their idolatrous ways and foreign alliances.

Verse 3. As in 20:47, God began His judgment oracle with **"Behold."** This time, God plainly announced, **"I am against you."** The people's investment in idolatry was about to reap the anger of God. This anger would be realized in the awesome sword of the Lord. He said, **"I will draw My sword out of its sheath."** "The sword of the Lord" is a concept found in a number of prophetic passages against the enemies of God's people (Deut. 32:41; Is. 31:8; 34:5–8; 66:16; Jer. 25:31; 50:35–37; Zeph. 2:12).

Now the sword of God's judgment was directed toward Jerusalem and the land of Israel. This sword would **cut off . . . the righteous** [the green trees of 20:47] **and the wicked** [the dry trees of 20:47]. The sword of the Lord was being placed in the hands of Nebuchadnezzar. He was to serve as God's instrument of destruction against Israel and Ammon in this chapter, and against the Egyptians in chapter 32. The punishment of the righteous with the wicked is not a contradiction of Ezekiel's earlier teaching (see 14:12–20; 18:20) or of Genesis 18:23, 25. When the armies of Babylon came upon Jerusalem, both good and bad would lose their lives in the battle.

Ezekiel 18 focuses on the responsibility of the individual for individual guilt. That is one side of the coin. But the Bible also recognizes the reality of the concept of corporate responsibility when it comes to accounting for the effect of some individual sins. The case of Achan in Joshua 7:1–26 is the best example of corporate solidarity, for when Achan sinned, it was said that all Israel had sinned as well.[1]

Verses 4, 5. God's judgment was **against all flesh** (see 7:2; 20:47; Jer. 12:12), meaning all of the people who remained in the land, **from south to north** (v. 4). His judgment would not overlook anyone; all were to **know that I, the LORD, have drawn My sword out of its sheath** (v. 5). God would not return the sword to its sheath until judgment was complete—then, and only then, could it be returned (21:30).

21:6, 7
⁶"As for you, son of man, groan with breaking heart and bitter grief, groan in their sight. ⁷And when they say to you, 'Why do you groan?' you shall say, 'Because of the news that is coming; and every heart will melt, all hands will be feeble, every spirit will faint and all knees will be weak as water. Behold, it comes and it will happen,' declares the Lord GOD."

Verses 6, 7. Ezekiel was told to **groan with breaking heart** (v. 6). Whereas Jeremiah frequently expressed his personal feelings of suffering, Ezekiel's sufferings were wrapped up in the words of God. A question from those around him made it necessary for him to give a public explanation for his expression of grief. The question "Why do you groan?" has its counterpart in 12:9; 24:19; and 37:18 (see 20:49). The act of groaning is another of the prophet's signs (see 12:17–20). The command to groan would certainly have been easy for Ezekiel to obey. His love for the people and for his city caused him great anguish. This was a

---

[1] Walter C. Kaiser, Jr., Peter H. Davids, F. F. Bruce, and Manfred T. Brauch, *Hard Sayings of the Bible* (Downers Grove, Ill.: InterVarsity Press, 1996), 315.

time of great sadness for the righteous among God's people; their hearts were breaking to see the demise of their nation. Walther Zimmerli wrote,

> That this judgement is not simply an appointed fate, but an act of suffering, is made clear in the concluding sign-action, once again in a very harshly objective way. Yahweh commands the prophet to groan. . . . The verb אנח ["to groan"] . . . expresses, according to 24:17, an overwhelming experience of pain which precludes any outward expression. Such pain the prophet is commanded to show "before their eyes" with "breaking loins" and in "bitter pain." The loins, on which men fasten a sword for battle or a sackcloth for lamentation, are the center of physical strength (Job 40:16; Nah 2:2). When they are "broken" (מחץ Dtn 33:11), seized with trembling (חלחלה Nah 2:11; Is 21:3), brought to tottering (29:7), then this strength has gone.[2]

Ezekiel was sure to be asked the meaning of his groan-sign. The answer had to do with **the news that [was] coming** regarding Israel (v. 7). The arrival of that news would bring four reactions. God said,

1. **"Every heart will melt."** Hope for restoration would be shattered. Rather than having an attitude of courage and strength, their hearts would "melt."
2. **"All hands will be feeble."** The desire to work would vanish.
3. **"Every spirit will faint."** Literally, spirits would "be dim." Optimistic attitudes were gone; the people's reason for living was lost.
4. **"All knees will be weak as water."** The news of the complete destruction of Jerusalem would leave the exiles unable to stand.

---

[2]Walther Zimmerli, *Ezekiel 1: A Commentary on the Book of the Prophet Ezekiel, Chapters 1—24*, trans. Ronald E. Clements, Hermeneia (Philadelphia: Fortress Press, 1979), 425.

"Behold, it comes and it will happen," God declared. Some might have been comforting themselves with the thought "It will not really be that bad; God is only trying to scare us." To the contrary, God warned that these events would happen exactly as He had described.

The Song of the Sword (21:8–17)

21:8–13

⁸Again the word of the Lord came to me, saying, ⁹"Son of man, prophesy and say, 'Thus says the Lord.' Say,

'A sword, a sword sharpened
And also polished!
¹⁰Sharpened to make a slaughter,
Polished to flash like lightning!'

Or shall we rejoice, the rod of My son despising every tree? ¹¹It is given to be polished, that it may be handled; the sword is sharpened and polished, to give it into the hand of the slayer. ¹²Cry out and wail, son of man; for it is against My people, it is against all the officials of Israel. They are delivered over to the sword with My people, therefore strike your thigh. ¹³For there is a testing; and what if even the rod which despises will be no more?" declares the Lord God.

Verses 8–10. God instructed Ezekiel to describe the **sword** of the Lord (v. 9), and he used two descriptive words: **sharpened** and **polished** (v. 10a). As a soldier preparing to go to battle would sharpen his sword, the Lord had sharpened His sword so that it might have maximum effectiveness. His intent was not to injure, but to kill, to **slaughter**. Next is the idea of a soldier who has extended great effort in preparing his weapon, not only sharpening it, but polishing it, so that, when wielded, it will **flash like lightning**.

Verse 10b asks, **"Or shall we rejoice, the rod of My son despising every tree?"** This is extremely difficult to interpret, especially since we cannot know exactly who was speaking. Two predominant theories are offered.

First, the people of Israel could have been speaking. If this is correct, what might they have been saying? Perhaps it was "We are not terrified at the sight of the Lord's sword, because it is not drawn against us, but only against our enemies [**despising every tree**, meaning enemy nations]." Maybe they were saying, "Now that the Lord's sword is drawn, it is not time for us to be indifferent, but rather to rejoice that the Lord is acting." S. Fisch wrote,

> At once comes the Divine retort destructive of such complacency. There can be no occasion here for self-satisfaction. The sharpened and flashing sword is destined for use only against Judea; it rejects any other people. There is nothing in the Hebrew to correspond with *against* and the verb *ma'as* means "to reject" as well as "to despise." The translation may . . . be: "(the sword) is the rod of My son, it rejecteth every (other) tree." The word *rod* is commonly used for God's chastisement (cf. Isa. x. 24; xxx. 31; Lam. iii. 1), and the instrument of human punishment (cf. Prov. xiii. 24 . . .). Since Jerusalem is compared to a forest (verse 2), the nations are referred to as "trees."[3]

Second, the Lord could have been speaking to the sword, saying, "Shall God 'rejoice' with the sword now that it is removed from its sheath?" The sword is the "rod" (instrument of punishment) of "My son" (Nebuchadnezzar) who was "despising every tree" (allowing his armies to move indiscriminately through the land, killing everyone and everything in sight).

Verse 11. God had drawn the sword out of its sheath (v. 5). Now He instructed that it be polished, made ready, and then handed over to His executioner (Nebuchadnezzar).

---

[3] S. Fisch, *Ezekiel: Hebrew Text and English Translation with an Introduction and Commentary*, Soncino Books of the Bible (London: Soncino Press, 1950), 135.

Verse 12. The prophet was instructed to demonstrate his anguish openly, to **cry out and wail**, because this judgment was **against all the officials of Israel**. Israel's leaders had failed bitterly. This judgment was an indictment against them. Ezekiel was told, **"Strike your thigh."** (Though some versions read "breast," "thigh" is more accurate.) This was a gesture of deep sorrow and remorse (see Jer. 31:19).

Verse 13. For there is a testing. The people of Judah had been tested and found wanting. It was not the sword that was being tested, but God's people. The people had failed this test and now were subject to the sword.[4]

21:14–17

¹⁴"You therefore, son of man, prophesy and clap your hands together; and let the sword be doubled the third time, the sword for the slain. It is the sword for the great one slain, which surrounds them, ¹⁵that their hearts may melt, and many fall at all their gates. I have given the glittering sword. Ah! It is made for striking like lightning, it is wrapped up in readiness for slaughter. ¹⁶Show yourself sharp, go to the right; set yourself; go to the left, wherever your edge is appointed. ¹⁷I will also clap My hands together, and I will appease My wrath; I, the LORD, have spoken."

Verse 14. In a public show of approval for God's decision, Ezekiel was to **clap** [his] **hands**. He agreed with the judicial decision made by the Lord because of the sins of Judah (v. 14a; see 6:11; 22:13; 25:6). God also instructed **the sword** [to] **be doubled the third time**. This has been interpreted as follows: The sword had been doubled, and it would come the third time. Nebuchadnezzar came against Judea three times: against Jehoiakim, Jehoiachin (or Jeconiah), and then Zedekiah. The sword had already been doubled; it was to come the "third time" against Zedekiah. Another interpretation is that the sword was already

---

[4]The verb בֹּחַן (*bochan*, "testing") cannot refer to the feminine חֶרֶב (*chereb*, "sword"), but must refer contextually to the near masculine singular antecedent עָם (*'am*, "people").

at ideal effectiveness, being sharpened on its double edges. However, God wanted it to be even more effective, tripling its power (making it three times more effective than normal). The sword would be wielded with such force and swiftness that it would produce two to three times the normal slaughter.

No one would be able to escape, because the sword of God's judgment would be everywhere, It **"surrounds them,"** God said. Zedekiah and others thought that they could flee under the cover of darkness and escape Nebuchadnezzar's sword. Such was not the case, because God did not will it so. The king and all of the people of Jerusalem were surrounded.

Verse 15. God seems to have been showing the **sword** to those who would soon feel its sharp edge. The people reacted upon seeing this impressive instrument: It made **their hearts ... melt** (they were without courage and strength), **and many** [fell] **at all their gates**. Perhaps these intended to escape but were caught before they got out of the city.

Verse 16. The command given to the sword was, "**. . . go to the right . . . go to the left.**" The sharp sword was instructed to **set** itself and then begin its work in various directions. To the right was Jerusalem; to the left lay Ammon. Again, we see that God's judgment was to be thorough and complete.

Verse 17. The Lord gave His approval by clapping. He declared that His **wrath** would cease only when this judgment was complete.

The Sword of Nebuchadnezzar En Route to Jerusalem (21:18–27)

21:18–20
¹⁸**The word of the LORD came to me saying,** ¹⁹**"As for you, son of man, make two ways for the sword of the king of Babylon to come; both of them will go out of one land. And make a signpost; make it at the head of the way to the city.** ²⁰**You shall mark a way for the sword to come to Rabbah of the sons of Ammon, and to Judah into fortified Jerusalem."**

Verses 18, 19. The next instruction was to **make two ways**

(v. 18). Ezekiel was told to build some road signs, telling the sword which way to go. The one bearing **the sword, the king of Babylon** (**the one land**) would come with two missions (two ways for the sword). As Nebuchadnezzar and his army approached, he was given directions to Jerusalem (v. 19). John B. Taylor said,

> The word which occurs most frequently in this section is the word *appoint* (AV; 19, 20, 22 twice). The Hebrew word is the more modest *sum* or *sim*, which simply means "to put" or "to place". It does however suggest once again that Ezekiel is intended to combine his message here with a symbolical performance of the advance of the Babylonian king along the road to Jerusalem, with suitable routes mapped out upon the ground. The first act is to mark out the road stemming from Babylon, or probably from the north, shaped like an inverted Y, with Jerusalem and Rabbath Ammon (suitably sign-posted) at the end of its two prongs. Then the various kinds of divination practised by the king as he stood at the parting of the ways are re-enacted. The alternatives were an assault on the Ammonite capital city (modern Amman) or a siege of Jerusalem.[5]

Verse 20. As if guiding a confused traveler, Ezekiel was to **mark a way for the sword**. It had two appointed destinations, and Ezekiel had to make sure it would arrive at both places.

21:21–23
21"For the king of Babylon stands at the parting of the way, at the head of the two ways, to use divination; he shakes the arrows, he consults the household idols, he looks at the liver. 22Into his right hand came the divination, 'Jerusalem,' to set battering rams, to open the mouth for slaughter, to lift up the voice with a battle cry, to set battering rams against the gates,

---

[5]John B. Taylor, *Ezekiel: An Introduction and Commentary*, Tyndale Old Testament Commentaries (Downers Grove, Ill.: Inter-Varsity Press, 1969), 163.

to cast up ramps, to build a siege wall. ²³And it will be to them like a false divination in their eyes; they have sworn solemn oaths. But he brings iniquity to remembrance, that they may be seized."

Verse 21. When Nebuchadnezzar reached the fork in the road that Ezekiel had marked, he used three methods of **divination** to determine which way he should go first: (1) **He shakes the arrows**—Arrows were marked with names or places, shaken up in a quiver, and then drawn out. The markings on the arrow drawn determined the place or person chosen. (2) **He consults the household idols**—Literally, these were the "teraphim" (תְּרָפִים, *th⁰rapim*). They were small images of pagan gods, used not only for personal worship, but also for legal matters (see Gen. 31:19–35). It is not known exactly how this household idol would be "consulted," but presumably it would be in a rite in which an answer was discernible through a series of "signs" established before the worship rite was begun. (3) **He looks at the liver**— This refers to hepatoscopy, an ancient practice of examining the liver or entrails of a sacrificial victim. It was a common practice in Babylonian divination and was carried into ancient Rome as well. The interpretation of markings on such organs was one of the skills in which Ancient Near Eastern soothsayers were instructed, as numbers of clay models unearthed by archaeologists appear to indicate.[6] This is the only time this practice is alluded to in the Old Testament.

Verse 22. The answer was given: Nebuchadnezzar was to attack **Jerusalem**. Perhaps Nebuchadnezzar drew out of the quiver the arrow that had "Jerusalem" written on it. Further instructions were supplied on the military tactics to be used. Whether or not this was also a part of the divination process is not stated. Nebuchadnezzar was to . . .

1. **Set battering rams.** This was done to break down the city gates or make a breach in the city wall. A battering

---

[6]J. D. Douglas, ed., "Marks," *New Bible Dictionary*, 2d ed. (Wheaton, Ill.: Tyndale House Publishers, 1982), 742.

ram was a tall tower that had a beam extending from ropes below. The beam, with a reinforced head (sometimes bronze cast in the shape of a ram), would swing back and forth, beating against the gate until its hinges were weakened or its planks broken.
2. **Open the mouth for slaughter.** That is, he was to give the order to slaughter.
3. **Lift up the voice with a battle cry.** The commanders were urging the solders to fight bravely and to secure victory.
4. **Set battering rams against the gates.**
5. **Cast up ramps.** Ramps ("mounds"; ASV) of rock and sand were piled against the city wall to enable the army to enter the city or attack the soldiers of the city.
6. **Build a siege wall.**[7]

Verse 23. These events would be **to them like a false divination**. The people of Jerusalem would not believe in the legitimacy of the "divination" but would be convinced that it was "false." They would be encouraged in this view by the false prophets in the city, who were continually pronouncing messages of peace. In addition, they would believe the divination to be false because they had **sworn solemn oaths**. This oath has been interpreted as follows:

(1) It could have been part of the covenant they had with the Lord. They did not believe He would let Nebuchadnezzar come against them.

(2) It could have been a peace treaty signed with Nebuchadnezzar. Even though they had been unfaithful to earlier promises to Nebuchadnezzar, they now believed their relationship with him to be secure. They did not think that he had any reason to come against them. Ralph H. Alexander wrote,

> The phrase "sworn allegiance" ["solemn oaths"] has led to two basic interpretations. Some maintain that the oaths were involved in the Mosaic covenant, for Judah had

---
[7]See the discussion on 4:2.

already broken her agreements with Nebuchadnezzar and would not be relying on them. Others maintain that the treaty-oaths were those made with Babylonia, for contextually the two participants are Babylonia and Judah. One could argue that the Mosaic covenant had already been broken; so Judah would not be relying on it. Perhaps the argument of the entire passage and the prophet's earlier invective against breaking political treaties (cf. 17:16–18) lends greater weight to the treaty concept with Babylonia. Regardless of which view we accept, Judah was placing unfounded confidence in treaties she had broken. This provided no security at all. Judah was deluded. On the contrary, Nebuchadnezzar ("he") would bring Judah's iniquity to remembrance when he, as God's instrument of wrath, destroyed the nation.[8]

21:24–27

^{24}"Therefore, thus says the Lord GOD, 'Because you have made your iniquity to be remembered, in that your transgressions are uncovered, so that in all your deeds your sins appear—because you have come to remembrance, you will be seized with the hand. ^{25}And you, O slain, wicked one, the prince of Israel, whose day has come, in the time of the punishment of the end,' ^{26}thus says the Lord GOD, 'Remove the turban and take off the crown; this will no longer be the same. Exalt that which is low and abase that which is high. ^{27}A ruin, a ruin, a ruin, I will make it. This also will be no more until He comes whose right it is, and I will give it to Him.'"

Verse 24. God was willing to forget sins of which the people had repented. However, those left unaddressed (and added to) would be **remembered**. Judah's sins had not been hidden. Her transgressions were in the open for all to see; therefore, she was

---

[8]Ralph H. Alexander, "Ezekiel," in *The Expositor's Bible Commentary*, ed. Frank E. Gaebelein (Grand Rapids, Mich.: Zondervan Publishing House, 1986), 6:844.

to be **seized with the hand**. She might try to escape, but Nebuchadnezzar would catch her.

Verse 25. Here is a reference to the **slain, wicked one, the prince of Israel**. The evil king of Judah, Zedekiah, was classified as the "wicked one" and was portrayed as already "slain." This was fulfilled in 587(6) B.C. It is thought that Zedekiah hastened this fate when he tried to make an alliance with Ammon, hoping they would join with him to fight against Babylon.

Verse 26. God described the end of both the monarchy (**the crown**) and the priesthood (the high priest's **turban**). (See Ex. 28:4, 37, 39; 29:6; 39:28, 31; Lev. 8:9; 16:4.[9]) The phrase **this will no longer be the same** is troublesome. It appears to be a declaration from God that, with the removal of the crown and the turban, a permanent end was coming to Judah—both politically and religiously. There would be "no more" kings or priests until God brought in one who was truly qualified. Presumably, this would mean until God reestablished His people in the land, or until the coming of Christ—who is both Priest and King (Zech. 6:12, 13). God's judgment would throw everything into confusion. The people were to **exalt that which is low and abase that which is high**. In captivity, all previous positions were worthless.

Verse 27. A ruin, a ruin, a ruin is what God would make of the city. This type of terminology is always emphatic in Hebrew (see Is. 6:3; Jer. 7:4). The triple emphasis spells out that God would make "a ruin" of the city and its king. This would stay in effect **until He comes whose right it is, and I will give it to Him**. This seems to be an allusion to Genesis 49:10, which says that God's true king will be placed on the throne. If this is referring to the Christ (and no one can be certain that it is), it is a sort of enthronement announcement similar to that in Psalm 2. Nevertheless, this mysterious phrase still offers a glimmer of hope.

---

[9]"Zedekiah is addressed typically, not as king, *melek*, but as prince, *nasi*, a word without Messianic overtones. The *mitre* (RV; *diadem* in AV) is the *turban* (from a word meaning 'to wind' . . . RSV) worn by the high priest (Ex. 28:4, 37, 39; 29:6; 39:28, 31; Lv. 8:9; 16:4). It is used only here as a symbol of royalty. There is no evidence that Zedekiah had added to his crimes by usurping priestly functions" (Taylor, 164).

All was not lost. Eventually, God would give the kingdom to a more worthy king.

The Sword of the Chaldean Conquest (21:28–32)

²⁸"And you, son of man, prophesy and say, 'Thus says the Lord GOD concerning the sons of Ammon and concerning their reproach,' and say: 'A sword, a sword is drawn, polished for the slaughter, to cause it to consume, that it may be like lightning—²⁹while they see for you false visions, while they divine lies for you—to place you on the necks of the wicked who are slain, whose day has come, in the time of the punishment of the end. ³⁰Return it to its sheath. In the place where you were created, in the land of your origin, I will judge you. ³¹I will pour out My indignation on you; I will blow on you with the fire of My wrath, and I will give you into the hand of brutal men, skilled in destruction. ³²You will be fuel for the fire; your blood will be in the midst of the land. You will not be remembered, for I, the LORD, have spoken.'"

Verse 28. If the Ammonites thought they could escape God's wrath (which came through Nebuchadnezzar) when the Babylonian army went to Jerusalem first, they were wrong. The **drawn** and **polished** sword was soon to begin its work against Judah's neighbor to the east.

Verse 29. Ammon delighted in the demise of Judah, yet the leaders of this nation had been deceived by those who would **see . . . false visions** and **divine lies** for them. They believed that they would be able to attack and defeat Judah. However, **the wicked who are slain** is a reference to those killed by Babylon, not by Ammon.

Verse 30. God determined to stay the execution of Ammon temporarily. He commanded that the sword be returned **to its sheath**. The reason for this delay is not stated. The eventual end of Ammon would come on their own soil. God said, **"Where you were created, in the land of your origin, I will judge you."** (See 25:1–7.)

Verse 31. When God's day of judgment finally arrived for Ammon, they would experience the full fury of His anger. He would **pour out** [His] **indignation** and **wrath**, giving the Ammonites into the hands of a vicious and destructive army. Identified as "the sons of the East" in 25:4, these were marauding bands living in the desert. If Ammon thought that the Lord was a local Judean deity, they were terribly mistaken. They, too, would have to answer to the Judge of the universe.

Verse 32. History records that Nebuchadnezzar did, in fact, return to conquer Ammon. After destroying Jerusalem in 586 B.C., he turned his attention to Ammon. In 581 B.C. Nebuchadnezzar succeeded in destroying the chief Ammonite city, Rabbah. While this did not completely eliminate the Ammonites (they still existed in intertestamental times), they eventually died out. Today there is no such nationality. Taylor said,

> Their ultimate fate will be worse than Israel's and worse even than Egypt's, for they will be *no more remembered*. To the Semitic mind nothing could be more terrible: no prospect of restoration, no continuance in succeeding generations, no memorial, not even a memory. Oblivion.[10]

APPLICATION

Israel and God's Divine Purpose

All nations are under the control of God. He can and will use them to accomplish His divine purposes. Romans 13:1–4 says,

> Every person is to be in subjection to the governing authorities. For there is no authority except from God, and those which exist are established by God. Therefore whoever resists authority has opposed the ordinance of God; and they who have opposed will receive condemnation upon themselves. For rulers are not a cause of fear for good behavior, but for evil. Do you want to

---

[10]Ibid., 165.

have no fear of authority? Do what is good and you will have praise from the same; for it is a minister of God to you for good. But if you do what is evil, be afraid; for it does not bear the sword for nothing; for it is a minister of God, an avenger who brings wrath on the one who practices evil.

True people of God are grieved by the sins of others (21:12). Jesus said, "Blessed are those who mourn, for they shall be comforted" (Mt. 5:4).

D.P.

Growing in Captivity

Nothing can limit God's work through man and circumstances. Joseph spent years in prison, but God used him even during this confinement. Paul wrote Ephesians, Philippians, Colossians, and Philemon while in prison (Acts 28:30, 31). He taught that even chains can glorify God.

From this viewpoint, the Captivity was a healthy experience for the southern kingdom. Being taken to another land, far away from Jerusalem, taught Judah that (1) sin does not pay, (2) idolatry is wrong and must not be practiced, (3) God cannot fellowship sin, (4) God keeps His promises, and (5) God can chastise without destroying His eternal purpose.

Judgment Facts (21:1–14)

God instructed Ezekiel to announce His judgment against His people. He said, "Son of man, set your face toward Jerusalem, and speak against the sanctuaries and prophesy against the land of Israel" (v. 2). The capital city of Jerusalem, the places of worship, and the land were to receive the brunt of His sentence. Wickedness was flourishing in all of these places, and it was time for the sword of the Lord to be unsheathed.

Embedded in this judgment oracle are the divine principles of eternal judgment. God's condemnation of sin does not waver. He is constant and unchanging in all His attributes. The expression of His wrath in this passage was for a specific time and place, but the elements of that expression will also be incorporated into His judgment of all people at the end of the Christian Age.

His judgment is certain. As surely as He is the Lord, judgment will come. His righteousness and holiness demand a day of reckoning for sin. We see this truth conceptualized and demonstrated in the Old Testament. It then reaches its climax in the New Testament. (See Rom. 14:12; 2 Cor. 5:10; Rev. 20:9, 10.)

His judgment is comprehensive. No one will be excused from it; every accountable person will stand before Him. Ezekiel is told to cry because of its completeness and thoroughness. God said, "Cry out and wail, son of man; for it is against My people, it is against all the officials of Israel" (v. 12). He further said, "Because I will cut off from you the righteous and the wicked, therefore My sword will go forth from its sheath against all flesh from south to north" (v. 4; see Mt. 25:31–34).

His judgment is severe. It will be the eternal judgment of God. Nothing can compare to His judgment. God said, ". . . when they say to you, 'Why do you groan?' you shall say, 'Because of the news that is coming; and every heart will melt, all hands will be feeble, every spirit will faint and all knees will be weak as water. Behold, it comes and it will happen,' declares the Lord GOD" (vv. 6, 7). God's people were to face a time of testing unlike any previous time. In a similar way, the final judgment will be the climax of human history (see Heb. 9:27).

His judgment is righteous. When His judgment is understood, all will say, "God is righteous. Just and right are all His ways." God's actions are never needless or unnecessary. They are mandatory because they grow out of His truth and character. Ezekiel was not only to groan, but he was to clap his hands—he was to groan in grief and clap his hands in gladness. While he agonized over its coming, he was to applaud the righteous character of God for His appropriate judgment sentence.

God's sword glittered. It was sharpened and polished—available and ready. It was to be placed in the hand of Nebuchadnezzar, and he would use it. Likewise, God's eternal judgment has been designated and recorded on His calendar. His judgment has been announced and described in His Word, and it will come suddenly and swiftly at God's bidding. At the time of His appearing, Jesus will occupy the judgment seat, and the execution of judgment will be placed in the hand.

From the Dust of Disaster (21:18–32)

All things are not good, and all things do not work together for good. However, in behalf of His people, God can bring good out of all things, even disasters like the fall of Jerusalem. He used Nebuchadnezzar, a pagan king, to discipline the nation He had chosen; but from that discipline, His people learned repentance and turned from their idolatry.

God said to His people, "I will pour out My indignation on you; I will blow on you with the fire of My wrath, and I will give you into the hand of brutal men, skilled in destruction" (v. 31). A bright and polished sword was placed in Nebuchadnezzar's hand, and he was directed to Jerusalem to administer their chastisement. Two signposts were put up, one of which had the name "Jerusalem" on it. Nebuchadnezzar would be guided by that signpost to Jerusalem and would wage war against the city. The prophet was told, "Into his right hand came the divination, 'Jerusalem,' to set battering rams, to open the mouth for slaughter, to lift up the voice with a battle cry, to set battering rams against the gates, to cast up ramps, to build a siege wall" (v. 22).

Could good come from the destruction of Jerusalem? What vital lessons rise up from the dust of this disaster?

First, we learn that sins can be forgiven, but they will not be overlooked. What an important lesson to learn! Judah's sins were in plain sight, public and visible. They would be seen and remembered: "Because you have made your iniquity to be remembered, in that your transgressions are uncovered, . . . you will be seized with the hand" (v. 24). God will forgive the sins of anyone who comes to Him in trusting obedience, but the sins of the impenitent will be punished. Solomon said, "He who conceals his transgressions will not prosper, but he who confesses and forsakes them will find compassion" (Prov. 28:13).

Second, we learn that leaders will give an account for their leadership. Let us not miss this lesson. Zedekiah, an evil king of Judah, was made to answer for his sins. Of him it was said, "And you,

O slain, wicked one, the prince of Israel, whose day has come, in the time of the punishment of the end" (v. 25). He was to be God's representative, but he sided with evil; he was to be God's servant, but he became the devil's henchman. Leadership positions bring with them high privileges, but they also bring grave responsibilities. God will hold every leader accountable for the way he handles his position.

Third, we learn that God exalts the humble and abases the exalted. Pity the person who fails to learn this lesson. Zedekiah had received a place of honor; but God said, "Remove the turban and take off the crown; this will no longer be the same. Exalt that which is low and abase that which is high" (v. 26).

Paul named three groups out of which "not many" are called by the gospel: ". . . not many wise according to the flesh, not many mighty, not many noble" (1 Cor. 1:26). The worldly wise, the people in powerful positions, and the aristocrat will not humble themselves and receive the gospel. Jesus added a fourth group, the rich (Mt. 19:23). Paul further said, "God has chosen the foolish things of the world to shame the wise, and God has chosen the weak things of the world to shame the things which are strong" (1 Cor. 1:27). God looks for a heart that humbles itself before His Word. He then lifts up this heart with His grace.

We should read God's instructions, take them to heart, and apply them to life. This kind of obedience requires no divine punishment and brings great rewards. However, when God's instructions are ignored, He attempts to get our attention in other ways, as He did Judah's. He puts a bridle on us and *makes* us take notice of our foolishness. In Psalm 32, David urged the readers not to be like rebellious horses and mules: "Do not be as the horse or as the mule which have no understanding, whose trappings include bit and bridle to hold them in check, otherwise they will not come near to you" (v. 9). One becomes like a horse or mule when he is stubborn and must be made to obey.

E.C.

Chapter 22

The Oracle Against Jerusalem

Chapter 22 falls into three sections dealing with the impurity of Jerusalem and the people of Judah. The first section (vv. 1–16) is an indictment of the city with her sins of bloodshed, idolatry, adultery, and oppression. It includes a judgment from God that exile and dispersion were inevitable. The second section (vv. 17–22) speaks of the refiner's furnace (God's judgment) being used to purify the city. As a fire burns the dross from the ore, so God's punishment would consume the wicked. The third section (vv. 23–31) reveals the evildoing of the whole population of Judah, including leaders, priests, princes, and prophets. No righteous souls were found to spare the city. The doom of Jerusalem was sealed. The repetition of words like "blood" and "bloodshed" is noticeable (vv. 2, 3, 4, 6, 9, 12, 13, 27). Her judgment was obviously related to her being "the bloody city."

THE SINS OF JERUSALEM (22)

An Indictment of the City (22:1–16)

22:1–6

¹Then the word of the LORD came to me, saying, ²"And you, son of man, will you judge, will you judge the bloody city? Then cause her to know all her abominations. ³You shall say, 'Thus says the Lord GOD, "A city shedding blood in her midst, so that her time will come, and that makes idols, contrary to her interest, for defilement! ⁴You have become guilty by the

blood which you have shed, and defiled by your idols which you have made. Thus you have brought your day near and have come to your years; therefore I have made you a reproach to the nations and a mocking to all the lands. ⁵Those who are near and those who are far from you will mock you, you of ill repute, full of turmoil.

⁶""'Behold, the rulers of Israel, each according to his power, have been in you for the purpose of shedding blood."'"

Verses 1, 2. "Will you judge the bloody city?" God asked Ezekiel (v. 2). He assigned Ezekiel the job of "judge" and prosecutor, saying, "**. . . cause her to know all her abominations.**" Ezekiel already had eyewitness evidence against the city, having seen the four abominable acts mentioned in chapter 8. He was charged with the task of presenting the evidence, then announcing the sentence to be decreed as a result of her sins.

Verse 3. If ever there could be a "holy city," it should have been Jerusalem. She should have been a shining example to the nations of what God wanted from His people, yet this was **a city shedding blood.** With the Law, the prophets, and her glorious history, Jerusalem had every advantage. What else could she possibly want or need in order to be a faithful city? Her needs had been supplied by God.

Instead of being a holy city, she became the opposite. She became "the bloody city" (v. 2) of **defilement** (v. 3). Her choices were **contrary to her interest**—that is, they were not in the best interests of her future, her security, or, foremost, her relationship with God. Chapter 22 lists the sins of the bloody city: idolatry (vv. 3, 4); irreverence (vv. 7, 8); contempt for parents (vv. 7a, 10); injustice to the helpless (vv. 7b, 12); Sabbath-breaking (v. 8); sexual abominations (vv. 10, 11); extortion (vv. 12, 13); and greed among the leaders (vv. 26, 27).

Verse 4. Verses 4 through 6 link the worshiping of **idols** and the bloodshed. The worship to the god Molech involved child sacrifice, thereby shedding the blood of innocent children (see 16:21; 20:26, 31; 23:37). However, blood had also been shed in other ways, including murder and violence. As adultery shatters the foundation of the relationship between husband and wife, so idolatry destroyed the relationship between God and His people. Instead of being a glorious city, the envy of all the nations, she became **a reproach**—an object of ridicule and mockery among them.

Verse 5. The message for Ezekiel to give to Jerusalem was "[People] **will mock you.**" Others knew the city's reputation, whether they lived **near** or **far**. She could have made a positive impact, even in faraway places. Instead, she became nationally known for her wickedness. She was a city of **ill repute** that was **full of turmoil**. This was not a desirable place to live or to have a family!

Verse 6. The rulers of Israel, who received their **power** from the Lord, abused that power. Each, exercising the privilege of power, used it to do evil deeds (**for the purpose of shedding blood**).

22:7–12

⁷"'"**They have treated father and mother lightly within you. The alien they have oppressed in your midst; the fatherless and the widow they have wronged in you. ⁸You have despised My holy things and profaned My sabbaths. ⁹Slanderous men have been in you for the purpose of shedding blood, and in you they have eaten at the mountain shrines. In your midst they have committed acts of lewdness. ¹⁰In you they have uncovered their fathers' nakedness; in you they have humbled her who was unclean in her menstrual impurity. ¹¹One has committed abomination with his neighbor's wife and another has lewdly defiled his daughter-in-law. And another in you has humbled his sister, his father's daughter. ¹²In you they have taken bribes to shed blood; you have taken interest and profits, and you have injured your neighbors for gain by oppression, and you have forgotten Me," declares the Lord God.'"**

Verse 7. They have treated father and mother lightly. The subject "they" does not refer to "the rulers of Israel" in verse 6, but to the people of Judea generally. They were faithless to the Law which repeatedly commanded them to honor their parents (Ex. 20:12; Lev. 19:3) and give fair treatment to **the alien . . . the**

fatherless and the widow. Those in need of assistance should have been able to go to Jerusalem for help. Instead, it was a place that the poor and oppressed wanted to avoid.

Verse 8. God's ordinances were not only ignored, but they were even **despised**. The various elements of God's temple and the **holy things** there were counted as rubbish. God's instructions regarding the **sabbaths** were openly profaned (disobeyed and spoken against).

Verse 9. Slanderous men found a haven within the city walls of Jerusalem, **for the purpose of shedding blood**. Lying and bearing false witness were in themselves forbidden by the Law (see Lev. 19:16); but the purpose of these slanders was to secure the death penalty of innocent people. This sin was a double evil. Within the city there was no integrity, no honesty, and apparently no safety for the righteous.

Verse 10. The expression **uncovered their fathers' nakedness** is a reference to incestuous marriage with a stepmother, prohibited in Leviticus 18:7, 8. **Humbled her ... in her menstrual impurity** may refer to a dual sin—not only rape (see Ezek. 18:6; Lev. 18:19; 20:18), but also having relations with a woman who was **unclean** (because of her menstrual cycle).

Verse 11. Neglecting God's instructions about the purity of marriage and the law of love, citizens of Jerusalem had frequently committed the **abomination** of adultery and incest. They had no moral reservations, but conducted themselves **lewdly**—with behavior that normally would be considered unthinkable, exceptionally depraved.

Verse 12. "You have forgotten Me," God declared. Those engaging in such activities did not have God on their minds. Their conduct had taken them far away from Him, His law, and His worship. Like those to whom Jeremiah prophesied, they had forgotten the Lord, for "days without number," not treating people as He had commanded (Jer. 2:32; see 5:7–9; 6:13; 7:5, 6; 22:3). Walther Zimmerli said,

> Thus it now becomes quite clear that we are dealing in the whole full listing of laws that have been broken, not with several things, but ultimately with one thing:

the turning away from the Lord, who gives to everything in life its order. Ezekiel loves to express this elsewhere more sharply with the word מרה "to be rebellious," (cf. 20:8, 13, 21).... In essence he stands exactly where Hosea stood in his list of offenses in Hos 4:2, or Jeremiah with his list in 7:9. In both prophets more is meant than the summing up of individual offenses. They both, together now with Ezekiel as a third, want to accuse the people of disobedience against an overall will.... They "forget" God and thereby dishonor him, who looks for obedience, not in any hidden "spirituality," but in the multiplicity of concrete situations in life. In the heightened accusation of sin, which goes far beyond Hos 4:2 and Jer 7:9, we can see the radical sharpening of the "accusation" which Ezekiel makes.[1]

God had witnessed the many ways they had oppressed others. They had (1) **taken bribes** and even injuring or killing others; (2) **taken interest**, which was forbidden in the Law; (3) "taken" [unlawful] **profits**; and (4) **injured** [their] **neighbors for gain by oppression.**

22:13–16

[13]"""Behold, then, I smite My hand at your dishonest gain which you have acquired and at the bloodshed which is among you. [14]Can your heart endure, or can your hands be strong in the days that I will deal with you? I, the LORD, have spoken and will act. [15]I will scatter you among the nations and I will disperse you through the lands, and I will consume your uncleanness from you. [16]You will profane yourself in the sight of the nations, and you will know that I am the LORD.""""

Carl Howie made three important observations from verses 13 through 16:

---

[1]Walther Zimmerli, *Ezekiel 1: A Commentary on the Book of the Prophet Ezekiel, Chapters 1—24*, trans. Ronald E. Clements, Hermeneia (Philadelphia: Fortress Press, 1979), 459.

[1] First, the Lord will punish those whose prime purposes are dishonest gain and shedding of blood. Economic and moral factors affect God's relationship to men. The Lord will not support a nation whose god is gain and whose only moral law is license. [2] The second implication is even more compelling: "Can your courage endure, or can your hands be strong, in the days that I shall deal with you?" The answer of experience is: No. Righteousness alone is the source of national strength; apart from it, social order is debilitated by sin and courage is diluted by immorality and duplicity. [3] Finally, the Almighty makes clear that he cannot and will not be neutral under these circumstances, but will punish the culprits and destroy their "filthiness." His name will be profaned among the nations, yet even in the face of this unfortunate result he will send them into exile. Ordinarily Ezekiel explains much of God's action on the supposition that the Almighty wishes at all costs to avoid profanation of his name; that is, misunderstanding of his Person and purpose.[2]

Verse 13. The Lord said, **"Behold, then."** He was calling for attention; it was time for Israel to listen carefully. He was about to speak, announcing His decision in light of the evidence presented against her: He would **smite** [His] **hand** at Israel's **dishonest gain.** This gesture is to be understood here as one illustrating total disgust and anger. It may be, however, that the loud "smack" made when the hand was struck was to awaken Israel.

Verses 14–16. The powerful repetition of the pronoun **I** dominates this section. It is used five times in announcing what God was going to do to Israel. As predicted before, God again declared that He would **scatter** the people among the nations and **disperse** them through the lands (v. 15). The idea of a united people living together in their own land was lost. God's reason

---

[2]Carl G. Howie, *The Book of Ezekiel, The Book of Daniel,* The Layman's Bible Commentary, vol. 13 (Richmond, Va.: John Knox Press, 1961), 52–53.

for this was made clear: **"I will consume your uncleanness from you."** The only way to get rid of the evil was to root it out and permanently remove it. The fires which would consume Jerusalem would also burn up the idolatrous shrines set up in her city streets. Again, God declared the main reason for this judgment: **". . . you will know that I am the Lord"** (v. 16).

The Refiner's Furnace
(22:17–22)

¹⁷And the word of the Lord came to me, saying, ¹⁸"Son of man, the house of Israel has become dross to Me; all of them are bronze and tin and iron and lead in the furnace; they are the dross of silver. ¹⁹Therefore, thus says the Lord God, 'Because all of you have become dross, therefore, behold, I am going to gather you into the midst of Jerusalem. ²⁰As they gather silver and bronze and iron and lead and tin into the furnace to blow fire on it in order to melt it, so I will gather you in My anger and in My wrath and I will lay you there and melt you. ²¹I will gather you and blow on you with the fire of My wrath, and you will be melted in the midst of it. ²²As silver is melted in the furnace, so you will be melted in the midst of it; and you will know that I, the Lord, have poured out My wrath on you.'"

Verses 17, 18. God expanded the thought given in verse 15—that He would "consume" the uncleanness from Israel. A common process in ancient Israel was that of purifying metal by melting it down and removing the **dross** that rises to the top of liquefied metal (see Is. 1:22, 25; 48:10; Jer. 6:27–30; 9:7; Zech. 13:9; Mal. 3:2, 3). When God "melted" Israel, He would find nothing worth keeping: Israel was nothing but dross! Whereas the people were once like precious metals, like silver and bronze, they had become totally worthless.

Verse 19. Beginning with **therefore**, God drew a logical conclusion. What is done with dross? Does it have any value or purpose? Is there any reason to preserve it? No! Therefore, since **all** of Israel had become **dross**, God would gather them **into the**

midst of Jerusalem, making that formerly holy city the boiling pot where the dross would be consumed.

Verses 20–22. In the midst of this boiling pot, Jerusalem, God would **melt** them (v. 20). Since God had already declared that the entire nation was dross, this seems like an unnecessary process. However, as an illustration of God's thorough judgment—and for the sake of fairness—He would go through this process. Perhaps, buried in the middle of the dross might be a piece of precious metal. Could someone in the midst of the nation have remained as **silver**? It appears, sadly, that the only "good" that would come from this process was to teach Israel to **know that I, the LORD, have poured out My wrath on you** (v. 22). This judgment did not come from the gods of Babylon.

The Evil of the Whole Population (22:23–31)

22:23–25

²³And the word of the LORD came to me, saying, ²⁴"Son of man, say to her, 'You are a land that is not cleansed or rained on in the day of indignation.' ²⁵There is a conspiracy of her prophets in her midst like a roaring lion tearing the prey. They have devoured lives; they have taken treasure and precious things; they have made many widows in the midst of her."

Verses 23, 24. "You are a land that is not cleansed," Judah was told (v. 23). The Bible often speaks of the land being defiled by the iniquities of its inhabitants (see 36:17, 18; Num. 35:34; Deut. 21:23). The Jews made no effort to purify their land. Therefore, they would not receive one of God's discernible blessings: rain (v. 24).

Verse 25. Ezekiel had given a scathing rebuke of the **prophets** in chapter 13. The NIV has "princes"; there is confusion as to which is meant here. These prophets or princes had taken advantage of their position by oppression and bloodshed (**they have made many widows**; see Jer. 15:8).

22:26–28

26"Her priests have done violence to My law and have profaned My holy things; they have made no distinction between the holy and the profane, and they have not taught the difference between the unclean and the clean; and they hide their eyes from My sabbaths, and I am profaned among them. ²⁷Her princes within her are like wolves tearing the prey, by shedding blood and destroying lives in order to get dishonest gain. ²⁸Her prophets have smeared whitewash for them, seeing false visions and divining lies for them, saying, 'Thus says the Lord God,' when the Lord has not spoken."

Next, God identified every part of Israel's society: "her priests" (v. 26), "her princes" (v. 27), "her prophets" (v. 28), and "the people" (v. 29). None were without guilt. Individual responsibility is seen again here. Regardless of what the religious leaders (the priests and prophets) or the political leaders (the princes) were doing, God expected the people to remain faithful.

Verse 26. They have made no distinction between the holy and the profane. The priests had the divine commission to teach the people and to practice personally the duty of separating the "holy" and the "profane." God had identified some things as strange (unapproved) and some as recognized. The priests, who were to study the law diligently so as to be able to make such a "distinction," failed to do so.

Verse 27. Ezekiel referred to **her princes within her**. The word for "prince" (נָשִׂיא, *naśi'*) is different from that used here, where the Hebrew word is שָׂרִים (*śarim*, "nobles"). The former refers to members of the royal house; the latter is used for leaders or chiefs of the people.[3] Whereas they were compared to lions in verse 25, here they are likened to **wolves**, tearing apart their victims. Why did they act this way? **To get dishonest gain.** Indeed, wealth is a motivating factor for all sorts of evil.

Verse 28. As in chapter 13, the **prophets** are said to have **smeared whitewash**. They had covered up the obvious sins of

---

[3]Francis Brown, S. R. Driver, and Charles A. Briggs, *A Hebrew and English Lexicon of the Old Testament* (Oxford: Clarendon Press, 1972), 672.

the nation with lies and false prophecies. They claimed to be speaking a word from God when, in fact, God had not spoken to them at all. This was an intentional and malicious attempt to deceive and mislead.

22:29–31

²⁹"The people of the land have practiced oppression and committed robbery, and they have wronged the poor and needy and have oppressed the sojourner without justice. ³⁰I searched for a man among them who would build up the wall and stand in the gap before Me for the land, so that I would not destroy it; but I found no one. ³¹Thus I have poured out My indignation on them; I have consumed them with the fire of My wrath; their way I have brought upon their heads," declares the Lord God.

Verse 29. The final group to fall under God's condemnation was **the people of the land**. What were their sins? (1) They **practiced oppression**. The verb "practiced" indicates a repeated activity with some degree of proficiency. (2) They **committed robbery**. (3) They **wronged the poor and needy**. (4) They **oppressed the sojourner without justice**. While on foreign soil, a person still deserves "justice." Certainly, fair treatment would be expected among God's people, but such was not the case. There was no concern for fairness and equity in dealing with the sojourner.

Verse 30. "I searched for a man . . . but I found no one," God said. Having named four classes of people, He declared that He had examined them all yet found "no one" living righteously. The ills of the society were being left unattended because no one was willing to **build up the wall** that had broken down; none would **stand in the gap** and represent the people with righteousness (see 13:5; Jer. 15:1). Here God is portrayed as one about to enter the city through a hole in the protective wall, and no one was concerned enough to keep Him from entering the city to destroy it.

The truth taught in this passage is different from the one in 14:14. There the presence of righteous men (such as Noah, Daniel, and Job) was said to be insufficient to save the city. One's righteousness would only be sufficient to save himself. Here, the concern is whether or not a righteous person would even have attempted to save the city. Corruption was so widespread that Israel had no champions to represent her to the Lord or try to dissuade the people from their wickedness.[4]

Verse 31. The chapter closes with the statement **Thus I have poured out My indignation....** The tense of the three verbs ("have poured out" ... **have consumed ... have brought**) makes some think that this passage is misplaced and should actually have come after the fall of Jerusalem. However, this is an example of a prophecy so certain to be fulfilled that it is spoken of as having already been fulfilled. These prophecies demonstrate the surety of God's Word.

APPLICATION

Living as God's Family

Just being in the family of God is no assurance of proper behavior. God's children must always be alert to the world around them, while being sensitive to the laws of God. This is the only way they can keep themselves pure.

Every person in God's family, whether a leader or not, is accountable to Him (vv. 26–31).

"Holy" vs. "Profane" (22:26)

The Jerusalem priests failed to distinguish between what was "holy" and "profane." This tendency has always existed among God's people. We do not want to cause trouble or appear unloving. We do not want to seem intolerant. Meanwhile, what *God wants* is ignored.

The Scriptures teach that we should "respect what is right in the sight of all men" and that we should try to "be at peace with all men" (Rom. 12:17, 18). Did God mean, though, that we

---

[4]Obviously, Jeremiah was an exception to this. However, Jeremiah himself was looking for such a righteous man (Jer. 5:1).

should forfeit doctrine in order to get along? Those in Ezekiel's day tried that approach, and it did not work. They were forcefully rebuked and punished by God for trying it.

We *must* lift high the doctrine of God. The church has the responsibility to be a "pillar and support *of the truth*" (1 Tim. 3:15; emphasis added), not to be the most popular church in the area. Let us say, along with Paul, "If I were still trying to please men, I would not be a bond-servant of Christ" (Gal. 1:10).

D.P.

Failure in Spite of Privileges

Israel was especially blessed. Think of the privileges she had:

She had divine resources. She was planted by the waters. God was with her, supplying her strength and needs. She should have been able to do what God had asked her to do.

She had a wonderful heritage. Great kings, such as David and Solomon, had ruled Israel. Her height was raised above the clouds of heaven.

She had countless opportunities. God was at her side and would have enabled her to excel above any other nation.

She had popularity. Her notoriety had spread throughout the earth. She was becoming known for her commitment to God.

If there was any nation that should have succeeded, Israel was that nation. However, with all of these privileges, she turned her back on God and failed.

E.C.

CHAPTER 23
AN ALLEGORY OF TWO SISTERS: OHOLAH AND OHOLIBAH

In the same vivid and graphic style used by Ezekiel in chapter 16, this chapter portrays the history of two kingdoms: Samaria (representing the northern kingdom of Israel) and Jerusalem (representing the southern kingdom of Judah). In an extended allegory, these two kingdoms are compared to two sisters. John B. Taylor explained,

> The introductory details of the allegory must not be over-pressed. The sisters represent cities and their inhabitants, rather than tribes. In any case Judah and Ephraim were not even brothers, for Ephraim was one of the two sons of Joseph and was therefore Judah's nephew. The points being made are simply that the two cities have a close affinity from the distant past, that their origins were in Egypt, and that the beginning of their subsequent conduct can be traced back to Egyptian prehistory.[1]

Both sisters were unfaithful to their husbands and lived as adulteresses (thereby furthering the discussion of ch. 16). Beginning with the older sister, the prophet detailed how she ignored the teachings of God and sought foreign alliances with various nations. In the process, she adopted the idolatrous practices of those nations. This proved to be disastrous for the nation,

---

[1] John B. Taylor, *Ezekiel: An Introduction and Commentary*, Tyndale Old Testament Commentaries (Downers Grove, Ill.: Inter-Varsity Press, 1969), 171.

plummeting her into moral decay and political unrest. Moving then to the younger sister, Ezekiel described how she failed to learn the lessons of history by observing her older sister. Instead, she imitated the idolatrous ways of her older sister and doomed herself to suffer the same fate.

There are some differences between this chapter and chapter 16. The discussion in chapter 16 revolves around the beginning of the nation and then her fall into adultery, while this chapter focuses on the later years of both kingdoms. Whereas the focus of chapter 16 is on religious decay (idolatry), this chapter concentrates on the consequences of political alliances.

THE PARABLE OF JUDGMENT ON JERUSALEM: THE TWO SISTERS (23)

Introduction to the Two Sisters (23:1–4)

¹**The word of the LORD came to me again, saying,** ²**"Son of man, there were two women, the daughters of one mother;** ³**and they played the harlot in Egypt. They played the harlot in their youth; there their breasts were pressed and there their virgin bosom was handled.** ⁴**Their names were Oholah the elder and Oholibah her sister. And they became Mine, and they bore sons and daughters. And as for their names, Samaria is Oholah and Jerusalem is Oholibah."**

Verses 1, 2. Samaria and Jerusalem were **daughters of one mother**. They were both the product of the once united kingdom of Israel, encompassing all twelve tribes (16:46; Jer. 3:7–10).

Verse 3. In the days when God first took Israel to be His people (Ex. 6:7), she **played the harlot**. When the nation was young, she learned from the Egyptians the ways of idolatry and prostitution (see 16:26; 20:7, 8; Num. 25:3–9; Josh. 24:14; 2 Kings 21:15; Hos. 1:2). In blunt, straightforward language, Ezekiel described how the people entered into sexual relations with other "lovers" (foreign nations and their gods), beginning a lifetime of perversion and corruption. There can be no misunderstanding with this vivid language. The perversion and sinfulness of

Israel began early and happened frequently. She became practiced in the art of prostitution.

Verse 4. These two sisters became the people of God. He adopted them and took them to be His (see ch. 16). The covenant relationship between God and Israel is often symbolized as a marriage (see Hos. 2:19, 20). As God's possession, the nation was given blessings that were only a dream to other nations. She was the select people of the one true and living God. He names the two sisters **Oholah** and **Oholibah**.

(1) Oholah is **Samaria**, the capital of the northern kingdom. She is called **the elder**, not because she became a nation before Judah did, but because she indulged in perversion before her sister did. The name "Oholah" means "her tent." The significance of this name seems to be that Oholah was often identified with the idolatrous tent-shrines of the pagan nations. (Archaeologists have discovered platforms for these tent-shrines on Mount Gerizim as well as in other locations.)

(2) Oholibah is **Jerusalem**. Her name means "my tent is in her." The possessive "my" seems to refer to God, since He had His temple/tent/tabernacle in Jerusalem. In contrast to Samaria (who had her own tent), Jerusalem had the privilege of being selected to be the city where God would dwell.

It is wise not to run too far in interpreting allegories. If the text does not specifically provide details (and perhaps the meanings of those details), the interpreter would do better to leave the text as it is. The fundamental point is clear. Samaria and Jerusalem were the two prominent cities of the kingdoms of Israel and Judah. These cities were inhabited by God's children, but they chose to forsake their relationship with Him and go after foreign alliances. Taylor said,

> The names, Oholah and Oholibah, derive from the Hebrew 'ohel, meaning a "tent". It could be a reference to a tented place of worship, but it is not clear whether this is Israel's tabernacle in the wilderness or a pagan shrine. The name of Esau's wife, Oholibamah (Gn. 36:2), or "tent of the high place", suggests the latter, as do the tents of the gods described in the Ugaritic texts. On the

other hand, Oholah could mean "her tent" and Oholibah almost certainly means "my tent (is) in her", which suggests Yahweh's sponsorship of Jerusalem. But again the details must not be pressed too far. It is enough that the names had a cultic flavour.[2]

Oholah's Harlotries (23:5–10)

⁵"**Oholah played the harlot while she was Mine; and she lusted after her lovers, after the Assyrians, her neighbors,** ⁶**who were clothed in purple, governors and officials, all of them desirable young men, horsemen riding on horses.** ⁷**She bestowed her harlotries on them, all of whom were the choicest men of Assyria; and with all whom she lusted after, with all their idols she defiled herself.** ⁸**She did not forsake her harlotries from the time in Egypt; for in her youth men had lain with her, and they handled her virgin bosom and poured out their lust on her.** ⁹**Therefore, I gave her into the hand of her lovers, into the hand of the Assyrians, after whom she lusted.** ¹⁰**They uncovered her nakedness; they took her sons and her daughters, but they slew her with the sword. Thus she became a byword among women, and they executed judgments on her.**"

Verse 5. Dealing first with the older sister, Oholah, God showed the sorrow of being forsaken by His bride. She **played the harlot** even though she belonged to the Lord (**she was Mine**). The sadness of such a statement is apparent. A husband enters into a marriage covenant with the hope and intention of keeping "the marriage bed . . . undefiled" (see Heb. 13:4). Oholah **lusted after her lovers, after the Assyrians**. The depravity of Samaria is shown by Oholah's initiative in offering herself to her Assyrian lovers. Hosea, too, had made insinuations of this sort: "They have gone up to Assyria, like a wild donkey all alone; Ephraim has hired lovers" (Hos. 8:9; see 5:13; 7:11; 12:1). The historicity of this charge is borne out by a good deal of evidence.

---

[2]Ibid., 171.

The Black Obelisk of Shalmaneser III illustrates Jehu prostrating himself before the Assyrian king (the date would be about 840 B.C., at the beginning of Jehu's reign) and offering gifts, possibly with a view to buying support against Hazael of Damascus. Adad-Nirari III (c. 812–782 B.C.), in an inscription found at Nimrud, also claimed to have received tribute from "the territory of Omri", ... 2 Kings also describes the paying of tribute by Israel to Assyria in the reigns of Menahem (c. 745–738 B.C.) and Hoshea (c. 732–724 B.C.); see 2 Kings 15:19ff.; 17:3.[3]

Verses 6, 7. The Assyrians **were clothed in purple** (v. 6). The Israelites found the more sophisticated civilizations very attractive, from the elaborate clothing to the impressive military forces. The kind of life that the Lord had provided was not as attractive as "the ways of the world." This attraction led to her defiling herself by worshiping the **idols** of Assyria (v. 7).

Verse 8. Since she had already experienced such harlotries **in Egypt**, God had hoped that Israel would now be a faithful wife. The perverted lifestyle she had learned **in her youth** had now become part of her character. Paul stated that "bad company corrupts good morals" (1 Cor. 15:33). Israel's association with pagan nations tainted her character. As she grew older, she found it difficult to break that pattern of idolatry.

Verse 9. According to the law of Moses, the innocent husband had the right to put the unfaithful wife to death (Lev. 20:10). God had every reason to destroy the nation and find a new "wife" (nation) to be His. Instead, God **gave her into the hand of her lovers . . . after whom she lusted**. In a way, this was a sort of punishment, because her alliances only made things worse for her; but it also was an act of resolution on God's part. He knew how badly she wanted these foreign lovers, so He allowed her to go after them (see Ps. 106:15).

Verse 10. In 722(1) B.C., the Assyrian army captured the cit-

---

[3]Ibid., 172. The obelisk is discussed in D. Winton Thomas, ed., *Documents from Old Testament Times* (New York: Harper & Brothers, 1958), 48–49, plate 3.

ies of the northern kingdom and carried the people into captivity (**took her sons and her daughters**). **She became a byword among women** (literally, "a name to women"). The fate of this harlot at the hand of her lovers served as a warning to others; she became a "byword," a symbol of immorality and perversion (similar to the way the name "Jezebel" is used today). What happened to Samaria should have been a deterrent to Jerusalem. What Israel expected from these alliances was very different from what she received. She was used, abused, and exposed to public ridicule.

Oholibah's Harlotries (23:11–21)

23:11–13
¹¹"**Now her sister Oholibah saw this, yet she was more corrupt in her lust than she, and her harlotries were more than the harlotries of her sister. ¹²She lusted after the Assyrians, governors and officials, the ones near, magnificently dressed, horsemen riding on horses, all of them desirable young men. ¹³I saw that she had defiled herself; they both took the same way.**"

Verse 11. Verses 11 through 21 speak of Oholibah's harlotries. While the older sister was engaging in adulterous behavior, the younger sister was watching. Did she see how her sister's life was being destroyed by her lovers? Did she observe how they "executed judgments on her" (v. 10)? Did she fear losing all that she had and being carried into captivity along with her sister? No. Instead, **she was more corrupt in her lust than she**. Though Judah saw what happened to Samaria as the result of her reliance on foreign powers and disloyalty to God, she adopted the same policy and even intensified it (see Jer. 3:8, 11). Ahaz attempted to make an alliance with Assyria (2 Kings 16:8) and was strongly condemned by Isaiah (7:17–19; see 10:5–11).

Verses 12, 13. The little sister saw the relationship her older sister had with **the Assyrians**, and **she lusted after** them as well (in spite of the way the Assyrians had mistreated the northern kingdom). The Assyrians were impressive and alluring with their powerful men and lavishly dressed horsemen. As God witnessed the entire affair, He saw that Judah **defiled herself**, going **the same way** her sister had gone (v. 13), making foreign alliances and participating in idolatry. Therefore, Judah's first "affair" was with the Assyrians.

23:14–16
¹⁴"So she increased her harlotries. And she saw men portrayed on the wall, images of the Chaldeans portrayed with vermilion, ¹⁵girded with belts on their loins, with flowing turbans on their heads, all of them looking like officers, like the Babylonians in Chaldea, the land of their birth. ¹⁶When she saw them she lusted after them and sent messengers to them in Chaldea."

Verses 14, 15. While one might hope that Judah's sinful behavior would eventually end, it did not. Rather, **she increased her harlotries** (v. 14). **She saw men portrayed on the wall.** Bas-relief artwork was common in ancient times, especially in palaces and temples of the Middle East. The monuments of Nineveh show how palace walls were adorned with figures portraying the dress and styles of these ancient peoples. These sculptures were very colorful (**vermilion**). While it is not known how or where Judah saw these handsomely portrayed **Chaldeans** (Babylonians) in such paintings, she desired them. S. Fisch wrote,

> ... an oriental woman of good position would never see strange men save in pictures; and though Hebrew women had more freedom, Ezekiel compares Judah's desire for closer acquaintance with Babylon to a wanton girl's desire for a world from which she would naturally be secluded. Not satisfied with Assyrians as a "lover," Judea also lusted after Babylon.[4]

Her relationship with Assyria was not enough; now she wanted one with Chaldea. **The land of their birth** (v. 15) emphasizes

---

[4]S. Fisch, *Ezekiel: Hebrew Text and English Translation with an Introduction and Commentary*, Soncino Books of the Bible (London: Soncino Press, 1950), 152.

that these men were foreigners. The people of Israel were attracted by foreign customs and sought to imitate them. In contrast, the Babylonians strictly conformed to their own national dress.

Verse 16. Seeing the Chaldeans in these colorful wall paintings, Judah **lusted after them**. Fisch explained, "The sight of the martial Chaldeans at once aroused an ardent desire to be allied with them. Another rendering is: 'and she doted upon them after the sight of her eyes.'"[5] Both Jehoahaz and Jehoiakim attempted to establish relations with the Babylonians.

23:17-21
[17]"The Babylonians came to her to the bed of love and defiled her with their harlotry. And when she had been defiled by them, she became disgusted with them. [18]She uncovered her harlotries and uncovered her nakedness; then I became disgusted with her, as I had become disgusted with her sister. [19]Yet she multiplied her harlotries, remembering the days of her youth, when she played the harlot in the land of Egypt. [20]She lusted after their paramours, whose flesh is like the flesh of donkeys and whose issue is like the issue of horses. [21]Thus you longed for the lewdness of your youth, when the Egyptians handled your bosom because of the breasts of your youth."

Verse 17. Babylon took advantage of the opportunity presented by the alliance with Judah. While Babylon profited financially by this alliance, it was disastrous for Judah. She became more corrupt and defiled through this political alliance. Rather than trusting in God to care for her and protect her, she leaned upon the might of Babylon. When Judah realized (after she had become subservient to Babylon) that this alliance was a mistake, **she became disgusted with them**.

Verse 18. Judah was now exposed for what she really was—an unfaithful harlot. This being the case, God became **disgusted with her**, as He had been **disgusted with her sister** (the northern kingdom).

---

[5]Ibid., 153.

Such degrading national behaviour had the same consequence as with Samaria. God decided to withdraw His protection and leave her to her fate, as a husband does with a faithless wife. Jeremiah uses the same phrase in vi. 8. "God is interwoven with Israel, as it were, but sin will wrench Him away from the people—a striking metaphor expressing God's love on the one hand, and the powerful effect of sin on the other" (Soncino Bible, *Jeremiah*, p. 45).[6]

God's disgust with Israel brought about her captivity by the Assyrians (722[1] B.C.). His disgust with Judah would lead to the destruction of Jerusalem and the Babylonian Captivity in 587(6) B.C.

Verses 19–21. One would think that being "disgusted" with the Babylonians would have brought about a reformation in Judah's character. Sadly, she only turned away from Babylon so she could go after the Egyptians (Jer. 2:18). In a pitiful irony, she returned to her first lover—the one who had exploited her in **the days of her youth** (v. 19). As the Babylonians had attracted Judah, so did the Egyptians. Their **paramours** are portrayed as lustful **donkeys** and "horses" (v. 20; see Jer. 2:24; 5:8; 13:27). (The **issue of horses** is a reference to the seminal issue. The image of a horse was the Egyptian hieroglyphic for a lustful person.) Zedekiah rebelled against Babylon and sent envoys to Egypt, hoping that they would provide "horses and many troops" (Ezek. 17:15).

The Fate of Oholibah (23:22–35)

23:22–27

²²"**Therefore, O Oholibah, thus says the Lord God, 'Behold I will arouse your lovers against you, from whom you were alienated, and I will bring them against you from every side: ²³the Babylonians and all the Chaldeans, Pekod and Shoa and Koa, and all the Assyrians with them; desirable young men,**

---

[6]Ibid.

governors and officials all of them, officers and men of renown, all of them riding on horses. ²⁴They will come against you with weapons, chariots and wagons, and with a company of peoples. They will set themselves against you on every side with buckler and shield and helmet; and I will commit the judgment to them, and they will judge you according to their customs. ²⁵I will set My jealousy against you, that they may deal with you in wrath. They will remove your nose and your ears; and your survivors will fall by the sword. They will take your sons and your daughters; and your survivors will be consumed by the fire. ²⁶They will also strip you of your clothes and take away your beautiful jewels. ²⁷Thus I will make your lewdness and your harlotry brought from the land of Egypt to cease from you, so that you will not lift up your eyes to them or remember Egypt anymore.'"

Verse 22. The phrase **thus says the Lord GOD** signals the beginning of four judgment oracles, all introduced with this phrase (vv. 22, 28, 32, 35). The very nations that were Judah's partners became her enemies.

Verse 23. Pekod and Shoa and Koa are identified with Pukudu, Sutu, and Kutu, Aramean races inhabiting the land east of the Tigris River, bordering on Elam or Persia. "*Pekod* was a powerful Chaldean tribe dwelling near the mouth of the river Tigris. The other two tribes have not been clearly identified."[7] The phrase **all the Assyrians with them** (literally "sons of Assyria") is thought by some to be a later addition. However, the phrase means that the Babylonians, having assimilated the military might of the Assyrians, would bring about the defeat of Jerusalem.

Verse 24. The Babylonian army was strong and impressive—one of the most efficient military machines in the ancient world.

Verse 25. I will set My jealousy against you. Ezekiel had spoken of God's jealousy, or "zeal" before (5:13), identifying that jealousy as the motivating factor for God's punishment. God

---

[7]Keith W. Carley, *The Book of the Prophet Ezekiel*, The Cambridge Bible Commentary (Cambridge: Cambridge University Press, 1974), 157.

would loose the fury of the Babylonians upon Jerusalem. The Babylonians were noted as being especially cruel and inhumane. God warned, **"They will remove your nose and your ears."** Walther Zimmerli said,

> In their wrath Yahweh's jealousy (קנאה 5:13; 16:38, 42) will be let loose upon Oholibah. The laws for the conduct of war in Dtn 20 show that Israel, in its wars, was conscious of being under the authority of its God, and thereby a certain law of humanity. Thus there is almost completely lacking in Israel's law any punishment involving mutilation. But things were different in the surrounding nations. The Assyrian illustrations of war show quite freely flaying, impaling, blinding, and physical mutilation which was the order of the day for prisoners. Oholibah will be delivered up to this grim practice of Babylonian victory for mutilation and the killing of her children. . . . The punishment of cutting off the nose and ears is attested in Egypt in connection with the punishment of a plot against Rameses III (Turin Papyrus), and among the Hittites as a punishment for a negligent temple servant.[8]

Verse 26. God had bestowed abundant gifts upon His people, His bride (ch. 16), but now the Babylonians would **strip** off those clothes and **take away** the **beautiful jewels**. All of the wonderful benefits given to them now belonged to their enemies.

Verse 27. Drastic action was necessary. God said, **"I will make your lewdness and your harlotry brought from the land of Egypt to cease."** He would end their idolatrous ways and their foreign alliances. This was done in an unimaginable way— seventy years of exile in Babylon and the destruction of their

---

[8]Walther Zimmerli, *Ezekiel 1: A Commentary on the Book of the Prophet Ezekiel, Chapters 1—24,* trans. Ronald E. Clements, Hermeneia (Philadelphia: Fortress Press, 1979), 488–89. Zimmerli's sources include James B. Pritchard, ed., *Ancient Near Eastern Text*s (Princeton, N.J.: Princeton University Press, 1969), 207, 215.

beloved city. God did not want to resort to this; but their continual forays into idolatry left Him no option. Like a jilted husband, exasperated by his attempts to restore his wandering wife, God eventually turned to desperate measures.

This completes the first oracle (vv. 22–27). God depicted Oholibah as one who, because of her continued unfaithfulness to God, was to suffer His judgment at the hands of her foreign lovers. These lovers (nations) would surround her (v. 24) so that there would be no possibility of escaping their wrath. With a huge army, fully prepared and equipped for battle, the Babylonians would lay siege to Jerusalem. She would not escape.

23:28–31
²⁸**"For thus says the Lord God, 'Behold, I will give you into the hand of those whom you hate, into the hand of those from whom you were alienated. ²⁹They will deal with you in hatred, take all your property, and leave you naked and bare. And the nakedness of your harlotries will be uncovered, both your lewdness and your harlotries. ³⁰These things will be done to you because you have played the harlot with the nations, because you have defiled yourself with their idols. ³¹You have walked in the way of your sister; therefore I will give her cup into your hand.'"**

Verses 28, 29. The second oracle (vv. 28–31) also begins with the phrase **For thus says the Lord God.**

Normally, a woman might not feel threatened by the thought of being turned over to a former lover. After all, they had been lovers. However, after coming to see the Babylonians for what they were, Judah had become "disgusted with them" (23:17). That disgust had turned into **hate**; the two were **alienated** (v. 28). This being the case, the prospect of being given to the Babylonians would be terrifying indeed—yet this is what Judah deserved after her centuries of harlotry. She was told, **"They will deal with you in hatred"** (v. 29). The thought of being given to someone who is filled with violence and rage is not inviting. The Babylonians' hatred for Judah would lead them to pillage Jerusalem, leaving her **naked and bare.** She would return to her original condition described in 16:7, when she had nothing. (The word "bare" should be understood to mean "defenseless.") Judah could do nothing to stop the rage of the Babylonians. She had insufficient military strength, and the Egyptians would not come to her defense.

Verses 30, 31. God gave definitive reasons for this judgment: **". . . you have played the harlot with the nations"** (figurative language) and **"because you have defiled yourself with their idols"** (literal language) (v. 30); **"You have walked in the way of your sister"** (v. 31). As is so often noted, those who do not learn from history are doomed to repeat it. Judah repeated Israel's history, and this angered God. Jim McGuiggan noted,

> He emphasizes that this judgment is severe to this degree, in part, because she had refused to pay attention to the misconduct of her sister and her punishment (verses 30ff). She wanted to follow in her sister's ways and so she must drink her sister's cup (verse 32) which is a violent one indeed (verses 33–34). And then He makes the real charge, the one which you and I ought to take especially to heart. Her crime was that: "Thou hast forgotten me, and cast me behind thy back. . . ."[9]

Samaria (Israel) had to drink the cup of God's wrath, and now Judah would have to do the same.

Judah's enemy—ironically a former lover who was now full of hatred and rage—would take everything of value away from Jerusalem. She would be left with nothing. Why was her punishment to be so severe? There were two reasons: (1) She defiled herself with idols, and (2) she failed to learn from history—that of her older sister.

23:32–34
[32]**"Thus says the Lord G**OD**,
'You will drink your sister's cup,**

---

[9]Jim McGuiggan, *The Book of Ezekiel*, Looking Into The Bible Series (Lubbock, Tex.: Montex Publishing Co., 1979), 251–52.

Which is deep and wide.
You will be laughed at and held in derision;
It contains much.
³³You will be filled with drunkenness and sorrow,
The cup of horror and desolation,
The cup of your sister Samaria.
³⁴You will drink it and drain it.
Then you will gnaw its fragments
And tear your breasts;

for I have spoken,' declares the Lord GOD."

Verse 32. The phrase **Thus says the Lord GOD** begins the third oracle (vv. 32–34). Judah, because she housed the temple of the Lord, thought that her punishment would be lighter than that given to Samaria. This was not the case. The same **cup** was to be given to her, and God said, **"It contains much."** The cup was a large one, **deep and wide**. When she drank the cup of God's wrath, various responses would follow. First, God revealed how others would react:

"You will be laughed at." Judah should have been the envy of surrounding nations. Instead, she would be the subject of jokes.

"You will be . . . held in derision." Her fate would evoke no pity or sympathy. Others would see her as getting what she deserved. They would ridicule, scorn, and disdain her.

Verses 33, 34. Next, God told how Judah herself would respond:

"You will be filled with drunkenness" (v. 33). Judah would be required to drink all of the cup. In so doing, she would become drunk. She would have no control over her environment. She would be powerless to stop the rage of the Babylonians.

"You will be filled with . . . sorrow" (v. 33). Perhaps only now, for the first time, Judah would be saddened by her terrible choices. Memories of the good days when the Lord blessed her would fill her heart with remorse, distress, unhappiness and regret.

"You will gnaw . . . fragments [of the cup]" (v. 34). This difficult phrase seems to describe Judah as shattering the cup the way a drunk man would throw his glass against the wall after consuming its contents. (The NIV has "you will dash it to pieces.") The word "gnaw" gives the idea of an animal breaking apart its victim and consuming even the bones. The sense here may be that Judah would not only drink the contents of the cup, but—in order to receive all of God's wrath—would be forced to consume the cup itself. The RSV ignores the MT in favor of the reading of the Syriac "and you shall pluck out your hair." This particular reading, however, is without support.

"You will . . . **tear your breasts**" (v. 34). Recognizing the breasts as instruments of her infidelity, she would remove them. Some see this as equivalent to "beating the breast," an action of deep sorrow and mourning.

In this third oracle, God announced that Jerusalem would have to consume all of His wrath. Any hope that her punishment would be lighter than her sister's was false hope. She would suffer severe consequences as a result of her sin.

23:35

35"Therefore, thus says the Lord GOD, 'Because you have forgotten Me and cast Me behind your back, bear now the punishment of your lewdness and your harlotries.'"

Verse 35. In this fourth and final oracle (v. 35), God described two more sins of Judah: "**. . . you have forgotten Me**" and "**you have . . . cast Me behind your back.**" With the first charge, God demonstrated one of the fundamental causes of infidelity—a failure to remember the covenant made with one's partner. Judah did not do the things necessary to keep God fresh in her mind. She failed to invest in her marriage to the Lord. With the second charge, God showed the logical consequence of "not remembering." When one is "out of sight, out of mind," it is easy to throw away all that was part of that relationship. Jerusalem threw "behind her back" the laws of God and the covenant she had made with God. McGuiggan said,

> Israel didn't find God completely satisfying so they

went in search of someone who could supply their wants. *This is the real crime in spiritual whoredom.* God is fine for some things, . . . the Jews thought (much of the time) when it comes to . . . religion. . . . But when it comes to matters of everyday living, when it comes to war and politics, survival and prosperity, he just can't match the job. NOW, ANYONE who adopts this attitude toward God *as a settled conviction* is in the process of committing spiritual whoredom. It doesn't make any difference what area we're dealing with, be it, finances, health, domestic or marital problems, business, religious, emotional or any other such area. If I draw the settled conviction that God cannot handle my problem I have the conviction that led these Jews into foreign alliances and idolatry.

I don't have to bow down to literal idols to be guilty of their crime. Putting God behind my back believing that he is incapable of supplying all my needs is the basis of the crime for which they were judged. And make no mistake, if one partner won't do, there's no guarantee that two will do any better.[10]

God's Judgment (23:36–49)

Verses 22 through 35 repeat much of what was stated earlier. Beginning with verse 36, however, God put the two sisters together—as if they were being brought before the judgment seat together—to hear the charges against them and the subsequent punishment. (The crimes committed and the punishment were the same for each.)

23:36–39

³⁶Moreover, the Lord said to me, "Son of man, will you judge Oholah and Oholibah? Then declare to them their abominations. ³⁷For they have committed adultery, and blood is on their hands. Thus they have committed adultery with their idols and even caused their sons, whom they bore to Me,

---

[10]Ibid., 252.

to pass through the fire to them as food. ³⁸Again, they have done this to Me: they have defiled My sanctuary on the same day and have profaned My sabbaths. ³⁹For when they had slaughtered their children for their idols, they entered My sanctuary on the same day to profane it; and lo, thus they did within My house."

Verse 36. Again, God asked Ezekiel to **judge** (see 20:4; 22:2). To "judge" is to consider the evidence given, then to **declare** publicly an assessment of the evidence. The deeds of these sisters were, upon examination, declared **abominations**.

Verses 37–39. As if in a courtroom scene, God detailed the religious sins of the two sisters (nations):

1. **"They have committed adultery,"** which was idolatry (v. 37). Part of this idolatry was the shedding of **blood**, the blood of their children whom they offered in child sacrifice.
2. **"They have defiled My sanctuary"** (v. 38). God's temple was defiled by open neglect of His laws. People entered it with the blood of child sacrifices on their hands. The northern kingdom was also charged with defiling the Jerusalem sanctuary, perhaps reflecting the times that—even after the division of the kingdom—people from the north still brought their idolatrous practices to Jerusalem (see Jer. 7:9–11).
3. "[They] **have profaned My sabbaths"** (v. 38). The profaning of God's sabbaths took place when they performed these child sacrifices on the Sabbath day.

23:40–45

⁴⁰"Furthermore, they have even sent for men who come from afar, to whom a messenger was sent; and lo, they came—for whom you bathed, painted your eyes and decorated yourselves with ornaments; ⁴¹and you sat on a splendid couch with a table arranged before it on which you had set My incense and My oil. ⁴²The sound of a carefree multitude was with her; and drunkards were brought from the wilderness with men

of the common sort. And they put bracelets on the hands of the women and beautiful crowns on their heads.

⁴³"Then I said concerning her who was worn out by adulteries, 'Will they now commit adultery with her when she is thus?' ⁴⁴But they went in to her as they would go in to a harlot. Thus they went in to Oholah and to Oholibah, the lewd women. ⁴⁵But they, righteous men, will judge them with the judgment of adulteresses and with the judgment of women who shed blood, because they are adulteresses and blood is on their hands."

Verses 40, 41. Verse 40 begins, **"Furthermore. . . ."** Were the three sins listed earlier not enough for a conviction? Yes, but, as in a courtroom of law, all of the evidence had to be presented. God used a figure of a prostitute who had prepared herself for her lover in these ways: (1) She **painted** [her] **eyes** using makeup (v. 40).[11] (2) She **decorated** [herself] **with ornaments** (v. 40)—putting on jewelry such as bracelets, rings, and crowns. (3) She **sat on a splendid couch with a table arranged** (v. 41). She had not only prepared herself but had straightened her house, as well, cleaning it and then using God's **incense** and **oil** to make herself and the air around her smell good. The "couch" (bed) is where she would "entertain" her guests.

Verse 42. Only the singular personal pronoun is used here, limiting God's comments to Judah. She had become so involved in her prostitution as to be associated with **drunkards** and **men of the common sort** (meaning despicable characters of base lifestyles). The Bible records that Judah established relations with other nations such as Arabia, Moab, Edom, and the Sabeans (from southern Arabia). These "lovers" presented to Judah **bracelets** and **crowns** as payment for her harlotries.

Verses 43, 44. Judah is portrayed as a harlot who had been so long involved in marketing herself that she was **worn out** by

---

[11]"The verb *kachal* occurs only here. The powdered antimony (*puch* in Hebrew) which was employed for the purpose is called *kohl* by the Arabs and the word appears in the English noun 'alcohol.' The effect was to enlarge the eye and add lustre to it (cf. 2 Kings ix. 30; Jer. iv. 30)" (Fisch, 158).

these adulteries (v. 43). Could anyone desire her now, when she was old and haggard? Even in this condition, she was able to find suitors (implying men [nations] desperate for a relationship with anybody).

Verse 45. Righteous men, will judge them. This is not a reference to the suitors of the previous verses, although those nations would eventually be used to punish Judah. This refers to men such as Ezekiel and Jeremiah, who were asked to judge (see v. 36). Being righteous men, they would be able to give a fair verdict. The verdict is given in verse 45: They were **adulteresses**, they had **shed blood**, and the evidence was **on their hands!**

23:46–49

⁴⁶"For thus says the Lord GOD, 'Bring up a company against them and give them over to terror and plunder. ⁴⁷The company will stone them with stones and cut them down with their swords; they will slay their sons and their daughters and burn their houses with fire. ⁴⁸Thus I will make lewdness cease from the land, that all women may be admonished and not commit lewdness as you have done. ⁴⁹Your lewdness will be requited upon you, and you will bear the penalty of worshiping your idols; thus you will know that I am the Lord GOD.'"

Verses 46, 47. Calling up images of Old Testament life, when the guilty parties were surrounded by those prepared to stone them, God said that **a company** had been brought up **against them** (v. 46). They would, through the dispensing of the punishment, create **terror and plunder**. The instruments of punishment would be stoning, slaying with swords, and burning their houses down. These three actions perfectly describe a city under siege (v. 47). **Stones** would be flying into the city from the catapults—sometimes covered with flammable materials. **Swords** would be used by the soldiers entering the city, destroying all life, including **their sons and their daughters**. The soldiers would then **burn** the **houses** in the conquered city.

Verse 48. God had said earlier, in verse 27, that He would bring these sinful activities to an end. Now, His acts of judgment (through invading armies) had removed the **lewdness** of Judah. Her fate serves as an object lesson to **all women** not to follow her evil path. God would not lighten the punishment. Judah had practiced "lewdness"; therefore, she was to receive the full sentence for such behavior.

Verse 49. The recurring phrase **thus you will know that I am the Lord God** provides a powerful ending to section 4 of the chapter. Why did Israel not know her God? Why did it take such drastic measures from God to teach them about Him? Salvation for those under the new covenant is also dependent upon knowing God (Jn. 17:3). Jesus, as the *Logos*, the Word, has revealed the Father to us (Jn. 1:14–18).

APPLICATION

Knowing God

When one forsakes the Word of God and goes after the things of the world, it will bring about a spiritual (and perhaps physical) demise (vv. 6, 7; see 1 Jn. 2:15–17).

Evil companions corrupt good morals (v. 8; 1 Cor. 15:33).

It is imperative for young people to learn that habits formed in their youth can adversely affect the rest of their lives (v. 8).

If our hearts are inclined toward evil, God will not stop us. He will allow us to immerse ourselves in sinful behavior (v. 9).

God expects us to learn from history and not make the same mistakes of those before us (v. 31; see 1 Cor. 10:1–13).

It is imperative for God's people to know Him (v. 49; Jn. 17:3; 1 Thess. 1:7–9).

The Ways of the World

Israel was drawn to the attractiveness of the Assyrian civilization. In the New Testament, John warned Christians, "Do not love the world nor the things in the world . . ." (1 Jn. 2:15–17). When one neglects to look beyond the physical into the spiritual, to see things the way God sees them, he is doomed for failure. Israel failed to keep her eyes on her own husband (the Lord). Let us not make the same mistake!

D.P.

The Voices of the Two Women

Two women were used as an allegory for the northern and the southern kingdoms, showing the tragedy of the fall of both kingdoms. What do we see in this figurative depiction?

We see the depth of human rebellion. A graphic picture of sin is given. Women who had great potential fell into the worst type of sin and debauchery.

We see the humiliation and degradation of sin. Individuals chosen by God fell to the level of brute beasts, desiring the love of pagans.

We see the pervasive power of sin. It dominates and destroys. If given a small place in our lives, it eventually reigns as lord.

We see the necessity of judgment. God sought to correct His people, to no avail. Finally, an accounting was demanded.

We see that the price paid for iniquity is always high. The reverberations of these sins are still being felt in the world.

E.C.

Chapter 24

The End of Jerusalem

Chapter 24 is marked by one of the most important dates in Judah's history, January 10, 588 B.C. On this day, Nebuchadnezzar began the siege of Jerusalem. This event had such an impact that it is recorded three other times in the Scriptures (2 Kings 25:1; Jer. 39:1; 52:4).

God had Ezekiel speak a parable to illustrate the siege (vv. 1–14). As in a figure used in 11:4, the city of Jerusalem was depicted as a pot and the inhabitants as the flesh within the pot. However, in the earlier passage, this image was given by "those who devise iniquity" (11:2) to illustrate how the flesh was safe within the iron walls of the pot. In this illustration, the flesh—the people of Jerusalem—were not safe. They would be consumed by the fire (that is, the Babylonian army). God commanded that the pot be put on the fire again, and this time the entire pot would be consumed.

John B. Taylor summarized the significance of this section with the following words:

> With these verses we come to the climax of all that Ezekiel has been trying to say in the previous twelve chapters. His main purpose, as we have noted, has been to justify the coming judgment upon Jerusalem. We called this collection of oracles "Objections to Judgment", . . . and we have seen arguments raised and demolished one by one and accusations made against both the past and the present conduct of the people of Jerusalem. There is

hardly anything more that can be said. The hour has come. Judgment is about to fall.[1]

After the parable was given, the sadness of the event touched Ezekiel in a personal way. On the evening of the siege, Ezekiel's wife died (vv. 15–27). Ezekiel was instructed not to mourn her death, for the people would be unable to mourn the destruction of Jerusalem. This monumental catastrophe would leave them too numb to grieve.

THE PARABLE OF JUDGMENT ON JERUSALEM: THE BOILING POT (24:1–14)

The Seige Begun; The Date (24:1, 2)

¹And the word of the LORD came to me in the ninth year, in the tenth month, on the tenth of the month, saying, ²"Son of man, write the name of the day, this very day. The king of Babylon has laid siege to Jerusalem this very day."

Verses 1, 2. "Write the name of the day," Ezekiel was commanded (v. 2). The date was January 10, 588 B.C. **The ninth year** (v. 1) refers to the reign of Zedekiah[2] (see 2 Kings 25:1, 2; Jer. 52:3, 4). This date became a day of fasting for the exiles (Zech. 8:19), commemorating one of the most significant events in their history: the fall of the holy city. It is still recognized on the Jewish calendar. Naturalists offer various explanations as to how Ezekiel could have known the exact date of an event taking place seven hundred miles away. Some have suggested that he was actually in Judah at the time; others, that this passage was written well after the fact. However, through the avenue of divine revelation, God gave Ezekiel this up-to-the-minute news.

---

[1]John B. Taylor, *Ezekiel: An Introduction and Commentary,* Tyndale Old Testament Commentaries (Downers Grove, Ill.: Inter-Varsity Press, 1969), 176–77.

[2]The number could also refer to the number of years Jehoiachin had been in exile, which was the same.

The **siege** (v. 2) that Nebuchadnezzar laid against Jerusalem was one that would last eighteen months, until a breach was made in the wall and the city was finally taken in 587(6) B.C.

The Seige Illustrated (24:3–14)

24:3–5
³"**Speak a parable to the rebellious house and say to them,** '**Thus says the Lord God,**

> "**Put on the pot, put it on and also pour water in it;**
> ⁴**Put in it the pieces,**
> **Every good piece, the thigh and the shoulder;**
> **Fill it with choice bones.**
> ⁵**Take the choicest of the flock,**
> **And also pile wood under the pot.**
> **Make it boil vigorously.**
> **Also seethe its bones in it.**"'"

Verse 3. God instructed Ezekiel to **speak a parable** and **put on the pot**. The imagery of the caldron, previously used by the inhabitants of Jerusalem for their deceptive hopes (11:3), was reinterpreted by God's prophet. Using the medium of a "parable," Ezekiel was told to get the "pot" ready for cooking. The Hebrew word for "pot" (סִיר, *sir*) refers to a large iron or ceramic utensil used for washing, cooking, or storing water.³ This pot was made of bronze (v. 11).

Verses 4, 5. Everything was being done to prepare the pot for cooking. This illustrated an invading army preparing to lay siege and conquer a city. After filling the pot with water, various pieces of meat were placed into the pot: **good** pieces of meat, **choice bones**, and **the choicest of the flock** (vv. 4, 5). This seems to represent the totality of God's people, both good and evil.

24:6–8
⁶"'**Therefore, thus says the Lord God,**

---

³Francis Brown, S. R. Driver, and Charles A. Briggs, *A Hebrew and English Lexicon of the Old Testament* (Oxford: Clarendon Press, 1972), 696.

"Woe to the bloody city,
To the pot in which there is rust
And whose rust has not gone out of it!
Take out of it piece after piece,
Without making a choice.
⁷For her blood is in her midst;
She placed it on the bare rock;
She did not pour it on the ground
To cover it with dust.
⁸That it may cause wrath to come up to take vengeance,
I have put her blood on the bare rock,
That it may not be covered."'"

Verse 6. Two oracles of **woe** were now given **to the bloody city** (vv. 6–8, 9–14). Both were based upon the parable of the boiling pot, a **pot in which there is rust**. The Hebrew word for "rust" (חֶלְאָתָה, *chel'athah*, from חָלָא, *chala'*) normally means "sick or diseased." It also has been translated "filthy," which may be the meaning here.⁴ This filthy rust had **not gone out of it**—indicating that whatever was wrong with Jerusalem remained. She had not purified herself (which is, in part, why this punishment was being given). Each **piece** of meat was indiscriminately withdrawn from the pot—illustrating how the people of Jerusalem would be taken from the city and scattered in *all directions*.

Verse 7. The statement **blood is in her midst** may explain the filthy "rust" referred to in verse 6. Jerusalem was a city of bloodshed—as documented several times already in this book ("blood" is a key word of the book, occurring fifty-five times). She did not even have enough respect to cover up her murderous ways. The evidence of her bloodshed was **on the bare rock** for everyone to see.

Verse 8. God declared, "**I have put her blood on the bare rock.**" Like the saying "What goes around comes around," Jerusalem was going to have her blood shed openly, and God Himself intended to make sure that it was not covered. When He saw the blood, God would be moved to **cause wrath** and

---

⁴Ibid., 316.

take vengeance (see Gen. 4:10; Is. 26:21). Walther Zimmerli said,

> Verse 8 gives the statement a surprising twist with reference to God—he himself has therefore seen to it that the blood was not covered over and thereby the call for his avenging action silenced. He himself was concerned that he should be provoked by the blood so that his anger should flare up and seek vengeance—a striking counterpart to the divine remembrance of his own mercy in the rainbow in Gen 9:12–17. The threatening application of this idea, according to which in the guilt mirrored by man's uncovered blood Yahweh himself is already at work in punishment (kindling his anger), recalls 3:20 and 14:9.[5]

24:9–11

⁹"'Therefore, thus says the Lord G<small>OD</small>,
"Woe to the bloody city!
I also will make the pile great.
¹⁰Heap on the wood, kindle the fire,
Boil the flesh well
And mix in the spices,
And let the bones be burned.
¹¹Then set it empty on its coals
So that it may be hot
And its bronze may glow
And its filthiness may be melted in it,
Its rust consumed."'"

Verse 9. A second **woe** oracle is given (vv. 9–14). In the first oracle (vv. 6–8), the emphasis was on the elements *in* the pot. In this second oracle, God wanted the fire rekindled for the purpose of destroying the pot itself. God said, **"I . . . will make the pile great."** This image suggests loading up an extra large pile of firewood—far more than what would normally be necessary.

---

[5]Walther Zimmerli, *Ezekiel 1: A Commentary on the Book of the Prophet Ezekiel, Chapters 1—24*, trans. Ronald E. Clements, Hermeneia (Philadelphia: Fortress Press, 1979), 500–1.

Verse 10. As the wood was **heap**[ed] **on,** the fire burned at full force, **boil**[ing] everything in the pot to the point that it was being **burned.** Those inhabitants of Jerusalem who had not earlier been removed from the city and taken into captivity would die in the city.

Verse 11. Next, the empty pot was set on coals, but there was nothing left in the pot itself. With the fire still flaring, the empty pot began to **glow,** becoming red-hot. This consumed all of the **filthiness** and **rust** that was in the pot.

24:12–14

¹²"'"She has wearied Me with toil,
Yet her great rust has not gone from her;
Let her rust be in the fire!
¹³In your filthiness is lewdness.
Because I would have cleansed you,
Yet you are not clean,
You will not be cleansed from your filthiness again
Until I have spent My wrath on you.

¹⁴I, the Lord, have spoken; it is coming and I will act. I will not relent, and I will not pity and I will not be sorry; according to your ways and according to your deeds I will judge you," declares the Lord God.'"

Verse 12. The deep-rooted sinfulness of Jerusalem had **wearied** the Lord. Even though the pot was made scorching hot, it was insufficient to remove the rust and scum from the pot. Therefore, another order was given: **Let her rust be in the fire!** God ordered the pot itself to be consumed by the heat.

Verse 13. God would willingly have **cleansed** Jerusalem, but her filthiness was so ingrained that she was beyond the point of cleansing. So deep was the rust that even the fire could not consume it. God had another plan: He determined to punish Jerusalem completely—until He had **spent** [His] **wrath** on her. Once that wrath had been spent, her **filthiness** would **be cleansed.** Many of the sins that had plagued the Jews (such as idolatry and forbidden foreign alliances) were no longer a problem after the people returned to the land (538 B.C.). The Captivity had, in fact, cleansed this evil from the people.

Verse 14. **"I will not relent,"** God said. The sixfold repetition of the pronoun "I" demonstrates God's resolve to carry through with this punishment. He would not change His mind. While the discipline was difficult, God said, **"I will not be sorry."** This, unquestionably, was the right thing to do. Nothing else was possible at this point.

EZEKIEL HIMSELF A SIGN UPON THE DEATH OF HIS WIFE (24:15–27)

Her Death and Ezekiel's Reactions (24:15–18)

¹⁵And the word of the LORD came to me saying, ¹⁶"Son of man, behold, I am about to take from you the desire of your eyes with a blow; but you shall not mourn and you shall not weep, and your tears shall not come. ¹⁷Groan silently; make no mourning for the dead. Bind on your turban and put your shoes on your feet, and do not cover your mustache and do not eat the bread of men." ¹⁸So I spoke to the people in the morning, and in the evening my wife died. And in the morning I did as I was commanded.

Verses 15–17. The parable of the pot was over. Next, God would involve Ezekiel personally in the message. He warned, **"I am about to take from you the desire of your eyes"** (v. 16). God alerted Ezekiel that in a short time (on the same day) his beloved wife would die. While we have observed the bold preaching of Ezekiel and the hardheadedness that God promised to give him, this gives us a new perspective concerning the character of this great man. His wife was "the desire of [his] eyes." What a wonderful description of this man's marriage! He loved his wife deeply; in his eyes she was his one and only. Taylor said,

In these verses we catch a glimpse of the inner Ezekiel which rarely appears through his apparently harsh and unyielding exterior. His austerity and rigid self-discipline, his passion for truth and for the honour of God's holy name, very nearly conceal the tender heart that lies within. While not wishing to romanticize Ezekiel in any way, it is worth commenting that often a man is seen for what he really is only when he is seen in conjunction with his wife. Whereas in the other forty-seven chapters we are impressed, if not overawed, by Ezekiel's personality, in this chapter at the heart of the book which bears his name we meet him and find him attractive with human emotions like our own. This is borne out by the phrase he uses to describe his wife: "the desire of his eyes, the one in whom his eyes delight." Skinner writes: "That phrase alone reveals that there was a fountain of tears sealed up within the breast of this stern preacher."[6]

Nevertheless, as a prophet—a true man of God—he gave his all to God and His work. His wife was to die **with a blow**. While this terminology does not demand an immediate or sudden death, the flow of the text seems to suggest it. Ezekiel was told a few hours before she actually died, but there were no physical warning signs of this coming tragedy.

God gave Ezekiel strict instructions on his behavior once his wife died:

1. **"You shall not mourn"** (v. 16). Public wailing was forbidden.
2. **"You shall not weep, and your tears shall not come"** (v. 16). His tears were not allowed to flow; he was to exhibit no watery eyes, no show of sorrow at all.
3. **"Groan silently"** (v. 17). God realized there would be a tremendous flow of emotion. Ezekiel was to remain silent; others were not to hear him groan.

---

[6]Taylor, 180; John Skinner, *The Book of Ezekiel* (New York: A. C. Armstrong and Sons, 1901), 210.

4. **"Make no mourning for the dead"** (v. 17). The typical procedure on the day of a death was to be avoided. Funeral songs were not to be sung; lamentations were not to be made.
5. **"Bind on your turban"** (v. 17). He was to prepare himself for a normal day, wearing the typical priestly garb (Ex. 39:28; Ezek. 44:18).
6. **"Put your shoes on your feet"** (v. 17). Those in distress traditionally removed their shoes (2 Sam. 15:30; Is. 20:2).
7. **"Do not cover your mustache"** (v. 17). Covering the lower half of the face was a sign of sorrow or disgrace (Mic. 3:7) and was required of the leper (Lev. 13:45).
8. **"Do not eat the bread of men"** (v. 17). The RSV reads "nor eat the bread of mourners"; the NIV reads "or eat the customary food [of mourners]." The sense seems to be that Ezekiel was not to eat the common meal eaten during a funeral period (see Jer. 16:5–8).

Verse 18. Ezekiel was speaking **to the people in the morning**. God had only told Ezekiel that his wife was "about" to die; there is no indication that Ezekiel knew it was going to happen that very day. Either way, Ezekiel began the day in a normal fashion, preaching the word of God to the people. Then, that very evening (presumably the day God told him she was going to die), she died. The very next "morning," Ezekiel had a number of visitors, no doubt to offer comfort and consolation to the prophet. What they found upon their arrival at his house surprised them. Ezekiel was behaving as if everything were normal, exactly as he had been **commanded**. His home showed absolutely no signs of grief or mourning.

The Meaning of the Sign (24:19–21)

¹⁹**The people said to me, "Will you not tell us what these things that you are doing mean for us?" ²⁰Then I said to them, "The word of the LORD came to me saying, ²¹'Speak to the house of Israel, "Thus says the Lord GOD, 'Behold, I am about to profane**

My sanctuary, the pride of your power, the desire of your eyes and the delight of your soul; and your sons and your daughters whom you have left behind will fall by the sword."'"

Verse 19. "Will you not tell us what these things . . . mean for us?" his visitors asked. Those who knew Ezekiel certainly knew of his wonderful marriage. They were aware of his deep love for his wife, the **desire of** [his] **eyes**. Therefore, approaching the prophet's house, they no doubt anticipated weeping and mourning—indications of a man who has suffered a tremendous loss. However, such was not the case. They knew that there must be a reason for Ezekiel to be acting normally, so they inquired of the prophet, in effect, "What does all of this mean to us?" According to S. Fisch, "he prefaces his message with the assurance that he was obeying God's command in what he did, and they rightly thought that his sudden loss and consequent behavior had a symbolic significance for the nation."[7]

Verses 20, 21. Their question gave Ezekiel an opportunity to explain the meaning of the sign. Notice that he did not succumb to the emotion of the moment and speak his own thoughts. When **the word of the LORD** came to him, he spoke. As Ezekiel had lost the desire of his eyes, his wife, so the people of God would lose something precious (v. 21):

1. **The pride of your power**—the stronghold of Jerusalem, with her fortified walls (see v. 25; Ps. 48:1–3).
2. **The desire of your eyes and the delight of your soul**—the temple, the **sanctuary** of the Lord.
3. **Your sons and your daughters.** The children would die by **the sword**.

---

[7]S. Fisch, *Ezekiel: Hebrew Text and English Translation with an Introduction and Commentary*, Soncino Books of the Bible (London: Soncino Press, 1950), 165–66.

The Application and Ezekiel's Message
(24:22–27; see 33:21, 22; 34—39)

24:22-24
²²"'"'You will do as I have done; you will not cover your mustache and you will not eat the bread of men. ²³Your turbans will be on your heads and your shoes on your feet. You will not mourn and you will not weep, but you will rot away in your iniquities and you will groan to one another. ²⁴Thus Ezekiel will be a sign to you; according to all that he has done you will do; when it comes, then you will know that I am the Lord GOD.'"'"

Verses 22, 23. "You will do as I have done," Ezekiel told them (v. 22). As he had refrained from visible signs of mourning, so would they—with one exception: **You will rot away in your iniquities** (v. 23). The fact that this tragedy was occurring because of their "iniquities" added more cause to despair.

Verse 24. Thus Ezekiel will be a sign to you. Ezekiel perfectly performed what God had asked of him, thereby proving to be "a sign" to the people. This, however, does not explain the lack of mourning by the people of Israel. Two explanations have been offered.

First, the people were indifferent to events in Jerusalem: Their hearts were so insensitive that they would not mourn when they heard the news. The uncaring people would continue their lives as if nothing had happened. This view cannot stand in light of God's description of what they were about to lose: their "power," "desire," and "delight" (v. 21). This event was sure to have a profound impact on them.

The second explanation is that the magnitude of this tragedy was so monumental that normal procedures of mourning would be inadequate. How could the people convey, through their words and actions, how awful and tragic this destruction was? Unable to express their deep grief over the loss, they would do no mourning.

24:25-27

25"'As for you, son of man, will it not be on the day when I take from them their stronghold, the joy of their pride, the desire of their eyes and their heart's delight, their sons and their daughters, 26that on that day he who escapes will come to you with information for your ears? 27On that day your mouth will be opened to him who escaped, and you will speak and be mute no longer. Thus you will be a sign to them, and they will know that I am the LORD.'"

Verse 25. While some have seen the **stronghold** as a reference to the temple itself, it seems best to understand it as the fortified city.[8] However, since the city and the temple within were all a part of the whole, a fine distinction need not be made.

Verse 26. God had announced that more people would be removed from Jerusalem in this final assault. Indeed, once Jerusalem was captured in 587(6) B.C., Nebuchadnezzar removed a large number of those who remained in the city, leaving only the poorest in the land. (Jeremiah chose to stay there as well; Jer. 39:9, 10.) This verse speaks of one **who escapes**. He was to make his way to Ezekiel and provide **information** regarding the siege, capture, and destruction of Jerusalem.

Verse 27. On that day, Ezekiel's **mouth** [would] **be opened.** The trip from Jerusalem to Babylon took approximately three months. When the escapee arrived, Ezekiel would be able to speak freely. In 3:26, 27, God had made Ezekiel mute, allowing him to speak only when he received a word from the Lord. When the city fell and the escapee arrived, Ezekiel would be mute no more and could return to a more normal lifestyle. He could once again move among the people and freely proclaim the Lord's message. In 33:21, 22, the escapee arrived in Babylon. On that day, Ezekiel was allowed to deliver a message of hope for the future of Israel (chs. 34—39). There was no longer a need to preach a message of doom, because the day of doom was over. The people would logically ask, "What will happen now?" and

---

[8]See 2 Sam. 5:7, 9; 1 Chron. 11:5, 7; Ps. 18:2; Prov. 21:22; Zech. 9:12. In Ezekiel 30:15 this word refers to a city in Egypt.

Ezekiel was allowed to tell them. Moreover, they would want to listen to Ezekiel. His prophecies had all come true; he had established himself as a genuine prophet of God.

APPLICATION

The Cost of Service vs. the Cost of Sin

People who truly love God and want to serve Him are willing to pay any price. Ezekiel was such a man. Jesus calls upon us to count the cost of being one of His disciples (see Mt. 16:24).

Passages such as 1 John 4:8 ("God is love") lead some to believe that God will not bring punishment upon the unfaithful. On the contrary, when people persist in sin, our righteous God will act (Ezek. 24:21). The doctrine of "universalism" (the idea that all will be saved, regardless of how they have lived) is false.

We need to behold both the "kindness and severity of God" (Rom. 11:22).

D.P.

Why the Fall?

One of the greatest events in the Old Testament is the destruction of Jerusalem by Nebuchadnezzar in 587(6) B.C. Much space is given to this tragedy because God wanted us to think about it. One important question is this: Why would Jerusalem fall? Several reasons are given in the Scriptures.

She had given herself to sin. Idolatry, mistreatment of each other, foreign alliances, and a host of other sins are mentioned. Judah opened the door to evil. She welcomed sin and gave her heart to it.

She had refused to repent. Much of the work of the prophets involved pleading for the repentance of the nation. Warning after warning was given. When we read the Prophets, God takes us behind the scenes and shows us how he pleaded through them for the nation to come back to Him.

She had exhausted the patience of the Lord. God's lovingkindness reaches to the heavens, but eventually it runs out. God will not wait forever for us to make up our minds about sin. Witnesses to this truth include the great flood (Gen. 6 and 7) and the destruction of Sodom and Gomorrah (Gen. 24).

Can we learn from this fall? Have we welcomed sin? Have we turned a deaf ear to God's call to repentance? Are we exhausting the patience of God?

E.C.

PART II

THE PROPHECIES AGAINST FOREIGN NATIONS (25—32)

1. The Prophecies Against Four Surrounding Nations (25)
2. The Prophecies Against Tyre (and Sidon) (26—28)
3. The Prophecies Against Egypt (29—32)

Chapter 25
Prophecies Against Ammon, Moab, Edom, and Philistia

Chapter 24 is a major turning point in the Book of Ezekiel. God had His prophet focus on the sins of Judah and the coming destruction as a result of those sins. In that chapter, Jerusalem was put under siege by the Babylonians (and was eventually destroyed, in 587[6] B.C.). Convinced that the city was safe and that their exile would be short, only two or so years, the people had thought Ezekiel was lying.

Nevertheless, Ezekiel was right. His prophecies and illustrations were accurate. As a result, the people came to see Ezekiel differently. He was gaining credibility as a genuine prophet of God.

The people would naturally have been interested in hearing about their future, if they were to have one, now that Jerusalem had been destroyed. However, God had other work for Ezekiel first.[1] He wanted Ezekiel to target seven specific heathen nations and announce His judgment and condemnation on them. They gloated and rejoiced over the fall of Judah, but they were making a serious mistake. They failed to realize that God was bringing them into judgment as well. In chapters 25 through 32, the seven nations to which Ezekiel gave his attention are divided into two groups: (1) nations near Israel, including Am-

---

[1] As readers, we see a powerful literary tactic being used. We, like the exiles, are anxious to move to the next stage. We find ourselves asking, "What will be next for God's people?" Since we must wait until chapter 33 to receive an answer, some curiosity and intrigue is developed. Besides, Ezekiel was not confirmed as God's prophet until the refugees from Jerusalem verified the accuracy of his prophetic message (33:21).

mon, Moab, Edom, and Philistia (ch. 25), and (2) nations farther away: Tyre, Sidon, and Egypt (chs. 26—32).

In condemning the seven nations, Ezekiel's presentation moved in a logical geographical sequence. Beginning with Ammon, to the northeast of Jerusalem, Ezekiel proceeded southward through Moab and Edom, and then made a half-circle to cover Philistia, to the west. Continuing northward along the coast of the Mediterranean Sea, he covered Tyre and Sidon (in Phoenicia). Finally, he dealt with the most distant power, Egypt, to the extreme south.

Scholars are amazed that Babylon was not included in this list of condemned nations. Perhaps the reason is that she was an instrument that God used to bring punishment on these other nations. Therefore, her judgment was to come later (see Hab.).

Giving such detailed attention to foreign nations is not unusual for God's prophets. Logically, they would have devoted a majority of their attention, work, and writings to God's people. However, God gave them a global outlook as well. Isaiah (chs. 13—23), Jeremiah (chs. 46—51), and Amos (ch. 1; 2:1–3) offered similar words of judgment and punishment for these nations. They were about to receive God's wrath for four basic reasons:

1. They were guilty of inhumane treatment of others, animals, and the land.
2. They violated covenants made with other men and nations, showing attitudes of pride and arrogance.
3. They continually worked against Israel and Judah, causing extra turmoil for God's people.
4. They rejoiced at the demise of God's people and, like vultures, were prepared to take advantage of them at every opportunity.

In God's dealings with these sinful nations, we can learn several lessons. First, God is truly the "God of all the earth." Every person, everywhere, will answer to Him. Polytheism has always been false. Second, God is the One who sets up kingdoms and removes kingdoms (see Dan. 2:20–22; 4:17; Rom. 13:1–7). Third, the Gentile nations were not judged by the law of

Moses, but by the moral law discussed by Paul in Romans 2:14, 15. Nevertheless, there is a divine standard for all people. (This amplifies the significance of the gospel, for now everyone is accountable to one system; Acts 17:30, 31; 2 Thess. 1:7–9; 1 Pet. 4:17.) The fact that exactly seven nations were condemned at this time may have symbolic significance, representing the thoroughness and perfection of God's judgment.

THE PROPHECIES AGAINST FOUR SURROUNDING NATIONS (25)[2]

Ammon (25:1–7)

25:1, 2

¹**And the word of the L**ORD **came to me saying,** ²**"Son of man, set your face toward the sons of Ammon and prophesy against them."**

Verses 1, 2. As the nations received the Lord's condemnation through Ezekiel, God first told him, **"Set your face toward the sons of Ammon"** (v. 2). The Ammonites lived on the east side of the Jordan River, northeast of Jerusalem. Being descendants of Ammon (or Ben-Ammi), the son of Lot's younger daughter, they were racially linked with Israel (Gen. 19:30, 38). God instructed the Israelites to avoid the Ammonites on their way to the Promised Land because that land had been given to the sons of Lot, not to the Israelites (Deut. 2:19, 37).

---

[2]"Most commentators remark on the colourless prose of these four oracles . . . , and this is true in comparison with the poetic splendour of the oracles on Tyre and Egypt. It does not follow from this, however, that they are secondary material. As with Amos's oracles (Am. 1:3—2:3), they were written in a stereotyped form, and they follow the 'because . . . therefore . . .' pattern of the invective oracle (*cf.* 26:2; 34:8–10; 36:2, *etc.*) which appears to be peculiar to Ezekiel. They have many phrases also which are typical of Ezekiel's style, such as 'profaning my sanctuary', 'stretching out my hand', 'executing judgments', and of course the ever-present 'you shall know that I am the Lord'" (John B. Taylor, *Ezekiel: An Introduction and Commentary*, Tyndale Old Testament Commentaries [Downers Grove, Ill.: Inter-Varsity Press, 1969], 186).

The Old Testament tells of Israel's ongoing struggles against the Ammonites, from the period of the judges onward. There were frequent wars and continual animosity between Israel and Ammon (see Judg. 10:11; 1 Sam. 11; 2 Sam. 10). In 722(1) B.C., when the Assyrians carried away the tribes located on the east side of the Jordan (Reuben, Gad, and part of Manasseh), the Ammonites were ready to take their land (Jer. 49:1). When Jehoiakim rebelled against Babylon, God sent marauding bands of Ammonites to help destroy him (2 Kings 24:2). Then, when Jerusalem fell, the Ammonite king Baalis encouraged Ishmael, the son of Nethaniah, to assassinate Gedaliah (the governor of Judah appointed by Nebuchadnezzar; Jer. 40:14).

The Ammonites later stood as adversaries to the rebuilding projects of Nehemiah in Jerusalem (Neh. 2:19, 20; 4:1–3). They also assisted the Syrians against the Jews in the Maccabean war.[3]

25:3–7

3"And say to the sons of Ammon, 'Hear the word of the Lord God! Thus says the Lord God, "Because you said, 'Aha!' against My sanctuary when it was profaned, and against the land of Israel when it was made desolate, and against the house of Judah when they went into exile, 4therefore, behold, I am going to give you to the sons of the east for a possession, and they will set their encampments among you and make their dwellings among you; they will eat your fruit and drink your milk. 5I will make Rabbah a pasture for camels and the sons of Ammon a resting place for flocks. Thus you will know that I am the Lord." 6For thus says the Lord God, "Because you have clapped your hands and stamped your feet and rejoiced with all the scorn of your soul against the land of Israel, 7therefore, behold, I have stretched out My hand against you and I will give you for spoil to the nations. And I will cut you off from the peoples and make you perish from the lands; I will destroy you. Thus you will know that I am the Lord."'"

---

[3] 1 Maccabees 5:6.

Verses 3–7. Ammon said, **"Aha!"** against Israel (v. 3). This word was evidence of gloating and happiness on the part of the Ammonites when they learned about the destruction of "Israel" (here referring to Judah, for the northern kingdom of Israel had been gone for a long time).

Two oracles follow, each beginning with **thus says the Lord God, "Because you . . ."** (vv. 3–5; vv. 6, 7). God was addressing the sin and the punishment of the Ammonites. First, He mentioned three ways they were guilty of gloating in verse 3:

1. **Against [His] sanctuary**—The Ammonites rejoiced to see the most holy place of the Jews **profaned**. When men do not share religious beliefs, one has no respect for the holy sites of the other. When the Ammonites received word that the temple had been desecrated by the Babylonians, they were delighted.
2. **Against the land of Israel**—The Israelites were very proud and boastful of their land. Their enemies rejoiced to see the Babylonians remove the people from the land they loved, making the land **desolate**.
3. **Against the house of Judah**—The Ammonites did not like the people of Judah, and their hatred was not veiled. When God's people were taken into **exile**, there was tremendous celebration among the Ammonites, who enjoyed seeing their neighboring nation fall.

Second, God continued His accusation against Ammon's bombastic behavior: **You have clapped your hands and stamped your feet and rejoiced** (v. 6). Seeing Judah destroyed, Ammon danced with delight. The phrase "with all the scorn of your soul" indicates the level of their joy. The NIV has "rejoicing with all the malice of your heart against the land of Israel."

God then specified her punishment (vv. 4–7):

"I am going to give you to the sons of the east" (v. 4). These people have nowhere been positively identified. They are, presumably, nomadic tribes of the Arabian desert. Josephus recorded that Nebuchadnezzar, five years after hia defeat of Jerusalem, brought Ammon (and Moab) into subjection. This would date around 582(1) B.C.[4] In chapter 21 Nebuchadnezzar was faced with the decision of whom to attack first: Jerusalem or Ammon. Through intervention by the Lord, Nebuchadnezzar first attacked Jerusalem; but God promised that the Ammonites would eventually feel Nebuchadnezzar's sword (21:20–32). Apparently, after their defeat by Nebuchadnezzar, the Ammonites were so weak that the smaller tribes to their east were easily able to defeat them—or perhaps God was referring to their eventual defeat at the hands of the Medes and Persians (who were northeast of Ammon). Regardless of the details, the Ammonites would be unable to stop their enemies' settling among them or from taking whatever they wanted.

"I will make Rabbah a pasture for camels" (v. 5). This once proud capital of Ammon would not only be reduced to rubble, but would never be rebuilt. Her ideal location would instead become "a pasture for camels." This city was located in the mountainous region east of the Jordan. Its ruins are used today by the Arabs as a place to lodge camels.

"I will give you for spoil to the nations" (v. 7). All that the proud Ammonites had been able to accumulate through the centuries by their warfare and thievery would become the treasure of others.

"I will cut you off from the peoples and make you perish from the lands; I will destroy you" (v. 7). No Ammonites exist today. They are known only through history.

What was the final result of this punishment? He said, **"Thus you will know that I am the Lord."**

Concerning this second oracle, Taylor wrote,

> The second oracle (6, 7) has the same form and deals with the same offence as the first, for clapping the hands and stamping the feet was obviously [an expression of "malicious delight"]. The punishment, however, is more specific: the Ammonites will become a prey to foreign peoples and will be completely destroyed as a nation. How the final phrase of verse 7 fits in with this is not

---

[4] Josephus *Antiquities* 10.9.7.

easy to see. It may be that a knowledge of the Lord will be experienced only in the calamity of final destruction. [Herbert G.] May compares the promises of restoration *after* destruction that are found in Jeremiah (48:47; 49:6, 39) and thinks that this hints at pagans eventually worshipping Yahweh as the true God.[5]

Moab (25:8–11)

⁸"'Thus says the Lord GOD, "Because Moab and Seir say, 'Behold, the house of Judah is like all the nations,' ⁹therefore, behold, I am going to deprive the flank of Moab of its cities, of its cities which are on its frontiers, the glory of the land, Beth-jeshimoth, Baal-meon and Kiriathaim, ¹⁰and I will give it for a possession along with the sons of Ammon to the sons of the east, so that the sons of Ammon will not be remembered among the nations. ¹¹Thus I will execute judgments on Moab, and they will know that I am the LORD."'"

Verse 8. The next two nations mentioned are **Moab and Seir**. The land of Moab is east of the Dead Sea. "Seir" stands for Edom, a close ally of Moab. (This nation was to receive its own condemnation, beginning in verse 12.) Like the Ammonites, the Moabites were kin to the Israelites. They came from Moab, the son of Lot's older daughter (Gen. 19:37). Hostility between Israel and Moab began in the days of Moses and Balak (Num. 22—24). The Moabites rebelled against Israel during the days of Elisha (2 Kings 3:5–12) and joined the Babylonians in the attack on Judah (2 Kings 24:2). Only one charge was made against Moab: She said that **the house of Judah is like all the nations**. Moab held Judah in contempt, openly rejecting and ridiculing her claim to be the chosen people of the Lord. As far as the Moabites were concerned, nothing was special about Judah. In their eyes, she was no different than the rest of the nations.

---

[5]Taylor, 187; Herbert G. May, "The Book of Ezekiel," in *The Interpreter's Bible*, ed. George Arthur Buttrick (Nashville: Abingdon Press, 1956), 6:202.

Oracles against Moab also occur in the writings of several other prophets (see Is. 15; 16; Jer. 48; Amos 2:1–3; Zeph. 2:8–11).

The judgment oracle of verses 9 and 10 begins with the dreaded "therefore." God listed three punishments for Moab.

Verse 9. I am going to deprive the flank of Moab of its cities. Moab was to be invaded by enemy armies who would conquer her fortified cities on the **frontiers**, which served as protection from attack. Three specific fortified cities of Moab are mentioned: **Beth-jeshimoth** was located on the southern plains of Moab, northeast of the Dead Sea (see Num. 33:49; Josh. 12:3; 13:20). **Baal-meon**, named Beth-baal-meon in Joshua 13:17, was located near the Dead Sea (see Num. 32:3, 38; 1 Chron. 5:8; Jer. 48:23). **Kiriathaim** was located a few miles south of Baal-meon (see Num. 32:37; Josh. 13:19; Jer. 48:1, 23). The last two cities are named on the famous Moabite Stone.[6]

Verses 10, 11. I will give it for a possession . . . to the sons of the east (v. 10). Not long after this prophecy, the Moabites (along with the Ammonites) were conquered by Nabatean tribesmen,[7] the Babylonians (582[1] B.C.), or perhaps the Medes. They ceased to exist as an independent nation.

These people would **not be remembered among the nations**. As with Ammon, the Moabites were to be defeated and their land left desolate (Is. 11:11, 14; Jer. 48:7–9).

Edom (25:12–14)

[12]"'Thus says the Lord GOD, "Because Edom has acted against the house of Judah by taking vengeance, and has incurred grievous guilt, and avenged themselves upon them," [13]therefore thus says the Lord GOD, "I will also stretch out My hand against Edom and cut off man and beast from it. And I

---

[6]The Moabite Stone is an inscribed slab of basalt with thirty-nine lines of Hebrew-like script. The inscription, by Mesha', king of Moab (mentioned in 2 Kings 3:4, 5), tells of his victory over Israel and of certain building projects. It provides historical, linguistic, religious, and economic insights regarding the Moabites.

[7]Taylor, 187.

will lay it waste; from Teman even to Dedan they will fall by the sword. ¹⁴I will lay My vengeance on Edom by the hand of My people Israel. Therefore, they will act in Edom according to My anger and according to My wrath; thus they will know My vengeance," declares the Lord GOD.'"

Verse 12. The nation of **Edom** normally inhabited the region south of the Dead Sea. Antagonism existed between Edom and Israel beginning with their two ancestors, Jacob (Israel) and Esau (Edom) (Gen. 25:23, 30; 27:41–46; 32:4). Since this nation was a "twin brother" to Israel, they should have had better relations; yet animosity existed throughout their histories (36:1–7; Lam. 4:21, 22; Amos 1:11, 12). Edom's hatred for Israel is seen in that she joined forces with Ammon and Moab in mocking Israel (see v. 8; 36:5). They evidently took advantage of every opportunity to oppress Israel, evoking frequent condemnation by God (Ps. 137; Is. 34:5–7; Jer. 49:7–22; Lam. 4:21, 22; Ezek. 35; Amos 1:11, 12; Obad.; Mal. 1:3–5). In addition, the Edomites participated in the Babylonian attack on Jerusalem and perhaps even occupied territory in southern Judah.[8]

The sins of Edom are given here. First, she **acted against the house of Judah by taking vengeance**. The NIV says, "Because Edom took revenge on the house of Judah and became very guilty by doing so." The RSV says that "Edom acted revengefully" and "grievously offended in taking vengeance upon them." These strong terms of condemnation show that Edom was holding a grudge against Judah. When the opportunity presented itself (perhaps in the attack of Nebuchadnezzar) she took "vengeance."

Next, God said that she had **incurred grievous guilt**. Her actions against Judah were inexcusable. Whatever Judah had done to Edom did not warrant this kind of violent response. Therefore, God was holding Edom guilty of this "grievous" sin. She had **avenged** [herself] **upon them**. Apparently, there were no legitimate reasons to avenge herself as she did.

---

[8]W. F. Albright, "Ostracon No. 6043 from Ezion-Geber," *Bulletin of the American Schools of Oriental Research* 82 (1941): 11–15.

Verses 13, 14. Beginning with the word of judicial decision, **therefore**, God announced the punishment. He would **stretch out [His] hand against Edom**. The punishment was severe. God said,

"I will . . . cut off man and beast" (v. 13). God would remove humans and cattle from the land, virtually making it desolate.

"I will lay it [the land] **waste"** (v. 13). Not only did God plan to remove man and beast, but He would also strike against the land, making it a wasteland, a desolation. This devastation would be thorough, **from Teman even to Dedan**. Although the exact locations of these two places are unknown, available evidence indicates that they were situated on the extreme northern and southern points of the nation.

"I will lay My vengeance on Edom by the hand of My people Israel" (v. 14). After this prophecy, the situation went from bad to worse for the Edomites. They were conquered by the Babylonians (see Jer. 27:1–11) and then the Nabateans. What was left of the nation was subdued by Judas Maccabeus and then John Hyrcanus (around 150 B.C.), who "incorporated them into the Jewish race by compulsory circumcision."[9] Those who would argue that Ezekiel's prophecies were written "after the fact" have difficulty with this prediction. There is no way that this prophecy could have been a later addition; for it existed in the MT and the LXX, and its fulfillment took place well after the book was written (c. 570 B.C.). Other prophets declared that Israel would possess Edom in the end time as well (see 35:1—36:15; Is. 11:14; Amos 9:12; Obad. 18).

In contrast to His message for the other nations, God did not declare here, "Thus you will know that I am the Lord." God's final statement to Edom is, **"Thus they will know My vengeance."** They would see the hand of God in their defeat and their incorporation by the Israelites. Further prophecies against Edom are given in 32:29 and chapter 35 (see Mal. 1:2–5). Edom cursed the people of God. Because of that arrogance and pride, God was full of "vengeance."

---

[9]Taylor, 188.

Philistia (25:15–17)

¹⁵"'Thus says the Lord GOD, "Because the Philistines have acted in revenge and have taken vengeance with scorn of soul to destroy with everlasting enmity," ¹⁶therefore thus says the Lord GOD, "Behold, I will stretch out My hand against the Philistines, even cut off the Cherethites and destroy the remnant of the seacoast. ¹⁷I will execute great vengeance on them with wrathful rebukes; and they will know that I am the LORD when I lay My vengeance on them."'"

Verse 15. Ezekiel made a half-circle in verse 15, moving to the west side of Jerusalem. This continued the pattern of condemning the closest nations first. Living along the coast of the Mediterranean Sea, the Philistines were known as the "sea people." Unlike the nations previously mentioned, the Philistines had no kinship tie to Israel. The Old Testament is full of recorded conflicts between Israel and Philistia. Consider the accounts of Samson (Judg. 13—16), Eli (1 Sam. 4), Saul (1 Sam. 13; 31), David (2 Sam. 5), Hezekiah (2 Kings 18:8), Jehoram (2 Chron. 21:16, 17), and Ahaz (2 Chron. 28:16, 18). God charged the Philistines with the following sins:

1. "[You] **have acted in revenge.**" The Philistines believed that they were oppressed by Israel through the centuries; therefore, they sought "revenge." They were given that opportunity by joining forces with the Babylonian army against Jerusalem.
2. "[You have] **taken vengeance.**" The Philistines took advantage of Judah's weakness and attacked with **scorn of soul**. Their deep-seated hatred and animosity against Israel is described as **everlasting enmity**.

Verses 16, 17. God announced the punishment for Philistia. As He had told Edom, God said, **"I will stretch out My hand."** He said that He would do the following:

"I will . . . **cut off the Cherethites.**" Scholars believe that these people were a subgroup of the Philistines or else had a treaty with Philistia (see 1 Sam. 30:14; Zeph. 2:5). The LXX translates this as "Cretans," perhaps indicating that the Philistines were originally settlers from Crete, who entered Palestine about 1200 B.C.

"I will . . . **destroy the remnant of the seacoast."** The nation itself, along with its seacoast dwellings, would be destroyed. The exact timing of this destruction is unknown. Philistia's demise presumably occurred around the same time as that of the previous three nations—falling to the Babylonians (see Jer. 47). The last record of the Philistines is during the time of the Maccabeans. They ceased to exist as a people. The prophets predicted that eventually Israel would possess the land of Philistia (Is. 11:14; Joel 3:1–4; Obad. 19; Zeph. 2:4–7).

"I will execute great vengeance on them." The Philistines had acted in revenge against God's people; now it was time for God to return vengeance upon them. They were deserving of the Lord's **wrathful rebukes** (see Jer. 25:17, 20).

APPLICATION

God's Protective Nature
God is jealous for His people. They are His family (see 1 Tim. 3:15).

If God is for us, who can be against us? (Rom. 8:31–39).

D.P.

Ammon's "Aha!" (25:1–7)
A righteous judgment was to be meted out to Ammon. The sons of the East would be allowed to come against this nation. They would take over Ammon's property, eat their food, and totally dominate them. Rabbah, the capital of Ammon, would be humbled and made desolate. It would become "pasture for camels" and "a resting place for flocks."

Any evaluation of this judgment sentence would mark it down as extremely severe. It prompts us to ask, "What was their crime? What was their transgression?"

Their great sin is summarized with the one word "Aha!" They uttered it in derision and sinister joy over the humiliation of Israel and Judah. The word is an outgrowth of wicked hearts. Three attitudes are depicted by it.

There is the "Aha!" of desecration. They rejoiced when the sanctuary of the Lord was profaned (v. 3). Respect for God and His place of worship is a serious matter. Even pagan people, worshipers of other gods, were not excused from recognizing God and His temple. Let us remember that reverence is the beginning of knowledge (Prov. 1:7).

There is the "Aha!" of desolation. They found godless joy in the desolation of the land of Israel. God said, "Because you have clapped your hands and stamped your feet and rejoiced with all the scorn of your soul against the land of Israel. . . . I have stretched out My hand against you . . ." (v. 6). The people of Israel had sinned, and God permitted them to be overtaken; however the rejoicing over their being removed from their land by the Assyrians was a wickedness that deserved judgment. Let us remember that the removal of a people from its land is a time for weeping and prayer, not mockery and ridicule.

There is the "Aha!" of deportation. They celebrated when Judah was taken into captivity. The Lord allowed Judah to be overtaken and removed to captivity for her idolatries and other sins; but Ammon had no right to laugh at her calamity. Edom received a similar judgment for a similar sin (see Obad.).

Let us remember that God judges anyone who rejoices over someone else's pain. Human pain, even when deserved, should bring sadness and sympathy, not gladness and celebration.

The writer of Ecclesiastes tells us that there is "a time to weep and a time to laugh" (Eccles. 3:4). We come under the wrath of God when we turn the first part of this truth around: God judges those who laugh when they should be weeping.

Who Is God? (25:8–15)

These judgment oracles give us an opportunity to look into the nature and attributes of God. They do not provide the most pleasant reading in the Old Testament, but they give us a clear picture of God that may not be seen in other passages.

What does this judgment sentence upon Moab, Edom, and Philistia say about God? What does it say God is like?

He is the true God. Twice in this short passage we see the familiar phrase, Ezekiel's dominate affirmation, "They will know that I am the LORD." God will bring swift judgment upon Moab, Edom, and Philistia, not because He is a tyrannical God of capricious terror, but because He wants them and all other nations to know that He is the true God and that He judges righteously. Our business as believers is to let the world know that God is the true God.

He is the God who acts. He is not a silent, passive God, like the pagan gods of stone and wood who never move or speak. He acts in judgment of all the nations. His actions are swift and terrible toward the wicked; yet, they are compassionate and loving toward the righteous. Whether a nation recognizes Him as God or not, that nation will have to deal with Him. It is on a collision course with Him. Let us teach the world that God is active in human affairs and rules over His world with providential wisdom.

He is the God who judges sin. Those who trust in Him and walk in His ways will have His salvation and grace; but those who defy His laws and mistreat others will receive His wrath. Throughout the history of the Old Testament, God has left the telltale signs for all to see that He does and will condemn sin and He does and will judge those who live in it. Have we told the world that God is the God of judgment as well as grace?

We did not make God; He made us. We do not choose Him to be the God that we want; He reveals to us who He is. We must either acknowledge Him, submit to His will, and live under His grace; or we can refuse the knowledge of Him and live under His wrath. He is the true God, the God of every human being, the God of judgment, and the God of grace and glory.

E.C.

Chapter 26
The Fall of Tyre

Moving north on the coast of the Mediterranean Sea, Ezekiel next dealt with the Phoenician city of Tyre. Tyre was located one hundred miles from Jerusalem and about thirty miles from the Sea of Galilee. Tyre had two superior harbors: one on the mainland, where the major portion of the city was built, and a second on an island located less than one mile from the coast. These two harbors, plus Tyre's excellent location, made her a key city in trade and commerce in the ancient world. The island and mainland were connected by a causeway built in the tenth century B.C. by Hiram I.[1] The island became a fortress whenever Tyre was besieged. The island fortress was easily defended and for centuries proved too great for enemy armies to conquer.

Some main points of the history of Tyre follow:

- Tyre rose to prominence in 1200 B.C.
- The merchants grew rich (Is. 23:8).
- With their wealth, the people created a "fortress of Tyre" (2 Sam. 24:7).
- Tyre paid tribute to powerful nations to keep peace.
- Since Tyre was only one hundred miles from Jerusalem, the merchants traded with Israel.
- King David used resources from Tyre to build his royal palace (2 Sam. 5:11).

---

[1]The causeway built by Hiram was used for commercial purposes. (Charles F. Pfeiffer, ed., "Tyre," in *The Biblical World: A Dictionary of Biblical Archaeology* [Grand Rapids, Mich.: Baker Book House, 1966], 591.)

- King Solomon granted Tyre territory in exchange for goods to build the great temple (1 Kings 9:11).
- Tyre stood at the crossroads of a worldwide trading network stretching from Europe to the Far East, from Asia Minor to Egypt.
- Products from Tyre included glassware and fine purple cloth (favored by royalty, dyed with an extract of the local murex marine snail).
- When the exiles returned to Jerusalem, they purchased materials from Tyre (Ezra 3:7).

Here are some additional facts about the evil kingdom of Phoenicia:

- The people were motivated by materialism and greed; they had no problem taking advantage of others.
- The nation frequently made alliances with the enemies of Israel.
- They took advantage of Israel in times of weakness.
- One of Tyre's rulers claimed to be a god (Ezek. 28:2).
- Several of Israel's prophets prophesied against Tyre, including Isaiah (23), Amos (1:9, 10), Joel (3:4–6), and Zechariah (9:3, 4).
- Ahab established an alliance with Tyre, marrying the evil woman Jezebel (daughter of Ethbaal, king of the Sidonians. This marriage not only violated the law of Moses, but also created fatal consequences for Samaria and Sidon (see 1 Kings 16:30–33; 21:25, 26).

In chapters 26 through 28, the prophecies against Tyre may be divided into five sections, each beginning with some variation of the phrase "the word of the LORD came to me":

1. The predicted destruction of Tyre (26:1–21).
2. A lamentation for Tyre (27:1–36).
3. A woe oracle for the prince of Tyre (28:1–10).
4. A lamentation for the king of Tyre (28:11–19).
5. A prophecy against Sidon (28:20–26).

THE OVERALL DESCRIPTION OF THE DESTRUCTION OF TYRE (26:1–6)

26:1, 2
¹Now in the eleventh year, on the first of the month, the word of the LORD came to me saying, ²"Son of man, because Tyre has said concerning Jerusalem, 'Aha, the gateway of the peoples is broken; it has opened to me. I shall be filled, now that she is laid waste.'"

Verse 1. This prophecy on Tyre came about **in the eleventh year** of the reign of Zedekiah, the year in which Jerusalem was captured. Since the month is not stated, the reference is probably to the eleventh month of the Jewish religious calendar (corresponding to February), in which the fate of Jerusalem was sealed. This was the year 587 or 586 B.C. There are some difficulties with the date. According to an earlier section, those in Babylon did not learn of the destruction of Jerusalem until the tenth month of the twelfth year (33:21). Therefore, some have attempted to resolve this dilemma by re-dating the passage in 33:21 to "the eleventh year" (following the MT). This would make the date of this prophecy on Tyre approximately one month after the exiles heard the news about Jerusalem.

However, if all dates stood as recorded, there would remain a viable explanation for Tyre's comments in verse 2. Tyre was only one hundred miles from Jerusalem. She would have received news of Jerusalem's demise long before those in Babylon. God, then, was revealing to Ezekiel what was going on among the Phoenician people—both their words and their deeds.

Verse 2. Upon hearing of the destruction of Jerusalem, Tyre rejoiced greatly (v. 2). She considered Jerusalem to be **the gateway of the peoples**—meaning that the prominent location of Jerusalem for trade routes allowed the residents to exact tolls from merchants. Tyre wanted these tolls for herself. Now that Jerusalem had fallen, Tyre believed those trade opportunities (and tolls) had **opened** to her. Now she expected to **be filled** with the profits that had been pouring into Jerusalem. Ralph H. Alexander wrote,

Tyre's major desire was to be filled with the spoils of Jerusalem and with the opportunities that would then be hers in western Asia, since Jerusalem "lies in ruins." ... It was this incessant desire for wealth and riches, now expressed toward God's holy city and its people, that brought God's wrath on Tyre in fulfillment of his promise in Genesis 12:3.[2]

26:3-6

³"Therefore thus says the Lord GOD, 'Behold, I am against you, O Tyre, and I will bring up many nations against you, as the sea brings up its waves. ⁴They will destroy the walls of Tyre and break down her towers; and I will scrape her debris from her and make her a bare rock. ⁵She will be a place for the spreading of nets in the midst of the sea, for I have spoken,' declares the Lord GOD, 'and she will become spoil for the nations. ⁶Also her daughters who are on the mainland will be slain by the sword, and they will know that I am the LORD.'"

Seven distinct prophecies were pronounced concerning the destruction of Tyre in this chapter:

1. Nebuchadnezzar's armies would attack Tyre (v. 7).
2. Other nations would help in her capture (v. 3).
3. Her stones and timbers would be laid in the sea (v. 12).
4. Tyre would be scraped as flat as the top of a rock (v. 4).
5. Other cities would fear and give up (v. 16).
6. Tyre would become a place for spreading nets (v. 5).
7. The old city was never to be rebuilt (v. 14).

Verse 3. "I am against you, O Tyre," God declared. These words spelled certain doom for any individual or nation. It is a terrifying thing to fall into the hands of the living God (see Heb. 10:31), and Tyre had just done that. Tyre had paid heavy tribute

---

[2]Ralph H. Alexander, "Ezekiel," in *The Expositor's Bible Commentary*, ed. Frank E. Gaebelein (Grand Rapids, Mich.: Zondervan Publishing House, 1986), 6:870.

to various nations in order to remain at peace. She thought, because of all the friends she had bought, that she was safe from attack. However, God decreed that He would **bring up many nations against** Tyre. History records that the Babylonians (586–573 B.C.), the Persians (525 B.C.), the Greeks led by Alexander the Great (c. 330 B.C.), the Seleucids (160 B.C.), the Romans (c. 100 B.C. to A.D. 400), and finally the Saracens[3] (A.D. 1290) fought against Tyre. Indeed, God did bring "many nations" against Tyre—in a series of battles through the centuries.[4]

More than 240 years after Nebuchadnezzar reigned, Alexander the Great fought against Tyre. Doubting that his navy could defeat the fleet of Tyre, he captured the fleets of other "nations" and used them to attack the island. This effort failed, but it was yet another fulfillment of Ezekiel's prophecy.

Verses 4–6. Those attacking Tyre would **destroy [her] walls** and **break down her towers** (v. 4). God declared that He would **scrape her debris from her and make her a bare rock**. Nebuchadnezzar (who is specifically named in v. 7) laid siege to Tyre for thirteen years (586–573 B.C.). During this time, the inhabitants transferred most of their valuables to the island fortress. While the Babylonians were able to seize Tyre's mainland territories, they were unable to conquer the island fortress (see 29:18). Tyre, weakened by the conflict, soon recognized Babylonian authority. Under King Ba'ali II, Tyre accepted Babylonian suzerainty and was ruled by judges. In 29:17-20, God foretold Babylon's failure to conquer Tyre completely. Later, when the Babylonians' dominance weakened, Tyre reclaimed her independence.

Nebuchadnezzar never "scrape[d] her debris" or made her "a bare rock." Does that mean this prophecy failed? The careful student will notice that God nowhere said these deeds were to be done by Nebuchadnezzar. As seen in verse 14, some specific events were fulfilled much later—by Alexander the Great.

---

[3]The Saracens were Muslims—Arab and Turkish conquerors of the Medieval Period.

[4]See Trevor Major, "The Fall of Tyre," *Reason and Revelation* 16 (December 1996): 95.

The **daughters** were the various villages **on the mainland** (v. 6). These peoples were easily defeated **by the sword**, which was wielded by the vast army of Nebuchadnezzar.

THE SPECIFIC MILITARY CAMPAIGN OF NEBUCHADNEZZAR (26:7–11)

⁷For thus says the Lord God, "Behold, I will bring upon Tyre from the north Nebuchadnezzar king of Babylon, king of kings, with horses, chariots, cavalry and a great army. ⁸He will slay your daughters on the mainland with the sword; and he will make siege walls against you, cast up a ramp against you and raise up a large shield against you. ⁹The blow of his battering rams he will direct against your walls, and with his axes he will break down your towers. ¹⁰Because of the multitude of his horses, the dust raised by them will cover you; your walls will shake at the noise of cavalry and wagons and chariots when he enters your gates as men enter a city that is breached. ¹¹With the hoofs of his horses he will trample all your streets. He will slay your people with the sword; and your strong pillars will come down to the ground."

Verses 7–9. God said, "**I will bring upon Tyre from the north Nebuchadnezzar king of Babylon**" (v. 7). The spelling of this name by Ezekiel in the Hebrew text, "Nebuchadrezzar" (which is also found in the Book of Jeremiah), is nearer the Babylonian Nabu-kudurri-usur, meaning "Nebo protect (my) labor." Nebuchadnezzar is here referred to as **king of kings**. He had dominion over many vassal kings (see Dan. 2:37; Ezra 7:12). Thus God specifically named His instrument to destroy the mainland city of Tyre. The impressiveness of Nebuchadnezzar's army is seen here. His army was an efficient military machine. God said, "**He will slay your daughters on the mainland . . .**" (v. 8). The attack against Tyre is given with precision. S. Fisch wrote,

> The Babylonian military operation against Tyre is described in chronological order. The first to suffer were

the cities on the mainland. Then came the attack on the island-city by means of *forts* or movable towers, mounds and bucklers, the last being probably large shields which gave cover to the besiegers. Finally the battering rams came into operation (verse 9).[5]

Verses 10, 11. The mention of **horses**, **cavalry**, **wagons**, and **chariots** demonstrates that the troops marching against Tyre had brought the instruments used in a land battle. God knew that the Babylonian army would be unable to fight against the island city. Nebuchadnezzar did enter into the **gates** of the mainland city of Tyre; however, a large number of people and the wealth of the city had already been moved to the island fortress. Therefore, the words of 29:18 came true:

"Son of man, Nebuchadnezzar king of Babylon made his army labor hard against Tyre; every head was made bald and every shoulder was rubbed bare. But he and his army had no wages from Tyre for the labor that he had performed against it."

THE FUTURE DESTRUCTION OF TYRE (26:12–21)

26:12–14
¹²"Also they will make a spoil of your riches and a prey of your merchandise, break down your walls and destroy your pleasant houses, and throw your stones and your timbers and your debris into the water. ¹³So I will silence the sound of your songs, and the sound of your harps will be heard no more. ¹⁴I will make you a bare rock; you will be a place for the spreading of nets. You will be built no more, for I the LORD have spoken," declares the Lord GOD.

---

[5]S. Fisch, *Ezekiel: Hebrew Text and English Translation with an Introduction and Commentary*, Soncino Books of the Bible (London: Soncino Press, 1950), 174.

Verses 12, 13. History shows no record of Nebuchadnezzar's having thrown **stones and . . . timbers and . . . debris** of the city into the sea (v. 12). This has led some to believe that the prophecy was false. However, notice the use of the personal pronouns. God clearly spoke of Nebuchadnezzar, using the pronouns "he" and "his" several times in verses 7 through 11. In verse 12 the pronoun changes to **they,** and God did not again identify Nebuchadnezzar (either by name or by a singular personal pronoun). The reason for this is that the prophecy in verses 12 through 21 refers to the army of Alexander the Great. In addition, the remaining portion of this prophecy focuses on what *God* would do to Tyre ("I will . . ."). Further, Nebuchadnezzar was not the one to **silence the sound of . . . songs** in Tyre (v. 13). In fact, the people on the island were able to continue their festivities after Nebuchadnezzar failed to complete his conquest. Alexander the Great, however, did silence their songs when he conquered the island fortress.

Verse 14. As in verse 4, God said that the city would be made

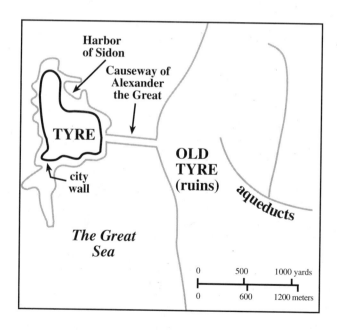

Tyre: The Island Fortress (c. 330 B.C.)

like **a bare rock** and become **a place for the spreading of nets**. This is a play on Tyre's name (צֹר, *tsor*, meaning "rock"). Like Nebuchadnezzar, Alexander the Great was hindered by Tyre's island fortress. His weak navy was unable to overtake the defenses of the island city. However, the brilliance of the Greek general is seen in what he did next. He knew that somehow he must get his army on this island. He used the building materials of the mainland city, even scraping the dust from the ground, to build a massive causeway, or "mole," from the mainland to the island. When this causeway was completed, his army marched to the island and quickly captured the stronghold. The complete conquest of Tyre took only seven months. Today the location of the old city of Tyre is "a place for the spreading of nets." The modern city of Tyre is built on a different spot. God announced that the city of Tyre would **be built no more**, and this prediction came true, even though the location of the ancient city seems ideally suited to support a modern city. Neither was the city-fortress ever rebuilt on the island. Gleason L. Archer, Jr., noted, "Exasperated by the long delay in his invasion schedule, Alexander resolved to make a fearsome example of Tyre; so he had the island city totally destroyed so that it should never be rebuilt (v. 14)."[6]

26:15–21

¹⁵**Thus says the Lord God to Tyre, "Shall not the coastlands shake at the sound of your fall when the wounded groan, when the slaughter occurs in your midst? ¹⁶Then all the princes of the sea will go down from their thrones, remove their robes and strip off their embroidered garments. They will clothe themselves with trembling; they will sit on the ground, tremble every moment and be appalled at you. ¹⁷They will take up a lamentation over you and say to you,**

> **'How you have perished, O inhabited one,
> From the seas, O renowned city,**

---

[6]Gleason L. Archer, Jr., *Encyclopedia of Bible Difficulties* (Grand Rapids, Mich.: Zondervan Publishing House, 1982), 276.

> Which was mighty on the sea,
> She and her inhabitants,
> Who imposed her terror
> On all her inhabitants!
> ¹⁸Now the coastlands will tremble
> On the day of your fall;
> Yes, the coastlands which are by the sea
> Will be terrified at your passing.'"

> ¹⁹For thus says the Lord GOD, "When I make you a desolate city, like the cities which are not inhabited, when I bring up the deep over you and the great waters cover you, ²⁰then I will bring you down with those who go down to the pit, to the people of old, and I will make you dwell in the lower parts of the earth, like the ancient waste places, with those who go down to the pit, so that you will not be inhabited; but I will set glory in the land of the living. ²¹I will bring terrors on you and you will be no more; though you will be sought, you will never be found again," declares the Lord GOD.

Verse 15. Tyre gloated over her invincibility, but God said that the coastlands would **shake at the sound of** [her] **fall**. The people believed that some fortresses could be brought down, but not this one. Neighbors who depended upon Tyre for their own goods (and prosperity) would have been shocked at her fall. Isaiah recorded that Tyre was a "bestower of crowns, whose merchants were princes, whose traders were the honored of the earth" (Is. 23:8).

Verse 16. Seeing the fall of Tyre convinced other nations to give up. They recognized that they had no chance of withstanding the invading army. This particular statement had a dual fulfillment. When Nebuchadnezzar conquered the mainland city, it led additional fortified cities to surrender to him. However, in a fuller sense, this applies to Alexander. "Many fortified cities in the region capitulated to Alexander after they saw the genius and relative ease with which he captured Tyre."[7]

---

[7]Major, 95.

Verses 17, 18. People would **tremble** (v. 18) at the fall of Tyre: both the "princes of the sea" (v. 16) and **the coastlands** (v. 18). Tyre had rejoiced at the fall of Jerusalem, but we see a powerful contrast between that reaction and the response of surrounding nations when Tyre fell. They recognized that Tyre's demise meant certain doom for them.

Verses 19, 20. God described the end of Tyre like the death of a man, like one who goes **down to the pit** (v. 20). This phrase is a common one meaning "death" in the Prophets (see 31:14–16; 32:18, 23–25; Is. 14:15; 38:18).

Verse 21. "**You will be no more,**" God declared to Tyre. The ancient city of Tyre, with its world influence through trade and great wealth, would be forever lost. Alexander the Great sold almost all of Tyre's inhabitants into slavery, and the city forever lost its importance on the world stage. Any vestiges of strength and power disappeared with the destruction of the Crusader fortress. Soûr, as it is known by Arabs today, is a small town in southern Lebanon with a population of about 14,000 (1990 estimate; refugees have since increased that number significantly).[8]

APPLICATION

God's Judgment

Nations that oppose the Lord or His people will be defeated.

While Jesus was healing the sick in this Gentile region, He used Tyre and Sidon as illustrations to show how wicked the cities of His day had become. He said, ". . . it will be more tolerable for Tyre and Sidon in the judgment than for you" (Lk. 10:13, 14; see Mt. 11:21, 22).

Jesus' audience was aware of the destruction of Tyre, which was foretold by Ezekiel. The fulfillment of prophecy—especially specific prophecies like this one—clearly demonstrates the inspiration of the Bible.

D.P.

---

[8]Ibid.

Tyre Before God's Tribunal

When Jerusalem was attacked, Tyre rejoiced because she saw this attack as allowing her to acquire the land of Judah for her own possession. Because of her sinful attitude, God pronounced a detailed judgment—a description in two chapters—upon her.

Her judgment would come in the form of the ruthless Babylonians. They would overcome Tyre and leave her to become a desert waste. Tyre was located on the seacoast and was considered to be invincible. Her fall, however, would proclaim to all seacoast cities that they, too, could fall.

What do we learn from her fall?

We see that God's judgment comes to all people—even to pagans. Tyre did not worship Yahweh, the true God, but she answered to Him anyway. Tyre sinned, and God called her into account.

We see that human energy cannot save. Tyre was a powerful city that had strength, money, and prestige. "No one can defeat Tyre," they said. "She is too strong." They had overlooked the truth that human energy alone cannot save. Tyre would fight against God with the arm of flesh and would lose.

We see that God controls all things. All nations and cities answer to His commands and judgments. He raises up nations, and He tears them down according to His wisdom and truth. He builds cities, and He destroys them.

God holds the future in His hands. He knows what will happen tomorrow. He does not look into a crystal ball and forecast the future. He determines the future, according to His divine judgments and providence.

These four truths spring from one basic truth: All people will, in one way or another, answer to God. Whether Tyre, the city being judged, Nebuchadnezzar, the instrument of judgment, or any other city, nation, or ruler, this judgment of Tyre affirms that all will be brought before the eternal tribunal of God.

E.C.

CHAPTER 27

A LAMENTATION FOR TYRE

In chapter 27 Tyre is depicted as a merchant ship, perfectly constructed and having a superior crew of sailors. However, in a great storm, the weight of the merchandise sank the ship to the depths of the sea. This great loss was mourned by many people, from seamen to kings.

THE DESCRIPTION OF TYRE AS A SHIP (27:1–9)

27:1–3
¹Moreover, the word of the LORD came to me saying, ²"And you, son of man, take up a lamentation over Tyre; ³and say to Tyre, who dwells at the entrance to the sea, merchant of the peoples to many coastlands, 'Thus says the Lord GOD,

"O Tyre, you have said, 'I am perfect in beauty.'""'

Verses 1, 2. God told Ezekiel, ". . . son of man, take up a lamentation[1] over Tyre" (v. 2). S. Fisch wrote, "'Take up' is literally 'raise.' 'This verb is always used in connection with a lamentation, because it was uttered in a loud voice.'"[2]

In chapter 26 neighboring "princes of the sea" (v. 16) are

---

[1] A "lamentation" is a mournful song or poem, usually presented at a funeral.
[2] S. Fisch, *Ezekiel: Hebrew Text and English Translation with an Introduction and Commentary*, Soncino Books of the Bible (London: Soncino Press, 1950), 178.

depicted as singing the dirge for Tyre. Now God instructed Ezekiel to sing a song noting Tyre's death.

Verse 3. Who dwells at the entrance to the sea notes the geographical location of Tyre. The Hebrew literally means "entrances," referring to the two harbors of Tyre. One was known as "the Sidonian" because it faced north, toward the city of Sidon. Tyre had said, **"I am perfect in beauty."** While this region of the Mediterranean was very beautiful, Tyre demonstrated a prideful, arrogant attitude. She considered herself superior to those around her—and did not hesitate to say so.

27:4–9

> 4"'"Your borders are in the heart of the seas;
> Your builders have perfected your beauty.
> 5They have made all your planks of fir trees from Senir;
> They have taken a cedar from Lebanon to make a mast for you.
> 6Of oaks from Bashan they have made your oars;
> With ivory they have inlaid your deck of boxwood from the coastlands of Cyprus.
> 7Your sail was of fine embroidered linen from Egypt
> So that it became your distinguishing mark;
> Your awning was blue and purple from the coastlands of Elishah.
> 8The inhabitants of Sidon and Arvad were your rowers;
> Your wise men, O Tyre, were aboard; they were your pilots.
> 9The elders of Gebal and her wise men were with you repairing your seams;
> All the ships of the sea and their sailors were
> with you in order to deal in your merchandise."'"

Verse 4. Ezekiel began by describing a ship, representative of Tyre (v. 4).[3] This description is not to be applied to a particular person (such as a king); rather, it described Tyre as a whole. As a nation (illustrated as a great ocean vessel), Tyre was con-

---

[3]This metaphor is explained in Edwin M. Good, "Ezekiel's Ship: Some Extended Metaphors in the Old Testament," *Semitics* 1 (1970): 79–103.

structed by expert **builders** who were able to capture fully the **beauty** of the area. Indeed, the deep blue waters of the Mediterranean Sea made this area exceptionally beautiful.

Verses 5, 6. The expert builders used only the best materials to construct Tyre (v. 5). The **planks** of the ship were made from the **fir trees from Senir**. "Senir" is the Amorite name for Hermon (see Deut. 3:9). The **mast** was made from **a cedar from Lebanon**, a resource frequently discussed in the Scriptures (Ps. 72:16; Is. 14:8; Hos. 14:5, 6). The **oars** (v. 6) were made **of oaks**, and the **deck** was made **of boxwood** ("cyprus wood"; NIV) inlaid with **ivory**.

Verse 7. The ship's sail, a beautifully colored fabric made from Egyptian linen, was **embroidered**. Her **awning** was brightly colored with blue and purple fabric which came **from the coastlands of Elishah**. Elishah, a son of Javan, became the founder of a people (Gen. 10:4). Italy, Sicily, and Greece have been suggested as possible locations of their territory. There are other possibilities, including Carthage and, more generally, the North African coastland. Racial and commercial ties between Carthage and Tyre were close.[4]

Verse 8. The ship had a most skillful crew of **rowers—the inhabitants of Sidon and Arvad**. Most scholars believe that "Sidon" was at this time a vassal of Tyre. This coastal city north of Tyre is considered to have been one of the oldest Phoenician cities. Sidon was the firstborn son of Canaan (Gen. 10:15; see Josh. 19:28). Arvad was also a son of Canaan (see Gen. 10:18). This name was given to an island town one hundred miles north of Tyre (just north of Tripoli).

Tyre was famous for the ships she built. Her **pilots** were highly skilled men, experts in directing a vessel (meaning that the governors of the city were highly proficient in guiding its political affairs).

Verse 9. The elders of Gebal (modern-day Byblos) were also on board, having the skill and equipment for **repairing your seams**. This illustrates that Tyre was prepared for trouble; she had wise men skilled in dealing with disruptive influences in

---

[4]Fisch, 180.

her society—from within or from without. In addition, she had a full complement of skilled tradesmen to handle her **merchandise**, which was the lifeblood of the city.

THE DIRECTORY OF TYRE'S TRADE PARTNERS (27:10–25)

27:10, 11

¹⁰"'"Persia and Lud and Put were in your army, your men of war. They hung shield and helmet in you; they set forth your splendor. ¹¹The sons of Arvad and your army were on your walls, all around, and the Gammadim were in your towers. They hung their shields on your walls all around; they perfected your beauty."'"

Verses 10, 11. Next, Ezekiel listed Tyre's trade partners. **Persia and Lud and Put were in [the] army** of Tyre (v. 10). Tyre had such proficient merchants and traders that she was able to purchase her military protection. Mercenaries came from faraway places, three of which are named here: (1) "Persia"—This is the first reference to Persia in the Bible. The Persians (along with the Medes) are prominent in the prophecies of Daniel. (2) "Lud"—The people of Lud are sometimes identified with the Lydians of western Asia Minor, or perhaps the Lubdi tribe who lived in the Upper Tigris region. (3) "Put"—Most likely, these people were from North Africa on the western coast of the Red Sea. Other mercenaries came from **Arvad** and were joined by **the Gammadim**, a people who have not been positively identified (v. 11).

27:12–18

¹²"'"Tarshish was your customer because of the abundance of all kinds of wealth; with silver, iron, tin and lead they paid for your wares. ¹³Javan, Tubal and Meshech, they were your traders; with the lives of men and vessels of bronze they paid for your merchandise. ¹⁴Those from Beth-togarmah gave horses and war horses and mules for your wares. ¹⁵The sons of Dedan were your traders. Many coastlands were your market; ivory

tusks and ebony they brought as your payment. ¹⁶Aram was your customer because of the abundance of your goods; they paid for your wares with emeralds, purple, embroidered work, fine linen, coral and rubies. ¹⁷Judah and the land of Israel, they were your traders; with the wheat of Minnith, cakes, honey, oil and balm they paid for your merchandise. ¹⁸Damascus was your customer because of the abundance of your goods, . . . because of the wine of Helbon and white wool.""

Ezekiel listed in geographical order some cities that traded with Tyre. While the naming of these cities and countries may seem tedious and extraneous, they provide valuable information on the following: the geography of the ancient world, the extent of trade routes, the relations established as a result of trade, the type of goods each place was noted for producing, and the extent of Tyre's influence in the ancient world—which certainly is the main point being made here.

Verse 12. Beginning with **Tarshish** in the west, Ezekiel moved to the eastern Mediterranean, then traveled north toward "Damascus" (v. 18), ending with "Arabia" (v. 21) and Mesopotamia (vv. 22–24). Tarshish is generally thought to be Tartessus (in Spain, near the straits of Gibraltar), but it could refer to the Phoenician city Nora in Sardinia. (See the map of "Composite of Places in Ezekiel's Prophecies" in Appendix 2.) Ralph H. Alexander wrote,

> When these various places are located on a map of the ancient Near East, it can be seen that Tyre traded with almost every region: from Tarshish (Spain) to northeast Anatolia (Tubal, Beth Togarmah) on an east-west axis (through the Aegean), and from Arabia through Syria and Palestine on a north-south axis. Each area brought the products of its land to trade with Tyre. Certainly the commercial operations of Tyre were vast!⁵

---

⁵Ralph H. Alexander, "Ezekiel," in *The Expositor's Bible Commentary*, ed. Frank E. Gaebelein (Grand Rapids, Mich.: Zondervan Publishing House, 1986), 6:876.

Verse 13. Javan, Tubal, and **Meshech** are between the Black Sea and the Caspian. Fisch noted,

> Names of three sons of Japheth (Gen. x. 2). *Javan* is the Hebrew term for the Ionians, the Greeks of Asia Minor. *Tubal* and *Meshech* are usually identified with the Tibareni and Maschi who lived south-east and south respectively of the Black Sea. These peoples supplied Tyre with slaves and copper.[6]

This region had a long history of slave trade (**with the lives of men**). The merchandising of human beings is a sad story: Usually, these were not men who chose to be slaves, but who were made slaves by compulsion. "Tubal" and "Meshech" (see chs. 38; 39) are also known from cuneiform inscriptions and from the writings of the Greek historian Herodotus (c. 484–425 B.C.).

Verse 14. Those from Beth-togarmah gave horses and war horses and mules for your wares. "Togarmah" was the name of one of the sons of Gomer (Gen. 10:3). The Hebrew word for "beth," בַּיִת (*bayith*), means "house." Beth-togarmah was located in the extreme north (see 38:6) and probably corresponds to Armenia. Herodotus mentioned this city as being famous for its horses and mules.

Verse 15. In the RSV, **Dedan** is translated as "Rhodes" (following the LXX), which is probably correct since "Dedan" is repeated in verse 20. It is possible that this refers to the "Dedan" (from Cush) near the Persian Sea, which was an avenue to the commerce of India.

Verse 16. Aram (Syria) is mentioned, but this is probably better understood to be Edom. The area was known for its precious stones. **Emeralds** found there were among the most beautiful of all gem stones, having a natural bright green color.

Verse 17. We are given a glimpse of the goods Judah and Israel traded with other nations. **Wheat** came from **Minnith**. This city was in Ammon, a country famous for wheat (2 Chron. 27:5). Other references to Minnith are in Joshua 12:2 and

---

[6]Fisch, 182.

Judges 11:33. The wheat was carried through the land of Israel to Tyre. **Cakes** (פַּנַּג, *pannag*) is a word that occurs only here. Some understand the word to refer to sweets, while others think it is the name of a place (perhaps Pingi, on the road from Baalbec to Damascus).

Verse 18. Damascus, which already was rich in goods, also sought out Tyre for trade. **Helbon**, near Damascus, produced a wine that was a favorite with Persian kings. **White wool** was a product of flocks that grazed in the wastelands of Syria and Arabia.

27:19–25

¹⁹"'"Vedan and Javan paid for your wares from Uzal; wrought iron, cassia and sweet cane were among your merchandise. ²⁰Dedan traded with you in saddlecloths for riding. ²¹Arabia and all the princes of Kedar, they were your customers for lambs, rams and goats; for these they were your customers. ²²The traders of Sheba and Raamah, they traded with you; they paid for your wares with the best of all kinds of spices, and with all kinds of precious stones and gold. ²³Haran, Canneh, Eden, the traders of Sheba, Asshur and Chilmad traded with you. ²⁴They traded with you in choice garments, in clothes of blue and embroidered work, and in carpets of many colors and tightly wound cords, which were among your merchandise. ²⁵The ships of Tarshish were the carriers for your merchandise.

> And you were filled and were very glorious
> In the heart of the seas."'"

Verse 19. Uzal is thought to be modern Sana, the capital of Yemen. **Cassia** was a perfume made from the bark of trees. It was used with **sweet cane** (see Is. 43:24; Jer. 6:20) to make the oil with which the priests were anointed (Ex. 20:23, 24).

Verses 20, 21. Dedan (v. 20) was one of the descendants of Abraham by Keturah, who dwelt in Arabia (see Gen. 25:3). This Dedan was a place located in **Arabia** (v. 21), or the Arabian Desert east of the Dead Sea.

Verses 22–24. Sheba and **Raamah** (v. 22) were situated at the entrance to the Persian Gulf. Verse 23 adds to the list of trade partners: **Haran, Canneh, Eden, the traders of Sheba, Asshur and Chilmad.** "Haran" was an ancient and well-known city in Mesopotamia. Because of its geographical position, on the route from Babylon to Syria, it was an important commercial center. It was from Haran that Abraham migrated to Canaan (Gen. 12:4). "Canneh" is sometimes identified with "Calneh" (Gen. 10:10), otherwise called "Calno" (Is. 10:9), a city in Babylon. "Eden" (or "Beth-eden"; see 2 Kings 19:12; Is. 37:12; Amos 1:5) is situated on either side of the Euphrates, due south of Haran. On Assyrian inscriptions, this city is called Bit-Adini.

The peoples of Haran, Canneh, and Eden, who traded also with Sheba, brought their wares to Phoenicia. "Asshur" is a name normally used to refer to Assyria, but that is inappropriate in this connection since that people had long been on the decline. Some identify Asshur with Sura on the Euphrates, or with a town situated on the west side of the Tigris, now the ruined site of Halat Serkat.[7]

Verse 25. The people **were filled and were very glorious in the heart of the seas.** Tyre was completely filled with these wares from the nations. Ezekiel, in naming these countries, vividly illustrated the extent of Tyre's influence. Peoples from all over the ancient world knew of Tyre. Nearly everyone would have owned something that had gone through the harbors of this city!

THE SHIPWRECK OF TYRE (27:26–36)

²⁶""'Your rowers have brought you
Into great waters;
The east wind has broken you
In the heart of the seas.
²⁷Your wealth, your wares, your merchandise,
Your sailors and your pilots,
Your repairers of seams, your dealers in merchandise

---

[7]Ibid., 184–85.

And all your men of war who are in you,
With all your company that is in your midst,
Will fall into the heart of the seas
On the day of your overthrow.
²⁸At the sound of the cry of your pilots
The pasture lands will shake.
²⁹All who handle the oar,
The sailors and all the pilots of the sea
Will come down from their ships;
They will stand on the land,
³⁰And they will make their voice heard over you
And will cry bitterly.
They will cast dust on their heads,
They will wallow in ashes.
³¹Also they will make themselves bald for you
And gird themselves with sackcloth;
And they will weep for you in bitterness of soul
With bitter mourning.
³²Moreover, in their wailing they will take up a lamentation for you
And lament over you:
'Who is like Tyre,
Like her who is silent in the midst of the sea?
³³When your wares went out from the seas,
You satisfied many peoples;
With the abundance of your wealth and your merchandise
You enriched the kings of earth.
³⁴Now that you are broken by the seas
In the depths of the waters,
Your merchandise and all your company
Have fallen in the midst of you.
³⁵All the inhabitants of the coastlands
Are appalled at you,
And their kings are horribly afraid;
They are troubled in countenance.
³⁶The merchants among the peoples hiss at you;
You have become terrified
And you will cease to be forever.'"'"

Verse 26. The shipwreck of Tyre is described (vv. 26–36). Tyre's expert **rowers** had brought her to a place in which she reigned supreme—the **great waters**. She was most comfortable here. For centuries, she had been the biggest ship on the sea as far as merchant enterprises were concerned. The meaning of this lamentation, therefore, is that Tyre had it all. She was blessed beyond most of her contemporary cities, yet she failed to account for **the east wind** (see Ps. 48:7). God used the Babylonian army first, then the Greek army (under Alexander the Great), to sink this city—and it was never to be raised again!

Verse 27. Tyre had tried to account for just about everything; she thought that she had every concern covered. However, she forgot one very important truth: God will judge. No matter how great a company of professionals she assembled, these could not help when the time came for God to bring judgment upon her. God did judge, and Tyre was to go **into the heart of the seas**. (This is the third time such a phrase has been used; see vv. 25, 26.)

Verses 28–31. Upon hearing about the fall of Tyre, **sailors** from all over would gather on the seashore (v. 29) and **cry bitterly** (v. 30). For them, this would be a tragic event, resulting in grief expressed through various acts of mourning. They would **cast dust on their heads** and **wallow in ashes**. They would shave their heads (**make themselves bald**) and **gird themselves with sackcloth** to go along with their weeping (v. 31).

Verse 32. The Lord added, **"Moreover, in their wailing they will take up a lamentation for you."** The lament of the sailors is given here. They would ask, **"Who is like Tyre?"** Certainly, there was no comparable city in the ancient world. They would be saddened to think of this fine "vessel" lying on the bottom of the sea.

Verses 33–36. One reason Tyre was so popular was that she **satisfied many peoples** and **enriched the kings of earth** (v. 33). She traded with so many nations that they all benefited from her wares. Knowing the wrath of Nebuchadnezzar, they could not be seen lamenting her death for long—or else they would receive the same fate. Thus they turned on Tyre, disowning her, and they **hiss**[ed] (v. 36) at her (a derogatory act).

APPLICATION

The Price of Pride

Tyre was a city full of arrogance and pride. The Lord hates pride, even when it is found in a pagan people (Prov. 8:13). Pride goes before destruction (Prov. 16:18) and keeps one from seeking God (Ps. 10:4). Since this described the people of Tyre (Ezek. 27:3), God brought the city down.

"From everyone who has been given much, much will be required" (Lk. 12:48b). Tyre was blessed with tremendous goods and a beautiful location. She used these blessings for her selfish purposes and materialistic ways.

Because of Tyre's great influence with so many countries in the ancient world, she had a unique opportunity to be a positive force for good. Instead, she became the symbol of evil and corruption—and therefore worthy of a lengthy rebuke of three chapters in the Book of Ezekiel! We today must use what the Lord has given us for His kingdom. We will be held accountable for the use of our gifts (see Mt. 25:14–30).

God does not base the value of a person (or nation) on how others view him. While the ancient world adored Tyre, God was filled with wrath toward her and brought her down. On the Day of Judgment, we will stand or fall only in the eyes of God. He is the One we should please (see Jn. 12:48; 2 Cor. 5:10).

Wealth seems desirable and attractive, yet it is often the very thing that dooms men—in this life *and* in the life to come! (1 Tim. 6:6–10).

D.P.

Pride Expressed

Tyre is figuratively described in Ezekiel 27 as a merchant ship that sinks in a great storm. The description is actually a funeral service for this great city on the coast. The dirge for Tyre gives a vivid picture of the expressions of pride:

Living without God. Tyre did not worship Yahweh. The city had its own gods and saw no need to seek the true and living God. Do we see the need for God?

Directing one's own way. Tyre felt no need for guidance. They saw themselves as having the wisdom and understanding to deal with any situation. Have we humbled ourselves before God's Word? Do we see the need for it?

Believing in one's own strength. The people of Tyre believed that they could handle anything that came along. They had the finest soldiers and the best ships of that day. Humanism says, "We can deal with anything, great or small."

Thinking oneself invincible. Due to their situation on the coast, those in Tyre believed that their city could never be overcome by anyone, that no army was powerful enough to overtake them. Do we believe that we are impregnable? "Pride goes before destruction, and a haughty spirit before stumbling" (Prov. 16:18).

E.C.

Chapter 28
Judgment of Tyre's Leaders and Sidon

Chapter 28 concludes the three-chapter block dedicated to Tyre. Why did God judge this city so harshly? Ultimately, the blame belongs to the corrupt leadership of Tyre: her prince. Through his leadership, Tyre became totally focused on wealth—an obsession which defined who she was as a people and a city. S. Fisch said, "Spiritual values had no place in the minds of her population; self-glorification and self-sufficiency reigned supreme. Such arrogance and demoralization must lead to destruction."[1]

The arrogance of the prince is seen in his boastful claim to be God. Therefore the Lord dispatched Ezekiel to present a scathing rebuke in not-so-veiled references. However, the rebuke was not just for him. He represented the totality of the people of Tyre. The view these people had of themselves is rarely matched elsewhere in the Old Testament. They saw themselves as being so far superior to others that it was laughable even to compare them with anyone else. They were superior in all areas, from wealth to wisdom. Their island fortress was impenetrable. Into the midst of this arrogance came God's prophet, delivering bad news: Tyre would fall (along with her sister city Sidon), never to rise again. When that came about, Tyre and the world would recognize the true God: "Then they will know that I am the Lord when I execute judgments in her" (v. 22).

---

[1] S. Fisch, *Ezekiel: Hebrew Text and English Translation with an Introduction and Commentary,* Soncino Books of the Bible (London: Soncino Press, 1950), 188.

JUDGMENT AGAINST THE PRINCE OF TYRE (28:1–10)

28:1, 2
¹The word of the LORD came again to me, saying, ²"Son of man, say to the leader of Tyre, 'Thus says the Lord GOD,

"Because your heart is lifted up
And you have said, 'I am a god,
I sit in the seat of gods
In the heart of the seas';
Yet you are a man and not God,
Although you make your heart like the heart of God—"'"

Verses 1, 2. God sent Ezekiel with a message for **the leader of Tyre** (vv. 1, 2a). The word translated "leader" is נָגִיד (*nagid*). This is a different word than "king" (מֶלֶךְ, *melek*), found in verse 12. The leader (prince) of Tyre was probably Ethbaal II, who reigned from 574 B.C. to 564 B.C. (Others have been suggested, but he best fits the description and the chronology.)

The prince had said, **"I am a god"** (v. 2b). This claim, which is repeated in various ways throughout the chapter (see vv. 2c, 6, 9), was the basis of God's condemnation. The prince may have even thought of himself as El, the chief deity of the Canaanite pantheon. Ancient Near Eastern thought often viewed the king as the embodiment of the god(s).[2] Nothing in history verifies that the Phoenicians believed in man-gods. However, this belief was certainly found in other cultures and could easily have been among these people as well.

The arrogant boast of the prince probably stemmed from the belief (by him and the people) that Tyre was self-sufficient, absolute, and accountable to no one. The prince said, **"I sit in the seat of gods."** He regarded his beautiful island fortress as a divine dwelling. Since there was nothing else like it on the earth

---

[2]John Gray, "Canaanite Kingship in Theory and Practice," *Vetus Testamentum* 2 (July 1952): 193–200.

(in his opinion), it had to be the place where the gods lived. **"You make your heart like the heart of God,"** he was told, but God informed him clearly that he was **a man and not God**. The prince of Tyre considered his "heart" (intellect) to be the heart of God; he viewed himself as having supernatural knowledge—that is, omniscience. His great wisdom is verified in verses 4 and 5, yet to equate that with the wisdom of God was foolish arrogance.

28:3–5

> ³"'"Behold, you are wiser than Daniel;
> There is no secret that is a match for you.
> ⁴By your wisdom and understanding
> You have acquired riches for yourself
> And have acquired gold and silver for your treasuries.
> ⁵By your great wisdom, by your trade
> You have increased your riches
> And your heart is lifted up because of your riches—"'"

Verse 3. The sarcastic reference to being **wiser than Daniel** (v. 3) shows the foolishness of the prince of Tyre. Compared to the great "Daniel," the leader of Tyre was nothing. Daniel was mentioned earlier for his righteousness (14:14, 20). While some doubt that this can be talking about the Daniel of the Old Testament, there is no legitimate reason to believe that it could refer to any other man. Daniel was noted for his righteousness and his wisdom, and both of these qualities are stressed in Ezekiel (see Dan. 1:17–20; 2:47; 4:18).

The great prophets of God were known and recognized in their own time. Therefore, anything that Daniel wrote would have been immediately accepted by God's people. Modern critics suggest that the Bible books were made a part of the canon of Scripture centuries after the authors lived, and that these books were voted into the canon by later rabbis. There is no evidence to suggest this. Instead, the Bible indicates that when a recognized prophet of God wrote, his writings were instantly and immediately accepted as being from God (see Ex. 24:4–8).

Verses 4, 5. Tyre had regarded herself as superior to all nations. Her pride equaled that of Edom, who was condemned by the prophet Obadiah. Especially noted were the **wisdom** and **understanding** of the prince (and by extension, the people). The text does not dispute the existence of wisdom and understanding. Certainly, Ethbaal was wise; he built and maintained an incredible empire through his wisdom. However, that very wisdom inflated his pride to the point that he foolishly considered himself equal with God.

28:6–10

> ⁶"'"Therefore thus says the Lord G<small>OD</small>,
> 'Because you have made your heart
> Like the heart of God,
> ⁷Therefore, behold, I will bring strangers upon you,
> The most ruthless of the nations.
> And they will draw their swords
> Against the beauty of your wisdom
> And defile your splendor.
> ⁸They will bring you down to the pit,
> And you will die the death of those who are slain
> In the heart of the seas.
> ⁹Will you still say, "I am a god,"
> In the presence of your slayer,
> Though you are a man and not God,
> In the hands of those who wound you?
> ¹⁰You will die the death of the uncircumcised
> By the hand of strangers,
> For I have spoken!' declares the Lord G<small>OD</small>!"'"

Verse 6. The phrase **heart like the heart of God** in verse 2 is used again. Here, the point was "*you have made* **your** heart like the heart of God" (emphasis added), showing that this was something the prince of Tyre created within himself. He did not humble himself when others praised and glorified him. It is dangerous to allow the accolades of others to affect our pride and make us view ourselves as more important than we really are. Paul said, "I say to everyone among you not to think more highly of himself than he ought to think" (Rom. 12:3a; see v. 16).

Verses 7, 8. God would bring against Tyre **the most ruthless of the nations** (v. 7): the Babylonians (see 30:11; 31:12; 32:12). They would **draw their swords**. "Sword" is a key word in the Book of Ezekiel, usually referring to the military might of the Babylonians—but only as an instrument in the hand of God (see 21:3–5, 15, 19). These swords would be brought **against the beauty of your wisdom**. When God puts His sword in the hand of man, no human wisdom can defend against it. If the people of Tyre thought they had escaped God's fury when they left the mainland city (which Nebuchadnezzar destroyed in 587[6] B.C.), they were wrong. God's promise to **bring you down to the pit** (v. 8) was fulfilled—through Alexander the Great's army (c. 330 B.C.).

Verses 9, 10. Tyre had thought of herself as eternal and indestructible. How quickly and easily God was able to bring about her end! What would she say to the one who was about to slay her: **"I am a god"** (v. 9)? No. In that fatal instant, the prince of Tyre (and the people) would finally realize the truth of the statement **you are a man and not God**.

A FUNERAL SONG FOR THE KING OF TYRE (28:11–19)

What God Had Given to Tyre (28:11–15)

¹¹Again the word of the Lord came to me saying, ¹²"Son of man, take up a lamentation over the king of Tyre and say to him, 'Thus says the Lord God,

"You had the seal of perfection,
Full of wisdom and perfect in beauty.
¹³You were in Eden, the garden of God;
Every precious stone was your covering:
The ruby, the topaz and the diamond;
The beryl, the onyx and the jasper;
The lapis lazuli, the turquoise and the emerald;

> And the gold, the workmanship of your settings and sockets,
> Was in you.
> On the day that you were created
> They were prepared.
> ¹⁴You were the anointed cherub who covers,
> And I placed you there.
> You were on the holy mountain of God;
> You walked in the midst of the stones of fire.
> ¹⁵You were blameless in your ways
> From the day you were created
> Until unrighteousness was found in you."'"

Verses 11–15. God next commissioned Ezekiel to sing a specific **lamentation** against the **king of Tyre** (v. 12). Verses 12 through 19 have been the subject of much discussion. Some people claim that the passage alludes to Satan.[3] It is clear, however, that the main subject of the discussion is as stated: the king of Tyre. Tyre had become the standard for business success, and her ability to rise above other cities in profitable trade enterprises filled her with pride. She considered herself "wiser than Daniel" and without rival on earth (v. 3). She had developed the most materialistic, pleasure-driven society in the ancient world. The amount of wealth that poured into the coffers of Tyre was unequaled. That wealth enabled her to purchase anything she wanted, including military protection. Meanwhile, the king of Tyre had promoted himself to "god" status. This foolish self-deification led the Lord to declare the end of Tyre. The king was addressed specifically in this lamentation. The section falls into two parts: (1) what God had given to Tyre (vv. 12–15) and (2) the judgment of God that would fall upon Tyre (vv. 16–19).

That which is said contains much exaggeration and irony. To take these images literally is to miss the function of the dirge. First, note what God said regarding Tyre and her king:

"You had the seal of perfection" (v. 12). She was the "per-

---

[3]See "Was 'the King of Tyre' an Allusion to Satan?" in "For Further Study" at the end of this chapter.

fect" city, having an ideal location, beautiful surroundings, and unimaginable wealth. What more could people want?[4]

"[You were] **full of wisdom**" (v. 12). She considered herself unrivaled, "wiser than Daniel." She succeeded in acquiring great wealth by her "great wisdom" (vv. 3–5). The text does not challenge the presence of wisdom in the king of Tyre or the people, but considering that wisdom equal to God's would bring about her downfall.

"[You were] **perfect in beauty**" (v. 12). The location of this island paradise, situated in the beautiful waters of the Mediterranean, made the people view their city as heavenly. No other place could match her beauty. As wealth poured into the city, she purchased the best of everything. No doubt, the city was magnificent.

"You were in Eden, the garden of God" (v. 13). An unquestioned allusion is made here to the paradise that Adam and Eve enjoyed (Gen. 2; 3). When God designed a location for the first man and woman, it was certainly beautiful beyond description. The phrase "the garden of God" lends itself to images of untold beauty. The idea is that Tyre had everything that Adam had been given when God placed him in Eden. If Adam was the epitome of the perfect primeval man, then so was the king of Tyre.

"Every precious stone was your covering" (v. 13). Moving to another Old Testament allusion, God said that the king was decorated with the same precious stones that adorned the breastplate of the high priest (Ex. 28:17–20). Every stone that was considered valuable was to be found in Tyre. The king had all of this on the day he was **created**—a term that applies to the day

---

[4]The "seal of perfection," according to Fisch, is "a phrase of doubtful meaning. The noun *tochnith* (*most accurate*) appears to be akin to *tochen* and *mathkoneth*, 'measurement.' If translated, 'thou wert one who sealeth measurement,' the sense is: he was perfect in physical form" (Fisch, 191). "The word 'perfect' does not imply 'sinless perfection.' It was used to show that one was blameless or unobjectionable in a given area. This would then mean that the king of Tyre was a good king against whom objections were not raised from the moment of his coronation till pride possessed him and he sinned" (Ralph H. Alexander, "Ezekiel," in *The Expositor's Bible Commentary*, ed. Frank E. Gaebelein [Grand Rapids, Mich.: Zondervan Publishing House, 1986], 6:884).

the king assumed the throne of Tyre. Since God created everything, the king of Tyre was able to be king only because God placed him in this position (see Dan. 2:20–23; 4:17, 25).

"You were the anointed cherub who covers" (v. 14). The king is compared to the cherubim whose wings extended out, covering the ark of the covenant in the Most Holy Place. These extended wings "cover[ed]," or protected, the ark. The king was the protector of several smaller states around his empire.

"You were on the holy mountain of God" (v. 14). What is meant by "the holy mountain of God" is uncertain. It may refer to Jerusalem. This is the most common meaning of such phrases in the Old Testament (see Ps. 99:9; Is. 56:7). If this is the meaning, then the phrase could be referring to the king of Tyre as he walked through the ruins of the city after the Babylonian devastation in 587(6) B.C. and gloated over her destruction (see 26:2). This would make **the stones of fire** refer to the smoldering rubble of the burned city.

Another possibility is that "the holy mountain of God [אֱלֹהִים, *ᵉlohim*, meaning "God" or "gods"]" is a reference to the home of the gods. Canaanite mythology often used the phrase "the mountain of god" to refer to the supposed dwelling place of a pagan god. This would make the king of Tyre a guardian cherub (perhaps of the god Melkart). Alexander said,

> Perhaps this phrase then implied that Tyre's king was in the domain of the pagan deities since he himself claimed to be a god and was perhaps a guardian cherub of the god Melkart.
>
> If the latter position concerning the meaning of the phrase "the holy mount of god" is taken, then one must explain the meaning of walking "among the fiery stones." The ritual of burning a god has been discovered on a bowl from Sidon and is recorded in the cult of Melkart at Tyre. . . . Melkart's resurrection was celebrated by a "burning in effigy," from which he would then be revitalized through the fire and the smelling of the burnt offering. Again, in keeping with the Phoenician religious-cultural background with which the passage is so closely

tied by the king's claim of deity, perhaps the explanation of walking among the fiery stones is a reference to the king's self-exaltation of himself even as the god Melkart—even to the extent of his claiming resurrection after burning by fire.[5]

"The stones of fire" could refer to the precious stones of verse 13, so brilliant that they appeared to be on fire.

"You were blameless in your ways" (v. 15). Every business action by the king and his people seemed to be the right decision. Such ability in trade was the reason for Tyre's untold wealth.

At the end of verse 15, the story changes: **until unrighteousness was found in you.** The king of Tyre was filled with pride for his accomplishments, and his people were living in haughtiness and conceit—definite attributes of "unrighteousness." The fact that this quality was found "in you" illustrates two truths. First, like a judge looking at discovered evidence, the Lord gave a thorough examination. Second, the unrighteousness was deeply imbedded within the king and his people.

God's Judgment That Would Fall upon Tyre (28:16–19)

> [16]"'**By the abundance of your trade**
> **You were internally filled with violence,**
> **And you sinned;**
> **Therefore I have cast you as profane**
> **From the mountain of God.**
> **And I have destroyed you, O covering cherub,**
> **From the midst of the stones of fire.**
> [17]**Your heart was lifted up because of your beauty;**
> **You corrupted your wisdom by reason of your splendor.**
> **I cast you to the ground;**
> **I put you before kings,**
> **That they may see you.**

---

[5]Ibid., 884.

> ¹⁸By the multitude of your iniquities,
> In the unrighteousness of your trade
> You profaned your sanctuaries.
> Therefore I have brought fire from the midst of you;
> It has consumed you,
> And I have turned you to ashes on the earth
> In the eyes of all who see you.
> ¹⁹All who know you among the peoples
> Are appalled at you;
> You have become terrified
> And you will cease to be forever."'"

Verses 16–18. With all of the described blessings afforded to the king of Tyre (and his people), he did not maintain a humble attitude. Instead, he became unrighteous. As a result, God declared seven judgments against him:

1. **"You sinned"** (v. 16). The sins of Tyre are specifically identified as being **filled with violence** as a result of **the abundance of your trade**. Their successful trade practices made them violent—however, the violence came not from without, but from within (**internally**).
2. **"[You were] profane"** (v. 16). The swaggering and bragging of Tyre were exposed by the Lord. This king had desecrated the holy things of God.
3. **"Your heart was lifted up because of your beauty"** (v. 17). Admiring his own beauty, the king (along with Tyre) was filled with smugness and self-importance.
4. **"You corrupted your wisdom"** (v. 17). Their God-endowed wisdom was not used properly, but rather was used to magnify Tyre's own **splendor.**
5. **"[You committed a] multitude of ... iniquities"** (v. 18). Untold wealth and unbridled power led Tyre to add sin upon sin. She committed a long list of sins, from abuse of power to arrogant pride.
6. **"[You were guilty] in the unrighteousness of your trade"** (v. 18). Tyre took advantage of others in her business practices, manipulating and abusing them.

EZEKIEL 28

7. **"You profaned your sanctuaries"** (v. 18). The terminology here is confusing. However, since the text says "your" sanctuaries, it would logically refer to the holy places found in the city of Tyre. The king, believing himself to be a god, demonstrated no respect for anyone or anything. He even scorned his own gods. While the God of all the earth would take no thought of one profaning the sanctuaries of idolatrous temples, this statement does demonstrate a sinful attitude for which God will hold man accountable—pride.[6]

In light of these seven charges, the penalty was given. God declared,

"I have cast you . . . from the mountain of God" (v. 16). In his own mind, the king had made himself God; now the Lord would remove him from this position of self-deification.

"I have destroyed you" (v. 16). The king, seeing himself as God, viewed himself as immortal and indestructible. Nevertheless, God would bring about his destruction. The **covering cherub** would no longer be able to protect himself or anyone else.

"I cast you to the ground" (v. 17). The king was exalted because of his "beauty," "wisdom," and "splendor." These three "corrupted" him. Therefore, God would humiliate him by bringing him down and having him lie in the dirt **before kings**. Other powerful monarchs were to witness the humiliation of the king of Tyre.

"I have brought fire from the midst of you; it has consumed you" (v. 18). The fire of God was to come "from the midst of you," indicating that there would be tremendous internal strife

---

[6]"The allusion is obscure. Rashi explains the Hebrew *mikdashĕcha* (*thy sanctuaries*) as 'thy holiness'; while Kimchi, quoting Amos vii. 13, *the king's sanctuary*, gives it in both passages the meaning of 'palaces.' This, however, is doubtful. The term [may] . . . be connected with *the garden of God* and *the holy mountain of God* which had been used in the description of Tyre. She once deserved to be called 'thy holy places' over which the prince bore sway; but through moral debasement that title can no longer be applied and the city will be destroyed" (Fisch, 193).

in the latter days of this king's reign. While some have suspected that this means traitors enabled Nebuchadnezzar (and later Alexander the Great) to conquer the city, such events have not been confirmed by any historical documents. It is also possible to see this as a reference to verse 14, where the king "walked in the midst of the stones of fire." The king, through his trade enterprises, brought great wealth into the city. This wealth—these stones of fire—caused corruption from within and eventually led to the city's destruction. Restated, then, their thirst for wealth eventually led to their downfall. "The seeds of a nation's destruction are usually to be found within herself."[7]

"I have turned you to ashes" (v. 18). The glorious kingdom is now reduced to nothing. All that remained of the beauty and splendor of the city would be found in the piles of "ashes." Nebuchadnezzar burned the mainland city to the ground, and Alexander the Great burned the island fortress to the ground.

Verse 19. The fall of Tyre sent a ripple of fear throughout the ancient world. Others were **appalled** at what happened to her. It was a shocking and unpredictable event. Instead of being a city envied and adored, Tyre would be a **terrified** city—meaning that this seemingly impenetrable city would be cowering in fear as they saw her certain doom. It is also possible to translate this "you have become a city of terrors" (see 26:18). God declared, **"You will cease to be forever."** While there is a modern city of Tyre, it is not located on the ancient site, nor has the island fortress ever been rebuilt (see the discussions on 26:14–21 and 27:36).

GOD'S JUDGMENT AGAINST SIDON (28:20–24)

²⁰And the word of the Lord came to me saying, ²¹"Son of man, set your face toward Sidon, prophesy against her ²²and say, 'Thus says the Lord God,

---

[7]John B. Taylor, *Ezekiel: An Introduction and Commentary,* Tyndale Old Testament Commentaries (Downers Grove, Ill.: Inter-Varsity Press, 1969), 197.

"Behold, I am against you, O Sidon,
And I will be glorified in your midst.
Then they will know that I am the LORD when I execute judgments in her,
And I will manifest My holiness in her.
²³For I will send pestilence to her
And blood to her streets,
And the wounded will fall in her midst
By the sword upon her on every side;
Then they will know that I am the LORD.

²⁴And there will be no more for the house of Israel a prickling brier or a painful thorn from any round about them who scorned them; then they will know that I am the Lord GOD."'"

Verses 20, 21. Sidon was also a city situated on the Mediterranean coast, about twenty-five miles north of Tyre. It had once been more prominent than the city of Tyre; and after Tyre's defeat, it rose to prominence again.

Verse 22. Following the same basic format as the condemnation of the Ammonites (25:1, 2), God declared, **"Behold, I am against you."** Interestingly, God did not here reveal His charges against this Phoenician city. However, He did state three purposes of His judgment, reminiscent of His purposes for the ten plagues brought upon Egypt:

1. **"I will be glorified in your midst."** The people of Sidon did not appreciate the Lord or His greatness. They offered no praise to Him. However, once His judgments were enacted, He would be "glorified" throughout the city ("in your midst").
2. **"I [will] execute judgments in her."** God found sin in the camp of the Sidonians. His judgments were based upon evidence.
3. **"I will manifest My holiness in her."** This phraseology normally refers to the uniqueness of the Lord as compared to other gods. Certainly, pagan nations saw the God of Israel as being no different from any

other god, or perhaps weaker than certain other gods. The true God of heaven and earth was about to "manifest" (publicly display) His "holiness"—and this was to be done "in her."

Verse 23. How would God accomplish His judgment and display His holiness? God said, **"I will send pestilence to her."** A virus, plague, or epidemic would devastate the city. Then He said, "I will send . . . **blood to her streets."** This would be done **by the sword.** (Again, history records that the Babylonians took Sidon; see Is. 23:1–4.) Her soldiers would die on home soil (**in her midst**). This was the very place that God said He would be glorified.

Verse 24. The fall of Sidon would end the oppression of Israel by her neighboring countries. They had been, for centuries **a prickling brier** and **a painful thorn**—not something powerful enough to destroy Israel single-handedly, but a constant irritation. As each prophecy of doom was fulfilled, it would confirm the fundamental truth taught in the Book of Ezekiel: **Then they will know that I am the Lord God.**

THE RESTORATION OF ISRAEL (28:25, 26)

²⁵"'Thus says the Lord God, "When I gather the house of Israel from the peoples among whom they are scattered, and will manifest My holiness in them in the sight of the nations, then they will live in their land which I gave to My servant Jacob. ²⁶They will live in it securely; and they will build houses, plant vineyards and live securely when I execute judgments upon all who scorn them round about them. Then they will know that I am the Lord their God."'"

Verse 25. All of the nations around Israel perished by the hand of the Lord, yet Israel survived. Upon returning to **their land**, God's people would realize how amazing it was that they still existed, and they would recognize the work of God in these marvelous events. Note that God planned to **manifest** [His] **holiness.** Unfortunately, the holiness of Israel could not be dis-

played to the other nations. Still, God's name was vindicated in what He did, and His love for His people was demonstrated.

Verse 26. The neighboring nations had been destroyed; God had fulfilled His plan to **execute judgments** upon them. With this completed, the returning exiles would be able to live **securely** in the land—allowing them to **build** and **plant**. These activities are representative of a nation at peace. John B. Taylor wrote,

> Finally, in a forward look beyond the exile to the days of the return, Ezekiel foretells the gathering together of the dispersed exiles and their dwelling in safety in their own land once again. This act of God will be His way of manifesting His holiness in and through His people before the nations of the world. The holy people are the channel through whom the Holy God reveals Himself. There is no mention of judgments upon Israel: that is presumably thought of as a thing of the past. The nations against whom these oracles have been uttered will be judged, and Israel will dwell securely in simple, agricultural prosperity.[8]

FOR FURTHER STUDY: WAS "THE KING OF TYRE" AN ALLUSION TO SATAN? (28:11–19)

Undeniably, Ezekiel 28:11–19 is filled with unique language. Some say that it is a reference to Satan. They offer the following similarities between the phrasing in this section and what happened to Satan:

- He was made "perfect" as one of the created angelic forces (v. 12).
- Being witness to God's creative genius, he was full of wisdom (v. 12).
- He was, along with the rest of the angelic host, present in Eden (v. 13).

---

[8]Ibid., 197–98.

- He was a "cherub" (v. 14).
- As with the other host of heaven, he dwelt in the "mountain of God" (v. 14).
- He fell because of pride—believing that he was equal with God in both wisdom and power (v. 17).
- He will face his doom with the fire of judgment (v. 18; see Rev. 19:20).

There are problems in attaching some of these descriptions to any man. Further, no known king of Tyre (not even Ethbaal II) fits this description.

Consider this argument for saying it is an allusion to Satan:

The historic fall of Satan, otherwise not directly described in the Bible but alluded to in a number of passages, supplied the background terminology and metaphor for this text, just as it did for Isaiah 14. His fall from heaven back, apparently, before time began will supply the model for the fall of the king of Tyre, as it had for the king of Babylon.

But in keeping with the concept of inaugurated eschatology, in which both the near and the distant future are brought together in one horizon, the fall of the king of Tyre will be but a small indication of what the fall of Satan will be like in the final day.

The king of Tyre was compared to the Evil One himself, who was in the Garden of Eden, the Garden of God. But this exalted one became corrupt and lost his position in heaven. Similarly, the king of Tyre is about to lose his position for the same reasons: he exalted himself above God. Thus the description seems to shift back and forth from the king of Tyre to Satan himself, but that fluidity of language can be seen elsewhere as the near fulfillments of many prophecies do not embrace the totality of the language as the final fulfillment does.

Thus, the mastermind behind God's enemies is not always recognized, but here is clearly the devil himself. He is the one that finally must suffer a fiery judgment, thereby appalling the nations who knew him, just as the nation of Tyre will suffer a fiery judgment from God prior to God's dealing with their sponsor.[9]

As compelling as these points might be, the claim that this is a reference to Satan may be rejected based upon the following reasoning:

(1) Nothing in the text gives any indication that an allusion is being made to Satan.

(2) The text states whom the figure represents: the king of Tyre. To suggest anything beyond this is to wander beyond textual support.

(3) Other passages that clearly refer to Satan do not support the ideas being presented here.

(4) Each description given here can be applied to the illusionary visions of grandeur and self-worth of the king of Tyre.

(5) Too many points made within this text cannot be applied to Satan: (a) The "mountain of God" is nowhere used to refer to heaven in the Scriptures. (b) No biblical passage describes Satan or any angel as one of the cherubim. Alexander said,

> To assume that the stones were the garment of Satan in the Garden of Eden and that Satan was a guardian cherub of Eden would be purely hypotheses without any exegetical basis elsewhere in Scripture. In fact, neither Michael nor Gabriel are described as cherubim, and one might expect that Satan was on the same level as these before his fall.[10]

(c) The judgment described in verses 16b through 19 does not fit the judgment to be given to Satan. Gleason L. Archer, Jr., said,

> As for a relationship with Satan, there does not seem to be any decisive evidence in the text that the Prince of Hell is being indirectly addressed through the prince of

---

[9]Walter C. Kaiser, Jr., Peter H. Davids, F. F. Bruce, and Manfred T. Brauch, *Hard Sayings of the Bible* (Downers Grove, Ill.: InterVarsity Press, 1996), 316.
[10]Alexander, 883.

Tyre. There is hardly a verse to be found that could be applied to the Devil alone rather than to the human rulers of the city itself. Certainly the theory advanced by some writers that this chapter contains a flashback to Satan's personal career prior to his rebellion and expulsion from heaven is at best an unsupported conjecture. All the hyperbolic language employed in the verses discussed above can best be understood as the flattering self-delusion of the Tyrian millionaires and their money-loving leaders, whose concept of heaven rose no higher than their treasures of rubies and gold, and whose yardstick for virtue consisted of material wealth.[11]

The view that this passage teaches us more about the heart of Satan and the reasons for his fall should be rejected. It does establish one fundamental point: All sin ultimately traces its roots back to Satan. The king of Tyre and his people were dominated by the temptations of Satan and will unquestionably share in the judgment that he will receive. Alexander wrote,

> Therefore, it is concluded that Tyre's king is best understood as the literal human contemporary king of that city in Ezekiel's day. Each characteristic given about him in these verses can be explained in light of the cultural and religious context of that day. Contrarily, the identification of the king as Satan must be done to a large extent on a presupposition that the descriptions here refer to Satan. Most of these descriptions—if they do in fact relate to Satan—are revealed nowhere else in Scripture. In light of the logical flow of the context and the explanations of the king's character given above, it is concluded that a human king is described herein.[12]

---

[11]Gleason L. Archer, Jr., *Encyclopedia of Bible Difficulties* (Grand Rapids, Mich.: Zondervan Publishing House, 1982), 279–80.
[12]Alexander, 885.

APPLICATION

Pride and Destruction

Pride goes before a fall. The leader of Tyre had an inflated view of himself, so God had to bring him down. We, too, face the danger of being puffed up because of pride. We need to learn humility (1 Pet. 5:6).

Those who participate in materialism are engulfed by pride. Ultimately, both materialism and pride are attributed to Satan.

The king of Tyre and his people were given an abundance of blessings—wealth untold, prosperity unrivaled. However, they used those gifts for their own hedonistic pleasures rather than for the glory of God. God has enriched us today. We will be held accountable for what we have done with His gifts. "Is it time for you yourselves to dwell in your paneled houses while this house lies desolate?" (see Hag. 1:4).

D.P.

What Saves?

The leaders of the great city of Tyre came under the judgment of God. We can learn from their judgment sentences.

We see that beauty does not save. Tyre's unusual beauty and splendor made the city "perfect," like the Garden of Eden (v. 12). The people gloried in that beauty; however, it did not prevent their destruction. They would be brought down to the pit (v. 8).

We see that wisdom does not save. They thought they were wiser than Daniel. God made them what they were, but they did not recognize it (v. 14). Their wisdom did not deliver them.

We see that wealth does not save. They had acquired great riches, silver, and gold (vv. 11, 12). Their treasures made their hearts proud and confident, but their money could not save them.

We see that reputation does not save. They were known in the ancient world as one of the greatest of cities, but that greatness was to no avail.

Only submission to God's Word can save. Obedience brings us to God, and God saves us. The people of Tyre gave themselves to pride, violence, and sin. God eventually judged them.

E.C.

CHAPTER 29

THE PROPHECY AGAINST EGYPT

One of Israel's perpetual tormentors was Egypt. Therefore, it seems fitting for such a large section of Scripture (chs. 29—32) to be devoted to this world power.

Six dated prophecies are given against Egypt, plus one undated, making a total of seven (a full, complete prophecy of destruction) against her.

(1) The first prophecy given is dated "the tenth year, in the tenth month" (v. 1)—January 587 B.C., almost exactly one year after Jerusalem was attacked (24:1), seven months before Jerusalem fell, and thirteen months earlier than the dated oracle against Tyre. It comes *after* the oracle against Tyre in the Book of Ezekiel because the defeat of Tyre took place chronologically before Egypt was defeated by Nebuchadnezzar.

(2) The second prophecy (29:17) is dated as the twenty-seventh year, the first month, the first day. This refers to a time twenty-seven years after the exile of Jehoiachin in 598 B.C. (April 571 B.C., the latest date for an oracle in the Book of Ezekiel).

(3) An undated oracle is given in 30:1–19.

(4) The third dated prophecy (30:20) is on the seventh day of the first month in the eleventh year (April 587 B.C.)—the time when Jerusalem was destroyed.

(5) The fourth dated prophecy (31:1) is on the first day of the third month in the eleventh year (June 587 B.C.).

(6) The fifth dated prophecy (32:1) is the first day of the twelfth month in the twelfth year (March 585 B.C.).

(7) The sixth dated prophecy (32:17) is the fifteenth day of the twelfth year (March 585 B.C.). See the following chart:

> **SEVEN DATES GIVEN DURING ORACLES AGAINST THE NATIONS (25—32)**[1]
>
> | Judgment on: | Scripture Reference: | Date Given: |
> |---|---|---|
> | Tyre | 26:1 | February 12, 586 B.C. |
> | Egypt | 29:1 | January 7, 587 B.C. |
> | Egypt | 29:17 | April 26, 571 B.C.* |
> | Egypt | 30:20 | April 29, 587 B.C. |
> | Egypt | 31:1 | June 21, 587 B.C. |
> | Egypt | 32:1 | March 3, 585 B.C. |
> | Egypt | 32:17 | March 17, 585 B.C. |
>
> *The oracle of 29:1, the latest dated prophecy in the Book of Ezekiel, fits here because it links the destruction of Egypt, which had just been prophesied, with the work of Nebuchadnezzar. When the long siege of Tyre ended in 574(3) B.C., the Babylonians were left without compensation for their labor for God. Therefore, in 571 B.C., God promised Egypt to Nebuchadnezzar.

The oracles against Egypt are powerful and blunt. As a world power, she exercised dominion over Israel in abusive and evil ways. She took advantage of this tiny Hebrew nation in every way possible. When Israel had secured an alliance with Egypt, she failed to respond when called upon to help fight against Babylon. She, like Tyre, was prideful. In addition, she was devoid of conscience, frequently making promises she had no intention of keeping. Israel was just a pawn in her hand—a bar-

---

[1] John B. Taylor, *Ezekiel: An Introduction and Commentary*, Tyndale Old Testament Commentaries (Downers Grove, Ill.: Inter-Varsity Press, 1969), 36.

gaining chip at times—but never a true friend. The prophets of God continually warned Israel of the futility of seeking alliances with Egypt. She was not, and would not be, dependable. Only God was a constant help in time of trouble, yet the people failed to see His strength. Like the adulterous wife (see 16:26), Israel sought a relationship with Egypt. This proved to be disastrous for her, both religiously and politically. The anger of the Lord came against Egypt because of her failure to meet her obligations. Therefore, as pronounced in these vivid chapters, Egypt must be punished. Ironically, she would be punished by the "little god" of the little, insignificant nation of Israel! John B. Taylor wrote,

> What Ezekiel was at pains to point out, however, was that the final say in Israel's destiny was not theirs but God's—and God was Israel's God! More than that, he said that even the destiny of the great powers, such as Egypt, was in the hands of Israel's God. Yahweh controlled everything. The situation was in fact the very reverse of what appeared to be the case. The secular historian saw Israel dwarfed into insignificance by mighty neighbours; the religious commentator, the prophet, saw the great powers held firmly in the hand of little Israel's mighty God. The lesson for the Christian minority is not difficult to draw.[2]

THE SINS OF EGYPT (29:1–16)

29:1, 2
¹In the tenth year, in the tenth month, on the twelfth of the month, the word of the LORD came to me saying, ²"Son of man, set your face against Pharaoh king of Egypt and prophesy against him and against all Egypt."

Verse 1. This prophecy came to Ezekiel **in the tenth year** of the reign of Zedekiah (in January 587 B.C.), about seven months

---

[2]Ibid., 198–99.

before the fall of Jerusalem (one year after the siege of Jerusalem began). The prophet delivered several prophecies against Egypt at various times later than the tenth year of the reign of Zedekiah. These are grouped together in one series, even though the first is dated before the oracle against Tyre in 26:1.

Verse 2. God's message was **Set your face against Pharaoh king of Egypt.** This pharaoh was Hophra (see Jer. 37:7; 44:30), the fourth king of the Twenty-sixth Dynasty. He reigned from 589(8) to 570(69) B.C. Zedekiah had appealed to him for help, but Egypt had failed to respond with much assistance (see vv. 6, 7). This one act, however, hardly seems to justify the extended rebuke and condemnation of Egypt. More likely, this judgment was the culmination of years of Egyptian hostility against Israel.

29:3–5

³"Speak and say, 'Thus says the Lord G<small>OD</small>,

"Behold, I am against you, Pharaoh king of Egypt,
The great monster that lies in the midst of his rivers,
That has said, 'My Nile is mine, and I myself have made it.'
⁴I will put hooks in your jaws
And make the fish of your rivers cling to your scales.
And I will bring you up out of the midst of your rivers,
And all the fish of your rivers will cling to your scales.
⁵I will abandon you to the wilderness, you and all the fish of your rivers;
You will fall on the open field; you will not be brought together or gathered.
I have given you for food to the beasts of the earth and to the birds of the sky.""'"

Verse 3. The great monster that lies in the midst of his rivers is a reference to Pharaoh. He was being likened to a "great monster" lurking in the "rivers." The Nile was the great river of Egypt. The word translated "monster" is תַּנִּין (*thannin*). This word occurs frequently in the Old Testament and can also be rendered "serpent" or "dragon." By analogy, *thannin* may refer to "Leviathan" or "Rahab" (see Is. 27:1; 51:9). It is presented as a feared creature (frequently thought to be the crocodile), but its power was no match for the Lord's. Ronald L. Giese, Jr., said,

> The [verb] in Ezek 32:2 is in the third of a four-line glorification of Pharaoh as [תַּנִּין] monster. . . . In this passage as well as 29:3, where Pharaoh is also called [תַּנִּין], the taunt consists of the removal of [תַּנִּין] from the source of his power, the water. Inside the world of water he is powerful: he flaunts his control by stirring the waters and mocks Yahweh by creating chaos (in large part the lack of a firm boundary to land). Outside the world of water he is powerless and does not affect his environment, but rather is affected by it (he is dried by the sun and eaten by animals).[3]

In his arrogance, Pharaoh considered himself the creator of the Nile and then made the Nile his home. **"I myself have made it,"** he declared. Like the prince of Tyre, Pharaoh thought of himself as more than human, the creator of the strength and productivity of Egypt. The exalted position which his country occupied in the world at that time was due—in his own estimation—to his exceptional powers.

Verse 4. While Pharaoh considered himself the indestructible king of the rivers, God intended to prove Himself more powerful, drawing him out with **hooks**. The concept of **fish** [that] **cling to your scales** represents the tiny nations or mercenaries that depended upon Egypt for protection and support. These would likewise suffer God's judgment.

Verse 5. Like a fish out of water, Pharaoh would be removed from the comforts of the Nile and could not survive. God would give this powerful ruler to be **food** for **the beasts** and **the birds**. The crocodile was typically caught with hooks and pulled to

---

[3]Ronald L. Giese, Jr., "דָּלַח" in *New International Dictionary of Old Testament Theology & Exegesis*, ed. Willem A. VanGemeren (Grand Rapids, Mich.: Zondervan Publishing House, 1997), 1:950.

dry land, where it could be killed.[4] The Egyptians had a crocodile god, Sebek, that was considered the protector of Egypt's river system. This god was sometimes linked with the sun god Ra (apparently referred to as "Rahab" in the Scriptures; the same word, *thannin*, is used in Ps. 74:13 and Is. 51:9).

29:6–9

> ⁶"'"Then all the inhabitants of Egypt will know that I am the LORD,
> Because they have been only a staff made of reed to the house of Israel.
> ⁷When they took hold of you with the hand,
> You broke and tore all their hands;
> And when they leaned on you,
> You broke and made all their loins quake."
>
> ⁸"'Therefore thus says the Lord GOD, "Behold, I will bring upon you a sword and I will cut off from you man and beast. ⁹The land of Egypt will become a desolation and waste. Then they will know that I am the LORD.
> Because you said, 'The Nile is mine, and I have made it.'"'"

Verse 6. "They have been only a staff made of reed to the house of Israel," God said. A second appropriate metaphor for Egypt, "the land of reeds," is now used. Egypt was a broken "reed," failing all who trusted in her. Rabshakeh's words to Hezekiah (Is. 36:6; 2 Kings 18:21) suggest that the description was almost proverbial. A few incidents can establish a reputation for unreliability, and Egypt well deserved such a reputation.

Verse 7. When they leaned on you, you broke. Zedekiah had appealed to Pharaoh Hophra for help when the Babylonians attacked. While little is known about the events that transpired, Hophra obviously did not offer much support—only enough to create a temporary lifting of the siege of Jerusalem (see Jer. 37:7). As already discussed, Nebuchadnezzar returned to finish the destruction of Jerusalem, and Egypt was nowhere to be found.

---

[4]Herodotus *History* 2.70; Diodorus *Diodorus of Sicily* 1.35.

She offered no assistance; she "broke" when God's people leaned on her. Of course, Israel should not have been leaning on Egypt in the first place!

Verses 8, 9. Great significance is found in the phrase **Therefore thus says the Lord God** (v. 8). Egypt did not feel the need to bother herself with a puny nation like Israel. Why jeopardize her own national security for such a nation? However, the all-powerful God of that nation now clearly pronounced judgment against her: **"I will cut off from you man and beast. The land of Egypt will become a desolation and waste."** The point of these prophecies would be difficult to overlook.

29:10–12

¹⁰"'"Therefore, behold, I am against you and against your rivers, and I will make the land of Egypt an utter waste and desolation, from Migdol to Syene and even to the border of Ethiopia. ¹¹A man's foot will not pass through it, and the foot of a beast will not pass through it, and it will not be inhabited for forty years. ¹²So I will make the land of Egypt a desolation in the midst of desolated lands. And her cities, in the midst of cities that are laid waste, will be desolate forty years; and I will scatter the Egyptians among the nations and disperse them among the lands."'"

Verse 10. Pharaoh had said, "The Nile is mine, and I have made it" (v. 9; see v. 3). This statement shows the arrogance of the nation, which provided the basis for God's words: **Behold, I am against you** (v. 10). This phrase has been a frequent refrain in God's judgments. He uttered this against Jerusalem (21:3), Tyre (26:3), and Sidon (28:22). He made the same pronouncement against the false prophets in 13:8. A close parallel is the phrase "I have stretched out My hand against you" (25:7; see vv. 13, 16). Egypt's punishment was to be thorough and far-reaching, **from Migdol** (in the delta area) **to Syene** (modern Aswan, opposite Elephantine Island on the east bank near the first cataract) to the southern **border of Ethiopia**.

Verses 11, 12. Unlike His previous prophecies against the nations, this pronouncement from God did not call for the permanent destruction of Egypt. Her punishment would be relatively brief, but long enough to establish the truthfulness of the Lord's word. God declared that Egypt would **not be inhabited for forty years** (v. 11), reminding us of the length of Judah's exile in 4:6. Attempts to establish the exact period when Egypt was **desolate** (v. 12) have proven futile, mainly because of the absence of significant historical data. Also, it is possible that this number is used representatively and is not intended to mean a literal forty years. Ralph H. Alexander said,

> If Egypt fell to the Babylonians about 568 B.C., as implied in the chronicles of the Babylonian kings, then a forty-year "captivity" of Egypt would end under the Persians. Since it was the Persians' practice to return many peoples displaced by the Babylonians, this very well may be the case. Sources for Egyptian and Babylonian history of this period are sparse. In addition, kings of the ancient Near East did not normally admit failure. Just because there is no direct statement in ancient history concerning this dispersion does not mean that it did not occur. God's word is more valid than our conjectures or ignorance.[5]

29:13–16

[13]"'For thus says the Lord God, "At the end of forty years I will gather the Egyptians from the peoples among whom they were scattered. [14]I will turn the fortunes of Egypt and make them return to the land of Pathros, to the land of their origin, and there they will be a lowly kingdom. [15]It will be the lowest of the kingdoms, and it will never again lift itself up above the nations. And I will make them so small that they will not rule over the nations. [16]And it will never again be the confidence of the house of Israel, bringing to mind the iniquity of their having turned to Egypt. Then they will know that I am the Lord God."'"

---

[5]Ralph H. Alexander, "Ezekiel," in *The Expositor's Bible Commentary*, ed. Frank E. Gaebelein (Grand Rapids, Mich.: Zondervan Publishing House, 1986), 6:891.

Verses 13, 14. God promised that Egypt's punishment would have a termination point—**at the end of forty years** (v. 13). At that point, God would allow the people to return to their land, but only in a limited fashion—**to the land of Pathros** (v. 14). "Pathros" was the northern part of Egypt. Upon their return, they could only rule over this limited area. Egypt's previous domination was extensive, but that would not be so after the Lord's judgment. After the forty years, she would return, but as **a lowly kingdom**. Time has verified the accuracy of this prophecy. The annals of Scripture and history verify the greatness of Egypt in the centuries preceding the days of Ezekiel. Now, thousands of years later, we can see that Egypt has never again achieved greatness. She has been, and remains, "a lowly kingdom" compared to her former grandeur.

Verses 15, 16. While Egyptian rulers may attempt to regain her supremacy, God will not allow her to succeed. He promised to **make them so small** (v. 15) that they would not rule again. In addition, the fate of Egypt served as a reminder of Israel's own **iniquity** in having turned to Egypt for help in the first place (v. 16). Apparently, this means that when the Israelites saw how small and insignificant the kingdom of Egypt was, they were to remember God's word and their own foolishness for seeking an alliance with Egypt.

EGYPT BECOMES COMPENSATION FOR BABYLON (29:17–21)

29:17–20

¹⁷Now in the twenty-seventh year, in the first month, on the first of the month, the word of the Lord came to me saying, ¹⁸"Son of man, Nebuchadnezzar king of Babylon made his army labor hard against Tyre; every head was made bald and every shoulder was rubbed bare. But he and his army had no wages from Tyre for the labor that he had performed against it." ¹⁹Therefore thus says the Lord God, "Behold, I will give the land of Egypt to Nebuchadnezzar king of Babylon. And he will carry off her wealth and capture her spoil and seize her plunder; and it will be wages for his army. ²⁰I have given

him the land of Egypt for his labor which he performed, because they acted for Me," declares the Lord God.

Verse 17. In the twenty-seventh year refers to April 571 B.C., easily the latest date for an oracle in the book. However, it fits here because it links the destruction of Egypt (which had just been prophesied) with the work of Nebuchadnezzar.

Verse 18. Nebuchadnezzar laid siege to Tyre for thirteen years, according to Josephus.[6] From historical records, it appears that Pharaoh Hophra and Ethbaal II of Tyre had made an alliance, which may account for the length of the siege. (Perhaps Tyre received the aid from Egypt that Israel did not.) When Nebuchadnezzar was finally able to breach the fortified walls of the mainland city and secure a surrender (in 574[3] B.C.), all the wealth had been moved to the island fortress or carried away by the Egyptian navy.[7] The Babylonian soldiers had worked hard for the treasures of the mainland city. The spoils of war were to be their payment for the extensive labor in capturing the city. God told Ezekiel that, in the course of the siege, **every head was made bald and every shoulder was rubbed bare.** Chafing from helmets and carrying heavy loads (to build the siege towers and battering rams) took its toll on the Babylonian soldiers' bodies.

Verses 19, 20. What Nebuchadnezzar was doing was for the Lord (v. 20). Since the thirteen years of work against Tyre were not sufficiently compensated, God would reward the Babylonians with wealth from the coffers of Egypt. Taylor wrote,

> In point of fact the Babylonian expeditionary force did not attack Egypt until after the date of this oracle (c. 568–567 BC) and we have no contemporary records of its measure of success, because the Babylonian inscriptions recording the campaign have been damaged. Ahmose II (Amasis), who had supplanted Pharaoh Hophra in 571 BC, had to come to terms with the invaders, so we may

---

[6]Josephus *Antiquities* 10.11.1; *Against Apion* 1.21.
[7]Such is the position argued by J. D. Newsome, *By the Waters of Babylon* (Atlanta: John Knox Press, 1979), 159.

presume that Nebuchadrezzar won the tribute to pay his armies as Ezekiel had prophesied. Jeremiah also foretold Nebuchadrezzar's campaign (*cf.* Je. 43:8–13; 46:1–25).[8]

Questions have been raised about these verses in comparison with the prophecy of chapter 26. In chapter 26 it was predicted that Nebuchadnezzar would succeed in his attack on Tyre. This has led some to argue that Ezekiel was mistaken in the previous prediction and was now trying to correct the error. History verifies the successful campaign forged by the Babylonian soldiers against Tyre. Everything that Ezekiel specified would be done by Nebuchadnezzar came true exactly as predicted. Nothing in the prophecy that deals specifically with Nebuchadnezzar (26:7–11) says that the conqueror would leave Tyre with great wealth. That honor was reserved for Alexander the Great, when he fulfilled the part of the prophecy relating to him (beginning in 26:12).

Ezekiel's words were carefully chosen to convey the accuracy of both attacks. Nothing in the account in chapter 26 contradicts the statements in 29:17–20. Alexander wrote,

> Though some perceive that this passage demonstrates the incomplete fulfillment of Ezekiel's prophecies against Tyre, such a position rests on silence. On the contrary, these verses demonstrate that God faithfully executed his word against Tyre through Babylonia as he promised. The Scriptures do not demand that complete fulfillment lay in this one siege alone.[9]

What about the dates? If Egypt fell in 568 B.C., how do we account for the predicted forty years of exile? That would have the Egyptians returning to Pathros in 528 B.C., nearly eight years after Cyrus' decree to the exiles that they could return home. Several explanations can be offered:

---

[8]Taylor, 201.
[9]Alexander, 893.

(1) Dating in this book, as with historical records, is an inexact science. For example, if we took the "twenty-seventh year" (29:17) and applied it to the years of Nebuchadnezzar's reign (he began in 605 B.C.), this would date the prophecy around 578 B.C.; it would describe an earlier attack (and exile) of Egypt by Nebuchadnezzar. According to Josephus, Nebuchadnezzar conquered Egypt five years after the destruction of Jerusalem—that is, around 582 B.C.[10] The forty years would then lead to 537(6) B.C., which is when the Chaldean domination of Egypt (and Israel) came to an end.

(2) History verifies that Egyptian pharaohs continued to have a limited reign during the following periods: Hophra (Uah-ib-Ra) 589(8) to 570(69) B.C.; and Amasis (Ahmose II) 570(69) to 527(6) B.C. It is conceivable that a significant number of exiles returned to Egypt at the end of Amasis' reign (around 527[6] B.C.).

(3) As recorded in the Books of Ezra and Nehemiah, not all of the Jews returned to Israel when they were first allowed to do so. Possibly, the Egyptians remained in the scattered lands of Chaldea until 528 B.C. As mentioned above, this was eight years after Cyrus decreed the release of all exiles. Some of the people did not return to Jerusalem until 445 B.C.—ninety-one years after the Jews were free to return!

Gleason L. Archer, Jr., wrote,

> More recent discoveries of documentation in both Babylonian cuneiform and Egyptian hieroglyphics confirm Josephus in a remarkable way....
>
> These contemporary records from Babylon and Egypt serve to belie the skepticism of Ezekiel's detractors. But even they will have to concede that Ezekiel's long range prediction concerning Egypt came true as stated in 29:15. After the forty years of Chaldean oppression were over and Babylon itself had succumbed to the Medo-Persian empire in 539, there was but little respite for Egypt before Cambyses, the son of Cyrus, launched his invasion and

---

[10]Josephus *Antiquities* 10.9.5–7.

proceeded to annex Egypt to his empire in 525. Despite a few brief intervals of independence, the Egyptians remained subjects of the Persian Empire right up until 332 B.C., when they were taken over by Alexander the Great and the Ptolemaic Dynasty that came into power after his death in 323. The Ptolemies ruled Egypt until Cleopatra's navy was defeated by Augustus at the Battle of Actium in 31 B.C. From that point on the Romans retained control right down to the Byzantine era, until finally the Arabs overwhelmed the Nile Valley in the A.D. 630s. In other words, there was no strong or enduring native Egyptian dynasty on the throne of Egypt from the time of Nebuchadnezzar until our present millennium; and in that sense it could be regarded as the "basest of kingdoms," according to Ezekiel 29:15.[11]

29:21

[21]"On that day I will make a horn sprout for the house of Israel, and I will open your mouth in their midst. Then they will know that I am the LORD."

Verse 21. In biblical terminology, **a horn** is a symbol for power and strength, or in some cases a reference to a ruler (see 1 Sam. 2:1; 1 Kings 22:11; Jer. 48:25). Therefore, this verse indicates that the time was coming when God would raise up a power **for the house of Israel**, rather than raising up those who had been against His people. To what does **on that day** refer? Two logical explanations are possible regarding what "day" this might be:

(1) The day when Nebuchadnezzar would humble Egypt. If this is correct, then Nebuchadnezzar himself would be the "horn" that God raised up for Israel. This would mean that God used him to defeat the enemies of Israel (Tyre, Ammon, and Egypt), just as he had used him to humble Israel. Alexander wrote,

---

[11]Gleason L. Archer, Jr., *Encyclopedia of Bible Difficulties* (Grand Rapids, Mich.: Zondervan Publishing House, 1982), 277–78.

God used Babylonia's conquest of Egypt to strengthen and encourage Israel in exile (v. 21). The phrase "make a horn [sprout]" can be understood when two aspects of the horn symbolism are grasped: (1) strength and (2) a leader or ruler. Some think "horn" refers here to the Messiah because of comparison with Psalm 132:17. However, the context of Ezekiel 29 argues against the messianic interpretation. The passage treats the judgment on Egypt and states that at the time of Nebuchadnezzar's invasion "a horn" will grow for Israel. No Messiah—or any other ruler—came in Israel around 586 B.C. The symbol must refer to the strength and encouragement that Israel was to receive when she observed God's faithfulness to execute his judgment on her enemy, Egypt, in accord with both these prophecies and the Abrahamic covenant (Gen 12:3).[12]

(2) The day when Cyrus, king of Persia, gave the decree for the exiles to return home (538 B.C.). This would make Cyrus the "horn" or power that God raised up on behalf of Israel. Ezra 1:2 says, "'Thus says Cyrus king of Persia, "The LORD, the God of heaven, has given me all the kingdoms of the earth and He has appointed me to build Him a house in Jerusalem, which is in Judah."'"

APPLICATION

Opportunities from God

People are given repeated opportunities to repent. God had offered warnings to Egypt for centuries through His prophets. Likewise, He provides us with every opportunity to hear His Word. Are we listening? He makes sure that those who seek will find—but we must be seeking (Mt. 7:7, 8). We must have "the love of the truth so as to be saved" (2 Thess. 2:10).

God told the Egyptians He would take away their source of pride—the Nile. He controls nature. If people love the creation

---

[12] Alexander, 893.

more than the Creator, He may resort to drastic measures and take away that which we love (see Rom. 1:18–32).

God wants everyone to "know the Lord." Our salvation is dependent upon that knowledge. John wrote, "This is eternal life, that they may know You, the only true God, and Jesus Christ whom You have sent" (Jn. 17:3). Paul described the scene of "the Lord Jesus [being] revealed from heaven with His mighty angels in flaming fire, dealing out retribution to those who do not know God and to those who do not obey the gospel of our Lord Jesus . . ." (2 Thess. 1:7–9).

D.P.

A Picture of God

In the prophecy concerning Egypt in chapter 29, we are given an inspiring picture of God. What characteristics are attributed to Him?

He is the Lord God. Five times God affirmed that He was acting in judgment of Egypt so that they might know Him to be the Lord God. He is the only true and living God, and He wants the entire world to know it.

He is sovereign Lord of all the earth. His judgment on Egypt illustrates that He is the Ruler of all nations, cities, and peoples. He raises up nations and brings them down.

He is the Judge of all people. He had the right to judge Egypt. He made all people, and every individual must answer to Him. He has sovereign control over all the earth.

He controls the future. God determines what will happen in the days ahead. He puts princes on the throne and deposes men and nations. We do not know what the future holds, but we do know who holds the future.

Egypt learned that Yahweh is God—the only God. Have we learned this lesson?

E.C.

CHAPTER 30

THE INVASION OF EGYPT

The oracle in 30:1–19 is undated, but it would logically fit with the oracle in 29:1 (January 587[6] B.C.) because of the specific reference to Nebuchadnezzar in 30:10. Three months later, another oracle would be given (30:20).

This section continues the rebuke and the divine judgment of Egypt that began in chapter 29 (and continues to 32:32). As a world power, Egypt had corrupted herself in her thirst for power and prestige. Her domination over the ancient world established her "foundation" and "wealth" among all the nations (v. 4). By God's decree, Egypt was to fall, having a tremendous impact upon all of her sub-states and allies alike.

NEBUCHADNEZZAR'S INVASION OF EGYPT (30:1–19)

30:1–4
¹The word of the LORD came again to me saying, ²"Son of man, prophesy and say, 'Thus says the Lord GOD,

"Wail, 'Alas for the day!'
³For the day is near,
Even the day of the LORD is near;
It will be a day of clouds,
A time of doom for the nations.
⁴A sword will come upon Egypt,
And anguish will be in Ethiopia;
When the slain fall in Egypt,

> They take away her wealth,
> And her foundations are torn down."'"

The first twelve verses present God's judgments against Egypt (vv. 1–4), her allies (vv. 5–9), and her multitude (vv. 10–12).

Verses 1–3. God wanted Ezekiel to prophesy and call upon people to **wail** (v. 2). Why were they to wait on that **day**? The reason is explained in verse 3:

1. **The day of the LORD is near.** "The day of the Lord" is popular Old Testament terminology representing a day of judgment. It sometimes is a terrible day for God's people because He is coming against them. At other times, the day of the Lord is a day of victory because He is coming to save His people. In this case, the "day of the LORD" is judgment against an enemy of God's people—Egypt. (See Is. 2:12–17; 13:6; Joel 1:15; 2:1, 2; Amos 5:18–20; Zeph. 1:7, 14–18.)
2. **It will be a day of clouds.** Clouds are frequently associated with judgment in apocalyptic phraseology (v. 18; 32:7; 34:12; Ps. 104:3; Is. 19:1; Lam. 2:1; Mt. 24:30).
3. [It will be] **a time of doom for the nations.** While this oracle was given against Egypt, the day would also bring doom to Egypt's allies. They, too, would fall under the judgment of God.

Verse 4. The coming **sword** refers to Nebuchadnezzar's Babylonian armies. Frequently in Ezekiel, the "sword" is a reference to the military might of the Chaldean army—an instrument in the hand of God (see ch. 21).

30:5–9

> ⁵"'"Ethiopia, Put, Lud, all Arabia, Libya and the people of the land that is in league will fall with them by the sword."
> ⁶Thus says the LORD,
>
> > "Indeed, those who support Egypt will fall
> > And the pride of her power will come down;
> > From Migdol to Syene

They will fall within her by the sword,"
Declares the Lord GOD.
⁷"They will be desolate
In the midst of the desolated lands;
And her cities will be
In the midst of the devastated cities.
⁸And they will know that I am the LORD,
When I set a fire in Egypt
And all her helpers are broken.

⁹On that day messengers will go forth from Me in ships to frighten secure Ethiopia; and anguish will be on them as on the day of Egypt; for behold, it comes!"'"

Verse 5. Egypt's allies would also fall, including **Ethiopia** (Cush), **Put** (Africa), **Lud** (Libya), **Arabia** (in the East), and all of **Libya** (probably Lydia, in western Anatolia, or modern Turkey). Everyone who might be **in league** with Egypt would fall. The literal rendering here is "the people of the covenant," referring to people from Judea who had rejected the word of Jeremiah and fled to Egypt after the assassination of Gedaliah (2 Kings 25:23–26; Jer. 44:1).

Verses 6–8. The land of **Egypt** would become **desolate**, and the **cities** would be **devastated** (v. 7). The land from north to south (**Migdol to Syene**) would **fall** (v. 6; see the discussion on 29:10). The fact that they would fall **within her** indicates that these allies were mixed with the Egyptian forces to oppose Nebuchadnezzar when he came into Egypt. Their combined army of **helpers** (v. 8) would not be able to withstand the Lord's instrument—Nebuchadnezzar. They would go down to defeat, **broken**.

Verse 9. God said, "**On that day messengers will go forth from Me.**" On this "day of the Lord," He would dispatch His workers ("messengers"). This was to become **the day of Egypt**—that is, the day of her destruction. The "messengers" were to deliver an announcement of judgment from the Lord.

30:10–12
   ¹⁰"'Thus says the Lord God,

"I will also make the hordes of Egypt cease
By the hand of Nebuchadnezzar king of Babylon.
¹¹He and his people with him,
The most ruthless of the nations,
Will be brought in to destroy the land;
And they will draw their swords against Egypt
And fill the land with the slain.
¹²Moreover, I will make the Nile canals dry
And sell the land into the hands of evil men.
And I will make the land desolate
And all that is in it,
By the hand of strangers; I the Lord have spoken."'"

Verses 10, 11. God specifically named His instrument: Nebuchadnezzar. He said, **"I will also make the hordes of Egypt cease by the hand of Nebuchadnezzar"** (v. 10). Jeremiah likewise predicted the fall of Egypt by the hand of Nebuchadnezzar. As mentioned previously, the Babylonian armies destroyed Egypt and her allies in 568 B.C. Even though Egypt, in anticipation of the arrival of the Chaldean forces, amassed a great counter-army, it was unable to stop the Babylonian military machine. God would **fill the land with the slain** (v. 11).

The Babylonians are again called **the most ruthless of the nations**, demonstrating the inhumane way the Babylonian soldiers went about their destructive conquests.[1]

Verse 12. Next, God declared, **"I will make the Nile canals dry and sell the land into the hands of evil men. And I will make the land desolate."** The overflowing of the Nile was the source of fertility in Egypt. When the "canals" were made "dry," the surrounding area faced doom. Numerous canals were dug in ancient times to transfer water from the Nile to various regions. Without men to service and maintain them, these canals would fall into disrepair; then water would no longer flow. In

---

[1]See 28:7; 31:12; 32:12; Deut. 28:50; Is. 14:4–6; Jer. 51:20–23; Hab. 1:6–9.

addition, God may have intended to reduce the flow of the Nile, preventing water from filling the canals.

30:13–19
> ¹³"'Thus says the Lord GOD,
>
> "I will also destroy the idols
> And make the images cease from Memphis.
> And there will no longer be a prince in the land of Egypt;
> And I will put fear in the land of Egypt.
> ¹⁴I will make Pathros desolate,
> Set a fire in Zoan
> And execute judgments on Thebes.
> ¹⁵I will pour out My wrath on Sin,
> The stronghold of Egypt;
> I will also cut off the hordes of Thebes.
> ¹⁶I will set a fire in Egypt;
> Sin will writhe in anguish,
> Thebes will be breached
> And Memphis will have distresses daily.
> ¹⁷The young men of On and of Pi-beseth
> Will fall by the sword,
> And the women will go into captivity.
> ¹⁸In Tehaphnehes the day will be dark
> When I break there the yoke bars of Egypt.
> Then the pride of her power will cease in her;
> A cloud will cover her,
> And her daughters will go into captivity.
> ¹⁹Thus I will execute judgments on Egypt,
> And they will know that I am the LORD."'"

Verses 13–15. God pronounced judgment on the Egyptian gods, destroying **idols** and **images** (v. 13). Egypt was noted for having dozens—maybe even hundreds—of gods. To illustrate a point made earlier (v. 6), God would demonstrate how literally *all* of the land would be devastated. This passage has been lauded as one of the most accurate geographical pictures of ancient Egypt. **Memphis** (modern Mit Rahneh) used to be the capital of

Lower Egypt and remained an important center until it was defeated by Alexander the Great (c. 330 B.C.). Some of the Jews who rejected the prophecies of Jeremiah had relocated to this city (Jer. 44:1). **Pathros** (v. 14; see 29:14) was located in the Upper Egypt region that extended south to Aswan. **Zoan** (or Tanis) was in the eastern region of the Nile delta. **Thebes** ("No"; KJV) was the capital of Egypt for most of the nation's history. It was the center for the worship of Amon (the sun-god, also called "No-Amon"; Nahum 3:8). The ancient city consisted of three areas known today as Luxor, Karnak, and the West Bank. **Sin** (v. 15; "Pelusium"; NIV) is the modern Tel Farama, on the Mediterranean coast near Port Said—an important defense point. Located on the northeastern border, this was the residence of the ruling Twenty-sixth Dynasty of Ezekiel's day.

Verses 16–18. God repeated the names of several cities, emphasizing that, in contrast to their current greatness, He would bring them to destruction. **On** (Aven) is Heliopolis, one of the oldest cities of Egypt (v. 17). This was the "city of the sun-god" and, therefore, one of the major religious centers of the nation. (Potiphera, Joseph's father-in-law, was a priest of On; Gen. 41:45). **Pi-beseth** corresponds to the modern Basta, northeast of Cairo. God mentioned here that **the women** from these cities would be taken into captivity; this is one of the few references to women in these judgment oracles. **Tehaphnehes** (v. 18), or "Tahpanhes" (Jer. 2:16; 44:1; 46:14), is the modern Tel Defenneh, ten miles west of Qantara on the Suez Canal. Jeremiah was taken here after Gedeliah was assassinated (Jer. 43:7; see 44:1).

Verse 19. Egypt and her great cities—plus her allies—would fall to the Babylonians. These are the **judgments** of God that He would **execute**. Through these tragic events, the Egyptian people would learn the identity of **the Lord**.

THE DEFEAT OF PHAROAH (30:20–26)

²⁰In the eleventh year, in the first month, on the seventh of the month, the word of the Lord came to me saying, ²¹"Son of man, I have broken the arm of Pharaoh king of Egypt; and, behold, it has not been bound up for healing or wrapped with

a bandage, that it may be strong to hold the sword. ²²Therefore thus says the Lord GOD, 'Behold, I am against Pharaoh king of Egypt and will break his arms, both the strong and the broken; and I will make the sword fall from his hand. ²³I will scatter the Egyptians among the nations and disperse them among the lands. ²⁴For I will strengthen the arms of the king of Babylon and put My sword in his hand; and I will break the arms of Pharaoh, so that he will groan before him with the groanings of a wounded man. ²⁵Thus I will strengthen the arms of the king of Babylon, but the arms of Pharaoh will fall. Then they will know that I am the LORD, when I put My sword into the hand of the king of Babylon and he stretches it out against the land of Egypt. ²⁶When I scatter the Egyptians among the nations and disperse them among the lands, then they will know that I am the LORD.'"

Verse 20. In yet another dated oracle, God returned to His judgments against Egypt. This time, He focused on the leader of Egypt, the pharaoh. This oracle was given **in the eleventh year** of the reign of Zedekiah (April 587 B.C.), about four months before the fall of Jerusalem.

Verses 21, 22. "**I have broken the arm of Pharaoh,**" God said (v. 21). This refers to Pharaoh Hophra, the pharaoh who failed to provide sufficient support to Zedekiah, even though an alliance had been made between Judah and Egypt. The arm frequently represents a man's strength in the Scriptures. God would reduce the strength of Pharaoh by breaking his arm; he would be unable **to hold the sword** and incapable of defending his nation. God eliminated the strength of Pharaoh by breaking both of his arms. Ralph H. Alexander explained,

> The flexed arm was a common Egyptian symbol for the Pharaoh's strength. Often statues or images of the Pharaoh have this arm flexed, wielding a sword in battle. A king with great biceps was especially a popular concept under the Saites Dynasty of Ezekiel's day. In addition Hophra took a second formal title that meant "possessed of a muscular arm" or "strong-armed" (Freedy and Red-

ford, pp. 482–83). Therefore Hophra's defeat was most suitably represented by "breaking his arm." Ezekiel then takes the imagery further by declaring that, Hophra's arm had not been splinted so that it might heal. Hophra's strength had been broken, and he had not regained that strength. He was unable to wield the sword.[2]

Now he was completely helpless. Notice the repetition of the pronoun "I" in 30:21–26, declaring what God would do.
Verses 23, 24. With their pharaoh incapacitated, the people would be forced to **scatter** when the nation fell to the Babylonians. These people, like those of Judah, were taken into exile by the Babylonians and dispersed throughout the nations.
Verses 25, 26. After defeating Tyre, Nebuchadnezzar turned his attention to Egypt. (She would provide spoil for his soldiers.) However, by the time Nebuchadnezzar reached Egypt, Hophra had already died in a civil war. John B. Taylor said,

> He had conducted a disastrous campaign in Libya, which brought on a major revolt from a rival faction under Ahmose, who was eventually responsible for [putting] him to death. We are not to interpret an oracle like this one of Ezekiel in too personal terms, but it clearly fits in admirably with Hophra's fate.[3]

APPLICATION

Making Wise Choices
Evil companions corrupt good morals. Those who joined forces with the evil empire of Egypt would fall alongside Egypt.

---

[2] Ralph H. Alexander, "Ezekiel," in *The Expositor's Bible Commentary*, ed. Frank E. Gaebelein (Grand Rapids, Mich.: Zondervan Publishing House, 1986), 6:897–98; K. S. Freedy and D. B. Redford, "The Dates in Ezekiel in Relation to Biblical, Babylonian and Egyptian Sources," *Journal of the American Oriental Society* 90 (1970): 482–83.

[3] John B. Taylor, *Ezekiel: An Introduction and Commentary*, Tyndale Old Testament Commentaries (Downers Grove, Ill.: Inter-Varsity Press, 1969), 204.

In the same way, we must choose our friends carefully, not allowing others to influence us toward evil (1 Cor. 15:33).

D.P.

When God Judges

The invasion of Egypt is prophesied in chapter 30. The text reveals some enlightening truths about God's judgment of mankind.

God determines the time of judgment. In Old Testament times, when He brought judgments upon cities and nations, these times were referred to as "the day of the Lord." Prophets often told the city or nation when the time was near. The New Testament mentions a day of eternal judgment (1 Thess. 5:2; 2 Pet. 3:10), also called "the day of the Lord." However, the time of its coming has not been revealed. We are always to be ready (Mt. 24:46).

Nothing can prevent His judgment. When God comes in His judgment, nothing can stop Him. An exception is the case of Nineveh (Jon. 3): The people repented in response to the judgment announcement, and God withdrew the punishment. Every person is subject to the judgment of God (Rom. 14:12; 2 Cor. 5:10). No one will miss the appointment.

His judgment will be accurate. God, who knows everything, will judge us flawlessly. In the Old Testament, He required faith and obedience for salvation. Acts 2 presents God's last will and testament for all nations. His plan still involves faith and obedience, but these are expressed by believing in Jesus (Jn. 8:24), repentance of sin (Acts 17:30, 31), confession of Jesus (Rom. 10:10), and baptism for the forgiveness of sins (Acts 2:38; 22:16). Faith and obedience bring one into the church that Jesus purchased (Acts 20:28), and they are expressed in daily living for Christ.

No one can escape it. God's judgment is all-inclusive and complete. Every human being is accountable to Him, and no one will be overlooked. We will all be brought before God in judgment. However, those in Christ, covered by the blood and mercy of heaven, need not be afraid. God wants to be our Savior; only out of necessity does He serve as our Judge.

E.C.

Chapter 31
Pharoah Is Judged:
The Allegory of the Cedar

Assyria had long been recognized as one of the great powers of the ancient world. At the height of her power in the seventh century B.C., Assyria held sway over Babylonia, parts of Media, Armenia, Syria, Cyprus, Arabia, and Egypt. Her army, her fortresses, and her powerful leaders meant world domination for decades. There was no end in sight for the mighty Assyrian Empire. Seemingly, she could rule for centuries to come.

Suddenly, without anticipation, her empire was shattered. How could this have happened? The Lord, the God of the Israelites, brought Assyria down. Egypt's turn was next. Her years of power and her long line of mighty pharaohs was about to be brought to an alarming end. Just as ruin came to Assyria when no one thought it possible, so Egypt would fall.

In chapter 31 Assyria is likened to a mighty cedar tree—strong, stable, and too great to fall. Nevertheless, it fell. Pharaoh Hophra is then likened to this mighty cedar. As it came down, so also would he and his Egyptian empire be brought down—to Sheol.

31:1-4

¹**In the eleventh year, in the third month, on the first of the month, the word of the Lord came to me saying,** ²**"Son of man, say to Pharaoh king of Egypt and to his hordes,**

'Whom are you like in your greatness?
³Behold, Assyria was a cedar in Lebanon
With beautiful branches and forest shade,

And very high,
And its top was among the clouds.
⁴The waters made it grow, the deep made it high.
With its rivers it continually extended all around its planting place,
And sent out its channels to all the trees of the field.'"

Verse 1. This oracle is dated in June 587 B.C., two months after the previous oracle (30:20).

Verse 2. Egypt was so great that she saw no parallels to herself. Was any nation a match for her? Could anyone compare with her **greatness**? She thought not. To convince her otherwise, God had Ezekiel present an allegory to her.

Verses 3, 4. The allegory began, **Assyria was a cedar in Lebanon** (v. 3). Those familiar with the Old Testament are aware of the frequent use of the cedars of Lebanon as an illustration of greatness and strength (see 17:1-10, 22-24; tree analogies are used in Is. 14:4-21; Dan. 4:1-12, 19-27; Mt. 13:31, 32). Assyria shared these eight characteristics with the great cedar:

(1) [It had] **beautiful branches** (v. 3). Assyria extended its strong arm of power far and wide.

(2) [It had] **forest shade** (v. 3). Assyria was the overshadowing nation for many smaller, less significant nations.

(3) [It was] **very high** (v. 3). No nation had previously risen to the prominence of Assyria. She was taller—greater—than all the rest.

(4) **Its top was among the clouds** (v. 3). Assyria considered herself blessed by the gods. In her idolatry, she believed herself to be the chosen nation.

(5) **Waters made it grow** (v. 4). Everything Assyria needed to remain strong was amply supplied. This may be an allusion to Assyria's great water sources, the Tigris and Euphrates rivers. Egypt was equally boastful of her great river, the Nile.

(6) **The deep** ["deep springs"; NIV] **made it high** (v. 4). Assyria had abundant resources. She did not need anything or anyone. She was self-sufficient.

(7) **Its rivers ... continually extended all around** (v. 4). With its "water supply," Assyria continued to grow even stronger.

(8) [It] **sent out its channels to all the trees of the field** (v. 4). Other nations were under the control of Assyria and dependent upon her for their sustenance.

31:5–9

> ⁵"'Therefore its height was loftier than all the trees of the field
> And its boughs became many and its branches long
> Because of many waters as it spread them out.
> ⁶All the birds of the heavens nested in its boughs,
> And under its branches all the beasts of the field gave birth,
> And all great nations lived under its shade.
> ⁷So it was beautiful in its greatness, in the length of its branches;
> For its roots extended to many waters.
> ⁸The cedars in God's garden could not match it;
> The cypresses could not compare with its boughs,
> And the plane trees could not match its branches.
> No tree in God's garden could compare with it in its beauty.
> ⁹I made it beautiful with the multitude of its branches,
> And all the trees of Eden, which were in the garden of God, were jealous of it.'"

Verses 5, 6. Having established the greatness of the tree (the nation of Assyria), God noted that **all the birds of the heavens nested in its boughs** (v. 6). Lesser powers were subjugated to the Assyrian dynasty. She controlled everything, and other kingdoms had to answer to her. She ruled supreme.

Verses 7–9. Using the force of poetic exaggeration, God described Assyria as greater than all other nations, even those in **God's garden** (v. 8). This hyperbolic statement suggests that even the perfect environment God created in the Garden of Eden could not match the beauty and splendor of this cedar. (In other words, no kingdom—including Israel—enjoyed glory equivalent to that of Assyria.) John B. Taylor said,

> The flattering language of verses 7–9 must not be taken too literally, unless it is intended to reflect the adulation

which a Pharaoh like Hophra received from his satellites, Zedekiah included. Its effect, however, is to heighten the sense of downfall when eventually this takes place, as with the similarly extravagant description of the good ship Tyre (27:3–9). Nothing whatsoever could compare with it in beauty, not even the finest trees in Eden, *the garden of God*. Here is another echo of the Genesis narrative (Gn. 2:8f), which appeared also in the lamentation on the king of Tyre (28:12–19), and it further illustrates Ezekiel's willingness to draw on the symbolism of the past, a symbolism which his readers or hearers were presumably expected to understand.[1]

31:10–14

10"'Therefore thus says the Lord GOD, "Because it is high in stature and has set its top among the clouds, and its heart is haughty in its loftiness, 11therefore I will give it into the hand of a despot of the nations; he will thoroughly deal with it. According to its wickedness I have driven it away. 12Alien tyrants of the nations have cut it down and left it; on the mountains and in all the valleys its branches have fallen and its boughs have been broken in all the ravines of the land. And all the peoples of the earth have gone down from its shade and left it. 13On its ruin all the birds of the heavens will dwell, and all the beasts of the field will be on its fallen branches 14so that all the trees by the waters may not be exalted in their stature, nor set their top among the clouds, nor their well-watered mighty ones stand erect in their height. For they have all been given over to death, to the earth beneath, among the sons of men, with those who go down to the pit."'"

Verse 10. As is typical in judgment oracles, God began with the word **therefore**. Based on the reasons given earlier, God was ready to act. Verse 10 provides the foundational reason for Assyria's fall: **Its heart is haughty**. How often this was the pri-

---

[1]John B. Taylor, *Ezekiel: An Introduction and Commentary*, Tyndale Old Testament Commentaries (Downers Grove, Ill.: Inter-Varsity Press, 1969), 206.

mary reason that God condemned a nation! Truly, it is easy for power to turn into sinful pride. (See the examples of Tyre in 28:2 and Babel in Gen. 11:4.)

Verses 11, 12. God declared that He would give Assyria **into the hand of a despot of the nations** (v. 11). **Alien tyrants** (v. 12) would bring down this empire. Assyria would be **cut . . . down and left**—a phrase demonstrating that the Assyrian dynasty would have no lasting legacy. According to S. Fisch, "In Hebrew the verb is the same as 'do leave him' at the end of the verse and may be similarly translated. The fallen cedar is left abandoned as something useless."[2] The Assyrians were excessively brutal in the way they treated conquered peoples. Now the situation would be reversed: They would be treated as they had treated others (see 28:7; 30:11; 32:12). History confirms that the Babylonians succeeded in bringing about the end of the Assyrian Empire—and with relative ease.

Verses 13, 14. Those who had enjoyed the protection of Assyria and had relied upon her power would consume what remained of the fallen empire. Verse 14 warned other nations not to aspire to the greatness of Assyria; for, in so doing, they would likely fall prey to the same sin of pride. Assyria was going the way of all men—death (**the pit**). Taylor wrote,

> Death is the great equalizer and the surest antidote to an excess of ambition. Even the Egypts of this world, who have success-stories despite their godlessness, need to be taught the lesson that may be hidden in verse 9 that *I (Yahweh) made it beautiful.* The prosperity of the wicked is, in the last analysis, all due to the mercy and goodness of God.[3]

What happened to Assyria? The Assyrian Empire, having been supreme in the ancient world for almost four centuries,

---

[2]S. Fisch, *Ezekiel: Hebrew Text and English Translation with an Introduction and Commentary*, Soncino Books of the Bible (London: Soncino Press, 1950), 210.
[3]Taylor, 206–7.

was overthrown by the united forces of the Babylonians (Nabopolassar) and the Medes (Cyaxares). The great Assyrian city of Nineveh fell in 612 B.C. (as predicted by Nahum), and the Assyrians were finally extinguished in the battle of Carchemish (605 B.C.) by Nebuchadnezzar.

31:15–18

¹⁵"'Thus says the Lord GOD, "On the day when it went down to Sheol I caused lamentations; I closed the deep over it and held back its rivers. And its many waters were stopped up, and I made Lebanon mourn for it, and all the trees of the field wilted away on account of it. ¹⁶I made the nations quake at the sound of its fall when I made it go down to Sheol with those who go down to the pit; and all the well-watered trees of Eden, the choicest and best of Lebanon, were comforted in the earth beneath. ¹⁷They also went down with it to Sheol to those who were slain by the sword; and those who were its strength lived under its shade among the nations.

¹⁸To which among the trees of Eden are you thus equal in glory and greatness? Yet you will be brought down with the trees of Eden to the earth beneath; you will lie in the midst of the uncircumcised, with those who were slain by the sword. So is Pharaoh and all his hordes!"' declares the Lord GOD."

Verse 15. The fall of the Assyrians sent shock waves throughout the empire. How could such a great nation be brought down so easily? If the Assyrians could be defeated, then every lesser nation could be as well. Like the sinking of Tyre, the fall of Assyria caused **lamentations** from many nations (v. 15).

Verses 16, 17. Assyria's allies would be defeated along with her. The partnership that had served them well for so long would turn on them, and they would join Assyria in **Sheol**.

Verse 18. The application to this extended allegory is given as the chapter closes. If Egypt thought that she had more advantages than Assyria had, she was terribly mistaken. Like most ancient peoples, the thought of an improper burial (being left in the open to be consumed by the beasts and birds, for example) haunted the proud Egyptian people. Nevertheless, they would die in disgrace, like **uncircumcised** pagans. Just as God brought down the powerful Assyrians, so He would destroy the mighty **Pharaoh and all his hordes.**

APPLICATION

The Danger of Pride
The Assyrians and the Egyptians trusted in their great strength. As a result, God had to bring them down. We must learn to lean on God, not on our own strength or wisdom (Jer. 10:23; Mt. 6:24–34).

"Pride goes before destruction" (Prov. 16:18a). Assyria was filled with sinful pride because of the great things she had accomplished. We also can let pride destroy us. It is one of the foundational sins of mankind (1 Jn. 2:15–17).

An adage says, "What goes around comes around." Assyria was excessively brutal and merciless in her treatment of conquered nations. Now God was ready to let her reap what she had sown.

D.P.

Look What Happened to the Titanic!
The Titanic was the latest in design, engineering, and technology of her time. She was heralded as the unsinkable ship, but she sank on her maiden voyage.

God began His announcement of Egypt's judgment by telling them about Assyria, the Titanic of its time, the unsinkable nation. Egypt, too, was big, powerful, and seen by many as invincible. The people needed to know that Assyria had possessed a similar reputation and yet was brought down by God. If He chose to judge Egypt, He would be able to humble her as easily as He destroyed Assyria.

What do we learn from His recounting of Assyria's status, strength, and spirit?

First, we see that pride does not pay. Assyria was proud. God said that it was because of her pride that He brought her down. In verse 10, God said that He destroyed her because her "heart is haughty in its loftiness."

The world teaches us to intimidate others, to believe in ourselves, to strut, and to brag; but God leads us to humble ourselves before His mighty hand.

Second, we see that power cannot preserve. Assyria had every advantage. To use the figurative language of the text, she was like a cedar in Lebanon with beautiful branches and a top that reached to the clouds. She had water and resources for growth. The birds of the heavens nested in her boughs. Under her branches all the beasts of field lived, and all great nations lived under her shade.

Assyria had power, prestige, and position. She was great in everyone's sight, except God's. She had sin, cruelty, and violence in her midst. When God turned His hand of judgment toward her, nothing she had could stay it.

Third, we learn that popular sentiment is not always a true assessment. Everyone stood in awe of Assyria. Her strength and victories were the envy of the world.

God saw through the outer shell of physical traits and evaluated the spiritual life of that nation. He weighed them in the balance of divine truth and found that they came out wanting.

Fourth, we see that physical resources do not assure a future. If a nation has conquered territories, material possessions, and storehouses of grain and food, will this not protect her people from judgment? No, a nation cannot live unless she recognizes God and serves Him.

When God brought the fall of Assyria, everyone heard of it. She was no match for God, who said,

> I made the nations quake at the sound of its fall when I made it go down to Sheol with those who go down to the pit; and all the well-watered trees of Eden, the choicest and best of Lebanon, were comforted in the earth beneath. They also went down with it to Sheol to those who were slain by the sword; and those who were its strength lived under its shade among the nations (31:16, 17).

E.C.

Chapter 32
A Lamentation for Pharaoh and Egypt

Chapter 32 concludes the extended discussion regarding God's judgment against seven nations. It is dated a few months after the news of the fall of Jerusalem reached the exiles (see 33:21). A powerful lesson is found within the events of the fall and this prediction of doom for Egypt. The nation of Judah had sought an alliance with Egypt. The people might even have held a conviction that if Egypt had come to their aid, the nation would not have fallen. Now, however, Egypt was predicted to be near its end. How foolish it was for Judah to trust in Egypt, who was unable even to defend herself!

As noted in earlier chapters, Babylon was recognized as God's instrument to bring about the destruction of Egypt. The powerful Babylonian army would quickly and easily defeat Egypt. A mournful song was to be lifted up for her and her mighty pharaoh. God commissioned Ezekiel to raise the lamentation on behalf of the pending death of Egypt.

A LAMENT FOR PHARAOH (32:1–16)

32:1–10

¹In the twelfth year, in the twelfth month, on the first of the month, the word of the LORD came to me saying, ²"Son of man, take up a lamentation over Pharaoh king of Egypt and say to him,

'You compared yourself to a young lion of the nations,
Yet you are like the monster in the seas;

And you burst forth in your rivers
And muddied the waters with your feet
And fouled their rivers."'

³Thus says the Lord GOD,
"Now I will spread My net over you
With a company of many peoples,
And they shall lift you up in My net.
⁴I will leave you on the land;
I will cast you on the open field.
And I will cause all the birds of the heavens to dwell on you,
And I will satisfy the beasts of the whole earth with you.
⁵I will lay your flesh on the mountains
And fill the valleys with your refuse.
⁶I will also make the land drink the discharge of your blood
As far as the mountains,
And the ravines will be full of you.
⁷And when I extinguish you,
I will cover the heavens and darken their stars;
I will cover the sun with a cloud
And the moon will not give its light.
⁸All the shining lights in the heavens
I will darken over you
And will set darkness on your land,"
Declares the Lord GOD.

⁹"I will also trouble the hearts of many peoples when I bring your destruction among the nations, into lands which you have not known. ¹⁰I will make many peoples appalled at you, and their kings will be horribly afraid of you when I brandish My sword before them; and they will tremble every moment, every man for his own life, on the day of your fall."

Verse 1. This dated oracle came **in the twelfth year, in the twelfth month, on the first of the month.** This was March 585 B.C., two months after the exiles received word of the fall of Jerusalem (33:21), which had occurred about eighteen months earlier. Meanwhile, back in Judah, some serious events had taken place. The Babylonian-appointed governor, Gedaliah, had been assassinated, and the remaining Jews had fled to Egypt. The prophet Jeremiah had been taken with them to Egypt (Jer. 44). While Jeremiah was predicting Egyptian doom in Egypt, Ezekiel was delivering the same message in Babylon.

Verse 2. God called upon Ezekiel to **take up a lamentation over Pharaoh king of Egypt**. This would refer to Pharaoh Hophra (589[8]–570[69] B.C.). While Pharaoh considered himself to be like **a young lion** (king of beasts over all the other nations), he was more like **the monster in the seas** (תַּנִּין, *thannin*). (See the discussion on 29:3.) He was likened to a crocodile that only **muddied the waters** of the Nile **and fouled their rivers**. John B. Taylor said,

> Ezekiel's point is that Pharaoh is not the lion-like creature that he fancied himself to be, but a *thannin*, a *dragon*. The word is the same as is used in 29:3, and again shares the double inference of the Egyptian crocodile and the mythological chaos-monster, Tiamat, which was slain by the god Marduk after being captured in a net.... Neither simile is intended to be flattering. Like a crocodile, the king of Egypt wallows in the muddy waters of the Nile, making them even muddier by his movements, and like Tiamat, he is going to be ensnared and hauled out on to dry ground, where his carcase will be a prey for the scavengers of the earth and sky.[1]

Verses 3, 4. God was going to spread his **net** over Pharaoh (v. 3) and **cast** [him into] **the open field** (v. 4), where he could not possibly survive. Both **the birds** and **the beasts** would feast on him.

Verses 5–8. The widespread destruction of Egypt would fill

---

[1] John B. Taylor, *Ezekiel: An Introduction and Commentary*, Tyndale Old Testament Commentaries (Downers Grove, Ill.: Inter-Varsity Press, 1969), 208–9. The story of the Tiamat monster is told in *Enuma Elish* 4; quoted in D. Winton Thomas, ed., *Documents from Old Testament Times* (New York: Harper & Brothers, 1958), 9.

the whole land with the blood of the nation (v. 5). Even **the mountains** and **the ravines** (v. 6) would be filled with blood. The number of slain would be massive. Even the luminaries of heaven would **darken** (vv. 7, 8). This is typical apocalyptic terminology, representing the Lord's coming in judgment (Is. 13:10; Joel 2:30, 31; 3:15; Amos 8:9). The phrasing is also reminiscent of the plagues God sent upon Egypt (Ex. 7:20–24; 10:21–23). Further, this prophecy can be seen as an attack upon the Egyptian sun and moon gods.

Verses 9, 10. The destruction of Egypt seemed inconceivable to **the nations** (v. 9). The imminent destruction of the great nation would leave the people **appalled** (v. 10) and their kings filled with fear. As is typical in this book, **My sword** refers to the Babylonians, the instrument of punishment in the hand of the Lord.

32:11–16

¹¹For thus says the Lord God, "The sword of the king of Babylon will come upon you. ¹²By the swords of the mighty ones I will cause your hordes to fall; all of them are tyrants of the nations,

> And they will devastate the pride of Egypt,
> And all its hordes will be destroyed.
> ¹³I will also destroy all its cattle from beside many waters;
> And the foot of man will not muddy them anymore
> And the hoofs of beasts will not muddy them.
> ¹⁴Then I will make their waters settle
> And will cause their rivers to run like oil,"
> Declares the Lord God.
> ¹⁵"When I make the land of Egypt a desolation,
> And the land is destitute of that which filled it,
> When I smite all those who live in it,
> Then they shall know that I am the Lord."

¹⁶This is a lamentation and they shall chant it. The daughters of the nations shall chant it. Over Egypt and over all her hordes they shall chant it," declares the Lord God.

Verses 11, 12. Leaving the figurative language of the earlier verses, the Lord spoke plainly about the fate of Egypt in verses 11 through 16. **The swords of** God's **mighty ones** (v. 12), would cause widespread death and destruction. They would **devastate the pride of Egypt**—her great wealth and her powerful leaders.

Verses 13–15. The **waters** of Egypt, which were frequently stirred with the passing of man and beast, were to become eerily silent (vv. 13, 14). God would make Egypt a **destitute** land where neither man nor beast would live (v. 15). God planned to **smite all those who live in it** for the purpose of teaching them **that I am the** LORD.

Verse 16. God provided the **lamentation** to be sung regarding Egypt. The pagan nations (**the daughters of the nations**) were to sing this dirge. Much had been given to Egypt; but because she was a nation filled with pride (instead of gratitude), she had to be brought low.

FINAL LAMENTATION FOR EGYPT AND HER ALLIES (32:17–32)

32:17–21

¹⁷In the twelfth year, on the fifteenth of the month, the word of the LORD came to me saying, ¹⁸"Son of man, wail for the hordes of Egypt and bring it down, her and the daughters of the powerful nations, to the nether world, with those who go down to the pit;

¹⁹'Whom do you surpass in beauty?
Go down and make your bed with the uncircumcised.'

²⁰They shall fall in the midst of those who are slain by the sword. She is given over to the sword; they have drawn her and all her hordes away. ²¹The strong among the mighty ones shall speak of him and his helpers from the midst of Sheol, 'They have gone down, they lie still, the uncircumcised, slain by the sword.'"

EZEKIEL 32

Verse 17. In the twelfth year, on the fifteenth of the month, Ezekiel concluded his prophecy of doom on Egypt. The date would have been March or April 585 B.C. This also marked the end of his prophecies against the nations (that began in ch. 25).

Verses 18, 19. Egypt and her allies were sent to the grave. She was joined there by **the daughters of the powerful nations** (v. 18), pagan nations that had also faced the wrath of God and met their end. Egypt had scorned other nations, thinking her **beauty** greater than theirs. In Sheol, she was just like all of the other condemned nations (**the uncircumcised**; v. 19).

Verses 20, 21. The fatal **sword** (v. 20) had found yet another victim. Egypt, who considered herself vastly superior to others who had succumbed to the sword, was now joining them. Her proud allies had considered themselves safe under the protective wing of Egypt, but they were also going to **Sheol** (v. 21). Additional **strong** nations that had joined Egypt are listed in the following verses.

32:22–30

²²"Assyria is there and all her company; her graves are round about her. All of them are slain, fallen by the sword, ²³whose graves are set in the remotest parts of the pit and her company is round about her grave. All of them are slain, fallen by the sword, who spread terror in the land of the living.

²⁴Elam is there and all her hordes around her grave; all of them slain, fallen by the sword, who went down uncircumcised to the lower parts of the earth, who instilled their terror in the land of the living and bore their disgrace with those who went down to the pit. ²⁵They have made a bed for her among the slain with all her hordes. Her graves are around it, they are all uncircumcised, slain by the sword (although their terror was instilled in the land of the living), and they bore their disgrace with those who go down to the pit; they were put in the midst of the slain.

²⁶Meshech, Tubal and all their hordes are there; their graves surround them. All of them were slain by the sword uncircumcised, though they instilled their terror in the land of the living. ²⁷Nor do they lie beside the fallen heroes of the

uncircumcised, who went down to Sheol with their weapons of war and whose swords were laid under their heads; but the punishment for their iniquity rested on their bones, though the terror of these heroes was once in the land of the living. ²⁸But in the midst of the uncircumcised you will be broken and lie with those slain by the sword.

²⁹There also is Edom, its kings and all its princes, who for all their might are laid with those slain by the sword; they will lie with the uncircumcised and with those who go down to the pit.

³⁰There also are the chiefs of the north, all of them, and all the Sidonians, who in spite of the terror resulting from their might, in shame went down with the slain. So they lay down uncircumcised with those slain by the sword and bore their disgrace with those who go down to the pit."

Beginning in this section, an impressive list of defeated nations is given. While listing defeated nations is not unusual, the nations listed here all fell within a century. Never in the history of mankind have so many world powers fallen from prominence in such rapid succession. The great Babylon—who brought about the death of all these others—would soon (in 539 B.C.) join the others in Sheol.

Verses 22, 23. The first nation listed as preceding Egypt to Sheol is **Assyria** (v. 22). Assyria had met her doom at the hands of the Babylonians just a few decades ago, falling in 612 B.C. and being completely eliminated in 605 B.C. (v. 23). **Her company** refers to Assyria's numerous allies.

Verses 24, 25. The second nation that had preceded Egypt to Sheol was **Elam** (v. 24). Elam, also known as Elymais, was southeast of Assyria. The Elamites were famous warriors, proud and vicious. They **instilled their terror** in the hearts of other nations. When the Assyrian king Ashurbanipal defeated the Elamites, he considered the victory one of his proudest moments. After the decline of Assyria, Elam again asserted itself—only to be defeated by the Babylonians. Their demise was prophesied in Isaiah 11:11 and Jeremiah 49:34–39. When one who is filled with pride is brought down, he is filled with "disgrace" (v. 30).

Verses 26–28. The third nation to face defeat and precede Egypt to Sheol is listed as **Meshech, Tubal and all their hordes** (v. 26). Located in northeastern Anatolia (modern Turkey), this nation is a surprising addition to the list. History does not credit Meshech-Tubal as being a great nation, yet it is presented as a formidable power in 38:2, 3 and 39:1. While the text is difficult to ascertain, it appears that this nation was not placed in the same position of humiliation as the others. (Verse 27a says, **"Nor do they lie beside the fallen heroes of the uncircumcised."**) The NIV eliminates the difficulty, turning this into a question: "Do they not lie with the other uncircumcised warriors . . . ?" If the NASB, KJV, RSV, and ASV are correct, the statement indicates a lesser punishment for this nation than that received by the others. Verse 28 is not talking about Meshech-Tubal; rather, the **you** refers to Pharaoh. He was to be **broken** and join the others who had died by the sword.

Verse 29. The fourth nation to be named is **Edom** (see 25:12–14; Jer. 49:7–22; Obad. 8). This longtime tormentor of Israel, located south of the Dead Sea, joined the other great nations in defeat and death.

Verse 30. The fifth and final nation listed is **the Sidonians**, the people of the great Phoenician kingdom that inhabited the land north of Israel (along the coastline of the Mediterranean Sea). They and all **the chiefs of the north** (the rulers of the various Phoenician cities) were brought to **disgrace** by **the sword** of the Lord (see 28:20–23).

32:31, 32

³¹**"These Pharaoh will see, and he will be comforted for all his hordes slain by the sword, even Pharaoh and all his army,"** declares the Lord God. ³²**"Though I instilled a terror of him in the land of the living, yet he will be made to lie down among the uncircumcised along with those slain by the sword, even Pharaoh and all his hordes,"** declares the Lord God.

Verse 31. Having listed these five great nations, God said that Egypt was now going to join them. They would be **comforted** to see the other nations that preceded them to Sheol—a

testimony to the adage "misery loves company." Pharaoh would be glad to see that others were suffering the same fate as he.

Verse 32. While Egypt was still **in the land of the living**, God made others fear her greatly. Such was not to be the case in Sheol. Egypt would be **made to lie down among the uncircumcised**, with all those who had perished by the Babylonian **sword**. While it may seem strange that Babylon herself is not named among those nations who had been (or would be) brought down, the exiles would know from other prophetic messages (such as Is. 46:1, 2; Jer. 50:1–3) that Babylon's day was coming as well. Habakkuk clearly predicted the fall of Babylon. She would not escape God's wrath.

EGYPT	JUDAH	ASSYRIA
		612 B.C. Nineveh captured and empire fell
	608–605 B.C. A vassal of Egypt	
		BABYLONIA
605 B.C. Battle of Carchemish: Neco routed by Babylon	605 B.C. First deportation to exile	605 B.C. Battle of Carchemish: Neco routed and Assyria extinguished by Babylon
	605–601 B.C. Gave tribute to Babylon	
589(8)–570(69) B.C. Hophra reigned		
	588 B.C. Babylon began siege of Jerusalem	
	587(6) B.C. Jerusalem destroyed	
		539 B.C. Persians conquered Babylon
	538 B.C. People in exile returned to Judah	
525 B.C. Persians conquered Egypt		

The Fall of Egypt and Other Events

FOR FURTHER STUDY: "SHEOL," THE REALM OF THE DEAD

The word "Sheol" (שְׁאוֹל, *sheʾol*) occurs sixty-seven times in the Old Testament, five times in Ezekiel (31:15–17; 32:21, 27). This word signifies a dark[2] "realm of the dead,"[3] located beneath the earth (Gen. 37:35; 42:38; Job 26:5; Is. 14:11, 15; Ezek. 31:15). While several passages connect Sheol and the grave, the two are not always synonymous. A person was said to go to Sheol at death. "Sheol is the Old Testament manner of asserting that death does not terminate human existence."[4] To render "Sheol" in Greek, the LXX translators always used "Hades" (ᾅδης, *hadēs*). This word is found only ten times in the Greek New Testament. It comes from ἰδεῖν (*idein*) ("to see") and means "the unseen realm."[5] A study of the words "Sheol" and "Hades" results in the following observations:

(1) *Sheol, or Hades, is a place where all go, whether they have been righteous or unrighteous.* It is the "house of meeting for all living" (Job 30:23), a place that never says, "Enough" (Prov. 30:15, 16). Wicked Korah and his followers were swallowed by the earth and sent to Sheol (Num. 16:30–33). God sent the evil pharaoh and his Egyptian people "down to Sheol" (Ezek. 31:15), yet the righteous Jacob recognized that he also would go down to Sheol (Gen. 37:35). The psalmist said concerning the wicked, ". . . they are appointed for Sheol" and "their form shall be for Sheol to consume" (Ps. 49:14). Psalm 16:10 says, "For You will not abandon my soul to Sheol; nor will You allow Your Holy One to undergo decay." While perhaps seeing an application for himself, the psalmist was also making a prophecy that would later be applied to the resurrection of Christ (Acts 2:27, 31), indicating that Jesus Himself went to Sheol when He died.

---

[2] See Job 10:21, 22.
[3] Joachim Jeremias, "Hades," in *Theological Dictionary of the New Testament*, ed. Gerhard Kittel, trans. Geoffrey W. Bromiley (Grand Rapids, Mich.: Wm. B. Eerdmans Publishing Co., 1964), 1:146.
[4] George Eldon Ladd, *A Theology of the New Testament* (Grand Rapids, Mich.: Wm. B. Eerdmans Publishing Co., 1974; reprint, 1989), 194.
[5] Jack P. Lewis, "The Intermediate State of the Dead," in *Exegesis of Difficult Passages* (Searcy, Ark.: Resource Publications, 1988), 182.

(2) *It is a place of consciousness.* In perhaps the clearest passage illustrating what happens after death, the rich man of Luke 16 is shown to be aware of his own pain, the presence of Lazarus and Abraham, and a memory of his brothers. David knew that even in Sheol he would recognize the presence of God (Ps. 139:8). In Revelation 6:9–11, the "souls under the altar" who had been martyred for the gospel were aware that their blood had not been avenged. Ezekiel 32:21 indicates that Pharaoh and the Egyptians would be recognized by other powerful nations that preceded them to Sheol.

(3) *Its inhabitants are no longer aware of earthly events.* Solomon stated that "the dead do not know anything, . . . for their memory is forgotten" (Eccles. 9:5). While the dead will remember circumstances on the earth (see Lk. 16:27, 28), they will have no knowledge of events that have taken place there since they died.

(4) *It is a place where there are no longer opportunities to change one's eternal destiny.* Those in Sheol cannot praise God (Is. 38:18; Ps. 6:5; 30:9; 88:10–12; 115:17) or hope to change their eternal destiny. Solomon perhaps gave the best overall description of Sheol: "Whatever your hand finds to do, do it with all your might; for there is no activity or planning or knowledge or wisdom in Sheol where you are going" (Eccles. 9:10). Although the rich man in Luke 16 realized that he could do nothing to bring either comfort or a change of location, Ezekiel 32 says that Pharaoh would "be comforted" in Sheol when he saw that he was not alone in this place of the slain (v. 31).

(5) *It is a place of no return.* Job observed that "he who goes down to Sheol does not come up. He will not return again to his house . . ." (Job 7:9, 10; see 10:21; 16:22; 20:9). Once a person dies, he cannot return to earth as himself, as someone else, or even as an animal or insect. Hebrews 9:27 affirms that after death every person will face the judgment. According to 1 Thessalonians 4:13–17, the dead rest (are "asleep") until Jesus comes.

APPLICATION

The Need for Humility

The fall of Egypt came because she was puffed up with pride (32:12). This should serve as a continual reminder to people today that God will humble those who are filled with pride. It is better to "humble yourselves under the mighty hand of God" (1 Pet. 5:6).

In Sheol there were many nations—an impressive list, all brought down by God. In hell, there will be an impressive list of men and women who were made heroes and were widely admired by others. However, in God's eyes, they were evil and corrupt; therefore, they must face His wrath. Indeed, the "great and the small" will appear before His judgment seat (Rev. 20:11–14). We should re-evaluate our views of people and try to see them as God sees them.

D.P.

PART III

THE PROPHECY OF ISRAEL'S RESTORATION—THE RETURN OF THE GLORY OF THE LORD (33—48)

1. The Fall of Jerusalem and the Promised Restoration of Israel (33—37)
2. Gog of Magog Defeated and God's People Delivered (38; 39)
3. The New Temple and God's Kingdom (40—48)

An Overview of Ezekiel 33—39
Six Messages from God

Using the prophetic formula "Then the word of the LORD came to me saying," Ezekiel delivered six messages from God in 33:23—39:29, beginning on the night before the refugees arrived in Babylon with the news of Jerusalem's destruction:

(1) God described the state of those remaining in Judah. He also talked about Ezekiel's reputation as a spokesman for God from this point forward (33:23–33).

(2) God had Ezekiel pronounce judgment against Judah's evil leaders, whose unrighteous leadership had brought about the destruction. This was followed by a divine proclamation that God Himself would be their Shepherd, and that He would personally select a leader (the Messiah) worthy to lead His people (34:1–31).

(3) The children of Israel were naturally curious about the state of the holy land, especially since their enemies, the Edomites, had moved into the land. God declared that He would permanently remove the Edomites (35:1—36:15).

(4) God described the need for a complete makeover of Israel, with divine cleansing, a new heart, and a rebuilding (36:16—37:14).

(5) Ezekiel presented a visual aid: He was told by God to put two sticks together—representing the northern kingdom (Israel) and the southern kingdom (Judah). This prophecy announced a time when Israel would have one king and be reunited as one nation (37:15–28).

(6) The last message contains seven distinct oracles, each marked by the opening phrase "Thus says the Lord." Continu-

ing the theme of the previous five messages, the sixth one describes how God would care for His people. This prophecy, simply stated, tells about an enemy called "Gog," who was forming a massive army to attack the exiles who had been restored to their land. However, God would intervene, defeating these enemies in a great slaughter. Then God's people would be able to live in peace and security (38:1—39:29).

APPLICATION

The Message for Us

The focus of Ezekiel 33—39 is God's desire for His people to return to the safe place He had prepared for them and to be faithful to His will. His desire for us is the same, even though the plan is different. What is God's plan for His people today? Like Israel, we have been separated from God by sin (Rom. 3:23); but He has prepared for us a safe place—Christ's body, the church. We can be saved (added to the church) by believing (Mk. 16:16), repenting (Acts 3:19), confessing our faith in Christ as God's Son and our risen Savior (Rom. 10:9), and being baptized for the forgiveness of our sins (Acts 2:38).

E.C.

Chapter 33

The Watchman and News Of the Fall of Jerusalem

In the first twenty-four chapters of his prophecy, Ezekiel had the difficult job of predicting the destruction of his beloved city and the exile of his people. After a brief excursion (chs. 25—32), which detailed the destruction of several foreign nations, God had Ezekiel to devote his attention to his own people. What did the future hold for them? Now that Jerusalem had been destroyed, what did God have planned for them, if anything? Since Ezekiel's earlier predictions had come true, the exiles would now have been listening to him with greater interest and respect.

Chapter 33 first lays a foundation that echoes some of Ezekiel's earlier messages: the duties of the watchman (vv. 1–9; see 3:16–21) and the importance of individual responsibility (vv. 10–20; see 18:21–29). These two sections are followed with the devastating news from the refugees from Jerusalem. Their message was clear: "The city has been taken" (v. 21). This message offered powerful confirmation to what Ezekiel had stated in 24:1, 2. These refugees then heard a word from the Lord through Ezekiel's mouth (vv. 22–29). This was followed by the Lord's telling Ezekiel that, by virtue of his true prophecies, he would become a popular prophet with the people (vv. 30–33).

The prophet was given the great task of reintroducing the people to God. They had to go through a process of learning about Him all over again. They had woefully miscalculated what He would do—and not do—in regard to their nation and their city. Therefore, Ezekiel assumed, once again, his position of watchman. As watchman, he warned the people not to be guilty of the sin of blaming others for what had happened. It was time to look at their own hearts, time to establish a deep-seated faith and reliance in their God. Only then would all the blessings that God had in store for them become reality.

THE WATCHMAN'S DUTIES RESTATED (33:1–20)

The Watchman's Duties (33:1–9)

33:1–6

¹And the word of the LORD came to me, saying, ²"Son of man, speak to the sons of your people and say to them, 'If I bring a sword upon a land, and the people of the land take one man from among them and make him their watchman, ³and he sees the sword coming upon the land and blows on the trumpet and warns the people, ⁴then he who hears the sound of the trumpet and does not take warning, and a sword comes and takes him away, his blood will be on his own head. ⁵He heard the sound of the trumpet but did not take warning; his blood will be on himself. But had he taken warning, he would have delivered his life. ⁶But if the watchman sees the sword coming and does not blow the trumpet and the people are not warned, and a sword comes and takes a person from them, he is taken away in his iniquity; but his blood I will require from the watchman's hand.'"

Verses 1–3. The people were fearful of **a sword** coming upon the land (compare 33:1–3 with 3:16–21). In order that they might be prepared when an attack was imminent, they relied upon a designated **watchman** to warn them. This watchman had one primary qualification: to be vigilant. He could not be lax on the job; the people were counting on him. From a spiritual standpoint, Ezekiel was the designated watchman for the people of God. In his first example, the prophet faithfully fulfilled his duty. He saw the "sword" coming upon the land and alerted the people. Ezekiel had blown the trumpet; he had warned the people of the approaching sword—that is, the Babylonians.

Verses 4, 5. A man might be foolish enough to ignore the warning of the watchman. Then, when the **sword** came and took him away, he would have no one to blame but himself. The people of Jerusalem ignored the warnings—and as a result they failed to prepare themselves for the invaders. Ezekiel was not talking collectively here as much as individually. Each person was responsible for his own reaction to the message. Any person could have **delivered his life** by heeding the warning.

Verse 6. In the earlier example, the watchman faithfully fulfilled his duty. This verse says that he saw the coming sword but, for unexplained reasons, did **not blow the trumpet**. Therefore, the people were not warned (by him), and **the sword** came and took them away. The reason for a person's being taken away was not the watchman's failure to warn, for each captive was **taken away in his iniquity**. One's judgment was not based upon the failure of others, but strictly upon his own sins. Nevertheless, the watchman would be held responsible for the **blood** of the people he had failed to warn. According to S. Fisch, "Though he was worthy of death on account of his sins, nevertheless the watchman who had failed in his duty is held guilty by God of that man's violent end."[1]

33:7–9

7"Now as for you, son of man, I have appointed you a watchman for the house of Israel; so you will hear a message from My mouth and give them warning from Me. ⁸When I say to the wicked, 'O wicked man, you will surely die,' and you do not speak to warn the wicked from his way, that wicked man shall die in his iniquity, but his blood I will require from your hand. ⁹But if you on your part warn a wicked man to turn from his way and he does not turn from his way, he will die in his iniquity, but you have delivered your life."

Verse 7. God reminded Ezekiel that he had been personally appointed by God to be **a watchman for the house of Israel**.

---

[1] S. Fisch, *Ezekiel: Hebrew Text and English Translation with an Introduction and Commentary*, Soncino Books of the Bible (London: Soncino Press, 1950), 222.

Their city had been destroyed, and they were in exile in Babylon, but they were still cared for by the Lord. Ezekiel was charged with taking the message from the **mouth** of God and **warning** the people. Jim McGuiggan explained,

> These verses are addressed to the prophet. He is about to enter into a new phase of his ministry. He is now known as a true prophet (i.e., when word filters through that the city has indeed fallen) but that doesn't mean he will be listened to by people whose hearts have radically changed. He will still have to speak some scalding words.[2]

Verse 8. God gave a message to **the wicked man**. He was to be told, **"You will surely die."** God intended for the one who chose a life of sin to know the consequences of that choice. It is possible for one to be so self-deluded, so self-deceived, that he does not think his sinful life will reap eternal consequences. That is why God sends His watchman to alert him to the truth. If Ezekiel failed to fulfill his duty and give God's message to the people, God would hold him responsible for his failure.

Verse 9. Ezekiel was not responsible for the way his listeners reacted to God's message. The person who rejected it would **die in his iniquity**. That would not affect the life of the watchman: God told him, **". . . you have delivered your life."**

The Importance of Individual Responsibility (33:10–20)

33:10

¹⁰"Now as for you, son of man, say to the house of Israel, 'Thus you have spoken, saying, "Surely our transgressions and our sins are upon us, and we are rotting away in them; how then can we survive?"'"

Verse 10. For the first time in this book, the exiles were ad-

---

[2]Jim McGuiggan, *The Book of Ezekiel*, Looking Into The Bible Series (Lubbock, Tex.: Montex Publishing Co., 1979), 279.

mitting their guilt. How could Ezekiel proceed with his ministry until the exiles faced the reality of their sinfulness? They were no longer claiming (as in 18:2) that they were suffering for their fathers' sins. The exiles admitted, **"Our transgressions and our sins are upon us."** They saw how they were **rotting away** because of their sins (see 4:17; 24:23; Lev. 26:39). The people began to ask, **"How then can we survive?"** They had come to realize that their sins were so bad that they had no hope of survival. Then Ezekiel's task was to demonstrate God's forgiving nature. Before people can be taught about His forgiveness, they must confess their own sinfulness. John B. Taylor wrote,

> They are neither to trust in their own righteousness nor to despair and with a fatalistic shrug of the shoulders to give in to their unhappy circumstances. Nor are they to take the easy way out by blaming all their misfortunes on the injustice of God. Every man has his chance and every man must act according to God's word to him. These are Ezekiel's terms of reference, and only when they have been clearly enunciated does the news break upon the waiting exiles that the city has fallen and Ezekiel's word has been proved true.[3]

33:11, 12

[11]"Say to them, 'As I live!' declares the Lord God, 'I take no pleasure in the death of the wicked, but rather that the wicked turn from his way and live. Turn back, turn back from your evil ways! Why then will you die, O house of Israel?' [12]And you, son of man, say to your fellow citizens, 'The righteousness of a righteous man will not deliver him in the day of his transgression, and as for the wickedness of the wicked, he will not stumble because of it in the day when he turns from his wickedness; whereas a righteous man will not be able to live by his righteousness on the day when he commits sin.'"

---

[3]John B. Taylor, *Ezekiel: An Introduction and Commentary*, Tyndale Old Testament Commentaries (Downers Grove, Ill.: Inter-Varsity Press, 1969), 213–14.

Verse 11. "**I take no pleasure in the death of the wicked,**" God said. Our God is not a vindictive God who finds "pleasure" in seeing wicked people die. Genuine sadness fills His heart when that day of death comes—because it seals that person's fate for eternity. His loving preference is that **the wicked turn from his way and live.** God wants all men to be saved. Therefore, He offers the urgent appeal to **turn back, turn back.** As long as there is life, there is hope of repentance.

God asked, "**Why then will you die, O house of Israel?**" This is a powerful question with several possible answers. An exile might believe that he would not die, no matter how he lived, because of being an "Israelite" (a descendant of Abraham; see Jn. 8:33–44; Mt. 3:9). Hearing mixed messages from other (false) prophets led many to believe that they did not need to do anything. Perhaps others had excuses that are still common. Why would anyone today choose death instead of repentance? Some believe that they have plenty of time to repent—that there is no urgency (Heb. 3:13; 2 Cor. 6:1, 2). Others, seeing the wicked prosper, doubt that their behavior will bring consequences (Eccles. 8:11; Ps. 73; see Jn. 5:28, 29). While some think that their former righteous deeds will atone for their sins (v. 12), others are stubborn and rebellious, refusing to change no matter what the consequences may be. Still others believe that they are hopelessly lost and that it would do them no good to repent.

Verse 12. Two scenarios are given in verse 12. From a negative perspective, the righteous deeds of a man who returns to sin **will not deliver him.** Despite teachings to the contrary, it is possible for a person, once saved, to become lost. If he enters into **transgression,** his former saved condition will be of no benefit to him. This passage teaches the possibility of apostasy. On a positive note, the wicked man who turns from his wickedness **will not stumble because of it.** God's grace is extended to him; he is forgiven of past sins and will suffer no consequences for his previous wicked choices. The very **day** he repents is the day God saves him.

33:13–16

¹³"When I say to the righteous he will surely live, and he so trusts in his righteousness that he commits iniquity, none of his righteous deeds will be remembered; but in that same iniquity of his which he has committed he will die. ¹⁴But when I say to the wicked, 'You will surely die,' and he turns from his sin and practices justice and righteousness, ¹⁵if a wicked man restores a pledge, pays back what he has taken by robbery, walks by the statutes which ensure life without committing iniquity, he shall surely live; he shall not die. ¹⁶None of his sins that he has committed will be remembered against him. He has practiced justice and righteousness; he shall surely live."

Verse 13. Complacency and indifference can affect a **righteous** man. Once this man heard God say of him, "**. . . he will surely live,**" he made the foolish mistake of trusting in his own **righteousness.** In his vanity, he sinned. God then declared that **none** of his previous righteous acts would be remembered. All was lost on the day he entered into sin. A. B. Davidson wrote,

> His purpose is to teach also the general truth that the past of one's life does not of necessity determine the future either in itself or in the judgment of God. This, next to the assurance of God's gracious will regarding men (*v.* 11), was the truth most needed to comfort the people and awaken them out of the stupor which lay on them into a moral life and activity again.[4]

Verses 14–16. The positive side of how God deals with mankind is discussed. In this scenario, **a wicked man** listened to the warning and determined to change his life's direction. Ezekiel illustrated six positive steps—the fruits of repentance (see Lk. 3:8)—in a person's life:

---

[4] A. B. Davidson, *The Book of the Prophet Ezekiel: With Notes and Introduction* (Cambridge: Cambridge University Press, 1892), 242.

1. **Turns from his sin** (v. 14)—He honors God's law and avoids acts condemned by God.
2. **Practices justice** (v. 14)—He treats others with respect. His word is true, and he treats other people with honor and integrity.
3. **[Practices] righteousness** (v. 14)—He obeys all of God's laws; he does not pick and choose (Mt. 5:20; 6:33; 23:23).
4. **Restores a pledge** (v. 15)—He determines to honor his previous promises and commitments.
5. **Pays back what he has taken by robbery** (v. 15)—Righteousness demands that he amend the wrongs he has committed. This involves going to anyone from whom he has stolen, admitting his thievery, and making restitution according to the law.
6. **Walks by the statutes which ensure life** (v. 15)—By devoting himself to God's laws, he is ensured "life," on the condition that he stops **committing iniquity**. God expects faithfulness; He does not want followers who drift back and forth between obedience and disobedience.

33:17–20

¹⁷"Yet your fellow citizens say, 'The way of the Lord is not right,' when it is their own way that is not right. ¹⁸When the righteous turns from his righteousness and commits iniquity, then he shall die in it. ¹⁹But when the wicked turns from his wickedness and practices justice and righteousness, he will live by them. ²⁰Yet you say, 'The way of the Lord is not right.' O house of Israel, I will judge each of you according to his ways."

Verse 17. The people were saying, **"The way of the Lord is not right."** They had earlier charged that "the way of the Lord" was at fault (see 18:25–30); but now God showed them that, instead, they were the ones who were not doing "right." As discussed in chapter 18, the people disagreed with God's judgment. They believed He was unfair to forget the righteous deeds of one who turned from righteousness and to overlook sins committed by one who repented. They had considered themselves to be paying the price for others' sins—but now they were finding out that God does not hold one person responsible for the sins of another.

Verses 18, 19. God repeated the basic premise of His judgment. The concept of individual responsibility is clear, as is the necessity of continued faithfulness. (Notice the word **practices**; 1 Jn. 3:8–10.)

Verse 20. Even in the midst of God's announcement of how He judges, the people continued to argue that His **way ... is not right**. They were not interested in truth; they wanted to blame their condition on others or on the way the Lord dealt with them. God clarified His approach: **"I will judge each of you according to his ways."** If the exiles, individually, turned from sin, they would live. This concluded God's appeal; He would offer no more warnings.

EZEKIEL'S REPUTATION ESTABLISHED BY THE REPORT OF THE FALL OF JERSUALEM (33:21–33)

33:21, 22

²¹Now in the twelfth year of our exile, on the fifth of the tenth month, the refugees from Jerusalem came to me, saying, "The city has been taken." ²²Now the hand of the LORD had been upon me in the evening, before the refugees came. And He opened my mouth at the time they came to me in the morning; so my mouth was opened and I was no longer speechless.

Verse 21. The date given here (January 585 B.C.) was a full eighteen months after Jerusalem had been taken. That date seems unlikely because it would not have taken **the refugees from Jerusalem** so long to travel to Babylon. Ezra and his companions arrived in only four months (Ezra 7:9), which would have been a normal amount of time to make this journey in Old Testament times. Therefore, most scholars adjust the wording to read the "eleventh year" (following some manuscripts and the Syriac version of the Bible). "This is much more likely, especially as the two words differ only by one consonant in written Hebrew and hardly at all in speech."[5] If the amended date is correct, it would mean that the escapees took six months to reach the exiles in Babylon.[6]

When the refugees arrived, they had one major message: **The city has been taken.** When Nebuchadnezzar laid siege to the city (see 24:1, 2), his armies took eighteen months to make a breach in the wall and capture the city. Once that happened, the refugees escaped and began the journey to Babylon.

Verse 22. Ezekiel had prepared the people for the news of Jerusalem's fall; but until **the refugees** confirmed its happening, it was difficult for them to believe. In addition, God had imposed a silence on Ezekiel that was to last until the arrival of the refugees (24:25–27). Now that the day had arrived, Ezekiel could engage in the normal work of a prophet, speaking freely and publicly the messages from God (33:22). He no longer had to work from his home (3:24–27). Ezekiel's first public prophecies after this included God's message for those left in Judah (vv. 23–29) and God's message for the exiles (vv. 30–33).

33:23–29

[23]Then the word of the LORD came to me saying, [24]"Son of man, they who live in these waste places in the land of Israel are saying, 'Abraham was only one, yet he possessed the land; so to us who are many the land has been given as a possession.' [25]Therefore say to them, 'Thus says the Lord GOD, "You eat meat with the blood in it, lift up your eyes to your idols as you shed blood. Should you then possess the land? [26]You rely on your sword, you commit abominations and each of you defiles

---

[5]Taylor, 216.

[6]Several other explanations were presented by S. Fisch, who concluded, "There is thus a dual system of reckoning: one which regards the year as a series of months beginning with Nisan in the spring, the other regarding the year as a period beginning in the autumn on the first day of the seventh month. Accordingly, the interval between the fourth month in the eleventh year (586) and the tenth month in the twelfth year (585) is only six months" (Fisch, 225).

his neighbor's wife. Should you then possess the land?"' ²⁷Thus you shall say to them, 'Thus says the Lord GOD, "As I live, surely those who are in the waste places will fall by the sword, and whoever is in the open field I will give to the beasts to be devoured, and those who are in the strongholds and in the caves will die of pestilence. ²⁸I will make the land a desolation and a waste, and the pride of her power will cease; and the mountains of Israel will be desolate so that no one will pass through. ²⁹Then they will know that I am the LORD, when I make the land a desolation and a waste because of all their abominations which they have committed."'"

Verses 23, 24. The poorest of the land, whom Nebuchadnezzar had allowed to remain, had developed a false view of themselves. Their theology was expressed in one sentence: **Abraham was only one, yet he possessed the land** (v. 24). Since God had given the entire land to one righteous man, they assumed that He was now giving it to **us who are many**. In their arrogance, they had failed to comprehend Jeremiah's message. He had prophesied not only the reason for the defeat, but also why these few would be allowed to remain in the land (to be "vinedressers and plowmen"; Jer. 52:16). He had told them that they were not God's choice; God's remnant would come from among the exiles. However, as a result of their faulty view of themselves, they began annexing property left by those exiled or killed. They considered themselves the new heirs of the land.[7] They viewed the exiles as wicked and likened themselves to "Abraham," their righteous forefather whom God had blessed.

Verses 25, 26. Ezekiel established that these few were far from righteous. He listed their offenses; and after each group, he asked, **"Should you then possess the land?"** These people engaged in a variety of sins, from eating unclean meats to idolatry to adultery. They were the ones to whom Jeremiah was prophesying. The poor were as involved in wickedness as were the wealthy and powerful.

---

[7]They were basically imitating what the remnant had done after the second deportation in 598(7) B.C. (see Ezek. 11:15).

Verse 27. Those . . . in the waste places (the land of Israel) would not enjoy the land for themselves. Instead, God planned to bring death upon those arrogant few, by a variety of methods: **sword, beasts,** and **pestilence.**

Verses 28, 29. Rather than allowing these people to possess **the land,** God determined to make it **a desolation and a waste** (v. 28). The land, **the pride of** [Israel's] **power** was to be taken away. When this happened, the people would learn a very important lesson: **Then they will know that I am the LORD** (v. 29).

33:30–33

³⁰"**But as for you, son of man, your fellow citizens who talk about you by the walls and in the doorways of the houses, speak to one another, each to his brother, saying, 'Come now and hear what the message is which comes forth from the LORD.' ³¹They come to you as people come, and sit before you as My people and hear your words, but they do not do them, for they do the lustful desires expressed by their mouth, and their heart goes after their gain. ³²Behold, you are to them like a sensual song by one who has a beautiful voice and plays well on an instrument; for they hear your words but they do not practice them. ³³So when it comes to pass—as surely it will—then they will know that a prophet has been in their midst."**

Verses 30, 31. Ezekiel was the subject of much conversation among the exiles. His accurate predictions had established his reputation as a true prophet among them, and they began inviting others to go and sit at his feet. However, the people were not sincere in listening to his messages. They would **hear** Ezekiel's words but **not do them.** Instead, the people were following their own **lustful desires.** They were bold in their desires; **their heart** was longing for more wealth, and **their mouth** talked openly about it.

Verses 32, 33. Ezekiel was an excellent speaker, and the people appreciated his gift (v. 32); but they did not listen sincerely. They would compliment the preacher on his good sermon but then ignore everything that he had said. Ezekiel would have his ultimate vindication, however, when his words had [come] **to pass** (v. 33).

APPLICATION

Preaching, Hearing, and Obeying the Truth

The watchman's responsibility is to be alert and warn of coming dangers. God appoints Christians as His watchmen today. We are to warn the ungodly (Gal. 6:1; 1 Tim. 4:16; Jas. 5:19, 20). This is especially the task of elders (Tit. 1:9; 1 Pet. 5:1–5; Heb. 13:17).

Each person is responsible for his or her own soul. God provides warnings of the coming judgment, and we must listen (Rom. 10:17). We are to "pay close attention to [ourselves]" (1 Tim. 4:16), and "test [ourselves] to see if [we] are in the faith" (2 Cor. 13:5).

One may become so self-deceived that he does not think he will suffer the consequences of his sins. God wants all to know that sin has eternal consequences (Rom. 6:23).

God does not hold preachers or teachers responsible for people who refuse to listen to and obey the message (as long as the preacher preaches the truth). Each person who hears the Word must respond to it. People must not listen to ear-tickling preachers (2 Tim. 4:2–4).

God disciplines us to encourage us to repent. He does not want anyone to perish, but desires for all to come to salvation (Ezek. 33:11; 1 Tim. 2:4; 2 Pet. 3:9). Fisch said, "Unlike man who punishes his enemy for the sake of revenge, God's purpose in chastening the wicked is to move them to penitence and so escape the full consequences of their guilt."[8]

Recognizing one's sinfulness and confessing that sinfulness are necessary steps toward renewal and forgiveness (see 1 Jn. 1:8–10).

The people who were left in the land considered themselves righteous and the exiles wicked (Ezek. 33:24). Comparing our-

---

[8] Fisch, 223.

selves to others is dangerous. God does not save or condemn a person based on how he compares to others, but on how that individual obeys His Word.

Good sermons are great, and polished orators are nice. However, God expects the listener to respond to His message when it is preached (2 Tim. 4:3, 4; Jas. 1:22–25).

D.P.

How Does One Repent? (33:13–16)

Ezekiel urged the people to repent. His message to them is a good example of how one goes about repenting:

First, he puts away his sin. Repentance is deciding to turn from sin and forsaking it.

Second, he begins to treat others right. True repentance issues forth in our treating others the way a righteous person should.

Third, he submits to the will of God. Real repentance is not just the negative aspect of turning *away*. It also has a positive thrust, seen in one's commitment to walk in the light of God's Word.

E.C.

Chapter 34

The Return of Israel To Their Own Land: The Good Shepherd

In the Scriptures, leaders are frequently referred to as "shepherds," a term providing a comprehensive description of what leaders are and what they do. God is the ultimate "shepherd" of His people (Ps. 23; see Gen. 48:15). Cyrus, Moses, David, Jesus, and elders of the church are all referred to as shepherds. (See Is. 44:28; 63:11; 2 Sam. 5:2; Jn. 10:11; Acts 20:28; 1 Pet. 5:1–3.)

While many leaders of God's people were shepherds, they were not necessarily good ones. God entrusted them with His flock. Those who took their responsibility lightly brought harm upon the people of God. Their failures resulted in the Exile and the destruction of their beloved city, Jerusalem.

To demonstrate the importance of good leadership, Ezekiel made a vivid comparison between the bad shepherds of the past and God, who would become their Shepherd. God planned to gather the flock, which had been scattered among the nations, and lead them back to Israel. Under His leadership, they would enjoy peace and security. He also promised to appoint for them a new Shepherd, One who would be faithful to His calling.

THE TRUE SHEPHERD, THE FALSE SHEPHERDS, AND THE FLOCK OF GOD (34:1–24)

The Evil Shepherds (34:1–10)

34:1–3

¹Then the word of the Lord came to me saying, ²"Son of

man, prophesy against the shepherds of Israel. Prophesy and say to those shepherds, 'Thus says the Lord GOD, "Woe, shepherds of Israel who have been feeding themselves! Should not the shepherds feed the flock? ³You eat the fat and clothe yourselves with the wool, you slaughter the fat sheep without feeding the flock."'"

Verses 1, 2. Ezekiel was commissioned to **prophesy against** the kings of Israel, to issue a **woe** against them. These evil shepherds were so busy caring for their own needs that they completely neglected the needs of the sheep. Leaders were called upon to give the people spiritual direction that would keep them strong as God's people. They should have frequently and openly exalted the law of the Lord before the people.

Verse 3. God made four charges against the shepherds, the kings of Israel:

1. **"You eat the fat,"** instead of providing the best for the people.
2. **"You . . . clothe yourselves with the wool,"** instead of providing for the sheep.
3. **"You slaughter the fat sheep"** in times of prosperity.
4. "You [do all this] **without feeding the flock."** Even in their corruption, these leaders could have fed the flock by providing some positive direction, but the kings of Israel did not.

34:4–6
⁴"'"Those who are sickly you have not strengthened, the diseased you have not healed, the broken you have not bound up, the scattered you have not brought back, nor have you sought for the lost; but with force and with severity you have dominated them. ⁵They were scattered for lack of a shepherd, and they became food for every beast of the field and were scattered. ⁶My flock wandered through all the mountains and on every high hill; My flock was scattered over all the surface of the earth, and there was no one to search or seek for them."'"

Verse 4. Condemnation of the shepherds is found in the words "you have not....": **Those who are sickly you have not strengthened, the diseased you have not healed, the broken you have not bound up, the scattered you have not brought back, nor have you sought for the lost.** This is followed by a powerful description of what they *had* done: **With force and with severity you have dominated them.**

The leaders had failed to care for the downtrodden, poor, oppressed, widows, and orphans—the people of society who need those of power and position to come to their aid. Instead, the leaders furthered the oppression. These evil shepherds were selfish, compassionless, merciless, and cruel.

Verses 5, 6. God's people were **scattered** throughout the nations as a result of poor leadership. They became easy prey to **every beast of the field** (v. 5), the cruel nations. The repetition of the phrase **My flock** (v. 6) demonstrates how the leadership had failed—not with their own possession, but with the possession of the Lord.

34:7–10

⁷Therefore, you shepherds, hear the word of the Lord: ⁸"As I live," declares the Lord God, "surely because My flock has become a prey, My flock has even become food for all the beasts of the field for lack of a shepherd, and My shepherds did not search for My flock, but rather the shepherds fed themselves and did not feed My flock; ⁹therefore, you shepherds, hear the word of the Lord: ¹⁰'Thus says the Lord God, "Behold, I am against the shepherds, and I will demand My sheep from them and make them cease from feeding sheep. So the shepherds will not feed themselves anymore, but I will deliver My flock from their mouth, so that they will not be food for them."'"

Verses 7–10. As established in Daniel 4:17, 25 (see Rom. 13:1–4), these rulers had been given their authority by God, who called them **My shepherds** (v. 8). They had failed in their divine commission; therefore, God was **against the shepherds** (v. 10). His opposition would bring three results. First, God would **demand**

[His] **sheep from them**. These evil leaders had forfeited their right to lead. Second, He would **make them cease from feeding sheep**. As noted earlier, they were not really feeding the sheep anyway. If they were feeding the sheep anything, it was cruelty and oppression. Third, He would **deliver** [His] **flock from their mouth**. Before the nation was consumed, God would snatch them from the mouths of the evil rulers. This suggests that their rule would come to an end.

The Concerned Shepherd (34:11–16)

¹¹**For thus says the Lord God, "Behold, I Myself will search for My sheep and seek them out.** ¹²**As a shepherd cares for his herd in the day when he is among his scattered sheep, so I will care for My sheep and will deliver them from all the places to which they were scattered on a cloudy and gloomy day.** ¹³**I will bring them out from the peoples and gather them from the countries and bring them to their own land; and I will feed them on the mountains of Israel, by the streams, and in all the inhabited places of the land.** ¹⁴**I will feed them in a good pasture, and their grazing ground will be on the mountain heights of Israel. There they will lie down on good grazing ground and feed in rich pasture on the mountains of Israel.** ¹⁵**I will feed My flock and I will lead them to rest," declares the Lord God.** ¹⁶**"I will seek the lost, bring back the scattered, bind up the broken and strengthen the sick; but the fat and the strong I will destroy. I will feed them with judgment."**

Verse 11. Next, God said, **"I Myself will search for My sheep and seek them out."** God, as the Chief Shepherd and Guardian of men's souls (see 1 Pet. 2:25; 5:4), was determined to "search" for His sheep. He Himself would do the job that He had entrusted others to do. John B. Taylor further elaborated on the use of this imagery:

> The picture of the shepherd searching out the wanderer, in verse 12, is a remarkable foreshadowing of the parable

of the lost sheep (Lk. 15:4ff.), which our Lord doubtless based on this passage in Ezekiel. It illustrates as clearly as anything can do the tender, loving qualities of the God of the Old Testament, and strikes a death-blow at those who try to drive a wedge between Yahweh, God of Israel, and the God and Father of our Lord Jesus Christ. Nor is it the only passage that speaks of the tender shepherd (*cf.* Pss. 78:52f.; 79:13; 80:1; Is. 40:11; 49:9f.; Je. 31:10).[1]

Verses 12, 13. What would a good shepherd do upon realizing that his herd had been **scattered** (v. 12)? The key word here is **care**. The rulers of Israel did not care for the people. God did, and He promised to do something about their problems. The action of the verbs in verses 12 and 13 vividly illustrate what God said He would do:

1. **"I will care for My sheep."**
2. **"I will ... deliver them."**
3. **"I will bring them out."** They would no longer be among **peoples** foreign to them—strangers who practiced idolatry, contrary to God's will.
4. **"I will ... gather them."** He would deliver them from these **countries** where they did not belong.
5. **"I will ... bring them to their own land."** God intended for them to dwell in the land they had once inhabited. They had lost their land because of their unfaithfulness; but, because of His mercy, God would allow them to return.
6. **"I will feed them."** He would provide "green pastures" and "quiet waters" to make the sheep thrive (see Ps. 23:1, 2).

Verses 14, 15. In words reminiscent of Psalm 23, God said that He would feed His people and bring them to **good grazing**

---

[1] John B. Taylor, *Ezekiel: An Introduction and Commentary*, Tyndale Old Testament Commentaries (Downers Grove, Ill.: Inter-Varsity Press, 1969), 220–21.

ground and allow them to **feed in rich pasture** (v. 14). This would not be in the land of Babylon or Assyria, but **on the mountain heights of Israel**. He vowed to lead His flock to **rest** (v. 15).

Verse 16. God promised to care for His people—to **seek, bring back, bind up,** and **strengthen** them. In stark contrast, He would punish those who had fattened themselves by feeding off of the people and who had gained power through oppression and injustice. Those who refused to be fair or kind to the people would encounter God's **judgment**.

The Good Shepherd
(34:17–24)

34:17–19
¹⁷"As for you, My flock, thus says the Lord GOD, 'Behold, I will judge between one sheep and another, between the rams and the male goats. ¹⁸Is it too slight a thing for you that you should feed in the good pasture, that you must tread down with your feet the rest of your pastures? Or that you should drink of the clear waters, that you must foul the rest with your feet? ¹⁹As for My flock, they must eat what you tread down with your feet and drink what you foul with your feet!'"

Verse 17. "I will judge between one sheep and another," the Lord continued. To this point, the judgment had been only against the kings, who were the bad shepherds. Certainly, many others shared the blame for Israel's unfaithfulness. Each "sheep" was to be judged individually, including **the rams and the male goats**. These represent the elite of the society, the rich and powerful, who were able to use their position to oppress others (thereby imitating the king under whom they served). Also included were dishonest merchants, as well as commoners who preyed upon the weak and helpless.

Verses 18, 19. Continuing His address to the ruling classes (and others who oppressed the people), God made two charges against them. They were guilty of (1) **feed**[ing] **in the good pasture**, greedily taking the best for themselves, and (2) **foul**[ing] **the rest with** [their] **feet**—that is, destroying everything that might have been valuable to anyone else. This amplifies the thoughtlessness, selfishness, and cruelty of the ruling classes. They simply did not care that they left nothing for others. Metaphorically speaking, they were leaving their tables, fully fed, and allowing the remains to spoil rather than giving anything to the starving masses.

34:20–24
²⁰Therefore, thus says the Lord God to them, "Behold, I, even I, will judge between the fat sheep and the lean sheep. ²¹Because you push with side and with shoulder, and thrust at all the weak with your horns until you have scattered them abroad, ²²therefore, I will deliver My flock, and they will no longer be a prey; and I will judge between one sheep and another.
²³"Then I will set over them one shepherd, My servant David, and he will feed them; he will feed them himself and be their shepherd. ²⁴And I, the Lord, will be their God, and My servant David will be prince among them; I the Lord have spoken."

Verses 20–22. God vowed to purge the flock of the evil sheep—the wicked leaders who had oppressed Israel for centuries and the wicked members of the nation. The terminology **I, even I, will judge** (v. 20) is emphatic in the Hebrew. Others, such as God's prophets, had judged these evil kings and people in the past. However, the prophets had been scorned or ignored, being nothing more than a mere irritation to these men of power. Since the leaders had not hearkened to the cries and warnings of God's prophets, they would have to deal with the Lord Himself. Such a thought is not a pleasant one. God does not view lightly the discarding of His messengers. The charges were clear: The leaders had oppressed and bullied the people to get their way (v. 21). Social injustice has always been a primary concern with God, and these leaders had strayed far from acceptable principles of integrity and decency. The Lord would deliver the people from oppression and judge their dealings with one another (v. 22).

Verse 23. The Shepherd is described as **My servant David**. There are several ways to interpret this designation, but the most reasonable explanation is that "My servant David" refers to Christ.[2]

What will the Shepherd do for the sheep, in contrast to the evil rulers?

1. **He will feed them.** Jesus was the "bread of life" (Jn. 6:35, 48). He fed the people His words, which came from heaven (Jn. 6:33). By partaking of (obeying) Jesus' words, one could live (Jn. 6:63). When Jesus departed, He sent the Holy Spirit upon the apostles, enabling them to "feed" the people the truth (Jn. 15:26; 16:13).
2. **He will feed them himself.** This is not an allusion to Jesus' flesh and His blood (Jn. 6:51–58). Rather, it means that the God-appointed shepherd would *personally* feed the people. Christ became flesh and dwelt among men to feed them the words of God (Jn. 1:14–18; see Is. 40:11; Jn. 21:15–17; Rev. 7:17).
3. "He will" . . . **be their shepherd.** He was to be their *true* shepherd. He would do everything that a shepherd is supposed to do. Jesus frequently wept, recognizing the people as sheep without a shepherd (Mt. 9:36; Mk. 6:34).

Verse 24. Next, a division of responsibilities is given. God would be **their God**; but His **servant David**, identified as the shepherd in verse 23, is now called the **prince**. Jesus was to be a ruler. Just as the kings of Israel were shepherds, so Jesus would be the Good Shepherd but would also be King. The New Testament identifies Jesus as King (Mt. 2:2; 27:42; 28:18; Jn. 1:49; 12:13; 18:36, 37; Rev. 1:5, 6).

One question remains: When was Jesus to fulfill this passage? It is a misapplication of this text to project it to some future period when Christ will serve as the messianic David-King

---

[2]See "My Servant David" in "For Further Study" at the end of this chapter.

in Jerusalem. The New Testament shows that Jesus was the Good Shepherd during His ministry in the flesh. He became King when His kingdom, the church, was established on the Day of Pentecost (Acts 2).

A COVENANT OF PEACE
(34:25–31)

^{25}"I will make a covenant of peace with them and eliminate harmful beasts from the land so that they may live securely in the wilderness and sleep in the woods. ^{26}I will make them and the places around My hill a blessing. And I will cause showers to come down in their season; they will be showers of blessing. ^{27}Also the tree of the field will yield its fruit and the earth will yield its increase, and they will be secure on their land. Then they will know that I am the LORD, when I have broken the bars of their yoke and have delivered them from the hand of those who enslaved them. ^{28}They will no longer be a prey to the nations, and the beasts of the earth will not devour them; but they will live securely, and no one will make them afraid. ^{29}I will establish for them a renowned planting place, and they will not again be victims of famine in the land, and they will not endure the insults of the nations anymore. ^{30}Then they will know that I, the LORD their God, am with them, and that they, the house of Israel, are My people," declares the Lord GOD. ^{31}"As for you, My sheep, the sheep of My pasture, you are men, and I am your God," declares the Lord GOD.

Verses 25–29. Under the direction of the wicked kings, the people knew only insecurity, poverty, and warfare. Ultimately, they lost what remained of their hope for peace when they were violently removed from their land and placed in a foreign land. God promised to make a new covenant, **a covenant of peace** (v. 25; see 37:26–28; 38:11–13; 39:25–29). Taylor explained,

> Relationships are frequently described in terms of covenant, and the phrase *covenant of peace* (25; *cf.* 37:26; Is. 54:10) means simply "a covenant that works". The

word *peace* is used to describe the harmony that exists when covenant obligations are being fulfilled and the relationship is sound. It is not a negative concept, implying absence of conflict or worry or noise, as we use it, but a thoroughly positive state in which all is functioning well. The area of safety promised to God's people includes both the *wilderness*, the uncultivated pastureland, and the *woods*, the scrubland which was usually a place of some danger by reason of wild beasts. But it was centred on Mount Zion (*my hill*, 26), as in most prophecies about the Messianic age.[3]

This covenant would provide peace in a number of ways. First, it would **eliminate harmful beasts**. Wild animals frequently attacked the people; they were a source of fear and a constant concern of parents (Lev. 26:6, 22). However, it is conceivable that this is not to be taken literally, but figuratively. The "beasts" could be the evil rulers who devoured the people (see Ezek. 34:3; 22:25, 27). By removing this danger, God would enable the people to **live securely**, even in areas previously viewed as extremely dangerous—**the wilderness** and **the woods**.

Second, God would send **showers of blessing** upon the land (v. 26). That land which was cursed because of their unfaithfulness would again be fruitful (v. 27; see Hos. 2:22; Joel 3:18; Amos 9:13, 14; Zech. 8:12). While some see in this a reference to the coming of the Holy Spirit, that is not what Ezekiel was referring to here. This is in the context of God's people enjoying His blessings under the leadership of the Shepherd. To insert the concept of the Holy Spirit would be a leap in the flow of this passage. Further, verse 27 was never referred to by any New Testament writer in the context of the giving of the Holy Spirit; nor is the giving of the Holy Spirit anywhere referred to in this way.

The third benefit is that God's people would **no longer be a prey to the nations** (v. 28). The history of Israel reveals how often they fell prey to other nations. Finally, they were

---

[3]Taylor, 223–24.

devour[ed] by the Assyrians (who conquered Israel in 722[1] B.C.) and the Babylonians (who conquered Judah in 587[6] B.C.).

The fourth benefit given is . . . **they will live securely**. God's covenant would provide security unlike anything the people had enjoyed for centuries. The threats of invasion, plague, and famine had undermined their ability to live securely. Such threats had made the people **afraid**, but God was about to remove the atmosphere of fear.

Fifth, He would **establish . . . a renowned planting place** (v. 29). The productivity of the land was to become world famous.

This would lead to the sixth blessing: **They will not again be victims of famine in the land** (see 36:29). Famines, which had ravaged the land and brought poverty and starvation, would no longer victimize the people.

Seventh, God's people would **not endure the insults of the nations anymore**. Ezekiel frequently mentioned how Israel had become a joke to the nations (25:6; 36:6, 15; see Ps. 74:10; 123:3, 4). This shame was about to end.

Verse 30. As Israel enjoyed all these blessings of the covenant of peace, she would have to acknowledge the hand of God in them. The people would realize that the Lord had been **their God** all along. They would begin to understand that, because of their sinfulness, He had to discipline them. Eventually, however, His love would be seen through restoration. God was going to prove that He was **with them** and that He still viewed **the house of Israel** as **My people**. While some literal, temporary promises may be seen in this "covenant of peace" (for example, the work of Zerubbabel, Ezra, and Nehemiah), that meaning is unlikely. Rather, it is better to view this section as continuing the discussion of the work and results of the God-appointed shepherd. This covenant is much the same as the one given in Jeremiah 31:31–34, promising that Jesus would provide peace, blessings, and security through the gospel (Heb. 8:6).

Verse 31. Of course, God was not really talking about **sheep** in this section, but about **men**. Still, the gentle, loving image of God's people as His sheep, **the sheep of My pasture**, presents a beautiful picture. What made these people special was being in His fold. The same is true today. Our value is not seen in what we have done or accumulated; rather, our worth is seen when we are conformed to the image of the Son of God (Rom. 8:29, 30).

This message of peace provides a foundation for the next five chapters (35—39), in which various threats to Israel's peace are addressed and eliminated, one by one:

> This announcement of the peace covenant provides a transition to the following messages delivered in this series of six oracles. Each of the next four speeches elaborates an aspect of the peace covenant. Ezekiel 35:1—36:15 describes how the foreign plundering nations would be removed and judged in preparation for Israel's return to her own land. The message in 36:16—37:14 provides a beautiful and descriptive account of God's restoration of Israel to her land. Ezekiel 37:15-28 stresses the full reunion of the nation and the fulfillment of her covenants when this peace covenant is established. Finally, Ezekiel 38—39 develops the concept of Israel's permanent and complete security in the Lord, for he would thwart the final attempt by a foreign power (Gog) to possess Israel's land and to plunder God's people.
>
> Israel could rejoice; for though she had experienced the cruel and incompetent leadership of recent rulers, she now was assured that God would provide perfect leadership through the Good Shepherd, the Messiah, who would care for her as a shepherd should. There was hope![4]

FOR FURTHER STUDY: "MY SERVANT DAVID"

Who is "My servant David" in 34:23? Here are some possibilities that have been suggested:

Is it David reincarnated? This cannot be the case. No biblical

---

[4]Ralph H. Alexander, "Ezekiel," in *The Expositor's Bible Commentary*, ed. Frank E. Gaebelein (Grand Rapids, Mich.: Zondervan Publishing House, 1986), 6:914.

passage even hints of a reincarnated David. Besides, the Bible teaches that the doctrine of reincarnation is false. Once men die, they face God in judgment. He does not return them to earth (Heb. 9:27).

Is it some unnamed, future ruler of Israel from the lineage of David? Again, this cannot be the case. The shepherd mentioned was to reign forever (Ezek. 37:24–28).

Could it be a concept rather than a literal person? This theory suggests that God was merely promising to bring back the peace and security enjoyed during the Davidic reign, not referring to a literal person. However, the text is pointing to a God-selected individual who would stand in contrast to the evil shepherds of old. He was to be everything they were not.

Is the reference to Christ? The reasons for adopting this position are many:

(1) The Messiah is frequently linked to David (Jer. 23:5, 6; 30:9; Ezek. 37:24, 25; Hos. 3:5; Mt. 1:1; 22:41–46).

(2) The Messiah linked to David is also called "the righteous branch." The "branch" terminology refers to Jesus (Is. 11:1–5; Zech. 6:12, 13; Rev. 22:16). Jeremiah called this branch "the LORD our righteousness" (Jer. 23:5, 6). The inspired writers never used Yahweh in reference to any man, but here it refers to Christ.

(3) Christ's reign is forever (Ezek. 37:24–28; Dan. 2:44; Ps. 110:4; Heb. 7:17; Rev. 1:5, 6).

(4) Jesus referred to Himself as "the good shepherd" (Jn. 10:14). His terminology is similar to that of this chapter. The God-appointed leader here is called a shepherd, and Jesus called Himself the shepherd. He saw Himself as the fulfillment of this passage.

(5) The text says that God would appoint "one" shepherd. No other single individual would fit this description. Micah 5:2–5, an obvious prophecy of Jesus, says, "He will arise and shepherd His flock . . ." (v. 4; see Mt. 2:6). Zechariah 13:7 reads, "Awake, O sword, against My Shepherd." Jesus applied this Scripture to Himself in Matthew 26:31 and Mark 14:27. Hebrews 13:20 says, "Now the God of peace . . . brought up from the dead the great Shepherd of the sheep. . . ." The New Testament is plain: The Shepherd is Jesus (1 Pet. 5:4).

APPLICATION

Strong Leadership Needed

The Lord places men in power, but He expects them to lead honorably. He will hold accountable those leaders who fail in their God-given responsibility.

Good leaders care for the whole flock, even with its varied problems and weaknesses. The church is full of people with assorted needs. Wise leaders address each and every one of those needs (see 1 Thess. 5:14).

God holds leaders responsible for people's souls. Elders, in particular, are shepherds of God's flock today (see Acts 20:28; Heb. 13:17). They are to watch over and care for the souls of the congregation.

This chapter depicts God as our Shepherd. He loves us, nurtures us, feeds us, and seeks the lost (see Lk. 19:10; Jn. 3:14–16; 1 Tim. 1:15). Still, it is our responsibility to respond to God's call (Is. 55:6; Mt. 7:7).

Jesus demonstrated the ultimate care in being our Good Shepherd: He was willing to lay down His life for the sheep (Jn. 10:15–18).

Shepherds of the Church (34:4)

By considering the responsibilities that the leaders of Israel neglected (v. 4), we can learn much about the work of elders, the shepherds of the Lord's church today:

- They strengthen the spiritually sick and take the Lord's healing teachings to those who are diseased with sin.
- They bind up and encourage the broken and discouraged.
- They seek those who have left the body of Christ and lovingly lead them back to the safety of the Lord's church.
- They are zealous in seeking the lost, recognizing the urgency of the situation.

D.P.

The Traits of a True Shepherd

Ezekiel was told to rebuke the shepherds (leaders) of the sheep (the people of Israel). Although Ezekiel was not talking about elders, the characteristics of a shepherd may also be applied to a good elder.

He puts his flock before himself. He does not live off the sheep; he lives for the sheep. If necessary, he will even lay down his life for the flock.

He acts with compassion toward those in trouble. When he sees a wounded lamb or sheep, he immediately cares for it. With tender compassion, he binds up its wounds and restores it to life.

He sees that the flock is properly fed. He keeps the flock from evil—not only by watching for wolves from without, but also by protecting it against tragedy from within.

He goes after those who have strayed. When he discovers that some have wandered away from the flock, he searches until they are found.

He sees himself as doing the work of God. God works through him. He is a steward, a superintendent for the Lord.

He recognizes his accountability to God. His responsibility is God-given, and he will answer to Him.

E.C.

Chapter 35

The Return of Israel To Their Own Land: Edom to Be Destroyed

A logical question to ask here is "Why was this section against Edom placed in chapter 35 instead of being with the other prophecies against Edom in 25:12–14?" The answer adopted by a number of commentators is that the section was misplaced in the text by some redactor. However, there are several reasons why this section belongs here.

First, Edom was viewed by the exiles as the number-one threat to a peaceful return to their land. After the people were exiled to Babylon, the Edomites were like vultures preying upon the land; they would be unlikely to give up that land peacefully upon the Israelites' return. Therefore, this section serves as a prelude to the discussion in the following chapters. Before Israel returned to their land, this primary enemy had to be addressed. (The Edomites may conceivably be the "harmful beasts" of 34:25; see 2 Chron. 28:17.) According to S. Fisch,

> After denouncing the evil shepherds of the past and promising ideal rulership as the first step along the path of restoration, Ezekiel proceeds to the next obstruction which must be removed if a restored Israel is to prosper. All the nations which oppressed Israel and retarded his progress must vanish from the stage of history. Edom, in particular, the archenemy of Israel, had forfeited his right to national existence, and his fall is an essential preliminary to Israel's final redemption and the universal recognition of God's Sovereignty. The prophet Obadiah proclaimed the same message with striking emphasis:

And saviours shall come up on mount Zion to judge the mount of Esau; and the kingdom shall be the Lord's (Obad. 21).[1]

Second, the fact that the Edomites were so quick to take advantage of Jerusalem's collapse became a relevant theme once that collapse had been announced to the exiles. They knew that the Edomites "lusted after their land" (35:10; see Ps. 83:1–18).

Third, a clear link exists between this section and 36:2. The "enemy" spoken of there is the same enemy discussed in chapter 35. Edom is even mentioned by name in 36:5. (Note the contrast between the mountains of Edom in 35:3 and the mountains of Judah in 36:9.)

The Edomites were the descendants of Esau, Jacob's older twin brother. As mentioned earlier in Ezekiel (see also Gen. 25:22–26), constant friction and open hostility existed between the two nations. The Edomites lived in the region south of the Dead Sea, including the city of Sela (modern-day Petra). The famous mountain range that graced that area, featuring Mount Seir, provided the terminology Ezekiel used to refer to Edom in this chapter. (Strangely, he did not use the word "Edom" at all.) Numerous biblical references are made to the Edomites; and one book, Obadiah, is devoted entirely to them.[2]

REMOVAL OF A THREAT TO PEACE: EDOM (35)

35:1–4
¹Moreover, the word of the Lord came to me saying, ²"Son of man, set your face against Mount Seir, and prophesy against it ³and say to it, 'Thus says the Lord God,

"Behold, I am against you, Mount Seir,
And I will stretch out My hand against you

---

[1] S. Fisch, *Ezekiel: Hebrew Text and English Translation with an Introduction and Commentary*, Soncino Books of the Bible (London: Soncino Press, 1950), 235.

[2] See Gen. 27:1–41; Num. 20:14–21; 2 Sam. 8:13, 14; 2 Kings 8:20–22; 14:7; 1 Chron. 18:12, 13; 2 Chron. 21:8; Ps. 137:7; Is. 34:5; Jer. 49:7–22; Lam. 4:21, 22; Amos 1:11, 12; Mal. 1:2–5.

And make you a desolation and a waste.
⁴I will lay waste your cities
And you will become a desolation.
Then you will know that I am the LORD."'"

Verses 1, 2. God commissioned Ezekiel to **set** [his] **face against Mount Seir.** This arrogant nation, which should have been a friend to Israel (since they were closely related nations), was about to receive God's prophecy against her.

Verses 3, 4. The exiles might mistakenly believe that God was against them and for Edom. After all, while Israel had been taken into captivity, the Edomites had been allowed to remain in their own land. If that was not bad enough, now the Edomites virtually had free reign over Israel's beloved Promised Land.

The thought of this was nauseating to the Israelites, especially in view of their constant problems with the Edomites. Ralph H. Alexander said,

> Edom, perhaps more than any other nation had continually detested and resented Israel. It started with the conflict between Jacob (Israel) and Esau (Edom) (Gen 25:22–34; 27; 36:1). Edom had sought to block Israel's first entrance into the Promised Land (Num 20:14–21; 24:15–19), though Edom would not do so again. There were conflicts during the times of Saul (1 Sam 14:47), Solomon (1 Kings 11:14–22), Jehoshaphat (2 Chron 20:1–23), Jehoram (2 Kings 8:21), and Ahaz (2 Chron 28:17). The prophets regularly made reference to Edom's antagonism toward Israel and the resulting judgment they would receive (Isa 11:11–16; Dan 11:41; Amos 2:1). Malachi demonstrated that the hatred between these nations was still common in his day (Mal 1:2–5). Therefore, it was fitting that Ezekiel used Edom as the epitome of nations that sought to overrun and acquire Israel's land for themselves.[3]

---

[3]Ralph H. Alexander, "Ezekiel," in *The Expositor's Bible Commentary*, ed. Frank E. Gaebelein (Grand Rapids, Mich.: Zondervan Publishing House, 1986), 6:916.

By taking advantage of the vacated land of Israel, Edom was sure to grow and prosper. It appeared that she would become a far greater nation than she could ever have been without the unintentional help from the Israelite assets. However, that was not to be the case. God assured the captives that He would **lay waste** the well-fortified and seemingly impenetrable cities of Edom (v. 4; see Obad. 3, 4). These would become **a desolation** and **a waste** (v. 3) in order to prove a primary truth: **Then you will know that I am the Lord** (v. 4).

35:5–9

⁵″″"Because you have had everlasting enmity and have delivered the sons of Israel to the power of the sword at the time of their calamity, at the time of the punishment of the end, ⁶therefore as I live," declares the Lord God, "I will give you over to bloodshed, and bloodshed will pursue you; since you have not hated bloodshed, therefore bloodshed will pursue you. ⁷I will make Mount Seir a waste and a desolation and I will cut off from it the one who passes through and returns. ⁸I will fill its mountains with its slain; on your hills and in your valleys and in all your ravines those slain by the sword will fall. ⁹I will make you an everlasting desolation and your cities will not be inhabited. Then you will know that I am the Lord.""″

This section announces God's judgment against Mount Seir (the Edomites), based upon the following charges:

- Edom harbored "everlasting enmity" against Israel (v. 5).
- She gladly betrayed her neighbor, delivering her to the "power of the sword" (v. 5). This probably indicates a willingness to help the Babylonians in their demolition of Jerusalem.
- She continually sought to "possess" the land of Israel (v. 10), no doubt motivating her to assist the Babylonians in achieving that end (see Obad. 10–14; Lam. 4:21, 22).
- She made arrogant statements against the "mountains of Israel" (v. 12) and against the God of Israel (v. 13).

Verse 5. At the time of their calamity refers to the siege of Jerusalem (589[8] B.C.) and its eventual fall to the Babylonians (587[6] B.C.). This is the only time period that fits the overall context of Ezekiel. When that time of "calamity" came, there was no remorse on Edom's part, no thought that she could be destroyed next. Her bitter, **everlasting** hatred for Israel was such that she would do anything to encourage the demise of Israel. She rejoiced to see Jerusalem fall. This **time of the punishment of the end** of the nation of Judah ("the time of their final punishment"; RSV) refers to the events of 587–585 B.C.

Verse 6. The fourfold repetition of the word **bloodshed** brings God's powerful judgment into clear view. Edom was not charged with any religious transgression, but with an inexcusable disregard for human life. God expected all people—Jew and Gentile alike—to hate "bloodshed." This is a foundation of decency and civility. Edom, however, loved to see blood flow. God said, in effect, "Do you like to see blood? Then I will show you some of your own!"

Verse 7. The words **waste** and **desolation** indicate the extent of the coming destruction. Edom's beautiful land would be destroyed. She would lose the tribute collected from travelers whose only choice was to go through the narrow mountain roads of Edom. Normal trade relations would be brought to an abrupt end. No one would remain in the cities!

Verses 8, 9. Since Edom liked blood (v. 6), her land was to be drenched with her own. The **mountains** would be filled with Edom's **slain**, as would her **hills, valleys,** and **ravines.** As God announced in 25:13, she would become **an everlasting desolation**. God was declaring the eternal death of Edom as a people. This prophecy came true: The Edomites today are nothing but a memory (see the notes on 25:13).

35:10–15

[10]"'"Because you have said, 'These two nations and these two lands will be mine, and we will possess them,' although the LORD was there, [11]therefore as I live," declares the Lord GOD, "I will deal with you according to your anger and according to your envy which you showed because of your

hatred against them; so I will make Myself known among them when I judge you. ¹²Then you will know that I, the LORD, have heard all your revilings which you have spoken against the mountains of Israel saying, 'They are laid desolate; they are given to us for food.' ¹³And you have spoken arrogantly against Me and have multiplied your words against Me; I have heard it." ¹⁴Thus says the Lord GOD, "As all the earth rejoices, I will make you a desolation. ¹⁵As you rejoiced over the inheritance of the house of Israel because it was desolate, so I will do to you. You will be a desolation, O Mount Seir, and all Edom, all of it. Then they will know that I am the LORD."'"

Verse 10. "These two lands will be mine," the Edomites declared. They had long dreamed of merging their nation with Israel and Judah (the **two nations**), gaining control of the entire region. The dream appeared as if it might become a reality when Edom assisted the Babylonians in conquering Judah. Her aid to Babylon was fueled by a hatred of Israel and a strong desire for the land she owned. However, she overlooked one significant truth: that **the LORD was there**. What an unfortunate oversight! Instead of absorbing Israel's land, she encountered Israel's angry God! What was God doing there? He may have sent His people to Babylon and Assyria, and He may have departed from the temple in Jerusalem (see 11:23), but this land was still special to God. He intended to maintain complete control over it. (Notice what happened to those who moved into the northern kingdom; 2 Kings 17:24–28.) Besides, God's plan was to give the land back to Judah in a few years (a total of seventy years; Jer. 25:11). The Captivity ended in 536 B.C.; when Ezekiel penned these words, that was perhaps only fifty years away.

Verse 11. In an Old Testament foreshadowing of the words of Jesus (Mt. 7:1–5), God declared that He would dispense judgment to the same degree that they dispensed it to others. He would judge the Edomites based on their **anger** toward Israel and their **envy** of her land and assets.

Verses 12, 13. Since the Edomites viewed Israel's God as a *local* deity, they assumed that the Lord would not be aware of their **revilings** of Israel (v. 12). Therefore, Edom engaged in vicious attacks on Israel, frequently and openly expressing her hatred. She disparaged, ridiculed, and mocked Israel—and God **heard it** (v. 13). Since they did not believe God could hear them, they thought that He was incapable of doing anything about their insults. It was time for them to learn a lesson about Yahweh, the God of Israel. He would "make [Him]self known" (v. 11) among them when they faced His "judgment." They were foolish in thinking that Israel would be **food** (v. 12) for them to enjoy.

Edom overlooked one significant truth: What was spoken against God's people was also an affront to God Himself (v. 13). Edom probably had fun mocking the great God of Israel, the God about whom the Israelites continually bragged—the God who now seemed unable to deliver them (see 1 Sam. 2:3; Rev. 13:6).

Verse 14. Edom was not popular among the nations. Her predicted demise was good news for **all the earth**. What a sad commentary on a people! They were despised by others for their evil ways and inhumane activities; no one liked them. What an indictment on the people and the leaders who governed them!

Verse 15. Edom had **rejoiced over** the destruction of others, and now the nations would rejoice over her destruction. She had been happy to see others **desolate**, so now she would endure **desolation**.

APPLICATION

Living in Peace and Decency

God has always expected decency and humane treatment of one's fellow man. There is no place for rejoicing in the demise of others.

Lusting for the possessions of others can lead to a variety of sins (anger, hatred, envy, murder). It is essential for God's people to defeat their lusts (Jas. 1:13, 14; 1 Jn. 2:15–17).

An attack against God's people is an attack on God Himself (see Ezek. 35:13). Any action against the body of Christ, the church, is an attack on the Son of God. He will arise to defend and save His people (Mt. 25:45; Acts 9:2–5).

The Edomites foolishly thought that God did not hear what

they said about Him. Likewise, people today say (and do) things which they foolishly think the Lord does not see. In truth, He sees all that we do, and He will judge us accordingly (Eccles. 12:13; 1 Tim. 5:24, 25; Ps. 139:12).

The Bible encourages us, so far as it depends upon us, to "be at peace with all men" (Rom. 12:18). The Edomites were despised by everyone because of their unwillingness to "try to get along."

D.P.

Crimes That Bring God's Judgment

Ezekiel was given an oracle against Mount Seir, a mountain in Edom, but why? For this reason: As one of the major mountains of Edom, it had come to stand for this country. It was such an integral part of the life of Edom that its name was given to the nation, just as Jerusalem often stands in the Scriptures for Judah, or the southern kingdom.

The oracle is a severe pronouncement of judgment. Its message is similar to the message of the entire Book of Obadiah. The judgment from God had far-reaching consequences. In fact, He was telling them that they would be removed from the land of the living. Their nation, in God's own time, would be completely destroyed.

Their sentence causes us to ask, "What were their crimes? What did they do that was so serious that God decreed that they must be totally eliminated?"

First, they were guilty of greed. The Edomites saw the beautiful land of Judah, coveted it, and resolved that when the opportunity came, they would get it. Because they said, "These two nations and these two lands will be mine, and we will possess them," they fell under God's judgment (Ezek. 35:10). Apparently, they were ready to do anything in order to get the lands they sought.

We may think that greed is just a childish immaturity, a little sin that all commit; but God sees it as a devastating sin that leads to other vicious sins. It is like the love of money. Paul said, "For the love of money is a root of all sorts of evil" (1 Tim. 6:10). Greed can motivate a person to commit almost any kind of evil to satisfy his lust.

When a nation develops an attitude of greed toward others' possessions, God will not allow this crime to go unpunished. He said to Edom, "I will deal with you according to your anger and according to your envy which you showed because of your hatred against them; so I will make Myself known among them when I judge you" (Ezek. 35:11).

Envy and love cannot dwell in the same heart. When we fill our hearts with love, greed dies; when we allow greed to dominate us, love dies.

Second, they were guilty of mistreating their brethren. Verse 5 pictures God telling them why they would be judged: "Because you have had everlasting enmity and have delivered the sons of Israel to the power of the sword at the time of their calamity, at the time of the punishment of the end. . . ."

The Edomites sprang from Esau, and the Israelites sprang from Jacob. God regarded these two nations as brothers. However, enmity had existed between them through the years. When tragedy came to Judah—when Jerusalem was destroyed by the Babylonians—the Edomites stood with the Babylonians, the enemy! Obadiah said of Edom, "Because of violence to your brother Jacob, you will be covered with shame. . . . On the day that you stood aloof, on the day that strangers carried off his wealth, and foreigners entered his gate and cast lots for Jerusalem—you too were as one of them" (Obad. 10, 11).

This crime was serious in the eyes of God. He told them that they would be treated as they had treated Judah. What we send out to others returns to us in the same form in which it was sent. God said, "As you rejoiced over the inheritance of the house of Israel because it was desolate, so I will do to you. You will be a desolation, O Mount Seir, and all Edom, all of it. Then they will know that I am the LORD'" (Ezek. 35:15). Obadiah further said, "As you have done, it will be done to you. Your dealings will return on your own head" (Obad. 15).

God would repay this nation because He is God. He cannot betray Himself. He, in His righteousness, will deal with sin, whether it is found in a nation or in an individual.

Here is a truth that should cause us to pause and meditate: We will receive what we have given to others. God, because of

His righteous character, will see that what we get in the end will be in harmony with what we have given.

Edom's third crime, perhaps the most serious of all, was that they were arrogant against God. He said to them, "And you have spoken arrogantly against Me and have multiplied your words against Me; I have heard it" (Ezek. 35:13). They had not only rejected His will, but also had reviled Him. The Edomites said, "We do not have to be afraid of God. What can He do to us? Who is God that we should have to obey Him? Why should we respect and revere Him?"

One trait that no one, not even a nation, can get away with for long is the horrible trait of irreverence against God. Such an attitude pervades human activities. It affects everything we do—our relationships, morality, home-life, and everything else. If one does not respect God, he cannot have the kind of respect that God wants him to have for other authority—whether it be parental, school, state, or national.

In verses 14 and 15, God said to the Edomites, in effect, "I am going to treat you the way you have treated My people. Then you will know that I am the Lord.'" As they experienced the hot judgment of God's wrath, they would recognize God and pay the proper respect to Him, even though it would be too late.

We might say, "Sin is sin. What difference does it make?" In one sense, that statement is right. Sin is sin, but there are some sins that lead to other sins, creating much pain and suffering in the world. Any sin will hurt, for it is the nature of sin to hurt; but some sins hurt more than others. These sins, because of their influence, are especially repulsive to God. Inordinate desire, insensitivity, and impertinence are three such sins. Greed leads to all types of evil. Insensitivity can be cruel when others are in great need, and impertinence can lead us to be disobedient to all of God's commands.

Treated as We Have Treated Others

The Edomites had been unfeeling and wicked toward their relatives, the people of Judah. In response to their cruelty, God said to them, "As you rejoiced over the inheritance of the house of Israel because it was desolate, so I will do to you" (Ezek. 35:15).

He also said, "Because you have had everlasting enmity and have delivered the sons of Israel to the power of the sword at the time of their calamity, at the time of the punishment of the end, therefore as I live . . . 'I will give you over to bloodshed, and bloodshed will pursue you; since you have not hated bloodshed, therefore bloodshed will pursue you" (vv. 5, 6). God promised them that they would receive what they had handed out to Judah and to others.

Jesus gave us the golden rule that says, "In everything, therefore, treat people the same way you want them to treat you . . ." (Mt. 7:12). However, people do not always listen to Jesus. They would rather live by the "nedlog" rule, the reverse of the "golden" rule. It says, "Treat others the way you do not want to be treated."

In God's own time, those who have mistreated others will receive His judgment. Realizing this fact should motivate us to adopt the golden rule as our standard of life.

Solemn justice is reflected in this fact: God is just, and He will administer judgment with equity. Paul said, "God is not mocked; for whatever a man sows, this he will also reap" (Gal. 6:7). Solomon rhetorically asked, "Can a man take fire in his bosom and his clothes not be burned? Or can a man walk on hot coals and his feet not be scorched?" (Prov. 6:27, 28). Moses said, "Your sin will find you out" (Num. 32:23b). Hosea said, "For they sow the wind and they reap the whirlwind" (Hos. 8:7).

Sin is reflected in this fact. The "nedlog" approach to life is obviously the wrong way to live. In Ezekiel 35, God said that He had observed the Edomites living this way and He would judge them for it. Treating others the way we do not want to be treated is a crass and heartless way to live. No one, not even the wicked, deep down in their souls, appreciate this lifestyle.

Amos said that judgment was coming to Tyre "because they delivered up an entire population to Edom and did not remember the covenant of brotherhood" (Amos 1:9). When one treats others wickedly, he forgets that he is part of the brotherhood of human beings and has a responsibility to assist others.

Sadness is reflected in this fact. We do not have to receive God's retribution, since we do not have to live evil lives. How tragic it was for the Edomites! They came to a dismal end, but it was an end they had chosen for themselves.

Any human being can choose to treat others as he would like to be treated. If we have spread goodness around and brought the blessings of peace and joy to others, goodness and blessings will come to us. Paul said, "For the one who sows to his own flesh will from the flesh reap corruption, but the one who sows to the Spirit will from the Spirit reap eternal life" (Gal. 6:8).

The divine hand of judgment treated the Edomites the way they had mistreated others. God said that He would see to their undoing, and He did. He spread it out over a period of time, but He did exactly what He said He would do.

Ask yourself, "Do I want to relive their experience?" Do I want God to say, "I will treat you the way you have mistreated others?" If not, then become a Christian and live according to the golden rule for the rest of your life.

E.C.

Chapter 36

The Return of Israel To Their Own Land: Restoration

The thought from chapter 35 flows into chapter 36. Ezekiel was prophesying to the mountain ranges: first, to Mount Seir (35:1, 2), then to "the mountains of Israel" (36:1). As noted in the last chapter, any hope of Israel's returning to the land would be dashed if the Edomites were there. Having announced that the Edomites would be removed (ch. 35), Ezekiel could devote his attention to the future of Israel (a topic begun in ch. 34). However, God was not just concerned with Israel's physical environment. The nation's spirituality had to be addressed, for the land would again be out of reach if the people's hearts were not dedicated to God. Ezekiel dealt with this dual concern as follows:

1. Israel was again assured that Edom and "the rest of the nations" would face the wrath of the Lord (vv. 1–7).
2. Ezekiel specifically addressed the land of Israel, promising a future of fruitfulness and repopulating of the cities (vv. 8–15).
3. The children of Israel were challenged not to repeat the past sins that caused them to lose their land (vv. 16–21).
4. Three "Thus says the Lord" statements are given, promising a bright future for the people of God (vv. 22–32; 33–36; 37, 38).

JUDGMENT ON HER ENEMIES
(36:1–7)

36:1–3
¹"And you, son of man, prophesy to the mountains of Israel and say, 'O mountains of Israel, hear the word of the LORD. ²Thus says the Lord GOD, "Because the enemy has spoken against you, 'Aha!' and, 'The everlasting heights have become our possession,' ³therefore prophesy and say, 'Thus says the Lord GOD, "For good reason they have made you desolate and crushed you from every side, that you would become a possession of the rest of the nations and you have been taken up in the talk and the whispering of the people."'"'"

Verse 1. As Ezekiel was told earlier to prophesy "against" Mount Seir, he was told here to **prophesy to the mountains of Israel**. No longer was he delivering words of doom and destruction to the land of Israel. God now had a message of hope for His people.

Verse 2. The enemy of God's land had **spoken against** it, claiming, **"The everlasting heights have become our possession."** Upon the Israelites' removal from the land (when they were exiled to Babylon), the Edomites had rejoiced that finally the land of Canaan could become theirs. Why did they call it "the everlasting heights"? One possibility is that they were referring to the idolatrous high places, which they could use to worship their gods forever. The Edomites liked high places, and those in Israel were desirable locations. A second possibility is that these words were mocking the Israelites, who had bragged that this land was theirs for eternity. In scorn, the enemies were saying, "Their eternal land has now become *ours!*"

Verse 3. The NASB translates the first clause **for good reason**, indicating that, in the minds of Israel's enemies, they had just cause to hate Israel and to work for her destruction. Other translations simply render this difficult clause in a way that indicates the nations were determined to destroy Israel. (For example, the RSV has "Because, yea, because they made you desolate, and crushed you from all sides. . . .") These nations worked to bring about the desolation of God's people. They wanted to see Israel **crushed** and her land possessed by aggressive nations. In addition, Israel became the favorite **talk** of the nations and **the whispering of** [their] **people**. "Talk" is actually translated from the phrase "the lip of the tongue." It refers to the lips of the slanderer, one who mocked and derided Israel, fulfilling God's prediction in Deuteronomy 28:37: "You shall become a horror, a proverb, and a taunt among all the people where the LORD drives you."

36:4–7

⁴"'Therefore, O mountains of Israel, hear the word of the Lord GOD. Thus says the Lord GOD to the mountains and to the hills, to the ravines and to the valleys, to the desolate wastes and to the forsaken cities which have become a prey and a derision to the rest of the nations which are round about, ⁵therefore thus says the Lord GOD, "Surely in the fire of My jealousy I have spoken against the rest of the nations, and against all Edom, who appropriated My land for themselves as a possession with wholehearted joy and with scorn of soul, to drive it out for a prey." ⁶Therefore prophesy concerning the land of Israel and say to the mountains and to the hills, to the ravines and to the valleys, "Thus says the Lord GOD, 'Behold, I have spoken in My jealousy and in My wrath because you have endured the insults of the nations.' ⁷Therefore thus says the Lord GOD, 'I have sworn that surely the nations which are around you will themselves endure their insults.'"'"

Verse 4. God called for the complete attention of six specific areas of the land: **mountains, hills, ravines, valleys, desolate wastes,** and **forsaken cities**. These areas are depicted as suffering when the nations made their taunts, as if they were animate and able to hear the insults. God wanted them to hear what He had to say regarding their future.

Verse 5. The taunts and heckling done by the nations had stirred up God's intense **jealousy**. These words of derision angered God until He arose to act. He specifically targeted **Edom**, the subject of chapter 35, and "the rest of the nations" (see v. 3) who had **appropriated** God's land (**My land**) for themselves. Stealing is sinful, but trying to take something from the Lord is foolishness. The nations had reacted to the opportunity to seize the Promised Land with "wholehearted joy" (see 35:15). This had been their dream. Along with their thrill at possessing the land, they expressed their **scorn of soul**—their contempt for Israel. This hatred provided their motivation to **drive** Israel out of the land and then **prey** upon it themselves.

Verse 6. By insulting Israel, the nations were offending God. Because the land had **endured the insults of the nations**, God would speak to them out of **jealousy** and **wrath**. Such a situation would not be pleasant for these nations. Running headlong into God's anger leads to certain doom.

Verse 7. God took a sworn oath that what the nations wished upon Israel would, instead, come upon them. They would taste the suffering they wanted Israel to experience and would **endure** their own insults. What happened to Israel was only for a time; the doom of these godless nations would last for all eternity.

GOD PROMISES TO BLESS THE LAND
(36:8–15)

36:8–11
⁸"'"'But you, O mountains of Israel, you will put forth your branches and bear your fruit for My people Israel; for they will soon come. ⁹For, behold, I am for you, and I will turn to you, and you will be cultivated and sown. ¹⁰I will multiply men on you, all the house of Israel, all of it; and the cities will be inhabited and the waste places will be rebuilt. ¹¹I will multiply on you man and beast; and they will increase and be fruitful; and I will cause you to be inhabited as you were formerly and will treat you better than at the first. Thus you will know that I am the Lord.'"'"

Verses 8, 9. The **mountains of Israel** are addressed again (v. 8). The productivity that the nations had envisioned for themselves in the land of Israel was not to be realized. They would not be alive to usurp the land; rather, God ordered the land to begin its productive rise on behalf of Israel, **My people**. This is stated in terminology that might depict a hostess getting ready for the arrival of guests who would **soon come**. Indeed, in about forty years, the exiles would be released to inhabit the land once again. (Forty years is the length of time that Ezekiel had lain on his right side, figuratively bearing the iniquity of Judah; see 4:6.) This wonderful promise was given because God was now on Israel's side: **"Behold, I am for you,"** He said (v. 9). This is in stark contrast to 21:3, where God had said to the land of Israel, "Behold, I am against you." Now that she had endured her punishment, God would be compassionate and forgiving toward her.

Verses 10, 11. The emptied **cities** (v. 10) would again be bustling with people; the destroyed places (such as farms and vineyards) were to be **rebuilt**. We are given here a picture of a nation coming back to life—a prelude to chapter 37. In addition, God was demonstrating how the enemies' dream for Judah would become their nightmare. They wished for Israel to be desolate, but their own land would be desolate (see v. 3; 35:3). They wanted to eliminate the inhabitants of Judah, but their own cities would be empty (see 35:9). They desired to appropriate Israel's land, but they themselves were about to be dispossessed (see v. 12; 35:10). The glory days of Israel, when the nation was strong and prosperous, would return. God planned to restore the nation **as you were formerly** (v. 11). In fact, He would go beyond that: He would make their situation better than it had been before the Exile. God promised to **multiply on you man and beast**; the growing population would use beasts of burden for travel and for agriculture.

36:12–15

¹²""'Yes, I will cause men—My people Israel—to walk on you and possess you, so that you will become their inheritance and never again bereave them of children.'

¹³""'Thus says the Lord God, 'Because they say to you, "You are a devourer of men and have bereaved your nation of children," ¹⁴therefore you will no longer devour men and no longer

bereave your nation of children,' declares the Lord God. ¹⁵I will not let you hear insults from the nations anymore, nor will you bear disgrace from the peoples any longer, nor will you cause your nation to stumble any longer," declares the Lord God.'"

Verses 12–14. The mountains of Israel would indeed be walked upon, but not by the feet of foreigners. God's people—**My people Israel** (v. 12)—would walk on those mountains and possess them. Also, in a phrase difficult to interpret with certainty, God declared that the mountains would **no longer devour men** or **bereave your nation of children** (v. 14). Possible interpretations of this statement include the following:

1. Because of sin, God had sent famine and drought, causing the deaths of men, women, and children through starvation.
2. The densely forested mountains frequently claimed lives; perhaps many fell victim to the wild beasts.
3. The land lost many inhabitants, with nation after nation claiming the land, then vanishing into history. The Israelite spies had described Canaan as "a land that devours its inhabitants" (Num. 13:32).
4. The land, by the will of God, responded in vengeance toward inhabitants who turned to wickedness. Idolatrous rites occurred on these high places; children were sacrificed there, and men died there when God caused various nations to purge the land of its evil inhabitants. (The Israelites purged the land of the Canaanites; the Assyrians purged the land of the people of Israel, the northern kingdom; and the Babylonians purged the land of the people of Judah.)

God intended to change the disposition of the land, making her more hospitable to the returning exiles. She would be a blessing and become abundantly fruitful rather than remaining a place of casualties. The only way for this to happen was for the inhabitants—unlike those who had dwelt there before—to be righteous.

Verse 15. As God concluded this section regarding the future of the land, He issued three mandates:

1. **"I will not let you hear insults from the nations anymore."** The constant mocking of Israel was over. Most of the mockers would be gone, and those who lived would see Israel vindicated. Her God proved to be the true God.
2. **"Nor will you bear disgrace from the peoples any longer."** Reminiscent of what happened in the Garden of Eden, the land suffered when man's sin brought a "curse" upon the ground. Now God promised that the land would bring Israel praise because of its fruitfulness, rather than "disgrace" because of its unfruitfulness.
3. **"Nor will you cause your nation to stumble any longer."** Perhaps this phrase means that the mountains would cease to tempt Israel to construct "high places" of idolatry. A better view may be that, instead of being an instrument of punishment in the hand of God (through famine and wild beast), the land would help to stabilize the nation and prevent future stumbling (see Is. 63:13; Jer. 13:16; 18:15).

The discussion of "land" is significant. According to Taylor there was an "inseparable relationship between a people and the physical contours of the land where they dwelt." Furthermore,

> . . . It does not necessarily imply a belief in localized deities, though the Old Testament did have a high regard for the locations of sanctuaries where God appeared to their forefathers, *e.g.* El Beth-el, the God of Bethel (Gn. 31:13; 35:7). But it is to be set alongside such facts as the place of Canaan, the promised land, in the Abrahamic and Mosaic covenants, and the selection of Jerusalem or

Mount Zion as the place where the Lord was thought particularly to dwell and where His worship was to be carried on.... Authority over the whole is witnessed to by the surrender of the part. So the Hebrews regarded the actual land where they lived, the mountains, the valleys, the plains and the rivers, as a kind of God's acre in the world, and its welfare was intimately bound up with the welfare of God's people who lived in it.[1]

PROTECTING GOD'S NAME: AN HISTORICAL REVIEW (36:16–23)

36:16–21
¹⁶Then the word of the LORD came to me saying, ¹⁷"Son of man, when the house of Israel was living in their own land, they defiled it by their ways and their deeds; their way before Me was like the uncleanness of a woman in her impurity. ¹⁸Therefore I poured out My wrath on them for the blood which they had shed on the land, because they had defiled it with their idols. ¹⁹Also I scattered them among the nations and they were dispersed throughout the lands. According to their ways and their deeds I judged them. ²⁰When they came to the nations where they went, they profaned My holy name, because it was said of them, 'These are the people of the LORD; yet they have come out of His land.' ²¹But I had concern for My holy name, which the house of Israel had profaned among the nations where they went."

Verses 16, 17. When everything was going well for Israel, the nation developed a smugness, an overconfidence, that this land was their land for eternity. (In truth, this seemed to be God's original intention; see Gen. 17:8; 48:4.) Then, they were comfortably **living in their own land** (Ezek. 36:17). This was a powerful thought, since these words were spoken when the people

---

[1] John B. Taylor, *Ezekiel: An Introduction and Commentary,* Tyndale Old Testament Commentaries (Downers Grove, Ill.: Inter-Varsity Press, 1969), 227–28.

were in captivity, living in someone else's land. The people of Israel had failed to appreciate what they had. Repeatedly, they had broken the nation's covenant to be faithful to the Lord. A review of **their ways and their deeds** indicates that Israel did little right and much wrong. Their conduct was such an abomination to God that He compared it to the **impurity** of **a woman** during her menstrual cycle (18:6; 22:10; Lev. 12:2–5; 15:19–30).[2]

Verse 18. Again and again, God detailed the reasons why Israel lost the land and was taken into captivity. This repetition, however, was necessary for two reasons. First, it was vital that the people come to a full understanding of the reasons why this disaster happened and humbly return to God in obedience. Only realizing the gravity of their sins—and accepting responsibility—would allow them to develop the new heart God wanted them to have. Second, the removal of the people from the land created a false view of God and His power. When the people were defeated, surrounding nations ascribed weakness and ineffectiveness to the Lord. It was important to re-establish God's reputation.

While the sins of Israel were many, these offenses fall into the two categories given:

1. **They had shed** [blood] **on the land.** Through tyranny, domination, cruelty, and oppression, the rich and powerful shed the blood of innocent victims (widows, orphans, and the poor). They did this to their own people!
2. **They had defiled** [the land] **with their idols.** The prophets painted a terrible picture of corruption, noting the people's love for idolatry. On every high hill and under every green tree, an idolatrous shrine was erected (Jer. 3:6; 17:2). Urban centers were likewise inundated with idols (Jer. 2:28; 7:17, 18; 11:12, 13; Ezek. 6:6).

---

[2]See David Kimchi, notes on Ezekiel in the Rabbinic Bible (New York: Columbia University Press, 1929), 212.

Verse 19. Their continued unfaithfulness left God with no option but to remove the people from their precious land. This should not have surprised Israel. God had said in the Mosaic covenant that He would do this (Deut. 29:22–28; 30:18). God judges all people **according to their ways and their deeds.**

Verse 20. Because of the need for discipline and punishment, God "scattered them among the nations" (v. 19). Did they learn their lesson? In the lands of captivity, did the people of Israel put away their idols forever? Sadly, the answer is no. Instead, in captivity, they **profaned** God's **holy name.** Their being taken into exile was an affront to the reputation of God. The repetition of the word "name" (four times in vv. 20–23) is significant. God's name is "holy"—unique, exalted, pure, and great. It should have been the name extolled among the nations. However, because of Israel's unfaithfulness, God's name was blasphemed. The nations' words regarding Israel were painful: **"These are the people of the LORD; yet they have come out of His land."** Was the Lord unable to protect them? Was He unable to keep them from leaving? In the nations' eyes, Yahweh was a small, localized, powerless God.

Verse 21. God had **concern** for His **holy name.** The word translated "concern" is חָמַל (*chamal*), meaning to "spare, bear, become responsible, ... have compassion."[3] God's primary concern here was for His own name, His own reputation. While this may seem harsh (as if lacking compassion for His people), it was essential for God to re-establish His own name before He could rebuild the nation. He had to have "compassion" for His own name first. Only then could He rebuild the nation of Israel. John B. Taylor said,

> The doctrine expressed in the phrase *I had concern for my holy name* (21, RSV), represents the utmost humiliation for the sinner. There is no consideration for him, no respect for his feelings, no love for him as a human being. He stands condemned because of his sins, and he forfeits

---

[3]Francis Brown, S. R. Driver, and Charles A. Briggs, *A Hebrew and English Lexicon of the Old Testament* (Oxford: Clarendon Press, 1972), 328.

all claim on God. He is simply a pawn on the chess-board of the world, in which God's prime concern is that all men and nations may know that He is the Lord. To put it like this in all its starkness may seem harsh and a contradiction of Christianity, but it is an aspect of the truth of God as revealed in the Old Testament. It is the aspect which is basic to Paul's statement in Romans 5:8, "While we were yet sinners . . ." We had no claim on God, we were His enemies, we were helpless to do anything to save ourselves: but God acted in salvation. In so doing He showed His love to us, and to all the world. But the humiliation of Ezekiel's doctrine is needed first, in order that we may appreciate the amazing grace of Romans 5.[4]

At this point, God's name was being **profaned**. This word (חָלַל, *chalal*) can mean "to defile, pollute, or desecrate."[5] The word is used this way more than thirty times in Ezekiel, obviously emphasizing an important message in the book. The people had committed a grievous sin; foremost was the damage done to the holy name of their God. In an amazing section, 20:9-14, God declared that He had delayed pouring out His wrath on Israel during their exodus from Egypt for the sake of His name. He did not want His name profaned by other nations. Chapter 39 declares that God would no longer permit the profaning of His holy name. He would punish Israel, making His people a public display before the other nations.[6]

36:22, 23

[22]"Therefore say to the house of Israel, 'Thus says the Lord God, "It is not for your sake, O house of Israel, that I am about to act, but for My holy name, which you have profaned among

---

[4]Taylor, 230–31.
[5]Brown, Driver, and Briggs, 320.
[6]A good study of this subject is given in W. Dommershausen, "חלל," in *Theological Dictionary of the Old Testament*, ed. G. Johannes Botterweck and Helmer Ringgren, trans. David E. Green (Grand Rapids, Mich.: Wm. B. Eerdmans Publishing Co., 1980), 4:410–17.

the nations where you went. ²³I will vindicate the holiness of My great name which has been profaned among the nations, which you have profaned in their midst. Then the nations will know that I am the LORD," declares the Lord GOD, "when I prove Myself holy among you in their sight."'"

Verse 22. "It is not for your sake, O house of Israel, that I am about to act," God said. He would have preferred to establish His name among the nations through the righteous acts of His people, but they did not give Him that opportunity. Therefore, God had to "act" in His own behalf—not because Israel deserved anything, but **for [His] holy name**. In effect, God was saying, "You have severely damaged my reputation, and now I must repair it." He planned to do this by restoring Israel to the land. This was a tremendous blessing for Israel, and one wholly undeserved.[7]

Verse 23. God's **great name** had been made small and insignificant in the eyes of the nations. His name had endured ridicule, mockery, insults, and blasphemy. Now it was time to **vindicate** the name Israel had **profaned** (a word used five times in vv. 16–23). Why was this vindication so important?

First, the truth is important. God is the only God, the almighty God of the universe. Other nations needed to realize this truth. They believed Him to be nothing more than a local god, effective only in the land of Israel—and not very effective there.

---

[7]"God was so concerned that Israel be restored to a proper relationship with him that he sent his people out of the Promised Land so that they might learn the importance of following his ways. God's ways are always best; for he, the Creator of life, knows how life can best be lived. But in disciplining Israel in this manner, the Lord risked his own reputation in the world. A nation was unique[ly] tied to its land in the ancient Near East. If a people were forced off their land, whether by conquest, famine, disease, or any other reason, this was a demonstration that their god was not sufficiently strong to protect and care for them. Therefore, when God scattered Israel among the nations, they perceived that Israel's God was weak; thereby the name of the Lord was profaned among them" (Ralph H. Alexander, "Ezekiel," in *The Expositor's Bible Commentary*, ed. Frank E. Gaebelein [Grand Rapids, Mich.: Zondervan Publishing House, 1986], 6:920).

Second, Yahweh seeks to be the God of all peoples. These nations would never turn to Him as long as they had this tainted view of Him. Israel had not brought about the glorification of His name, but had caused the opposite. They should have led people to God; instead, they turned people away from Him. God wanted what He had always wanted: **Then the nations will know that I am the LORD.**

Third, God wanted to **prove [Him]self holy** in the eyes of Israel and the nations. His own people had a false view of Him. They needed to relearn the truth. God would use the punishment inflicted upon Israel as a steppingstone in rescuing His reputation. Taylor said,

> It must have been very difficult for Israel to accept this role, and the only hint that some in Israel were able to accept it is to be found in the so-called Servant Songs of Isaiah 40—55, where Israel as the Servant of the Lord fulfils His mission among the Gentiles through suffering. [This does not of course exhaust the interpretation of these songs (viz. Is. 42:1–4; 49:1–6; 50:4–9; 52:13—53:12), for they have strong Messianic overtones, but this is an element which must not be overlooked in the desire to see them solely as prefigurings of Christ.] The church also finds it a difficult role to accept, but in an age when God's power is all too often discredited by reason of His people's failures, the church needs to be prepared to be treated harshly for the sake of God's greater glory in the world.[8]

GOD PROMISES TO CLEANSE ISRAEL (36:24–32)

[24]"'"For I will take you from the nations, gather you from all the lands and bring you into your own land. [25]Then I will sprinkle clean water on you, and you will be clean; I will cleanse you from all your filthiness and from all your idols.

---

[8]Taylor, 231.

²⁶Moreover, I will give you a new heart and put a new spirit within you; and I will remove the heart of stone from your flesh and give you a heart of flesh. ²⁷I will put My Spirit within you and cause you to walk in My statutes, and you will be careful to observe My ordinances. ²⁸You will live in the land that I gave to your forefathers; so you will be My people, and I will be your God. ²⁹Moreover, I will save you from all your uncleanness; and I will call for the grain and multiply it, and I will not bring a famine on you. ³⁰I will multiply the fruit of the tree and the produce of the field, so that you will not receive again the disgrace of famine among the nations. ³¹Then you will remember your evil ways and your deeds that were not good, and you will loathe yourselves in your own sight for your iniquities and your abominations. ³²I am not doing this for your sake," declares the Lord God, "let it be known to you. Be ashamed and confounded for your ways, O house of Israel!"'"

Verses 24–30. How was God to vindicate His name? It would not be through a great show of power, as with the plagues brought upon Egypt (Ex. 7—11); not by fire from heaven, as with Elijah (2 Kings 1:9–15). It would be done by restoring Israel back to their "own land." Notice the progression of what God said He would do:

"**I will . . . gather you . . . and bring you into your own land**" (v. 24). It was a shame and disgrace for God's people not to be in God's Promised Land. It discredited them and profaned His name. The reputation of God could only be re-established if the people were once again living in Israel.

"**I will sprinkle clean water on you**" (v. 25). A physical restoration to the land without a spiritual renewal would be worthless. The people had to be cleansed. This cleansing would begin with forgiveness and then would be followed by "bringing forth fruits of repentance" (see Lk. 3:8) by their living according to the divine covenant. The imagery of sprinkling water refers to the ceremonial washings that removed their uncleanness (Ex. 30:17–21; Lev. 14:52; Num. 19:17–19; Ps. 51:7; see Tit. 3:5, 6; Heb. 9:13, 19; 10:22). As a priest, Ezekiel would have been trained in the method of cleansing an unclean person; but this refers to a divine cleansing, not a ceremonial cleansing. As a prophet, Ezekiel was privileged to announce the divine cleansing of an unholy people. This sin could not be removed through any animal sacrifice; it required a direct act of God.

"I will cleanse you from all your filthiness and from all your idols" (v. 25). The cleansing brought forgiveness of their idolatrous ways and required the permanent removal of those idols.

"I will give you a new heart" (v. 26). The old heart was hopelessly corrupted by sin. As David asked God to "create in [him] a clean heart" (Ps. 51:10), so Israel required this new creation. (See the discussion on 16:30.) By saying that they would receive a new heart, God was declaring a renewed mind or intellect, as well as an emotional makeover. From the heart flow the "springs of life" (Prov. 4:23); if the heart is not maintained, it will lead (flow) away from the Lord.

"I will . . . put a new spirit within you" (v. 26). The spirit is the life force of the individual. It is what drives him, motivates him, and governs him.

"I will remove the heart of stone" (v. 26). The people had become obstinate, stubborn, and rebellious. Their hearts had become completely insensitive to the will of God; their ears were deaf to His cries.

"I will . . . give you a heart of flesh" (v. 26). Now the people would be sensitive, alive, and alert to the word of the Lord (11:19). They would be able to feel His pain when they disobeyed and comprehend His joy when they served Him. To assume that the Israelites could not turn this heart of flesh into another heart of stone would be to misunderstand how God operates in this world. Their first heart was of flesh, and they ruined it. If they returned to sinful living, they could harden this one as well.

"I will put My Spirit within you" (v. 27). This phrase has been interpreted in two ways. First, it may refer to the outpouring of the Holy Spirit, as prophesied by Joel (Joel 2:28, 29) and fulfilled in Acts 2 (see Is. 42:1; 44:3; 59:21; Hag. 2:5; Joel 3:1, 2). Second, it may refer to an act by which God gave the people a spirit or attitude like His own. This would not have been a miraculous event, but a providential one, such as could have occurred through God's discipline and the work of God's prophets. In view of the results from the giving of this spirit (the people would "walk in [God's] statutes" and "be careful to observe [His] ordinances"), it seems best to adopt the second interpretation (see also 37:14; 39:29). God was faithful to His covenant; with the same "spirit," the people would be equally committed. (A similar prophecy is given in Jer. 31:31–34.)

"I will . . . **cause you to walk in My statutes**" (v. 27). Once the people received the "spirit of God," they would have a renewed enthusiasm for God's laws. To see predestination in this section is to miss the flow of the text and the truth already established in chapter 18. God intended to create an environment that would encourage faithfulness to His "statutes" and "ordinances." Would God be glorified if people were *made* to obey Him instead of choosing to obey Him out of their own free will? Of course not! God does not want puppets; He wants hearts that love Him and willingly obey Him.

"**You will live in the land that I gave to your forefathers**" (v. 28). The land that was promised to Abraham and was then given to the Israelites in the days of Joshua would be theirs again. Sometimes people's choices prove disastrous for a lifetime. In this case, God allowed Judah's sins to have only a temporary consequence. Old men who remembered the former glory of Jerusalem wept as they saw the new start God was giving to His people (Ezra 3:12).

"**I will be your God**" (v. 28). Israel had abandoned Him while still living in the land—worshiping, instead, other gods known in Assyria, Babylon, Egypt, Moab, and Ammon. Their return to God, as opposed to the abominable polytheism they had practiced, allowed God to declare, "**So you will be My people.**" God does not claim as His own those who worship other gods and are thereby unfaithful to Him.

"**I will save you from all your uncleanness**" (v. 29). The people had made themselves unclean through their shedding of blood and their idolatry. Once the uncleanness was removed, they were saved. Baptism provides the same result under the new covenant: Before, we are unclean—dead in sin. After baptism, we are new creatures, washed and declared clean by the Lord (2 Cor. 5:17; Tit. 3:5; 1 Pet. 3:21).

"I will call for the grain and multiply it" (v. 29). This statement, reminiscent of the promise in verse 11, returns to the theme of a blessed and productive land. The earth would answer God's "call"—His command to be productive (see Jer. 31:12). This echoes what was done at the Creation (Gen. 1).

"I will not bring a famine on you" (v. 29). God's punishment upon Israel involved the decimation of the land through plague and famine. Other nations frequently commented on the barrenness of Canaan (see 5:14, 15).

"I will multiply the fruit of the tree and the produce of the field" (v. 30). God was not promising marginal productivity, but abundant crops. Unproductive land had been a **disgrace** to Israel, affecting her reputation among the nations. The land would respond to God's command by producing to an extent beyond what the people would have dreamed.

Verse 31. Upon receiving these fifteen blessings, the Israelites would respond in three ways. God described these reactions:

"You will remember your evil ways." The only way for the people to avoid returning to a life of sin was to "remember." One of Israel's problems was the failure to remember what the nation was like before God "entered into a covenant" with her (see 16:8, 22). In 16:60-63, God wanted the people to remember so that they would be ashamed and not commit abominations any more.

"You will remember . . . your deeds that were not good." Their deeds were not good in the sense that they were unhealthy for the spiritual and physical health of the nation. God had promised that His laws were for their benefit (Deut. 6:24; 10:13; 30:9).

"You will loathe yourselves in your own sight." In remembering the past and her remarkable plunge into wickedness, Israel would not feel good about herself. Thinking of her own wickedness in contrast with the goodness of God, whom she had rejected, would result in a high degree of self-loathing (see 20:43). However, good could result from this self-hatred: Israel would learn from it and develop the appreciation for God which she had lacked before.

Verse 32. God said, **"I am not doing this for your sake."** His goodness and blessings were undeserved. The Israelites were the fortunate recipients of God's determination to exalt His name among the nations. Knowing that they were receiving this undeserved benefit should have made them **ashamed and confounded.** Why? Because of their **ways.** God should not have had to take such measures to protect His holy name.

GOD REBUILDS THE NATION AND REPOPULATES THE LAND (36:33–38)

36:33–36
³³"'Thus says the Lord GOD, "On the day that I cleanse you from all your iniquities, I will cause the cities to be inhabited, and the waste places will be rebuilt. ³⁴The desolate land will be cultivated instead of being a desolation in the sight of everyone who passes by. ³⁵They will say, 'This desolate land has become like the garden of Eden; and the waste, desolate and ruined cities are fortified and inhabited.' ³⁶Then the nations that are left round about you will know that I, the LORD, have rebuilt the ruined places and planted that which was desolate; I, the LORD, have spoken and will do it."'"

Verses 33, 34. The benefits of God's cleansing are repeated. God would turn the deserted towns into thriving cities again. Uncultivated fields and vineyards would be replanted and rebuilt. Travelers who passed through the region had been appalled at what **a desolation** it was; but when the Israelites returned, they would find the land growing and **cultivated** (v. 34).

Verses 35, 36. Passersby who remembered the land as it had been before would be impressed with the change, comparing its beauty and productivity to that of **the garden of Eden** (v. 35; see Is. 51:3; Joel 3:18; Amos 9:13–15). Ezekiel's threefold description of the current state of the cities is vivid: **waste, desolate and ruined.** The Babylonians had not just depopulated the cities; they had also ransacked them, burned them, and torn down their walls. Rebuilding would be a major project; if anyone attempted it, the Babylonians would hear about the effort and respond with an attempt to stop it. Nevertheless, these cities would be **fortified and inhabited**; and **the nations** would know they were rebuilt because of God's blessings (v. 36). This prediction is literal (unlike the apocalyptic description in 38:11); for when the exiles returned, they did refortify their cities (Neh. 6:15, 16).

36:37, 38

³⁷"'Thus says the Lord G<small>OD</small>, "This also I will let the house of Israel ask Me to do for them: I will increase their men like a flock. ³⁸Like the flock for sacrifices, like the flock at Jerusalem during her appointed feasts, so will the waste cities be filled with flocks of men. Then they will know that I am the L<small>ORD</small>."'"

Verse 37. God had not been listening to Israel's prayers, for they had turned their ears away from the Law (see Prov. 28:9). That was not the relationship God wanted with His children; He wanted to hear and answer their prayers. Now He would listen, and He would **increase** them.

Verse 38. Thousands of animals would be brought to Jerusalem during the **appointed feasts**. This is a vivid analogy of what God would do to their **waste cities**, which would be **filled with flocks of men**. God's ultimate point would be made: **Then they will know that I am the L<small>ORD</small>**.

APPLICATION

The Consequences of Sin

When one sins, discipline and punishment are necessary. After the period of discipline, God demonstrates compassion and forgiveness (36:9).

God provides numerous physical blessings for His people. However, persistent sinful behavior may force God to remove those blessings. We are but stewards of God's gifts. Failure to use them properly will bring His wrath (see 2 Cor. 8; 9).

People have always been judged by God according to their deeds (36:19). The final judgment will be no different. Each individual will face God solely on the basis of what he has done in the body, whether good or evil (Eccles. 12:13, 14; Jn. 5:28, 29; Rom. 2:6; 2 Cor. 5:10; Rev. 20:11–13).

God is concerned about how He is perceived in the world. Israel's evil conduct caused God's name to be profaned (36:21). Paul criticized the Jews, saying, "The name of God is blasphemed among the Gentiles because of you" (Rom. 2:24; Is. 52:5). Today, the reputation of God—and Christ—is based on the behavior of His people. As Christians, we are to strive to be holy as He is holy (1 Pet. 1:14–16; 2:12).

There is value in remembering our past and our sins. Even though they have been forgiven and we should forgive ourselves, we should remember for the purpose of learning—learning never to commit those sins again (36:31).

D.P.

God and the Trusting Soul

Chapter 36 shows what God does for those who put their faith in Him. Many of God's blessings in the Old Testament concerned land, actual battles, and physical sustenance. New Testament promises are more spiritual than physical. However, we can apply Old Testament promises in a spiritual way to the faithful in the Christian Age. What does God do for them?

He gives them prosperity. To His people under the Old Testament, God promised the restoration of the land they had lost. Today, He grants Christians all spiritual blessings (Eph. 1:3).

He protects them from evil. Judah would be delivered from those who had oppressed them. New Testament Christians will be delivered from the evil one.

He sustains them with His daily strength. God provided for the people of Israel, as He does for us, by supplying daily bread and the spiritual and physical ability to do His will.

He points them to a glorious future. His Word describes a glorious tomorrow. The Israelites were told about the coming of the Messiah, and we are told about the coming of eternal life with God in heaven.

E.C.

Chapter 37

The Return of Israel To Their Own Land: A New Life

Chapter 37 is probably the most famous chapter in the Book of Ezekiel. It answers a question that was asked in 33:10: "Surely our transgressions and our sins are upon us . . . ; how then can we survive?" The answer is given in a graphic and intriguing way. Ezekiel had emphasized the "desolation" that had occurred in the land (5:14; 12:20; 23:33; 36:34). How could this dead nation live again? God's Spirit would reconstruct the dead bones of the nation, giving them sinews, flesh, skin, and finally the breath of life.

What does this represent? Sadly, some have used this material to teach the doctrine of the bodily resurrection—a gross misapplication of this chapter. Others have championed the view that the two sticks in 37:16 refer to the British Israelites.[1] The verses themselves, however, are inseparable from the message begun in chapter 34. Starting there, the Lord spoke of a new shepherd (leadership) and new opportunities in the land of Israel (ch. 35), with renewed hope of growth and prosperity (ch. 36).

Such glowing promises were naturally met with suspicion and disbelief. A number of the exiles had witnessed the utter devastation of their cities. In addition, they lived under the iron grip of the Babylonians—a nation so powerful that a change in world domination seemed impossible for centuries to come.

---

[1] "British Israelites" refers to an unscriptural view that Britain and the US constitute the ten lost tribes of Israel who were carried away as captives by the Assyrians in 722(1) B.C. It argues that one of the "sticks" of Ezekiel 37 represents Britain and the US, who will be joined with the present Jews to form again the nation of God's people.

These people saw too many negatives to hope for a renewed nation. How could restoration come? Only through the power of God. God would regenerate the nation, making it strong and powerful. The second half of chapter 37 (vv. 15–28) tells how Ezekiel brought two "sticks" together, illustrating that the divided nations of Israel and Judah would emerge as one. This one nation was to be led by "David, My servant" (v. 25).

THE VISION OF THE VALLEY OF DRY BONES (37:1–14)

37:1, 2
¹The hand of the Lord was upon me, and He brought me out by the Spirit of the Lord and set me down in the middle of the valley; and it was full of bones. ²He caused me to pass among them round about, and behold, there were very many on the surface of the valley; and lo, they were very dry.

Verse 1. The statements **The hand of the Lord was upon me** (see 1:3; 33:22; 40:1) and **He brought me out by the Spirit** indicate that Ezekiel was having a vision. The Spirit set Ezekiel **down in the middle of the valley.** This valley had been the scene of a great battle. The dead remained where they had fallen—unburied.

Notice these three truths: (1) A tremendous slaughter had occurred—the valley was **full of bones.** (2) No one had cared enough to bury the dead, nor had God covered their bones. (3) God would not continue to tolerate sin—He would eventually bring judgment.

Verse 2. God had Ezekiel pass among the bones **round about.** He wanted the prophet to grasp the number of casualties and to understand that no life was left there. The bones represented the exiles in Babylon, who had been in captivity for at least ten years—some for as many as twenty years (since the first deportation in 606[5] B.C.). False prophets had predicted a short, two-year stay in Babylon. As the years passed, the exiles' hope faded.

Regarding the bones, Ezekiel noted that **there were very many.** The large number of Israelites in exile is illustrated here.

The once-powerful nation was now a valley of bones. Also, the bones were **very dry**. They were bleached from exposure to the sun. There was seemingly no hope of restoration.

37:3–6
³He said to me, "Son of man, can these bones live?" And I answered, "O Lord GOD, You know." ⁴Again He said to me, "Prophesy over these bones and say to them, 'O dry bones, hear the word of the LORD.' ⁵Thus says the Lord GOD to these bones, 'Behold, I will cause breath to enter you that you may come to life. ⁶I will put sinews on you, make flesh grow back on you, cover you with skin and put breath in you that you may come alive; and you will know that I am the LORD.'"

Verse 3. God asked Ezekiel, **"Son of man, can these bones live?"** The answer to the question seems obvious. However, Ezekiel knew the awesome power of God and therefore responded, in effect, "I don't know, but You do." Common sense said that it was impossible; but reverence answered, **"O Lord GOD, You know."**

Verse 4. As seen in the Creation and throughout the Scriptures, God's word has tremendous power. He spoke the world into existence, and His word will bring its end (2 Pet. 3:7). God told Ezekiel to **prophesy over these bones**. Ironically, Ezekiel would get better results by prophesying to these bones than by preaching to living beings.

Verses 5, 6. **"I will cause breath to enter you that you may come to life,"** God said to the bones (v. 5). The word for "breath," רוּחַ (*ruach*), is used repeatedly in this section. It is sometimes translated as "breath" (vv. 5, 6, 8, 9, 10), sometimes as "spirit" (vv. 1, 14), and once as "winds" (v. 9).[2] The word occurs 378 times in the Hebrew Old Testament,[3] fifty-two times in Ezekiel. The spirit in Ezekiel was a God-sent power which energized the

---

[2] A thorough discussion on Ezekiel's use of the word "spirit" is given in Daniel I. Block, "The Prophet of the Spirit: The Use of *RWH* in the Book of Ezekiel," *Journal of the Evangelical Theological Society* 32 (March 1989): 27–49.

[3] Ibid., 29. According to Block, the Aramaic sections of Daniel contain an additional eleven occurrences.

prophet, induced visions, and revitalized Israel (see 11:19; 36:26; 39:29).

37:7–10

⁷So I prophesied as I was commanded; and as I prophesied, there was a noise, and behold, a rattling; and the bones came together, bone to its bone. ⁸And I looked, and behold, sinews were on them, and flesh grew and skin covered them; but there was no breath in them. ⁹Then He said to me, "Prophesy to the breath, prophesy, son of man, and say to the breath, 'Thus says the Lord GOD, "Come from the four winds, O breath, and breathe on these slain, that they come to life."'" ¹⁰So I prophesied as He commanded me, and the breath came into them, and they came to life and stood on their feet, an exceedingly great army.

Verse 7. Ezekiel faithfully fulfilled his commission as a prophet, delivering God's word. Carl G. Howie said,

> The Hebrews thought of God's word as a creative agent working through his prophet. The word was more than a sound disturbing the tranquillity of the air; it carried with it the full power of the speaker. So God's creative word re-created life where death had been. As the prophet spoke, the Spirit ("breath") of God possessed dry bones, making them into a mighty army (vss. 7–10). Life is meaningless existence until it is given meaning by the indwelling Spirit of God.[4]

The thought of preaching to a pile of bones may seem foolish or humorous to us. However, this prophet had played in the dirt, lain on his side for long periods of time, cut off his hair and chased it with a sword, and preached to mountain ranges. Perhaps to him this did not seem so unusual. During Ezekiel's sermon, a commotion occurred. **A rattling** disrupted his message:

---

[4]Carl G. Howie, *The Book of Ezekiel, The Book of Daniel*, The Layman's Bible Commentary (Richmond, Va.: John Knox Press, 1961), 73–74.

the **noise** of dry bones clicking as they **came together**, each moving to its appropriate location in the body. The ASV translates this, "So I prophesied as I was commanded: and as I prophesied, there was a noise, and, behold, an earthquake; and the bones came together, bone to its bone." The "noise" described was not an earthquake, but the sound of the bones assembling. The phrase **bone to its bone** represents a complete restoration, not a crippled nation.

Verses 8, 9. At this point, **there was no breath in them** (v. 8). Remarkable things had happened, but the audience still consisted of dead men. So it was with other great prophets of God who had preached great messages that fell on deaf ears (see Is. 6:10). In the same way, men of God today may be called upon to preach to a "dead" church. Nevertheless, faithful men preach their sermons, believing in the power of God's Word to bring life to those who are dead. As God lovingly breathed into the nostrils of Adam the "breath of life" so that he became a living being (Gen. 2:7), God here called upon the four winds to energize this vast army of cadavers (v. 9). The winds came obediently from every direction—from the four corners of the earth (see 7:2)—to instill the breath of life.

Verse 10. The faithful prophet did as he was **commanded** and, as with his other prophecies, saw immediate results. The wind did its job, and the **exceedingly great army** came alive, standing at attention. Thus the vision was complete. John B. Taylor said,

> Notice that, throughout this vision, Ezekiel has acted under orders and has even described his own implicit obedience to God's commands (7, 10). In so doing he emphasizes that this work of revival is God's work from start to finish. If man plays any part in it himself, it is only in obedience to God's direction. The same can be said of man's contribution to any spiritual revival.[5]

---

[5]John B. Taylor, *Ezekiel: An Introduction and Commentary,* Tyndale Old Testament Commentaries (Downers Grove, Ill.: Inter-Varsity Press, 1969), 238.

The figure presented does not teach the doctrine of the bodily resurrection of the dead. We have no reason to suspect from this or any other passage in Ezekiel that the prophet held this belief. God Himself gave the interpretation of what Ezekiel had witnessed.

37:11–14

¹¹Then He said to me, "Son of man, these bones are the whole house of Israel; behold, they say, 'Our bones are dried up and our hope has perished. We are completely cut off.' ¹²Therefore prophesy and say to them, 'Thus says the Lord God, "Behold, I will open your graves and cause you to come up out of your graves, My people; and I will bring you into the land of Israel. ¹³Then you will know that I am the Lord, when I have opened your graves and caused you to come up out of your graves, My people. ¹⁴I will put My Spirit within you and you will come to life, and I will place you on your own land. Then you will know that I, the Lord, have spoken and done it," declares the Lord.'"

Verse 11. God explained that **these bones** [were] **the whole house of Israel**. They represented the multitude of His people. The application was to the *whole* house of Israel—both the northern and southern kingdoms. This nation's view of itself is seen in three statements. They said,

1. **"Our bones are dried up."** The time the people had spent in captivity had destroyed their hope for restoration.
2. **"Our hope has perished."** Even in captivity, the people had at first hoped for a quick return. That hope had been dashed—not only by the preaching of Jeremiah and Ezekiel, but also by years in exile.
3. **"We are completely cut off."** As evidenced in the Books of Jeremiah and 2 Kings, the people were scattered throughout the nations and cut off from one another. Their situation defeated any vision of being a "transplanted nation."

Verse 12. The application continues. God would energize His dead people and **bring** them back to the land of Israel. "Bring" (בּוֹא, *bo'*) is a key word, appearing frequently in this book (fifty-six times) and in Jeremiah (about forty times). Its significance is seen in that this event would occur through divine intervention; only God could bring the Israelites back to their land.

Verse 13. Repeating one of the key phrases in the Book of Ezekiel, God declared that this action would teach Israel **that I am the Lord**. They admitted that they had no hope, that all seemed lost. When God caused them to **come up out of** [their] **graves**, no one else could claim the credit: This was an act of God.

Verse 14. God declared that He would place His **Spirit** within the people. Human power could not bring to life the dead nation. Through the power of the Spirit, they would be freed from their graveyards of captivity, restored to divine favor, and returned to their beloved land. These events would teach them the all-important lesson that God is Lord.

The plan was now complete. First, there had to be *physical restoration*, which God secured when He resurrected the dead nation. Second, *spiritual restoration* was needed—with the people alive spiritually, obeying the stipulations of their covenant with Yahweh (see 36:27).

THE TWO STICKS: REUNITING THE TWO KINGDOMS UNDER ONE HEAD (37:15–28)

37:15–21

¹⁵The word of the Lord came again to me saying, ¹⁶"And you, son of man, take for yourself one stick and write on it, 'For Judah and for the sons of Israel, his companions'; then take another stick and write on it, 'For Joseph, the stick of Ephraim and all the house of Israel, his companions.' ¹⁷Then join them for yourself one to another into one stick, that they may become one in your hand. ¹⁸When the sons of your people speak to you saying, 'Will you not declare to us what you mean

by these?' ¹⁹say to them, 'Thus says the Lord GOD, "Behold, I will take the stick of Joseph, which is in the hand of Ephraim, and the tribes of Israel, his companions; and I will put them with it, with the stick of Judah, and make them one stick, and they will be one in My hand."' ²⁰The sticks on which you write will be in your hand before their eyes. ²¹Say to them, 'Thus says the Lord GOD, "Behold, I will take the sons of Israel from among the nations where they have gone, and I will gather them from every side and bring them into their own land."'"

Verses 15, 16. As in 4:1 and 5:1, God had Ezekiel prepare a visual aid to teach the next lesson. The prophet was instructed to take two sticks and write on them (v. 16). On the first one, he was to write, **For Judah.** This represented the southern kingdom, made up of two tribes (Judah and Benjamin). On the second stick, he was to write, **For Joseph,** meaning the northern kingdom, which included ten tribes. This kingdom is sometimes called "Joseph" or **Ephraim,** because its first king, Jeroboam (see 1 Kings 11:31), came from that tribe. Sometimes it is called Samaria, because that was the capital city of the northern kingdom. (Oholah represented "Samaria" in 23:4.)

Writing on sticks occurred on two other occasions. Moses did it in Numbers 17:2–7, to determine whom God had selected as His high priest. Zechariah also wrote on two sticks, inscribing "favor" on one and "union" on the other (Zech. 11:7–14).

Verses 17–20. God next instructed Ezekiel to **join . . . one to another into one stick** (v. 17). Such a sight would be a curiosity to the onlookers, and they would inquire as to its meaning (v. 18). Ezekiel was to make sure they saw the writing on both sticks—for that was crucial to understanding the meaning of the lesson. He declared that God would make them **one stick** (v. 19), and then he held it up **before their eyes** (v. 20). All they saw was one long stick. (Most likely, Ezekiel was holding them together, end to end, with his fist in the middle so that he appeared to be holding only one long stick. There is no reason to interject a miracle here.)

Verse 21. God explained the meaning of the sticks. He intended to reunite the scattered people in **their own land.** Hope for the political reunion of the two nations was proclaimed by a few other prophets (Is. 11:16; Jer. 3:18; Hos. 1:11), yet none did so as dramatically as did Ezekiel. Such a reunion seemed impossible, for the northern kingdom of Israel had lost her identity as a nation after being defeated and dispersed by the Assyrian king Tiglath-pileser III (722[1] B.C.; see 2 Kings 15:29; 16:9).

The idea of Israel being reunited with Judah has created a great deal of discussion. A literal application of verses 15 through 21 seems to be demanded, for such was the whole purpose of the stick illustration. The application might be explained in any of the following ways:

(1) When the Medo-Persian Empire conquered Babylon (which had conquered Assyria about eighty years earlier), the king decreed that all foreign people were to return to their own lands (Ezra 1:1–4). While the Books of Ezra and Nehemiah focus primarily on the exiles in Babylon, many Israelites from the northern kingdom could have maintained their identity throughout the 180 years of exile.

(2) Numerous Israelites had left the northern kingdom and joined the southern kingdom. People from the tribes of Ephraim, Manasseh, Zebulun, Asher, and Issachar—tribes of the northern kingdom—"humbled themselves and came to Jerusalem" (2 Chron. 30:11; see vv. 10, 18). The people offered "twelve bulls for all Israel" because each tribe was represented at the sacrifice (Ezra 8:35; see 6:17).

(3) This reuniting is fulfilled allegorically in the church, the new Israel, where all people are united under the cross of Christ (Gal. 6:16; Eph. 2:13–16).

(4) The prophecy remains unfulfilled, to be fulfilled at some future date.

(5) It is a prophecy that failed. It will never come true.

While the first and second interpretations have merit, they must be rejected on the basis of what follows. The united kingdom was to have "My servant David" as king (v. 24). This is messianic terminology (see the discussion on 34:23, 24) and does not apply to any leader who would come in the near future (for example, Zerubbabel, Ezra, or Nehemiah). The fourth should also be rejected, for two reasons. First, it overlooks Christ's work during His earthly ministry. The Old Testament was to lead us *to* Christ, not to look past His earthly ministry to unforeseen events in the future. Second, no New Testament writer repeated or renewed the promise of a literal uniting of Israel and Judah.

Number five must certainly be rejected, considering the inspiration and inerrancy of the Scriptures. Therefore, the third interpretation is the most logical and contextually satisfying. As Paul declared in Romans 2:28, 29 and 9:6 that all who have obeyed the gospel of Christ are "Israel." The cross united all men under the Lordship of Christ (2:12–16). These truths correspond with the promises made in Ezekiel 37. Albert Barnes said,

> The restoration of Israel to their native soil will lead the way to the coming of the promised King, the Son of David, Who will gather into His kingdom the true Israel, all who shall by faith be acknowledged as the Israel of God. The reign of the One King David is the reign of Christ in His kingdom, the Church.[6]

37:22, 23

²²""'And I will make them one nation in the land, on the mountains of Israel; and one king will be king for all of them; and they will no longer be two nations and no longer be divided into two kingdoms. ²³They will no longer defile themselves with their idols, or with their detestable things, or with any of their transgressions; but I will deliver them from all their dwelling places in which they have sinned, and will cleanse them. And they will be My people, and I will be their God.'"""

The children of Israel would be gathered from the nations where they had been scattered. Once reunited, they would repopulate the land as one nation (v. 22a), having one king and one kingdom (v. 22b). They would no longer worship idols

---

[6]Albert Barnes, *The Bible Commentary: Proverbs to Ezekiel*, Barnes' Notes, ed. F. C. Cook, abr. and ed. J. M. Fuller (Grand Rapids, Mich.: Baker Book House, 1983), 390.

(v. 23a), but would be a holy (v. 23b) and obedient people (v. 24).

Verse 22. God revealed the meaning of the two sticks: Israel and Judah would be brought together as **one nation**. One of the most tragic days in Israel's history was when the nation was split under two kings, with ten tribes following Jeroboam and two tribes following Solomon's son Rehoboam (1 Kings 12). Their best days were when they had "one king" over them—David, the son of Jesse. God promised to renew the glory of that time by reuniting them.

Verse 23. Idols had brought about the fall of both nations (Israel in 2 Kings 17; Judah in Ezek. 16). Their days of **defil[ing]** themselves with these idols was to end, along with other **transgressions**. When the exiles returned to Israel, they no longer had the problem of idolatry—even to the time of Jesus. God restated His intent: **"They will be My people, and I will be their God."** Variations of this statement occur at least seventeen times in the Scriptures.[7] The occurrence in Jeremiah 31:31–34, in the prophecy of the new covenant, provides another reason to see the ultimate fulfillment of these words in the gospel of Christ (see Heb. 8; 10).

37:24–28

24"'"My servant David will be king over them, and they will all have one shepherd; and they will walk in My ordinances and keep My statutes and observe them. 25They will live on the land that I gave to Jacob My servant, in which your fathers lived; and they will live on it, they, and their sons and their sons' sons, forever; and David My servant will be their prince forever. 26I will make a covenant of peace with them; it will be an everlasting covenant with them. And I will place them and multiply them, and will set My sanctuary in their midst forever. 27My dwelling place also will be with them; and I will be their God, and they will be My people. 28And the nations will know that I am the LORD who sanctifies Israel, when My sanctuary is in their midst forever."'"

---

[7]See Gen. 17:8; Ex. 29:45; Lev. 26:44, 45; Jer. 24:7; 31:33; 32:38; Ezek. 11:20; 14:11; 34:24; 37:23, 27; Zech. 8:8; 10:6; 2 Cor. 6:16; Heb. 8:10; Rev. 21:3.

Verse 24. God declared, **"My servant David will be king over them."** This is a messianic title (see the discussion on 34:23, 24) and should be so understood here. In addition, two other titles belonging to Christ are used: "king" and **shepherd**. This means that the leader of God's people would be both their political king and their religious shepherd. He would unite them under both offices. (Notice the concepts of priest and king in Zech. 6:12, 13.) The leadership of this king was to be such that the people would **observe** [His] **ordinances** and **statutes** (see the discussion on 5:6).

Verse 25. Further, God said, **"They will live on the land that I gave to Jacob My servant."** Only the land promise given to Jacob is mentioned here. S. Fisch wrote,

> Though Abraham and Isaac were also promised the land, only Jacob is mentioned in this connection because he was the ancestor of Israel alone, whereas the other two patriarchs were also the ancestors of Ishmael and Esau respectively, who were not included in the promise.[8]

This promise was fulfilled when the exiles returned to the land; but it was a conditional promise, dependent upon their continued faithfulness (see Deut. 4:25, 26). The inherited land in which the righteous are to dwell with Jesus as King is the "new earth" (2 Pet. 3:13; Rev. 21:1). Jesus was not concerned with His people's possession of literal property, for His kingdom was "not of this world" (Jn. 18:36). He has prepared a place in His Father's house for the faithful (Jn. 14:1, 2)—a place not located on this earth (for the earth will someday be destroyed; 2 Pet. 3:10–12).

Verse 26. The **covenant of peace** (see 16:62; 20:37; 34:25) is mentioned again. This covenant was to be governed by the "prince of peace" (Is. 9:6) in a kingdom of peace (Phil. 4:7). This is not peace from external conflict (Jn. 14:27), but peace that comes from a good relationship with God. This covenant will also be an **everlasting** one. Those under the banner of the Davidic

---

[8]S. Fisch, *Ezekiel: Hebrew Text and English Translation with an Introduction and Commentary*, Soncino Books of the Bible (London: Soncino Press, 1950), 251–52.

king will always enjoy peace. The phrase **will set My sanctuary in their midst forever** refers not only to protection, but also to divine selection.

Verse 27. God said, "**My dwelling place also will be with them.**" Jesus was truly Emmanuel—"God with us" (see Jn. 1:14). Again, God stated His intention through Ezekiel: "**I will be their God, and they will be My people**" (see 1 Cor. 3:16, 17; 2 Cor. 6:16; Heb. 8:10).

Verse 28. The fulfillment of these events would prove to the nations that the Lord had sanctified Israel. Only God could cleanse the evil from His people (see 36:25), setting them apart from the other nations. His **sanctuary** would be in the midst of the people **forever**. The kingdom established by God's king was to be an eternal one. That description fits the kingdom of Christ, the church (Dan. 2:44; 7:13, 14; Mt. 16:16–18; Heb. 1:8).

All of this could take place only when the nation became whole again. Its ultimate fulfillment is the church, in which all of God's people are brought together under the reign of Christ. Some elements of this kingdom are supported in the New Testament. God said,

1. "I . . . will set My sanctuary in their midst forever" (v. 26; see 1 Cor. 3:16, 17).
2. "My dwelling place also will be with them" (v. 27; see Jn. 1:14).
3. "I will be their God, and they will be My people" (v. 27; see 2 Cor. 6:16).
4. "My sanctuary is in their midst forever" (v. 28; see Mt. 28:20; 1 Thess. 4:17).

Five times in the Hebrew, Ezekiel used the word 'olam (עוֹלָם), which means "forever" (v. 25, twice; v. 26, twice; v. 28, once). These events were not temporary. The promised security was not to be short-lived. The prophesied kingdom would never end. The word 'olam is the same one used to describe the Passover (Ex. 12:14), incense (Ex. 30:8), the Sabbath (Ex. 31:16), burnt offerings (Ex. 29:42), the Aaronic priesthood (Ex. 40:15), and the earth itself (Eccles. 1:4). The Bible teaches about the end of each of these. (Some have already been brought to an end, while the end of the earth is yet in the future; see 2 Pet. 3:10–12.) The word refers to something that lasts for ages or seems continual to *mankind*. God, and only God, can cause these things to cease. Only God could bring an end to the offering of incense or animal sacrifices, and only God can decree the end of this present earth. Likewise, He could end Israel's dwelling "forever" in the land.

It is neither logical nor biblical to claim that the promises in Ezekiel 37:26–28 were made solely to physical Israel. Did Israel ever again possess the land as promised here? They did not, and they never will—because the land promise was dependent on their obedience. God made that plain when the Israelites were brought into the land the first time (Deut. 4:25–27), and they were reminded of the condition when they returned from the Babylonian Exile (Jer. 18:5–12; Hag. 1:3–11). The Book of Ezekiel explains that God brought the people back to the land in order to protect His name, not because Israel was righteous (Ezek. 36:22).

God's promises are conditional. If Israel returned to her unfaithful ways, would God keep the people in their land anyway? Of course not! (See Jer. 18:5–12.) Before the coming of Christ, the Israelites were given 1,400 years in which to prove their faithfulness. They failed again and again. Then, when their longed-for Messiah finally appeared, they crucified Him. Paul specified that the only people who are special to God now are those who have conformed to the image of His Son (Rom. 8:29, 30) and have obeyed the gospel (Rom. 11; see 2 Thess. 1:7–9; 1 Pet. 4:17, 18). Those who are obedient to the gospel are the "chosen race" (1 Pet. 2:9, 10).

FOR FURTHER STUDY: THE TWO STICKS AND MORMON DOCTRINE

Mormons claim that Ezekiel's illustration of the two sticks prophesies the uniting of the Bible and the Book of Mormon. Their doctrine says that Ezekiel 37:16–23 teaches God's intention for both books, or "scrolls," to be obeyed by His people. Such cannot be the case for the following reasons:

1. A "stick" is not a "scroll." The Hebrew word for "stick" is עֵץ (*'ets*), while "scroll" is סֵפֶר (*sepher*). The Bible never interchanges the words "stick" and "scroll."[9]
2. Ezekiel was told what to write on the sticks: "For Judah" and "For Joseph," not "The Bible" on one and "The Book of Mormon" on the other.
3. Ezekiel is not the author of the Bible and the Book of Mormon—as he would technically have to be, according to the Mormon line of thinking.
4. The context of this passage is about Israel and Judah (vv. 20–22). To make such an application to the Bible and the Book of Mormon would make the entire message of hope—from the valley of dry bones to the coming "one nation"—meaningless to the exiles.

APPLICATION

God's Patience, Punishment, and Redeeming Power

The disobedient will be punished. Because of her continued wickedness, God brought an end to Israel. He will not tolerate sin forever.

God is longsuffering. The fact that He waited so long to bring judgment shows His patient nature (see Rom. 2:3, 4; 2 Pet. 3:9).

One who appears spiritually dead can be raised by God (see Jn. 5:24–27).

Preachers (and all Christians) should learn a lesson from Ezekiel. When the situation looked hopeless, Ezekiel allowed God to do His work before making a judgment. Many people in our world seem out of reach of the gospel, hopelessly dead in sin—but we must not underestimate the power of God's Word. God can make them live!

The Word of God has tremendous power, even when it is preached by "earthen vessels" (see Rom. 1:16; 1 Cor. 1:18).

D.P.

---

[9]Francis Brown, S. R. Driver, and Charles A. Briggs, *A Hebrew and English Lexicon of the Old Testament* (Oxford: Clarendon Press, 1972), 706–7, 781–82.

With God in the Cemetery

Ezekiel was brought to a valley of dry bones, a vast graveyard. God wanted to teach him a vital lesson. To talk about life, He took Ezekiel to a special classroom: a mortuary. What did He teach Ezekiel about Himself there?

God can do the impossible. He can raise the dead. He can make dry bones receive flesh and come to life.

God will keep His promises. Not even death can keep God from fulfilling each of His promises.

God is the God of eternal hope. When everything seems to be lost, there is hope in God.

God wants us to know of His power. This dramatic event took place to illustrate to the world who God is. We cannot find comfort in God unless we understand what He can do.

These truths are carried into the New Testament. God can do the impossible: He can forgive our sins through Jesus. He will keep His promises; not one promise made by Him will be broken. He surrounds us with hope. Under His care, even the darkest night turns to day. He wants everyone on earth to know what He can do!

E.C.

CHAPTER 38
ORACLES 1–4 AGAINST GOG AND MAGOG[1]

Chapters 38 and 39 are well organized. They present seven distinct oracles, each beginning with the phrase "Thus says the Lord GOD" (38:3–9, 10–13, 14–16, 17–23; 39:1–16, 17–24, 25–29). The oracles chronicle how Gog, the chief prince of Meshech and Tubal, gathered terrific forces in the north and came to conquer the land of Judah. His intention was to destroy the people who were living in peace with unfortified cities. However, God intervened, destroying the invading armies with a huge slaughter, so that the land was filled with corpses and littered with implements of warfare. The bodies served as food for the wild beasts, and the weapons provided Israel with a seven-year supply of firewood. John B. Taylor wrote,

> Now the idea of a huge eschatological battle between the forces of evil, or the north, and the faithful people of God was no new one. Ezekiel was aware that he spoke of a fulfilment of events which earlier spokesmen had prophesied (38:17; 39:8), and his words echoed the language of others, especially Jeremiah (Je. 4:5—6:26; *cf.* Joel 2:20). He was in fact representing the last days in terms of the "day of the Lord" imagery which dominated the future for prophets like Joel (Joel 2:28–32), Amos (Am. 5:18–20) and Zephaniah (Zp. 1:14–18), and which appears strongly in parts of Isaiah (Is. 29:5–8; 66:15ff.) and Zechariah (Zc. 12:1–9; 14:1–15). This is a totally different

---

[1]See "The Oracles Against Gog and Magog" in Appendix 1.

picture from the "golden age" motif, in terms of which the return from exile to the promised land had been couched. How possible it is to reconcile the two approaches into a consistent chronological scheme must be left to others to judge, on the basis of the efforts of those who have tried. The important thing to note is that Ezekiel was apparently able to use both forms of imagery without a sense of contradiction, though he does not give any clear guidance as to how they may be balanced against each other.[2]

ORACLE 1: THE DESCRIPTION OF GOG AND HIS FORCES (38:1–9)

38:1–6
¹**And the word of the L**ORD **came to me saying,** ²**"Son of man, set your face toward Gog of the land of Magog, the prince of Rosh, Meshech and Tubal, and prophesy against him** ³**and say, 'Thus says the Lord G**OD**, "Behold, I am against you, O Gog, prince of Rosh, Meshech and Tubal.** ⁴**I will turn you about and put hooks into your jaws, and I will bring you out, and all your army, horses and horsemen, all of them splendidly attired, a great company with buckler and shield, all of them wielding swords;** ⁵**Persia, Ethiopia and Put with them, all of them with shield and helmet;** ⁶**Gomer with all its troops; Beth-togarmah from the remote parts of the north with all its troops—many peoples with you."'"**

Verses 1, 2. Gog of the land of Magog (v. 2) has been the topic of much discussion. Part of the difficulty with this section can be attributed to works such as *The Scofield Reference Bible*,[3] which says, "That the primary reference is to the Northern (European) powers headed up by Russia, all agree. . . . The ref-

---

[2]John B. Taylor, *Ezekiel: An Introduction and Commentary*, Tyndale Old Testament Commentaries (Downers Grove, Ill.: Inter-Varsity Press, 1969), 243.
[3]C. I. Scofield, ed., *The Scofield Reference Bible* (New York: Oxford University Press, 1986), 883.

erence to Meshech and Tubal (Moscow and Tobolsk) is a clear mark of identification." In truth, commentators are far from agreement. With the demise of the Soviet Union, many commentators abandoned this view. Some have reinterpreted the section, attempting to associate Gog and Magog with modern nations, while others refuse to rethink the position.

This section was written to re-establish confidence in the Lord. He would now fight for His people rather than withdraw from them (as He had in 587[6] B.C.; ch. 11). As in the days of conquering Canaan, God would once again fight for Israel. Most likely, these terms do not refer to any literal nation or people, but were used by the prophet to represent the enemies of God's people. According to Taylor, "The . . . origin of the name is less significant than what it symbolizes, namely the personified head of the forces of evil which are intent on destroying the people of God."[4] This would explain why John could easily adopt these names in Revelation 20, again referring to the enemies of God and His people. Nevertheless, numerous suggestions have been made regarding the historical identity of "Gog,"[5] "Magog,"[6] **Meshech**, and **Tubal**.

Verses 3, 4. The seven oracles begin in verse 3. In the first oracle, God described Gog and his forces. The Lord vowed to **put hooks into [his] jaws** and **bring . . . out** Gog with his **army** (v. 4). This terminology is similar to the description of the capture of the sea monster in 29:3–5, adding support to the theory

---

[4]Taylor, 244.

[5]"*Gog* has been variously identified with Gyges, king of Lydia, who is called Gugu in the records of Ashurbanipal, and with the place-name, Gagaia, referred to in the Tell el-Amarna letters as a land of barbarians. From Ras Shamra writings there has been found a god, Gaga, and this identification too has been suggested (*Enuma Elish*, III: line 2). Others have seen in Gog a historical figure like Alexander the Great" (Ibid.). Thorough discussions are given in Edwin Yamauchi, "Meshech, Tubal, and Company: A Review Article," *Journal of the Evangelical Theological Society* 19 (Summer 1976): 239–47, and Clyde E. Billington, "The Rosh People in History and Prophecy (Part One)," *Master's Theological Journal* 3 (Spring 1992): 54–64.

[6]"Since the location of Magog was unknown, interpreters have had a field day in identifying Gog and Magog with successive nomadic hordes from the steppes of Russia" (Yamauchi, 246).

that these forces are metaphorical. The weaponry described is that of ancient peoples, much different from the technological weapons used today. This army is said to ride **horses** (see v. 15) and carry **swords**, along with **buckler and shield**. These implements of warfare were made of so much wood that Israel could use them for firewood for seven years (39:9, 10).

Verse 5. Israel's enemies are listed. Gog is portrayed as amassing great forces to join his already powerful army. Being added to his number were **Persia, Ethiopia and Put** (northern Africa). Carl G. Howie noted, "It goes without saying that the names of these ancient places do not contain any references to modern nations and states."[7] Gog's forces now included two southern allies, Ethiopia and Put. With their help, encircling Israel would be easier.

Verse 6. Gomer with all its troops is another force named but not clearly identified. The eldest son of Japheth was named Gomer (Gen. 10:2). Some scholars link Gomer with the Assyrians; others associate him with the Cimmerians (the Greek name for Armenians).[8] **Beth-togarmah** is thought to be ancient Armenia (see 27:14; Gen. 10:3).

38:7–9

⁷"'"Be prepared, and prepare yourself, you and all your companies that are assembled about you, and be a guard for them. ⁸After many days you will be summoned; in the latter years you will come into the land that is restored from the sword, whose inhabitants have been gathered from many nations to the mountains of Israel which had been a continual waste; but its people were brought out from the nations, and they are living securely, all of them. ⁹You will go up, you will

---

[7]Carl G. Howie, *The Book of Ezekiel, The Book of Daniel*, The Layman's Bible Commentary, vol. 13 (Richmond, Va.: John Knox Press, 1961), 75–76.

[8]The Cimmerians, a people from Ukraine, later migrated into what is now eastern Turkey and became foes of the Assyrians. They are also associated with the Galatians. The word "Galatia" is thought to be derived from "Gomer." Extensive information on these people is given in Yamauchi (242–43).

come like a storm; you will be like a cloud covering the land, you and all your troops, and many peoples with you."'"

Verse 7. Using powerful irony, God called upon these nations to **prepare**. He knew that their efforts would be in vain. God was saying, "Go ahead and try"—but the army had no chance of victory against God.

Verse 8. **"After many days you will be summoned,"** the prophecy continued. This event was to take place in the future, **in the latter years**. (Notice the phrase "the last days" in verse 16.) Some scholars have incorrectly taken great pains to establish this time as the period just before the second coming of Christ. The phrase has wide application in the Old Testament and therefore cannot be said to pinpoint a particular period of time (see Gen. 49:1; Num. 24:14; Jer. 23:20; Dan. 2:28; 8:17, 19, 26; 10:14; Is. 2:2; Hos. 3:5). What is evident from this text is that "the latter years" describes a time when Israel would be **restored from the sword**. The word "sword" has most often referred to Babylon in the Book of Ezekiel (see 21:1–19). This being the case, we may understand this to mean "restored from Babylon." It would not make sense, therefore, to apply this prophecy to a time thousands of years in the future, far removed from the days of the Babylonian Captivity. The phrases **gathered from many nations** (36:24; 37:21) and **to the mountains of Israel** (34:13; 36:1–8) are familiar in Ezekiel and do not refer to the end of time.

The fact that Israel was **living securely** is an important concept in this section (see 38:11, 14). The phrase cannot be reconciled with the position of Dispensational Premillennialism, which places the battle against Gog somewhere in the midst of the Tribulation (certainly not a period of security). The phrase does remind us of the promised security with the coming Messiah (34:25, 28). It would logically describe the peace enjoyed by those in Christ (see Jn. 14:27; Phil. 4:4–7; Rom. 5:1).

Verse 9. The vastness of Gog's army is seen here. **Like a storm** that covers **the land** and quickly converges on it, Gog's army would blanket the land, **covering** it with his vast **troops, and many peoples**.

ORACLE 2: GOG'S EVIL PLAN (38:10–13)

¹⁰"'Thus says the Lord GOD, "It will come about on that day, that thoughts will come into your mind and you will devise an evil plan, ¹¹and you will say, 'I will go up against the land of unwalled villages. I will go against those who are at rest, that live securely, all of them living without walls and having no bars or gates, ¹²to capture spoil and to seize plunder, to turn your hand against the waste places which are now inhabited, and against the people who are gathered from the nations, who have acquired cattle and goods, who live at the center of the world.' ¹³Sheba and Dedan and the merchants of Tarshish with all its villages will say to you, 'Have you come to capture spoil? Have you assembled your company to seize plunder, to carry away silver and gold, to take away cattle and goods, to capture great spoil?'"'"

Verse 10. The second oracle reveals Gog's "evil plan." Gog wanted to cause trouble, and the peaceful Israelite nation appeared to be worthy of his evil plan. He wanted to kill and pillage, and Israel was an easy target (having no fortified cities). This verse verifies the free will of Gog. He was not being forced to come against Israel, but was doing so by his own evil thoughts which led him to **devise an evil plan**. (This verse clarifies the statements of verses 4 and 16 regarding the actions of God.) S. Fisch said, "The gravity of Gog's crime will lie in the fact that his attack was directed against a land which had been desolated and whose people have been redeemed from the countries of their dispersion."[9]

Verse 11. Gog's strategy was to attack **unwalled villages**, areas that were not defended. The barbaric nature of the enemy is revealed here: They wanted to kill and plunder the unprotected. Ezekiel talked about fortified (walled) cities in 36:35. Zechariah 2:4, 5 also mentions that Jerusalem would be "inhab-

---

[9] S. Fisch, *Ezekiel: Hebrew Text and English Translation with an Introduction and Commentary*, Soncino Books of the Bible (London: Soncino Press, 1950), 254.

ited without walls," indicating that God would be her protection.

Verse 12. The intentions of Gog are revealed. He wanted to . . .

1. **Capture spoil**—Soldiers were allowed to take whatever they could find from homes in the cities they conquered.
2. **Seize plunder**—The coffers of Israel had been filled by conquering other nations and plundering their riches. This phrase is also thought to refer to the treasures of the temple, which the enemy soldiers would not be allowed to take for themselves. Such items would be seized by the king of the conquering army.
3. **Turn [his] hand against the waste places which are now inhabited**—The land had seen troubled times, and Gog brought more trouble. Gog showed no interest in the land itself, but intended to plunder its riches and then return home.
4. **[Turn] against the people**—These people had seen days of hardship and struggle. After their captivity, they had been **gathered from the nations** to live in peace once again, in their own land. Since returning to the land, they had enjoyed prosperity, acquiring **cattle and goods**—some of the spoil the soldiers coveted.

God's people are described as living **at the center of the world**—literally "in the navel of the earth" (see Judg. 9:37). With the powerful Egyptians to the south, and the Assyrians and Babylonians to the north, Israel was in the middle (see 5:5). Gog (in the distant north) perceived no threat to him or his kingdom. His intentions grew out of lust and greed.

Verse 13. Additional nations joined Gog, including **Sheba** (to the south; see 27:22, 23), **Dedan** (to the east; see 25:13; 27:15, 20), and **Tarshish** (to the west; see 27:12), **with all its villages**. These greedy nations wanted to take part in the plundering, because Israel looked like easy prey.

ORACLE 3: GOG'S ARMY MOBILIZED (38:14–16)

¹⁴"Therefore prophesy, son of man, and say to Gog, 'Thus says the Lord GOD, "On that day when My people Israel are living securely, will you not know it? ¹⁵You will come from your place out of the remote parts of the north, you and many peoples with you, all of them riding on horses, a great assembly and a mighty army; ¹⁶and you will come up against My people Israel like a cloud to cover the land. It shall come about in the last days that I will bring you against My land, so that the nations may know Me when I am sanctified through you before their eyes, O Gog."'"

Verses 14, 15. In the third oracle, God described the mobilizing of a great army but declared that Gog's attack would result in the Lord's being "sanctified." When Gog and his forces arrived in Israel, the people were **living securely**. As he had anticipated, they were unsuspecting of an enemy invasion. God's question **". . . will you not know it?"** probably refers to the scouting and preparation done by Gog's forces. His spies had brought back a favorable report: The people were rich and unprotected. Gog deployed an army with an incredible number of soldiers—all with lust and greed in their eyes.

Verse 16. The phrase **in the last days** is equivalent to "after many days" and "in the latter years" (v. 8).[10] **"I will bring you against My land,"** God said. Gog had already devised evil (v. 10), and God was using that evil decision against him. Gog's free will was not removed, but it was being used to bring him under the wrath of God. Taylor said,

> Whereas the previous oracle regards Gog as fully responsible for planning the operation, these verses show that God is bringing him against Israel. There is no inconsistency here: "a divine purpose overrules while it

---

[10]See the discussion of "the last days" in "The Oracles Against Gog and Magog" in Appendix 1.

makes use of, the base human motive" (Cooke). The same paradox marks Isaiah's teaching on the Assyrian invasion (Is. 10:5–19) and Habakkuk's attitude to the Chaldean menace (Hab. 1:5–11). It does not mean that Gog is a luckless pawn in the hand of an all-powerful but immoral God. Gog freely acts according to the evil dictates of his lust for conquest and easy spoil, but behind everything in the universe (and especially as it relates to God's people) there is the controlling hand of God, who orders all things with a view to the ultimate vindication of His honour among the nations. What Gog imagines to be a victory for himself, the Lord turns into an opportunity for His glory....[11]

By God's providence, Gog's massive army made its way to Israel to become an object lesson. The utter wickedness of Gog stands in stark contrast to the nature of God, who would be **sanctified through** Gog's destruction. Anyone who thought that God would overlook evil—or considered Him powerless to do anything about it—would be proven wrong. God's name was to be vindicated, and His character established.

ORACLE 4: THE DESTRUCTION OF GOG (38:17–23)

[17]*"***Thus says the Lord G**OD**, "Are you the one of whom I spoke in former days through My servants the prophets of Israel, who prophesied in those days for many years that I would bring you against them?** [18]**It will come about on that day, when Gog comes against the land of Israel," declares the Lord G**OD**, "that My fury will mount up in My anger.** [19]**In My zeal and in My blazing wrath I declare that on that day there will surely be a great earthquake in the land of Israel.** [20]**The

---

[11]Taylor, 246. Taylor cited G. A. Cooke, *A Critical and Exegetical Commentary on the Book of Ezekiel,* International Critical Commentary (Edinburgh: T. & T. Clark, 1936), n.p.

fish of the sea, the birds of the heavens, the beasts of the field, all the creeping things that creep on the earth, and all the men who are on the face of the earth will shake at My presence; the mountains also will be thrown down, the steep pathways will collapse and every wall will fall to the ground. ²¹I will call for a sword against him on all My mountains," declares the Lord God. "Every man's sword will be against his brother. ²²With pestilence and with blood I will enter into judgment with him; and I will rain on him and on his troops, and on the many peoples who are with him, a torrential rain, with hailstones, fire and brimstone. ²³I will magnify Myself, sanctify Myself, and make Myself known in the sight of many nations; and they will know that I am the Lord."'"

Verse 17. In the fourth oracle, God spoke of His fury and zeal, promising to make Himself known through the destruction of His enemies. The ultimate destruction of Gog had been prophesied **through My servants the prophets of Israel**. They had predicted (**for many years**) Gog's ultimate end. While some commentators minimize this statement (saying that prophets had predicted the demise of God's enemies in general, not Gog specifically), the thought is not so easily dismissed. The verse indicates that *this* force of evil was the subject of prophetic work. (**Are you the one of whom I spoke in former days . . . ?**) Therefore, the Bible student should consider what nation was continually condemned by the prophets. Babylon is the clear choice, having been the subject of prophecies by Isaiah (47:1, 5; 48:14–20), Jeremiah (25:12; 50:35, 45; 51:1–45), Daniel (5:7–30), and Habakkuk (1:5–11).

Verse 18. While Gog's heart was filled with lustful thoughts of wealth and plunder, God's thoughts were of **fury**, which would **mount up in [His] anger**. There was no legitimate reason for this aggression against God's people. They were peace-loving people who posed no threat. Gog's desire to take advantage of their security was an outrage to the almighty God.

Verse 19. Gog considered himself unbeatable with his massive army, equipped and trained for warfare. He was sure of victory—yet he miscalculated. He failed to understand the reason the people lived in unfortified cities: They had a divine Protector, who would be filled with **zeal** and **blazing wrath** against Gog and his hoards. The word for "zeal" (קִנְאָה, *qin'ah*), when used of God, refers to His being provoked beyond tolerance. There was no longer room for compassion. His character had been challenged, and His beloved people were in danger. Gog's action provoked God to the point that His anger was boiling over. The word "zeal," therefore, includes the need for divine vindication of God's nature and power.[12]

Verses 20–22. The apocalyptic nature of this section is clearly demonstrated. In highly figurative and symbolic language, God described the horror of the created world upon encountering His awesome **presence**. The creatures **of the sea, the heavens,** and **the field,** along **with creeping things, men,** and even **the mountains** would **shake** and be **thrown down**. The **pathways** would **collapse,** and **every wall** would **fall** down before God (v. 20). Everything—animate or inanimate—would respond to God. What other power in the universe can generate such a response? Gog was unaware of what he was bringing upon himself.

Gog's forces intended to use the **sword** against the people of Israel, but their own weapons would be used against them (v. 21). In their confusion, with everything collapsing around them, they would turn against each other. Unlike Gog, the Lord has the natural elements at His disposal. His weapons are many, and any one of them could defeat Gog. This arsenal is listed:

- "Earthquakes" of such magnitude (see v. 19) that even mountains would collapse (see Is. 24:18–20; Joel 3:16; Hag. 2:6, 7).
- "Swords" brought against Israel but used by God to destroy Gog (see 21:3–5).
- **Pestilence**, plagues, and deadly epidemics sent against these forces (see Num. 14:12; Jer. 27:8; Hab. 3:5).
- **Torrential rain** that would sweep away the enemy. Horses

---

[12]Francis Brown, S. R. Driver, and Charles A. Briggs, *A Hebrew and English Lexicon of the Old Testament* (Oxford: Clarendon Press, 1972), 888.

and foot soldiers would be unable to proceed in the floods (see Gen. 6:17).
- **Hailstones** which would kill those on whom they fell (see Josh. 10:11; Ps. 11:6; 18:12–14; Is. 28:17).
- **Fire** like that which God rained down upon Sodom and Gomorrah (Gen. 19:1–25; Lev. 10:1, 2; Ps. 11:6; Is. 30:30).
- **Brimstone** like burning rocks that spew out of a volcano (see Gen. 19:24; Ps. 11:6; Is. 34:9).

Taylor wrote concerning the many weapons,

> All of these, except the sword, are non-human agents frequently associated with God's judgments, and this is partly why RSV follows LXX in emending 21 to *I will summon every kind of terror* against him. But despite the difficult Hebrew, the AV rendering is fully consonant with passages such as 5:17; 6:3; 11:8; 12:14, *etc.*, and it alone makes sense of the consequent *every man's sword shall be against his brother*, as the demoralized heathen slay each other in their panic and add to the general destruction (*cf.* Jdg. 7:22; 1 Sa. 14:20; Hg. 2:22; Zc. 14:13).[13]

Verse 23. God's intent was threefold. First, He wanted to **magnify [Him]self**. This means that He would enable the nations to see His greatness and might. At this point, He was recognized as nothing more than a small, localized god with limited power and influence. He would show Himself to be the God of the universe. Second, He would **sanctify [Him]self**. God had been grouped with other gods—small, ineffective, and weak. Through this awesome display of power, God would vindicate Himself and demonstrate the difference between Himself and so-called gods: He is the only true God. Third, He would **make [Him]self known**—not to just a few, but **in the sight of many nations**. Those who considered the Lord to be just the God of Israel were about to learn a valuable theology lesson. God declared, **"They will know that I am the Lord."** His displayed

---

[13]Taylor, 246–47.

power would convince the nations of the existence of only one God; they would come to a knowledge of the Lord.

APPLICATION

Vanquishing the Enemy

As long as this earth remains, God's people will have enemies. It is imperative that we remain alert. Forewarned, we should be forearmed (see 1 Pet. 5:8).

The forces of Gog were motivated by evil thoughts and desires (38:10). Our sins begin with our own uncontrolled lusts (Jas. 1:13–15).

Greed motivates people and nations to join forces with others, even those with whom they would normally not associate. God's people must choose their associates carefully (see 1 Cor. 15:33; 2 Cor. 6:14–18).

God will glorify His name. He wants His people to "magnify," "sanctify," and "make . . . known" His name (38:23; see 1 Pet. 2:9). The time will come when every knee will bow and all will confess the greatness of God and His Son (Phil. 2:9–11).

D.P.

How God Protects His People

Some powerful army was coming against Israel. God allowed this to happen because He wanted to show Israel that He was their God and that He would watch over them.

He prepared them. God gave them detailed instructions about what He was going to do. He also prepares us.

He strengthened them. During the battle, God provides the strength and the energy needed.

He delivered them. The battle belongs to the Lord. He gives the victory.

E.C.

CHAPTER 39

ORACLES 5–7 AGAINST GOG AND MAGOG

After describing the tremendous forces of Gog and his certain fall to the power of the Lord (ch. 38), Ezekiel recounted God's decisive victory in a fuller, more vivid way. Retelling accounts was not unusual in Hebrew literature. (For example, Genesis 2 recounts the Creation story of chapter 1, detailing the creation of Adam and Eve.) In this apocalyptic account, the huge multitudes of Gog were defeated—to the extent that the land was filled with the dead, and it took seven months to bury them all. In addition, Gog's massive army had been well-armed—so much so that the wood from their weapons would provide the Israelites with fuel to burn for seven years. In the time it took to bury the dead, God offered a tremendous feast to the beasts and birds, as they devoured the flesh and blood of the mighty soldiers from "Gog of the land of Magog" (38:2). This victory was to have a powerful impact upon the children of Israel, who were assured of God's love for them and His willingness to forgive their iniquities.

ORACLE 5: THE DEFEAT AND BURIAL OF GOG (39:1–16)

39:1–6
¹"And you, son of man, prophesy against Gog and say, 'Thus says the Lord GOD, "Behold, I am against you, O Gog, prince of Rosh, Meshech and Tubal; ²and I will turn you around, drive you on, take you up from the remotest parts of the north and bring you against the mountains of Israel. ³I

will strike your bow from your left hand and dash down your arrows from your right hand. ⁴**You will fall on the mountains of Israel, you and all your troops and the peoples who are with you; I will give you as food to every kind of predatory bird and beast of the field.** ⁵**You will fall on the open field; for it is I who have spoken," declares the Lord God.** ⁶**"And I will send fire upon Magog and those who inhabit the coastlands in safety; and they will know that I am the Lord."'"**

Verse 1. As in chapter 38, God told Ezekiel to **prophesy against Gog**—a task the prophet would have been glad to perform, since Gog was the great enemy of his people. The message against Gog was simple: **Behold, I am against you.** This message, given already in 38:3, meant certain doom for any enemy of God. *Here, it becomes the fifth oracle, telling of the defeat and burial of Gog.*

Verse 2. Basically repeating 38:6, God led Gog **from the remotest parts of the north** to come to Israel. It was time for judgment to take place against the evil nations, and God would **bring** them to **the mountains of Israel** to be slaughtered. This is a reminder of what God did to the inhabitants of Canaan:

> For it was of the Lord to harden their hearts, to meet Israel in battle in order that he might utterly destroy them, that they might receive no mercy, but that he might destroy them, just as the Lord had commanded Moses (Josh. 11:20).

This time, however, the enemies would not even meet Israel in battle. God would defeat them with His many weapons (38:22).

Verse 3. God reduced the soldiers to uselessness by removing their weapons from their hands. The terminology used here is similar to what God said He would do to the great Pharaoh of Egypt (30:21–24; see Ps. 76:3). The weapons that men intended to use against God's people would be eliminated by God.

Verses 4, 5. As the armies of Gog filled **the mountains** (v. 4), God defeated them (see 38:21). The vast **troops** and the numerous **peoples** who had enjoyed visions of feasting on Israel became the feast for every kind of **predatory bird and beast of the field**. There was no dignified burial of the dead, no honor in death. Their bodies lay in **the open field** (v. 5). In ancient cultures, the ultimate dread was to be denied a decent burial. Gog's forces would suffer that fate.

Verse 6. Not only were the invading forces destroyed, but God sent **fire** to destroy their homelands as well. **Magog** and **the coastlands** considered themselves far removed from trouble (as had Judah; 38:8), yet their security was taken away from them. Again, the notion that Israel's God was only a local god was removed. God is the Lord of the universe. Every nation is accountable to Him.

39:7, 8
⁷""**"My holy name I will make known in the midst of My people Israel; and I will not let My holy name be profaned anymore. And the nations will know that I am the** Lord, **the Holy One in Israel.** ⁸**Behold, it is coming and it shall be done,"** **declares the Lord** God. **"That is the day of which I have spoken.""**"

Verse 7. "**I will not let My holy name be profaned anymore**," God announced. This is the key to God's actions. He was not defending Israel because of their righteousness (see vv. 23, 24). God declared to all nations that He was **the Holy One in Israel**. God's holy name had been "profaned" because the nations considered Him weak and ineffective. In their eyes, He was no match for their pagan gods because He had failed to protect His people from captivity and prevent the Holy City from being destroyed. However, God intended to teach these nations that He had brought His people into captivity as punishment for their sins (see 36:19).

Verse 8. We find a divine guarantee: **It is coming and it shall be done.** God declared that this destruction was **the day of which** [He had] **spoken.** Previously, God had issued warnings, saying, "I will . . ." or "I shall. . . ." He wanted everyone to remember how He had spoken of this day.

39:9, 10

⁹"'"Then those who inhabit the cities of Israel will go out and make fires with the weapons and burn them, both shields and bucklers, bows and arrows, war clubs and spears, and for seven years they will make fires of them. ¹⁰They will not take wood from the field or gather firewood from the forests, for they will make fires with the weapons; and they will take the spoil of those who despoiled them and seize the plunder of those who plundered them," declares the Lord God.'"

Verses 9, 10. "**Those who inhabit the cities of Israel will go out**," the prophecy continued (v. 9). God did not require His people to engage the enemy. All they were asked to do was clean up the remains of the great army. They found implements of warfare scattered throughout the land. They gathered immense numbers of **shields and bucklers, bows and arrows, war clubs and spears**—evidence of a well-armed and well-trained army. As Isaiah had said years earlier, "No weapon that is formed against you will prosper" (Is. 54:17a). The security of the people was sure; there was no reason to save these weapons for future battles. They had value only as firewood—enough **for seven years**. Gog's forces had intended to plunder Israel, but they themselves were **plundered** (v. 10).

Scholars of apocalyptic/symbolic literature understand the figurative use of the "seven years." This is not a literal amount of time, but—consistent with the meaning of the number "seven"—represents the amount of time needed to *complete* the job. God had destroyed the enemies of His people. (There is no literal Gog and no literal battle to identify.) John B. Taylor said, "The repeated reference to the number 'seven' is a reminder that we are here dealing with apocalyptic symbolism, and that therefore literal fulfilment of these details is not to be sought."[1]

---

[1]John B. Taylor, *Ezekiel: An Introduction and Commentary*, Tyndale Old Testament Commentaries (Downers Grove, Ill.: Inter-Varsity Press, 1969), 247–48.

39:11–16

¹¹"'"On that day I will give Gog a burial ground there in Israel, the valley of those who pass by east of the sea, and it will block off those who would pass by. So they will bury Gog there with all his horde, and they will call it the valley of Hamon-gog. ¹²For seven months the house of Israel will be burying them in order to cleanse the land. ¹³Even all the people of the land will bury them; and it will be to their renown on the day that I glorify Myself," declares the Lord GOD. ¹⁴"They will set apart men who will constantly pass through the land, burying those who were passing through, even those left on the surface of the ground, in order to cleanse it. At the end of seven months they will make a search. ¹⁵As those who pass through the land pass through and anyone sees a man's bone, then he will set up a marker by it until the buriers have buried it in the valley of Hamon-gog. ¹⁶And even the name of the city will be Hamonah. So they will cleanse the land."'"

Verse 11. The forces of Gog came to Israel to gain riches; instead, the land of Israel became their grave. Ezekiel said that the masses would be buried in a **valley** located **east of the sea**. This terminology is vague—no doubt, on purpose, because Ezekiel had no literal burial ground in mind. A great slaughter was being described—so great that if all the soldiers were buried in one valley, that valley would be blocked off and no traveler could pass.

If Ezekiel had meant a literal valley, there would be two possibilities:

First, "the sea" could be the Dead Sea. Even this position presents two possibilities, because of the way the Hebrew can be translated. Translating the clause "the valley of those *who pass east toward the sea*" would make it refer to a valley usually traveled in the direction of the Dead Sea. In this case, it would most likely refer to the Esdraelon Valley in lower Galilee. Ralph H. Alexander wrote,

> Though one might see the Esdraelon Valley as an essential east-west valley that was well traveled throughout

history and would fit the text well, none of the theories of identification of this valley can be substantiated without question because of the sparse data.[2]

Translating the clause "the valley of those *who pass by east of the sea*" would make it refer to a valley outside of Israel's territory. This valley would be one that led travelers to the Dead Sea from the east (traveling west). What valley this could be is open to much speculation.

Second, "the sea" could be the Mediterranean Sea. In this case, it could refer to several valleys found "east" of that sea.

The unidentified valley, filled with the slain, would be renamed **Hamon-gog**, which means "the multitude of Gog," or "the hoard of Gog."

Verse 12. The land was defiled with the dead. The cleanup process was an extensive one: **Seven months** were required to bury the slain. By completing this burial process, the people would **cleanse** [their] **land**. This was in accordance with the law of Moses (Deut. 21:23; Lev. 5:2; 21:1–4). In view of the great flesheater feast described in verses 17 through 20, the sequence of events seems to be as follows: The soldiers were killed, and the people began burying the dead. In the meantime, the birds and beasts enjoyed feasting on bodies not yet buried. They scattered the body parts, complicating the process of burial and necessitating the system described in verse 15.

Verse 13. Burying the slain was a nationwide effort involving **all the people**. This task was gladly undertaken by Israel, because each burial was a symbol of victory. Every dead soldier of Gog represented the degree of love God had for Israel, showing their importance in His eyes. The defeat of Gog was to **glorify** the Lord, but it also established the **renown** of Israel.

Verse 14. The bodies that had fallen in well-traveled areas would be found and buried immediately. However, certain men had to be assigned full-time jobs to find those who might have

---

[2]Ralph H. Alexander, "Ezekiel," in *The Expositor's Bible Commentary*, ed. Frank E. Gaebelein (Grand Rapids, Mich.: Zondervan Publishing House, 1986), 6:936.

died in rough terrain or desert areas. Their constant task was to **pass through the land**, seeking bodies to bury. For **seven months**, they would bury **those left on the surface of the ground**.

Verse 15. After the seven months, travelers (**those who pass through the land**) joined in the search for what was left of the mighty soldiers. The objective was to "cleanse the land" (v. 16). Identifying markers were left so that the men assigned to do the burying could locate every **bone** and transport all the remains to the burial ground of **Hamon-gog**.

Verse 16. To commemorate the great victory, a city was to be named **Hamonah**, meaning "multitude" or "horde." What city is meant is unclear. Several theories have been proposed: (1) Perhaps Jerusalem would be called "Hamonah" by other nations, identifying it as the great city that defeated the multitude of invaders. (2) A city in the area of Hamon-gog might have been renamed to serve as a reminder of the great victory secured—and evidenced by the multitudes buried nearby.[3] (3) The burial ground was as vast as a city—a city of the dead.

When the battle was over, four things had been accomplished. First, God's holy name had been glorified (v. 13) rather than profaned (v. 7). Through this battle, God undid the damage Israel had brought to His reputation (v. 23). Second, through accurate prophecies, God had demonstrated Himself to be the one true God (38:17; 39:5, 8). Third, God had confirmed His love for His people (v. 13). Fourth, God had taught the nations about Yahweh, the "Holy One in Israel" (vv. 6, 7).

---

[3] "A city shall also be built in commemoration of Gog's overthrow; naturally the city must be supposed situated near the valley of Hamon-gog, because its name Hamonah (multitude), if the city were situated elsewhere, would not of itself suggest any connection with Gog" (A. B. Davidson, *The Book of the Prophet Ezekiel: With Notes and Introduction* [Cambridge: Cambridge University Press, 1892], 287); "This concluding clause provides the reason for the great care taken to remove the corpses and name the city after the vast burial-place. The city would help to cleanse the land, because it would serve as a reminder to keep away from the defiled area" (S. Fisch, *Ezekiel: Hebrew Text and English Translation with an Introduction and Commentary*, Soncino Books of the Bible [London: Soncino Press, 1950], 262).

ORACLE 6: GOD'S GREAT BIRD FEAST
(39:17–24)

39:17–20
¹⁷"As for you, son of man, thus says the Lord GOD, 'Speak to every kind of bird and to every beast of the field, "Assemble and come, gather from every side to My sacrifice which I am going to sacrifice for you, as a great sacrifice on the mountains of Israel, that you may eat flesh and drink blood. ¹⁸You will eat the flesh of mighty men and drink the blood of the princes of the earth, as though they were rams, lambs, goats and bulls, all of them fatlings of Bashan. ¹⁹So you will eat fat until you are glutted, and drink blood until you are drunk, from My sacrifice which I have sacrificed for you. ²⁰You will be glutted at My table with horses and charioteers, with mighty men and all the men of war," declares the Lord GOD.'"

Verse 17. The sixth oracle tells of God's great bird feast. God had announced in verse 4 that this feast would soon take place; now the time had arrived. God speaks of His **sacrifice**. The enemy is portrayed as a sacrificial meal, prepared by God, for the flesh-eaters. They would gorge themselves because there was so much to eat! This gory feast reminds us of Isaiah 34:6, 7; 63:1–6; Jeremiah 46:10; and Zephaniah 1:1–9. John used the same images in Revelation 19:17–21.

Verse 18. The flesh-eating birds and beasts were invited to feast upon **the flesh of mighty men** and **drink the blood of the princes**. Logic would have suggested that these "mighty men" would win the battle, that "the princes" would be victorious. However, God overcame them. The time for their destruction had come, so they were caught in the Lord's net (see Eccles. 9:11, 12).

Verses 19, 20. The carrion-eaters would gorge themselves until they were **glutted** because there was so much to eat. This vivid description shows the greatness of God's victory. We would not appreciate the scope of it without Ezekiel's apocalyptic imagery. According to Taylor,

It is a graphic, though gruesome, picture; but the squeamish need to be reminded that atrocious acts have to be expressed in corresponding imagery, just as the blessings of God's righteous reign are symbolized by the language of the golden age. Judgment *is* a horrifying thing, and the more devastating its description is, the more men will fear it.[4]

There is no reason to believe that the great bird feast of Revelation 19 is the same event as the one in Ezekiel 39:17–20. To argue that they are the same is to ignore dozens of apocalyptic figures which were borrowed by later speakers and writers. (For example, Jesus used numerous apocalyptic symbols to speak of the destruction of Jerusalem; Mt. 24:29–31.) This account in Ezekiel symbolizes the great victory of God over evil. The one in Revelation has the same general meaning. Attempts to equate the two events have led to dozens of conflicting views.

39:21–24
²¹"'"And I will set My glory among the nations; and all the nations will see My judgment which I have executed and My hand which I have laid on them. ²²And the house of Israel will know that I am the LORD their God from that day onward. ²³The nations will know that the house of Israel went into exile for their iniquity because they acted treacherously against Me, and I hid My face from them; so I gave them into the hand of their adversaries, and all of them fell by the sword. ²⁴According to their uncleanness and according to their transgressions I dealt with them, and I hid My face from them."'"**

God set forth clear goals which He intended to achieve through the annihilation of Gog and his hordes:
Verse 21. "I will set My glory among the nations." The "glory" of God here is equivalent to all of His attributes, especially His omnipotence, omnipresence, and omniscience. The

---

[4]Taylor, 248.

pagan nations would see the attributes of the true God, in comparison to their false gods that were made in the images of human beings, beasts, and birds.

"All the nations will see My judgment." The nations would come to understand and appreciate the Lord's ways. They would grasp the evil nature of their own ways and see how His judgment, their destruction, was deserved. They would see that the Lord was the One who had **executed** this judgment.

"All the nations will see . . . **My hand which I have laid on them."** This was not the work of some pagan god. It was done by the one true God. The enemy may have believed that Israel's God could not harm them. Perhaps they believed that their gods would protect them from the hand of Israel's deity. They would see, however, that no idol was a match for God.

Verse 22. "Israel will know that I am the LORD their God from that day onward." What did Israel think of God before this? They had been quick to turn to the gods of other nations (even gods of nations whom they had conquered). They had been eager to pollute His land with pagan idols and willing to shed the blood of their innocent children in the abomination of child sacrifice. Apparently, they did not know God at all. They did not understand about His love, His attributes, His covenant, or His promises. Ignorance had brought doom upon them. The same will be true for people today (see Jn. 17:3).

Ezekiel said that they would know the Lord "from that day onward." To what "day" was he referring? Several possibilities are discussed as follows:

(1) Was he referring to the day when the Lord defeated Gog and his forces? If so, then Israel was "living securely" in the land (38:8, 11, 14) but did not yet know the Lord! This view obviously presents difficulties for the Post-millennialists, who consider Ezekiel 38 and 39 to refer to the end of the thousand-year reign of Christ, just before the destruction of Gog/Satan. It is inconceivable that, during a millennial reign of Christ, the people of God would not know God. It also presents problems for the Premillennialists, who see Ezekiel 38 and 39 as describing the conflict just before the millennial reign of Christ. If such were the case, how would the people be "living securely" in the land

during the "Tribulation"? Both of these positions lack biblical authority; assumptions and inferences abound.

(2) Is the "day" referring to the time just before God restored the people in their land? (See v. 27.) If so, it has no direct connection with the defeat of Gog. This view is based upon the fact that the people were "living securely" in the land (ch. 38)—but then this section has them being returned to the land, so it had to begin before they lived in the land. Taylor said,

> The reference to the Exile in verse 23 leads Ezekiel back in this final oracle to his present situation. Some would say that these verses have no place in the Gog apocalypse, and it is quite true that their style and content are no longer eschatological. But they appear to be a deliberate attempt to round off the Gog oracles and to relate their message to the immediate needs of the post 587 B.C. generation of exiles. Nothing new is added to what Ezekiel has said on previous occasions, but as a summary of his teaching they represent a convenient conclusion to chapters 1—39, before the vision of the new temple is added in chapter 40.[5]

(3) Is the "day" referring to a non-specific period in the future (for example, after the return from exile)? The promised blessings would be dependent upon Israel's obedience.

(4) Is the "day" referring to a period during the messianic kingdom (the Church Age), when God's people were to be restored to the "land"—that is, the church? It may be best to see the "day" as a generic reference to the time when God would restore His people in the land, serve as their Shepherd, and select the David-like King.

Verses 23, 24. "The nations will know that the house of Israel went into exile for their iniquity." The repetition of this point (see 36:18, 19) shows its importance to the Lord. Israel's removal from the land and Jerusalem's destruction reflected upon God Himself, making Him appear weak and ineffective

---

[5]Ibid., 249.

before the nations. God did not like leaving this false impression, yet He had to discipline His sinful people. By allowing them to go into captivity, He accomplished *the first goal:* to discipline Israel for their "iniquity" and for **act**[ing] **treacherously** against the Lord. God could not look favorably upon **their uncleanness** and **transgressions** (v. 24), so He **hid** [His] **face from them** (see Is. 1:15; 59:1, 2). The people had to be punished. By bringing them back to the land, He accomplished *the second goal:* to re-establish His reputation, specifically His holiness and glory.

ORACLE 7: THE RESTORATION OF ISRAEL (39:25-29)

²⁵Therefore thus says the Lord God, "Now I will restore the fortunes of Jacob and have mercy on the whole house of Israel; and I will be jealous for My holy name. ²⁶They will forget their disgrace and all their treachery which they perpetrated against Me, when they live securely on their own land with no one to make them afraid. ²⁷When I bring them back from the peoples and gather them from the lands of their enemies, then I shall be sanctified through them in the sight of the many nations. ²⁸Then they will know that I am the Lord their God because I made them go into exile among the nations, and then gathered them again to their own land; and I will leave none of them there any longer. ²⁹I will not hide My face from them any longer, for I will have poured out My Spirit on the house of Israel," declares the Lord God.

Verse 25. In the seventh and final oracle, God promised restoration for Israel. He said, **"I will restore the fortunes of Jacob"** (see 16:53; 29:14; Job 42:10; Ps. 14:7; 85:1; 126:1; Amos 9:14). This refers to the time when God would again bless His people. It illustrates God's great **mercy**—not to just a few, but to **the whole house of Israel**, both the northern kingdom and the southern kingdom. While it could be said that this promise was partially fulfilled when the exiles returned in 536 B.C., the complete fulfillment came in the time of Christ. Then all of God's people, Jew and Gentile alike, were united under the banner of the cross

(see Eph. 2:12–14). Nothing in the Bible indicates a future blessing of physical Israel (after the time of Christ).[6]

God is **jealous** for His **holy name**. This jealousy moved God to take an active role in protecting His reputation. Never again would God punish His people at the expense of His own reputation among the nations.

Verse 26. As time passed, the people of God would **forget** what they had done against God; they would grow in their love and devotion to Him. The phrasing here can also be translated, "And they shall bear their disgrace. . . ." This idea is supported elsewhere (6:9; 16:61; 20:43; 36:31) and appears in the MT. Israel felt guilty for abandoning God in the first place. She was living in peace and security, with only God to thank. She would "bear" the burden of knowing that she had left the one true God and had no right to return to the land.

Verses 27, 28. By bringing the people back to the land, God would be **sanctified** (v. 27). His name had been profaned and blasphemed among the nations (v. 7). God wanted Israel—and all the nations—to recognize Him as the one true God (v. 28). S. Fisch said, "God's dealings with Israel will bring home to the nations that He reveals Himself in history no less than in Nature, and there is a Divine plan in human affairs which gradually unfolds itself in time."[7] Emphasizing His resolve to save His people, God said, **"I will leave none of them there any longer."** It was repulsive to the God of the universe to have His people dwelling on foreign soil. He wanted them to come home.

Verse 29. Because of their sin, God had to **hide** [His] **face**, allowing them to suffer their consequences. He turned away, withdrawing His blessings and protection. When the Spirit left the temple (ch. 11), God's loving protection was withdrawn. However, God **poured out** [His] **Spirit**, blessing them in abundance when He brought them back to the land. Taylor wrote,

The oracle concludes by promising a complete re-

---

[6]For more on this, see the discussion on 37:28 and "An Overview of Ezekiel 40—48."
[7]Fisch, 264.

versal of the exile. The exiles will be gathered into their own land; not one of them will be left among the nations (the fact that many preferred to stay in Babylon after Cyrus's edict is immaterial); and, greatest of all, *I will not hide my face any more from them*, a promise of blessing and favour in perpetuity. Finally, 36:27 is reiterated with the powerful statement, put in the prophetic perfect tense, that *I have poured out my spirit upon the house of Israel* (RV). To put this in the future (as RSV) weakens the dramatic force of this assertion. True, God had not yet done this in reality; but it was such an assured word that it could be spoken by Ezekiel as if it were an accomplished fact.[8]

Nothing indicates that God gave His Spirit to the Israelites in the Old Testament; therefore, this either has a figurative application (representing the blessings of God), or it finds its ultimate fulfillment in the outpouring of the Holy Spirit in the New Testament (Acts 2).

APPLICATION

God Will Prevail

The enemies of God's people will use all sorts of weapons against them, yet God can eliminate the danger (39:3). Satan will attack Christians with his "fiery missiles," but the "armor of God" provides protection (Eph. 6:10–17).

No matter how great the forces of evil may appear, God will win. Christians must stay on course and be faithful to the end. In so doing, they will secure the victory for themselves (Mt. 24:13; Rev. 2:10).

The defeat of evil is always a triumph for God's name and a victory for His people (39:13). God's ultimate vindication will come on the Day of Judgment.

God will not look upon wickedness. When one enters a life

---

[8]Taylor, 249–50.

of sin, God will "hide [His] face"—that is, He will remove His providential blessings (see Is. 1:15; 59:1, 2; 1 Pet. 3:10–12).

Israel failed to teach her children about the Lord (see Deut. 6:4–9). Her failure to know God led to all sorts of lawlessness and abominations. If we do not know God and Christ, we will not have eternal life (Jn. 17:3; see 8:24, 32). Let us pray, with Paul, that the Lord's people might "know" the hope of His calling, the riches of His inheritance in the saints, and the surpassing greatness of His power toward believers (Eph. 1:18, 19).

D.P.

When Vengeance Belongs to the Lord

Paul wrote in Romans 12:19, "Never take your own revenge ... leave room for the wrath of God, for it is written, 'Vengeance is Mine; I will repay,' says the Lord" (see Deut. 32:35). When we are mistreated, we know that we ought to respond patiently and lovingly, but sometimes it is difficult to allow God to be the Lord of vengeance. Ezekiel 39 uses metaphorical language to emphasize how horrid God's vengeance against Gog would be.

"I will strike your bow from your left hand and dash down your arrows from your right hand" (v. 3). God leaves His enemies defenseless. Woe to the ones who oppose the Lord!

"Those who inhabit the cities of Israel will go out and make fires with the weapons" (v. 9). The enemy's defeat is emphasized further by Israel's burning these weapons for firewood.

"They will bury Gog there with all his horde, and they will call it the valley of Hamon-gog" (v. 11). According to the prophet, the enemy's casualties would be so great that it would take seven months to bury the bodies.

Speaking to wild birds and animals, God said, "You will eat the flesh of mighty men" (v. 18) "as a great sacrifice" (v. 17). Imagine God feeding the birds a sacrifice of human flesh!

As Christians, we do not wish these nightmares on anyone, but perhaps verses like these reassure us that God is in control. When we believe that everyone is against us, we should not take vengeance into our own hands. Instead, we should trust in the One who willingly bears our burdens and protects us.

T.P.W.

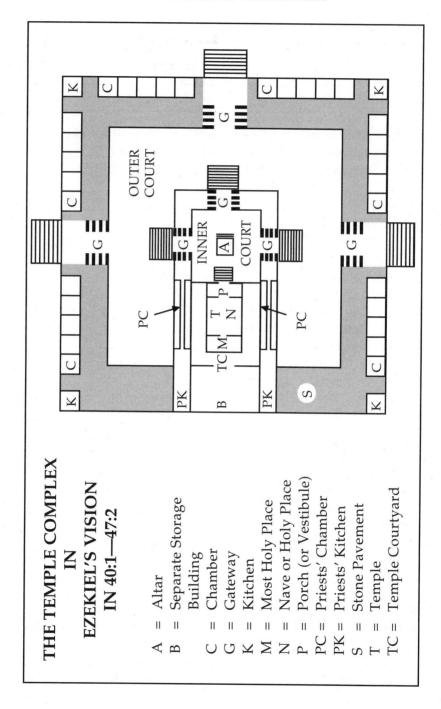

An Overview of Ezekiel 40—48:
The New Temple and God's Kingdom

THE CONTENT

The last nine chapters of Ezekiel are a unit which describes a vision of the new temple and all of its buildings, walls, and sacrificial implements, along with priestly allotments of land and the priests' sacrificial duties. These chapters were written after the other portions of the book (the vision is dated around 573 B.C.), and they provide an important conclusion to Ezekiel's prophecy, especially in one key area: the return of the glory of the Lord. John B. Taylor wrote, "They are therefore to be thought of not as a completely independent composition, only loosely tacked on to the end of the main body of Ezekiel's work, but as a real climax to his thought as it has been maturing through twenty years of prayer, meditation and ministry."[1] In 11:22, 23, God had withdrawn from the evils so prevalent in the temple and the city of Jerusalem. Was there any hope of His returning? Had He abandoned His people forever? Chapters 40 through 48 provide a fitting answer to these all-important questions.

In showing Ezekiel the "four abominations" centered in the temple, God provided substantial reason why He should abandon the temple. It had become hopelessly corrupt. The Holy One of Israel could not continue to inhabit such a place. When He departed, His protection of this place also departed. Its destruction was inevitable, and it came to pass in 587(6) B.C.

---

[1] John B. Taylor, *Ezekiel: An Introduction and Commentary,* Tyndale Old Testament Commentaries (Downers Grove, Ill.: Inter-Varsity Press, 1969), 250.

However, just as Ezekiel began his book with the magnificent vision of the glory of the Lord, the book appropriately ends with another prolonged vision. This time, Ezekiel saw the Lord returning to dwell with His people.

THE PURPOSES

1. It encouraged the exiles, showing that they would again be recipients of God's blessings, dwelling in a beautiful and productive land. It created a dream for a discouraged people.
2. It showed that God had not forsaken His people forever. He would return to them, cleanse them, and dwell with them once again.
3. It underscores the importance of covenant obedience. The people were expected to be faithful to God's statutes and ordinances (see 43:11; 37:24).
4. It demonstrates that even those without hope can come to God and receive His blessings.
5. It shows how all of God's people have a place in His kingdom and how He has work for all to do (see Eph. 2:10; 1 Cor. 15:58; Gal. 6:9, 10).

THE INTERPRETATION

Literal: Those who hold this view of interpretation strive to apply literally all of the numbers, buildings, and priesthood duties in these chapters. This section is seen as a divine blueprint which God expects the faithful to follow meticulously as they construct His future dwelling.

Dispensational/Premillennial: This view was made popular by *The Scofield Reference Bible*, which titled this section "Israel in the Land during the Kingdom-Age." It points to a future time when a messianic kingdom is set up, a thousand-year reign is about to begin, and Ezekiel's temple will be literally constructed.[2]

---

[2]This is the position presented in Ralph H. Alexander, "Ezekiel," in *The Expositor's Bible Commentary*, ed. Frank E. Gaebelein (Grand Rapids, Mich.: Zondervan Publishing House, 1986), 6:942–52.

Symbolic Christian: This position sees the fulfillment in the church and the work of Christians as priests of God. It seeks to define the various measurements and descriptions by using symbols.

Apocalyptic: This view presents the section as a vivid symbolic prophecy, describing the glorious return of the exiles to the Promised Land. It includes the idea that they would again enjoy the presence of God, the beauty of a rebuilt city and temple, and land ownership. This is the most logical position. It honors the type of literature Ezekiel was using (chs. 40—48) and allows for immediate application to the discouraged exiles.

FOR FURTHER STUDY: AN ANALYSIS OF FOUR VIEWS FOR INTERPRETING EZEKIEL 40—48

Literal

Strengths

1. Ezekiel had prophesied a return to the land and anticipated a future rebuilding of the temple.

2. Logically, God would provide guidance concerning the holy edifice the returning exiles would have to reconstruct.

3. Ezekiel, as a priest, was surely the one to predict the glorious future of the Lord's temple.

4. It provides a framework for the holiness of the Lord to be re-established. Ezekiel connected the building of the new temple with the return of the exiles, which in turn established the holiness of the name of Yahweh.

Weaknesses

1. The exiles did not attempt to use the "blueprint" when they returned. Apparently, they did not view this literally. The builders of Herod's temple did not attempt to follow these specifications either.

2. Unlike the description of the temple in Exodus, this temple has many measurements that are nonspecific, thereby casting doubt that this was ever intended to be a literal "blueprint."

3. Certain details would be impossible to construct.

4. Other vital parts of the temple are not addressed, which leaves to the imagination how they might be constructed. Such omissions are out of character for the way God instructed His people.

5. Some details are unfeasible—for example, the size of the temple and its location on "a very high mountain" (40:2). The literal placement of the temple would be outside the city, and the tribal allotments do not match the topography of Israel (47:13—48:29). The function and location of the river (47:1–12) are also unlikely.

6. This view fails to appreciate the conditional nature of biblical prophecy. Even if the description of the temple were to be taken literally, it could not serve as a divine guarantee—because its fulfillment required faithfulness on the part of the people (see Jer. 18:5–10).

Dispensational/Premillennial

Strengths

1. It provides legitimacy for the theme of God's glory and its return. God's glory left because of wickedness, but Ezekiel said that it would return once God's people returned to the land and purified themselves. This cleansing is intimately connected with the new temple.

2. Since God's holiness was to be established only when God's people were brought back to the land (36:20–24), a future return to the land was necessary.

3. Ezekiel 43:6, 7 says that when God's glory returned He would "dwell among the sons of Israel forever." This terminology lends itself to a literal premillennial fulfillment because God said that He would dwell with them when He returned Israel to the land.[3]

4. The entire tenor of the section seems to imply that these events could describe the end of history and the onset of the

---

[3]Gleason L. Archer, Jr., *A Survey of Old Testament Introduction* (Chicago: Moody Press, 1964), 363.

messianic kingdom. In 47:12 Ezekiel described a river of life, as did Moses in Genesis 2:8–14 and John in Revelation 22:1. This river that was lost in the beginning will be regained in the end.

5. The idea of God's dwelling with His people is predominant in this temple (48:35) and is a part of the end time description in Revelation 22:1–6.[4]

Weaknesses

1. It requires switching back and forth between literal and figurative applications of the Ezekiel temple.[5]

2. Several aspects are incompatible with Christianity.

3. It fails to appreciate the atoning work of Christ, encouraging God's people to revert to inferior ways.

4. It overlooks the place of the church in the overall scheme of God.[6]

5. It requires a literal fulfillment of these chapters, thus hav-

---

[4]See Alexander, 944.

[5]Those embracing this view are aware of these difficulties. Therefore, they maintain that the sacrifices symbolize worship. Anthony A. Hoekema cited support from *The New Scofield Reference Bible*: "The reference to sacrifices is not to be taken literally, in view of the putting away of such offerings, but is rather to be regarded as a presentation of the worship of redeemed Israel, in her own land and in the millennial Temple, using the terms with which the Jews were familiar in Ezekiel's day" (C. I. Scofield, ed., *The New Scofield Reference Bible* [New York: Oxford University Press, 1967], 888; Anthony A. Hoekema, *The Bible and the Future* [Grand Rapids, Mich.: Wm. B. Eerdmans Publishing Co., 1979], 204). This statement is used to substantiate that even dispensationalists recognize a nonliteral approach to portions of Ezekiel 40—48. Admittedly, this is only one of two ways that *The New Scofield Reference Bible* declares the sacrifices could be interpreted. It is the deviating between "literal here" and "figurative there" exegesis that makes this view unacceptable.

[6]"A major fallacy of premillennialism is in its basic opposition to the redemption of the human race. If Christ *had* established the millennial kingdom, as millenarians maintain was his actual intention, then he would not have been rejected and crucified, and redemption could never have been offered to mankind. . . . The gospel of salvation becomes the unexpected and unplanned result of Christ's failure to establish the kingdom!" (Edward C. Wharton, "Interpreting Old Testament Prophecies: Premillennial Violations Exposed," in *Difficult Texts of the Old Testament Explained*, ed. Wendell Winkler [Montgomery, Ala.: Winkler Publications, 1982], 105–6).

ing many of the same weaknesses given previously regarding literal interpretation.[7]

6. It requires the text to skip the most significant time in history—the incarnation of Christ. How could a description of the new temple overlook the work of Christ? How could it describe the return of God to His people and neglect the "Immanuel," the literal presence of God with His people?

7. It fails to appreciate that the Old Testament was designed to lead us *to* Christ and the events of the first century, not to reach beyond that time.

8. It is based on the false doctrine that Christ failed to establish His kingdom during the first coming and will therefore return to establish His millennial kingdom (of which this temple would be a part). Jesus taught during His earthly ministry that the kingdom was "at hand" and that the time was "fulfilled" (Mk. 1:15). He said that the kingdom would be established before some of His hearers died (Mk. 9:1).

9. It fails to appreciate the fact that this section does not *have* to be fulfilled, because this prophecy—like others—was conditional upon faithfulness (see Jer. 18:5–12). Since Israel was untrue to the covenant (even after the return from exile), why should we expect God's plan for a glorious, new physical temple to proceed?[8]

---

[7]"If it follows from this that Old Testament festivals, blood sacrifices, priesthood and worship at a temple are to be reintroduced, after the New Testament revelation of Christ and His finished, fulfilling work, it shows how completely this view misinterprets the significance of Christ's salvation and how it casts doubt on the consistency of God's dealings with mankind. But its fault is basically in regarding Ezekiel 40—48 as prophecy and insisting on a literal fulfilment of it, if not in the past then in the future" (Taylor, 252–53).

[8]For example, Merrill F. Unger overlooked the possibility of prophecy unfulfilled because of disobedience: "Only one conclusion is possible. Non-premillennial views just do not supply any appropriate place for Ezekiel's temple. This great section of Old Testament prophecy must remain wrapped in darkness and confusion, unless some plan of prophetic interpretation is provided to give a fitting and suitable future fulfillment to all that is written in this vision" (Merrill F. Unger, *Great Neglected Bible Prophecies* [Chicago: Scripture Press, 1955], 62).

Symbolic Christian

Strengths

1. It utilizes the same type of symbolic terminology used by John in Revelation. John's new Jerusalem had numerous parallels to the temple described by Ezekiel.

2. It provides a framework for Christianity, with its connection and relationship to the Old Testament forms (in a way similar to type/antitype fulfillment).

3. It draws upon the promise of the Davidic king who will rule His people (as promised in 34:23, 24). The rule of the Messiah is seen through His church. (Jesus is head of the church that He built [Mt. 16:16–18; Eph. 1:22, 23]).

4. It provides an all-important prophecy of the church, which is otherwise absent in the Old Testament.

Weaknesses

1. It has no bearing or relevance to those of Ezekiel's day.

2. It is nowhere used or referred to by the inspired writers of the New Testament; there is no application of this to the church. If this were the glorious prediction of the church, there would be one or more direct quotes.

3. Even when applied to Christianity, the forms, the priesthood, and the tribal allotments in Ezekiel 40—48 do not fit logically with the pattern of Christianity. The interpreter has to stretch and make unsubstantiated parallels, leaving solid exegetical principles and engaging in speculation.

Apocalyptic

Strengths

1. It allows for a message given directly to the exiles. This section of prophecy, interpreted in such a way, would have filled them with hope for their future. It describes "the glorious future of the people of God in the age to come in terms which the Jews of that day would understand."[9]

---

[9]Hoekema, 205.

2. It fits with previous non-apocalyptic passages in which Ezekiel described a return to the land (see 34:11–19; 36:8–38; 37:1–10, 11–28).

3. It provides a logical connection with 39:21–29 and fits with the apocalyptic style of writing in chapters 38 and 39.

4. It was the view held by Jewish interpreters, who did not seek a literal application or fulfillment of these chapters.

5. Ezekiel was clearly using figurative and symbolic language (see 40:2, 3; 43:1–5).

6. He made no mention of the high priest, an inexcusable oversight if he intended for the temple to be built literally in the Old Testament or was giving a prophetic view of a millennium. (The work and function of the high priest is a key idea in the New Testament.)

7. There are contradictions to laws given by Moses (for example, in sizes, duties, and allotments).

Weaknesses

1. Apocalyptic language does not use this much detail. Opposing this position, Alexander wrote, "The many details of these chapters would be difficult to comment on if one took the approach just described, for such an approach can only deal in generalities. The details would have little or no meaning."[10]

2. It leaves many verses unanalyzed, because no application can be made. This appears to be a waste of space.

ADDITIONAL NOTES

Other Purposes

Other purposes of this section include the following, according to Taylor:[11]

1. The text illustrates "the perfection of God's plan for His restored people, symbolically expressed in the immaculate symmetry of the temple building."

---

[10] Alexander, 907.
[11] Taylor, 253.

2. It shows "the centrality of worship in the new age, its importance being expressed in the scrupulous concern for detail in the observance of its rites."

3. It reaffirms "the abiding presence of the Lord in the midst of His people."

4. It shows "the blessings that will flow from God's presence to the barren places of the earth (the river of life)."

5. It demonstrates "the orderly allocation of duties and privileges to all God's people, as shown both in the temple duties and in the apportionment of the land (a theme taken up in Rev. 7:4–8)."[12]

Dispensational/Premillennial View:
Practices Incompatible with Christianity

Here is a list of elements which make the dispensational/premillennial view incompatible with Christianity:

Animal blood sacrifices. The writer of Hebrews stated that "it is impossible for the blood of bulls and goats to take away sins" (10:4). Why would there be a return to this futile system? Only the blood of Jesus can wash away sin. These sacrifices were only a "shadow" and not the "very form of things" (Heb. 10:1).

The Aaronic/Levitical priesthood (44:10–31). The law of Christ declares all Christians to be priests (1 Pet. 2:5–9; Rev. 1:6). The priesthood of Christ is superior to that of the old covenant (Heb. 7:1–28).

Old Testament festivals (45:18—46:15). Paul declared that festivals, new moons, and Sabbath days are no more than "a mere shadow of what is to come; but the substance belongs to Christ" (Col. 2:16, 17; see Heb. 8:5; 10:1).

A physical temple. The New Testament shows the better way—that "the Most High does not dwell in houses made by human hands" (Acts 7:48). It teaches that the temple of God is the church

---

[12]"These are of course only the main themes which Ezekiel seems to be expressing in this apocalyptic sequence. There is much more which can be adduced through detailed exposition. But if the vision is interpreted on these lines, and not as prophecy in the conventional sense, readers will be spared the necessity of trying to look for some fulfillment of the words in past or future history" (Ibid., 254).

(1 Cor. 3:16), the bodies of Christians (1 Cor. 6:19, 20). Paul noted that the "Spirit of God" resides in these temples—in us, not in some physical edifice.

Temple worship. It was a part of the old system, which Jesus told the Samaritan woman was soon to pass (Jn. 4:20–24).

Tribal allotments (47:13—48:29). This concept is contrary to the "new heavens and a new earth" (2 Pet. 3:13) and the portrayal of our eternal abode (see Rev. 22:1–5).

Evidence That the Old Testament Leads to Christ

The following Scriptures show that the Old Testament was designed to lead us *to* Christ and the events of the first century, not to reach beyond it:

Luke 24:44–47. All of the divisions of the Old Testament, including the Prophets, were fulfilled in Jesus.

Matthew 11:13. The Law and the Prophets brought us *to* John's ministry, not beyond it.

Luke 16:16a. The Law and the Prophets "were proclaimed unto John; *since that time* the gospel of the kingdom of God has been preached" (emphasis added). The Old Testament did not proclaim events beyond the work and ministry of John, Jesus, and the apostles.

Acts 26:22, 23. The Old Testament predicted the ministry, death, and resurrection of Christ.

1 Peter 1:10–12. The prophets testified regarding the coming grace connected with "the sufferings of Christ, and the glories to follow."

2 Timothy 1:10. Jesus "brought life and immortality to light through the gospel." Teachings regarding future rewards were not found in the Old Testament. Such was not the intended purpose of the prophets; their job was to prepare people for Christ. Then Christ and His apostles would teach what was to come in the future.

Chapter 40

The New Temple: Its Outer and Inner Courts

THE OUTER COURT (40:1–27)

The Man with the Measuring Rod (40:1–4)

¹In the twenty-fifth year of our exile, at the beginning of the year, on the tenth of the month, in the fourteenth year after the city was taken, on that same day the hand of the LORD was upon me and He brought me there. ²In the visions of God He brought me into the land of Israel and set me on a very high mountain, and on it to the south there was a structure like a city. ³So He brought me there; and behold, there was a man whose appearance was like the appearance of bronze, with a line of flax and a measuring rod in his hand; and he was standing in the gateway. ⁴The man said to me, "Son of man, see with your eyes, hear with your ears, and give attention to all that I am going to show you; for you have been brought here in order to show it to you. Declare to the house of Israel all that you see."

Verse 1. The twenty-fifth year of our exile refers to the exile of Ezekiel (as well as King Jehoiachin), which took place in 598(7) B.C. Therefore, this prophecy may be dated around April 573 B.C. This would easily make it the next to the last prophecy in Ezekiel. (The prophecy against Egypt was dated in April 571 B.C.; see the discussion of 29:17.)

Verse 2. In the visions of God (see 1:1; 8:3), Ezekiel was taken to **a very high mountain**—terminology that does not describe any mountain near Jerusalem. Mount Zion is the most logical identification of the place mentioned, even though it is some three hundred feet lower than the Mount of Olives. The mountain here is spiritual rather than literal; it represents the place where God showed Ezekiel the new temple. Ezekiel saw **a structure like a city**. This is a reference to the temple.

Verse 3. Ezekiel met **a man whose appearance was like the appearance of bronze**. This probably refers to an angelic being. Some believe that it was the Lord Himself in human form, although this is unlikely. His "bronze" appearance suggests glowing or shining. In his hands were two items. **A line of flax** was a tool used for longer measurements (see Zech. 2:1). It served as a plumb line, a mason's line, to evaluate the integrity of a building and identify its defects. **A measuring rod** was used in house construction, for marking the straightness of the walls (see Rev. 21:15). This measuring rod was about 10.3 feet long (the thickness and the height of the solid wall surrounding the temple area).

Verse 4. Extensive information was about to be given to Ezekiel; therefore, he was called upon to **give attention**. The prophet received this commission: **Declare to the house of Israel all that you see**. It is fitting that Ezekiel, a priest, was able to see this glorious vision of the new temple. The vision serves as a conclusion to the message of his book.

God cared about His people and wanted to encourage them. He wanted to put in their hearts a dream of a brighter future. A legitimate question should be asked here: Would these chapters have to be literal in order to encourage Israel? If the answer is yes, then the description of the holy city in Revelation 21:9–27 must also be literal. Certainly, John's words in Revelation offer a view of a glorious abode in the future, without demanding a literal understanding. In the same way, Ezekiel's description of the temple—cloaked in apocalyptic terminology—offered the Israelites hope for a better future.

The Wall and the East Gate (40:5–16)

⁵**And behold, there was a wall on the outside of the temple**

all around, and in the man's hand was a measuring rod of six cubits, each of which was a cubit and a handbreadth. So he measured the thickness of the wall, one rod; and the height, one rod. ⁶Then he went to the gate which faced east, went up its steps and measured the threshold of the gate, one rod in width; and the other threshold was one rod in width. ⁷The guardroom was one rod long and one rod wide; and there were five cubits between the guardrooms. And the threshold of the gate by the porch of the gate facing inward was one rod. ⁸Then he measured the porch of the gate facing inward, one rod. ⁹He measured the porch of the gate, eight cubits; and its side pillars, two cubits. And the porch of the gate was faced inward. ¹⁰The guardrooms of the gate toward the east numbered three on each side; the three of them had the same measurement. The side pillars also had the same measurement on each side. ¹¹And he measured the width of the gateway, ten cubits, and the length of the gate, thirteen cubits. ¹²There was a barrier wall one cubit wide in front of the guardrooms on each side; and the guardrooms were six cubits square on each side. ¹³He measured the gate from the roof of the one guardroom to the roof of the other, a width of twenty-five cubits from one door to the door opposite. ¹⁴He made the side pillars sixty cubits high; the gate extended round about to the side pillar of the courtyard. ¹⁵From the front of the entrance gate to the front of the inner porch of the gate was fifty cubits. ¹⁶There were shuttered windows looking toward the guardrooms, and toward their side pillars within the gate all around, and likewise for the porches. And there were windows all around inside; and on each side pillar were palm tree ornaments.

Verse 5. Ezekiel first described the **wall** encircling the courts and the temple. The size of this wall, like the other measurements in this section, is open to much speculation. Normally, a "cubit" would be seventeen inches long, but the longer temple cubit is identified in verse 5 as **a cubit and a handbreadth** (about twenty-one inches long). Throughout this study of Ezekiel's vision, the longer cubit is used, along with the following units of measure:

Hebrew Measurement Equivalents

1 palm or handbreadth = 3.5 inches (⅙ cubit) = 8.97 cm.
1 long cubit = 21 inches (1.75 feet) = 53.9 cm.
1 rod = 10.3 feet (or 6 long cubits) = 3.14 m.
1 reed = 1 rod (10.3 feet or 6 long cubits) = 3.14 m.

The wall encircled a huge structure. The height of the wall **(one rod)** was approximately 10.3 feet high; **the thickness of the wall** was the same. These dimensions show that the wall was not intended to provide protection. Rather, it separated the temple from any defiling objects outside.

Verses 6, 7. The gate which faced east had **steps** at its entrance (v. 6). This gateway was like a hallway with three **guardrooms** (v. 7) on each side, actually making it more like a gate house. Each guardroom was 10.3 feet wide and long. After entering through this gate, one would be in the outer court. (See "The Temple Complex in Ezekiel's Vision" on page 586.) This place was used for general assemblies and for general worship

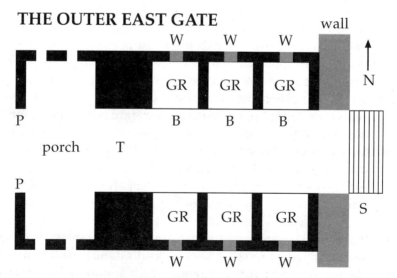

THE OUTER EAST GATE

P = Pillar   T = Threshold   W = Window   S = Steps
GR = Guardroom   B = Barrier (half-wall in front of guardroom)

by the people. The prophet saw three gates, each of the same design: a northern gate (see vv. 20–23), a southern gate (see vv. 24–27), and the eastern gate, which served as the pattern for the other gates. Leading to each gate were "seven steps" (vv. 22, 26), indicating that the entire temple was elevated on a huge terrace or platform. Only the west side of the wall had no gate. These gate-houses were typical of ancient cities. Archaeologists have discovered one very similar to this one at Megiddo (the military center of Solomon's kingdom).

The huge gateways, with six guardrooms, symbolize the protection the Lord provides for His people. He gives strength and refuge to those who are faithful to Him (see Ps. 91:1, 2).

Verses 8–12. Ezekiel was taken up the steps leading to **the porch** (v. 8). This was the area with the guardrooms on each side. Ezekiel noticed that each guardroom had **a barrier wall** (v. 12) in front of it (like a half-wall in front of each guardroom). After passing the guardrooms, Ezekiel came to a second large porch (8 x 20 cubits) leading to the outer court. Later, in 44:1–3, the eastern gate was closed (because the Lord had entered through it). "The prince" used "the porch" to enter the gate (from the inside). There, he would "eat bread before the LORD" (44:3).

Verse 13. The entire width of the east gate from door to door was **twenty-five cubits**. This would include the thickness of the wall (one cubit), plus the size of the room (six cubits), plus the hallway (eleven cubits), plus the opposite side guardroom (six cubits) and the other wall (one cubit).

Verses 14, 15. These verses are somewhat confusing. Scholars offer varying options as to the meaning. It is possible that the **sixty cubits** represent the total size of the porch, counting all measurements (width and height). Another possibility is that the door posts were sixty cubits high. The entire length from the external entrance to the porch of the outer court was **fifty cubits**.

Verse 16. The ancients had no glass, so the windows were **shuttered** or latticed. The only decorations mentioned in the temple are the **palm tree ornaments** that apparently were engraved on the door posts.

The Outer Court Itself (40:17-19)

¹⁷**Then he brought me into the outer court, and behold, there were chambers and a pavement made for the court all around; thirty chambers faced the pavement.** ¹⁸**The pavement (that is, the lower pavement) was by the side of the gates, corresponding to the length of the gates.** ¹⁹**Then he measured the width from the front of the lower gate to the front of the exterior of the inner court, a hundred cubits on the east and on the north.**

Verse 17. Ezekiel said, **Then he brought me into the outer court.** (See "The Temple Complex in Ezekiel's Vision" on page 586.) In his vision, the prophet had walked through the hallway of the east gate. Next, he entered through that gate into "the outer court." He called this the "outer" court because there was another court closer to the temple itself. The outer court surrounded the temple on all sides except the west side, where the temple was a part of the wall. In the Talmud this "outer court" is referred to as "the court of women." In addition, Ezekiel saw **thirty chambers** facing toward the inside, toward the outer court. In an actual structure of Ezekiel's day, such chambers might have been designed for worshipers who traveled to the temple or for Levites who were working their shift (see Jer. 35:2).

Verses 18, 19. The chambers were built on stone pavements which went alongside the north, east, and south walls. There were ten chambers on each side, divided by the gates. **The lower pavement** (on which the chambers were built) led to the next paved area, the raised inner court. Pavement was used in Solomon's temple (2 Chron. 7:3) and was perhaps a mosaic, a work of art, as at the palace of Ahasuerus (Esther 1:6).

The North and South Gates (40:20-27)

²⁰**As for the gate of the outer court which faced the north, he measured its length and its width.** ²¹**It had three guardrooms on each side; and its side pillars and its porches had the same measurement as the first gate. Its length was fifty cubits and**

the width twenty-five cubits. ²²Its windows and its porches and its palm tree ornaments had the same measurements as the gate which faced toward the east; and it was reached by seven steps, and its porch was in front of them. ²³The inner court had a gate opposite the gate on the north as well as the gate on the east; and he measured a hundred cubits from gate to gate.

²⁴Then he led me toward the south, and behold, there was a gate toward the south; and he measured its side pillars and its porches according to those same measurements. ²⁵The gate and its porches had windows all around like those other windows; the length was fifty cubits and the width twenty-five cubits. ²⁶There were seven steps going up to it, and its porches were in front of them; and it had palm tree ornaments on its side pillars, one on each side. ²⁷The inner court had a gate toward the south; and he measured from gate to gate toward the south, a hundred cubits.

Verses 20–25. The north and **south** gates **had the same measurements** as the east gate (vv. 20, 21, 24). There was no gate on the west, since that was the location of the temple itself. No new information is given in the next verses, except that **seven steps** (v. 22) led to the gate entrance. The details regarding the eastern gate did not mention the number "seven." As noted earlier, the symbolism of "seven" might demonstrate that these stairs led to the perfect place—the place where God was present. Similar emphasis is given to the numbers "three" and "twelve." "Three" represents the fullness of divinity (ultimately realized in the Godhead), and "twelve" represents the totality of God's people and His rule over them.

As in the earlier section, Ezekiel mentioned the **porches**. These hallway-type areas of the gates were part of Solomon's temple (1 Kings 6:3; 2 Chron. 3:4). Similar vestibules were located at the end of the gateway corridor and opened onto the outer court. The door for each gate (v. 11) was ten cubits in width and thirteen cubits in height. At each gateway, Ezekiel saw two pillars, two cubits thick and sixty cubits high (vv. 9, 14).

Verses 26, 27. The pillars were significantly engraved with

palm tree ornaments (v. 26). Palms were symbols of beauty (Song 7:7), righteousness, prosperity, and fruitfulness (Ps. 92:12-14), as well as salvation and victory (see Rev. 7:9). Palm branches were employed in the celebration of the Feast of Tabernacles. Extensive use of the palm in Solomon's temple (1 Kings 6:29, 32, 35) identifies it with the triumph and splendor of the rule of the one "greater than Solomon" (see Mt. 12:42; Lk. 11:31). During the Triumphal Entry, palms were used to welcome the Messiah to Jerusalem (Jn. 12:13; see Mt. 21:8).

THE INNER COURT (40:28-47)

The Three Gates (40:28-37)

²⁸Then he brought me to the inner court by the south gate; and he measured the south gate according to those same measurements. ²⁹Its guardrooms also, its side pillars and its porches were according to those same measurements. And the gate and its porches had windows all around; it was fifty cubits long and twenty-five cubits wide. ³⁰There were porches all around, twenty-five cubits long and five cubits wide. ³¹Its porches were toward the outer court; and palm tree ornaments were on its side pillars, and its stairway had eight steps.

³²He brought me into the inner court toward the east. And he measured the gate according to those same measurements. ³³Its guardrooms also, its side pillars and its porches were according to those same measurements. And the gate and its porches had windows all around; it was fifty cubits long and twenty-five cubits wide. ³⁴Its porches were toward the outer court; and palm tree ornaments were on its side pillars, on each side, and its stairway had eight steps.

³⁵Then he brought me to the north gate; and he measured it according to those same measurements, ³⁶with its guardrooms, its side pillars and its porches. And the gate had windows all around; the length was fifty cubits and the width twenty-five cubits. ³⁷Its side pillars were toward the outer court; and palm tree ornaments were on its side pillars on each side, and its stairway had eight steps.

Verses 28–30. The inner court (v. 28) was the place where the temple itself stood. It was one hundred cubits square. Although it is not specifically stated, there probably was a wall that surrounded this court, since the area was exclusively for the priests. It was here that God said they would perform their priestly duties, including those concerning the altar. In this area the priests would change their garments to minister to the people (see 42:14). This inner court was also entered through three gates—all facing the same directions as the outer gates.

Verses 31, 32. Ezekiel was brought into the temple by the "south gate." This gate, along with the "north gate" (v. 35) was the same size as the external gate, with two exceptions: (1) they had **eight steps** instead of the seven steps of the east gate (v. 31), and (2) the **porches** were reversed, this time being on the side of the outer court. The additional steps made the temple itself that much higher than the rest of the temple square. Therefore, it was easily visible from every direction (including outside, where the short wall would make it easy to see inside). Approaching the temple, one would continue to move higher. As the Lord was high and lifted up, so also was His temple.

Verses 33–37. The inner gates also had **guardrooms** (v. 33), three on each side of the hallway (as with the outer gates). The **porches** were on the side of the outer court. The **palm tree ornaments** (v. 34) were found on these inner pillars as well. (Therefore, one would see these carvings upon approaching the temple complex and then see them again after entering into the outer court heading through the gates into the inner court.)

Each gate was exactly aligned with the corresponding external gate (separated by one hundred cubits), demonstrating the beautiful symmetry of the whole complex.

The Equipment for Sacrifices (40:38–43)

[38]A chamber with its doorway was by the side pillars at the gates; there they rinse the burnt offering. [39]In the porch of the gate were two tables on each side, on which to slaughter the burnt offering, the sin offering and the guilt offering. [40]On the outer side, as one went up to the gateway toward the north,

were two tables; and on the other side of the porch of the gate were two tables. ⁴¹Four tables were on each side next to the gate; or, eight tables on which they slaughter sacrifices. ⁴²For the burnt offering there were four tables of hewn stone, a cubit and a half long, a cubit and a half wide and one cubit high, on which they lay the instruments with which they slaughter the burnt offering and the sacrifice. ⁴³The double hooks, one handbreadth in length, were installed in the house all around; and on the tables was the flesh of the offering.

Verses 38–40. As Ezekiel entered the gate into the temple itself, he came to the place where the priests would **rinse the burnt offering** (v. 38). In this area were **two tables on each side,** [used] **to slaughter the burnt offering, the sin offering and the guilt offering** (v. 39). There are three interpretations as to the location of these "tables":

1. They were in the porch area of the east gate (46:1, 2).
2. They were in the porch area of the north gate (40:40; 46:19, 20).
3. They were located at the entrances of all three gates.

Verses 41, 42. Exactly how the tables were arranged is unclear. It appears that there were a total of twelve tables, eight used for slaughtering sacrificial animals and four smaller tables used to hold the knives and other tools used in the slaughtering. If these tables were located only at the north gate, it would channel all of the worshipers to one location for sacrifices. (This would cause cramped conditions, both outside, with all the people, and inside, with a group of priests trying to navigate around so many tables. Again, we see that this was not meant to be a literal temple.) Some see spiritual significance in the north gate. For example, Unger wrote,

> But why is provision made for sacrifice in the northern gate? Scripture often associates the north with judgment. From that direction catastrophe fell upon both Israel and Judah. The "north" properly means "the

hidden, the dark," since the ancients regarded the north as the seat of gloom and darkness in contrast to the bright and sunny south. The concept of darkness is associated scripturally with judgment. It is "in everlasting chains" under "darkness" that the wicked angels are kept (Jude 6), unregenerate man is in darkness (Eph. 4:18; 5:8), the unsaved face an eternal doom of outer darkness, and Jesus paid the penalty for sin in the midnight darkness of Calvary. It is in connection, then, with the north gate that the truth and need of sacrifice are to be apprehended.[1]

Verse 43. The double hooks were fixed on the walls for the purpose of hanging the meat so that it could be roasted. Using the hooks made the job somewhat more orderly.

As noted earlier, one must question what possible connection such sacrifices would have either in the Gospel Age or in the premillennial position (which has this temple being literally built as part of the thousand-year reign of Christ). Premillennialists have certainly recognized the difficulty this presents and have proposed numerous solutions.[2] None of these solutions are satisfactory. There is simply no way to make this section literal without showing disregard for the atoning work of Christ.

The Priests' Chambers (40:44–47)

44From the outside to the inner gate were chambers for the singers in the inner court, one of which was at the side of the north gate, with its front toward the south, and one at the side of the south gate facing toward the north. 45He said to me, "This

---

[1] Merrill F. Unger, *Great Neglected Bible Prophecies* (Chicago: Scripture Press, 1955), 74–75.

[2] Unger's explanation is that "millennial sacrifices are in no sense propitiations, but are purely commemorative of the one all-sufficient sacrifice of Christ" (Ibid., 27). A full discussion is given in Jerry M. Hullinger, "The Problem of Animal Sacrifices in Ezekiel 40–48," *Bibliotheca Sacra* 152 (July 1995): 279–89.

is the chamber which faces toward the south, intended for the priests who keep charge of the temple; ⁴⁶but the chamber which faces toward the north is for the priests who keep charge of the altar. These are the sons of Zadok, who from the sons of Levi come near to the LORD to minister to Him." ⁴⁷He measured the court, a perfect square, a hundred cubits long and a hundred cubits wide; and the altar was in front of the temple.

Verse 44. The introduction of the word **singers** is a subject of some debate. The Hebrew does include the word שָׁרִים (*sharim*, "singers" or "song leaders"). However, the RSV, following the LXX, omitted the word.³ The translators of the NIV also omitted the word: "Outside the inner gate, within the inner court, were two rooms, one at the side of the north gate and facing south, and another at the side of the south gate and facing north." Nevertheless, the evidence is insufficient for omitting the word "singers." We know from the Old Testament that singing was a function of the priests in temple worship (see 1 Chron. 16:4–6; 23:5; 2 Chron. 29:25–30).

Verses 45, 46. Ezekiel was given an explanation of the significance of this area (information that would be especially interesting to a priest). The priests described in verse 45 (at **the south** chamber) were those in charge of the daily operations at **the temple** (see 44:10–14; Lev. 8:35; Num. 3:27, 28, 32, 38; 18:4; 1 Chron. 9:23; 2 Chron. 13:11; Ps. 134:1). The priests mentioned in verse 46 worked with the sacrifices connected with **the altar**. These priests would be **the sons of Zadok** (see 44:15, 16). Zadok was a descendant of Aaron and held the high priesthood during the days of Solomon (see 1 Kings 1:8).

Verse 47. The altar was located in the center of the square, which was **a perfect square**, measuring one hundred cubits on each side. Its dimensions are not given here, but they are discussed in 43:13–17. This altar would draw immediate attention as the first item one would see upon entering the inner gates.

---

³John B. Taylor agreed with this omission in *Ezekiel: An Introduction and Commentary*, Tyndale Old Testament Commentaries (Downers Grove, Ill.: Inter-Varsity Press, 1969), 259.

THE TEMPLE PORCH (OR VESTIBULE) (40:48, 49)

⁴⁸Then he brought me to the porch of the temple and measured each side pillar of the porch, five cubits on each side; and the width of the gate was three cubits on each side. ⁴⁹The length of the porch was twenty cubits and the width eleven cubits; and at the stairway by which it was ascended were columns belonging to the side pillars, one on each side.

Verses 48, 49. Entering through the gates of the inner square (those that led to the temple itself), Ezekiel came to **the porch of the temple** (v. 48). This porch had another flight of stairs (thought to have either eight or ten steps, as reads the LXX). The width of the porch is reported as **eleven cubits** (v. 49), but that is probably incorrect. The LXX has twelve—which is necessary for the other measurements to line up. (The RSV also translates it as "twelve.") The **columns** were freestanding pillars, next to **the side pillars** (see 1 Kings 7:15–22).

APPLICATION

God's Protection and Instruction

Like the impressive gates leading into the temple (with the six guardrooms), the Lord provides protection for His people (Ps. 91:1, 2; see Eph. 6:10–17; 2 Thess. 3:3).

The particulars of worship have always been of paramount importance to God. It is essential for God's people to pay attention to divine instruction concerning worship (see Jn. 4:23, 24).

D.P.

God's Perfection

God is perfect (Mt. 5:48). He makes no mistakes and has no character flaws. His love is perfect toward all people. He sends the rain upon the just and the unjust. He makes the sun to rise upon the evil and the good. How do we see His perfection highlighted in the Scriptures?

His works are perfect (Deut. 32:4). ". . . His work is perfect, for all His ways are just; a God of faithfulness and without injustice, righteous and upright is He." No one can improve upon what God does.

His words are perfect (Ps. 19:7a). "The law of the Lord is perfect, restoring the soul." His Word is complete, unerring, and perfectly suited to our needs. God has not told us everything we want to know, but He has told us all that we need to know.

His ways are perfect (Ps. 18:30). No one can bring an honest accusation against what He has done. He has never erred in judgment. He has never miscalculated. He has never forgotten.

If we stand with Him, we cannot lose. If we stand apart from Him, we cannot win.

The God Who Goes Before

God has always been the God who has gone before us. As a flower girl goes before a bride to toss flowers and decorate her path, God has gone before us to bless our paths with His grace.

He has gone before us in this life. When we came into this world, God had already prepared everything for us. He had a world that would sustain us, people who would love us, and opportunities for growth standing before us.

He has gone before us in the spiritual realm. He has been planning for us through two biblical ages and part of a third. He brought Christ into the world, He put the church here, and He has provided the everlasting gospel to be our means of salvation. All spiritual blessings were available for us when we made the decision to put on Jesus in baptism (Gal. 3:27; Eph. 1:3).

We can trust, on the basis of what He has done in the past, that He has gone before us in eternity. Jesus said, "I go and prepare a place for you" (Jn. 14:3). When we step over to life's other side, we will find that God is waiting for us with far greater blessings than we have seen in this life. Paul said that to depart and be with Christ is far better (Phil. 1:23).

God went before Israel, fighting their battles and giving their victories. He goes before us as well. He has charted a map for our journey so that we will not make a wrong turn. If we follow His leadership, all will be well—in life, in the church, and in eternity.

E.C.

Chapter 41

The Temple Itself

THE HOLY PLACE AND THE MOST HOLY PLACE (41:1–4)

¹Then he brought me to the nave and measured the side pillars; six cubits wide on each side was the width of the side pillar. ²The width of the entrance was ten cubits and the sides of the entrance were five cubits on each side. And he measured the length of the nave, forty cubits, and the width, twenty cubits. ³Then he went inside and measured each side pillar of the doorway, two cubits, and the doorway, six cubits high; and the width of the doorway, seven cubits. ⁴He measured its length, twenty cubits, and the width, twenty cubits, before the nave; and he said to me, "This is the most holy place."

Verses 1, 2. The temple in Ezekiel's vision was similar to Solomon's temple, with three principal parts: the porch, **the nave** (or holy place), and the "most holy place" (v. 4). (See "The Temple Complex in Ezekiel's Vision" on page 586.) The "nave" was due west of the altar and was approached by going up ten steps. Therefore, it took seven steps to reach the outer gate, eight more steps to the inner gate, and then ten steps to the temple itself. Ezekiel, being a priest, was qualified to enter the holy place (which was 40 x 20 cubits). Inside, there was one piece of furniture: the wooden table-altar consecrated to the Lord (see v. 22).

Verses 3, 4. Only Ezekiel's guide proceeded from there into the most holy place (see Lev. 16; Heb. 9:7). This was the innermost part of the temple, twenty cubits square. Notice that there is no mention of the ark of the covenant, the cherubim, the mercy seat, or the law of Moses. The absence of these elements further illustrates the non-literal nature of this vision.

THE SIDE CHAMBERS (41:5–12)

⁵Then he measured the wall of the temple, six cubits; and the width of the side chambers, four cubits, all around about the house on every side. ⁶The side chambers were in three stories, one above another, and thirty in each story; and the side chambers extended to the wall which stood on their inward side all around, that they might be fastened, and not be fastened into the wall of the temple itself. ⁷The side chambers surrounding the temple were wider at each successive story. Because the structure surrounding the temple went upward by stages on all sides of the temple, therefore the width of the temple increased as it went higher; and thus one went up from the lowest story to the highest by way of the second story. ⁸I saw also that the house had a raised platform all around; the foundations of the side chambers were a full rod of six long cubits in height. ⁹The thickness of the outer wall of the side chambers was five cubits. But the free space between the side chambers belonging to the temple ¹⁰and the outer chambers was twenty cubits in width all around the temple on every side. ¹¹The doorways of the side chambers toward the free space consisted of one doorway toward the north and another doorway toward the south; and the width of the free space was five cubits all around.

¹²The building that was in front of the separate area at the side toward the west was seventy cubits wide; and the wall of the building was five cubits thick all around, and its length was ninety cubits.

Verses 5–8. The side chambers are discussed in these verses. These rooms were probably for storage rather than for housing, although their exact purpose is not given. These rooms were on three sides of the temple—the north, west, and south sides. A total of thirty such rooms were located on each story, ninety in all. Perhaps this number is symbolic: 3 x 10 x 3 = 90. The usual theories center on the number "three" as representative of the Trinity and the number "ten" representing completeness. Thus the temple would exhibit the complete "house" of God. Such explanations of these numbers are widely varied and somewhat fanciful.

Josephus said that around Solomon's temple were chambers three stories high, each story consisting of thirty chambers.[1] It is supposed that twelve were placed to the north of the temple, twelve to the south, and six to the east. The chambers described here would be similar to those of Solomon's temple (1 Kings 6:5–10), although the measurements are not quite the same. The chambers on each level increased in size (four cubits on the first floor, five cubits on the second floor, and six cubits on the top floor). Each level was slightly recessed; the size difference was made up from the adjoining temple wall.

Verses 9–11. Each chamber had two entrances, one **doorway toward the north** side and another on **the south** side (v. 11). The walls opposite the doorway were those of the holy place and the most holy place.

Verse 12. On **the west** side was a large building (called **the separate area**), measuring 70 x 90 cubits. This building, most likely, was also used for storage, although some have suggested other functions. For example, this might have been a place where priests could go for a break, where animal remnants were stored until they could be hauled away, or where live animals were kept until they were needed as sacrifices. With its five-cubit wall on either side, plus its ninety-cubit length, the building was exactly one hundred cubits across from north to south. This made it exactly the same length as the inner courtyard and the inner court to the east of the temple itself (vv. 13–15).

---

[1] Josephus *Antiquities* 8.3.2.

THE MEASUREMENTS, FURNISHINGS, AND DECORATIONS (41:13–26)

¹³Then he measured the temple, a hundred cubits long; the separate area with the building and its walls were also a hundred cubits long. ¹⁴Also the width of the front of the temple and that of the separate areas along the east side totaled a hundred cubits.

¹⁵He measured the length of the building along the front of the separate area behind it, with a gallery on each side, a hundred cubits; he also measured the inner nave and the porches of the court. ¹⁶The thresholds, the latticed windows and the galleries round about their three stories, opposite the threshold, were paneled with wood all around, and from the ground to the windows (but the windows were covered), ¹⁷over the entrance, and to the inner house, and on the outside, and on all the wall all around inside and outside, by measurement. ¹⁸It was carved with cherubim and palm trees; and a palm tree was between cherub and cherub, and every cherub had two faces, ¹⁹a man's face toward the palm tree on one side and a young lion's face toward the palm tree on the other side; they were carved on all the house all around. ²⁰From the ground to above the entrance cherubim and palm trees were carved, as well as on the wall of the nave.

²¹The doorposts of the nave were square; as for the front of the sanctuary, the appearance of one doorpost was like that of the other. ²²The altar was of wood, three cubits high and its length two cubits; its corners, its base and its sides were of wood. And he said to me, "This is the table that is before the LORD." ²³The nave and the sanctuary each had a double door. ²⁴Each of the doors had two leaves, two swinging leaves; two leaves for one door and two leaves for the other. ²⁵Also there were carved on them, on the doors of the nave, cherubim and palm trees like those carved on the walls; and there was a threshold of wood on the front of the porch outside. ²⁶There were latticed windows and palm trees on one side and on the other, on the sides of the porch; thus were the side chambers of the house and the thresholds.

Verses 13–15. The temple was measured next, totaling **a hundred cubits** in length and one hundred cubits in width (including **the separate areas**; vv. 13, 14). The symmetry of the structure would have been pleasing to the eye and impressive to an architect. However, the overall idea seems to be the perfection of the dwelling of God, portrayed here in beautiful apocalyptic language.

Verse 16. The latticed windows provided light for the holy place, even though they had some sort of covering over them. The most holy place had no windows and was kept in darkness.

Verses 17–20. The descriptions given here are, at best, difficult to follow. Nevertheless, it appears that the interior was paneled or wainscoted with wood, with designs alternating between **palm trees** and **cherubim** with **two faces**. These were **carved** into the wood paneling. The two-faced cherubim were unique; such creatures were normally depicted with four faces (see 1:6–12). The two faces were those of **a man** and of **a young lion**. (The bull and the eagle faces of the cherub in chapter 1 are omitted.) The two faces of the cherubim were looking in opposite directions, each one facing toward the palm tree on the appropriate side.

Verses 21–23. The doorposts ... were square (v. 21), adding to the overall symmetry of the building. In front of those was an **altar** made **of wood, three cubits high** and **two cubits** long (about 3½ feet square and about 5 feet high). Ezekiel was specifically told that this altar was **the table that is before the Lord** (v. 22). This must certainly be referring to the table of showbread, or the table of "the bread of the Presence" (see Ex. 25:23–30; Lev. 24:5–9; 1 Kings 6:20), although some have considered it an altar of incense.[2] In comparison to Solomon's temple, which was lavishly overlaid with silver and gold, this temple was intentionally plain. External trappings of beauty and splendor were purposely omitted, emphasizing the simplicity of worship.

Verses 24–26. The doors separating the porch from the holy

---

[2]Merrill F. Unger, *Great Neglected Bible Prophecies* (Chicago: Scripture Press, 1955), 78.

place had **two swinging leaves** that swung freely and were hinged in the middle so they could be folded to half of their actual width (v. 24). These doors were also ornamented like the walls, with **cherubim and palm trees** (v. 25) engraved on them (similar to Solomon's temple; see 1 Kings 6:31–35). The phrase **threshold of wood** is from a Hebrew word of uncertain meaning. Some think that it referred to a wooden canopy which extended outward, providing shade and protection (see 1 Kings 7:6, where the same word is used).

APPLICATION

Worshiping a Great God

The closer one comes to God, the more appreciation he has of God's exalted nature.

Doors can serve either of two purposes: to let people in or to keep people out. If one is full of sin, he cannot reach God. However, those coming to Him through penitence and obedience can enter because of His grace.

D.P.

The Worshiper's Wish

The one who comes before God in worship has only one real ambition: to please God. This aspiration can be seen from three viewpoints.

"May what I say be pleasing to God." The words that we use in our worship of God are carefully chosen, just as we carefully choose the words we use to encourage our loved ones. We want to use the best words and the truest, most beautiful thoughts as we praise Him.

"May what I think be pleasing to God." We want holy minds and pure hearts as we worship. God not only hears our words, but He also sees the thoughts and meditations behind our words.

"May my worship be pleasing to God." We worship God to please Him. We desire for our worship to come before Him as a sweet-smelling sacrifice. Our worship will be acceptable only if we have right hearts and lips involved in it.

Our one wish should be that the thoughts of our hearts and

the words that we speak will be acceptable to God as we praise Him.

The Rewards of Worship

We worship because we desire to give God the honor and praise due Him. No one, however, does what is right without receiving benefits from it. What does the worshiper receive?

He receives the blessings of God. His Father bestows upon him favors that are in harmony with His will, grace, and wisdom. No one can praise God and not be made better in the process.

He receives the righteousness of God. He becomes like the One he worships. He is cleansed, molded, and made more usable by his worship.

He receives the approval of God. His living out the will of God brings the applause of heaven. To know that we have brought gladness to God's heart is one of life's greatest rewards.

We do not go to worship dominated by the question "What will I get out of this?" However, the sincere worshiper, as a kind of serendipity, is bathed in the glory of God as he praises Him.

E.C.

Chapter 42

The Priests' Chambers
And the Temple Measurements

THE PRIESTS' CHAMBER-BUILDINGS IN THE OUTER COURT (42:1–14)

¹Then he brought me out into the outer court, the way toward the north; and he brought me to the chamber which was opposite the separate area and opposite the building toward the north. ²Along the length, which was a hundred cubits, was the north door; the width was fifty cubits. ³Opposite the twenty cubits which belonged to the inner court, and opposite the pavement which belonged to the outer court, was gallery corresponding to gallery in three stories. ⁴Before the chambers was an inner walk ten cubits wide, a way of one hundred cubits; and their openings were on the north. ⁵Now the upper chambers were smaller because the galleries took more space away from them than from the lower and middle ones in the building. ⁶For they were in three stories and had no pillars like the pillars of the courts; therefore the upper chambers were set back from the ground upward, more than the lower and middle ones. ⁷As for the outer wall by the side of the chambers, toward the outer court facing the chambers, its length was fifty cubits. ⁸For the length of the chambers which were in the outer court was fifty cubits; and behold, the length of those facing the temple was a hundred cubits. ⁹Below these chambers was the entrance on the east side, as one enters them from the outer court.

¹⁰In the thickness of the wall of the court toward the east,

facing the separate area and facing the building, there were chambers. ¹¹The way in front of them was like the appearance of the chambers which were on the north, according to their length so was their width, and all their exits were both according to their arrangements and openings. ¹²Corresponding to the openings of the chambers which were toward the south was an opening at the head of the way, the way in front of the wall toward the east, as one enters them.

¹³Then he said to me, "The north chambers and the south chambers, which are opposite the separate area, they are the holy chambers where the priests who are near to the LORD shall eat the most holy things. There they shall lay the most holy things, the grain offering, the sin offering and the guilt offering; for the place is holy. ¹⁴When the priests enter, then they shall not go out into the outer court from the sanctuary without laying there their garments in which they minister, for they are holy. They shall put on other garments; then they shall approach that which is for the people."

Verses 1–9. Ezekiel next described the priests' chambers that faced toward the temple yard. (See "The Temple Complex in Ezekiel's Vision" on page 586.) These chambers were located on both the north and south sides of the temple. (He described the north side in some detail; the south was exactly like it.) These chambers were for the personal use of the priests, who would use the area to change as well as to "eat the most holy things" and to store other offerings given to them (see v. 13). A walkway went in front of the chambers. These chambers had **three stories** (v. 3), as did the side chambers described in 41:5–11 (the thirty storage rooms per floor). The exact layout of this section is difficult to discern. Scholars have depended upon the LXX to understand more clearly the MT; but even with that, no satisfactory understanding has been reached. What is clear is that the buildings were one hundred cubits long from east to west and fifty cubits wide from north to south. All of the rooms apparently had doors on the north side. Each floor was entered from the north as well, except for the main floor, which had an **entrance on the east side** (v. 9). In front of this east entrance was an **outer wall** (v. 7), fifty cubits in length. Such a structure might have provided privacy from the outer court.

Verses 10–12. The priests' chambers on the south were built exactly like those toward the north—again providing a squared effect and having perfect symmetry. Here a different set of rooms is described that faced directly toward the outer courtyard.

Verses 13, 14. The specific purposes of these rooms are given. The priests were to eat their sacrifices there, as well as to store other offerings that were given to them. The emphasis on the word **holy** (v. 13) serves as a vivid reminder of the importance of following the divine pattern. These regulations were not to be taken lightly. When the priests went to **the outer court**, they were first to remove the **garments** they wore while **minister**[ing] as priests—for these garments were **holy** (v. 14). They were to keep other clothing in their chambers, and that was to be worn when they went into the courtyard among the people.

THE MEASUREMENTS OF THE TEMPLE AREA (42:15–20)

¹⁵**Now when he had finished measuring the inner house, he brought me out by the way of the gate which faced toward the east and measured it all around. ¹⁶He measured on the east side with the measuring reed five hundred reeds by the measuring reed. ¹⁷He measured on the north side five hundred reeds by the measuring reed. ¹⁸On the south side he measured five hundred reeds with the measuring reed. ¹⁹He turned to the west side and measured five hundred reeds with the measuring reed. ²⁰He measured it on the four sides; it had a wall all around, the length five hundred and the width five hundred, to divide between the holy and the profane.**

Verse 15. Ezekiel was next taken outside of the temple, first going through the gate that was part of the inner court and then through the gate that was part of the outer court. These gates were in line with each other. There, he received the dimensions of the entire building (v. 15).

EZEKIEL 42

Verses 16–20. Like the Hebrew text, the NASB describes each side of the temple as measuring **five hundred reeds** (v. 16). Some versions have "rods" here. This measurement has been a subject of much debate, for the Hebrew clearly uses the word "reeds" (from קָנִים, *qanim*), whereas the LXX has the word "cubits."

If the measurement is accepted to be in "reeds" (as in the NASB) or "rods," the temple is of immense size, extending beyond the borders of Israel. (It would be seven miles across, with an area of more than sixty square miles—six times the size of the structure if measured in cubits). Accepting the measurement in "reeds" presents obvious difficulties for the millennial view, which attempts to make the text literal. However, it is almost essential for millennialists to take it literally, even with the difficulties; otherwise (changing it to "cubits"), the temple would be too small for a millennial kingdom. If the word "reeds" is adopted but understood figuratively (as part of an apocalyptic vision), then the text demonstrates the vastness of God's kingdom (indeed, so large that it is like a "city"; see 40:2).

Taking the measurement to be "cubits" (as in the NIV) is the more popular position among scholars today (even with some premillennialists). Besides the fact that this change was made by the LXX translators, it fits the measurements previously given (unless the temple area is but one small part of a great wall that has previously not been mentioned). The size of the temple, according to the cubit measurement, would be approximately 1½ square miles, larger than the entire city of ancient Jerusalem. This would be impressive, considering how much larger it was than the temple of Solomon. (However, it would still be too small for the premillennial view.[1]) Evidence for rejecting the normal reading of "reeds" is insufficient.

No attempt should be made to literalize this text; it is a vision demonstrating the greatness of God and His care for His people. His city is of enormous size, able to welcome all of the faithful. The fact that the dimensions would go beyond the borders of Israel might symbolize how God's grace has reached

---

[1] Merrill F. Unger, *Great Neglected Bible Prophecies* (Chicago: Scripture Press, 1955), 66.

beyond the nation of Israel, welcoming the "other sheep" into the fold (Jn. 10:16).

APPLICATION

Serving in the Presence of God

We can view God in many different ways. We understand Him to be our Father, our Provider, our Creator, and sometimes we may even think of Him as our Friend. Each of these descriptions brings us comfort and helps our understanding of His nature. However, we must remember that in the Old Testament, whenever people were in God's presence, the overwhelming sensation they often felt was reverence for His glory.

When Moses saw the burning bush, God told Moses to remove his sandals because the place where he was standing was holy (Ex. 3:5).

When the Israelites prepared to receive God's laws at Mount Sinai, they were told not to approach the mountain (Ex. 19:18–25).

When the Lord appeared to Isaiah, he recognized his own sinfulness and declared, "Woe is me, for I am ruined!" (Is. 6:5).

Although we may befriend God and approach Him through Christ's blood, He must be feared and revered. Our license to approach the Almighty does not allow us to bring Him down to our level. He is holy, and only because of grace and the blood of Christ are we able to stand before Him. As members of the royal priesthood (1 Pet. 2:9) who serve the Holy One, we are to "fear God and keep His commandments" (Eccles. 12:13) and live "in a manner worthy" of our calling (Eph. 4:1).

Many Rooms

One recurring theme or symbol in the vision of chapters 40 through 48 is that of the priests' chambers. These rooms were to be used by the priests to perform their priestly duties. Although these chambers are difficult to interpret, they may remind the reader of certain rooms that Jesus discussed.

Jesus comforted His disciples with the following words, "In My Father's house are many dwelling places; if it were not so, I would have told you; for I go to prepare a place for you"

(Jn. 14:2). At the time when Jesus gave this promise, He was moments away from His trial and crucifixion. On the eve of His suffering, He gave the disciples hope of a heavenly dwelling place.

Both texts provide hope for the future. As God's people, we have the assurance that we will be with Him. We can know that as citizens of the kingdom of God we have a place to call home as we dwell with our Father forever.

Gathering "Sheep into the Fold"

The apocalyptic city's extending beyond the borders of Israel may be an allusion to God's grace reaching beyond the people of Israel. This causes us to consider God's method of salvation. Newcomers to the Bible may be disturbed by wars and acts of judgment in the Old Testament. However, the Old Testament is filled with cases when God's mercy extended not only to the Israelites but also to the "aliens" who joined the community of Israel.

First, a "mixed multitude" joined the Israelites' exodus out of Egypt (Ex. 12:38). The word in Hebrew is עֶרֶב (*'ereb*), which can also be translated as "foreigner."

Second, Rahab and her family were saved from the destruction of Jericho because she hid the Israelite spies (Josh. 2; see Heb. 11:31). Rahab was a citizen of Jericho, a Moabite woman, and a prostitute.

Third, Ruth, also from Moab, was assimilated into the tribe of Judah through her marriage to Boaz. They became the great-grandparents of David (Ruth 4:17) and were specifically mentioned in the lineage of Jesus (Mt. 1:5).

Finally, Solomon prayed for the foreigner who would come to the temple to worship God (1 Kings 8:41–43): "Hear in heaven Your dwelling place, and do according to all for which the foreigner calls to You" (v. 43).

In many other examples in the Old Testament God showed mercy to the repentant foreigner. His mercy is not bound by nationality or race. God invites all to enter into a covenant relationship with Him.

T.P.W.

Chapter 43

God's Glory Returns To the Temple; The Altar of Burnt Offerings

THE RETURN OF THE GLORY OF GOD TO THE TEMPLE (43:1–12)

The greatest tragedy in the Book of Ezekiel was the departure of the Lord from the temple (10:18, 19; 11:22, 23). Nineteen years later, Ezekiel received a message the exiles were eager to hear: The Lord was returning! As with the temple built by Solomon, God would consecrate the new temple and make it His holy dwelling place. Ezekiel's vision of this temple was carefully described in chapters 40 through 42.

The Glory of the Lord Coming to the Temple (43:1–5)

¹Then he led me to the gate, the gate facing toward the east; ²and behold, the glory of the God of Israel was coming from the way of the east. And His voice was like the sound of many waters; and the earth shone with His glory. ³And it was like the appearance of the vision which I saw, like the vision which I saw when He came to destroy the city. And the visions were like the vision which I saw by the river Chebar; and I fell on my face. ⁴And the glory of the LORD came into the house by the way of the gate facing toward the east. ⁵And the Spirit lifted me up and brought me into the inner court; and behold, the glory of the LORD filled the house.

Verse 1. Ezekiel left by the east gate of the temple square and moved toward the main east gate. (See "The Temple Complex in Ezekiel's Vision" on page 586.) Here, he witnessed one of the most significant events in his ministry.

Verse 2. As Ezekiel was facing the east gate, he saw **the glory of the God of Israel** coming toward him. God had departed from that direction (11:23); and now, from that same direction, He was returning. Ezekiel heard a thunderous **voice**, as if God were announcing a glorious victory. The Lord's return made **the earth** [shine] **with His glory** (Deut. 33:2; Is. 60:1–3; Hab. 3:3, 4).

Verse 3. What Ezekiel **saw** was like the vision he had seen by the river Chebar in chapter 1. The prophet reminded his readers that it was not really the Babylonians who had destroyed their city. Rather, he said that God **came to destroy the city** (see 9:1–11). Even though he had seen all this before, Ezekiel had the same reaction described earlier: He **fell on** [his] **face.** The wonder of seeing God's greatness still had a tremendous impact on this humble servant.

Verse 4. As He had done when Solomon dedicated the first temple to Him, God demonstrated His approval of the new temple by coming **into the house** (see 1 Kings 8:10, 11; 2 Chron. 5:14). The entrance to the temple faced east, so the glory of God was coming from the east. It must have passed by the outer east gate and through the east entrance to the temple, entering directly into the sanctuary.

Verse 5. Ezekiel, who was outside the temple itself (in the outer court), was taken **into the inner court**. This enabled him to have a clear view of **the glory of the** Lord [which] **filled the house**. If God had not considered this place holy, He would not have inhabited it.

The Lord Speaking Within His Temple (43:6–12)

⁶Then I heard one speaking to me from the house, while a man was standing beside me. ⁷He said to me, "Son of man, this is the place of My throne and the place of the soles of My feet, where I will dwell among the sons of Israel forever. And the house of Israel will not again defile My holy name, neither they nor their kings, by their harlotry and by the corpses of

their kings when they die, ⁸by setting their threshold by My threshold and their door post beside My door post, with only the wall between Me and them. And they have defiled My holy name by their abominations which they have committed. So I have consumed them in My anger. ⁹Now let them put away their harlotry and the corpses of their kings far from Me; and I will dwell among them forever.

¹⁰"As for you, son of man, describe the temple to the house of Israel, that they may be ashamed of their iniquities; and let them measure the plan. ¹¹If they are ashamed of all that they have done, make known to them the design of the house, its structure, its exits, its entrances, all its designs, all its statutes, and all its laws. And write it in their sight, so that they may observe its whole design and all its statutes and do them. ¹²This is the law of the house: its entire area on the top of the mountain all around shall be most holy. Behold, this is the law of the house."

Verse 6. When Ezekiel said, **I heard one speaking to me from the house,** he could not have been referring to the messenger who was standing beside him. The Lord Himself must have been speaking.

Verse 7. God returned to the familiar terminology of **son of man**. He made some key statements regarding this new temple. First, He said, **"This is the place of My throne."** This unusual terminology in the Hebrew emphasizes the word "place." From this place, the Lord would rule. His "throne"—the one Ezekiel had seen in chapter 1—would now reside here. S. Fisch wrote,

> In contrast to the former Temple which was only God's *footstool*, His throne being in heaven (Isa. lx. 13; Ps. cxxxii. 7; Lam. ii. 1; 1 Chron. xxviii. 2), the new Temple will become in a complete sense the abode of the Divine Presence, indicated by the combination of *throne* and *soles of My feet*.[1]

---

[1] S. Fisch, *Ezekiel: Hebrew Text and English Translation with an Introduction and Commentary*, Soncino Books of the Bible (London: Soncino Press, 1950), 294.

The concept of the temple being the throne of God is repeated elsewhere (Jer. 3:17; 17:12).

Second, He said, "This is . . . **the place of the soles of My feet**"—terminology to speak of permanent habitation (see Ps. 99:5; 132:7). However, as Ezekiel would be shown, God is not bound to any one geographical place (see Is. 66:1, 2).

Third, God declared, **"I will dwell among the sons of Israel forever."** The redeemed people would forever enjoy the presence of God. This could only refer to those who have been cleansed and sanctified by the Lord.

Since God had returned to the temple, He would now make certain demands upon **the house of Israel**. They were not to go back to their old ways. God said that they must **not again defile** [His] **holy name**. They had done this frequently—by worshiping other gods and by showing their lack of faith in the Lord when they made foreign alliances. All of the people were guilty of these sins, from **their kings** to the poor. They were guilty of **harlotry** (going after pagan idols and the sacred prostitution that was part of the pagan rites). They had defiled the land with **the corpses of their kings**. Apparently, these kings had been buried in sacred areas, too close to the temple. John B. Taylor said,

> We know from the books of Kings that fourteen kings of Judah were buried "in the city of David", *i.e.* where the temple and royal palace were, and it appears as if the fault lay in the lack of any clear line of demarcation between what was sacred (the temple proper) and what was profane (the palace and any tombs associated with it). This separateness was Ezekiel's great plea, as we have already observed.[2]

Verse 8. The palace buildings or the burial plots of the kings had been placed too close to the Lord's **threshold** and by His **door post**. A clear separation was necessary, even in the build-

---

[2]John B. Taylor, *Ezekiel: An Introduction and Commentary,* Tyndale Old Testament Commentaries (Downers Grove, Ill.: Inter-Varsity Press, 1969), 265–66.

ings themselves. Solomon's temple had no wall separating the outer court from the temple. Ezekiel's temple solved this problem.

Verse 9. God promised to dwell with His people **forever**, but this promise was given with the condition that they must correct the two sins mentioned: (1) They must **put away their harlotry** (see 1 Kings 14:24), and (2) they were to relocate the burial places **of their kings** (see 2 Kings 21:18, 26). What if they failed to rectify these two sins? The answer is clear: God would not dwell with them forever—not even for a moment. These texts demonstrate the idea of *conditional* promises. God has never promised to dwell with people regardless of their spiritual state. His presence is always conditioned upon their faithfulness.

Verse 10. In verses 10 through 12, God clearly stated the purpose of the entire temple vision. Ezekiel was to **describe** (declare in its fullness) **the temple** (literally "house"—the house of the Lord) **to the house of Israel**. There were two reasons for him to do this.

(1) **That they may be ashamed of their iniquities.** What was it about this temple that would evoke shame? First, it would demonstrate the holiness of God in contrast to the sinfulness of humanity. The people had failed to make a distinction between the holy and the profane (see 22:26). Second, upon seeing God's compassion for them, despite their sinful past, they would be filled with shame. Third, they would see the absolute perfection of the buildings and be reminded of their own unworthiness even to have such a place.

(2) **Let them measure the plan.** The people needed to observe the way God wanted things to be (as opposed to the way the temple had been defiled in ch. 8). All of God's specifications are to be honored (although the specifications for this temple could not literally be honored). Chapters 40 through 42 describe how the most holy place was set apart by numerous walls and doors, emphasizing the separation between an unholy people and their holy God. This is why so many details were given. Without them, we would not have been able to "measure the plan" ourselves and see how this separation was made.

Verse 11. God said that **if** the people were **ashamed**, then

Ezekiel could continue in further detail. It was possible that the hardhearted Israelites were beyond caring. Perhaps being in exile had so embittered them against God that they were no longer interested in hearing from Him or His prophets. However, "if" they listened and were "ashamed," then there was hope. Their shame could lead them to genuine repentance. Only when they went back to hearing God's law could they appreciate the various aspects of the new temple, including **all its laws**. The very structure of the temple illustrated the existence of laws—laws on where people could go and could not go; laws concerning where priests could go and not go; laws regarding when, where, and how to offer sacrifices. God wanted them to follow the **whole design and all its statutes**. Nothing, this time, was to be neglected or overlooked. God demanded and expected complete obedience. It is sad that so many today seek to identify "major commands" to the neglect of lesser ones.

Verse 12. God declared that this was **the law of the house**. The predominant law, to keep it **most holy**, was to be respected. This is further illustrated by the fact that the temple was built on a very high **mountain** (see 40:2). This location would automatically have separated it from the people since the city itself was not on the mountain (45:1–6).

THE ALTAR OF BURNT OFFERINGS
(43:13–27)

The Description and Measurements
Of the Altar (43:13–17)

¹³"And these are the measurements of the altar by cubits (the cubit being a cubit and a handbreadth): the base shall be a cubit and the width a cubit, and its border on its edge round about one span; and this shall be the height of the base of the altar. ¹⁴From the base on the ground to the lower ledge shall be two cubits and the width one cubit; and from the smaller ledge to the larger ledge shall be four cubits and the width one cubit. ¹⁵The altar hearth shall be four cubits; and from the

altar hearth shall extend upwards four horns. ¹⁶Now the altar hearth shall be twelve cubits long by twelve wide, square in its four sides. ¹⁷The ledge shall be fourteen cubits long by fourteen wide in its four sides, the border around it shall be half a cubit and its base shall be a cubit round about; and its steps shall face the east."

Verse 13. The altar was mentioned earlier, in 40:47. It was located in the geometric center of the temple area. This altar, according to the longer cubit (**a cubit and a handbreadth**), would be about twenty-one inches long, as opposed to about seventeen inches long if the original measurement had been given in standard cubits. The exact length of the cubit, however, is unknown.

Verses 14–17. The altar was built upon a foundation that was inlaid into the ground and rose upward in three layers (v. 14). The bottom layer, or "ledge," was sixteen cubits square. The second layer was fourteen cubits long, and the top layer was twelve cubits long. However, the first layer (called **the lower ledge**) was thinner than the others, being two cubits thick. The next ledge was four cubits, and the top ledge was also four cubits (v. 15). Thus the total height of the altar was ten cubits (bottom layer, 2 + middle layer, 4 + top layer, 4 = 10 cubits). A priest would have constructed a stairway to **face the east** (v. 17), ascending to the top of the altar, more than seventeen feet high. **Four horns** projected upward (v. 15)—one on each corner, one cubit high each. The horns, composing the very top of the altar, were representative of the power to forgive sins. (Of course, in the New Testament, we learn that this power of forgiveness actually came through the blood of Christ; see Heb. 10:4.) The sacrificial blood was smeared on these horns (Ex. 29:12; Lev. 4:7; Ezek. 43:20). The people believed that one clutching these horns should not be put to death (see 1 Kings 1:50–53; 2:28–34).

The altar faced "east" (v. 17). Thus one who entered through the predominant east gate, upon coming through the temple gate, would immediately run into the altar. It would separate him from the sanctuary. One could not enter into the presence of God until his sins had been atoned at the altar of sacrifice.

In the same way, we cannot approach God except through the blood of Christ (Heb. 4:16; 10:19).

The overall appearance of the altar was like a Babylonian ziggurat, which rose up in a pyramid style, with each successive layer being small enough to leave a ledge around it.

The Statutes Concerning the Altar (43:18–27)

¹⁸And He said to me, "Son of man, thus says the Lord GOD, 'These are the statutes for the altar on the day it is built, to offer burnt offerings on it and to sprinkle blood on it. ¹⁹You shall give to the Levitical priests who are from the offspring of Zadok, who draw near to Me to minister to Me,' declares the Lord GOD, 'a young bull for a sin offering. ²⁰You shall take some of its blood and put it on its four horns and on the four corners of the ledge and on the border round about; thus you shall cleanse it and make atonement for it. ²¹You shall also take the bull for the sin offering, and it shall be burned in the appointed place of the house, outside the sanctuary.

²²"'On the second day you shall offer a male goat without blemish for a sin offering, and they shall cleanse the altar as they cleansed it with the bull. ²³When you have finished cleansing it, you shall present a young bull without blemish and a ram without blemish from the flock. ²⁴You shall present them before the LORD, and the priests shall throw salt on them, and they shall offer them up as a burnt offering to the LORD. ²⁵For seven days you shall prepare daily a goat for a sin offering; also a young bull and a ram from the flock, without blemish, shall be prepared. ²⁶For seven days they shall make atonement for the altar and purify it; so shall they consecrate it. ²⁷When they have completed the days, it shall be that on the eighth day and onward, the priests shall offer your burnt offerings on the altar, and your peace offerings; and I will accept you,' declares the Lord GOD."

Verse 18. The altar came with a number of regulations or **statutes**. Without the observance of these divine statutes, the sacrifices would be worthless. The priests had two duties in-

volving the altar: **to offer burnt offerings on it and to sprinkle blood on it**.

Verse 19. Not all priests were allowed to minister at the altar, but only **the Levitical priests . . . from the offspring of Zadok** (see 40:46; 44:15, 16). Zadok, a descendant of Phinehas, was the first high priest of Solomon's temple. He was given the covenant of an everlasting priesthood (Num. 25:13; 1 Kings 2:35). Priests from other families were not allowed to serve because of past idolatrous practices (44:10). They were relegated to menial tasks around the temple.

Verses 20–22. The first order of business was for the sons of Zadok to **cleanse** and **make atonement** for the altar itself (v. 20). The remnants of **the bull** that was used **for the sin offering** were to be **burned** outside of the entire temple complex (v. 21). **On the second day a male goat** was to be offered as **a sin offering** (v. 22). This practice was unique, not having been mentioned in the law of sacrifices. The same procedures followed in sacrificing the bull were to be followed with the goat. Once this was done, the priests were to "cleanse" the altar and get it ready for use on that day. It is interesting that Ezekiel did not detail the cleansing of the priest—a requirement that is heavily emphasized in the Mosaic law (see Ex. 29; Lev. 8).

Verses 23, 24. The Zadokite priests were to follow this ritual every day, or else the altar was not cleansed. After these two animals were sacrificed, the priests would then offer **a young bull** and **a ram**—both **without blemish**—as **a burnt offering**. A burnt offering consumed the entire animal. Thus, unlike the sin and trespass offerings (from which the priest received a portion) and the peace offerings (from which both the priest and the one offering the sacrifice received a portion), this entire animal was given to God. The throwing of **salt** (v. 24) is not unique to the laws of animal sacrifice. It was mentioned in regard to grain offerings in Leviticus 2:13.

Verses 25, 26. The initial cleansing of the altar would take **seven days** (v. 25). Failure to follow this procedure would prevent the altar from being **purif**[ied] or **consecrate**[d] (v. 26; see Ex. 29:37).

Verse 27. After the seven days of purifying, the altar could then be used for sacrifices of all kinds. The people were to make **burnt offerings** (which were to atone for sin in general) and **peace offerings** (which included the votive, freewill, and thank offerings). As noted above, the peace offerings were the only ones from which the offerer received a portion of the sacrifice. The three sin offerings (burnt offerings, sin offerings, and trespass offerings) provided no portion for the one making the offering. He was not to benefit in any way from his own sin.

APPLICATION

God's Holiness and Expectations

If God had not considered the temple holy, He would not have inhabited it. The same is true with our bodies (1 Cor. 6:19, 20) and the church (1 Cor. 3:16).

The judgments of God may seem harsh, but they serve a vital purpose: that God can ultimately save. God's return to the temple shows His true intent.

God promised to dwell with the people "forever" (v. 7). However, this promise was conditional upon their meeting His requirements. In eternity, "those who do not know God and . . . do not obey the gospel" will be sent "away from the presence of the Lord and from the glory of His power" (2 Thess. 1:8, 9).

God wanted His people to "measure the plan" for the new temple (v. 10). The word "plan" can mean "pattern." God has always had a divine blueprint for His people, and this is true regarding the new covenant. The gospel of Christ (given by the Lord and the apostles) provides the blueprint, pattern, or form for God's people to follow today. Paul wrote, "Hold fast the form of sound words, which thou hast heard of me, in faith and love which is in Christ Jesus" (2 Tim. 1:13; KJV; see Rom. 6:17).

He also expected the people to follow the "whole design and all its statutes" (v. 11). Today Jesus wants us to obey all of God's laws (Mt. 23:23).

The Israelites were to obey "the law of the house" (v. 12). Paul said that the church is "the household of God" (1 Tim. 3:15). It is His house; therefore, His rules must be followed. First Timothy gives testimony to God's "house laws," which include insisting on proper qualifications for elders and deacons, as well as the silence of women in public assemblies.

D.P.

When God Fills His House

The Lord's returning to His temple had great significance in Ezekiel's message. It provided hope and assurance that God would keep His promises and dwell with His people. This progressive theme is seen throughout the Scriptures.

Solomon's temple. Once the ark of the covenant was placed in the inner sanctuary of the temple, God's presence (in the appearance of a cloud) "filled the house of the LORD" (1 Kings 8:10, 11; see 2 Chron. 5:14). Solomon declared to the Lord, "I have surely built You a lofty house, a place for Your dwelling forever" (1 Kings 8:13).

Ezekiel's temple. Ezekiel was led in a vision to witness another spectacular event. With a sound like the rushing waters and with the earth reflecting His glory, the Lord returned to the temple and "filled the house" (43:2, 4). At this time, God reinstated His presence and declared, "I will dwell among the sons of Israel forever" (v. 7).

The Day of Pentecost. In a similar way, when God instituted the church, He sent the Holy Spirit with a rushing wind and "filled the whole house" where the disciples were meeting (Acts 2:2). This was the dawn of a new order, when the Spirit of God would fill His people (Rom. 8:11; 2 Tim. 1:14), who are His temple (1 Cor. 3:16) and His royal priesthood (1 Pet. 2:9). This new temple was not made of stones, but of people. The shift was made from God's presence in a building to God's presence in the individual lives of His followers.

The new heaven and earth. In Revelation, the temple imagery changed again. According to John's vision, in a new heaven and a new earth, "God Himself will be among" His people (Rev. 21:3). There will be no temple in the new Jerusalem, "for the Lord God the Almighty and the Lamb are its temple" (v. 22).

As followers of God, we have a promise and a hope for our eternal relationship with Him. After repentance and baptism, one receives forgiveness of sins and the gift of the Holy Spirit

(Acts 2:38). How wonderful it is to have the assurance from our Creator that He will dwell with us forever! Just as the imagery of God's returning to the temple gave hope to the readers of Ezekiel, we have the hope of being with God in heaven and a personal relationship with Him through His indwelling Spirit.

T.P.W.

The Throne of God in the Temple of God

In earlier days, God had resided in Jerusalem above the ark of the covenant. He had chosen Jerusalem as His dwelling place. However, because of the sins of the people, He had withdrawn His presence. Jerusalem had fallen, and the Babylonians had desecrated the temple. Now Ezekiel was being told the best of all news, the news that God would return and would once again make His throne in His temple. What would God's throne, His presence, in the temple mean to His people?

His people would have divine glory in their midst. When Jerusalem fell, the glory of God departed from the temple. The Jew could not think of a greater tragedy than this loss. Ezekiel was given the good news that His glory was returning to the new temple. Ezekiel said, "Then he led me to the gate, the gate facing toward the east; and behold, the glory of the God of Israel was coming from the way of the east. And His voice was like the sound of many waters; and the earth shone with His glory" (43:1, 2). Those who walk with God are surrounded by His glory. His glorious existence overshadows their lives.

They would be reminded by His presence of the purity that should characterize His people. God is a righteous God, and His throne is a righteous throne. Ezekiel was told, "And the house of Israel will not again defile My holy name, neither they nor their kings, by their harlotry and by the corpses of their kings when they die, by setting their threshold by My threshold and their door post beside My door post, with only the wall between Me and them" (vv. 7, 8). God has said to His people in all the ages, "be holy, for I am holy" (Lev. 11:44).

They would also be reminded that their walk with Him was predicated upon righteousness. Ezekiel was told,

> As for you, son of man, describe the temple to the house of Israel, that they may be ashamed of their iniquities; and let them measure the plan. If they are ashamed of all that they have done, make known to them the design of the house, its structure, its exits, its entrances, all its designs, all its statutes, and all its laws. And write it in their sight, so that they may observe its whole design and all its statutes and do them (vv. 10, 11).

The temple had been destroyed in the past because of the sin of God's people. Ezekiel was told to describe the temple to them so that they would understand that it was to be a place of obedience and truth. They were to walk with God through the righteous character of an obedient life.

His throne in the temple vividly portrayed that God would be among and near His people. They would be able to come near and worship Him. Ezekiel was told, "Son of man, this is the place of My throne and the place of the soles of My feet, where I will dwell among the sons of Israel forever" (v. 7). God would take up residence in His temple once again. It would be the place of His throne and the place where the soles of His feet would tread. As long as Israel remained faithful to Him, He would dwell among them.

God would be among them when they engaged in worship and praise. God gave instructions on how worship was to be offered to Him. "When you have finished cleansing it, you shall present a young bull without blemish and a ram without blemish from the flock. You shall present them before the Lord, and the priests shall throw salt on them, and they shall offer them up as a burnt offering to the Lord" (vv. 23, 24). In their worship, they were coming before God.

Nothing equals the presence of God. With Him, we have everything—peace, protection, and power. Without Him, we have nothing. God would be among His people. They would know His glory; they would be constantly reminded of His purity and righteousness. God would be near them, and they would have ample opportunities to worship and praise Him.

The Glory of the New Temple

Great significance was attached to this new temple. How encouraging the news of its coming would be to God's people!

It would be the place of His throne. God would place His throne in that temple and would rule from their midst.

It would be the place of His habitation. God would live among them. He would walk among His people.

It would be the place of His dwelling. He would take permanent residence among the people He had chosen as His own.

God would be their God, and they would be His people.

Walking with and Worshiping God

Being in God's fellowship brought important responsibilities to the people of Judah. Ezekiel was asked to tell them what they must do to maintain this relationship with God.

They were told that they could not go back to their old ways. Sin had brought the downfall of Jerusalem and Judah. They could not go back to that type of living.

They were told that they had to respect His house. They could not pollute or misuse it. As God's temple, it would have a reverent and holy aura about it.

They were told that they must obey Him. They must honor His statutes and keep them.

God is a God of grace, but He is also a God of righteousness. He is holy, and He requires His people to be holy.

E.C.

Chapter 44

The New Worship: Servants in the Temple

THE DUTIES AND INHERITANCE FOR THE PRIESTS (44:1—45:8)

The work of the priests had to be detailed, especially in regard to the various people who would come to the temple and the kinds of sacrifices that were to be offered. Only those priests who faithfully dispatched their duties would receive their "inheritance"—that is, the various payments given to them. The Levites received no land as a possession, because the Lord was "their possession" (44:28).

The Closed East Gate (44:1–3)

¹**Then He brought me back by the way of the outer gate of the sanctuary, which faces the east; and it was shut.** ²**The Lord said to me, "This gate shall be shut; it shall not be opened, and no one shall enter by it, for the Lord God of Israel has entered by it; therefore it shall be shut.** ³**As for the prince, he shall sit in it as prince to eat bread before the Lord; he shall enter by way of the porch of the gate and shall go out by the same way."**

Verses 1, 2. Ezekiel had earlier been standing in this location, by **the outer gate of the sanctuary**. (See "The Temple Complex in Ezekiel's Vision" on page 586.) That was before he was taken inside the east gate into the temple itself. In verse 1, he was brought back to the outer courtyard, where he had seen the glory of the Lord return. This time, however, he observed that the east gate **was shut**. Since the glory of the Lord entered through that gate, no one else (except for the prince) was ever to use it.[1] In this way, it would not be defiled.

Verse 3. One use was to be allowed for this east gate: **The prince** would be permitted to enter into the porch of the gate in order to eat his sacrificial meal (**eat bread before the Lord**). Notice that the Hebrew word used here is נָשִׂיא (naśi', "prince"), rather than מֶלֶךְ (melek, "king"), which was reserved for David as God's king (37:24). It is noteworthy that the leaders of God's people were to be respectful of God's laws and engage in worship to Him. They also were required to respect His ordinance regarding the sanctity of the temple, a place they were not allowed to enter. This prince could, however, enter the porch of the east gate (from the west end) and exit the same way. (See "The Outer East Gate" on page 600.)

The Qualifications for Service In the Temple (44:4–27)

Foreigners Excluded (44:4–9)

⁴**Then He brought me by way of the north gate to the front of the house; and I looked, and behold, the glory of the Lord filled the house of the Lord, and I fell on my face. ⁵The Lord said to me, "Son of man, mark well, see with your eyes and hear with your ears all that I say to you concerning all the statutes of the house of the Lord and concerning all its laws; and mark well the entrance of the house, with all exits of the sanctuary. ⁶You shall say to the rebellious ones, to the house**

---

[1] "There is no evidence that the east gate of either Zerubbabel's or Herod's Temple was closed, though its use may have been restricted to priests, and the walled-up Golden Gate in the present east wall of Jerusalem reflects a later tradition and should not be related to this passage" (John B. Taylor, *Ezekiel: An Introduction and Commentary,* Tyndale Old Testament Commentaries [Downers Grove, Ill.: Inter-Varsity Press, 1969], 270).

of Israel, 'Thus says the Lord GOD, "Enough of all your abominations, O house of Israel, ⁷when you brought in foreigners, uncircumcised in heart and uncircumcised in flesh, to be in My sanctuary to profane it, even My house, when you offered My food, the fat and the blood; for they made My covenant void—this in addition to all your abominations. ⁸And you have not kept charge of My holy things yourselves, but you have set foreigners to keep charge of My sanctuary."

⁹"'Thus says the Lord GOD, "No foreigner uncircumcised in heart and uncircumcised in flesh, of all the foreigners who are among the sons of Israel, shall enter My sanctuary."'"

Verses 4, 5. Next, Ezekiel was brought to the front of the structure through **the north gate** (v. 4). From this perspective, he again saw **the glory of the LORD** as it filled the temple. Ezekiel responded as he had in the past: **I fell on my face.** He was not reacting this way out of false humility; his was not fake reverence. Seeing the magnificence of God's glory elicited this humble response from the prophet. He was again challenged by God to pay careful attention to all that he had been shown, including **the statutes** and the **laws** (v. 5). The emphasis on these statutes and laws (see 43:11, 18) should be noted. God wanted the people to know that this new temple would not be defiled by their lawlessness.

Verses 6–9. The temple was a holy place, especially designed for the people of God. **Foreigners** who were **uncircumcised in heart and . . . flesh** were not part of the covenant family of God and therefore were to have no part in the temple. When the Israelites allowed such people to enter, they **profane**[d] the temple (v. 7). Service in the temple was a special duty of the priests and was to be performed *only* by the priests. They were given a sacred trust to keep the temple holy. God rebuked them because they had **not kept charge of** [His] **holy things** (v. 8). By allowing foreigners to participate in temple worship, they minimized the importance of proper worship to Yahweh. An example of this is found in 2 Kings 11:4, where Carites were serving as temple guards. The returning exiles paid particular attention to these regulations (Ezra 4:1–3; 10:10–44; Neh. 13:1–9; Hag. 2:13,

14). Near Herod's temple, the Jews posted a sign, warning Gentiles that if they should pass beyond a certain point they would immediately be put to death.[2]

Levites Given Only Menial Tasks (44:10–14)

¹⁰""'But the Levites who went far from Me when Israel went astray, who went astray from Me after their idols, shall bear the punishment for their iniquity. ¹¹Yet they shall be ministers in My sanctuary, having oversight at the gates of the house and ministering in the house; they shall slaughter the burnt offering and the sacrifice for the people, and they shall stand before them to minister to them. ¹²Because they ministered to them before their idols and became a stumbling block of iniquity to the house of Israel, therefore I have sworn against them," declares the Lord God, "that they shall bear the punishment for their iniquity. ¹³And they shall not come near to Me to serve as a priest to Me, nor come near to any of My holy things, to the things that are most holy; but they will bear their shame and their abominations which they have committed. ¹⁴Yet I will appoint them to keep charge of the house, of all its service and of all that shall be done in it."'"

Verse 10. The Levites were the hereditary priests of Israel (see Deut. 18:1). Upon them had been conferred the most sacred of all trusts: keeping the house of God pure. In this charge, they had failed bitterly. God said that they had gone **far from** [Him]. Not only had they failed to act as guides to the people (who were straying **after their idols**), but they had actually joined them in the abominations. The Levites would have to **bear the punishment for their iniquity**.

Verse 11. These priests are described generally as "ministers in My sanctuary." Their new responsibility was to act as special servants of God in His holy place. Their specific duties included the following:

---

[2]D. J. Wiseman, *Illustrations from Biblical Archaeology*, 3d ed. (London: Tyndale Press, 1966), 84, 92.

1. **Having oversight at the gates of the house and ministering in the house.** They were to perform the menial tasks of guarding the gates and controlling the crowd of worshipers, as well as sweeping and cleaning.
2. **Slaughter[ing] the burnt offering and the sacrifice for the people.** They assumed the most distasteful of the sacrificial duties.
3. **Stand[ing] before them** [the people and the other priests] **to minister to them.** That is, they were to assist the people so that their worship experiences would be according to the statutes of the Lord, as well as doing whatever was necessary for the other priests. Whereas these priests were to "stand before" the people, the sons of Zadok were to "stand before" the Lord (see v. 15).

Verse 12. The reason for this reduction in sacred responsibilities was the past sin of the Levites. Basically, their sin had been twofold.

First, they had **ministered to them before their idols**. For priests of the Lord to assist in idol worship was the gravest of abominations. They were so lacking in knowledge of the law of the Lord, or perhaps in their respect for it, that they had somehow justified promoting and encouraging idol worship. Why had they committed such acts? For money? For prestige? Whatever their reasons, their sin had brought the anger of the Lord upon them.

Second, they had become **a stumbling block of iniquity**. James warned Christians, "Let not many of you become teachers, my brethren, knowing that as such we will incur a stricter judgment" (Jas. 3:1). The priests of Judah had been given the ability, the power of influence, to direct the people back to God. Instead, they had become a stumbling block, actually encouraging more iniquity. Therefore, their **punishment** would be great.

Verse 13. Specifically, the punishment of these priests was their loss of special duties in the house of the Lord. God would not allow them to **come near** to Him. They could not approach

Him in worship—either in the sacrifice or in the ceremonies. Neither were they to **come near to any . . . holy things**, God said. The implements of sacrifice and the items found in the holy place were specifically forbidden to them. Every day that they performed their menial duties would serve as a reminder to them that they were forced to **bear their shame and their abominations**.

Verse 14. Nevertheless, they still had a divine appointment, which was more than the common citizen of Israel could claim. Although they were performing menial tasks, these priests were allowed to be in the temple. If their attitude was right, they would still count it an honor to serve—in any capacity.

Ezra 2 tells of more than four thousand priests among the nearly fifty thousand Israelites who returned from the Captivity. Of that number, only seventy-four were Levites (Ezra 2:40). As a result, it was necessary to call upon the priests to perform some of the menial services (Ezra 8:15–20). Apparently, the Levites who were in Babylon were unwilling to make the sacrifice to return to Jerusalem. Life for them had become quite comfortable in the pagan city. The seventy-four who did return to Judah were special men, willing to surrender to the will of their God (see Ps. 84:10).

Zadokites Selected to Serve as Priests (44:15–27)

¹⁵"'"**But the Levitical priests, the sons of Zadok, who kept charge of My sanctuary when the sons of Israel went astray from Me, shall come near to Me to minister to Me; and they shall stand before Me to offer Me the fat and the blood,**" declares the Lord God. ¹⁶"**They shall enter My sanctuary; they shall come near to My table to minister to Me and keep My charge.** ¹⁷**It shall be that when they enter at the gates of the inner court, they shall be clothed with linen garments; and wool shall not be on them while they are ministering in the gates of the inner court and in the house.** ¹⁸**Linen turbans shall be on their heads and linen undergarments shall be on their loins; they shall not gird themselves with anything which makes them sweat.** ¹⁹**When they go out into the outer court,**

into the outer court to the people, they shall put off their garments in which they have been ministering and lay them in the holy chambers; then they shall put on other garments so that they will not transmit holiness to the people with their garments. ²⁰Also they shall not shave their heads, yet they shall not let their locks grow long; they shall only trim the hair of their heads. ²¹Nor shall any of the priests drink wine when they enter the inner court. ²²And they shall not marry a widow or a divorced woman but shall take virgins from the offspring of the house of Israel, or a widow who is the widow of a priest. ²³Moreover, they shall teach My people the difference between the holy and the profane, and cause them to discern between the unclean and the clean. ²⁴In a dispute they shall take their stand to judge; they shall judge it according to My ordinances. They shall also keep My laws and My statutes in all My appointed feasts and sanctify My sabbaths. ²⁵They shall not go to a dead person to defile themselves; however, for father, for mother, for son, for daughter, for brother, or for a sister who has not had a husband, they may defile themselves. ²⁶After he is cleansed, seven days shall elapse for him. ²⁷On the day that he goes into the sanctuary, into the inner court to minister in the sanctuary, he shall offer his sin offering," declares the Lord God.'"

Verses 15, 16. The sons of Zadok (v. 15) were given the honor and responsibility to minister to the Lord. The name "Zadok" means "just or righteous." Zadok was a young warrior who helped to win the kingdom of Saul and David (1 Chron. 12:28). He was a descendant of Aaron (1 Chron. 6:50–53) and served as a priest during David's reign (2 Sam. 8:17; 15:24–35). After the events in 1 Kings 1:5–45 (see 2:26, 27; 4:4), the sons of Zadok were considered the only qualified priests in Jerusalem. God said, "[They] **kept charge of My sanctuary when the sons of Israel went astray from Me.**" This is not to suggest that there was no sin among the Zadokites (all practiced deceit, according to Jer. 8:1–10); but, in comparison to the other priests, there was far less overall corruption among them. What were their God-given responsibilities? He told them,

1. **"Come near to Me to minister to Me"** (v. 15). Only the Zadokites were able to approach God through the sacrifice. Their "ministry" was to serve Him in all aspects of worship and sacrifice. One must be holy to approach God—to "come near" to Him. This is a reminder of how Christians in the new covenant are the only ones able to draw near to God in worship through Christ (1 Pet. 2:5–8; Heb. 13:15, 16).
2. **"Stand before Me to offer Me the fat and the blood"** (v. 15). The atoning sacrifices could not be offered by just anyone. Those who stood before the Lord in worship had to meet His divine standards. The description of "the fat" and "the blood" would cover the six principal sacrifices.
3. **"Enter My sanctuary"** (v. 16). The people were not allowed to enter the sanctuary, but not every priest could enter either—only those chosen by the Lord. This sacred duty and honor was bestowed upon the Zadokites.
4. **"Come near to My table to minister to Me"** (v. 16). This means to place the showbread in the holy place (on the table mentioned in 41:22 and Mal. 1:7, 12).
5. **"Keep My charge"** (v. 16). They were to be knowledgeable of the Lord's statutes and ordinances and take special care to observe all of His laws regarding worship and sacrifice. They were entrusted to keep God's laws pure and holy, so as not to defile the holy place or the holy name of the Lord.

Verses 17–19. The Zadokite priests were to give special attention to how they were **clothed** (v. 17), for their clothing would represent the solemnity and importance of their work. They were commanded to wear **linen**, which was symbolic of purity. Also, it would allow them to stay cooler (since they were continually around fire) and perform their tasks more comfortably. **Wool** was not to be worn, because in the high temperatures of the east they would more readily **sweat** (v. 18). After they had finished their work, when they were going in among the people, the **garments** were to be removed and placed **in the holy chambers** (v. 19). It was forbidden for them to mingle with the people while wearing these holy garments, to prevent the garments from **transmit**[ting] **holiness** when touched. The people were not to think that they could become clean simply by touching these garments, as opposed to becoming clean according to the stipulations of the Law. God never wants anyone to be deceived into thinking that he can become holy simply by coming into contact with that which is holy. In Haggai 2:10–13, a different perspective is discussed. There, the question was asked if one's uncleanness could make unholy that which was holy. The priests answered in verse 13, "It will become unholy."

Verse 20. These priests were commanded to keep their hair neatly trimmed, but in moderation. They were not to **shave their heads**; this probably would have associated them with pagan practices (see Lev. 21:5). Neither were they to let the hair **grow long**, which might have confused them with Nazirites or otherwise caused them to be perceived as unkempt. In the New Testament Paul said that it is a shame for men to wear long hair; it is unnatural and effeminate (see 1 Cor. 11:14).

Verse 21. The priests were to stay away from **wine** when they were ministering in God's temple (see Lev. 10:9). It would be an abomination for a priest to come before the Lord drunk or impaired in any fashion. Such would be an insult to God, who deserves the very best, and to the people, who were depending upon the priest to carry out his duties faithfully.

Verse 22. A priest could **marry**, but he was to choose either a virgin from **the house of Israel** or **the widow of a priest**. Those ineligible for marriage included foreigners, widows who had not been married to priests, divorced women, and non-virgins. Even the mate of a priest could defile his sacred office before God. These regulations were stricter than the Mosaic legislation, which kept only the high priest from marrying a widow (see Lev. 21:7; Neh. 10:30; 13:23–30).

Verse 23. God expected the Zadokite priests to be learned in the law and to be capable teachers. Through them, the Lord would instruct the people (v. 23; see Deut. 33:10). Only God was to distinguish **between the holy and the profane**. This was not for man to decide. Man's task was to respect the laws of God. Isaiah had issued a woe to those who called "evil good, and good evil" (Is. 5:20). People have always had a tendency to circumvent God's laws or to minimize their importance.

Verse 24. The priests were also given judicial responsibilities (see Deut. 17:8, 9). They were to be men of the highest integrity, as well as being knowledgeable about God's legislation. This combination would make them ideal to render judgments when **a dispute** arose among God's people. Since the priests answered directly to God, their judgments had to be completely without bias. Buying the favor of a priest or a judge was abominable to the Lord (Prov. 17:8, 23; Eccles. 7:7; Ex. 23:8; Deut. 16:19). In addition, God instructed the priests, **"Keep My laws"**; **"Keep ... My statutes in all My appointed feasts"**; and **"Sanctify My sabbaths."**

Verses 25–27. God also gave His special servants some laws regarding personal purity, especially in regard to **defil**[ing] **themselves** by going near **a dead person** (v. 25). Certain exceptions (such as being the closest of kin) would allow them to go near, but all other situations would defile them. This is similar to the laws of the Nazirite vow (Num. 6:1–12) as well as the laws for priests in general (Lev. 21:1–9).

The Inheritance of Land for the Priests (44:28–31)

²⁸"'"**And it shall be with regard to an inheritance for them, that I am their inheritance; and you shall give them no possession in Israel—I am their possession. ²⁹They shall eat the grain offering, the sin offering and the guilt offering; and every devoted thing in Israel shall be theirs. ³⁰The first of all the first fruits of every kind and every contribution of every kind, from all your contributions, shall be for the priests; you shall also give to the priest the first of your dough to cause a blessing to rest on your house. ³¹The priests shall not eat any bird or beast that has died a natural death or has been torn to pieces."'"**

Verses 28–30. All other tribes among His people were to re-

ceive a land inheritance—but not the priests. God said, **"I am their inheritance . . . I am their possession"** (v. 28). What, then, did the priests receive? They were to eat of the various sacrifices made at the temple, as well as the various **contributions**—free will offerings donated to the priests (v. 30). The people would give such gifts because the Lord told them that doing so would **cause a blessing to rest on your house**. A similar principle is true in the new covenant: Christians are challenged to give liberally to God. No one can out-give God. He will repay (see 2 Cor. 8; 9).

God did not want the priests to be consumed with the concerns of land ownership and management. Their whole lives centered on the temple. That was their first and only concern. Those under the new covenant are to have a similar concern: "But seek first His kingdom and His righteousness, and all these things will be added to you" (Mt. 6:33). Some land was apportioned to the priests (see 48:10), but it was insufficient to do much. Christians today should maintain the attitude that "a little is enough" and not worry about food, clothing, or other worldly goods (Mt. 6:24–30).

Verse 31. The final command in this chapter, in verse 31, emphasizes the purity of the priesthood. Priests were not to eat **any bird or beast** that was defiled by natural death or by being **torn to pieces** by wild animals.

APPLICATION

Sacred Service to God

God's place of worship was profaned when foreigners were allowed to participate in the temple worship. Likewise, the Lord's church is exclusive to those who have obeyed the gospel of Christ. Just declaring that Jesus is Lord does not make a person a child of God. Jesus would say to such a one, "I never knew you" (Mt. 7:21–23).

Those who serve in God's house should consider it a sacred privilege (note vv. 7, 8). In the Lord's church men should lift up "holy hands" (1 Tim. 2:8) and should make sure that all those who serve are qualified.

Not all servants have the same tasks (v. 14). Everyone in the church of Christ should count it an honor to serve in whatever capacity possible. (Note the "body" descriptions of the work of the church in Rom. 12 and 1 Cor. 12.)

Only qualified priests could approach God in sacrifice. Equally, only those who offer worship to God through Christ will be accepted (Jn. 14:6; 1 Pet. 2:5–8; Heb. 13:15, 16).

The priests had the responsibility of teaching the people what was "holy" and what was "profane." Such was not for man to judge. Today people say, "God will accept this"—even without biblical authority. They may say, "Doing this is not so bad"—even though it may be profane in the eyes of the Lord. The only safe and logical way to live is to follow exactly the stipulations given by Him. Following any other course exposes one to rejection and condemnation by the Lord.

The priests in chapter 44 were to live off of the people's sacrifices and contributions. They received no inheritance (because God was their inheritance; v. 28). Christians today should avoid the trappings of materialism. Loving the world creates enmity with God (Jas. 4:4; 1 Jn. 2:15–17). If we have food and covering, we should be content (1 Tim. 6:6–10).

D.P.

Serving as God's Priests (44:15)

Chapter 44 emphasizes importance of holiness and duty in the lives of God's priests. With coming of the New Testament, the idea of the priesthood of all believers was introduced (1 Pet. 2:5, 9). What can the New Testament "priests" learn from this vision?

The priests were to "come near" to God. The first task that Christians have is to draw near to God. One cannot minister without having an intimate relationship with the Lord. The writer of Hebrews declared, "Let us draw near [to Him] with a sincere heart in full assurance of faith" (Heb. 10:21, 22a).

The priests were to "stand" before God. We may stand before God "with confidence" because of Christ (Heb. 4:16).

The priests were to "offer" sacrifices to God. With this confidence we have through Jesus to stand in the presence of the

Father, we may minister either by making a personal sacrifice (Rom. 12:1) or by serving and teaching others.

"Come near" and "offer" have the same Hebrew root (קָרַב, *qarab*). Approaching God implies serving in His presence. As members of the new priesthood, we must take full advantage of the opportunity to come near to God, to stand before Him, and to offer ourselves as living sacrifices.

T.P.W.

Chapter 45

The "Holy Portion" Allotted and Temple Regulations

Ezekiel had finished recording the Lord's instructions concerning the work of the priests and the locations where they were to do their work. Next, God provided His will concerning the division of the land for the people—the tribes of Israel—as well as choice locations for the priests, the Levites, and the prince. The division of the land is developed more fully in 47:13—48:35.

The Land Allotted as a "Holy Portion" (45:1–8)

¹"'And when you divide by lot the land for inheritance, you shall offer an allotment to the Lord, a holy portion of the land; the length shall be the length of 25,000 cubits, and the width shall be 20,000. It shall be holy within all its boundary round about. ²Out of this there shall be for the holy place a square round about five hundred by five hundred cubits, and fifty cubits for its open space round about. ³From this area you shall measure a length of 25,000 cubits and a width of 10,000 cubits; and in it shall be the sanctuary, the most holy place. ⁴It shall be the holy portion of the land; it shall be for the priests, the ministers of the sanctuary, who come near to minister to the Lord, and it shall be a place for their houses and a holy place for the sanctuary. ⁵An area 25,000 cubits in length and 10,000 in width shall be for the Levites, the ministers of the house, and for their possession cities to dwell in.

⁶You shall give the city possession of an area 5,000 cubits wide and 25,000 cubits long, alongside the allotment of the

holy portion; it shall be for the whole house of Israel. ⁷The prince shall have land on either side of the holy allotment and the property of the city, adjacent to the holy allotment and the property of the city, on the west side toward the west and on the east side toward the east, and in length comparable to one of the portions, from the west border to the east border. ⁸This shall be his land for a possession in Israel; so My princes shall no longer oppress My people, but they shall give the rest of the land to the house of Israel according to their tribes."'"

Verse 1. The illustration on the following page is laid out according to the description given in verses 1 through 8. Verse 1 describes **an allotment to the Lord, a holy portion of the land**. This would be the center section of the land. Ultimately, all of the land belonged to the Lord, but certain portions of it were allocated to the priests and the Levites. This land was to be divided **by lot**. Presumably, this is talking only about the "holy portion" and not the entire layout of the land. (The portions for the twelve tribes would also be divided by lot; see 47:22.) The size of this "holy portion" (the middle section) is given as **25,000 cubits** by **20,000**, although the word "cubits" is not in the Hebrew. This brings us back to the earlier discussion (in connection with 42:15–20) on whether the description of the land should be in "cubits" or in "reeds" (as in the KJV). The reading of that passage in the Hebrew is clear: "reeds" (קָנִים, *qanim*), translated "rods" in some versions. Therefore, the same measurement ought to be applied here. Dogmatism on this point is futile, especially when considering that the entire vision is apocalyptic and not literal. The omission of a unit of measurement here—whether cubits or reeds—is unusual. This could not be a mere oversight. Ezekiel, through inspiration, intentionally left off the most important measurement identification. Why? Probably because this was not to be applied literally. If measured in reeds, this area would extend beyond the borders of Israel on both sides—beyond the Jordan River to the east and into the Mediterranean Sea on the west. To make it cubits is to reduce it to an amazingly small area (about twelve miles across, five miles north to south).

Regarding this section, "25,000 cubits" is the dimension from east to west; the measurement north to south is given as "20,000" (v. 1).[1] This entire section, God declared, would **be holy within all its boundary round about.**

Verses 2–4. God's portion was to be subdivided, beginning with a **holy place** that is **square** in shape (v. 2). (This is labeled as "Sanctuary/Priests' Portion" in the diagram.) This square is the land allotment for the temple itself, 500 by 500 cubits, with **open space** around it **fifty cubits** in size (like a green belt surrounding the temple). The Hebrew does have the word "cubit" here. This area would separate the sanctuary from everything else. It was to be a holy place, separated from the other locations. In the middle of it would be **the sanctuary, the most holy place** (v. 3). In addition to the sanctuary being located here, the

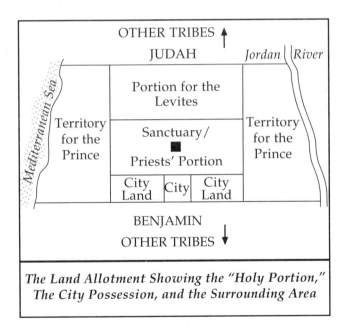

The Land Allotment Showing the "Holy Portion," The City Possession, and the Surrounding Area

---

[1] The number given here is in dispute. The LXX reading, "20,000," is the number accepted by many scholars. However, the use of the number "10,000" in verses 3 and 5 lends support to the idea that this number also was meant to be "10,000," as given in the KJV and earlier editions of the NASB.

remaining land was to be reserved **for the priests,** for them to build **their houses** in a place close to the temple (v. 4).

Verse 5. A second section of land, the same size as that described in verse 3, was allocated **for the Levites.** The Levites would also be able to build **cities.**

Verse 6. The city possession would be **5,000 cubits wide and 25,000 cubits long.** Further clarification of the city layout is given in 48:15, where the city[2] is said to be bordered by two lots of land on its west and east sides. This land would be for common use and for open spaces. (See the diagram on page 652.) This city would not belong to any one tribe; God said, **"It shall be for the whole house of Israel."** The plan located the city property "adjacent to the holy allotment"—directly to the south, located about three miles from the temple (if the measurement is understood to be given in "cubits"). The size of the city, including its open land, was only about one-fifth of the entire district.

Verses 7, 8. The prince (נָשִׂיא, *naśi'*) was to receive land on both sides **of the holy allotment and the property of the city** (v. 7). This was the only land he was to receive, the Lord explained, **"So My princes shall no longer oppress My people"** (v. 8; see 11:1–13; 14:1–11; 20:1—23:49; 34:1–10). They were to make sure the rest of the land belonged to the twelve tribes.

REGULATIONS REGARDING THE TEMPLE AND COMMUNITY (45:9—46:24)

A Plea to Deal Justly and Righteously (45:9–12)

⁹"'Thus says the Lord GOD, "Enough, you princes of Israel; put away violence and destruction, and practice justice and righteousness. Stop your expropriations from My people," declares the Lord GOD.

¹⁰You shall have just balances, a just ephah and a just bath.

---

[2]The Bible speaks of a "new Jerusalem," although no such name is used here.

¹¹"The ephah and the bath shall be the same quantity, so that the bath will contain a tenth of a homer and the ephah a tenth of a homer; their standard shall be according to the homer. ¹²The shekel shall be twenty gerahs; twenty shekels, twenty-five shekels, and fifteen shekels shall be your maneh."'"

Verse 9. God identified the abusive princes in times past as land-grabbing oppressors. Based on their moral responsibility, the **princes of Israel** were called upon by God to do the following:

1. **"Put away violence."** The way they treated their own people was shameful. They took what they wanted at whatever cost, even violence. The princes were accustomed to bullying the people.
2. **"Put away . . . destruction."** The princes did not do that which would build the nation, but made decisions which brought its destruction.
3. **"Practice justice."** Fair treatment of the people was expected. The princes should not have unjust balances that tipped all things in their favor (see v. 10). The people needed to know that their prince had their best interests in mind. They needed to know that they could trust him.
4. **"Practice . . . righteousness."** The prince should be truly committed to the Lord—a genuinely righteous man, one who would "practice" righteousness. He would observe even the "little laws" of God, not overlooking or minimizing any of God's commands or ordinances.
5. **"Stop your expropriations from My people."** The people had been oppressed with excessive taxation. The prince was to end such practices.

Verses 10–12. Ezekiel expanded the requirements for honesty in dealing with the people. The prince was to use proper standards of measurement. An **ephah** (approximately one bushel, or 35.2 liters) was a dry measurement; the **bath** (approximately five gallons, or 18.95 liters) was a liquid measure. A bath should **contain a tenth of a homer** (48.4 gallons, or 183.44 liters). The homer was to be used as the basic **standard** for all measurements, so that all business could be conducted fairly.

In addition to the above, Ezekiel's vision called upon the prince to establish just standards for weights (v. 12). One **shekel** (0.4 ounces, or 11.3 grams) would equal **twenty gerahs**. Sixty "shekels" was to equal one **maneh** (or "mina"). God demanded just weights! The days of oppression through unfair business dealings were over.

Sacrifices and Sacred Days (45:13—46:15)

The People's Obligations to the Prince (45:13–17)

¹³"'"This is the offering that you shall offer: a sixth of an ephah from a homer of wheat; a sixth of an ephah from a homer of barley; ¹⁴and the prescribed portion of oil (namely, the bath of oil), a tenth of a bath from each kor (which is ten baths or a homer, for ten baths are a homer); ¹⁵and one sheep from each flock of two hundred from the watering places of Israel—for a grain offering, for a burnt offering and for peace offerings, to make atonement for them," declares the Lord God. ¹⁶"All the people of the land shall give to this offering for the prince in Israel. ¹⁷It shall be the prince's part to provide the burnt offerings, the grain offerings and the drink offerings, at the feasts, on the new moons and on the sabbaths, at all the appointed feasts of the house of Israel; he shall provide the sin offering, the grain offering, the burnt offering and the peace offerings, to make atonement for the house of Israel."'"

Verses 13–16. The people were called upon to give to the **offering for the prince** (v. 16). This was probably associated with the festivals.

Verse 17. Next, the prince was given a specific responsibility for each festival: to provide the prescribed **offerings**. This commandment was not part of the Mosaic law; rather, each had been instructed to give proportionately, as he had been blessed. This new requirement shows that the Lord expected the prince to be actively involved in the religious festivals of the people. Israel's leader was to be a willing participant in the worship to the Lord, demonstrating his righteousness before the people.

Sin Offering Regulations (45:18–20)

¹⁸"'Thus says the Lord God, "In the first month, on the first of the month, you shall take a young bull without blemish and cleanse the sanctuary. ¹⁹The priest shall take some of the blood from the sin offering and put it on the door posts of the house, on the four corners of the ledge of the altar and on the posts of the gate of the inner court. ²⁰Thus you shall do on the seventh day of the month for everyone who goes astray or is naive; so you shall make atonement for the house."'"

Verse 18. It would be impossible for the worshipers to carry out these rituals without further instructions. Therefore, either the additional information was assumed or the details did not matter, since these instructions were never intended to be applied literally. The first regulation involved New Year's Day. On this day **a young bull** would be taken to **cleanse the sanctuary**.

Verses 19, 20. While some details are uncertain, it appears that this bull was used in a preliminary act to cleanse the sanctuary during the first and seventh months, at the beginning of each festival. (These two months included all of the major feasts except the Feast of Weeks.) Verse 20 gives a confusing regulation regarding **everyone who goes astray or is naive**: An additional sacrifice was to be made for them six days later. Perhaps this describes a "modified 'Day of Atonement.'"[3]

This section proved to be a major problem for the rabbis, because the burnt offering of verse 18 is called a **sin offering** in verse 19. As a result, the Talmud states, "R. Judah says, 'This passage will be interpreted by Elijah in the future.'"[4]

---

[3] John B. Taylor, *Ezekiel: An Introduction and Commentary*, Tyndale Old Testament Commentaries (Downers Grove, Ill.: Inter-Varsity Press, 1969), 275.
[4] b. Menahoth 45a.

The Passover (45:21-24)

²¹"'"In the first month, on the fourteenth day of the month, you shall have the Passover, a feast of seven days; unleavened bread shall be eaten. ²²On that day the prince shall provide for himself and all the people of the land a bull for a sin offering. ²³During the seven days of the feast he shall provide as a burnt offering to the LORD seven bulls and seven rams without blemish on every day of the seven days, and a male goat daily for a sin offering. ²⁴He shall provide as a grain offering an ephah with a bull, an ephah with a ram and a hin of oil with an ephah."'"

Verse 21. On the fourteenth day of the month, the feast of **the Passover** was to be observed. During this feast, which lasted **seven days, unleavened bread** was to be eaten. The specifics given here differ considerably from those in Mosaic legislation (see Deut. 16).

Verses 22-24. As noted in verse 17, the prince was to provide a number of sacrifices for the feast of the Passover. His sacrifices were **for himself** as well as for **all the people of the land** (v. 22). During the course of the Passover feast, he was to provide **seven bulls and seven rams** on each day, plus **a male goat** each day (v. 23).

The idea of offering these animal sacrifices presents tremendous difficulties for those who hold the premillennial view. (Review the discussion of 40:43.) Attempts have been made to justify the reintroduction of such animal sacrifices.[5] Arguments like this are weak and without scriptural support. The statement of Hebrews 10:4 cannot be ignored: "For it is impossible for the blood of bulls and goats to take away sins." The writer of the Book of Hebrews emphasized that animal blood never took away sins—even under the old covenant.

---

[5]See, for example, Merrill F. Unger, *Great Neglected Bible Prophecies* (Chicago: Scripture Press, 1955), 88-89.

The Feast of Tabernacles (45:25)

²⁵"'"'In the seventh month, on the fifteenth day of the month, at the feast, he shall provide like this, seven days for the sin offering, the burnt offering, the grain offering and the oil."'"'

Verse 25. The Feast of Weeks, surprisingly, was omitted. Ezekiel went directly to the feast **in the seventh month**, the Feast of Tabernacles. The overall purpose of this feast changed in the vision. No longer was it to commemorate deliverance from Egyptian bondage and divine blessings. Instead, it became a feast for the purpose of dealing with sin.

APPLICATION

All Centers in God

The temple was located in the center of the land. This demonstrates that man's primary concern is to worship God. The city, with its center for business, travel, and government, was not to be separated from God's "holy allotment." All of our activities should be considered in light of the fact that the Lord is near; He should be the center of everything.

God expects justice and fairness in all business dealings (vv. 9–12). People today are called upon to treat others with honesty and respect. Colossians 3:9–11 says,

> Do not lie to one another, since you laid aside the old self with its evil practices, and have put on the new self who is being renewed to a true knowledge according to the image of the One who created him—a renewal in which there is no distinction between Greek and Jew, circumcised and uncircumcised, barbarian, Scythian, slave and freeman, but Christ is all, and in all.

D.P.

Godly Leadership (45:8–25)

This section mentions "the prince" who was to rule the people justly and according to God's will. The theocratic leader would not oppress the nation. He was to offer sacrifices for himself and the people. He would also observe the Lord's holy days (see vv. 8, 17, 21). These acts reflected Israel's historical problems and future hopes, bearing significant meaning to the original readers. However, what do these examples offer us? What can we learn about Christian leaders from this vision?

They are fair. They lead according to the Lord's righteousness. Godly leaders make decisions based on the Scriptures and a fair assessment of the impending or current situation.

They make sacrifices. Jesus showed His disciples the true value of sacrifice when He humbly washed their feet (Jn. 13:3–16). Godly leaders are the first ones serving the flock, rather than expecting to be served. Realizing that they are responsible for the spiritual condition of the people they lead, these mentors readily demonstrate daily acts of humble service.

They honor God's time. In the context of the Book of Ezekiel, the prince observed sabbath rest and the Passover. Christians need time with their Father in personal and corporate worship. Godly leaders are aware of this need and provide opportunities for others to grow in spirit and truth.

Whether leading in the home, in the church, or in a business, those who desire to lead effectively will learn from biblical examples—that godly leadership is fair, humble in service, and respectful toward God's time with His people.

T.P.W.

CHAPTER 46

ADDITIONAL REGULATIONS

Sacrifices and Sacred Days (Continued) (45:13—46:15)

Sacrifices for the Sabbath and New Moon (46:1–8)

¹"'Thus says the Lord GOD, "The gate of the inner court facing east shall be shut the six working days; but it shall be opened on the sabbath day and opened on the day of the new moon. ²The prince shall enter by way of the porch of the gate from outside and stand by the post of the gate. Then the priests shall provide his burnt offering and his peace offerings, and he shall worship at the threshold of the gate and then go out; but the gate shall not be shut until the evening. ³The people of the land shall also worship at the doorway of that gate before the LORD on the sabbaths and on the new moons. ⁴The burnt offering which the prince shall offer to the LORD on the sabbath day shall be six lambs without blemish and a ram without blemish; ⁵and the grain offering shall be an ephah with the ram, and the grain offering with the lambs as much as he is able to give, and a hin of oil with an ephah. ⁶On the day of the new moon he shall offer a young bull without blemish, also six lambs and a ram, which shall be without blemish. ⁷And he shall provide a grain offering, an ephah with the bull and an ephah with the ram, and with the lambs as much as he is able, and a hin of oil with an ephah. ⁸When the prince enters, he shall go in by way of the porch of the gate and go out by the same way."'"

Verses 1, 2. In 44:2 the outer east gate was permanently closed after the glory of the Lord passed through it. In that section, the prince was afforded a special privilege: being allowed to eat in the porch of that gate. Here, the prince was given another blessing. He would be allowed to enter the inner east gate, as far as **the post of the gate**—the innermost part of the gate (v. 2). He would give to the priests the offerings he brought and then **worship** there. This would be a special blessing to the prince because he would be able to witness the workings of the priests at the main altar—something only the priests normally saw.

Verses 3, 4. The people were allowed to stand in the outer courtyard, just outside the entrance of the east (inner) gate—the one through which the prince entered and would also leave (see v. 8). The regulations given in verses 3 through 5 involve **six lambs** and **a ram** which were to be offered as sacrifices **on the sabbaths and on the new moons**. In contrast, the Mosaic law specified that two lambs were to be offered morning and evening as burnt offerings (see Num. 28:1–10).

Verses 5–8. The offerings for **the new moon** (the beginning of each month) also differed from those under the law of Moses (see Num. 28:11–15). The Law required two bulls, seven lambs, and one ram. Here the offering was to be **a young bull, six lambs, and a ram** (v. 6). The rabbis had difficulty explaining these changes in the divine ordinances given by the Lord.[1]

Crowd Control in the Temple
(46:9, 10)

⁹""'"But when the people of the land come before the Lord at the appointed feasts, he who enters by way of the north gate to worship shall go out by way of the south gate. And he who enters by way of the south gate shall go out by way of the north gate. No one shall return by way of the gate by which he

---

[1]These and other questions about Ezekiel 40—48 are discussed in Neale Pryor, "Ezekiel 40—48: Correctly Interpreting Ezekiel's New Temple," in *Difficult Texts of the Old Testament Explained*, ed. Wendell Winkler (Montgomery, Ala.: Winkler Publications, 1982), 372–81.

entered but shall go straight out. ¹⁰When they go in, the prince shall go in among them; and when they go out, he shall go out."'"

Verses 9, 10. Paul said, regarding Christian worship, "But all things must be done properly and in an orderly manner" (1 Cor. 14:40) because "God is not a God of confusion but of peace" (1 Cor. 14:33). When God's people gathered in the courtyard, they were to note which gate they used to enter, then proceed out the opposite gate. No one was to **return by way of the gate by which he entered** (v. 9), so that two flowing lines would filter past the inner east gate. Besides creating an orderly flow of people, this regulation caused each one to **go straight out**. In a symbolic act, the people were to stay straight, neither turning to the right nor to the left (see Josh. 1:7).

Further Regulations (46:11–15)

¹¹"'"At the festivals and the appointed feasts the grain offering shall be an ephah with a bull and an ephah with a ram, and with the lambs as much as one is able to give, and a hin of oil with an ephah. ¹²When the prince provides a freewill offering, a burnt offering, or peace offerings as a freewill offering to the LORD, the gate facing east shall be opened for him. And he shall provide his burnt offering and his peace offerings as he does on the sabbath day. Then he shall go out, and the gate shall be shut after he goes out. ¹³And you shall provide a lamb a year old without blemish for a burnt offering to the LORD daily; morning by morning you shall provide it. ¹⁴Also you shall provide a grain offering with it morning by morning, a sixth of an ephah and a third of a hin of oil to moisten the fine flour, a grain offering to the LORD continually by a perpetual ordinance. ¹⁵Thus they shall provide the lamb, the grain offering and the oil, morning by morning, for a continual burnt offering."'"

Verses 11–15. These verses focus on daily sacrifices, again specifying what the prince was to provide. When he made these sacrifices, **the gate facing east** was **opened for him** (v. 12). When he finished his sacrifice, the gate would be closed again. It may seem odd that the prince should be making **daily** sacrifices (v. 13) since that was not required of him under the Law. In addition, the prince was given regulations for making **a freewill offering** (v. 12). On top of all the offerings commanded, this prince would be interested in making freewill sacrifices not required by the Law.

Giving Land as Gifts (46:16–18)

¹⁶**"'Thus says the Lord God, "If the prince gives a gift out of his inheritance to any of his sons, it shall belong to his sons; it is their possession by inheritance. ¹⁷But if he gives a gift from his inheritance to one of his servants, it shall be his until the year of liberty; then it shall return to the prince. His inheritance shall be only his sons'; it shall belong to them. ¹⁸The prince shall not take from the people's inheritance, thrusting them out of their possession; he shall give his sons inheritance from his own possession so that My people will not be scattered, anyone from his possession."'"**

Verse 16. The prince might want to give land to his sons as **a gift**. Such a gift could come from only one source: **out of his inheritance**. He could not give land that belonged to others. (This regulation would prevent a recurrence of the old oppression mentioned in 45:8–12.)

Verse 17. If **one of his servants** had served him well, the prince might also wish to reward him with a land gift. However, the prince did not have the authority to give it to the servant permanently. The land would always return to the prince, thereby protecting it for future generations. The servant was entitled to keep it **until the year of liberty**—in the seventh year, when the Hebrew servant would be freed (see Jer. 34:14), or in the fiftieth year (the Year of Jubilee; see Lev. 25:10–13; 27:24).

Verse 18. The prince had no authority over the land of his people. It was their **inheritance**, and he had no right to it. The people knew that they would be **scattered** if they lost their land possession. For this reason, owning the land provided a unifying effect upon the nation.

Cooking Sacrificial Meals (46:19–24)

¹⁹Then he brought me through the entrance, which was at the side of the gate, into the holy chambers for the priests, which faced north; and behold, there was a place at the extreme rear toward the west. ²⁰He said to me, "This is the place where the priests shall boil the guilt offering and the sin offering and where they shall bake the grain offering, in order that they may not bring them out into the outer court to transmit holiness to the people."

²¹Then he brought me out into the outer court and led me across to the four corners of the court; and behold, in every corner of the court there was a small court. ²²In the four corners of the court there were enclosed courts, forty cubits long and thirty wide; these four in the corners were the same size. ²³There was a row of masonry round about in them, around the four of them, and boiling places were made under the rows round about. ²⁴Then he said to me, "These are the boiling places where the ministers of the house shall boil the sacrifices of the people."

Verses 19, 20. Ezekiel's guide is mentioned for the first time since 42:19. He took Ezekiel **through the entrance . . . into the holy chambers for the priests**. This is said to be the section to the northwest of the temple itself. Ezekiel the priest saw where the priests were to **boil the guilt offering and the sin offering**, as well as the place to **bake the grain offering**[s] (v. 20). These regulations were to be followed exactly; the priests were not to bring these offerings into the public courtyard, where they could **transmit holiness to the people**.

Verses 21–24. Ezekiel was next shown **the boiling places**, or kitchens, where the priests would prepare the sacrifices. (See "The Temple Complex in Ezekiel's Vision" on page 586.) The **four** kitchens indicate the amount of work the priests had to do in handling all of the sacrifices brought to them daily.

APPLICATION

"The Prince" and Sacrifice in Ezekiel

Ezekiel's reference to "the prince" in chapters 44 through 48 is sometimes interpreted as an allusion to Jesus, although a more likely messianic reference is 34:23–25. The prince of the temple would do the following:

- Eat bread before the Lord (44:3).
- Possess land on each side of the city (45:7).
- Receive the people's offering of wheat and oil (45:16).
- Provide a bull for a sin offering for himself and the people (45:22).
- Make burnt offerings to the Lord (46:2, 4, 12).
- Go in and out with the people (46:8, 10).
- Divide the inheritance with his son or a servant (46:16–18).
- Receive an allotment of property (48:21, 22).

If this prince is Jesus, then his activity must be considered figurative for at least five reasons. (1) The prince was to offer animal sacrifices, but Jesus sacrificed Himself (Heb. 9:26). (2) The prince would offer sacrifices repeatedly, while Jesus made a one-time offering for all times (Heb. 7:27; 9:12; 9:25–28; 10:10–12). (3) The prince was to have an earthly kingdom, but Jesus' kingdom is not an earthly one (Jn. 18:36). (4) The prince was to provide a bull as a sin offering for himself and the people (Ezek. 45:22). Jesus had no sin, so He would not need to make such an offering. (5) The prince was to own property, while Jesus owned no property (Mt. 8:20).

A literal fulfillment of this passage would contradict the truth that Jesus' sacrifice covers the sins of people of all times. The reinstitution of animal sacrifice would mean that His sacrifice was inadequate. If sacrifice under the law of Moses could not forgive sins (Heb. 10:4), why would it be reinstated? By one offering, Christ has perfected for all times those who are sanctified (Heb. 10:14).

The priestly work and rule of Jesus is heavenly. According

to Zechariah, the Messiah "will be a priest on His throne, and the counsel of peace will be between the two offices" (Zech. 6:13b). Hebrews 8:4a says, "Now if He were on earth, He would not be a priest at all." Rather, Jesus serves as a priest in heaven (Heb. 9:24).

Through Jesus' sacrifice, His blood is able to wash clean (Rev. 1:5b) those who obey Him (Heb. 5:8, 9). This cleansing comes through listening to Jesus (Acts 3:22, 23; Rom. 10:14), placing faith in His blood (Rom. 3:25), repenting (Acts 17:30), confessing Jesus (Rom. 10:9, 10), and being baptized (Acts 2:38; 22:16).

Those who accept the truth of Jesus' sacrifice should follow His example with their personal death to sin. They must crucify the old self in baptism, so as to live for Jesus (Rom. 6:4–7). Christians are to offer their bodies as living sacrifices (Rom. 12:1, 2) and give sacrifices of praise to God with their lips (Heb. 13:15).

O.D.O.

Chapter 47
The New Land (Part 1)

THE RIVER OF THE WATER OF LIFE FROM THE TEMPLE (47:1–12)

¹Then he brought me back to the door of the house; and behold, water was flowing from under the threshold of the house toward the east, for the house faced east. And the water was flowing down from under, from the right side of the house, from south of the altar. ²He brought me out by way of the north gate and led me around on the outside to the outer gate by way of the gate that faces east. And behold, water was trickling from the south side.

³When the man went out toward the east with a line in his hand, he measured a thousand cubits, and he led me through the water, water reaching the ankles. ⁴Again he measured a thousand and led me through the water, water reaching the knees. Again he measured a thousand and led me through the water, water reaching the loins. ⁵Again he measured a thousand; and it was a river that I could not ford, for the water had risen, enough water to swim in, a river that could not be forded. ⁶He said to me, "Son of man, have you seen this?" Then he brought me back to the bank of the river. ⁷Now when I had returned, behold, on the bank of the river there were very many trees on the one side and on the other. ⁸Then he said to me, "These waters go out toward the eastern region and go down into the Arabah; then they go toward the sea, being made to flow into the sea, and the waters of the sea become fresh. ⁹It

will come about that every living creature which swarms in every place where the river goes, will live. And there will be very many fish, for these waters go there and the others become fresh; so everything will live where the river goes. ¹⁰And it will come about that fishermen will stand beside it; from Engedi to Eneglaim there will be a place for the spreading of nets. Their fish will be according to their kinds, like the fish of the Great Sea, very many. ¹¹But its swamps and marshes will not become fresh; they will be left for salt. ¹²By the river on its bank, on one side and on the other, will grow all kinds of trees for food. Their leaves will not wither and their fruit will not fail. They will bear every month because their water flows from the sanctuary, and their fruit will be for food and their leaves for healing."

This section provides the clearest symbolic description yet. Ezekiel was shown how God would provide abundant blessings for His people. These blessings, represented by a river flowing from the temple, would fertilize all the land, bringing forth abundant crops and miraculous healings, and ultimately turning the Dead Sea into a freshwater haven.[1]

Verses 1, 2. Ezekiel was brought **to the door of the house** (v. 1)—that is, to the main entrance to the temple itself. He saw

---

[1]"To attempt to take this literally, as some have done, is to miss completely the point which is being made. So we need not pause over the traditions that suggest that Mount Zion, on which the temple was built, concealed beneath its rocky exterior 'an inexhaustible supply of water and underground reservoirs'. . . . No amount of water-divining will confirm Ezekiel 47. The fact that this represents an idealization of God's abundant blessings is confirmed by passages such as Psalms 46:4; 65:9; Isaiah 33:20f. Blessing, fertility and water are almost interchangeable ideas in the Old Testament. The commentator is, however, justified in looking for parallels to and antecedents for this kind of symbolism, and most turn to the creation narrative in Genesis 2. The former paradise which was watered by the four-streamed river (Gn. 2:10) is here paralleled by the new creation which also has its river and its trees (7). If we add to this the fact . . . that Ezekiel seems to have known of a paradise tradition linked to a 'holy mountain of God' (28:14, 16) as well as a 'garden of God', the parallel to our present passage is almost complete" (John B. Taylor, *Ezekiel: An Introduction and Commentary*, Tyndale Old Testament Commentaries [Downers Grove, Ill.: Inter-Varsity Press, 1969], 278–79).

water . . . flowing from under the threshold of the house toward the east. This was the direction the temple faced. The water flowed to the south side of the altar. Ezekiel exited through **the north gate** (v. 2). He could not go through the east gate, for it had been closed ever since God passed through it (44:2). The prophet proceeded to the east side of the gate facing **east**, where he saw that the **water was trickling from the south side** of the gate. Certainly, this was not a powerful, flowing river. It is interesting to compare this with other apocalyptic passages. Zechariah 14:8 depicts two rivers that flow both east and west. Joel spoke of a river watering "the valley of Shittim" (Joel 3:18), located east of the Jordan River. It seems clear that these river images are not intended to be understood literally. While each prophet applied them in his own unique way, all emphasize one fundamental point—God provides blessings for everyone.

Verses 3–8. The guide took Ezekiel alongside the river, measuring it as they went (vv. 3, 4). Every **thousand cubits** he measured it, and each measurement showed that the river was becoming deeper. Its depth began at **the ankles**, then reached **the knees**, then **the loins**. Finally, the river was too deep to be **forded**, but it looked like a good swimming place (v. 5). This type of description is certainly symbolic. The idea of underground tributaries (which are not mentioned) swelling the river would destroy the spiritual message being given here. Ezekiel was in the water for a time (perhaps swimming) and eventually returned **to the bank of the river** (v. 6). To his surprise, the river had so watered the barren land that—in the time he had spent in the river—the land was able to produce **very many trees** (v. 7), located on both sides of the river. The guide explained that this river would make its way to **the sea** (the Dead Sea), where the influx of its flow would transform the sea into **fresh** water (v. 8).

Verses 9–11. The river would provide life to all creatures that came in contact with its waters. **Fishermen** (v. 10) would benefit from fishing out of the waters of this river because it would hold **very many fish** (v. 9). As if to provide some ecological balance, God said that the **swamps and marshes** would not be transformed by the temple river (v. 11). These would be **left for salt**.

Verse 12. The guide then returned to the subject of the riverside trees. These trees, growing in abundance on both sides of the river, had some interesting qualities: (1) They could grow all kinds of **food**; (2) **their leaves** [would] **not wither** (see the description of the blessed man in Ps. 1) and could be used for **healing**; and (3) **their fruit** [would] **not fail**. They would be productive **every month**, providing a continual source of "food."

Why were these trees able to accomplish such feats? Because they were in contact with the **water** [which flowed] **from the sanctuary**.[2]

THE DIVISION OF THE LAND
(47:13—48:29)

The Boundaries (47:13–21)

¹³Thus says the Lord GOD, "This shall be the boundary by which you shall divide the land for an inheritance among the twelve tribes of Israel; Joseph shall have two portions. ¹⁴You shall divide it for an inheritance, each one equally with the other; for I swore to give it to your forefathers, and this land shall fall to you as an inheritance.

¹⁵This shall be the boundary of the land: on the north side, from the Great Sea by the way of Hethlon, to the entrance of Zedad; ¹⁶Hamath, Berothah, Sibraim, which is between the

---

[2] "Toward the close of Ezekiel's prophecy, the man of God reports the vision which he had of a stream of water issuing from the altar of the sanctuary and flowing out under the threshold of the house to the east, increasing as it went, though fed by no tributary streams, until it emptied its healing waters into the Dead Sea, transforming it and all the country through which it passed. Invited by his heavenly guide to walk with him through the waters, the prophet found them first only ankle-deep, but a distance beyond they reached the knees; still farther on they became waist-deep, and finally they were a river to swim in. What a parable of Christian experience! The stream of blessing starts from the altar, the place of sacrifice, the place where Christ took our sins upon Himself, and increasing with the very increase of God, as the Spirit multiplies its fulness, becomes a deep-flowing river that none can fathom" (Everett F. Harrison, "A Neglected Apologetic," *Bibliotheca Sacra* 95 [October-December 1938]: 444).

border of Damascus and the border of Hamath; Hazer-hatticon, which is by the border of Hauran. ¹⁷The boundary shall extend from the sea to Hazar-enan at the border of Damascus, and on the north toward the north is the border of Hamath. This is the north side.

¹⁸The east side, from between Hauran, Damascus, Gilead and the land of Israel, shall be the Jordan; from the north border to the eastern sea you shall measure. This is the east side.

¹⁹The south side toward the south shall extend from Tamar as far as the waters of Meribath-kadesh, to the brook of Egypt and to the Great Sea. This is the south side toward the south.

²⁰The west side shall be the Great Sea, from the south border to a point opposite Lebo-hamath. This is the west side.

²¹So you shall divide this land among yourselves according to the tribes of Israel."

Verses 13, 14. This continues the discussion which was begun in 37:15–28, although here it is more fully developed. Unlike other divisions of the land, Ezekiel's allotment provided each tribe with an even portion (except Levi, which would be given the portion of God's holy allotment [44:28; 45:5]). God declared that the portions were to be divided **each one equally with the other**. This was in accordance with the promise God had made to their **forefathers** (see Deut. 1:8). Also, God said, **"Joseph shall have two portions,"** bringing the number of tribes receiving land to twelve (since Levi did not receive one of these portions).

Verses 15–21. The place names given in verses 15 through 21 are difficult to identify with certainty. However, it is obvious that the typical boundaries were used: **the Great Sea** or Mediterranean on the west side (v. 20) and the Jordan River on the east (v. 18). The northern boundary was Hamath, the same as that used by Solomon (**the entrance of . . . Hamath**; 1 Kings 8:65). The southern border was **the brook of Egypt** (v. 19). The total amount of land was about 175 miles long, 100 miles wide on the southern edge, and 30 miles wide on the northern edge.

The fact that the land promise of old was never realized is

the foundational idea behind premillennialism. The view holds that the promise was a divine guarantee and must therefore be fulfilled at some future date. However, a careful study of Numbers 34:1–12; 1 Kings 8:65; Joshua 21:43–45; 23:14–16; and Nehemiah 9:5–8 reveals that God's people did, in fact, receive all the land that was promised to them. Nehemiah 9:8 says,

> "You found his heart faithful before You,
> And made a covenant with him
> To give him the land of the Canaanite,
> Of the Hittite and the Amorite,
> Of the Perizzite, the Jebusite and the Girgashite—
> To give it to his descendants.
> And You have fulfilled Your promise,
> For You are righteous."

Notice carefully the words "You have fulfilled Your promise." The inspired writer confirmed that the people had received the land which God promised they would possess as an inheritance (see Josh. 1:11).

An Inheritance for the Alien (47:22, 23)

²²"You shall divide it by lot for an inheritance among yourselves and among the aliens who stay in your midst, who bring forth sons in your midst. And they shall be to you as the native-born among the sons of Israel; they shall be allotted an inheritance with you among the tribes of Israel. ²³And in the tribe with which the alien stays, there you shall give him his inheritance," declares the Lord GOD.

Verses 22, 23. In this remarkable passage, God allowed something that would have been an abomination under Mosaic law: He permitted **aliens** who had moved into the land to receive a land inheritance. No provisions were made for aliens under the previous divisions. Now, if they were willing to comply fully with all of God's laws, they were **allotted an inheritance** with the Israelites (v. 22). This serves as a reminder of the unifying effect of the gospel, which brought Jews and Gentiles together under the cross of Christ (Eph. 2:12–22).

APPLICATION

Rivers of Life

Rivers are important sources of life and sustenance for both people and wildlife. Rivers are often mentioned in the Bible when God provides for His people.

In the Garden of Eden a river "flowed out of Eden" and became four rivers: Pishon, Gihon, Tigris, and Euphrates. The source of these rivers nourished the garden (Gen. 2:10–14).

In Ezekiel's vision water flowed from underneath the threshold of the temple. This water turned into a river too deep for Ezekiel to cross. The river provided life for many trees and fish and for "every living creature" that lived by the river (vv. 1–9).

In John's vision there was also a river; however, this river flowed "from the throne of God and of the Lamb" (Rev. 22:1). This "water of life" watered the "tree of life" and symbolized through prophecy the Christian's future hope of God's care in a new heaven and new earth.

God provides for His children. From the beginning of creation until the end of time, we can take comfort in Him as our source of refreshing and nourishment that lasts forever. May we thirst for God's living water! Indeed, as Jesus declared, "The water that I will give . . . will become . . . a well of water springing up to eternal life" (Jn. 4:14).

The Promise of Land

Ownership of property can mean a great deal to an individual's self-worth and sense of well-being. Owning a home may make a person feel stable and secure. The Bible is rich with "land theology," but when God provided His people with land, He always gave a condition: They were to keep His ordinances in order to remain in an inheritance. The symbol of "land" had great meaning for the Israelites and is applicable to the lives of Christians as well.

God instructed Adam to "cultivate and keep" the land (Gen. 2:15).

From the beginning, the first couple was given a place to live that was a gift from God. Planted in the garden were trees from which they could eat freely. However, after they ate fruit from the one tree that was forbidden, they were removed from paradise (3:24).

God promised the Israelites the land of Canaan. In preparation for their conquest of the land, they were instructed to "listen to the statutes and the judgments . . . so that [they] may . . . go in and take possession of the land." On the other hand, they were also warned that if they would not follow God's commands, they would "surely perish quickly from the land" (Deut. 4:1, 26).

God removed His people from their land after years of rebellion (see 2 Kings 17; 25). The Book of Ezekiel was set in a time when "the house of Israel" had been deemed "a rebellious house." God fulfilled His warning by once again cutting off the people from the land because of sin.

God reinstated His promise of land to His remnant. In this chapter, we see a restoration that echoed the promises of the past. He mentioned trees of all kinds, imagery resembling the Garden of Eden (v. 12). He described an inheritance for the tribes of Israel that was reminiscent of the conquest of Canaan (vv. 13–21). Although the people had lost their possession because of rebelliousness, God was merciful to them and provided a hope for the future.

As Christians we do not long for physical lands or kingdoms, but we do have hope for our spiritual home. The promise is available to all of God's people; however, we must be sure to keep His covenant. If we do so, we will receive our Promised Land, our inheritance.

T.P.W.

Chapter 48
The New Land (Part 2)

With the boundaries of the land having been determined, Ezekiel was now to divide the land equally among the tribes of Israel. Using the Jordan and the Mediterranean as the east-west borders, the land was divided from north to south in this order: Dan, Asher, Naphtali, Manasseh, Ephraim, Reuben, Judah, Benjamin, Simeon, Issachar, Zebulun, and Gad. The only break in these land blocks surrounded the holy portion for the Lord. In this area were located the temple, the city, and the land portions for the prince, the priests, and the Levites. This separated Benjamin from Judah.

The Tribal Allotments (48:1–29)

The Seven Northern Tribes (48:1–7)

¹"Now these are the names of the tribes: from the northern extremity, beside the way of Hethlon to Lebo-hamath, as far as Hazar-enan at the border of Damascus, toward the north beside Hamath, running from east to west, Dan, one portion. ²Beside the border of Dan, from the east side to the west side, Asher, one portion. ³Beside the border of Asher, from the east side to the west side, Naphtali, one portion. ⁴Beside the border of Naphtali, from the east side to the west side, Manasseh, one portion. ⁵Beside the border of Manasseh, from the east side to the west side, Ephraim, one portion. ⁶Beside the border of Ephraim, from the east side to the west side, Reuben, one portion. ⁷Beside the border of Reuben, from the east side to the west side, Judah, one portion."

Verses 1–7. The northern tribes (beginning from the north) were Dan, Asher, Naphtali, Manasseh, Ephraim, Reuben, and Judah. John B. Taylor wrote,

> Of these it is worth noting that the three which are farthest from the sanctuary are tribes descended from sons of Jacob's concubines, Dan and Naphtali having been born to Rachel's maid Bilhah, and Asher to Leah's maid Zilpah (Gn. 30:5–13). The fourth son by concubinage, Gad, is the farthest away from the sanctuary among the southern group of tribes (27). Judah has pride of place immediately to the north of the central portion, as being the inheritor of the Messianic promise through the blessing of Jacob (Gn. 49:8–12), and he supersedes Reuben, the first-born, who is in the next position away on the north side. The other two places are held by the two grandsons of Rachel, the children of Joseph.[1]

The phrase **from the east side to the west side** (used in vv. 2–8) demonstrates that the geography of the land was ignored. Straight borderlines were to be drawn across, making seven parallel, equal sections running from the north to the south. (See "The Land Allotment in Ezekiel's Vision" on the following page.)

The Central Tribe, "the Holy Portion,"
The City Possession, and the Surrounding Area (48:8–22)

⁸**"And beside the border of Judah, from the east side to the west side, shall be the allotment which you shall set apart, 25,000 cubits in width, and in length like one of the portions, from the east side to the west side; and the sanctuary shall be in the middle of it. ⁹The allotment that you shall set apart to the Lord shall be 25,000 cubits in length and 10,000 in width. ¹⁰The holy allotment shall be for these, namely for the priests,**

---

[1] John B. Taylor, *Ezekiel: An Introduction and Commentary*, Tyndale Old Testament Commentaries (Downers Grove, Ill.: Inter-Varsity Press, 1969), 282–83.

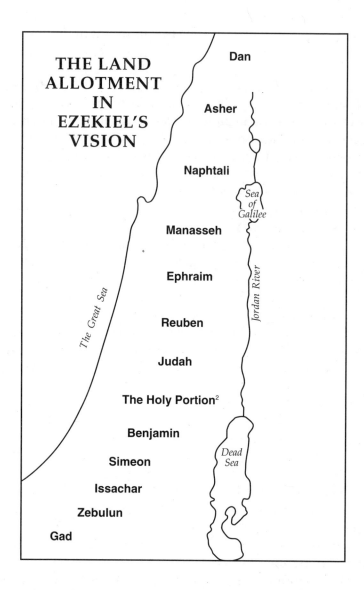

[2]The area surrounding the Holy Portion included the city possession, the land for the Levites, and the territory allotted to the prince. Remember that geography was not a consideration in the apportionment of land. This map is only a representation of the tribal arrangement.

toward the north 25,000 cubits in length, toward the west 10,000 in width, toward the east 10,000 in width, and toward the south 25,000 in length; and the sanctuary of the LORD shall be in its midst. ¹¹It shall be for the priests who are sanctified of the sons of Zadok, who have kept My charge, who did not go astray when the sons of Israel went astray as the Levites went astray. ¹²It shall be an allotment to them from the allotment of the land, a most holy place, by the border of the Levites. ¹³Alongside the border of the priests the Levites shall have 25,000 cubits in length and 10,000 in width. The whole length shall be 25,000 cubits and the width 10,000. ¹⁴Moreover, they shall not sell or exchange any of it, or alienate this choice portion of land; for it is holy to the LORD.

¹⁵The remainder, 5,000 cubits in width and 25,000 in length, shall be for common use for the city, for dwellings and for open spaces; and the city shall be in its midst. ¹⁶These shall be its measurements: the north side 4,500 cubits, the south side 4,500 cubits, the east side 4,500 cubits, and the west side 4,500 cubits. ¹⁷The city shall have open spaces: on the north 250 cubits, on the south 250 cubits, on the east 250 cubits, and on the west 250 cubits. ¹⁸The remainder of the length alongside the holy allotment shall be 10,000 cubits toward the east and 10,000 toward the west; and it shall be alongside the holy allotment. And its produce shall be food for the workers of the city. ¹⁹The workers of the city, out of all the tribes of Israel, shall cultivate it. ²⁰The whole allotment shall be 25,000 by 25,000 cubits; you shall set apart the holy allotment, a square, with the property of the city.

²¹The remainder shall be for the prince, on the one side and on the other of the holy allotment and of the property of the city; in front of the 25,000 cubits of the allotment toward the east border and westward in front of the 25,000 toward the west border, alongside the portions, it shall be for the prince. And the holy allotment and the sanctuary of the house shall be in the middle of it. ²²Exclusive of the property of the Levites and the property of the city, which are in the middle of that which belongs to the prince, everything between the border of Judah and the border of Benjamin shall be for the prince."

Verses 8–22. Virtually no new information is given here. The land encompassing the "holy portion" (45:1) is explained again. (For a better understanding of the division of these sections, review the discussion on 45:1–8.) Verse 15 provides a clearer picture of the layout of the city. Rather than running the entire width of the land allotment, the city would sit in the middle, with open spaces on each side.

The Five Southern Tribes
(48:23–29)

²³"As for the rest of the tribes: from the east side to the west side, Benjamin, one portion. ²⁴Beside the border of Benjamin, from the east side to the west side, Simeon, one portion. ²⁵Beside the border of Simeon, from the east side to the west side, Issachar, one portion. ²⁶Beside the border of Issachar, from the east side to the west side, Zebulun, one portion. ²⁷Beside the border of Zebulun, from the east side to the west side, Gad, one portion. ²⁸And beside the border of Gad, at the south side toward the south, the border shall be from Tamar to the waters of Meribath-kadesh, to the brook of Egypt, to the Great Sea. ²⁹This is the land which you shall divide by lot to the tribes of Israel for an inheritance, and these are their several portions," declares the Lord GOD.

Verses 23–28. Among the tribal land in the southern region, Benjamin was honored to have the northernmost portion, located directly south of the city. Judah (located just north of the "holy portion") and Benjamin (located just south of it) would be the only tribes to maintain the proximity to the city that they had enjoyed before, although their locations were reversed. The other tribes' former locations had no bearing on where their land allotments were.

Verse 29. After identifying the division of the land **by lot**, God acknowledged that all of the tribes received **their several portions**. No tribe received a lesser share. Equality was a feature of God's new plan, and each tribe was honored accordingly, with an equal amount of land.

THE CITY: THE SIZE, GATES, AND NAME (48:30–35)

The Size and the Gates (48:30–35a)

³⁰"These are the exits of the city: on the north side, 4,500 cubits by measurement, ³¹shall be the gates of the city, named for the tribes of Israel, three gates toward the north: the gate of Reuben, one; the gate of Judah, one; the gate of Levi, one. ³²On the east side, 4,500 cubits, shall be three gates: the gate of Joseph, one; the gate of Benjamin, one; the gate of Dan, one. ³³On the south side, 4,500 cubits by measurement, shall be three gates: the gate of Simeon, one; the gate of Issachar, one; the gate of Zebulun, one. ³⁴On the west side, 4,500 cubits, shall be three gates: the gate of Gad, one; the gate of Asher, one; the gate of Naphtali, one. ³⁵ᵃThe city shall be 18,000 cubits round about.'"

Verses 30–35a. The city was to have twelve **gates**, each named for one of **the tribes of Israel**. They are listed below:

North: Reuben, Judah, and Levi (the firstborn, the messianic tribe, and the priestly tribe).
East: Joseph, Benjamin, and Dan. (Since the tribe of Levi was included in this listing, Joseph was used instead of his sons Ephraim and Manasseh, keeping the number of gates/tribes at twelve.)
South: Simeon, Issachar, and Zebulun (all tribes given southerly land allotments).
West: Gad, Asher, and Naphtali (three of the concubine tribes).

No special significance is evident in the location of these gates or the tribes assigned to them.

The Name: "The Lord Is There" (48:35b)

35b"'And the name of the city from that day shall be, 'The Lord is there.'"

Verse 35b. This verse gives the name of the new city: שָׁמָּה יהוה, (*YHWH shammah*), meaning **The Lord is there**. This beautiful name fully encompasses the final messages of Ezekiel. The Lord, who had departed because of the excessive wickedness of His people, had finally returned. His city could have no more fitting name than one expressing His permanent dwelling there. The Lord dwells among the redeemed (see Jer. 3:17; Zech. 8:3; Is. 1:26; 62:2).

CONCLUSION

John, in writing Revelation, borrowed terminology from Ezekiel. Taylor explained, "The writer of Revelation owed much to Ezekiel's vivid imagery and was not afraid to Christianize it, because he saw that the symbolism still possessed meaning for the Christian church of his day as well as for the Jews of the exile."[3] Note the parallels between Ezekiel's city and the "new Jerusalem" of Revelation 21:

1. Twelve gates were named after the twelve tribes of Israel. The locations were given, three to a side (Ezek. 48:31–34; Rev. 21:12–14). (John's city also had twelve foundations named after the apostles.)
2. Both cities were "square" (Ezek. 48:20; Rev. 21:16).
3. As in Ezekiel's vision, a guide with a measuring rod showed John the city (Ezek. 40:3; Rev. 21:15).
4. John described a river of the water of life, flowing from the throne of God. By its waters grew trees that continually produced fruit and had healing leaves (Rev. 22:1, 2; see Ezek. 47:12).
5. John heard a voice that cried, "Behold, the tabernacle of God is among men, and He will dwell among them, and they

---

[3]Taylor, 285.

shall be His people, and God Himself will be among them" (Rev. 21:3). Indeed, the new Jerusalem could be called "The LORD is there" (as in Ezek. 48:35).

To say that John was describing the same city would be a stretch. Sin still existed in Ezekiel's city, but in John's city there would be no more sin (see Rev. 22:3). Ezekiel emphasized the temple, while John mentioned no temple at all (Rev. 21:22). John was describing the new heavens and new earth, of which the new Jerusalem would be a part. Ezekiel was speaking to a downtrodden people, violently removed from the land they loved, separated from the city they cherished.

What hope remained for the exiles? All had been ripped from beneath them. Then, however, the loving God sent His prophet. As Ezekiel conveyed his vision to the people, each wall of the new temple, each gate, restored hope. The ultimate good news was delivered when the city was named "The LORD is there."[4]

APPLICATION

God's Power

The Book of Ezekiel depicts God's great power. Although some doubted that He would act, He caused His holy city to be destroyed, sent His people into captivity, and then led them back to the Promised Land. Though we live under the new covenant and God works differently than He did under the old covenant, He has not lost any of His power.

Through the power of God, the spiritually dead can live. Paul saw the Jews' acceptance of Jesus as "life from the dead" (Rom. 11:14, 15). Likewise, the Ephesians were dead in their trespasses and sins until they were made alive with Christ (Eph. 2:1, 5, 6). Let us not join the faithless exiles in denying God's power to raise the dead. Jesus taught the possibility of passing out of death into life (Jn. 5:24, 25).

Through the power of God, the physically dead will live. The Book of Ezekiel does not deal specifically with the resurrection of the

---

[4]For further study, see "What Happened After the Exile" in Appendix 1.

dead at the last day; however, the same power of God which restores the spiritually dead will affect the resurrection. The people living under the Old Testament were not without information on the resurrection of the dead. (See Job 14:14; Dan. 12:2.) To us, God has given the words of John 5:28, 29, promising "a resurrection of life" to those who did good deeds and "a resurrection of judgment" for those who did evil.

The power of life and death are in God's hands. He uses His great power to supply all that we need (see Mt. 6:32). Faith in that power will allow Christians to overcome.

A.J.

APPENDIX 1
ADDITIONAL STUDIES

The Oracles Against Gog and Magog:
    Interpreting Ezekiel 38; 39   687
What Happened After the Exile?   696

THE ORACLES AGAINST GOG AND MAGOG: INTERPRETING EZEKIEL 38; 39

The amount of attention given to chapters 38 and 39 reminds one of Solomon's words in Ecclesiastes 12:12: "The writing of many books is endless, and excessive devotion to books is wearying to the body." The over-analysis of these chapters is wearying. Ralph H. Alexander has said, "One of the perennial enigmas of biblical prophecy has been the Gog and Magog event described in Ezekiel 38 and 39. The plethora of interpretations for this passage caution the student concerning dogmatism in his conclusions."[1]

While careful consideration of these two chapters is in order, we must not lose the fundamental message in the scholarly rhetoric. Five messages have been given since chapter 33. It is not essential to try to view these two chapters contextually. Ezekiel has jumped around before. Perhaps John B. Taylor offered a viable explanation:

> These chapters [38; 39] can be isolated from their context in much the same way as can the prophecies against the nations in chapters 25—32. They appear to interrupt the sequence of chapters 33—37 and 40—48, which give us a picture of renewed leadership for Israel, a restored land and a reborn people, leading on to the concluding vision of the design and organization of the temple worship of this new community. How does an

---

[1]Ralph H. Alexander, "A Fresh Look at Ezekiel 38 and 39," *Journal of the Evangelical Theological Society* 17 (Summer 1974): 157.

apocalyptic oracle of this order fit into such a pattern?
... It may be that, as 40—48 clearly hang together and are dated late ("in the twenty-fifth year of our exile", 40:1), this compels [Ezekiel] to place them at the end of the whole book, and that this chronological consideration has outweighed the logical one; for one might well argue that a final overthrow of the powers of darkness should come *after* the dawning of the new age and not *before* it.... Understood this way, the oracles against Gog were a suitable conclusion to chapters 1—39.[2]

The last message (38; 39) contains seven oracles against the enemies of God's people. This prophecy presents three puzzling questions:

1. Who is "Gog"?
2. To what place was Ezekiel alluding—that is, where is "Magog"?
3. When are "the last days" in which these events were to take place (38:16)?

The first two questions were addressed in the comments on chapter 38. However, the third question has given rise to such varied speculation that a separate discussion of "the last days" seems necessary.

NON-LITERAL VIEWS

The Symbolic View

The symbolic view of this prophecy says that the section is not to be specifically applied to any particular person or event but was designed to offer comfort to God's people by showing that He will defeat every enemy. Being a non-literal approach, it does not burden the student with scores of interpretations.

This view is most acceptable for a number of reasons.

---

[2]John B. Taylor, *Ezekiel: An Introduction and Commentary*, Tyndale Old Testament Commentaries (Downers Grove, Ill.: Inter-Varsity Press, 1969), 241–42.

APPENDIX 1: ADDITIONAL STUDIES

(1) It flows naturally from the previous five prophecies with a message of hope and certainty for the exiles. (2) It would have been meaningful to the exiles, rather than referring to an event which—more than 2,500 years later—still has not taken place. (3) Unlike other views, it does not skip over the most significant event of all time: the coming of the Messiah, with His earthly ministry and the establishment of the church. (4) It allows for events to take place after the destruction of God's enemies, a major point of difficulty for some interpretations. (5) Perhaps most important, it takes into consideration the type of writing in these chapters—apocalyptic literature, which is full of figures and symbols. Those who accept other views have spent countless hours of research and argumentation trying to explain the details of this prophecy (often making the mistake of literalizing the symbols).

Ezekiel had already dealt with the nations close to Israel, telling what God would do to them (chs. 25—32). What about distant nations or future threats? Gog and his hoard could represent any evil that might prey upon God's people. Perhaps these chapters were to assure Israel, in typical Jewish apocalyptic fashion, that any force which might come against them—even one as mighty as Gog and his host—would quickly and easily be defeated (see Rev. 16:14; 20:7–10). Therefore, Israel had nothing to worry about. Their complete trust was to be in God.

A further word of caution must be spoken about the interpretation of these two chapters. The language is apocalyptic language: It is largely symbolical and at times deliberately shadowy and even cryptic. Though the details are vague, the main thrust is boldly expressed. Interpretation, therefore, needs to correspond to contents. Attempts to read too much into the incidentals of the prophecy betray the ingenuity of the speculator rather than the sobriety of the exegete.[3]

Two problems are connected with symbolic interpretation: The prophecy seems too specific not to relate to a particular event, and it does not account for the direct reference to Gog and Magog in Revelation 20:8.

---

[3]Ibid., 243.

The "Church Age" View

Another non-literal approach, the "Church Age" view, asserts that the prophecy in Ezekiel 38; 39 refers to the uniting of God's people under the protective leadership of Jesus. All enemies of God's family will be defeated. Again, some problems arise: (1) Too many of the details do not fit church life. (2) The view does not account for the direct reference to Gog and Magog in Revelation 20:8. (3) No reference to the Messiah is made in these chapters.

Still, the "Church Age" view has several strengths. (1) It flows logically from chapter 37, a figure of the uniting of God's people (the two sticks) that takes place through the blood of the cross (Eph. 2:12–15). (2) Ezekiel 37:24 alludes to Jesus as the King over His people. While the absence of a messianic reference is a weakness of this view, the mention of "My servant David" in 37:24 provides a natural lead-in to chapter 38. (3) It best explains the idea of God's people "living securely." This terminology describes the time of the Messiah (34:25, 28). Those in the body of Christ, His church, have an unparalleled peace (Jn. 14:27; Phil. 4:4–7). (4) The Church Age had already been described in apocalyptic terms by God's prophets, so this would not be unusual (see Is. 2:1–4; Ezek. 34:20–24; Joel 2:28–32, compared to Acts 2:16–21; Dan. 7:13, 14). (5) It would allow flexibility within apocalyptic terminology. That is, it would allow the enemies of God's people—Gog and Magog—to be used in different contexts, even as the Scriptures use "Egypt" and "Babylon" to refer to the enemies of God's people. (6) The terminology "in the last days" (38:16) was used by other Old Testament prophets to refer to the Church Age (Is. 2:2; Hos. 3:5; Mic. 4:1). (7) The Jewish rabbis understood this to be a prophecy of the age before the coming of the Messiah.[4]

---

[4]"In Rabbinic literature, Gog and Magog (the latter as an individual) are frequently referred to as the leaders of a hostile army against Israel before the coming of the Messiah. The Midrash Tanchuma (Korach, end) interprets *Gog u-Magog* to mean the assembly of enemy nations [without trying to pinpoint these nations specifically]" (S. Fisch, *Ezekiel: Hebrew Text and English Translation with an Introduction and Commentary*, Soncino Books of the Bible [London: Soncino Press, 1950], 253).

Rabbinic literature also describes how "the numerical value of the two Hebrew words [Gog, Magog] is seventy, the supposed number of peoples in the ancient world."[5] This would be understood to represent the "perfect" army to come against God and His people, the totality of all peoples outside of God's chosen nation. Other writings identify Gog and Magog with pre-first-century nations.[6]

LITERAL VIEWS

The View of "Gog" as Babylon

For those who insist that this section should have a literal application, the most acceptable approach is to interpret "Gog" as a name for Babylon. Chapters 25 through 32 dealt with Israel's close neighbors. Those chapters detailed, nation by nation, how God would move each enemy out of the way so that Israel could enjoy peace and security. One listening to Ezekiel would likely have raised a logical question: "What about Babylon? Are they not the most likely to keep us from returning to our land?" Therefore, it seems reasonable that Ezekiel's last section would deal with the greatest threat of all, Babylon. In apocalyptic fashion, he would have avoided using the name "Babylon" (as he had used the names of other nations) because the Israelites were still living in Babylon. For the same reason, John, in writing Revelation, referred to the Roman Empire with a number of apocalyptic terms, never mentioning Rome by name.

Here are some observations that make a literal application of "Gog" to Babylon plausible:

Babylon had continually been referred to as the threat that comes from the "north" (9:2; 26:7; see Jer. 1:13, 14, 15; 4:6; 6:1, 22; 15:12; 46:20, 24; 50:3). Likewise, the forces of Gog are continually referenced as coming from the north (38:6, 15; 39:2). Some may

---

[5]Ibid.

[6]"The Palestinian Talmud ([*Megillah*] 71b) identifies Magog with Gothia, the land of the Goths (the reading in the Babylonian Talmud, Yoma 10a is "Kandia," perhaps Crete). Josephus (*Antiquities* I.vi.1) associates the Magogites with the Scythians, the ancestors of the Gothians who inhabited the region of the Caucasus mountains" (Ibid.).

object, noting that Ezekiel 38:6 says that Gog would come from "the remote parts" of the north—or farther north than Babylon. However, Jeremiah used the same Hebrew terminology to describe the location of Babylon (Jer. 6:22; 25:32). Rather than discrediting this point, the additional phrase "the remote parts of the north" strengthens the Babylon/Gog connection.

Babylon had an army that was feared by nations near and far (Hab. 1:5-11). Gog had gathered "a great assembly and a mighty army" (38:15). Just as no one thought that Babylon could be defeated, Gog considered himself invincible (38:10-13).

The army of Babylon is described in similar fashion to the army of Gog (compare 26:7 with 38:4, 15).

Babylon, to the shock of the nations, fell quickly and easily to the Medes and the Persians (who were instruments in God's hand; Jer. 51:7, 8; Dan. 5:30, 31). In the same way, Gog would be defeated quickly and easily by God (39:1-8). (Babylon fell in 539 B.C., about one generation after the date of this prophecy.)

God made the same powerful declaration against Babylon that He made against Gog: "Behold, I am against you" (38:3; 39:1; Jer. 51:25).

The account of Gog is tied with Israel's captivity and eventual return (39:23-25). This connection can only be made with the Babylonian Exile.

Gog is said to have been a topic of the prophets "in former days" (38:17). While no previous prophet of God had ever prophesied against "Gog," several prophets had prophesied against Babylon (Isaiah, Jeremiah, Daniel, and Habakkuk).

The View of Dispensational Premillennialists

This view claims that the section refers to an invasion during a period called the "Tribulation," immediately preceding the second coming of Christ. When Christ returns, according to this view, He will deliver His people in a monumental battle which will forever destroy His enemies. Then He will establish His kingdom in Jerusalem and embark upon His thousand-year reign. This position is based primarily upon the mention of the great "bird supper" in Revelation 19:17, 18, which corresponds to the description given in Ezekiel 39:17-20. This bird supper is

APPENDIX 1: ADDITIONAL STUDIES

expected to occur before Christ begins His thousand-year reign (Rev. 20:4).[7]

A number of problems arise in relation to this view:

1. It assumes the doctrines of the "Rapture" and the "Tribulation," neither of which is biblically supportable.

2. It does not sufficiently address how God's people could be "living securely" during the Tribulation (38:8, 11, 14).

3. It gives an insufficient explanation for the direct reference to Gog and Magog in Revelation 20:8.

4. It is based on such sparse evidence that adherents to this view are divided into countless sub-positions.[8]

5. The battle in Revelation 19 (other battles follow; see Rev. 20) does not fit with the battle described in Ezekiel 38; 39 (the final battle).

6. Those who place this battle in the midst of the Tribulation cannot reconcile their opinion with 39:22, which says that after the battle the house of Israel would know the Lord "from that day onward." Further, 39:2 says that the outcome of the battle would cause the Gentile nations to know the Lord as "the Holy One in Israel" (see 38:16, 23; 39:21). This could not be fulfilled in keeping with the Tribulation period described by Premillennialists.[9]

7. This interpretation makes the sixth message in chapters 38 and 39 an abrupt change from the previous five, not logically fitting with the context of those sections.

8. This view leaves the interpreter hopelessly lost in determining which parts of the prophecy are literal and which are figurative.

---

[7] "In this theological system so much emphasis has been placed upon an eschatological tribulation period that it was almost assumed that Ezekiel 38—39 belonged there" (J. Paul Tanner, "Rethinking Ezekiel's Invasion by Gog," *Journal of the Evangelical Theological Society* 39 [March 1996]: 29).

[8] "I would suggest that this seeming interpretive tension has spurred many a premillennialist to locate the battle of Gog and Magog in the tribulation so as to avoid the conflict that naturally arises by having it after the second coming. Rather than resolving the tension, however, I feel that this tendency to link the passage with the tribulation only results in a greater interpretive quagmire" (Ibid., 40).

[9] Ibid., 43.

The View of Post-millennialists

Post-millennialism (which states that Christ's second coming will follow the millennium) claims that this section applies to the great battle of Revelation 20, where Gog and Magog are mentioned. This battle is said to be the final one, in which Satan and his followers will be sentenced eternally to the lake of fire (Rev. 20:10). Problems with this view include the following:

1. In Ezekiel, the forces of Gog come from the north; in Revelation 20:8 the armies come from "the four corners of the earth."

2. Jerusalem is not mentioned as being the center of the battle in Ezekiel 38; 39, whereas it is the central location in Revelation 20:9.

3. The weaponry described in Ezekiel is ancient; it is not the type of warfare likely to be used today or in the future.

4. In Ezekiel, the slain cover the landscape to the extent that it takes seven months to bury the dead; in Revelation, the fire of God consumes all and leaves none to bury.

5. Ezekiel 39:17–20 describes the great "bird supper"; there is no place for such an occurrence in Revelation 20.

6. The seven months needed to bury the dead (39:12) and the seven years used to bury the weapons (39:9) do not match Revelation 20, which has neither weapons nor dead, but proceeds immediately into the judgment of all mankind (vv. 11–14). The passage in Revelation makes no mention of "time"—seven years, seven months, or otherwise.

7. Like the Premillennialists' position, this view fails to flow logically with the earlier five messages from God.

8. It does not sufficiently reconcile the purpose of the two battles. In Ezekiel, the battle is used as the springboard to reestablishing God's relationship with Israel. The battle in Revelation 20 is said to take place after God's people have been living in peace with Him for one thousand years.

9. This view does not provide adequate reason for interpreting some parts of the prophecy literally and other parts figuratively.

APPENDIX 1: ADDITIONAL STUDIES

CONCLUSION

Perhaps this quick description of positions will affirm the difficulties of interpretation. Some commentators, hoping to alleviate the conflict, suggest that more than one interpretation is correct—and that Ezekiel 38; 39 will have a dual fulfillment. Alexander wrote,

> The hermeneutical principle of "multiple fulfillment" declares that a given prophecy has one meaning applied in two or more ways. There may be a near and far fulfillment, two near fulfillments, or two far fulfillments. The latter is proposed here. Ezekiel 38 and 39 has a multiple fulfillment in 1) the demise of "the beast," the chief instrument of Satan (similar to Ezek 28:1–10), in Revelation 19:17–21 and in 2) the final fall of Satan, *the* Gog, the supreme enemy of Israel (similar to Ezek 28:11–19), who makes *the* final attempt to regain the land of Israel from God's chosen people. The multiple fulfillment is concentrated in two similar events with the last and greatest enemies of Israel. Both "the beast" and Satan seek to defeat Israel and acquire the land. Both attempts are thwarted by the Lord. The former, in one sense, prefigures the latter.[10]

---

[10] Alexander, 169–70.

What Happened After the Exile?

The number of persons taken into captivity in Babylon is difficult to determine. Only concerning the second deportation do the Scriptures give a number: "10,000." (This group included 7,000 men of might and 1,000 craftsmen; see 2 Kings 24:14–16.) Those taken in the first deportation included "youths in whom was no defect" (Dan. 1:4). During the third deportation, it is said that all were seized except "some of the poorest of the land" (2 Kings 25:12). That thousands were taken is indicated by the number who returned: 49,897 were led back by Sheshbazzar (Ezra 2:64, 65; Neh. 7:66, 67) and more by Ezra and Nehemiah.

Life during the Captivity was actually somewhat pleasant. The exiles were not kept in concentration camps; they were allowed freedom of movement within the land. They could write letters to friends and relatives in Judah (see Jer. 29:25). Favorable employment opportunities were open to the them. They were permitted to live on fertile land. In fact, when the Captivity was over, some did not want to leave their new homes.

However, the Captivity was punishment. Psalm 137 records the captives' sadness and bitterness about being separated from Jerusalem. Jeremiah had predicted that this punishment would last seventy years (Jer. 25:11, 12; see 29:10).

The Babylonian Captivity came to an end around 539 B.C., when the Babylonian world power was supplanted by the Medo-Persian world power. After the Persian king became the sole ruler of the Persian Empire, Cyrus, acting under a different policy than the Assyrians and the Babylonians, issued a decree that allowed displaced citizens to return to their homelands.

APPENDIX 1: ADDITIONAL STUDIES

Isaiah had said that Cyrus would be God's servant:

> "[God] says of Cyrus, 'He is My shepherd!
> And he will perform all My desire.'
> And he declares of Jerusalem, 'She will be built,'
> And of the temple, 'Your foundation will be laid'"
>   (Is. 44:28).

This prophecy was a name prophecy, which was fulfilled two hundred or so years after it was written. Isaiah began prophesying around 739 B.C., and Cyrus issued his decree around 536 B.C.:

> Thus says Cyrus king of Persia, "The LORD, the God of heaven, has given me all the kingdoms of the earth and He has appointed me to build Him a house in Jerusalem, which is in Judah. Whoever there is among you of all His people, may his God be with him! Let him go up to Jerusalem which is in Judah and rebuild the house of the LORD, the God of Israel; He is the God who is in Jerusalem. Every survivor, at whatever place he may live, let the men of that place support him with silver and gold, with goods and cattle, together with a freewill offering for the house of God which is in Jerusalem" (Ezra 1:2–4).

The first copy of the decree in Ezra was written in Hebrew and had the form of a royal proclamation (1:1). The second copy, in Aramaic, had the form of a memorandum or an oral royal decision (6:3–5). Another copy mentioned in 2 Chronicles 36:22, 23 is incomplete.

During his excavations at Babylon (1879–1882), Hormuzd Rassam discovered a clay barrel inscription in which Cyrus described and justified his policies. Concerning his conquest of Babylon, Cyrus said that Marduk looked through all the land for a world leader and chose him. Having taken Babylon, Cyrus allowed captive peoples to return to their homelands and rebuild their temples. The Cyrus Cylinder says, "I also gathered all their former inhabitants and returned to them their habitations." Cyrus seemed to have been in favor of all gods.[1]

What orders were given by Cyrus' decree? First, it said that Jerusalem was to be rebuilt. Second, the cost of rebuilding would be defrayed from Cyrus' own treasury. Third, all who wished to return to Jerusalem would be allowed to do so. Fourth, those who remained were urged to assist those who were going to Judah. The gold and silver vessels taken by Nebuchadnezzar when he destroyed Jerusalem were to be returned.

Ezra related the return of two groups of exiles; the Book of Nehemiah tells of the return of the third group. The first was the return by Sheshbazzar in 536 B.C. (1:1). The second came about eighty years later, in the seventh year of Artaxerxes Longimanus (458 B.C.; see 7:7). The third group, led by Nehemiah, returned thirteen years after the second, in the twentieth year of Artaxerxes Longimanus (445 B.C.; Neh. 2:1).

Not all transplanted Jews[2] returned. Freewill offerings were given to those whom God stirred to return (Ezra 1:5, 6). Their neighbors assisted them with articles of silver and gold, with goods and livestock, and with valuable gifts in addition to the freewill offerings.

Vessels taken from the temple by Nebuchadnezzar were given to Sheshbazzar by Cyrus (Ezra 1:7–11). All the vessels together numbered 5,400, according to the NASB.

THE FIRST RETURN

Those returning to Judah were led by Sheshbazzar and Zerubbabel (Ezra 1:8; 2:2). Sheshbazzar seems to have been the one in charge, although "Zerubbabel" and "Sheshbazzar" may simply be two names for the same person. Both are called "governor" of Judah (Ezra 5:14; Hag. 1:1). However, a more likely

---

[1]"Cyrus Cylinder," *The Biblical World: A Dictionary of Biblical Archaeology*, ed. Charles F. Pfeiffer (Grand Rapids, Mich.: Baker Book House, 1966), 178.

[2]From Ezra's time forward, the Israelites are commonly referred to as "Jews." Most of those who returned from captivity were of the tribe of Judah, and the word "Judah" gave rise to the name "Jew."

view is that Sheshbazzar was succeeded by Zerubbabel. They likely went to Jerusalem with the same group. Perhaps Sheshbazzar was the leader at the beginning of the return but died shortly after arriving in Jerusalem, and then Zerubbabel assumed the leadership position.

A total of 49,897 people left Babylon: 42,360 from the assembly of the Jews, 200 singers, and 7,337 servants. The livestock that were taken included 736 horses; 245 mules; 435 camels; and 6,720 donkeys, which would be a total of 8,136 animals (see Ezra 2:64–67; Neh. 7:66–69).

This was a large company, but it probably was not even a majority of the Jews in captivity. During the days of Esther, Jews were still living throughout the land of Persia. These were able to kill 75,000 of their enemies in two days (Esther 9:16). That kind of fighting would require a large number of Jews.

When the Jews reached their land, they dwelt in their respective cities. However, in the seventh month of the first year of their return, they gathered at Jerusalem. There, Zerubbabel and the high priest Jeshua erected an altar and offered burnt offerings upon it (Ezra 3:1–6). The people also kept the Feast of Tabernacles. From this time forward, they began to keep the feasts and the sacrifices of the law of Moses.

The foundation of the temple was laid in the second month of the second year (Ezra 3:7–13). They hired masons, carpenters, and men of Tyre and Sidon to bring cedar trees from Lebanon to Joppa, according to the grant of Cyrus (v. 7). When this foundation was laid, some rejoiced and others wept. The people could not distinguish the sound of rejoicing from weeping (vv. 12, 13).

Immediately, discouragement came from the Samaritans ("the people of the land"; Ezra 4:4), and work on the temple was stopped. The people turned from rebuilding the temple to building their own houses (Hag. 1:3–11). The temple foundation remained incomplete until 520 B.C., sixteen years later (Hag. 1:1).

At that time, Haggai began prophesying. Zechariah appeared shortly after Haggai. His message for the people, though more figurative, was basically the same as Haggai's. With the encouragement of these prophets, the people resumed the work of rebuilding the temple (Ezra 5:1–3).

Tattenai (or Tatnai), the governor, with his assistant Shethar-bozenai, asked why the work had started again. They were told to look at the decree of Cyrus, which gave the Jews the right to work on the temple. They wrote to Darius, who looked up Cyrus' decree and granted them the freedom to continue building. Cyrus' decree is even repeated at this point in the narrative of Ezra (6:3–5).

The work on the temple was resumed, then, in 520 B.C., during the reign of Darius (522 to 486 B.C.). The structure was completed in 516 B.C., the sixth year of the reign of Darius. Once the people started again, it took them only four years to complete the temple. This temple did not have the glory that Solomon's temple had, but at least it had been rebuilt.

A joyous celebration followed the completion of the temple. The people sacrificed one hundred bulls, two hundred rams, and four hundred lambs. Compare this with the dedication of Solomon's temple in 2 Chronicles 7:1–3.

Solomon offered 22,000 oxen and 120,000 sheep at this celebration (2 Chron. 7:5).

Those who returned to Judah also kept the Passover in the land:

> The exiles observed the Passover on the fourteenth of the first month. For the priests and the Levites had purified themselves together; all of them were pure. Then they slaughtered the Passover lamb for all the exiles, both for their brothers the priests and for themselves. The sons of Israel who returned from exile and all those who had separated themselves from the impurity of the nations of the land to join them, to seek the LORD God of Israel, ate the Passover. And they observed the Feast of Unleavened Bread seven days with joy, for the LORD had caused them to rejoice, and had turned the heart of the king of Assyria toward them to encourage them in the work of the house of God, the God of Israel (Ezra 6:19–22).

APPENDIX 1: ADDITIONAL STUDIES

THE SECOND RETURN

Fifty-eight years passed between the completion of the temple and the second return of the Jews. Only a few clues exist about what happened during the intervening years. However, the story of Esther must have occurred during these years, between the events of Ezra 6 and 7.

Artaxerxes Longimanus reigned over the Persian Empire from 465 to 424 B.C. Through some means, Ezra gained standing with this king and persuaded him to allow a group of Jews to go to Jerusalem. Thus Ezra led the second group back to Judah.

Like Sheshbazzar, eighty years before, Ezra received a letter from the king granting him permission to go (7:11–26). It contained authority for him to take as many of his fellow Jews as he wished.

A smaller number were part of this return: less than 1,800. No women or children were included in this count. Ezra assembled those who wished to go at the River Ahava (a river unknown today). The men numbered about 1,500 (8:1–14). When no Levites were found in the group, Ezra delayed the trip until thirty-eight Levites could be persuaded to go (8:15–19). These Levites were accompanied by 220 helpers (8:20). In about four months, the group arrived in Judah.

Ezra's task was to restore the spiritual life of the holy city. The main reform was to stop the intermarriage of the Jews with the surrounding people.

THE THIRD RETURN

A third group was led to Judah by Nehemiah. He was a cupbearer to King Artaxerxes. We do not know how many Jews went with Nehemiah. The fact that he was accompanied by the "army officers and cavalry" may suggest that a sizable group went with him.

Nehemiah arrived in Jerusalem twelve or thirteen years after Ezra's return. He stayed in Jerusalem twelve years, from the twentieth year to the thirty-second year of Artaxerxes' reign (445 to 433 B.C.; see Neh. 2:1; 5:14). Nehemiah's mission was to rebuild the walls of the city of Jerusalem. He returned to Susa in 433 B.C. Later, in 430 B.C., he made another trip to Jerusalem, during which time he launched various reforms (13:6–31).

During the time of Nehemiah, Malachi wrote to encourage the people by affirming that God still loved Israel. At the same time, he expounded doctrines of the Lord's holiness and righteousness. The zeal and excitement that had characterized the exiles at their return to Jerusalem had faded. The people had grown indifferent. They were sacrificing blemished animals to God; they were robbing Him in their tithes and offerings. They were not heeding marriage laws. Many were discouraged because the golden age that had been prophesied had not come.

However, a greater age was coming. Malachi closed his book, and thus the Old Testament, by describing the ultimate destruction of the wicked and the triumph of the righteous. No more messages came from God until Gabriel announced John's birth to Zacharias in the temple (Lk. 1). All had been said and done—nothing remained but to prepare for the coming of the promised Messiah.

E.C.

APPENDIX 2
CHARTS AND MAPS

A Timeline of Ezekiel — 704

Babylon in the Time of Ezekiel — 705

Composite of Places in Ezekiel's Prophecies — 706

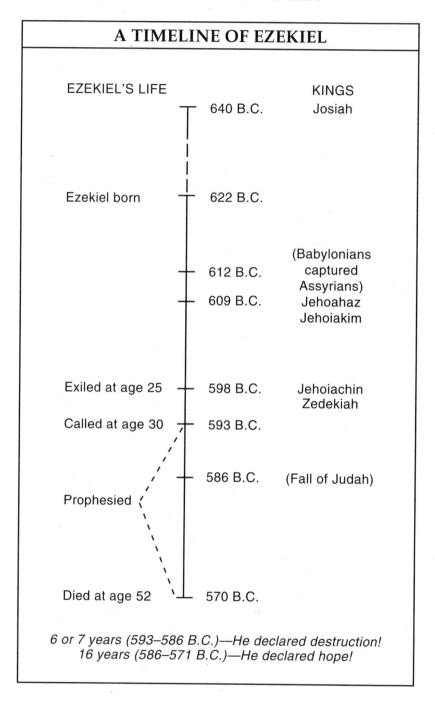

APPENDIX 2: CHARTS AND MAPS

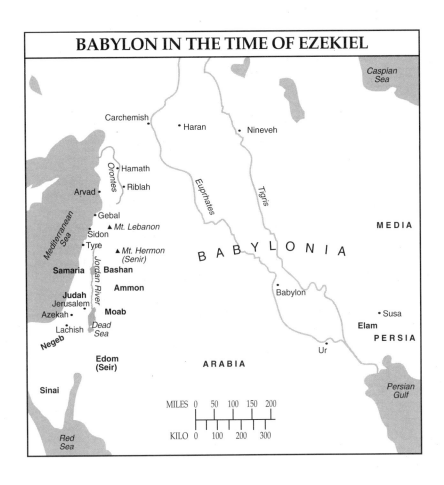

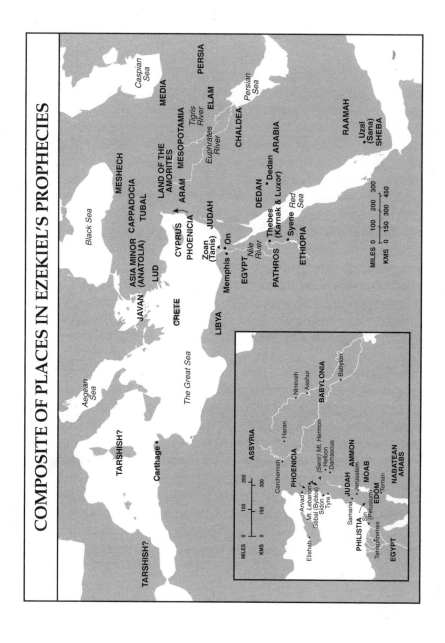

Selected Bibliography

GENERAL

Ralph H. Alexander. "Ezekiel." In *The Expositor's Bible Commentary*, ed. Frank E. Gaebelein, 6:737–996. Grand Rapids, Mich.: Zondervan Publishing House, 1986.

Archer, Gleason L., Jr. *Encyclopedia of Bible Difficulties*. Grand Rapids, Mich.: Zondervan Publishing House, 1982.

_____. *A Survey of Old Testament Introduction*. Chicago: Moody Press, 1974.

Barnes, Albert. *The Bible Commentary: Proverbs to Ezekiel*. Barnes' Notes, ed. F. C. Cook. Abridged and edited by J. M. Fuller. Grand Rapids, Mich.: Baker Book House, 1983.

Brownlee, William H. *Ezekiel 1—19*. Word Biblical Commentary, vol. 28. Waco, Tex.: Word Books, 1986.

Carley, Keith W. *The Book of the Prophet Ezekiel*. The Cambridge Bible Commentary. Cambridge: Cambridge University Press, 1974.

Clarke, Adam. *The Holy Bible with a Commentary and Critical Notes*, Vol. 4. *Isaiah to Malachi*. New York: Abingdon-Cokesbury Press, n.d.

Cooke, G. A. *A Critical and Exegetical Commentary on the Book of Ezekiel.* International Critical Commentary. Edinburgh: T. & T. Clark, 1936.

Davidson, A. B. *The Book of the Prophet Ezekiel: With Notes and Introduction.* Cambridge: Cambridge University Press, 1892.

Driver, S. R. *An Introduction to the Literature of the Old Testament.* New York: C. Scribner, 1891. Reprint, New York: Meridian Books, 1956.

Eichrodt, Walther. *Ezekiel: A Commentary.* Translated by Cosslett Quin. The Old Testament Library. Philadelphia: Westminster Press, 1970.

Ellison, Henry L. *Ezekiel: The Man and His Message.* Grand Rapids, Mich.: Wm. B. Eerdmans Publishing Co., 1956.

Feinberg, Charles Lee. *The Prophecy of Ezekiel: The Glory of the Lord.* Chicago: Moody Press, 1969.

Fisch, S. *Ezekiel: Hebrew Text and English Translation with an Introduction and Commentary.* Soncino Books of the Bible. London: Soncino Press, 1950.

Gaebelein, A. C. *The Prophet Ezekiel: An Analytical Exposition.* New York: Our Hope, 1918.

Greenberg, Moshe. *Ezekiel 1—20: A New Translation with Introduction and Commentary.* The Anchor Bible, vol. 22. Garden City, N.Y.: Doubleday & Company, 1983.

_____. *Ezekiel 21—37: A New Translation with Introduction and Commentary.* The Anchor Bible, vol. 22a. New York: Doubleday, 1997.

Hanson, Paul D. *The Dawn of Apocalyptic.* Philadelphia: Fortress Press, 1979.

SELECTED BIBLIOGRAPHY

Howie, Carl G. *The Book of Ezekiel, The Book of Daniel*. The Layman's Bible Commentary, vol. 13. Richmond, Va.: John Knox Press, 1961.

Ironside, H. A. *Ezekiel*. Neptune, N.J.: Loizeaux, 1949.

Irwin, William A. *The Problem of Ezekiel*. Chicago: University of Chicago Press, 1943.

Kaiser, Walter C., Jr., Peter H. Davids, F. F. Bruce, and Manfred T. Brauch. *Hard Sayings of the Bible*. Downers Grove, Ill.: InterVarsity Press, 1996.

Keil, Carl F. *Biblical Commentary on the Prophecies of Ezekiel*. 2 vols. Translated by James Martin. Biblical Commentary on the Old Testament. Grand Rapids, Mich.: Wm. B. Eerdmans Publishing Co., 1950.

Lewis, Jack P. *The Major Prophets*. Henderson, Tenn.: Hester Publications, 1999.

Matthews, I. G. *Ezekiel*. American Commentary on the Old Testament, vol. 21. Chicago: American Baptist Publication Society, 1939.

Mazar, Benjamin. *Jerusalem Through the Ages*. Jerusalem: Israel Exploration Society, 1964.

McGuiggan, Jim. *The Book of Ezekiel*. Looking Into The Bible Series. Lubbock, Tex.: Montext Publishing Company, 1979.

Parrot, Andre. *The Temple of Jerusalem*. New York: Philosophical Library, 1955.

Pentecost, J. Dwight. *Things to Come*. Findlay, Ohio: Dunham, 1958.

Pfeiffer, Charles F., ed. *The Biblical World*. Grand Rapids, Mich.: Baker Book House, 1966.

Pritchard, James B., ed. *Ancient Near Eastern Texts*. Princeton, N.J.: Princeton University Press, 1969.

Raitt, Thomas. *A Theology of Exile: Judgment/Deliverance in Jeremiah and Ezekiel*. Philadelphia: Fortress Press, 1977.

Russell, D. S. *The Method and Message of Jewish Apocalyptic*. Philadelphia: Westminster Press, 1964.

Skinner, John. *The Book of Ezekiel*. New York: A. C. Armstrong and Sons, 1901.

Taylor, John B. *Ezekiel: An Introduction and Commentary*. Tyndale Old Testament Commentaries. Downers Grove, Ill.: Inter-Varsity Press, 1969.

Thomas, D. Winton, ed. *Documents from Old Testament Times*. New York: Harper & Brothers, 1958.

Unger, Merrill F. *Great Neglected Bible Prophecies*. Chicago, Ill.: Scripture Press, 1955.

Van Dijk, H. J. *Ezekiel's Prophecy on Tyre*. Rome: Pontifical Bible Institute, 1968.

Wendell Winkler, ed. *Difficult Texts of the Old Testament Explained*. Montgomery, Ala.: Winkler Publications, 1982.

Wevers, John W. *Ezekiel*. London: Nelson, 1969.

Yamauchi, Edwin M. *Foes from the Northern Frontier*. Grand Rapids, Mich.: Baker Book House, 1982.

Zimmerli, Walther. *Ezekiel 1: A Commentary on the Book of the Prophet Ezekiel, Chapters 1—24*. Translated by Ronald E. Clements. Hermeneia. Philadelphia: Fortress Press, 1979.

BIBLE TRANSLATIONS

The Amplified Bible. Grand Rapids, Mich.: Zondervan Publishing House, 1987.

The Holy Bible; American Standard Version. Thomas Nelson & Sons, 1901.

The Holy Bible; Authorized King James Version. Colorado Springs, Colo.: International Bible Society, 1987.

The Holy Bible; New International Version. Grand Rapids, Mich.: Zondervan Publishing House, 1978.

The Holy Bible; New King James Version. New York: American Bible Society, 1990.

The Holy Bible; New Revised Standard Version. Grand Rapids, Mich.: Zondervan Bible Publishers, 1989.

New American Standard Bible. Anaheim, Calif.: Foundation Publications, 1995.

From the Editor
Have You Heard . . . About Truth for Today?

What are the big missionary needs of our time? Those who study missionary evangelism point to two paramount needs that are ever present in the mission field.

THE BIG NEEDS OF WORLD EVANGELISM

First, they tell us that educating and maturing the national Christian man so that he can preach to his own people in their own language is of supreme importance. Giving this type of assistance to the national man will help to make our missionary efforts more self-supporting and more enduring. We appreciate one of our own preaching to us, and so do other peoples of the world. When we consider the work "our work," we approach it with greater care and will sacrifice more for it. This principle holds true in all cultures.

Christianity can flourish in any nation and culture, in any time or circumstance, if we will let it. When it is established through national preachers, it is far more likely to grow and blossom in the lives of the national people and not become an effort that is totally dependent upon American support.

After the Restoration Movement began in America, it did not take the early preachers long to realize that they had to teach young men to preach if the movement was really to grow. Thus, very early in the history of the Restoration Movement, schools were established. Wisdom suggested that route.

Christians should be grateful for every mission effort that is going on, such as campaigns, medical missions, and television presentations. However, we must not overlook the surpassing value of providing educational opportunities overseas that will assist a man in becoming capable of preaching effectively to his own people. This approach is absolutely vital to the ongoing success of the overall missionary work of the church.

Second, those who have researched missionary evangelism tell us that we need to make available biblical literature that provides an understanding of the Bible on the level of the people. Those whom the missionary is seeking to teach need their own copies of the Bible and assistance in understanding the Scriptures. They require guidance so they can grow quickly and accurately in their comprehension of the Bible. (See Acts 8:30, 31.)

When Tex Williams, the director of World Bible School, was on Harding University's campus sometime ago, he spoke to students about mission work. As a guest lecturer, he told one of the mission classes that the greatest need of Africa is Christian literature. "Without this literature," he said, "they simply cannot become Christians and grow into Christian maturity as they should." There is possibly one exception to this principle. The exception would be places where there is the presence of well-grounded men of faith continually teaching and preaching. This exception obviously applies to only a few places around the world. Even then, biblical literature is needed to support the teaching done.

Let us all consider carefully these two obvious missionary needs. Our efforts must be geared to meeting them. Not to address them is to ignore the clear results of the research that has been done in mission evangelism.

ADDRESSING THESE NEEDS

An effort is currently being made to address both of these big missionary needs. It has been designated the Truth for Today World Mission School (TFTWMS). Started in 1990 as a work under the oversight of the Champions church of Christ in Houston, Texas, it has proven to be a wonderful way to combine three methods of evangelism and thus minister to these supreme needs.

First, TFTWMS is a unique preacher school. An education in the Scriptures is mailed to the national preacher. The work started with 1,460 native preachers enrolled from 110 nations. Now literature is mailed to 40,000 people in 150 nations. These preachers were recommended to the school by World Bible School teachers, missionaries, campaigners, and the national preachers themselves. The school has enjoyed amazing growth.

Second, it is a printed preacher school. Every two months, the men enrolled receive the equivalent of three hundred pages of expository studies on the Scriptures. It is believed that the expository type of study crosses cultures better than other types of study. The materials sent give a thorough treatment of the New Testament book or Old Testament book being studied. It is designed to keep the national preacher enrolled in the school until he receives a study of each of the New Testament and Old Testament books, as well as *Cruden's Concordance*, *Smith's Bible Dictionary*, and several important special studies.

Picture two normal-sized books that are 150 pages in length, and you have the equivalent of the amount of material that is sent to these men every two months. The entire curriculum calls for these men to receive books that are 150 pages in size, that cover the entire Bible, and that include special studies on leadership, building sermons and Bible lessons, and soul-winning.

Third, in addition to sending expository studies to these men, a flexible, on-site preacher school is sometimes used as a follow-up to the printed material. This on-site school is literally taken to where the men are. Preachers and teachers go into a country and study with the national preachers in that location for two or three weeks. Students are provided with food and a syllabus for the classes they attend. They stay at that location day and night for the entire length of the school. They thus enjoy fellowship with other preaching brethren and are given opportunities to ask questions and receive feedback on problems they are facing.

The printed preacher school and the on-site school answer the big need of giving the national man an opportunity to prepare himself to preach to his own people in their own language. Since this work is accomplished to some extent through the printed page, it also answers the need of providing Christian literature for these teachers and preachers who are in desperate need of it.

THE STRONG POINTS

This unique missionary effort has strong points that should be immediately recognized. First, it provides an education to national men inexpensively. Expository materials can be sent to each of these men every two months in a cost-efficient way. Money for missions is hard to find or raise; what missionary money we have should be used to the maximum. TFTWMS sends an education to hundreds of national men with a small amount of money.

Second, the thrust of this work is to educate national men in their own land. Bringing these men to the United States for an education is very expensive. Often, when the national man tastes of the blessings of America, he does not want to return to his land. It is almost essential that a way be found through which the national preacher can receive an education in his own country.

Third, this effort can reach out to hundreds of national men quickly. All of these men are in need of assistance now! How can we get it to them? This method is one of the most practical ways of immediately getting materials to them.

Fourth, it allows the national man to receive an education over a period of time. Because the education comes in the form of printed matter, they have access to the material for months and even years. These men need time to comprehend and assimilate the studies. The printed page offers them that opportunity. They can read and re-read it. They can easily store it. They can share it with others. It can be retained in their possession for as long as ten to fifteen years.

PICTURING THE EFFECTIVENESS

Picture 40,000 men (and thousands more as the work grows) in 150 nations of the world, going out to preach in their own languages to their own people. They are committed to Christ but have had little teaching upon which to build. Furthermore, these men will never have the opportunity to study in the United States to enable them to preach more accurately and faithfully. They have few books, if any. Picture yourself in this type of situation. What would you need?

Can you imagine how these men would be assisted if they received materials on every Old Testament and New Testament book? Can you imagine how encouraging it would be to them to be able to attend a two- to three-week preacher school in their community? Can you picture them in a school, taking several courses in Bible studies, having fellowship with other preachers, having opportunities to have their questions answered, and getting assistance regarding the problems they are facing? Can you not see how these opportunities would increase their effectiveness in leading souls to Christ and in edifying those who have become Christians?

HELPING THOSE WHO HAVE NOT HEARD

In order to help those who have never heard the gospel to become Christians, a special book was designed in 1998 by TFTWMS. It contains three hundred plus pages on how to become a Christian. The reader of the book is introduced to God, Christ, the Holy Spirit, the Bible, the earthly life of Jesus, the death, burial, and resurrection of Jesus, the establishment of the church, and how one can live for Christ today as a member of His church. Then, in the last two hundred pages of the book, there is a complete copy of the New Testament (NASB).

Thousands of these books have been sent to Africa, the Eastern European countries, India, and other places. The success rate has been very high—almost amazing. The book, 512 pages in length, can be printed and sent to someone in another country for $1.63. It is an attempt to bring together the very message that any Christian would want to provide for someone who has not heard the gospel.

Plans are being made every year to cover a large area of the earth with these books. Before printing, the book is culturally adapted for the specific area into which it is being sent.

HOW CAN YOU HELP?

Your help is needed to maintain this missionary effort that has become one of the largest, most cost-effective and productive efforts. Here is a two-part challenge for every Christian:

First, would you challenge the church where you worship and with whom you work to give a one-time contribution to this work?

Even a small contribution will go a long way in providing teaching materials and on-site training for these national preachers.

Second, could you give a one-time contribution to this work? This contribution, of course, would have to be above and beyond your regular contribution to the local congregation of which you are a part. We are not asking anyone to interrupt his commitment to the work of the local congregation. The church needs more works, not fewer works. This effort is designed to strengthen every missionary activity and does not seek to detract from any one of them.

You would be surprised how much can be done if we all do a little extra. No one person has a lot of light, but if we put our lights together, we can have a big light that will reach out into all of the world. Would you decide today to dig a little deeper and give a little extra for this wonderful method of world evangelization?

CONTRIBUTIONS NEEDED

Contributions should be made out to Truth for Today World Mission School and sent to 2209 S. Benton, Searcy, AR 72143. Will you assist us in providing study materials for national preachers? This work is under the oversight of the Champions church of Christ in Houston, Texas.

Eddie Cloer